International Regulatory Competition
and Coordination

International Regulatory Competition and Coordination

Perspectives on Economic Regulation in Europe and the United States

Edited by

William Bratton,
Joseph McCahery,
Sol Picciotto,
and
Colin Scott

CLARENDON PRESS · OXFORD

1996

Oxford University Press, Great Clarendon Street, Oxford OX2 6DP

Oxford New York

Athens Auckland Bangkok Bogota Bombay
Buenos Aires Calcutta Cape Town Dar es Salaam
Delhi Florence Hong Kong Istanbul Karachi
Kuala Lumpur Madras Madrid Melbourne
Mexico City Nairobi Paris Singapore
Taipei Tokyo Toronto

and associated companies in
Berlin Ibadan

Oxford is a trade mark of Oxford University Press

Published in the United States
by Oxford University Press Inc., New York

British Library Cataloguing in Publication Data

Data available

Library of Congress Cataloging in Publication Data

International regulatory competition and coordination: perspectives on
economic regulation in Europe and the United States / edited by
William Bratton . . . [et al].
p. cm.
Includes bibliographical references.
1. Trade regulation—United States. 2. Competition—United States.
3. Trade regulation—Europe. 4. Competition—Europe.
I. Bratton, William W., 1951– .
K3840.I58 1996 341.7'54—dc20 96–8697
ISBN 0–19–826035–0

1 3 5 7 9 10 8 6 4 2

Typeset by Hope Services (Abingdon) Ltd.
Printed in Great Britain
on acid-free paper by
Biddles Ltd.,
Guildford & King's Lynn

Preface

This volume began life as a Workshop on International Regulatory Competition and Coordination, organized jointly by the School of Law, University of Warwick, and the Cardozo School of Law, Yeshiva University, New York. The Workshop was held at Radcliffe House at the University of Warwick in July 1994. We were fortunate to have the generous financial assistance of the Samuel and Ronnie Heyman Center for Corporate Governance of the Benjamin N. Cardozo Law School and the Research and Innovations Fund of the University of Warwick.

We would like to acknowledge the large number of people who have provided us with advice, and invaluable forms of encouragement as the Workshop project has developed into this publication. They include Gavin Anderson, Davina Cooper, Yves Dezalay, Morten Hviid, Henk de Jong, Mike McConville, John McEldowney, Frank Macchiarola, Marius Messer, Han Somsen, Joel Trachtman, Geoffrey Underhill, and Geoffrey Wilson. We are grateful for the administrative support, in the form of a grant, provided by the Legal Research Institute of Warwick University. We would like to thank Barbara Gray, Valerie Innes, and Jill Watson for the administrative help.

We would like to thank all authors of papers, commentators, and chairs of sessions for their contributions at the Workshop. We are particularly grateful to the contributors whom we have worked with over many months before and after the Workshop to produce this collection.

We would like to thank Kristen Roberts and Toby O'Reilly for their help in preparing this volume. We give special thanks to Rhian Whitehead who did much of the difficult work of preparing the final submissions of disks and paper copy by contributors for submission to the Press. Finally, we would like to extend our thanks to our editors, Richard Hart and Elissa Soave.

April 1996   W.W.B.
                                                                                J.McC.
                                                                                S.P.
                                                                                C.S.

Contents

Notes on Contributors

Ian Ayres, William K. Townsend Professor of Law, Yale Law School.

Jennifer Gerarda Brown, Professor of Law, Quinnipiac College School of Law.

William W. Bratton, Jr., Professor of Law and Governor Woodrow Wilson Scholar, Rutgers Law School.

William J. Carney, Charles Howard Candler Professor of Law, Emory University.

Yves Dezalay, charge de recherches au C.N.R.S. (Centre National de la Recherche Scientifique), and associate, C.R.I.V. (Centre de Recherches Interdisciplinaires de Vaucresson).

Daniel Drache, Professor of Political Economy and Director, Robarts Centre for Canadian Studies, York University.

Henk W. de Jong, Professor of Economics, Emeritus, University of Amsterdam.

Brian A. Langille, Professor of Law, University of Toronto.

Joseph McCahery, Lecturer in Law, University of Warwick.

Graham Moffat, Senior Lecturer in Law, University of Warwick.

Joel R. Paul, Professor of Law, University of Connecticut.

Sol Picciotto, Professor of Law, Lancaster University.

Roberta Romano, Allen Duffy/Class of 1960 Professor of Law, Yale Law School and School of Organization and Management.

Colin Scott, Lecturer in Law, London School of Economics and Political Science.

Katherine Van Wezel Stone, Professor of Law, Cornell Law School and Cornell School of Industrial and Labor Relations.

Stephen Woolcock, Research Fellow, Centre for Research on the USA, London School of Economics and Political Science.

Table of Cases

Other countries

Table of Statutes

European Community Legislation and Treaties

International Conventions and Agreements

I

Introduction: Regulatory Competition and Institutional Evolution

WILLIAM W. BRATTON, JOSEPH McCAHERY, SOL PICCIOTTO, AND COLIN SCOTT

Reductions in border controls and other forms of state intervention have created a much greater potential for, if not always actual increases of, flows of goods, services, capital, and labour between jurisdictions. Talk of 'globalization' is widespread among observers, both popular and academic, who speculate about the implications of this increase in the fluidity and openness of the world economic system. The reduction in border controls has brought more sharply into focus the ways in which differences in national arrangements, including regulatory systems, may act as 'non-tariff-barriers' hindering cross-border flows. At the same time, the concept of competition has emerged in a more pervasive form, and is invoked as a counterweight to these institutional constraints. Competitive markets are no longer understood only as structuring private economic relations, but also as an actual or potential determinant of levels and modes of public provision and state activity. National governments are seen not only to respond to the politically-expressed wishes of their citizens, but to the exigencies of international market forces.[1]

The increased emphasis on competition has generally had a negative impact on existing regulatory processes, for a variety of reasons. Intense competitive jockeying for market access causes traditional regulatory requirements to be seen as costs and barriers. This view applies to a wide swathe of regulation, from product safety and other consumer protection laws, to disclosure requirements for firms and issuers of securities, as well as probity and capital adequacy conditions for financial services firms, and antitrust or competition laws and policies applied to business. Firms complain that the regulatory requirements of foreign countries hinder market access, but also that the requirements of home country regulators are an unfair burden to them vis-à-vis their foreign competitors. At the same time, greater public awareness and concern over matters such as environmental, health, and safety protection have raised the cost implications of regulatory

---

[1] See e.g. Krugman (1994) and the subsequent debate in *Foreign Affairs*.

requirements, sometimes astronomically. As the competitiveness of commodities has come to depend less on simple functionality and much more on cultural attributes, the mediation of control over such attributes through intellectual property rights has become more sharply contested. Finally, the divestment of state ownership through privatization has made it possible to revise the regulatory frameworks within which utilities and other firms operate.

Global competition can both challenge regulation and cause its withdrawal or alteration, or lead to the creation of new regulatory régimes. Struggles to open up markets entail extended processes of economic diplomacy focusing on regulatory requirements and enforcement. Economies based on well-established and relatively stringent regulatory systems are forced to re-evaluate or relax their requirements in response to threatened loss of business. But they also can pressure or attempt to persuade foreign regulators to adopt similar levels or modes of regulation. Regulators have also reacted to the threat that global mobility poses, and especially to highly publicised regulatory failures, by developing new modes of international coordination. Business firms themselves, co-operatively and through groupings and associations, can act to ensure international coordination and enforcement of regulation in their interest, with the support of professional brokers of norms, the lawyers and accountants. Finally, cities, regions, or countries wishing to attract investment offer a diversity of tailor-made features going far beyond the fiscal laxity of earlier 'offshore' havens. To be sure, low taxes, free movement of money, and a good location can still attract brass plates and some types of financial business. However, to induce investments in a wider range of activity and especially those offering jobs, public authorities must also provide more general 'infrastructure', particularly labour which is low-cost, high-skilled, or both—for example in attracting financial services firms to Dublin, or computer software subcontracting to India or Russia—or a high 'quality of life', offered by aspirant 'world cities' such as Barcelona or Toronto.

Three primary and interrelated concerns can be identified in debates about global regulation. First comes the question of how institutions emerge and evolve in mediating the dynamic of the global marketplace. Secondly, there is a functional policy concern—the problem of the appropriate level for public governance of economic activities. This has long been a question within federal systems, and is now posed at the international level. Thirdly, there is a problem of a democratic deficit. This stems from a perception that internationalized economic activities are no longer subject to control or facilitation by national governments acting alone, while international structures are institutionally underdeveloped.

Not surprisingly, there is also a form of competition among the paradigms which, with varying degrees of intensity and emphasis, address these concerns. The different paradigms or theories may, for our purposes, be grouped around two broad perspectives, that of markets and that of social structures. The market perspective follows from microeconomic thinking and is committed to the idea that distributed decision-making and spontaneous order enhance economic welfare. It considers that the dynamic of governance institutions may be explained in terms of the behaviour of rational economic actors and, by analogy to the activities of individuals transacting in markets, often concludes that optimal regulation is most likely to result from competition between institutional orders. In contrast, the social structures perspective emphasizes that social relations are historically and logically prior and that economic exchanges are always embedded in social relations and structured by normative expectations. Hence, 'markets' consist of the competitive strategies and practices of social groups and actors, which may be dysfunctional or at best disruptive, and change in both markets and governance institutions must be explained by the persistence and evolution of social norms and institutions. The two perspectives thus imply contrasting notions of regulatory competition. But both share an interest in emergence, endurance, and change among institutions, and each has a good deal to say about what regulatory action should occur, and by what means.

The chapters in this volume draw on both paradigms in discussing the connection between competition and regulation. Some emphatically follow from one or the other perspective, while others select ideas from both. Legal practices are a focal point for all, and commonalities emerge despite paradigmatic differences—market models adjust to institutional frameworks, and institutional explanations encompass competitive behaviour and outcomes. The chapters address all three of the main issues bound up in globalization debates. Some focus on the description and explanation of institutional settings in which competition influences results traditionally thought to lie in the discretion of sovereign regulators. Others consider economic and political theories that bear on the choice of regulatory strategies among multiple sovereigns. Still others concentrate on the ideas and institutions that confront or resolve tensions between the promise of enhanced economic welfare held out by a competitive global economy and the demands for social welfare registered within the democratic processes of nation states.

The collection makes what amounts to a substantive assertion: Globalization is not a leap into an economic cyberspace that renders obsolete existing frameworks for understanding the influence of markets on regulation and of regulation on markets. Factors that render intelligible the regulatory implications of global product competition can be identified in local, state, national, and international institutions and regulations, and in the mediative activities of the lawyers and other intermediaries. Indeed, much learning of immediate pertinence to the three leading concerns in debates about the global economy—institutional, functional, and political—has developed in discussions of subject matter within the United States of America federal system and the European Union's régime of harmonization. This volume, accordingly, makes an entry onto the global blank slate by juxtaposing chapters that discuss economic activity in global venues removed from strong sovereign controls (in part 1) and new sovereign controls designed to promote such economic activity (in part 4), with chapters on USA and EU topics that bear analytically on those discussions (in parts 2 and 3). The chapters in part 2 present a case study of the deployment of the market model of regulatory competition within the USA federal system. The chapters in part 3 address tensions between competition and coordination in the EU, which continues to occupy a central position as a catalyst and a precursor of global institutional developments.

More particularly, the chapters in part 1 bring the social structures perspective to global economic activity beyond the apparent reach of nation states. They teach us that, contrary to the popular view situating these economic relationships in a regulatory void, they are in fact embedded in regulatory institutions. To identify these institutions, the authors look to the technologically sophisticated lawyers who operate at the boundary between the state and the market. These actors sell services which are irretrievably connected to the operations of formal state régimes, but at the same time exploit their measure of independence to shift economic activity between alternative forms and locations to suit the interests of their clients and themselves. Global regulation, thus constituted, is less a denationalized phenomenon than a practice of competitive interaction among national legal systems. These regulatory intermediaries are not, however, at liberty to carry on their arbitrage operations without concern for consequences within national regulatory régimes. Responsive coordination between national régimes can occur, implemented by transnational networks of regulatory technicians, but influenced by nationally-based interest group conflicts.

Business lawyers and managers and arbitrage activities against a background of interest group conflict remain the focus of the chapters in part 2. But the venue changes from the transnational business deal to the corporate codes of the American states and the paradigmatic perspective shifts to the market side. These chapters follow an approach derived from a formal model of regulatory competition first developed in public sector economics (Tiebout 1956) and now widely applied in American federalism discussions. The model predicts, first, that given free mobility of individuals and factors of production, regulators in search of taxpayers will be forced into competition respecting the terms of regulation; and secondly, that regulation thus produced will enhance economic welfare because competitive conditions diminish interest group influence and foster innovation. USA corporate law, long produced in competitive conditions well-suited to application of this model, serves here as the laboratory for its evaluation. The chapters show, first, that a very precise set of juridical conditions permitted USA corporate law to evolve to provide a working example of the model's predictions, conditions not quite met in the closely analogous case of Canada, and largely absent in the EU. Secondly, institutional dynamics figure importantly in accounts of lawmaking in this context. Here, cutting-edge scholarship works towards a description of the precise alignment of the economic incentives of the lawmakers, professional intermediaries, and corporate managers who participate in this competitive lawmaking, and then seeks to determine the impact of that behaviour on the quality of the law produced. Thirdly, this causal connection between competitive behaviour and corporate lawmaking, once established, leads to a vigorous normative debate. Two such challenges are included here. One takes a public choice perspective and argues for central government intervention to cure perverse effects of interest group capture embedded in the structure of this regulatory market. The other looks to the economic theory of product innovation to suggest that a pure model of competition does not provide the best basis for designing the juridical structure within which states compete for legal business.

In part 3 the venue shifts from the USA, where the allocation of authority between states and federation is relatively settled, to the EU, where the exercise of describing the prevailing allocation of authority to its fledgling central institutions can prompt heated debate. In this more fluid structural environment, a process of conflict and accommodation between co-ordinative and competitive approaches to economic integration has figured prominently in the evolution of regulatory institutions and policies. Interestingly, the necessity of such a process probably would be conceded even by those who bring the strictest of market perspectives to problems of governmental organization. In their model, regulatory competition with wealth enhancing effects must rest on a structure of vigorous central controls on member states—whether in a federal system or in an international organization—so that borders are opened for the free movement of goods, services, factors of production, and individuals. The experience of the EU shows that defining the extent of those controls entails a process of selection from a range of alternatives—from a negative removal of barriers that leaves multiple regulatory régimes substantially in place, ranging through to thorough-going regulatory harmonization following from the notion that full mobility requires a level regulatory playing field. The EC pursued the latter alternative, but its program of harmonization through exhaustively detailed directives proved politically and technically problematic. Now the EU follows an intermediate path, pursuing the elimination of barriers to trade with a range of principles and policy instruments—subsidiarity, mutual recognition of national standards, harmonizing directives, and self-regulation—which contemplate continued vesting of significant economic regulatory authority at the national level. Within this redirected framework, the harmonization project continues to confront the problem of subject matter definition, including the difficult question of social regulation that bears directly on economic activity. These problems are compounded in an institutional framework that vests enforcement powers at the national level.

Regulatory competition thus very much remains an active element within the framework of EU harmonization. As in the contexts treated in parts 1 and 2 of this volume, it here presents a phenomenon that calls for description and appraisal. But in this complicated and fluid regulatory environment, it also has emerged as a policy prescription impacting on decisionmaking about the future structure and authority of central institutions. Accordingly, interest group and democratic politics—a background influence on the business actors and regulators in part 1 and a problem for technical solution in part 2—become a more prominent concern. The nature of the interrelationship between competition and coordination also takes on a distinctive character in the EU. Here, as institutional actors continue to work out the subject matter parameters and mode of execution of their harmonization project, competition and coordination can lose the appearance of starkly opposed meta-strategies and reemerge as functional policy alternatives jointly available for the treatment of particular regulatory problems.

The chapters in part 4 return to the global arena to consider the impact of new institutions of international trade regulation, the North American Free Trade Association (NAFTA) and the World Trade Organization (WTO). As in part 3, the institutional and technical problems presented by economic integration across national lines are addressed. But the discussion's primary emphasis changes along with the venue: Here the democratic deficit left by competitive regulation becomes the focal point. Although NAFTA and the WTO are distinguished by weak central institutions that hold out dialogic processes instead of weapons at the enforcement level, they nevertheless threaten the integrity of national regulatory and social settlements. This partly results from regulatory standards that they apply to their member states, and partly from the possibility that they will accomplish their intended purpose of facilitating enhanced international product competition. The resulting loss in national regulatory capability extends beyond the subject matter covered by the régimes themselves, such as tariffs and product standards, and spills over to social matters such as labour protection and environmental regulation. The chapters, sceptical of the benefits held out by global trade liberalization, make a number of strategic points in response. The first debunks the notion that economic integration enhances welfare, along with the suggested palliative of an international régime of social protection. The second takes up the problem of protecting the interests of labour and the integrity of existing labour protection regulations, and revives a point developed in part I—that national regulations overlap when applied to international transactions, and coordination takes a number of forms which also encompass competition. The final chapter returns to the market model of regulatory competition developed in part 2, and develops a two-sided critique. The first side, based on game theoretic analysis, deploys rational expectations methodology independent of market ideology; the second side points out that preferences for the market or the social structures perspective tend to be value-based.

The sections that follow contextualize and introduce the individual chapters in more detail.

I. GLOBAL (RE)VISIONS

Competition between market and social structures paradigms in discussions of economic regulation stems in part from competition between different academic disciplines with their own epistemological perspectives and professional practices. However, these disciplines in turn have been moulded by the social and institutional histories within which they originated and developed. There is therefore an intriguing interaction between theory and practice in these paradigmatic disputes, and a parallel between the competition between theories on the one hand and the practices on the other. Competition between different professional groups within agencies can follow a similar pattern. Policy shifts within agencies and inter-agency realignments result not only from top-down political decisions, but to a great extent from internal cultural and ideological changes, and the emergence and ascendancy of new professional perspectives and discourses (Eisner 1991). Of course the indeterminate, tentative, and contingent nature of scientific discourses allows for the emergence of new paradigms as a function of the search for truth (or efficiency). But these developments also are bound up in broader strategic rivalries among the learned communities which govern the reputational evaluation processes within and between these discourses.

Similar processes can also be identified as taking place on a global scale. International regulatory competition also has an important dimension of competition between paradigms and philosophies of regulation (Albert 1992). It is possible to take this perspective further, as does Yves Dezalay in chapter 2 of this volume, by conceptualizing this as a competitive process involving strategic behaviour between different groups of players. Dezalay begins by emphasizing that regulatory competition is not just between rules, but involves a much broader complex of social institutions and practices, embedded in cultural forms and underpinned by symbolic discourses. His chapter contrasts the legalism of the North American model of regulation with the state-centric approach more typical in Europe (focusing on France), and traces their cultural roots and the social and class strategies through which each was constructed. Further, the creation of a competition between these regulatory modes has also been a process of construction, in which neo-liberal ideologies have helped to destabilize the interventionist welfare-state structures. Dezalay argues that this has taken place through a process of reconstitution of the internal power relationships of professional classes, in which a rising business bourgeoisie has claimed a new privileged position by investing in a new type of professional expertise. This new expertise is characterized as cosmopolitan, in the sense that it is not wedded to state intervention, and its advocates do not derive their position and influence from controlling the distribution of benefits to achieve social consensus amongst conflicting groups or classes.

Dezalay focuses on lawyers, whose 'ambiguous position, poised between the public and the private, permits the mobilization of state or political resources, while claiming complete independence from the state'. This same ambiguous position also enables lawyers to operate trans-nationally, making use of their national legal capital and contact networks to facilitate transnational interpenetration. However, Dezalay goes further and suggests that their opportunism and double-dealing capacity also makes them instrumental in 'the construction of quasi-state arrangements to ensure the regulation of a market economy encircling the planet'. It is important to consider closely what is being argued here. First, it is the investment by lawyers in the appropriate skills and technologies which helps to construct a workable and attractive regulatory régime. Working on the boundaries between the state and the market, they can both contribute to the formalization of regulation in the state, while exploiting their apparent independence to keep open the possibilities of an opportunistic shift to alternative forms or locations. This dynamic offers a prospect of escape from arrangements which can be denigrated as ossified, in turn creating competitive pressures on the original regulatory forms. On the other hand, their relationship to the private sphere cannot be merely one of self-interest, since their credibility obliges them to invest in the elaboration of symbols incarnating universal values and to act as 'merchants of virtue'. Thus, within the private sphere they help to construct the public, supplying the normative glue which helps to structure economic activity.

The intriguing question opened up by Dezalay is whether these new professional practices can be denationalized, so as to build new forms of global governance independent of or transcending the traditional international state system. In his view, it is of the essence of the emerging new arrangements for global governance that they consist of competing and overlapping competences, both decentralized and delocalized. Taking as his example the construction of international commercial arbitration as a system of 'offshore justice', he shows that it is built on the basis of competitive rivalry between local arbitration centres, each offering special facilities or expertise in order to attract market share. However, Dezalay argues that the market for arbitration is relatively small, fragile, and far from competitive, and its practices bind the competitors closely together as a sort of private club. Although each locality may use the need to compete internationally as an argument towards its own state for greater autonomy and deregulation, international commercial arbitration forms a small world consisting of interpenetrating networks clustered around the diverse, nationally-based centres. Thus, 'the "international" is constructed largely from competition among national approaches' (Dezalay and Garth 1995: 61).

A slightly different approach to this question is taken by Sol Picciotto, in chapter 3, who looks more closely at the nature of the international arrangements for coordinating national jurisdiction, as they have developed historically, and at the tensions and contradictions (both national and international) that have led to the recent processes of transformation. He argues that the traditional inter-state arrangements for international coordination of national regulatory arrangements involved considerable overlapping and potential conflicts between the scope or jurisdiction of different regulatory bodies, and this interaction both relied on and facilitated the development of 'transnational' regulatory practices. These depended on exploiting the interaction between different national regulatory systems, as well as seeking out and developing convenient jurisdictional locations, to minimize the impact of regulation on international business activities. Pioneered by or for transnational corporations (TNCs), it was the generalization of these practices, the shift from ad hoc tailor-made arrangements to the routinized practices of regulatory arbitrage, that greatly contributed to the crisis of the international arrangements for coordination, often triggered by symbolic dramas highlighting regulatory failure, for example bank collapses such as BCCI and Barings, or 'insider dealing' scandals.

Focusing on the changing nature of international arrangements for coordination of regulation, Picciotto uses the concept of 'networks' to describe the growth of loosely coordinated and semi-legitimized international regulatory communities of specialists. However, Picciotto points out that competition and coordination between regulators are not opposed, but exist in a symbiotic relationship: the construction of new international co-operative arrangements results from battles between nationally-based interest groups and alliances, and once constructed they provide new arenas for competitive struggles. Although in some fields of regulation globally-agreed criteria or principles have gradually been devised (such as transfer-pricing rules for taxation, or capital-adequacy rules for banks), their inherent indeterminacy and the reliance on decentralized enforcement through national authorities leaves considerable scope for diversity. Picciotto's account suggests that the traditional forms of international coordination relying on inter-state diplomacy have been replaced by a far denser and more diverse system, in which new breeds of professionals and managers engage in a novel type of transnational regulatory diplomacy.

Thus, although it seems clear that there have been significant changes to the arrangements for international regulatory co-operation or coordination, these are not an alternative to but result from regulatory competition, and seem to take their character from the competitive and diverse nature of the regulatory landscape. Indeed, the very meaning of regulation and its origins in specific social practices should be seen in the mediation of market relations by normative practices generated by professionals, who themselves are engaged in competition, although one of a particular kind, which consists in generating the universals and symbols which help to structure markets and provide social consensus. These practices helped to construct the institutions, grouped around the different nation-states, which are now being re-envisioned and restructured, once again in a process of competition as much as coordination. It is therefore important to trace the origins of regulation within these national systems.

2. REGULATORY COMPETITION: LESSONS FROM THE USA FEDERAL SYSTEM

American federalism seeks to preserve political decentralization and social diversity and to encourage citizen participation in public life, and simultaneously to allow national solutions to national problems and to deter localized oppression (Stewart 1985). The cluster of federalism values serves as a mediative focal point in American politics—participants in regulatory debates invoke them routinely. They are historically rooted. But they also have a dynamic aspect, taking on different political colorations and synchronizing with different economic agendas from period to period. Regulatory competition has an established, albeit controversial, place among these federalism values. It came to American politics and jurisprudence from a theory developed in public sector economics in the early post-war period (Tiebout 1956), and now bears importantly on discussions of diverse subject matter, including local government authority (Briffault 1990), social welfare legislation (Stewart 1985), bankruptcy (Skeel 1994), products liability (McConnell 1988), environmental law (Revesz 1993), antitrust (Easterbrook 1983), and banking and securities regulation (Butler and Macey 1988; Coffee 1995). In its most successful application, the theory has explained and justified the state-based system of USA corporate law, a jurisprudence unique for its century-long susceptibility to competitive forces.

Regulatory competition theory also lends itself to deployment beyond the borders of the USA. Its basis in an abstract rational expectations model makes it prima facie applicable in any political context that poses a choice between central (or coordinated) regulatory authority and junior (or unco-ordinated) authority—local/national, state/federal, member state/EU, or national/international. These applications cover a variety of political and institutional settings. All nonetheless draw on a set of assertions developed in public sector economics and first applied in American contexts. The theory's deployment along parallel lines both inside and outside of the USA implies that lessons learned from USA applications may have relevance for international applications, despite differences of political and institutional context. There results an exercise in comparative law and economics in which the institutional and structural inquiries of traditional comparative law proceed together with inquiries into the feasibility of applying the universalized descriptions and predictions of economic theory in practice contexts.

The second part of this volume undertakes such a comparative exercise. Its chapters either address, draw on, or have normative implications for the competitive state-based system of USA corporate law. Taken together they enhance the basis for cross-reference between USA and international discussions of regulatory competition. Two contrasting themes emerge. Under one line of thinking, the USA corporate law system presents a productive model that usefully might be emulated abroad. Under the other line of thinking, significant sticking points show up in the application of regulatory competition theory to the USA corporate law system upon extended consideration of its economic and political attributes. This signals greater complexity for international applications.

The subsections that follow discuss, first, the theory's basic tenets and their place in American federalism debates, and, secondly, USA corporate law's special role as a laboratory for testing the theory's robustness.

2.1 Regulatory Competition and Political Theory

Regulatory competition theory came into circulation at the same time as a broader public choice critique of the interventionist theories of economic regulation that came to the fore in the USA in the immediate post-war period. The interventionist theories emphasized the government's role as a benevolent maximizer of social welfare both in the provision of traditional public goods and as an economic regulator (Laffont and Tirole 1993: 476). Their adherents tended to look to centralization as best means to the end of realizing the public interest, particularly in the case of market failures—which they deemed likely to occur. In their view, democratic processes were adequate to the task of checking any tendency on the part of the central government to expand to excess. They assumed that the process of competition among interest groups seeking to influence regulation would assure that regulatory results reflected citizen preferences.

Social choice and public choice theories of government countered this perspective. Social choice theory (Arrow 1951) asserted that regulation does not embody a 'public interest' in the sense of an aggregation of the preferences of the electorate. It posited that the public interest does not emerge in political practice because voting paradoxes prevent the emergence of a preference ordering for public goods, and predicted that no technical adjustment of democratic processes could solve the problem. Samuelson (1954) added that actors were likely to misrepresent their preferences in the discourse of democracy. The free rider problem that comes up in the arena of collective political action makes it rational for an actor to misstate the level of his or her demand for public goods.

Public choice theory went on to draw on these points in accounting for the substantive content of regulation as a reflection of multifarious private interests. The theory asserts that actors rationally employ the government and form groups to influence it. Lawmaking in turn follows the demand patterns of these interest groups as risk averse lawmakers respond to the dominant voices (Olson 1965). Deadweight social losses result. Furthermore, government actors, particularly central government actors, tend to assume a monopolist's position respecting the provision of public goods and try to maximize governmental revenues (Brennan and Buchanan 1980: 17–24). Given the uncertainties of majority rule cycling, the rational ignorance of voters, and confusion amongst politicians (ibid; Mueller 1990: 268), political controls will not be equal to the task of containing government growth. Thus, the provision of public goods will reflect not the utility level of the average taxpayer, but that of the expanding state.

Public choice theory, having thus diagnosed regulatory capture and unchecked central government growth as principal ailments of the USA federal system, looked in part [2] to the devolution of regulatory authority to junior levels of government for a cure. Reducing the size of the regulating unit narrows the variance in the distribution of preferences and reduces the likelihood that preferences will be bundled. Regulation, thus adapted to local conditions, is more likely to approach the ideal of consonance with citizen preferences. At the same time, decentralization increases the chance that a diverse range of preferences will come to be manifested in regulation promulgated by one or another jurisdiction. The localized experimentation thus fostered (Romano 1993: 4–5), makes it possible for a range of regulatory strategies to appear, while simultaneously limiting the negative impact of unsuccessful experiments. Finally, decentralization reduces the scope of

---

[2] Another line of public choice theory looks to the redesign of central government institutions (Weingast 1995; Weingast 1993; Macey 1992).

the central government monopoly and ameliorates the negative effects of regulatory capture. Capture[3] leads to bigger deadweight costs when authority is exercised at higher levels of government. Local authorities have less capacity to damage the economy: they cannot impose tariffs and quotas on imports; their licensing arrangements have a limited reach; their limited resources limit subsidies. Incentives to interest groups, accordingly, decrease as authority vests in junior levels (Easterbrook 1994: 127).

This localist programme faced one remaining problem. Junior units of government are as vulnerable to distortive influence activities as senior units, albeit on a smaller scale. The first model of regulatory competition (Tiebout 1956) offered a theoretical cure for the junior-level capture problem. Tiebout modelled citizen-voter tastes for local public goods in the hypothetical context of a city resident contemplating a move to the suburbs and choosing among a number of towns. The model makes three assertions. First, locational decisions will reveal individual preferences for public goods and levels of taxation: Rational forward-looking individuals, after surveying the range of available choices, will act in accordance with their preferences for location-specific bundles of public goods. Second, a local public goods equilibrium can be established if, like producers of private goods and services, local government units compete with their public goods offerings to attract in-migration. Third, the promotion of competition between local governments should lead to an optimal balance between the level of taxation and the provision of public goods.

This technical exercise had a stunning theoretical implication—its market-driven lawmaking equilibrium solves the problems of preference aggregation identified by Arrow and Samuelson. But, taken on its own terms, the model had policy implications for only a limited class of regulatory subject matter. It addressed the production of public goods in the narrow definition—actual goods and services produced by government for which citizens willingly pay rents, such as national defence, police protection, fire protection, education, roads, and sewers. Under this narrow definition, the model bears mostly on discussions of the powers and policies of local authorities. But an expansion of the concept of public goods gave the model policy implications as striking as its theoretical implications. In the expansive reading, public goods include government's output of regulation—the public consumes and pays for regulatory outcomes such as contract enforcement, clean air, safe products, and stable labour relations. Government becomes another producer in the overall economy, and law

---

[3] 'Capture' comes in two varieties. In some cases it denotes the public choice point that regulatory regimes are initiated for the purpose of serving the regulatees; in other cases it denotes the institutional phenomenon that occurs when regulatees acquire excess influence over the operations of an agency originally established to advance the public interest (Levine and Forrence 1990: 169 n. 4). The former meaning is intended here.

becomes product. If law is product, then microeconomic theory, formally manifested in the Tiebout model and its progeny, counsels that market transactions are its most accurate allocators. It follows that law should follow from the responses of at-the-margin producers rather than from discourse in a democratic political context. Just as price competition forces producers of private goods to come up with better products at lower prices for the benefit of consumers, so regulatory competition promises to discipline the governments that produce law, forcing them to abandon their capture arrangements and come up with laws that better satisfy the preferences of taxpaying citizens.

Two crucial points in this picture of competitive lawmaking should be underscored. First, the picture holds out two benefits—reduced regulatory capture and increased lawmaking innovation. Secondly, it relies on mobile individuals and factors of production to give to lawmakers an incentive to satisfy citizen preferences. Given mobility of people and factors, the imposition of costly and restrictive interest group legislation in one jurisdiction benefits a neighbouring jurisdiction with a less costly régime. Individuals and factors of production will vote with their feet, migrating to the less costly jurisdiction. They thereby affect lawmakers' incentives, making inefficient wealth transfers to favoured groups less attractive than regulations that enhance the wealth of the larger population (Easterbrook 1994: 126).

This leads to a strong prescription for the structure of government. Regulatory competition only can occur if individuals and factors can choose among distinct governmental units. In most regulatory contexts this means geographically separate units. Regulatory competition theory thus reinforced public choice theory's presumption favoring lawmaking at junior levels. Decentralization expands opportunities for competitive lawmaking by increasing the junior units' subject matter jurisdiction. Contrariwise, removal of subject matter to a central government eliminates competitors and diminishes the chance that regulation will be shaped by actors seeking to attract individuals and factors. In the USA federal system this means that the potential for competition increases with the field of authority allocated to the states. In international contexts, where economic globalization has sharpened competition among nation-states, this means scepticism respecting initiatives for transnational regulatory co-operation or coordination. Competition among governments, like that among firms, can be suppressed through vertical integration or coordination by a central agency—successful exercises in international coordination could reduce or eliminate it (Trachtman 1993: 48–9).

We come at last to regulatory competition theory's bottom line. Assuming the requisite degree of decentralization, the standard Darwinian evolutionary framework of microeconomics applies to support a prediction that competitive conditions force regulators to race to the top. In a dynamic environment, competition assures that only efficient regulation continues in effect (Reich 1992); over time, then, it makes all regulation more efficient.

2.2 USA Corporate Law as a Paradigm Case

The strong assertions just described have been met by a range of objections in USA debates. Those committed to democratic values and sceptical of functional analyses directed to the goal of economic welfare tend to reject applications of regulatory competition theory. In their view, competition causes the content of regulation and the level of public goods and taxation to be dictated by the private preferences of a narrow, arbitrarily identified class of itinerant at-the-margin consumers or investors, instead of following from decisionmaking processes benefitting from the participation of individuals committed to the polity's long-term interests. The competitive race goes not to the top but to the bottom because competition can force the pursuit of policies farther and farther removed from the public interest.[4]

A more receptive, but still critical line of response draws on an extensive body of public sector economics that refines and narrows the Tiebout model. Tiebout's public goods equilibrium rests on a series of heroic assumptions. These include costless mobility, perfect information, optimally sized communities, and an absence of externalities and spillovers. The model has not survived the process of relaxation of these assumptions in robust form. All who discuss its practical application agree, for example, that jurisdictional competition can lead to negative externalities, and that centralized suppression of such competition is justified. The exercise of relaxing the other assumptions leads to similar problems. Regulatory competition presupposes individual and factor mobility, but mobility varies among individuals and factors and among locales. Capital may be more mobile than people, or vice versa, depending on the case; even given mobility, some moves will be more feasible than others. In practice, information asymmetries may impair both the jurisdictional choices of individuals and factors and the competitive responses of units of government. And even given substantial mobility and adequate information, governments can be expected to be more responsive to the preferences of legal consumers when those preferences are homogenous and the context permits separate adoption of specific regulatory package. Finally, horizontal vesting of regulatory authority across jurisdictions does not by itself assure that regulatory actors operate in an incentive structure comparable to that of a market entrepreneur. Accordingly, competition for factors of production may not determine

---

[4] This counterstory can be told in rational expectations terms by placing the competing jurisdictions in a prisoners' dilemma framework (e.g., Stewart 1977). The prisoner's dilemma story has been sharply controverted in recent years. (Revesz 1993; Stewart 1993). Brian Langille offers a response in ch. 16.

the content of regulation even given transparency, mobility, and unbundled products. Even where the regulator's dominant motivation is entrepreneurial, capture can destroy the nexus between the regulation's content and the preferences of its consumers.

These limitations turn applications of the model to core USA subject matter such as local government (Sterk 1992; Been 1991), product safety (Rice 1985), and social welfare (Stewart 1985) into painstaking cost-benefit inquiries. But the model nevertheless exerts considerable influence on the prevailing disposition of USA federalism values—many credit it as a source for a general presumption favouring decentralization (Revesz 1993; cf. Weingast 1995: 3–4).

USA corporate law is a subject matter uniquely well-suited to the evaluation of this presumption, because it is a rare jurisprudence which manifestly has been shaped by competitive forces for an extended period. Of course, competitive forces actively shape many regulatory régimes, within the USA, the EU, and internationally. But these cases can be subdivided into two broad categories, with structural impediments to competition bearing more or less strongly depending on the category. In the first category, conflict of laws rules allow firms or individuals to select among a number of jurisdictions for the situs of a legal relationship, and the jurisdictions compete for their business. In the second category, public or private product competition across jurisdictional lines prompts competitive lawmaking by governments either pursuing new residents or factors of production or attempting to confer competitive advantages on existing factors. With the first category it is relatively easy to show that limited mobility, information asymmetries, product bundling, and government incentives present no insurmountable barriers to the realization of competition; with the second category no such presumption obtains and any showing will be situation specific. USA corporate chartering falls into the the first category, along with family law (as Brown's contribution in chapter 9 shows), and such phenomena as offshore tax havens and international ship registration.

American corporations may choose their state of incorporation without regard to the location of the firm's physical assets—the commerce clause of the federal constitution was interpreted to assure this result. At least as to larger firms, conditions for competitive lawmaking clearly obtain. Mobility, which is effectuated through reincorporation to another state, is not costless, but is relatively cheap for larger firms; large law firms effectively serve as information intermediaries; the legal product offered is unbundled because incorporation triggers only the application of the chartering states' corporate law; and an incentive to compete can be identified on the supply side, at least in the case of Delaware, the market leader. Delaware has been competing actively for chartering business for a century, along with a handful of less successful states. It offers reincorporating firms an attractive code and ancillary services in exchange for franchise tax revenues. Other states over time tend to bring their codes into line with that of the market leader.

A long-established division between federal and state regulatory functions has let this competitive process go forward without substantial interference from the central government. State competition began in the 1890s, when New Jersey, followed by Delaware (Grandy 1993: 43–45), enacted codes designed to appeal to the interests of the then new mass-producing corporations. Although some observers took a dim view of this management-friendly legal régime,[5] its effects were not generally deemed to be incompatible with the national economic policy pursued under antitrust and other federal régimes. But the climate became less favourable when ownership and trading of corporate securities became widespread beginning in the 1920s. A new centralization initiative occurred with the enactment of the federal securities laws in the 1930s. Even this, however, was structured so as to leave the state authority over internal corporate matters largely unimpaired (Bratton 1989: 1493).

Federal regulation of the securities markets coincided with a renewed debate over management legitimacy. This debate had negative implications for the competitive state system and its management customers. Berle and Means (1932) constructed an influential, politicized picture of the large corporation. They identified management as a powerful group, and showed that its power stemmed from a juridical model of corporate structure grounded in state law. The traditional state law model of corporate ownership and structure, when combined with the new development of widespread and passive security holding, had left management in an unintended position of strategic dominance and accountable to no one. Cary (1974) brought this Berle and Means perspective to bear on a study of Delaware's regulatory product and concluded that the race had indeed gone 'to the bottom.' To Cary, corporate law implicated the public interest; therefore, revenue maximization was an inappropriate motive for the state taking the leading role in its creation. He suggested federal preemption as a remedy.

Regulatory competition theory stood ready to provide the basis for a counterstory. Winter (1977) drew on it to assert that state charter competition had resulted in a 'race to the top.' Under this view, the chartering system is a market in which firms purchase corporate status and corporate codes in exchange for franchise tax payments. Reincorporating firms are the market's marginal consumers, with the firms presently incorporated in each state holding out a constant threat of departure through reincorporation. The result is a constraint on the ability of any state to impose inefficient

---

[5] Brandeis identified a 'race to the bottom' problem in a famous dissenting opinion in *Liggett* v. *Lee* (1932). In Brandeis's phrase, 'The race was one not of diligence but of laxity' (ibid. 559).

regulations and a system that efficiently matches the preferences of corporate consumers with the terms of regulation.

This 'race to the top' view strongly influences USA discussions of corporate regulation. Charter competition now is generally recognized to have desirable results. But significant negative effects on shareholder value also are acknowledged. During the 1980s the states raced to accommodate the management interest with antitakeover legislation, impairing the operation of the principal market check on the agency costs of corporate organization. Delaware, historically the leading jurisdiction respecting management-protective innovations, took an uncharacteristic follower's role with these and related innovations. These two developments—the system's ready provision of interest group legislation detrimental to the interests of equity investors and Delaware's position as a follower respecting these legislative innovations—present key problems for current discussions. The solutions eventually articulated will have important implications for regulatory competition theory as a whole. Here is a competitive lawmaking régime little impaired by problems of limited mobility, asymmetric information, bundling, and a lack of entrepreneurial incentive. Yet even the régime's proponents agree that it has not fulfilled the theory's promise of lawmaking free from undue influence. In addition, no consensus has emerged on a precise description of the incentive structure that determines regulatory outcomes within the system. Until that consensus emerges, debate will continue on the question whether the system makes good on the theory's promise of regulatory innovation directed to the preferences of the actors with interests at stake.

The chapters in this part of the volume bring a range of perspectives to bear on these issues. They also raise questions concerning the implications of the USA model for corporate law in the EU. The final chapter suggests a politically controversial extension of the corporate law model within the USA federal system—to family law so as to realign the incentives of the American states and effect an extension the juridical status of marriage to same-sex couples.

2.3 Charter Competition and Productivity

A. Charter Competition as Relational Contracting

Roberta Romano, the leading authority on USA charter competition, begins chapter 4 with a summary of her account of the system and the leading position of Delaware. She describes a relational contract between Delaware and its corporate customers, grounded in its credible commitment to put the corporations' interests first and refrain from exploiting their sunk investments in Delaware incorporation. A special rent incentive imports this credibility. Delaware's small population, when coupled with its success as a corporate legal centre, has caused franchise tax revenues to amount to a substantial proportion of its tax receipts—a result which would not obtain in a larger state or at the federal level. Delaware bonds this commitment with special process rules that insulate its corporate law from transient domestic political interference. In exchange for its customers' fees, Delaware offers special judicial and administrative expertise. Its legal product, along with the incentives that generate it, creates a store of reputational and human capital that would be difficult to replicate in a potential competing state. This capital, then, helps Delaware to preserve its lead.

Romano also is the system's leading defender against proponents of federal intervention. In a pathbreaking empirical study (Romano 1985), she showed that relocation to Delaware does not decrease the value of reincorporating firms. In this volume she restates this position, pointing out that her earlier study demonstrated that reincorporating firms look to product innovation when selecting a new domicile. Regulation at a higher level of government, she argues, is unlikely to create incentives to support investment in the research and development necessary for the continued servicing of the expertise developed in Delaware. But Romano also acknowledges that the state system can lead to suboptimal results, as occurred when most states adopted management-protective takeover legislation during the 1980s.

In chapter 5, William Carney builds on Romano's model and her supporting empirical studies by providing an empirically-based description of the pattern of lawmaking innovation in the remaining 49 states. He first addresses a question concerning the very existence of incentives to innovate in the other 49. The distribution of chartering business—with half of large firm incorporations in Delaware and the rest widely dispersed—makes it difficult to account for the appearance of innovation in the corporate codes of the other 49 states in classic public choice terms. Since these legislatures are not seeking to go into active competition, there is no apparent payoff for investments in corporate law reform. Yet these legislatures do take the time to keep their codes current. Carney looks to interest group influence for an explanation. He identifies lawyers and management as the two groups having incentives and resources sufficient to justify investment in local corporate law reform. Lawyers outside of Delaware, like the Delaware bar, have a financial incentive to provide flexible and modern legislation for locally incorporated clients. But, unlike Delaware lawyers, these lawyers do not compete for new incorporations in the national market. Their incentive, accordingly, will not support investment in cutting edge innovation on an ongoing basis. A pattern of statutory obsolescence results, with the local bar rousing itself to sponsor updated legislation only if local firms begin to defect by reincorporating in Delaware.

Carney also shows how local lawyers mitigate their incentive problems through their collective action institutions, the bar associations. His empir-

ical survey shows that statutory innovations lacking any obvious rent implications for either local lawyers or corporate managers have diffused widely
among the states in recent years. Here the states draw on the Revised Model
Business Corporation Act, a model statute drafted by an elite committee of
the American Bar Association. In effect, local bar groups surmount the collective action problem presented by investment in an updated code by free
riding on a document produced by the national organization, in much the
same way that individual lawyers rely on the efforts of the local bar association. The model statute facilitates ongoing servicing of local clients with a
minimal investment in research and development. Carney concludes with a
complex explanation of the incentives of both the lawyers responsible for
the model act and the lawyers who invest in its local implementation. The
leading role at both levels is taken by lawyers from the large law firms. This
implies a rent incentive: High profile law reform work directed to the satisfaction of their corporate clients' general interests enhances their reputations. But this payoff is indirect and these enterprises require a substantial
investment of human capital. This disparity leads Carney to take step outside the public choice framework to cite altruism as an additional motivation.[6]

B. Comparisons with Canada and Europe

Romano's chapter goes on to a comparative analysis of the régimes of
Canada and the EU. Here she uses her model to explain the absence of
American-style charter competition. In her Canadian discussion she considers the proposition that the diffusion among the provinces of the reform
provisions of the Canada Business Corporations Act after its 1975 enactment can be explained as a form of charter competition (Daniels 1991).
Romano, bringing components of her American model to bear, tends
towards the view that the federal innovations should be treated either as a
random event or a function of bureaucratic preferences (MacIntosh 1993).
She questions whether the Canadian national government has significant
incentives to compete for charters. At the provincial level, competitive
incentives are dampened by an uncongenial structure of authority sharing
arrangements among the provinces and between the provinces and the fed-

---

[6] In Carney's picture, management serves as a powerful prime mover in the innovation
process, but on a selective basis. His data on the rate of diffusion of statutory innovations show
that those bearing most immediately on management interests—limitations on potentially onerous sources of liability and antitakeover legislation—spread the fastest. Carney joins most
observers in characterizing the latter statutes as suboptimal interest group legislation. But, contrary to the views of some observers, for instance Bebchuk (1992) and Bratton and McCahery,
chapter 7 in this volume, Carney does not conclude that the development has negative implications for the system as a whole. In his view, the system is fundamentally sound because it works
well in the large areas of alignment between shareholder and management interests and remains
subject to market pressures exerted by shareholders when it privileges the management interest.

eral government. Finally, the ownership of larger Canadian firms tends to be concentrated, and controlling shareholders who have the voting power to opt out of default rules and have less incentive to pay a premium for a responsive régime.

In Europe, the fact for explanation is the virtual absence of any law-making behavior that even arguably resembles American charter competition. Romano sets out an accumulation of legal and institutional barriers. First, reincorporation costs in Europe make corporations immobile. Since European choice of law rules apply the law of the corporation's real rather than nominal domicile, changing domiciles entails new capital investment and the costs of transferring human capital. Also, European reincorporations trigger taxes on hidden reserves. Second, European patterns of corporate regulation and equity capitalization do not open up market opportunities for a revenue-seeking jurisdiction. European systems have not allowed for much shareholder litigation, and some restrict shareholder voting rights. This dampens demand for responsive lawmaking along American lines. Scant demand also results from the fact that the percentage of corporate capital embodied in publicly traded equity remains small. Outside of the UK, capital still tends to be raised privately from banks and equity ownership tends to be concentrated. Third, Europe's normative landscape is more complex. Labour codetermination in Germany and statutory worker participation structures elsewhere create a barrier to a regulatory system directed to the preferences of managers and shareholders.

C. Implications for Productivity

Both Romano and Carney express the view that the USA system holds out productivity advantages over its European counterparts. Romano reveals her preference for the USA system when discussing European codetermination schemes. In her view, worker participation schemes are unlikely to enhance shareholder value, and give rise to incentives that prevent the emergence of active charter competition. Romano takes a similarly negative view of the EC's corporate and securities law harmonization project. Carney sends a similar signal with an empirical investigation directed to two matters that figure in EU debates on the desirability of regulatory competition. It has been argued that the decentralization necessary for competition can lead to costly regulatory diversity; accordingly, harmonization initiatives that promote uniform standards can be cost-beneficial even though they inhibit competition (see Charny 1991). Carney's data support a contrary proposition—that competition in the USA has not in fact led to suboptimal diversity, even as it has facilitated a dynamic process of innovation.

Romano confronts a competing empirical claim. Some have evaluated the two systems against the yardstick of relative productivity growth. These comparisons have a negative implication for the USA system, since the USA figures have been lower during the postwar period. The argument is that corporate governance systems exhibiting the features of concentrated stock ownership (such as those of Germany and Japan) may have had some responsibility for the differential. Romano, however, argues that the USA's lower productivity performance does not imply superiority for the corporate governance systems of its competitors. Some of the disparity can be accounted for in terms of the inevitable catch up by economies which lagged behind that of the USA at the beginning of the period. Indeed, since absolute productivity measures depend upon national savings and investment in human capital and research and development, there exists little empirical evidence linking these factors with the selection of corporate governance rules. Romano closes her case with a reference to the accomplishments of the USA system in reducing agency costs. Despite her preference for the USA system, she concludes by noting that legal and institutional differences between North American and European capitalism make it unlikely that a superior system can be identified.

Is there a yardstick that effectively measures the relative merits of the different systems of corporate organization in advanced capitalist economies? This is an empirical question with significant policy implications. In chapter 6, Henk de Jong argues that such a yardstick now exists, and it is not the 'shareholder value' measure of market equity employed in USA studies. He provides a net value-added study that yields a relative performance measure of European firms under the three leading models of corporate organization, Anglo-Saxon, German, and Latin. De Jong argues that, despite the complexity of the task of measuring the impact of the different structures on firm performance, the value-added criterion offers a cogent methodology. Firms are now required to generate this result in all three régimes and it is possible to divide the net value added to obtain an accurate reflection of the productivity of the corporation.

De Jong's figures on the distribution of net value-added for 1991–1992 strikingly reflect the defining features of the underlying systems of corporate organization: Anglo-Saxon firms pay out a much lower share of net value-added to labour whereas with European firms, particularly German and Italian firms, labour has a relatively high share as compared with capital; French, Benelux, Scandinavian, and Swiss firms are located on a middle ground. De Jong's results on corporate performance are equally striking. The data tend to demonstrate that both the UK and Italy have a significant number of firms which perform below the European standard of productivity. In contrast, Germany, France, Switzerland, and the Benelux countries tend to have a greater number of firms operating at average and medium level productivity. The figures for 1992 confirm the earlier trend and indicate that corporations incorporated in the leading continental states are approximately twice as productive in the high performance range than are Anglo-Saxon corporations.

What conclusions should we draw from these results? De Jong suggests that we can learn something from the differences in productivity by reference to the nationality of the corporation. His review of the main productive sectors demonstrates that, with the some specific exceptions, Anglo-Saxon corporations perform less well than do continental corporations. He contends that the differences in productivity must be explained in terms of the performance of individual companies and is not nullified by the cyclical nature of sectoral production. Nor, looking for an explanation on a company by company basis, can we account for the results by reference to differences of relative management capabilities or to the success of certain business strategies (see generally Kay 1993). De Jong points instead to the different objectives that firms pursue in the different organizational frameworks. The study shows that the Anglo-Saxon corporation is more profitable than its continental counterpart, as it works to satisfy the structural demand for dividend payments. The continental corporation, in contrast, is generally larger than the Anglo-Saxon firm, and tends to invest more in production facilities and pursue maximum output. Furthermore, de Jong suggests that the continental firm enjoys the option of selecting either the profit-maximizing route or sticking with the typical strategy of capturing a high level of market share.

This last point implies that stakeholders use their influence in the decisionmaking processes of continental corporations to close off the option of pursuit of the Anglo-Saxon strategy. This result dovetails with Romano's observation that, due to a thin capital market and limited shareholders' rights, European corporations follow a strategy which is not shareholder value maximizing. But de Jong, with his different measure of firm value and showing of strong firm growth in the European core and decline for Italian and UK based firms, turns the point into a critique of the Anglo Saxon organization. The Anglo-Saxon system achieves greater profitability at the expense of a lower growth rate and net value-added. The continental system, in contrast, permits the pursuit of multiple goals, and a virtuous productivity cycle results.

De Jong's results represent a first entry in what promises to be an extended empirical discussion. Meanwhile, they send a somewhat mixed signal for the USA corporate law model. Charter competition played no role in shaping the organizational attributes of the British firms included in the study. But the results do have implications for the USA system because they bear on a closely-related debate over the agency costs attending different modes of organization. They imply that the deterrent approach to limiting management influence activities bound up in an active market for corporate control will not help to set an appropriate balance between productivity and profitability—institutionalized stakeholder representation works better than shareholder primacy. Ironically, the figures resonate well with recent legislative results of USA charter competition, which limit shareholder primacy on the justification that uninhibited takeovers inhibit long-term investment, and have their strongest negative implications for the academic views of charter competition represented by the other contributions to this volume. But even this point must be qualified. As Bratton and McCahery argue in chapter 7, charter competition consistently effects the results desired by American managers, and vigorous, institutionalized monitoring—whether by equity investors, debt investors, or labour representatives—has no place on that management agenda. In their view, any innovation along these lines would have to result from central government intervention.

2.3 Supply-Side Problems in the Production of USA Corporate Law

As noted above, regulatory competition theory promises diminished regulatory capture and product innovation. Questions about the charter competition system's delivery on the former promise have been asked since Cary (1974) leveled the charge of a race to the bottom. William Bratton and Joseph McCahery ask these questions again in chapter 7 and look to political theory for answers. The system's fulfillment of the promise to promote innovation has been less controversial. But in chapter 8 Ian Ayres draws on the economics of technological change to suggest that the system may be structured to lead to second best outcomes.

A. Regulatory Capture

Regulatory competition theory lost some of its explanatory credibility for corporate law when its proponents were forced to carve out an exception for the management-protective antitakeover legislation of the 1980s. Renewed allegations of regulatory capture followed. Bebchuk (1992) argued that transactions in the charter market are directed only to the preferences of the managers who control reincorporation decisions, and those preferences do not necessarily serve as proxies for the result that maximizes shareholder value. As a remedy, he revived Cary's suggestion of federal fiduciary standards. Bratton and McCahery expand on Bebchuk's analysis, but reach a different conclusion respecting the appropriate remedy.

They note that the conflicting interests of shareholders and managers make reincorporation a form of mobility that does not effect a matching of regulation and consumer preferences. Although firms can exit from unsatisfactory jurisdictions, their shareholders have no power to force them to do so. Most state codes contain mandatory process rules assuring this result. Bratton and McCahery look to capture theories of legislation and administration to explain this arrangement. With reincorporation as the at the margin transaction, process rules that vest that exit decision in management bond the chartering state to continued solicitude to the management interest. Given a state thus bonded, management has no collective action problem when it comes to securing legislation favouring its interests—the state's organized bar performs the job voluntarily. The system at the same time exacerbates the collective action problem of the shareholders. Dispersed in the first place, they have no necessary ties to the chartering state. The bar shares their interests only to the extent that litigable, fee-generating legal rights result, but has no stake in designing a legal system that minimizes agency costs. Meanwhile, a constant threat of federal intervention, a negative development in the eyes of the system's advocates, ameliorates the capture problem. A weak dual demand model results: Delaware, the state with most to lose in the event of federalization, makes gestures in the direction of shareholder protection in order to defuse the threat.

Bratton and McCahery, however, part company with the critics of the system who advocate that the federal government follow through on the threat and impose national fiduciary standards. They argue that this could destroy the principal benefit of the Delaware-based system. With state corporate codes in substantial harmony, Delaware maintains its position by providing a corporate dispute resolution center of extraordinary sophistication. The incentives and rents that support its position as an information repository would dissipate with federalization. They suggest that a dual demand model constituted of shareholder threats rather than federal threats would improve matters and that the federal government intervene to effect this result. Drawing on administrative law models that recommend interest group empowerment as a remedy for agency capture, they recommend federal preemption of process rules that prevent shareholder initiatives to amend corporate charters and effect reincorporation. They look to a new group of players on the American corporate stage—the politicized agents of investment institutions—to provide a class of entrepreneurs who would put such an initiative privilege to use. They project that a grant of standing to these shareholder representatives to set the legislative agenda within corporations would reorder the incentives of state politicians and lawyers, forcing them to listen to the shareholder voice. Corporate law would remain state subject matter, but managers no longer would have unilateral power to set the agenda. Bratton and McCahery argue that competition and the benefits following from it, far from being stifled by this central government mandate, would intensify.

B. Incentives to Innovate

Ian Ayres, in chapter 8, draws on economic theories of market failure to challenge the assertion that competing jurisdictions produce first-best law. Like

Bratton and McCahery, he takes a critical look at the supply side of the state competition framework. But instead of focusing on the distortions of interest group politics, he focuses on distortions that stem from competing states' strategic conduct vis-à-vis one another. His analysis suggests that a perfect competition model may not provide the most useful basis for understanding regulatory competition, and that a less restrictive notion of competition may work better (cf. Vickers 1995: 7). He makes an intriguing series of points. His first model indicates that competition in the charter market may be so free that it results too little innovation, and that legally imposed barriers to entry could improve matters. Then, in a second model, he suggests that the market leader may have a perverse incentive to imitate suboptimal innovations of follower jurisdictions. Finally, in his third model, the market leader propounds its own suboptimal innovations in order to lock in its customers.

Ayres' first model identifies a spillover problem stemming from the fact that legal products, unlike private sector products, are pure public goods. An innovative regulation produced in one jurisdiction, accordingly, can be copied by a rival state, depriving the innovating state of a return on its investment. It follows that states are unlikely to produce at an efficient rate to meet the demands of corporations because they lack the incentive to invest in a steady stream of statutory innovations. To back up this assertion, Ayres looks to the states' recent competitive production of anti-takeover statutes when follower states replicated the leaders' formulations without incurring significant costs.

To ameliorate this free rider problem, Ayres in effect suggests that we take the law as product analogy a step farther and look at law as technology. That step having been taken, we can constrain competition with property rights along lines already established in the private sector. Here he relies on the entry-deterrence framework of industrial organization theory, which contends that the monopoly provided by the rights in a patent gives the monopolist a high-powered incentive to innovate (Katz and Shapiro 1985; Gilbert and Newberry 1982). Under this view,[7] the efficient rate of innovation depends on the probability of a state having the optimal degree of patent protection. It should be noted that Ayres does make some concessions to those who might resist the idea of removing law from the domain of public goods. He admits, for example, that despite free-riding and the risky and contingent nature of the enterprise, some leading states in the

---

[7] The economics of product patents is based on the idea that a patent makes it more costly for a rival to enter a market. The view of patent as deterrent supports an analysis of monopolist competition (Gilbert and Newberry 1982; Vickers 1995). The patent prevents a rival from introducing a sufficiently close product. It does not, however, foreclose entry into the product area. The patent race literature, like the entry deterrence literature, is concerned with whether or not monopolists are more likely to innovate. It shows that the monopolist has more incentives to innovate and hence spends more capital on research and development (Fudenberg & Tirole 1986; Tirole 1988).

antitakeover race had incentives sufficient to induce investment. He also concedes that first-movers can get returns on investment without property rights, given a time lag between entry and copying by competitors. But Ayres concludes that, although some innovation at-the-margin is sustainable without patent protection,[8] it cannot be assumed that, based on grounds of competitive efficiency, the innovation is sustainable in the long run without property rights.

Ayres goes on to employ a first-mover advantage model to suggest that, in the context of USA charter competition, supply side inefficiencies can result if lead states deem it prudent to imitate the inefficient statutory innovations of follower states. He illustrates this point with a yachting story. In a race between two equally sailed boats, the lead boat will often choose to cover the trailing boat by mimicking its tack. This ensures that both boats have the same access to the wind and that the trailing boat is denied the potential advantage created by an innovative tack. If both boats are slowed by the move, it makes no difference to the leader in a two-boat race. This story, says Ayres, explains Delaware's response to the race for legislating antitakeover statutes: It had an incentive to cover because so many other states had moved in this direction. Finally, in his third model, Ayres considers whether Delaware successfully can employ product differentiation as an entry barrier strategy. In this model, Delaware is the first-mover and the follower states mimic its innovations in order to retain their current base of incorporations. He suggests that Delaware is inclined to make innocuous excessive innovations in order to deter reincorporations and at the same time to limit copy cat actions by following states.[9]

2.4 The Product Model and the Legal Status of Marriage

Since regulatory competition theory remits the substance of regulation to the preferences of the consumer with the means to pay the rent, it invites conflicts with those who view democracy in participatory terms as an appropriate agent of wealth redistribution. Ayres' chapter, for example, evinces this tension with its suggestion that new law be removed from the public domain. In the context of USA federalism this would traverse constitutional free speech values in the eyes of many observers.

But regulatory competition should not be dismissed as a lawmaking strat-

---

[8] Technological progress is not solely dependent upon patents. Tirole (1988: 400) contends that unpatented innovations will yield gains, at least for a short period of time. It is claimed that there is a lag time due to a delay in the observation time or because of problems associated with producing an imitation. Some industries do not use patents and there may be other mechanisms than patents which promote dynamic innovation, and technological competition may best be understood in terms of a dynamic process of rivalry (Vickers 1995: 17).

[9] Ayres here draws on the switching costs literature of locked-in monopoly (e.g., Klemperer 1987; Farrell and Shapiro 1988; Dixit 1980, Dixit 1979).

egy that is intrinsically inimical to progressive social agendas. Jennifer Gerarda Brown shows this in chapter 9. Brown takes a pathbreaking decision of the Supreme Court of Hawaii,[10] which ruled that the state's marriage statute discriminates on the basis of gender in allowing marriage only between a man and a women and may as a result violate the equal protection clause of Hawaii's constitution, as the opportunity to suggest that the legislature of Hawaii (or a similarly-situated state) can enhance the economic welfare of its citizens by authorizing same-sex marriage. Brown brings to bear the model of legislative incentives developed in the charter competition literature in making this dollars and cents case. Here, as there, a small state seeking rents modifies its code so as to package a legal status that meets a demand among monied outsiders, and competitive advantages accrue to the first-mover jurisdiction. Structural differences in the economics of the two cases complicate, but by no means prevent, the model's application—Brown's first-mover state must not only be small, it also must be an attractive tourist destination.[11]

Much of the interest in Brown's chapter lies in political and institutional factors that distinguish it from the charter competition literature. The USA corporate law discussion addresses the relative merits of an established, competitively-driven legal institution, dwelling on the relative costs and benefits of centralized and decentralized approaches to regulation, with democratic concerns usually coming to bear on the side of centralization. In contrast, centralized legal institutions come to bear on Brown's discussion only tangentially—domestic relations are state law subject matter in the constitutional system of the USA. Brown takes a particularly stable feature of that context, the legal institution of opposite-sex marriage, and deploys the rent incentive to destablize the embedded norms that support it. In her construct regulatory competition assists a social minority possessing the means to purchase legal status from a rent-seeking jurisdiction but, due to small numbers and normative resistance, lacking the influence to secure access to the status through the normal democratic processes. Her chapter, thus has a unique position in the literature that discusses regulatory competition and law reform. Here entrepreneurship and law reform overlap completely: Brown identifies an existing, unmet consumer demand, identifies suitable legislatures, and presents them an opportunity to open up a new legal market.

It also bears noting that Brown's discussion does not suggest that this legislative entrepreneurship could (or should) circumvent political discussions of the legitimacy of same-sex marriage. Conflict of laws is the legal institu-

---

[10] *Baehr* v. *Lewin*, 852 P. 2d 44 (1993).

[11] Brown's revenue estimates are impressive: On her base case, the present value of increased tourism revenue to Hawaii could exceed $4 billion in direct spending, translating into $440 million in tax revenues and $2.4 billion in household income.

tion that makes it feasible for one jurisdiction to sell a special status package to outsiders, and Brown's scenario turns at its bottom line to the conflict of laws issue that would be created by same-sex marriage in a single American state. Brown's maverick jurisdiction, with its economic motivation, in the end performs a political role in the evolution of American domestic relations and civil rights law. As married same-sex couples return to other states in the federation and seek recognition for their status, those states will be forced to confront the issue of the legitimacy of the marriage, a confrontation otherwise likely to be avoided at the level of local politics. Indeed, that confrontation already has occurred in many American states, well in advance of the appearance of any such same-sex couples, prompted by national attention paid to Hawaii's ongoing determination of the same-sex marriage issue.

3. INSTITUTIONS AND REGULATORY COORDINATION: THE CASE OF THE EU

3.1 A Novel Institutional Framework

From its beginnings, the European Economic Community (and its associated coal and steel and atomic power communities),[12] aimed at the creation of a common market rather than merely a free trade area, and was equipped with a supranational institutional order going beyond tradititional interstate arrangements (Sbragia 1992; Nugent 1994). In one perspective, it still remains an international organization of a well-developed character, founded on the basis of treaties between its constituent Member States (MS), and giving a key role to bodies consisting of representatives of governments of the MS: the Council of Ministers and its Committee of Permanent Representatives (Coreper), the European Council, and the Inter-Governmental Conferences (IGCs) which negotiate amendments to the constitutive treaties. From another angle, the EU resembles a confederal structure, with a high degree of pooling of sovereignty, and important roles given to centralized institutions, notably the European Commission and the European Court of Justice (ECJ). However, the 'federalism' of the EU is strictly limited, in that the centre has only the competences granted to it and lacks autonomous executive powers, so that that 'effective policy-making

---

[12] Under the Single European Act of 1986 the EEC was renamed The European Community (EC). The Treaty on European Union of Maastricht added two further 'pillars' of competence in Foreign and Security Policy and Justice and Home Affairs. These three pillars together are named The European Union (EU). Strictly, the main socio-economic jurisdiction is that of the EC, although it is common to refer generally to the EU.

can only result from negotiations between politically autonomous governments.' (Scharpf 1994: 221).

The Commission has distinctive roles, both as the sole initiator of
Community legislation, and as 'guardian of the treaties' with a duty to
enforce compliance (mainly by monitoring the MS although in the important area of competition law it has direct powers of enforcement against
firms and citizens). Initially designed as authoritative interpreter of the
treaties, the ECJ quickly became central in developing a jurisprudence of
European integration, developing the key concepts of the direct applicability and direct effect of Community law. This key integrative role, developed
within the context of an emerging European legal community and in co-
operation with national courts (Weiler 1993; Burley and Mattli 1993; Maher
1995), was especially important when the other institutions were deadlocked
in periods of 'Eurosclerosis'. In the post-Maastricht period, with increased
sensitivity about national sovereignty and reluctance to extend Community
competences (Dehousse 1994), the ECJ has been drawing in its horns as its
powers have become controversial. The European Parliament provides a
popularly-elected forum, but its powers in the legislative process have been
mainly consultative until they were expanded in relation to the Single
Market programme to 'co-operation' with the Council in some fields, and
further extended by Maastricht to virtual co-decision (Dashwood 1994).
Perhaps due to its limited powers, it has not generated sufficient public
identification to provide a strong central counterweight to national parlia-
ments, as in federal systems. Furthermore, the multi-tiered and fragmented
distribution of power within the EU has meant that, despite the extensive
lobbying and consultative processes which permeate the Brussels institutions, they have still failed to develop Euro-corporatism (Schmitter and
Streek 1991), and have stifled rather than stimulated the development of a
European 'civil society' (Lambert 1994).

In its first period, the Community was necessarily primarily concerned
with the staged removal of tariffs and other border barriers, and the elaboration of its common policies in related key areas such as agriculture and
competition. As barriers were progressively removed, commentators began
to identify the problems associated with the need to shift from 'negative' to
'positive' integration (Pinder 1968). The Treaty of Rome (art. 100) already
provided for agreement on harmonized Community standards to replace
distinctive national laws or administrative requirements which could be
regarded as creating barriers to trade or otherwise impede the functioning
of the common market. The harmonization approach, however, proved
problematic for a number of reasons. First, it required the development of
detailed legislative standards which could command unanimous agreement
among the MSs in the Council of Ministers. This process was slow and cumbersome, as proposals could be delayed many years by a failure to secure

the necessary consensus.[13] Secondly, the harmonization approach greatly added to the complexities of producing acceptable and workable rules, due to the need to synchronize the technical work of an enormous range of national and transnational committees and bodies. Thirdly, the across-the-board programmes of harmonization failed to focus on the initiatives that really mattered, and wasted energy on futile or marginal issues (Braithwaite 1993a: 3).

The general difficulties of EU decision-making were first and most directly felt in relation to the differences in national technical standards. These were considered by industrialists to be the single most important barrier to trade in the Community (Emerson 1988: 32, 39), yet the attempts to coordinate through harmonization were derided as entailing the imposition of pointless and undesirable uniformity, symbolized by the apocryphal 'Eurosausage'. Indeed, the problems of Euro-harmonization contributed to the growing counter-tendency within many MSs towards deregulation and the reduction of regulatory burdens.[14]

3.2 The New Approach to Harmonization and the Regulatory Competition Debate

In 1985 the EC project was revived and relaunched through the programme for completion of the Single European Market (SEM). Integral to this was the adoption of a 'new approach' to harmonization, outlined in the Commission's White Paper on the SEM. This aimed to limit harmonization efforts to the essential mimimum, tolerating a high degree of diversity both of national rules and of detailed technical standards set by industry or professional bodies. A key element here, as is shown by Woolcock in chapter 10, was the acceptance of the German performance-oriented approach to technical standards. This confines legal requirements to broad regulatory objectives, which may be met by compliance with the technical specifications formulated by the specialized standards-setting institutions, thus enabling the EC to recognize multiple standards as equivalent (e.g. the French AFNOR as well as German DIN standards), and displacing much of the complex and detailed technical work from the state to private bodies.

The second main element in the 'new approach' was the acceptance of the principle of Mutual Recognition, developed by the ECJ, especially in the

---

[13] The Single European Act (1986) ameliorated this problem by providing for qualified majority voting for measures necessary to complete the Single European Market (article 100a EC Treaty).

[14] Some economists have also argued that a unified approach to standards may be inefficient: for example, a single suboptimal standard can introduce 'lock-in' effects, delaying adoption of a superior standard, and impeding innovation (Arthur 1989; Katz and Shapiro 1986; David 1987).

Cassis de Dijon (1979) case. The Court decided that national regulatory requirements constituting barriers to trade were contrary to the Treaty of Rome, using a broad interpretation of the concept 'measures having an equivalent effect' to quantitative restrictions. Thus, a MS could maintain its own rules for its own producers, but could not impede the importation of goods validly produced under the rules of another state, unless they could be justified under specific criteria. This principle, once incorporated into the Commission's 'new approach', creates a dynamic of interaction between national rules and Community-level harmonized regulation (Dehousse 1989). The key to this strategy is the tension between mutual recognition of national rules and coordination at Community level. In cases where harmonized rules are in place, a MS can no longer block imports produced under a national system complying with those rules, although it still can choose different or higher requirements for its own producers. In cases where no harmonized rules apply, a state can be threatened with imports of goods produced under different and less costly regulatory systems, unless it can persuade the Commission and the Court that compliance with its rules is strictly necessary for health and safety or consumer protection. Thus, the threat of regulatory competition can act as a spur to persuade the MS to agree upon at least a basic floor of harmonized rules.

By introducing regulatory diversity and competition, the 'new approach' further increased the complexity of EC regulation and compliance arrangements. Even harmonization at EC level only produces a loose form of coordination, since it is generally done not by a European-level regulation directly applicable as law, but by directives which each MS must transform into and enforce as part of its own national law and practice. This entails a cumbersome process of monitoring of implementation by the Commission, which focuses on transposition into domestic law and is relatively powerless to ensure parity of enforcement or compliance. The ECJ's doctrine of 'direct effect' has done much to remedy this difficulty (Curtin 1990), and its *Francovitch* decision of 1991 opened up a new legal remedy for individuals and firms against a MS for damages caused by inadequate implementation of EC law (Bebr 1992). After 1992, however, the new central concerns became to reduce the complexity of EC regulation, and enhance coordination among the various authorities responsible for the implementation and enforcement of Community measures, improving the coordinating role of the Commission in relation to the national bureaucracies of the Member States.

The problem of complexity was highlighted in the Report of a high-level group appointed by the Commission (Sutherland 1992), which pointed out that by abandoning the imposition of uniformity, the 'new approach' had created intricate arrangements lacking transparency and requiring improved coordination. Although the Report accepted that in most areas enforcement must continue to be decentralized, for some matters a more centralized régime has been found necessary, notably for new product approval for pharmaceuticals (see Woolcock, ch. 10). Where a relatively centralized régime exists (e.g. competition)[15] or is emerging (utilities regulation), there is a debate about whether the powers of the Commission should be devolved to specialized functional agencies with rule-making and direct enforcement powers (Ehlermann 1995; Sauter 1994*a*). While the aim seems to be to insulate what are regarded as technical or specialist matters from harmful political influences, the MS would inevitably insist on national representation and involvement of national authorities, potentially producing unwieldy federal mini-bureaucracies.

Following the adoption of the 'new approach' to harmonization, the debates within the EU were affected by the importation of the regulatory competition concept and its 'race to the top' story from the USA (see e.g. Reich 1992, discussing Kitch 1981; Padoa-Schioppa 1987). That story, as noted above, indicated that uniform rules carried the risk of regulatory capture, while competitive diversity would lead to regulation tailored to local preferences, deter opportunism among national regulators, and encourage regulatory experimentation and innovation (Siebert and Koop 1993: 15–30). It followed for Europe that mutual recognition within the EC might be not just a device to stimulate harmonization, but desirable in itself. A European counter-argument also appeared, however. This echoed the USA 'race to the bottom' story, and feared that, in the absence of effective harmonization, national-level regulation would involve uncertainty, complexity, and undesirable competitive deregulation.

---

[15] The EC competition regime provides an instructive example of indirect harmonization and regulatory coordination. Formally, neither harmonization nor coordination are necessary, since the Treaty's competition rules for entrprises (arts. 85 and 86) apply in parallel with national laws and only to anti-competitive behaviour affecting trade between the MSs. However, the ECJ has given this a wide interpretation, and also held (*Walt Wilhelm* v. *Bundeskartellamt* [1969] ECR 1) that national laws cannot be applied in circumstances which would impede the effectiveness of EC law, e.g. against a trans-national cartel considered unduly restrictive at national level but beneficial to the EC market as a whole. Following this decision the Commission suggested that the the national authorities should be required to consult it over enforcement of their laws, but accepted instead an agreement to improve coordination. On the other hand, the Commission must notify the national authorities of its investigations and consult with them before taking decisions, including the exercise of enforcement powers. In practice, cooperation has been quite close among the relevant officials and mediated by the specialized lawyers, and a majority of the MSs have now enacted national laws in line with the Community rules. Coordination is especially important in the case of a pre-merger notification requirement, and this held up its introduction until the 1989 Mergers Regulation introduced a 'one-stop shop', described by its architect, Commisioner Sir Leon Brittan as a good example of subsidiarity. It gave the Commission exclusive jurisdiction over the largest mergers defined as having 'a Community dimension'. In practice this has operated permissively (only two have been refused), allowing the Commission to approve cross-border concentrations which might have been blocked by national resistance. However, the Commission's ambition to widen its jurisdiction by lowering the 'Community dimension' threshhold has been resisted, partly because it would increase the likelihood that it might prohibit mergers to create a 'national champion' and thus favoured by a MS.

In chapter 10, Stephen Woolcock evaluates these assertions in the context of the EC after completion of the SEM. Woolcock finds trends towards regulatory competition in some sectors, due to a preference for 'convergence from below', but he projects that the scope of such competition is likely to remain limited. Neither a race to the bottom nor to the top is to be expected. Against the race to the bottom, Woolcock points out, first, that there has already been significant harmonization as a result of the SEM program, setting a fairly high regulatory floor in most areas. Secondly, the existence of a blocking minority means that most proposals result in fairly high levels of regulation. Thirdly, national regulators have retained the capacity to maintain higher standards than are required by the EC floor, suggesting that deregulatory pressures from corporate lobbies either have not materialized or have been neutralized by governments hoping to maintain group consensus. Fourthly, regulation sometimes holds out competitive advantages for local producers: It has been argued, particularly for social policy and environmental protection, that the imposition of higher levels of regulation may increase competitiveness, by encouraging investment and improving productivity. High levels of regulation can also enhance reputation, as can be seen in the race to improve investor protection in European capital markets. Against the race to the top, Woolcock points to the general absence of the necessary background conditions in the EU: namely, an open market with factor mobility as well as transparency of the regulations among the competing jurisdictions. The persistence of local markets and limitations on mobility both of persons and factors (despite mutual recognition) suggests there will be little competition among régimes. Even if greater mobility develops, informational problems would make it very hard for individuals or most firms to understand, let alone evaluate, the effects of different national regulatory arrangements. Finally, the bundling of regulatory policies would make it hard to select among a menu of alternatives in different areas.

Woolcock also points to the institutional and political factors which inhibit the prospects for competitive lawmaking in the EU. The MS make regulatory decisions within various different, and path-dependent, institutional frameworks, and in many of these contexts factor movement is not a major factor in prompting a regulatory response. At the same time, and somewhat counter-intuitively, competition among national rules will not occur unless there is effective enforcement of the EC minimum standards. This is because, as discussed above, harmonization generally occurs through Directives, and while the Commission monitors their transformation into national law, actual enforcement is generally left to each MS. This gives rise to a risk of opportunism, which is compounded by the complexity of the regulatory arrangements allowed by mutual recognition. Woolcock argues that this incomplete system of enforcement inhibits prospects for regulatory competition, because a MS which does not trust the effectiveness of enforcement by others will be reluctant to accept mutual recognition, and will prefer a higher level of harmonized rules to ensure equivalent regulatory outcomes.

Woolcock concludes that those who make strong claims for regulatory competition in the EC wrongly tend to assume that competition among rules presents a complete alternative to the problems encountered in the EC's first phase of harmonization. On the contrary, Woolcock points out that in the EC regulatory competition and harmonization are complementary rather than alternatives. Harmonization is important, if only to avoid a reversion to regressive national tendencies. Competition among rules 'cannot be seen as an end in itself', but must be critically assessed against a range of possibilities such as the desirability of transferring power to common institutions. Nor, in the EC's institutional context, can competition result from the unilateral decision of a single state. Rather, the possibility or threat of such competition is a tactical element in the complex process of bargaining among MSs pursuing multiple objectives (Joerges 1994; Garrett 1992; Moravcsik 1993; Scharpf 1994).

3.3 The Single Market: Unity through Diversity?

Even if regulatory competition, as introduced by the mutual recognition principle, does not exist in a pure form in the EU, it has certainly greatly contributed to the dramatic shift away from a presumption of integration based on centralization or uniformity, to an emphasis on the preservation of diversity. In this context, the continuing and problematic dynamic of both EC institutions and Community-MS relations has generated a debate with two facets. First, what are the appropriate subjects of state intervention? In particular, is it possible to distinguish market-creating measures from social protection measures? Secondly, what is the appropriate level of state activity, local, national, or supranational? The following discussion highlights some of the main issues in recent discussions and the patterns that have emerged in the EU integration programme under the new approach.

A. Market Creation, Social Protection, and Subsidiarity

Generally, in the experience of the EC, it has been difficult to separate market-creation from social protection, and therefore to confine EC action entirely to the former and leave the latter to the MS. Nevertheless, the primary emphasis has inevitably been on market-creation, and social-protection is generally a poor second. Certainly, European social provision has developed in national welfare-state régimes of very disparate types and without a common policy tradition, and it has been argued that these differences make a bottom-up process of harmonization impossible and call for central or top-down initiatives (Leibfried 1992). Some conclude that the economic, social, and political diversity of the EU rules out centralized welfare policies of a redistributionist character, but that these in any case concern the social problems of the past, and that the EC is in fact addressing contemporary quality-of-life issues, such as environmental protection, consumer rights, and equal treatment between women and men (Majone 1993). Others emphasize that market-creation measures create 'spill-over' into social policy, but political initiative is needed to create a 'rights-based conception of social citizenship' (Leibfried and Pearson 1992). A much-overlooked success of the European social dimension is the women's policy, which has certainly brought substantial changes to national regulation on equal pay and non-discrimination; but while the strength of womens' politics since the 1970s succeeded in activating a provision on equal pay inserted into the Treaty to ensure French industry was not disadvantaged, it has had less success in broadening the agenda to social issues such as childcare (Hoskyns 1996).

The primary focus on market-creation has led to the 'rise of the regulatory state' in Europe (Majone 1993). The creation of European-wide markets has focused on regulatory harmonization aimed at least at establishing equivalent régimes in all the MSs. Positive functional arguments for Community coordinating activity are based on the potential for transnational externalities, in that a MS may regulate inadequately for the Community-wide effects of concentration of economic power, or for the transfrontier effects of problems such as environmental pollution, or may actively use regulatory requirements in a protectionist way (McGowan and Seabright 1995: 231–2). However, the regulatory competition concept has been deployed to argue that harmonization should be aimed at and confined to what is necessary to create a single market, and that otherwise diversity and competition among national rules may be encouraged. The principle of 'subsidiarity', enshrined by the Maastricht agreement in art. 3b of the EC Treaty, explicitly states that the Community shall take action only if and in so far as its objectives cannot be sufficiently achieved by the MS, due to the 'scale and effects' of the action. The concept of subsidiarity is far from clear in its application, and principles derived from the regulatory competition debate may be used to help clarify the appropriate circumstances for EU coordination or national diversity. Indeed, in the light of the 'subsidiarity' principle, the Commission has undertaken reviews of pending proposals to identify which could be withdrawn, or amended by harmonizing only to the extent strictly necessary.

Nevertheless, the view remains strong in Europe that markets must have a 'human face'. It is noteworthy that the 'objectives' of the EC, which justify coordination under the subsidiarity principle, are not defined in narrow, market-creation terms, and the Maastricht agreement also expanded Community competence in many areas where economic and social policy overlap, such as public health; the environment; education and training; and health and safety at work. Although the UK government blocked a further broadening of the provisions relating to labour and employment, the other eleven MSs adopted a separate Social Policy Agreement which allows them to use Community institutions to develop policy in this area, giving the UK an opt-out but also creating a shut-out.[16]

Thus, within the EC these issues are played out partly by negotiations and manoeuvres between pressure-groups and decision-makers at different locations over the development and refinement, as well as the monitoring and enforcement, of the various European regulatory systems. It is in this context that the regulatory competition argument has been deployed, and has succeeded to some extent in modifying the integrationist ideology underpinning the EU project. Nevertheless, there has been a notable reluctance to abandon, or even relax very far, the efforts to find agreed accommodations on institutional régimes governing markets. Although the Commission's White Paper of 1985 envisaged a wide application of the principle of mutual recognition, to cover for example financial services, it quickly met a significant obstacle in the ECJ decision of 1986 in the Insurance case (*Commission* v. *Germany* [1986] ECR 3755), which accepted that Germany could require compliance with its authorization requirements by foreign insurance firms, at least in the retail market, since the specially close relationship to the consumer justifies regulation by the host state in the 'general good'. This seemed to provide a broader scope to justify host state regulation than was authorized for goods in the *Cassis de Dijon* case, and consequently broadened the area in which harmonized rules would be necessary to remove regulatory obstacles to cross-border services. This led to a modified form of mutual recognition for services, referred to as the single passport principle (McGowan and Seabright 1995: 235). This implies that an authorization issued by the home state of a service-provider should provide entry to other states, but they may wish to scrutinize it, and may still require obedience to their general laws. Furthermore, some

---

[16] See Stone, ch. 15. A proposal may initially be formulated under the main treaty provisions, with UK participation, but if this proves obstructive it can be removed to the Social Policy Agreement procedure. The UK does not participate in this procedure, and so cannot influence but also need not apply it. However, firms operating on a European scale are likely to choose to apply a measure across all their plants, including those in the UK. This has been so in the case of the European Works Council Directive (the first to be adopted using this procedure): firms have rushed to set up such Councils ahead of the September 1996 deadline, since by doing so they have greater choice of format, and according to the Commission, all have chosen to include their UK workforces (*Financial Times*, 12th July 1995). Nevertheless, other labour-protective measures, such as those covering part-time or low-paid workers, may provide the UK with a more genuine opt-out, supporting the present government's policy of 'pricing workers into jobs', criticized by others as 'social dumping'.

commentators have pointed to the incentives for a MS under a mutual recognition régime to set standards at a low level which could create benefits for its firms, while most of the costs will fall on consumers or citizens in other MSs.

As a result, although the mutual recognition principle remains the cornerstone of the programme of harmonization aimed at opening up financial markets, it is significantly modified and limited in various ways in the many Directives which have been adopted, to cover banking and credit, investment services, insurance, and other financial market rules. In general, these Directives seek to establish a broad common definition for the activities or products permissible in the markets; to provide a 'single passport' by giving supervisory jurisdiction to the regulator in each firm's home state, subject to coordination with the regulator in the host state; while conceding to the host state a residual power to regulate these activities in the 'public good'. Thus, the Second Banking Directive (discussed by Woolcock) gives credit institutions licensed in their home MS the right to trade and set up branches in other MSs, subject to a procedure of notification and administrative cooperation among the home and host states, and to the residual right of the host state to regulate transactions in the 'public good'.[17] In practice, the harmonization of financial market regulation as part of the Single Market has produced a fairly comprehensive common framework of rules, including licensing requirements and detailed liquidity and solvency requirements. However, enforcement remains decentralized, and the Commission has a minimal role, so there is a complex and perhaps unstable interaction between the roles and responsibilities of the EC institutions and the home and host states.[18]

B. Facilitating Factor Mobility

The paradox, therefore, is that harmonization has been needed in order to create the preconditions for regulatory competition, particularly factor mobility. Without factor mobility there is no effective choice between 'exit, voice and loyalty' (Hirschman 1970; McGowan and Seabright 1995: 230), and the engine of regulatory competition, regulatory arbitrage, is not present (Siebert and Koop 1993: 16–17; Woolcock, ch. 10). It was indeed a central aim of the EC to create the conditions for free movement of goods,

---

[17] Although national restrictions on financial products can do as much to create barriers to entry as national financial regulations (Gatsios and Seabright 1989: 44), local banks have not lobbied for such protections, preferring to achieve competitive advantage through product innovation (Sun and Pelkmans 1995: 80–82).

[18] The European Central Bank, to be set up for the third stage of Economic and Monetary Union or by 1st July 1998, may provide some centralized coordination, since it may be given 'specific tasks concerning policies relating to the prudential supervision of credit institutions and other financial institutions with the exception of insurance undertakings' by the Council acting unanimously.

labour, services, and capital. Within the EU, however, the predominant ideology is that such mobility requires a 'level playing-field'. This implies an equivalence of regulatory régimes, and excludes the freedom to move to seek a regulatory advantage. In the words of a Commission official:

Some economists believe that different standards should co-exist and compete. I consider that this works better for tradeable goods and services than for legislation, because legislation comprises package deals. For example, a company cannot just opt for the company law of a Member State without also having to accept the tax laws and employment laws of that country, which might well distort competition between national company laws (Wolff, in Andenas and Kenyon-Slade 1993: 20).

The view that economic and social regulation must be considered an indivisible package involves narrowing the scope for regulatory arbitrage to exclude opportunistic choice among a menu of discrete regulatory régimes, and limiting it to the selection of a package offered by a single location. The corollary for the EU is that regulatory harmonization or coordination needs to be integrated across regulatory régimes. Certainly, the experience of the EC has been that topics are found to be interrelated, and one issue leads to another: it is hard, for example, to tackle banking separately from brokerage, or integrate financial markets without concerting monetary policy and taxation. Yet international liberalization is easier to accept for some matters than others.

There is certainly the perception of a qualitative difference between trade in goods and other international economic movements. Short-term money movements and foreign exchange transactions are clearly extremely fluid, and now take place globally on a virtual 24-hour basis. However, economic factors of production are far less mobile than would appear to be the case, and this for both cultural and regulatory reasons. International movements of labour or capital, and trade in 'services', do not take place as discrete transactions, and they therefore involve a much more direct interaction between the social and regulatory conditions of their countries of origin and destination. This is also because international 'movements' of factors other than goods take place in very different ways. At one extreme there is relocation, whether of labour or of capital; and at the other, an international transaction in 'invisibles'. Such transactions, however, generally involve closer relations between producer and consumer than in the case of the sale of goods, and therefore a closer integration or interaction between the two jurisdictions. For example, workers often do not permanently emigrate but maintain links with their home country; service providers may attract foreign clients through various agency arrangements or links of a co-operative character, such as airline inter-ticketing, or the tie-ups among European law firms.

Labour is generally regarded as relatively immobile mainly for cultural reasons, but much of labour's immobility is also related to regulatory embeddedness, or obstacles such as non-transferability of entitlements to social benefits of health-care, housing, and social security. Despite the EC's strong principle of non-discrimination or national-treatment, there has been some reluctance to liberalize the availability of benefits, expressed in fears of 'welfare tourism'. Further, freedom of movement has been limited to EC nationals: despite the use of the broad term 'worker' in the Treaty (art. 48), it has by convention been interpreted to apply only to nationals of a MS, excluding resident third-country nationals (O'Keefe 1992) and thus insulating each state's immigration régime. To achieve the ambition of abolition of border controls, there have been continuing negotiations and agreements to coordinate external immigration controls, although this has been on an inter-governmental basis and much criticized as secretive and restrictive.

Controls on the movement of capital within the EC were only gradually required to be relaxed, although this meant distinguishing capital from current payments, which from the beginning the MSs were required to authorize to the extent that the movements of goods, services, capital, and persons had been liberalized under the Treaty (original art. 106 EEC). The obligatory removal of direct controls was finally agreed with the adoption of the Capital Movements Directive of 1988 (88/361) and, under the Maastricht Treaty amendments, restrictions on both payments and movements of capital are now prohibited, both between the MS and with third states (new art. 73b). However, there has been concern within the EU that this liberalization should be paralleled by the harmonization of rules governing banks and other credit institutions, stock markets, and taxation of income from capital. It also brought sharply into focus the question of Economic and Monetary Union (EMU): the 1988 liberalization had also been made possible by the adoption of provisions for medium-term financial assistance for MSs with balance of payments difficulties (Usher 1994: 19), and at least pending the third stage of EMU powers to deal with balance of payments problems are given under the Treaty (arts. 109h and 109i).

A major area where diversity creates prospects for regulatory competition is individual and corporate income taxation, which has been regarded as an area of national sovereignty, and where measures can only be adopted by unanimity. Freedom of movement for savings and short-term capital was considered to create the threat of tax evasion or avoidance, and an exception to the freedom for capital and payments was allowed for anti-avoidance measures by states, provided they do not involve arbitrary discrimination or disguised restrictions on capital or payments (art. 73d). It was also recognized that concerted action would be necessary, and the 1988 Capital Movements Directive required proposals to be brought forward, but a Commission draft of 1989 for a harmonized minimum 15% withholding tax on dividend and interest income of EC residents was vetoed by London and Luxembourg, arguing that it would produce capital flight to non-EC offshore centres (Picciotto 1992: 74–5). National diversity in taxation and the need for unanimity for its harmonization allows some, such as a senior UK official, to contrast the 'glacial pace' of international discussions to harmonize direct taxation with 'the power of market forces to effect a real convergence' in tax systems (Isaac 1989). Market forces generally, however, exert a downward pressure on taxation. In particular, the mobility of short-term capital restricts national government action, notably defeating attempts by Germany to introduce a withholding tax on interest (in the absence of a harmonized EC requirement), due to immediate large outflows of deposits to Luxembourg.

Freedom to locate or relocate capital investment in the EU takes the form of the 'right of establishment' for nationals of a MS to carry out economic activities in any form within another MS without discrimination (art. 52, extended to companies registered or resident in a MS by art. 58). However, the ECJ has rejected arguments that this right should extend to the transfer of corporate residence, in a case where the motive was regulatory avoidance, in this case of tax (*Reg* v. *HM Treasury and CIR ex p Daily Mail and General Trust plc* (1988) 53 CMLR 713). For financial firms, the Directives allowed refusal of authorization where regulatory avoidance was suspected, and in the wake of the BCCI débacle this was strengthened by introducing a requirement that financial firms must be registered where their real headquarters are located (adopted on 21 June 1995). These rules reinforce the *siège réel* principle of several national laws, and restrict the scope for firms to choose a favoured corporate law régime. The main motive appears to be the fear that such choice would also permit avoidance of other regulation, such as corporate taxation or prudential supervision.

The blocking of competition for corporate charters is also complemented by the EC's programme of company law harmonization, which now encompasses many basic company law rules, including accounts, as well as related regulation on financial matters such as stock listing rules. However, there has been a significant move towards allowing greater diversity within the harmonized régimes being proposed, largely in order to facilitate adoption. Thus, in the 1991 version of its long-standing attempt to promulgate a statute for a European Company (SE = *societas europea*), the Commission abandoned the previous highly-detailed approach, specifying in the statute itself only basic principles which had mostly already been agreed in the series of company law Directives already adopted, and accepting that for other purposes the SE would come under the corporate law régime of the state of its registration. This was however subject to the firm principle that an SE must have its central administration in the state of registration (Wehlau 1992). Despite this, and the related attempt to defuse the politically difficult issue of two-tier boards and worker representation by allowing a wide range of options, neither proposal has yet been adopted. A proposed Directive on take-overs is also stalled, due to opposition to its mandatory bid requirement, and the UK's preference for its self-regulatory City Code. On the other hand, the Insider Dealing Directive (adopted as part of the financial markets programme), carefully fell short of specifying that insider dealing should be a criminal offence, since criminal law is considered to be outside the EC's competence, and Germany at that time defended its preference for self-regulation on this matter. Nevertheless, as part of the Finanzplatz Deutschland policy to upgrade its financial markets, criminal penalties were eventually introduced in 1995.

C. Competition and coordination in the EU: the Evolving Pattern

In relation to some areas, notably financial markets regulation, the EC harmonization programmes are well-developed, often providing more elaborate and even rigorous rules than those previously existing at national level. Here, what seems to be happening is that the introduction of rule-based régimes as a result of European harmonization is making entry easier for outsiders by opening up the exclusive domains formed by cozy relationships between national ministries or regulators and their local firms. However, the key position of the centralized supranational institutions has undeniably been greatly weakened by the force of the arguments for diversity and competition in regulatory arrangements, leading to what might be called a centrifugal centre in the European system. Even more important, however, these arguments have strengthened the positions of those who have attacked the capacity of national states to identify collective preferences and manage welfare programmes. Thus it has been argued that if there is an emerging supranational polity in Europe, it is neo-voluntarist one, which is taking the lead in moving national states 'away from hard obligations to soft incentives, from regulation to voluntarism, and from social-interventionism to liberal democracy' (Streeck 1995). It is the combined effects of the 'subversive liberalism' in which economic liberalization undermines national autonomy to make redistributionist welfare choices (Rhodes 1994), and the failure so far to develop stronger concepts of social citizenship and social-protection policies at the European level, that chart the parameters of European politics.

There remains also some scope for competition to attract investment on the basis of locational advantages, including regulatory difference, due especially to the inability to agree to greater harmonization of direct taxation. This is also facilitated by the relative weakness of harmonization on social protection matters, significantly undermined by the hostility of the present UK government to the emergence of a 'European corporatism'. The result is a dilemma, expressed in the UK's unique position in having opted out both of the Social Policy Agreement and of progression to the third stage of EMU.[19] The present UK government argues for a Europe with greater regulatory diversity, including possibilities for regulatory arbitrage, but a 'Europe à la carte' is generally rejected by the other MSs. Much will depend on whether EMU is achieved, in which case the UK would have to decide whether to accept a position as the only major state outside a cohesive monetary bloc, in order to maintain a competitive position based both on an independent monetary policy and lower social protection standards.

3.4 Case Studies

The volume includes three case-studies that illustrate the complexities of negotiating regulatory arrangements at multiple levels within EC institutional structures.

A. Pensions

In chapter 11 Graham Moffat shows how different regulatory concerns may converge so as to stimulate an effort to harmonize an area which in principle might be thought appropriate to be left to regulatory diversity, in this case non-state pensions. Here the clearest justification for harmonization is the improvement of labour mobility. But this has limited validity, since provision has already been made for transferability of state pensions in the EC and social and linguistic considerations have historically tied most workers to local areas in any case. Of greater relevance, as Moffat shows, is the increasing importance of private pension provision due to projections of the future inability of the state to finance full pensions for ageing populations. Thus, Moffat emphasizes that the labour mobility issue is intricately linked to both the freedom to establish services and the free movement of capital in the Community, in the former case because firms seeking to establish in another Member State may wish to bring over key personnel from the home state, and in the latter case because pension funds provide a key source of institutional capital in the Community. However, the complexity of the issues involved also make it much more difficult to concede the accommodations necessary to reach agreement.

The application of principles of mutual recognition to areas other than manufactured goods presents particular technical problems. Positive efforts to coordinate the financial services area include provision for mutual

---

[19] The third stage of EMU involves acceptance of irrevocably fixed exchange rates, a single currency, and a European Central Bank independent from political influence. The treaty provides that the third stage shall in any event start on 1st Jan. 1999, with whichever MSs have by 1 July 1998 met the convergence criteria laid down in the Treaty. Denmark and UK have the right to opt out, and are currently negotiating over what institutional role they may have if they do so. Transition before 1999 has virtually been ruled out, and it remains problematic whether the deadline of 1 July 1998 will be enforceable if only a minority of MSs meet the criteria (see generally Usher 1994: ch. 7; Snyder 1994).

recognition of operating licences. Negative integration may occur through the removal of rules which prevent freedom of establishment of services provision. Thus, there may be a degree of deregulation in the instruments of both positive and negative integration in the financial services area and the creation of a further dynamic towards deregulation captured in the idea of competition between rules. Moffat demonstrates that the complexity of EC pensions policy and the variety of interests involved is also reflected in the institutional competition between the Directorates General of the Commission which share responsibility for pensions. Furthermore considerable pressure from vested interests in the Member States has effectively slowed the development of Community-level policies inimical to the interests of these groups. Against these interests are ranged other arguments that the negative integration themes of the SEM should be balanced by a positive integrative agenda which has a more developed social dimension, concerned with the establishment of a floor of provision for Community workers. To some degree the tensions over policy being played out at Community level also reflect tensions at MS level, as for those who lose the argument at MS level there is the prospect of an 'appeal' to the higher level.

B. Waste Packaging

In chapter 12 Joel R. Paul studies the interplay between regulatory competition and harmonization in the regulation of waste packaging in the EC. To Paul, as to others before him, waste packaging presents a classic market failure because producers do not internalize the costs of processing their products' waste. Economists have responded by arguing that government should limit the externality's impact either through taxation at the point of production or through a subsidy to recycling firms. Paul, however, argues that these cost-benefit analyses lack neutrality since there is no single method for determining the price of welfare in this context. The cost-benefit outcome will vary, for example, depending on whether the asking price or the offering price is employed. A damaging problem remains even if a correct price could be obtained. The fact of a price helps little in assigning a figure to the marginal gain in consumer welfare that follows from an alteration in producer preferences leading to the elimination of non-recyclable packaging, and, since individuals have different preferences for pollution, it may be impossible to achieve a single value.

Paul carries this scepticism about cost-benefit assertions to his review of the evolution of EC waste packaging regulation. He endorses the broad outlines of the EU's new approach to harmonization on the grounds, first, that it can serve to ameliorate negative effects of regulatory competition, and, secondly, that its closer ties to national regulatory policy bring enhanced democratic legitimacy. Paul, however, also recognizes that the system leaves room for destructive competition, because it leaves legislators subject to a range of pressures to emulate other jurisdictions. His study further complicates this picture. Prior to the EC Directive on Packaging of 1994, the MSs had adopted a wide range of regulatory approaches which may have distorted trade, either through subsidies to recycled packaging products, which could threaten the economic basis of the packaging, or through mandatory requirements set at different levels in different MS. This uncoordinated régime proved conducive to an outbreak of regulatory competition, which in turn led to higher levels of regulation in some MSs. The 1994 Directive, which attempts to harmonize requirements as to the amount of recovered packaging, raises standards significantly in some MSs while simultaneously prohibiting some national requirements which exceed the standards (though the Commission may approve higher standards if accepted as consistent with both environmental and single market objectives).

These developments lead Paul to some critical observations about positions taken in regulatory competition debates. He observes that interactions among various institutional players create here an evolutionary picture that is more complex than those allowed by the race to the top and race to the bottom versions of regulatory competition theory. Parodoxically, competition among states led to stricter levels of regulation in this case, with the EC's harmonization machinery responding by lowering this competitively-driven level of regulation in some MS even as it raised the level in others. Environmental concerns, expressed through interest groups, were a key factor. But the Community Directive, which permits manufacturers to pass on costs to consumers without the fear of being undercut by other Community competitors, was achieved only through the exploitation of consumers' willingness to pay more for products perceived as environmentally friendly. Thus Paul's chapter highlights pressures that can lead to suboptimal outcomes in the name of harmonization.

C. Telecommunications

The provision of services in the Community is highly diffuse in character. Some services are necessarily provided with a degree of local or cultural specificity which makes inter-state competition implausible. Therefore the Community can take little legitimate interest in them, and MSs have no incentive to adjust regulatory régimes to compete to attract businesses conducting such activities. Other types of service may be provided on an international level by multinational enterprises. A paradigm example, of great importance to the economies of the Member States, is telecommunications. In chapter 13 Colin Scott compares the processes of liberalization of the telecommunication sectors in the United States of America and the European Community, arguing that competition between firms and between states, while it might offer some explanation for the broad thrust of policies of liberalization, fails to adequately take into account processes of institutional competition. In the United States of America allocation of powers between federal and state authorities is relatively stable, but this has not prevented considerable tension both between the federal and state jurisdictions, and between the various actors involved in the development of policy at federal level. The relatively centralized and coordinated federal régime has been the key force in liberalization of the sector, and it is only in very recent years that state regulatory authorities and courts have accepted arguments for widespread liberalization of intrastate services. At the federal level there has been a form of institutional competition in which key actors have deployed institutional resources, such as legal rules, constitutional norms, and cultural assumptions to advance their positions. There also has been a long period of judicial, as opposed to agency, administration of the federal liberalization programme. But it appears that the present Congress may succeed in legislating for the reestablishment of the dual regulatory and anti-trust régimes at the federal administrative level.

In the EC the jurisdictions of the Member States and the Community institutions are subject to continuing renegotiation through processes of litigation, legislation and treaty amendments. Scott shows that key actors in the liberalization process, such as DG IV of the Commission, have both had their perspectives shaped by their institutional position and the instruments available to advance such perspectives, but at the same time have sought to use these instruments innovatively to advance their perspectives. Thus whereas in the United States of America the federal competition jurisdiction is legally distinct from federal regulatory jurisdiction, the latter gradually giving way to the former, in the EC the competition jurisdiction has been deployed alongside the regulatory jurisdiction, the latter deriving from the Single Market objectives in the Treaty. As the completion of single market objectives is achieved in the telecommunications sector the attention of the Commission has turned towards the liberalizing potential of the competition jurisdiction. The Commission has been supported in these developments by representatives of large business users who see some advantage from liberalization in terms of lower business service charges. Those groups in the Commission and the Parliament which are more cautious about liberalization have recently developed a stronger institutional position. This discernible shift has resulted in a greater emphasis on the objective of coordinating universal service provision in the Member States, so that protection of social obligations will be mandated rather than merely tolerated as before. There also has been a movement to permit entry by telecommunications firms from third countries led by those Member States, such as the UK, which are the strongest advocates of policies of liberalization. Finally, telecommunications liberalization at the level of the Member States is accompanied by extensive new or re-regulation, which in turn provides a rationale for continuing extensive Community regulation through the Open

Network Provision legislation. This continuing involvement creates the prospect of a transfer of some of the Commission powers in this sector to an independent Community telecommunications regulator.

3.5 Future Expansion

The EU has been, and continues to be, of central importance both as a catalyst and a precursor for global institutional developments. Whatever its weaknesses and limitations, there is a lengthening queue of states at its doors claiming admission, which will further add to the institutional strains, requiring the reconciliation of 'deepening' with 'widening' of the EU framework. Indeed, one of the strongest arguments made by proponents of greater diversity and looser coordination of EC regulatory arrangements is that this must be inevitable as the Community grows to 25 or more members. Yet it can also be said that it is the stability offered by the strength of EU institutions that underpins the markets and offers the strongest attraction to aspirant members, from Turkey to the Baltic.

4. SHIFTS AND TRANSITIONS IN GLOBAL GOVERNANCE

The formation and development of the EU has made a major impact on global forums, if only due to its substantial weight as the world's largest trading organization, now also closely integrated with the states in the European Economic Area (EEA), and many associated states, including 69 parties to the Lomé Agreement. The success of the EEC as a common market, although initially viewed negatively by global free-trade advocates (Bhagwati 1993: 28), in practice stimulated a more general trade liberalization through the GATT, as trade conflicts tended to result in mutual concessions in the major negotiating rounds of the 1960s. However, the push to deeper integration through the Single Market programme widened the concerns of the EU's major partners and rivals. In a number of areas, especially in services, the process of re-regulation by the EC has favoured EU-based firms, or has involved explicit reciprocity requirements as a condition of entry by non-EU firms, creating accusations of 'fortress Europe'.

However, the broadening of the GATT agenda came at the same time as the slowdown in economic growth, and as domestic economies became vulnerable to trade and factor flows resulting from earlier liberalization through GATT. Thus, governments found it hard to resist domestic economic pressure groups, while collective action problems in GATT were enervated by the increased number of participants and the widening of the range of issues to be tackled. Thus, attention turned to regional and bilateral trade arrangements which seemed to have brought gains, and Europe's success had removed any basis for argument that regional trade blocs would undermine global liberalization (Dornbusch 1993: 185). It remains to be seen whether a dual track strategy of regionalism and multilateralism can be mutually supportive, but recent case studies of the EC and GATT suggest that there is convergence in approaches to liberalization (Woolcock 1993).

The dual process led to the formation of NAFTA at the same time that multilateralism regained its momentum with the Uruguay Round of negotiations and came forth with the ambitious programme for global economic governance manifested in the World Trade Organisation (WTO). Just as the EC has attracted its penumbra of associated states and queue of applicants, NAFTA has also generated proposals for expansion, as well as raising issues of coordination with related hemispheric organizations. More broadly, it helped administer a stimulus to other regional free-trade area negotiations in the Asia-Pacific, Caribbean, and Africa. It remains to be seen whether multilateral global trade liberalization under the aegis of the WTO can achieve its goals against a background of solidifying trade blocs. But the very prospect of a successful dual strategy, signalled by the coincidence of the formation of NAFTA and the WTO, necessitates confrontation with its social and political implications. The central critique of this new market-focus is that it destabilizes the mechanisms necessary to regulate markets, and therefore exposes the world's population much more directly to the potentially destructive effects of market forces, from increasing inequalities of power and income to environmental degradation. The chapters in part 4 of this volume contribute to this body of criticism.

4.1 The New Market-Focus

The WTO now brings under a single umbrella an enormous range of economic regulatory matters, ranging from agricultural support programmes to property rights in computer programs. This creates a stronger basis for harmonization or coordination at global level of many regulatory régimes previously dealt with through specific bilateral or multilateral treaty arrangements. Thus, as part of the Uruguay Round bargains on market access, present or aspirant members of the WTO are to be obliged to accept a wide range of international rules and standards. These may be contained in other international agreements (e.g. intellectual property rights for integrated circuits), or go beyond such agreements (e.g. copyright protection for computer programs), or are more restrictive than such agreements (e.g. remuneration standards for compulsory patent licences). States are also required to bring their national health or technical product requirements into line with international standards, or accept products complying with exporting country standards if these are shown to be equivalent, or to justify their higher standards by scientific criteria and prove that they are not disproportionately damaging to trade. These provisions require that any state which does not wish to be the potential target of trade sanctions by being deprived of the right to Most-Favoured-Nation (MFN) treatment conferred by WTO membership, must accept that a wide range of its domestic arrangements for regulating economic activity be submitted to scrutiny for conformity with internationally-agreed criteria, and through international negotiations including WTO dispute-settlement.

Thus, the establishment of the WTO very clearly reveals a more general transformation which has been taking place in global governance: the undermining of the postwar neo-Keynesian régime of 'embedded liberalism' (Ruggie 1982) by means of 'subversive liberalism' (Rhodes 1994). The loss by even the most powerful states of control over monetary policy exposes the whole gamut of national government policies to the judgements of international financial markets and the pressures of international trade competition, creating the conditions for new alliances around market-oriented policy agendas. If this can be seen as the increasing tendency in the EC since the Single Market programme (as discussed in the previous section), it is even more clearly the case both for the WTO and the NAFTA. The price for access to world markets, for finance or goods, is the surrender of national autonomy over political decisions on measures involving market regulation, from permitted food additives to telecommunications interconnection rights, and from agricultural support systems to local content requirements for industry.

The critics of this new market-focus are divided about the remedy, however. Some argue for a broadening of the scope of international competence to include social issues, notably labour and the environment, as well as a strengthening of the procedures and institutions of global governance. Others call for the continued defence of national political autonomy, since they fear that the international sphere will inevitably be dominated by the interests of money, and that open markets and competition mean the lowering of standards. Certainly, it has been the forces of competition, as much or more than political pressures, that have put the labour and environmental issues on the agenda of the WTO and NAFTA. Countries with higher standards and vociferous domestic lobbies, in particular the USA, have been accused of imposing their rules on others as disguised protectionism. Nevertheless, the linkage demonstrates, as was seen in the examination of the EC Single Market in the previous section, that market-creation cannot be kept separate from social-protection, since markets are embedded in diverse regulatory régimes. The central questions, therefore, are how are these linked, are the mechanisms for coordinating the evaluation of the balance between market-creation and social-protection capable of constructive outcomes, and what scope should there be for diversity and competition among regulatory régimes?

The recognition that national regulation may provide as much of an obstacle as tariffs to international trade is not new, and it has equally long been understood that this requires some mechanisms of inter-state coordination. Lawyers have generally complained of the weaknesses of the international machinery, and have argued for a stronger international legal framework. Thus, a recommendation of the 1933 London Monetary and Economic Conference that consultations should be required if government actions are claimed to be affecting commerce is said to have been the origin of the 'nullification and impairment' clause, used especially in USA treaties, and developed as the cornerstone of both the GATT/WTO and the NAFTA disputes processes. The 'nullification and impairment' principle has been criticized as helping to justify unilateral action without regard to whether the difficulties of access to foreign markets may be due to breach of an international obligation (Hudec 1975: ch. 3). This was reinforced in GATT by the emphasis on conciliation rather than litigation, and therefore on political negotiation of differences between states rather than legal adjudication or interpretation of their mutual obligations. Only slowly did adjudication by Panels become established as part of GATT practice and then formalized in the 1979 Tokyo Round Understanding, but the domination of political and economic considerations over law in GATT procedures continued, as expressed in the practice of taking Council decisions by consensus, thus allowing parties effectively a veto both over the appointment of a Panel and implementation of its Report.

Under the WTO there has been a significant legalization of the dispute-settlement system. Now a Panel must be set up (if consultations have failed) unless there is a consensus against doing so, adoption of a Panel report is also semi-automatic (Petersmann 1994: 1208), and there is also a right of appeal to a standing Appellate Body. Doubts have been expressed, however, as to whether the new procedures will succeed in imposing stronger discipline on states, especially the most powerful, and may therefore be 'over-ambitious' and 'unrealistic' (Vermulst and Driessen 1995: 153). They certainly fall far short of the situation in the EC, where (as discussed in the previous section) the domination of law has largely deprived governments of the power to override central decisions in the name of political legitimacy. This may partly be attributable to different conceptions and forms of law: Kenneth W. Dam, a legal academic later to turn lawyer-diplomat before returning to the academy, described the perceived tension in GATT between legalism and pragmatism as due to a naive view of law as substantive rules rather than procedures and process, particularly in the international arena (Dam 1970). Certainly, it is the USA-trained lawyers who have invested most heavily in realist doctrines aimed at understanding law flexibly and in harness with policy, and who may be best placed to navigate the intricate channels of these international procedures, which in the complex of agreements grouped together under the WTO involve different types of expert groups as well as Panels and the Appellate Body (Vermulst and Driessen 1995). However, this has not prevented the USA from coming under attack (including criticism from USA lawyers) for using its dominant position in world trade to threaten unilateral sanctions and pursue bilateral negotiations, in preference to established GATT/WTO procedures, in disputes with trading partners such as Japan, most recently over auto components. In offering themselves and their techniques as the brokers of a more harmonious international order, USA lawyers frequently need to distance themselves from the power-political stances of the USA government.

The weakness of the central institutions of the WTO are paralleled in NAFTA, which gives few powers to its ministerial-level Free Trade Commission, and provides a dispute-settlement procedure like that of the GATT/WTO, based on the 'nullification and impairment' principle (Huntington 1993).[20] Just as the EC has faced increasingly complex inter- and intra-organizational coordination problems as it has widened and deepened, the question of NAFTA's relationships with other regional hemispheric bodies, such as MERCOSUR and the Andean Pact immediately raises a range of issues, although it may be questioned whether this should take place under the central guidance of NAFTA, as some have assumed (O'Hop 1995). Thus, what is taking place is not a coalescence around fixed trading and political blocs, but a process of liberalization and re-regulation involving overlapping circles or networks of bodies, each with their own political and economic dynamics.

Daniel Drache, in chapter 14, challenges the project of regional trade blocs and global liberalization head-on. His wide-ranging critique argues that the dramatic shift, from the gradual reduction of direct barriers to some types of merchandize trade under GATT, to the sweeping elimination of all obstacles to every type of trade and investment now envisaged, holds out an impossible dream of harmonious global economic integration. Few, if any mechanisms have been established, even within the EU despite its strong institutional base, to deal with the major problems of equivalence of market-access, power asymmetries among members of blocs, and resource-transfer to deal with adjustment difficulties. He argues that the successes of trade liberalization took place mainly in an earlier period, especially in the EC, when it was driven primarily by a political agenda but accepted that social issues and adjustment could and should continue to be dealt with at national level. He questions whether European social-democrats have been misled by the success of managed integration into accepting that further

---

[20] The Labour and Environment Side Agreements have their own procedures, which focus on whether each party is adequately enforcing its own laws: See Garvey 1995 and Stone in chapter 15.

liberalization can ensure the long-term future of the welfare state and social democracy. In North America, by contrast, the gradual liberalization of USA-Canada economic relations led, in his view, to increasing concern to protect Canadian distinctiveness, which is now threatened by the comprehensive character of the NAFTA.

This analysis sharply identifies the dilemma posed by the current processes of integration, which are opening the market throttle while abandoning the social-protection controls. Those who favour the market perspective tend to welcome the dissolving effects of liberalization on arrangements which they regard as protecting privileged positions and hindering the efficient working of markets; and if they accept that there may be some market breakdowns and externality problems, assume that these will manifest themselves in due course, and lead to appropriate intervention at the relevant level of government. Those who regard liberalization as a strategy with a dangerously corrosive effect on social institutions which are essential to regulate markets, must however confront more directly the problem of identifying what type of regulation is needed, and at what level of government. Some, like Drache, emphasize that broadening the international agenda to include social protection issues merely undermines effective national regulation. Even more tellingly, Drache points to the major issue of international resource-transfers. Even if national deregulation can be replaced by more effective measures of international re-regulation, and social citizenship and environmental protection principles formulated at the international level can create a focus for social and political pressures, it is hard to envisage the emergence in the near future of any substantial measures of fiscal adjustment or resource transfers to deal with international asymmetries and adjustment.

4.2 Labour Relations and Environmental Concerns

If the extent of centralized coordination on global trade regulation issues is low, their integration with social-protection issues, notably labour and the environment, is even lower. Here a significant question is whether the political pressures behind such social protection demands are weakened or strengthened when they are thrust into the trade arena, where the dominant concern is competition for market access. Unilateral actions, in particular by powerful trade blocs, such as the EC's over its beef-hormone rules, or the imposition of the complex USA drift-net fishing rules on other nations as a condition of acceptance of their tinned tuna, have inevitably fuelled accusations that health or environmental concerns are being used as a mere cloak for trade protectionism. This may account for the reluctance of states to widen the WTO's trade agenda to address environmental questions, even though their interconnectedness has become evident due both to unilateral actions such as those just mentioned, and to the attempt to restrict such actions by the emphasis on trade criteria, for example in the Agreement on Sanitary and Phytosanitary Standards (Charnovitz 1995: 25). The establishment of the WTO Environment Committee seems an altogether inadequate way to bring the two sets of concerns into fruitful interaction. The WTO's action on labour standards has also quickly hit difficulties, although the importance of joint action in this area was identified as long ago as the Treaty of Versailles and the setting up of the ILO. In the case of the NAFTA, political opposition to the entire agreement was only overcome by the addition of the Side Agreements on Labour and the Environment. The emphasis of these Agreements on process rather than substance has been heralded as 'revolutionary in establishing . . . a procedural mechanism that provides for compromises between free trade and national labour, health and environmental regulation' (Garvey 1995: 442). Yet this optimistic evaluation is belied by a closer examination: The procedures provide for complaint only if one party is demonstrating egregious failure to enforce its own national standards, and although there is some opportunity for involvement in them by pressure groups expressing public concern, they are oriented to political conciliation, and procrastination, taking over three years before the possibility of penalty is reached.

Significant differences must also be acknowledged between environmental and labour issues, affecting their relationship to the trade agenda. Thus, Katherine Stone in chapter 15 begins by pointing out that labour and environmental issues differ, in that in the former the group that stands to benefit the most from regulation is also the group that has the most to lose from any resultant business flight. Capital's 'exit' is labour's loss of 'voice'. That is, labour regulation involves a different type of prisoner's dilemma than is present in the environmental area. With labour regulation there are not two opposed parties, each of which is able to articulate its own interest in a policy arena, but it is the same group which has the strongest concerns on both sides of the issue. Labour's dilemma is exacerbated if it is politically embedded within national regulatory arrangements, as is the case for USA unions within the highly-regulated collective bargaining framework, and Stone also points to the national orientation and significant differences in labour regulation between EU states.

Stone develops a typology of coordination, distinguishing between integrative and interpenetrative approaches. The former, exemplified by the EU, may take the form of pre-emptive legislation (in the EU, Regulations directly applicable as law) or harmonization (EU Directives), while the latter, characteristic of North America, may take the form of cross-border monitoring and enforcement, or of unilateral, extraterritorial application of regulation. This typology provides a basis for analysing the merits and problems with each approach, and evaluating whether they are likely to create an upward or downward ratchet on labour standards. While the integrative approaches favoured in the EU may seem more harmonious, the preservation of national standards and a national focus for labour organization and democracy are identified as valuable advantages of the interpenetrative modes. Further complications can, of course, be introduced by applying the models to actual political processes. The different opportunities of mobility open to different actors, as well as the possibility of combining different strategies, naturally create a more complex picture, but the model is extremely helpful in identifying what may influence the strategies and arguments adopted. Stone's chapter also reminds us, as Picciotto's discussion in chapter 3 equally demonstrated, that regulation does not apply only within the closed borders of states, but may follow transborder economic contacts and produce extraterritorial and interpenentrative effects. While states may engage in forms of regulatory warfare, this interaction is also a form of coordination, and may produce convergence, if not harmonization.

Brian Langille, in the final chapter, returns to the analysis of regulatory competition as a strategic game, and argues that one's analysis of the nature of the game depends first on assumptions about the interaction of factors and their mobility, and second on the values attached to outcomes. The most familiar race to the bottom argument is that competition among rent-seeking states gives rise to an incentive in each to loosen costly labour and environmental regulations so as to maximize the profits of local firms, putting the states into a prisoner's dilemma in which a sub-optimal strategy of regulatory laxity dominates an optimal solution of coordinated regulation. In an influential essay, Revesz (1992) presented a detailed refutation of this position. Langille, in turn, deconstructs Revesz's argument. Among other things, Langille points out that the Revesz position relies on an especially strong set of assumptions, and argues that the process of relaxing the assumptions increases the probability that there will in fact be a prisoner's dilemma respecting labour and environmental regulation. Revesz, for example, assumes jurisdictions which do not pursue policies of attracting additional employment and investment; Langille points out that real world states are not indifferent to further investment and that competition for increased employment will impact on environmental standards.[21] Revesz asserts that competing states choose optimal levels of pollution without con-

---

[21] Here Langille contends that Revesz incorrectly applies the public sector economics that undergird his theory, in particular the model of Oates and Schwab (1988). Oates and Schwab demonstrate that rational jurisdictions in competition, when faced with two policy choices-either raising tax on capital or lowering the environmental standard-will reach an optimal equilibrium if they set a tax rate of zero. The problem for Revesz is that states do not tax capital at zero; hence there is competition between states over environmental standards. For Langille, the upshot is that the Oates and Schwab model, properly interpreted, cannot assist Revesz's argument because it assumes full employment. Langille goes on to argue that Oates and

sidering the impact of spillovers; Langille asserts that spillovers materially skew the incentive picture. Protagonists from both perspectives often also assume that what is needed to attract capital is a reduction of labour protection; however, some may take the view (as does de Jong in his chapter in Section 2) that labour participation provisions such as co-determination in Germany enhance corporate efficiency and may therefore be attractive for capital investment.

Langille concludes that even with a model built on assumptions reasonably congruent with the real world, judgements on the desirable outcome of competition ultimately depend on values. The classic prisoner's dilemma does not demonstrate that competition to confess produces a 'bad' outcome, but that what is bad for the prisoners may be good for society more generally. Thus, the 'market' perspective not only assumes mobility of factors, but also that such mobility is 'good'; whereas the 'social structures' perspective not only assumes that regulatory embeddeness limits mobility, but also that embeddedness is 'good'. The basis for a pessimistic prognosis, in Langille's view, is that the emerging international system is unsuited to the mediation of such normative conflict. The increased mobility of capital has challenged the traditional corporatist position of labour. At the same time, the emergence of trade blocs has placed economic policies beyond the reach of the nation state's traditional interest group networks. Given greater competition among states, it is unlikely that there will emerge a new set of international political structures adequate to provide a platform for the representation of the preferences of labour.

5. CONCLUSION

If there is a merit, therefore, in the regulatory competition debate, it may be that it forces us to reconsider many of the assumptions on which different paradigms, social strategies, and social institutions are based. In the major changes and upheavals taking place in global governance during this last decade of the century, if the issues and problems can be identified, the likely or even desirable outcomes are very far from clear. For social scientists, this involves some difficult feats, to combine audacious analysis with tentative conclusions, cogent debate with reflective methodology. We hope that this collection will contribute something to these tasks.

Schwab's model supports the view that states are heavily invested in attracting new investments and employment. As this last point suggests, the race to the bottom exists because of states' pursuit of self interest, which the PD approach is well-suited to reveal

PART I

Global (Re)visions

2

Between the State, Law, and the Market: The Social and Professional Stakes in the Construction and Definition of a Regulatory Arena

YVES DEZALAY*

REGULATORY SHOPPING V. REGULATORY COORDINATION . . . 'RACE TO THE BOTTOM' V. 'RACE TO THE TOP' THEORIES

As a result of the opening up of borders, the rules, institutions, and more generally the whole framework for economic activity in capitalist countries have become one of the weapons, as well as one of the stakes, in increased international competition. These legal devices are also one of the objects of an entire export-oriented—and imperialist—service industry of symbolic production, which aims to substitute the market economy for the various more or less interventionist systems of planning erected by the communist régimes, as well as the welfare states and the 'developmental states' (Castells 1992).

It is therefore hardly surprising that the analysis of these regulatory devices has once again become the focus of academic debate, not only among lawyers, but also economists and sociologists, who after a short period of neglect have rediscovered the issue of the government of economic activity. Rules and institutions are in fashion, but each participant gives them a definition which suits his or her position in the academic arena and strategy in the arena of professional practices. Thus, regulatory competition is paralleled by competition over the representation of this regulatory arena. How should it be defined? Is it concerned with rules and legal institutions, as most lawyers suggest, at least implicitly? Or should it include 'markets, hierarchies, states, networks and associations' (Hollingsworth *et al.* 1994, p. 8), in other words a whole range of devices for governing the economy which are combined differently according to the country, the sector of activity, and the epoch, to make up an extraordinary variety of 'modes of regulation'?

* Translated from the French by Sol Picciotto.

These questions are of more than merely academic interest. These learned debates are also strategic arguments in the 'palace wars' between the different skills and the different fractions of the class which governs in this arena—or these arenas—of regulation, on the overlapping boundaries between the fields of state power and business. They involve both political and professional stakes, which internationalization has only raised: by shaking up the borders of markets and states, it compels the redefinition of these arenas, and more specifically of their interaction; thus, it sets off a giant game of musical chairs which is also played on the field of discourse about governance. This is what has sparked the revival of interest and heightened competition which add to the confusion about the meaning of this notion of regulation.[1]

This Babel-effect is further increased when the comparative dimension is added. There is such diversity in the histories of national structures in which the field of economic power is continually being refashioned that such basic notions as the state, professions and the law cover quite different realities. In particular, the structures of the law and its place in both the field of the state and that of business are very dissimilar on either side of the Atlantic. Hence, to compare these two models of regulation without taking account of the fact that they do not relate to the same social reality would lead to multiple confusions. Yet this international dimension cannot be ignored since this is precisely what has 'dealt the new hand' in these arenas of professional practices. These 'palace wars' are an inseparable part of a geopolitical battle. The exporting of the market economy, as has been said, involves symbolic imperialism.

The generalisation of the North American model of the lawyer as privileged operator of a 'regulatory process' defined in juridical terms is one of the stakes—and one of the supporting elements—in a process of 'globalization' which is also a battle for global domination. In exporting or imposing a mode of economic governance which it can dominate all the better for having been its inventor, the North American ruling class is giving itself the means of extending its hegemony over the whole of the planet. After all, it is no accident that the rise of this system of legal production invented in Wall Street and which we have called 'Cravathism' is part of the tidal wave of internationalisation (Trubek, Dezalay *et al.* 1993). These Wall Street lawyers, or the imitators which they have produced and trained almost everywhere, are the modern mercenaries of this new brand of symbolic imperialism[2] which has been called 'global unilateralism' (Whitman 1984, cited in Strange 1986: 152).

[1] To reduce the risk of such confusion—and yet without claiming to take a position in this debate, since my aim is precisely to define the social and professionals stakes which are involved—I will use the term regulation to refer to the ensemble of legal and social devices.

[2] Just as, in another age, the European legislators (at the side of the missionaries and teachers) took up the baton from the colonial armies to reinforce the subjugation of those populations by imposing on them a western legal system presented as universal and liberating.

In this context of symbolic struggle, how should *regulatory competition* be analysed? To think of it as limited to the creation of competition between different rules and legal institutions, and avoiding the question of their embeddedness (Granovetter 1985) in a whole system of more informal devices, whether statist or corporatist, is to be 'legal-centric' (Galanter 1981) and blindly mistake a part for the whole. But in this case, indeed, this perception is partial in both senses of the word. To privilege formal rules, without taking account of the social process which has allowed the law and lawyers to occupy a more or less central place in the ensemble of regulatory provisions, surely provides support for this new imperialism which advances under the banner of legalism?

These very real difficulties are not peculiar to this subject. As Bourdieu remarks, in attempting to think about any social subject-matter which presents itself with all the appearance of being natural, such as the state, the law, or the professions, the analysis is liable to be conducted on the basis of conceptual categories created by and for these institutions themselves. To escape this redundance effect, tied to the correspondence between objective and cognitive structures, he suggests that 'there is perhaps no more powerful instrument for providing rupture than the reconstruction of origins' which permits the identification of "discarded possibilities" (1993: 51).

Rather than speculate about whether the international market in regulation leads to a 'race to the bottom' or 'to the top', on the basis of political presuppositions,[3] or of one or another legal theory of regulation,[4] it seems to me more useful to try to clarify the political and professional stakes involved in this recomposition of national regulatory arenas, by reminding ourselves of the strategic game in—and by—which they were originally constructed.[5] This is indeed the source of their specificity, but also what gives them their 'competitive advantages' in this 'global market' for regulatory

---

[3] One should be wary of simplistic judgments which associate deregulation with right-wing politics, or the converse. Thus, in France, the deregulation of financial markets was carried out by a socialist Minister (Beregovoy), who cannot be said to have been part of the French financial establishment. One of the objectives was to upset the habits and positions of a banking and state establishment which was not too well-disposed towards the then socialist newcomers. 'Naori [the *chef de cabinet* of Beregovoy] wanted to throw a rock into this pool where the financial and administrative lobbies were each protecting the other' (Mamou 1987: 270). This finding has a more general applicability. For many reforms, the ostensible philosophy counts perhaps for less than the 'new hand' which it deals and the repositioning to which it leads within a field of practices. There is therefore no alternative but to analyse them pragmatically case-by-case.

[4] In any case, as McCraw suggests, after analysing the ancestry of the American regulatory model, 'all overarching theories and heroic generalizations about 'Regulation' (with a capital R) run an extremely high risk of being in error' (1984: 301). What price a global perspective!

[5] This historical approach is complementary to the work I have published elsewhere on the current confrontation between the 'American model' and the 'European model': in particular, on the management of the market for corporate control (Dezalay 1992, 1995*b*) and the constitution of a field of international arbitration (Dezalay & Garth, forthcoming).

know-how. Since I neither have the space, nor above all the knowledge, to develop a general theory of the social process of construction of regulatory arrangements, I will content myself with showing how, on either side of the Atlantic, they have been developed according to two quite different models: around the law (and lawyers), and around the state.

In contrast to the 'North American model', in which the lawyers play a central part in regulatory processes thanks to the multiplicity of positions they occupy in the fields of the state and politics as well as in business and the academy, in the French model it is the 'grands corps' of the elite groups, with their strong professional bonding based on their selection and training through the *grandes écoles*, which occupy the same positions and visibly play the same role of intermediary between the state and the market. Yet there is a major and significant difference: the former claim to represent the Rule of Law, while the latter to represent State Rule.[6] This difference of terms in fact reflects the ways in which these national arenas are built and structured, and the players and rules of the game. It also reveals what is at stake in the game now being played over the law.

The construction of Europe—and more generally the opening of borders—are indeed seen as an excellent opportunity to regain lost ground by a European legal elite which sees itself as having been outranked in the field of power. This demotion is related to its marginalization in the field of governance which has pushed judicial institutions to the sidelines by creating direct links between state agencies and corporate networks (Abel-Smith & Stevens 1967). The new ideologists' prediction that the law will stage a major come-back as a result of internationalization is also because the construction of the European Single Market and the acceleration of the process of economic concentration are reproducing in Europe the socio-political context which on the other side of the Atlantic facilitated the emergence of a legalist model of regulation of economic activity, making judges the umpires in the 'economic wars' between two modes of production: small business and monopoly capital.

I. THE 'NORTH AMERICAN MODEL': LEGALISM AND MOBILITY

To describe the North American model of regulation as a legalist one may today seem either obvious or banal. Yet this legalisation of economic relations is diametrically opposed to the 'non-contractual relations' revealed by Macaulay's classic study (1963). Could this legalism be a recent phenome-

[6] Translator's note: here the language difference also reflects the different histories and cultures: the English term *rule of law* divorces right entirely from the state, unlike the French *l'Etat de Droit* (equivalent to the German *Rechtstaat*); on the other hand the French term lends itself neatly to inversion as *le Droit de l'Etat,* which can only be imperfectly rendered in English.

non? Could legal regulation be limited strictly to the domain of intervention by federal agencies? In which case, what is the relationship between these law-based processes and the entire ensemble of social networks which daily ensure the regulation of a 'relational capitalism'?

A proper reply to these questions—especially the last one—requires a historical approach.[7] It does indeed seem to be the case that the role of law in these arrangements has greatly increased, especially in the past two or three decades. This is as much due to the intervention of federal agencies as to the specific dynamic of the legal field. My central hypothesis is precisely that these two types of phenomena are closely interrelated. The emergence, the rise, and more generally the impact of the federal agencies can only be understood if one takes into account the positions and strategies of their protagonists within the legal field. Conversely, it was by the deployment of the authority and state-derived legitimacy of the regulatory institutions that the business-law practitioners were able gradually to come to dominate the field of business as professionals in the formalization of economic relations. Relational capitalism as described by Macaulay still exists, but the management of these relations has been professionalized and they are increasingly cast in legal forms. Nevertheless, they have not lost their social and interpersonal dimension; but personal relations between lawyers have tended to replace personal relations between entrepreneurs.

In emphasizing the dynamics of the field of practices, I do not mean to deny the importance of external determinations, notably in relation to the transformation of the business field. These two aspects are indeed closely linked. As Bourdieu (1987b) has suggested, the degree of formalism in social relations—and hence of recourse to legal forms—is often a function of social distance. The market for law is partly a function of the degree of cohesion and of social proximity between economic agents. From this perspective, there are wide variations and the path of development is not reducible to an almost inevitable process of atomization and weakening of communitarian links. Political crises or technological innovations help to make and unmake social networks.

Thus, at the end of the last century, it was the relentless acceleration of the process of capitalist concentration and restructuring which allowed the anti-trust judge to impose himself as the umpire between two worlds which

---

[7] My aim here is neither to theorize the North American regulatory system nor to give an account of its history, but simply to recall the political and professional circumstances prevailing in the period of the development of some of its major institutions, anti-trust or SEC. These have certainly subsequently changed substantially (cf Eisner 1991). This may be due at least partly to the routinization of the practices, and therefore downgrading of the recruitment to these institutions, which began as pioneer ventures and gradually became integrated into the professional landscape and career patterns. Hence the radical critiques of 'capture' of regulatory bodies, which were put forward only shortly before their revival and reorientation under the auspices of the believers of neo-liberalism. However, as is often the case for state bodies, analysis of their origins reveals their main structural characteristics.

were ignorant of and hated each other, almost to the verge of a civil war. In contrast, in the relatively prosperous climate of the 1960s, the business community in Wisconsin studied by Macaulay was no doubt homogeneous enough to spare itself the expense of the law by taking advantage of the important personal links facilitated by social and spatial proximity. To a certain extent it was the same for relations between large firms, especially in periods of economic growth: the relative social homogeneity of the group of top managers facilitated arrangements 'between ourselves', far from the publicity generated by recourse to the courts. In any case, in this small world of business law, it was a social elite of corporate lawyers who played the role of mediators and intermediaries, relying essentially on their experience and their contacts. Just like their clients, these 'leading lights' of business law were suspicious of courts, with which they only had tenuous and somewhat mistrustful connections.[8] The exception was in periods of crisis when this 'low legality', such as that of the bankruptcy courts, turned out to be very useful for the 'lowly tasks' involved in the restructuring of capital (Gordon 1984).

In this model of regulation, judicial intervention in the regulation of economic activity was therefore fairly rare. Daily business matters—meaning those which did not involve major political stakes—were regulated 'in the shadow of the law'. It was only relatively late that this pattern began to be upset, and for various related reasons. From the 1970s, the oil crisis, and then the monetary upheavals and the intensification of international competition set off a profound and lasting restructuring of the business field, upsetting the stable alliances and networks which supported informal regulation. At the same time, the mushrooming of law schools and the rise of a market for regulation facilitated the entry into the market for business law of a meritocracy, which was especially enthusiastic to use the courts tactically in economic battles since those essentially were its special skills, as it did not have the wordly wisdom or the social capital of its elders. This meritocracy used the regulatory bodies for its apprenticeship both in the courts and in the business world. The emergence of a regulatory field therefore played a key role in the juridification of the field of business. Conversely, it

---

[8] It is in this context of mistrust and distance between the world of business and that of courts that what is called the 'Delaware effect' should be understood. This strategic choice gave the big business leaders (and their advisers) the assurance, in case of need, of access to a legality which would be, if not 'made to measure', at least specialized, in tune with their preoccupations and familiar with their arguments. This, according to Max Weber, is the main requirement of the business world as regards legality. The ad hoc courts set up during the big medieval fairs were the first manifestation of this. But there are many others, with more or less close relationships to state jurisdictions: the London Commercial Court, the French Tribunaux de Commerce, as well as all the forms of commercial arbitration, both domestic or international . . . In this last case, which is tending to become a sort of 'offshore justice' (Dezalay and Garth 1995), these relationships depend on the professional eminence of the arbitrators. This raises the question of whether the 'Delaware effect' might largely result from this factor — which would make it the equivalent of the Commercial Court.

is because the law and lawyers were for a long period at the centre of the political game that these new state regulatory devices were cast in a legal mould.

It was indeed very early when judges found themselves in the position of umpires between the different social groups fighting each other in the state arena. As Sklar has shown (Sklar 1988), the anti-trust laws made the judge the arbiter of a political equilibrium between the appetites of the big Wall Street financiers, who wanted to profit from carrying through the necessary rationalization of the apparatus of production, and the fears of a middle class of small entrepreneurs whose populist ideology expressed their desperation to fight off the threats to social structures and their mode of production.

Paradoxically, in putting themselves forward as strict defenders of the traditional conception of a competitive market in the face of a federal authority which was more responsive to new arguments in terms of macroeconomic equilibrium and efficiency, the Supreme Court judges were acting in conformity not only with a professional ideology and social origins which predisposed them to be defenders of the 'little' against the 'big', they were also contributing to the institutionalization of the power of the big Wall Street lawyers as intermediaries, as necessary as they were legitimate, in the market for corporate restructuring. The complexity and seriousness of the legal and juridical provisions made the former indispensable to the financiers who employed them; they also allowed them to demonstrate a certain autonomy in relation to those over-powerful clients who were always tempted to reduce them to the status of 'hired guns' (Gordon 1984).

This example already contains all the essential ingredients which characterise the American model and have ensured, if not its success, at least the prosperity and the social attainments of those who were both its inventors and its operators. What is striking is the complementarity of roles between those who appear as the guardians of the general interest and those who defend private interests. Indeed this structural complementarity is so strong that both these roles can be carried out by the same person—whether successively or even simultaneously. Gordon (1984) gives a perfect description of this 'institutional schizophrenia' of the elite of the New York Bar, attempting to preserve the ideals and the 'civic virtues' of the gentleman lawyer, while showing no embarassment or scruples in their mercenary activities in the service of the 'robber barons'.

In contributing to the development of an ideal of the law, the members of this professional elite developed rules to which they subjected themselves (and above all perhaps their collaborators and competitors who were even less scrupulous, being more careerist). These rules were just so many firebreaks to shelter them from the demands of clients who could have created dangers for their ultimate credibility and legitimacy by making them appear too openly as simple instruments in the service of capital. Their position condemned them to be 'double agents', now public servants, now mercenaries, fashioning with one hand the rules which they were striving to evade with the other. The more they undermined the image of the law by appearing as 'hired guns' in the service of the highest bidder, the more they had to augment in parallel the authority of the law which is the basis of their social power. Such a double game, although very profitable, is also a very delicate one to play. So it is confined to a small elite, skilled at accumulating positions and titles. This also explains the large contribution which these great business lawyers made to the growth of the great law schools. By subcontracting this double role of learned authority and moral conscience to a special category of professional, a solution was found to that dilemma, by transforming an 'institutional schizophrenia' into a rational division of symbolical labour.

The law schools therefore came to play a central role in the emergence of these arrangements of legal regulation. The great professors such as Pound or Frankfurter wanted to be reformers and 'social engineers'. They tried to inculcate this public service mission in their best pupils. Obviously, the moralism of this education was not enough to make the majority of these graduates turn aside from the career mapped out for them in the big Wall Street firms. At least it maintained the schizophrenic predispositions of these WASP gentleman lawyers who saw themselves as an enlightened elite. On the other hand, this appeal to build an 'alternative' elite ready to devote itself to the service of institutions embodying the general interest[9] was bound to strike a very strong chord among the minority fraction of the young graduates for whom, because of their social origins, the royal road to a legal career was closed. This was even more so in the periods of crisis when the Wall Street elite could give their prejudices free rein, due to the slowdown in the business law market.

During the New Deal period all these conditions came together.[10] Roosevelt could fish in this breeding-ground of brilliant social outsiders to recruit lawyers whose competence matched their predisposition to dress his reformist programme in legal clothes, the better to defend it from the attacks of the legal establishment.[11] It is true that the moral authority and

[9] Frankfurter's ambition was to set up in the United States of America an elite civil service on the British model (McCraw 1984). Thus he became a 'job-broker', directing his pupils towards those New Deal agencies which for this meritocracy represented a 'unique opportunity for upward professional and social mobility'.

[10] 'It [public service] attracted young, upwardly mobile, minority-group lawyers whose professional advancement within traditional channels was thwarted by the Depression and frustrated by the social structure of the bar' (Auerbach 1976: 173).

[11] 'The prototypical New Dealer was an upwardly mobile urbanite, a second-generation member of an ethnic minority group with superior academic credentials' (Auerbach 1976: 174).

the political power of this establishment were quite shaken by a crisis the depth of which underlined their powerlessness and the urgency of devising new solutions to the failures of the capitalist market.

If, contrary to what happened in Europe, the crisis of 1929 did not result in the United States of America in the disqualification of legal forms as a means of governing the market, the credit goes to this alternative elite. While opposing the political views of the legal notables, they shared their devotion to the law.[12] They were all the more legalist since they had to make up for the weakness of their social capital by an additional investment in legal techniques and belief in the virtues of the law.

This shared belief greatly facilitated the ultimate reconciliation of these opponents and the integration of this meritocracy of combative outsiders into the dominant institutions of the business law world. It is true that these 'prodigal sons' did not return empty handed. They were bearers of this entire new market of economic regulation, the intricacies of which they knew better than anyone since they had helped fashion them. By welcoming them as partners, the big law firms at the same stroke were acquiring a slice of expert capital and of contacts which ensured their mastery of this new and rapidly growing market, for the benefit of their big business clientele.

By putting the weight of their experience and reputation in the service of the entrepreneurs, the 'founding fathers' completely overturned the balance of forces which they had helped to establish in this space of legal regulation between the public and private poles. The reversal is all the greater since the successors of these 'pioneers' are not necessarily of the same calibre. Taking the side-road through the state agencies no longer smacks of that brave strategy, capable of attracting those very special individuals who are ready to opt for careers at the frontiers of law and politics, where the symbolic profits are commensurate with the risks taken. Their success stimulates imitators, but with a more ordinary profile. Once out of their formative period, the institutions do not need creators but managers. Neither the risks nor the profits are comparable.

So we come to the usual account in which these state agencies are used as a sort of 'passing lane' for those professionals who enter the market for regulation by the 'side-door'. Taking the detour through these institutions whose esteem is as low as their pay-rates provides a second chance for those young people who—for educational or social reasons—could not get access to the big firms where the most high-flying and prestigious careers are made.

[12] As Auerbach (1976) rightly remarks: 'the ideology of legalism had become the dominant ideology of decision-making in government (226) (. . .) lawyer's skills (drafting, negotiation, compromise) and lawyer's values (process divorced from substance, means over ends) permitted New Deal achievements, yet set New Deal boundaries. (. . .) Social problems were amenable to resolution by enacting a statute, creating an administrative agency and staffing it with law review editors' (227).

This apprenticeship allows them to acquire practical knowledge and contacts, which the more ambitious—or lucky—ones will be able to cash in by rejoining the private sector after some years of 'purgatory' in the service of the state.

The path taken by the leading lights of the law in the field of regulation is quite different from that of this hard-working meritocracy who only gain entry by the 'side door' after proving their worth in the arena. The royal road which allows you to play the role of 'power broker' in the regulatory field is that of lobbying in the wings—or sometimes also on the main stage—of the big federal institutions. What counts in this power strategy is the amassing of positions, relationships, and titles which allow a person always to be in the right place, while wielding the social resources and symbolic skills necessary to insert themselves everywhere as indispensable mediators. Due to the extraordinary mobility and multi-positioning of the Washingtonian elites, the lines of force between the public and private poles are extremely variable and fluctuating. However, to the extent that the great law firms function as a source of tactical support (and if necessary a fallback post) in these strategies, which unfold on the cross-roads of the legal and the political, commercial preoccupations are ever-present. These specialists who are at the heart of the regulatory machinery are above all dealers. Naturally, they are dealers who also know how to speak like 'statesmen', that is to say by taking into account preoccupations of a political nature. But is this not exactly what, properly understood, is needed in the interests of a clientele of big multinational firms which must take political factors into account in their investment decisions? In other words, the strategy of these eminent specialists in regulation who create an image for themselves as statesmen perfectly corresponds to the strategy of multinationals who, by dint of negotiating as equals with states, tend to behave like them.

These two career paths for regulatory agents—by the side door or the main entrance[13]—is therefore central to the North American regulatory system. It explains both the strengths and weaknesses of the system, as well as its dynamics. In fact, the history of the regulatory institutions is not a linear one. It consists of a series of innovations and retreats which provide newcomers with strategic opportunities to build their careers by taking advantage of the transformations of the social field to extend the regulatory field. But, outside the crisis periods when the creation of new regulatory

[13] This model is also what we have observed in the field of arbitration (Dezalay & Garth 1995). It is also a much more general one in all the symbolic fields which must simultaneously identify their specific identity and establish exchange networks with civil society. In studying this phenomenon in the religious or the cultural fields, Bourdieu (1982) came to distinguish between the 'lower orders' of monks (the *oblats*), who abandon all worldly goods and identity and devote themselves entirely to the worship and cultivation of the values of the field which they enter by the side door, and the 'high priests' from whom the institution in no way expects such a sacrifice, since it benefits from the social capital and eminence which they represent.

devices temporarily becomes law's 'new frontier', this field is structured in favour of the defenders of private interests. Nevertheless, the domination of this field of practices by the spokes-persons for private interests (or those who aspire to this role) should not be seen as simply the 'capture' of the regulatory agencies. If there is a capture, it has a double meaning. The mobility of the agents also entails a degree of dissemination of a public order logic—one which takes account of the major elements of social equilibrium—even into big business. In this scenario, the professionals play the main role of courtier, but also that of 'double agent', between the State and the market. So the intersection of these two worlds can be seen either as a delegation to the entrepreneurs of public authority—but also public responsibilities—or as the introduction of competition and of merchants into the world of the state and the constitution of a market in public order, indeed a market in expertise and state legitimacy (Dezalay 1993).

To summarize, the central place of law and lawyers in regulatory processes is in no way natural or immutable. It is continually reconstructed by a professional elite, which is both exclusive as well as relatively open to entry by the more successful of a meritocracy of social outsiders. In terms of imagery, it could be said that it is an order of legal knights which has managed to take advantage of crises periodically to re-gild its coat of arms at the cost of accepting some alliances with more lowly newcomers who had accumulated some valuable social capital by opening up new markets and new spaces of influence for the law. This strategy of forming lowly alliances has allowed it to keep its positions in the field of state power, as well as in that of economic power. The two are inseparable. It is vital, for a professional group which lays claim to the role of mediator, to keep a balance between these two poles of power, since they are mutually complementary. Law's authority—and hence the value of lawyers—in the field of business is based on the mastery of the spaces and the instruments where the regulation of economic activity takes place.

2. THE 'FRENCH MODEL': THE MARGINALIZATION OF LEGAL PROFESSIONALS IN A FAIRLY CLOSED REGULATORY SPACE

In comparison with this schema of the emergence of a field of regulation which expands until it merges with that of the practitioners of business law, the history of Europe[14] provides a sort of counter-example: one of regula-

---

[14] The warning previously given about this highly schematic version of history is even more important here due to the diversity of European histories as regards the relationships between entrepreneurs, law and the state (Siegrist 1993). Given the length of this paper, and to be able to go beyond generalities, it has seemed better to focus on the 'French model' since it is in sharp contrast to the 'American model'. However, it would be wrong to see this as exceptional in European terms. The enclosure of the regulatory arena, the marginalization of the legal

tory processes which develop at the margins of the law and largely avoid judicial institutions. There is a total contrast between the two sides of the Atlantic: on the one side, as we have just recounted, the circulation of members of the elite between its various fractions helps to ensure the relative homogeneity of a regulatory process which is both at the heart of the field of business law and closely involved with that of economic power; on the other side, by contrast, the distance between the state, the judicial institutions and the business world is so great that it is quite difficult to speak of a single field of regulation.

Due to these big differences, there is some danger in using the concept of regulation. There is a great risk—or temptation—to take a part for the whole, by acting as if regulation is identical with and limited to one or other of the elements of a divided world: the rule of law, state intervention, and the more or less informal processes of self-regulation. The misreading which results from this partial (in both senses of the word) perspective is all the more serious since the competitive battles between these different regulatory processes—and the antagonisms between the different categories of agents who represent them—make a major contribution to the dynamics of these arenas of practices.

These multiple processes of 'corporate governance' are defined and constructed by their opposition to each other. When they nationalize large firms, or intervene more or less directly in their management through the terms of credit, industrial policies, or 'indicative' planning, the supporters of the welfare state claim to correct or prevent market disequilibrium. They denounce the economic inefficiency and social injustice of a juridico-economic order which follows a strictly commercial and contractual logic. Indeed, often they do not stop at suspending or modifying the freedom of contractual relations, they also ensure that judicial institutions are kept in the background (Abel-Smith & Stevens 1967). According to the well-known formula, 'state rule replaces the rule of law'.

Conversely, 're-legalization' is directly tied to the success of neo-liberal policies in dismantling a state machinery which was denounced as costly, clumsy, and inefficient. The great majority of legal practitioners openly rejoice in this 'restoration' of the rule of law, which they expect will bring an end to a long period of political marginalization and social decline. At the same time, they have embarked on the 'reconquest'—or more accurately the conquest—of the position which they consider they deserve in the management of business. Depending on the positions they occupy, the learned lawyers contribute in various ways, direct or indirect, to this strategy of challenging, or even denouncing, 'relational capitalism'. The new generation

professions in the business field and the dominant role of state-based processes are present to various extents in most European countries, even if the routes towards them have been very different (cf Abel-Smith & Stevens 1967; Hall 1986).

of business lawyers, trained in the American style, is trying to profit from the process of restructuring of the field of economic power, accelerated by the crisis and internationalization, to promote a legalized, American-style managerial system. At the same time, the eminent lawyers are trying to extend the economic powers of state bodies by using the creation of the European Single Market and the establishment of a 'level playing-field' to press for powers of judicial review over the corporatist-style self-regulatory bodies (Bancaud & Boigeol 1995). Finally, even the learned lawyers who are apparently the furthest removed from the business world make their own contribution, although a more indirect one, to this attempt to juridify economic relations: especially by using the court bench to denounce as corruption the more or less hidden financial arrangements linking the political class with the world of business (*mani pulite* in Italy: Bergalli 1994).

Naturally, we should make allowances for rhetorical devices when considering these mutual denunciations. There has been frequent movement between these different levels of regulation of economic activity, and a small number of lawyers have played, as elsewhere, the role of broker between these different worlds to which they have had access. The state bureaucracies generally resorted to public law specialists to give their interventions legal legitimacy by clothing them in legal forms. Elsewhere, by accepting a few 'leading eminent lawyers' in those circles or networks which structured the world of economic rulers, the business establishment to some extent sheltered itself from the law; at least, it limited the right of oversight of ordinary courts into its 'gentlemen's codes' and prevented any attempt to interfere in what was no more than a form of 'private justice'.[15]

However, the relationships between these various regulatory bodies were exceptional and precarious. Far from being institutionalized, they remained unofficial and relied essentially on the goodwill of a few individuals, who were always somewhat suspected of being 'double agents'. The articulation between all these arrangements for governing the economy therefore was not based on any rational division of regulatory tasks, but rather on a competitive drive between agents who were more likely to denigrate each other than to co-operate. The major characteristic of this European market in regulation was—and remains—its closed nature, and only a small role is played in it by legal practitioners and juridical institutions, although for the past few years, due to the development of European integration and more generally of internationalization, they have been busy building up their positions.

To understand this phenomenon of exclusion and of marginalization, it is necessary to go back into the history of the legal field, all the more so

---

[15] The City Code and the Take-Over Panel were—and still are—a classic example of this type of self-regulation 'at the margins of the law' (Dezalay 1995*b*). But many other examples can be found, especially in the arbitral procedures which operated in the framework of the Chambers of Commerce and Industry.

since the same conflicts and accusations can be seen in the past. The problem comes from the fact that this professional field, like most institutions of
symbolic power, has a virtual monopoly on the social discourse about itself
(Charle 1992). History is continually rewritten to produce legitimacy, or for
tactical advantages in the internal struggles in the fields of power. Thus, in
France, where the legal professionals have found it hard to accommodate
to their loss of influence and prestige, there are repeated references to the
grand old days when the High Court of Paris (the *Parlement*) dared to stand
out against royal absolutism, and to that other 'golden age' of the *république
des avocats*. The implicit thesis is that the fortunes—and the misfortunes—
of the Bar are linked to its political and professional choices: cultivating
neutrality and renouncing business to become the spokesperson and
defender of public opinion in the face of the state's authoritarianism. By
deliberately cutting themselves off from the world of the economy, the practitioners of law tied their fate to that of their politics. The arrival of the
Third Republic (from the 1870s), on this account, was the apogee of the
activist struggles of a young republican Bar. Conversely, the marginalization of juridical institutions in the field of state power is said to be the heri-
tage of the old mistrust that both Royal and revolutionary power-holders
had of the High Courts (*Parlements*) of the *ancien régime*.

   While these versions undoubtedly have a kernel of truth, they are inadequate as a basis of understanding of the position of lawyers in the market(s)
of regulation, to the extent that they keep in the shadows all the struggles
between the different fractions of the dominant class played out at the
intersection of the state and civil society, and thus precisely on the legal
arena.

   As Charle (1992: 202) recalls, 'the main struggle of the High Court of
Paris was against anything which threatened its position as a *corps d'Etat*
[major state institution], that is to say the new bureaucrats with which the
monarchy was surrounding itself'. And the mobilization of public opinion
(which at that time was confined to the small circle of the Parisian bourgeoisie) essentially played a tactical support role in a battle waged at the
heart of the state. What was at stake was the relative position in the hierarchy within this field of power.

   A century later, the stakes and the competing institutions are almost the
same; but the bases of their recruitment and the social forces on which they
rely are changing. Certainly, during the whole of the 19th century the most
intellectual fractions of the Parisian bourgeoisie still provided the basis of
that public opinion of which the tenors of the republican bar made themselves the mouthpieces during the major political trials. But gradually the
elite of these well-heeled and well-educated classes distanced itself from the
main institutions of the legal field, which were increasingly identified with a
static or even conservative image.

Subjected to political power and recruited essentially from among provincial notables, the judiciary became a bastion of moral order. Even at the heart of the Bar, active republicans were only a small minority, more noisy than representative. More generally, apart from a minority gambling their careers on a political strategy—most frequently, indeed, on the side of the powers-that-be, in the Public Prosecutor's office[16]—the legal world shelters mainly notables, usually from the provinces, amateurish and conservative. Rentiers or careerists of modest origins, what these two fractions have in common is the distance that separates them from the world of business. This is what explains the ideology of neutrality which predominates in the Bar (Karpik 1992): whatever their other differences as regards class and divergences of opinion, the *avocats*-political activists and the rentier-notables of the Bar were agreed on the denunciation of any involvement in the business world as meddling with 'trade'. Even if it was for very different reasons, neither group was keen to strike out into a world which was very unfamiliar to them. Moreover, the emergence of a market in business law would have endangered—even more than today—the image of unity which the Bar carefully cultivates because it allows it to defend its collective prerogatives.

This denunciation of the practices of business law did not prevent them from prospering, but this success occured at the margins of the legal professional world in the strict sense of the term.[17] Rejected by their peers, the lawyers who became interested in the business world had no option but to join it officially by themselves becoming 'men of affairs'. This change of designation somewhat modified their role: they acted as intermediaries in commercial transactions which they helped to 'put into legal form' and in which they sometimes intervened for their own account; elsewhere, they could be called upon as mediators of conflicts, but most often informally.[18] In short, it was doubtless these rejects from the world of 'noble' legal practices who were largely responsible for the rise of the processes of self-regulation and of private justice 'in the shadow of the law'.

If the denunciation of involvement in 'trade' by the Bar shows the widening gulf between the 'active' and the rentier fractions of the bourgeoisie, the creation of the Free School of Political Sciences (1872) demonstrates that the most intellectual and dynamic layers of the ruling class also are keeping remote from a world of law that they are leaving to the provincial notables and the tribune-*avocats*. This project is openly elitist: its aims are to train statesmen, or more precisely to select and educate the scions of the ruling

---

[16] As Karpik remarks (1992 p. 309), the politicization of the courts primarily comes about through the activism of the representatives of government Ministries who hope by this means to obtain the favours of those with political power.

[17] Particularly by taking the part of banker or intermediary, or one related to less 'noble' professional groups such as accountants (Sugarman 1993).

[18] Although they might have the possibility of defending their clients in the commercial courts.

classes and turn them into 'government professionals' (Damamme 1987). But this project, the promoters of which are themselves situated at the intersection of the economic, intellectual and political fields, is aimed at the most intellectual or innovative fractions of the high bourgeoisie. Convinced that 'it was the University of Berlin that won the battle of Sadowa' (Damamme 1987: 33) these reformers are immersed in positivism and scientism, and intend to construct a modern bureaucracy, whose dowry includes the double legitimacy of birth and knowledge.

This School identifies itself with the political sciences also because it is designed as a weapon to wage war on the law faculties which are so 'rooted in their doctrinal traditionalism and their corporatism' that they have refused to open themselves up to these new fields of knowledge and new practices establishing themselves around the sciences of the state and the economy (Le Van-Lemesle 1983). This is precisely the gap which is aimed to be filled by this School sponsored by innovative scholars, top civil servants and the leading entrepreneurs in business or banking of the period.

The educational project and the political ambitions of these reformers conformed to their social positions: they were thus the very opposite of what the law faculties represented. The latter at that time were notorious for the weakness of their teaching and the absenteeism of their students.[19] The latter, it is true, had little reason to be motivated by their studies, since they mostly came from not very intellectual backgrounds and knew instinctively that their careers would be determined much more by the patronage that they could obtain than by the technical skills that they might acquire.[20]

By recruiting its students preferably from the most open and intellectual fraction of the Parisian bourgeoisie and by paying much more attention to their educational environment, the new institution quickly and easily came to dominate the market for training the new state elites. Ever since then, the fame of the 'sciences po' went along with that of the 'grands corps' which in many ways constituted the new learned nobility. More exactly, they are its heirs to the extent that they have facilitated the conversion of the old

[19] This description was still applied, according to Dahrendorf (1969), to the German law faculties in the sixties.

[20] Karady (1991) makes a similar observation about pre-war Hungary to which he attributes the relative scholarly mediocrity of the law faculties. Hierarchical position in the legal field owes much more to social capital than to educational capital. This generalization—which applies to France, as well as Germany (cf Dahrendorf, ibid.), and to Latin America (Perdomo 1981, 1988; Falcao 1979, 1988) leads to a reconsideration of the idea that the professors played a dominant role in these systems based on codified law, often described following Max Weber as the 'professorenrecht'. At the same time, the low-level educational recruitment characteristic of these institutions explains their increasing marginalization in the field of reproduction of elites, especially after the arrival of new institutions and the growth of competition creates a surplus of educational qualifications (Bourdieu 1987). The French situation is thus not as exceptional as might be thought. It only anticipates a more general development.

learned bourgeoisie into a 'state bourgeoisie' (Bourdieu). Indeed, not satisfied with coopting the most brilliant heirs of this fine old urbane and intellectual bourgeoisie which traditionally supplied the elite of the legal field, these 'grands corps' also borrowed the juridical model on which the learned lawyers had built their legitimacy. The Conseil d'Etat and the Cour des Comptes are organized along the lines of tribunals and the Inspection des Finances prosecutes its investigations on the lines of an adversarial hearing.[21] That is not all. Charle (1992: 197, 228) shows that the analogy goes much further. Just as the learned nobility claimed to 'constitute an autonomous social force in relation to its progenitor the king', this new state aristocracy allows itself to judge and censure the state. Today, as yesterday, their esprit de corps allows a small, privileged and high-born elite to pool their social and intellectual capital for a better defence of their positions in the field of power.

Just as in the past the landed wealth of the judiciary allowed it to maintain its independence, today the top civil servants and politicians carefully nurture their network of links and influence in the business world to ensure their access to lucrative livings which are also positions of power.[22] Thanks to their opportunities and strategies, they can be simultaneously inside and outside the state. In this dual role, they can ensure that the state's influence extends into the field of business much further than the already large area of it occupied by public enterprises.[23] Thus, they occupy this 'pivotal position between administration and politics, law and administration, or more generally between the state and civil society' which allows them to 'intercede in the complex game of interacting powers'. In short, they occupy a central position in what we have defined as the regulatory arena.

French-style planning perfectly illustrates this close interaction between the state and the economy where the legitimacy of the state nobility depends on its ability to handle the technological advances which underpin social progress. 'The plan itself became the high priest of high technology' (Hall 1986: 179). During the '30-year boom', the supremacy of this

---

[21] This formalism is mostly a facade. The interventions are essentially negotiated on the basis of the relations of power and networks of influence represented by former colleagues who have moved into cushy jobs at the head of the big public enterprises or firms controlled by the state and the *grands corps* (Mamou 1987: 77, 280; Bourdieu & de Saint Martin 1978). As Hall (1986: 153) points out, adapting a remark by Tocqueville, the government only passes strict and general laws to make it easier later to negotiate case-by-case exceptions which allow it to exercise its discretionary power. Naturally, these arrangements exclude any public debate and differing opinions.

[22] This phenomenon, which is referred to as 'pantouflage', has grown over time. In 1973, 43% of of directors of the 100 biggest firms were former top civil servants (Birnbaum 1977: 141).

[23] As is remarked by all observers (Birnbaum 1978: 85; Grémion 1974: 173) these top civil servants see no contradiction between these two roles. On the contrary, this symbiosis between state and business leaders is considered as a trump card contributing to the success of industrial policies favouring growth and technological progress.

interventionist state model was hardly challenged, except at the political level. The waves of poujadism expressed the dissatisfaction of artisans and small businesses condemned by this industrial policy which actively favours concentration based on large firm, which are considered to be 'national champions' in the economic and technological race. But the rise of this populism only increases the powerlessness of parliament in relation to this technostructure. At least until the oil shocks and the crisis of the Fordist model challenge the legitimacy of this 'developmental state' and forces this state nobility to restructure itself around new power bases . . . and perhaps to borrow, for this purpose, the clothes of the law, or more exactly of the North American lawyer.

3. 'LAWYERS VS TECHNOCRATS' OR THE CONVERSION OF STATE TECHNOCRATS INTO INTERNATIONAL EXPERTS

Having sketched out these very contrasting examples of the construction of national regulatory arenas, the logical next step would be to show how they are recomposing with the help of the increased pace of the process of internationalization, and especially of its institutionalization. And since these two models represent virtually the two extremities of the gamut of arrangements for governing the economy—the one legal and the other bureaucratic; the one managed by legal entrepreneurs, the other centralized or coordinated by the state—one can ask whether internationalization should not be analyzed also as the creation of competition between these two technologies of power. In short, the conflict between the market economy and the welfare-state could be summed up as a competition between lawyers and technocrats. Yet it is not so simple. Before proceeding to analyse this dual relationship, a brief precautionary theoretical reflection is necessary.

Indeed, it is enough to put forward this parallel to realise that it is far too simplistic. To be convinced of this, one has only to think of the meteoric rise of the 'Chicago boys', especially in Latin America (Silva 1991; Loureiro 1993), and more generally in most government bodies (Coates 1981; Markoff & Montecinos 1993). The world of economic technocracy no longer identifies itself only with state interventionism, even if in many cases this conversion to monetarist 'fundamentalism' has seemed to be nothing short of an institutional earthquake (Georges & Sabelli 1994: 97). On the other hand, in the public debates provoked by the ratification of free trade agreements such as the NAFTA, there were also many lawyers who denounced the attacks on the gains made through the welfare state (Buchanan 1995), although it is true that they were found on both sides of the argument. So what is the explanation for what appear to be manoeuvres in a double game or the conversion of experts: individual career moves or the structural logic of these fields of power?

3.1 Symbolic Structures and Social Positions

These examples—and many others—show that there are disjunctures, of varying extent, between the positioning of these different categories of expert in the field of power and the structures of regulatory bodies which political scientists call 'regulatory régimes' (Eisner 1993). It is certainly true that professional ideology or *esprit de corps* as well as 'turf battles' (Abbott 1988) are an essential element of the symbolic and ideological conflicts through which the social credibility of different regulatory modes are fought out. On the other hand, many experts develop a strong identification with the institutions, which are both technical and political, which they have helped to produce, and which define their means of intervention and their status in the power hierarchies. For this reason, many researchers tend to confuse these two levels of analysis: the arena of producers of expertise and that of their symbolic productions. Sociologists tend to deny the· specificity of legal forms and discourses, seeing them only as the means or ends of social struggles, or even of a confrontation between techniques. Conversely, legal commentaries accept the professional ideology which describes these symbolic structures as if they were natural and transcendant, helping to obscure the struggles and social compromises in and through which they were devised.

The confusion is all the worse because these learned commentators are themselves part of the political and professional game which they claim to describe 'objectively'. This rhetoric may be effective as a tactical argument; however, it is not very helpful in analysing the origins of these systems, and even less so their transformations. To understand how and why 'regulatory régimes' of apparently quite different inspiration come into being, they must be approached as constructions—continually being reconstructed—in a professional field which has as its principle of transformation its internal differences and struggles. These 'regulatory régimes' do not have an objective existence in themselves, they can only be understood and analyzed in relation to the 'palace wars' which retranscribe into symbolic language the confontational games of the field of economic power.[24]

---

[24] Thus, in 'The Force of Law', Bourdieu (1987: 212) points out the important distinction which must be made between on the one hand 'the juridical field [which] contains the principles of its own transformation in the struggle between objective interests' and on the other 'a symbolic order of norms . . . [which] does not contain within itself the principles of its own dynamic. I propose to distinguish this symbolic order from the order of objective relations between actors and institutions in competition with each other for the right to determine the law'.

This distinction is even more indispensable if the focus of interest is on the international competition played out, in part, on the terrain of institutions and techniques of government. At the national level, there may be many links between positional systems and symbolic structures, since institutions and techniques are rooted in patterns of *habitus* developed by a long structural history. It is not the same for international relations: the strategies of experts are only partly determined by their positions in their relevant national fields. The latter are in any case hard to evaluate, due to the distortion effects produced by a distance that is not only geographic but also social. There is more scope for individual career promotion strategies, as well as possibilities of playing a double game,[25] especially as international institutional arrangements are heavily involved with political imperatives, which the experts seek to clothe in learned technical terms. This enables them to bring professional considerations to the fore. Paradoxically, these political institutions thus devote most of their energies in asserting their autonomy from politics. There is therefore all the greater risk that those who study them fall into the trap of institutionalism: reinforcing the pseudo-learned appearance that these institutions are trying to conjure up, to justify their existence or reinforce their credibility.

In contrast to the rhetoric, which is very wide-spread, of 'globalization', it is helpful to describe the emergence of an international field of expertise by analysing what is nourishing it—and how it is transforming the various national fields from which it is constituting itself (Dezalay 1993*c*, 1993*d*). Far from sparing the necessity of an analysis of national specificities, this object of research on the contrary requires a deepening of the structural history of the national fields in which these internationalization strategies are inscribed. Hence, there is no split or contradiction in the ways in which the 'global' and the 'local' should be approached, nor any fundamental difference between these levels of analysis. Indeed, as the chapters in this book on 'forum shopping' and the 'Delaware effect' show, it is not only at the international level that there is competition between regulatory bodies proclaiming quite different rationalities.[26] However, as we will see below in

[25] It is true that these also exist at national level. As we have seen, both in the USA and in France, these strategies of playing a double game are common in the field of experts in governing the economy. Since they also facilitate conversions, it is easier to understand how apparently very different 'regulatory régimes' can coexist without too much conflict, or can succeed each other as a result of a mini-putsch within the field of economic power. Contrary to the picture sometimes painted by theorists of 'regulatory régimes', these symbolic structures do not spring up magically in the political field. Frequently, these 'new' bodies are only a recasting or recycling of professional techniques, dressed up in the fashion of the day by minor rhetorical changes.

[26] However, too much importance should not be attached to these proclaimed ideological differences, since quite often they are only marketing talk, borrowed from the register of political discourse, serving tactical purposes and the strategies of their promoters. Indeed, these proclaimed differences in no way prevent them from transferring their registration or becoming converted to another specialism, at least for the small elite of professionals who have

relation to international commercial arbitration, such 'regulatory competition' should also be seen as complementation, a sort of division of the labour of symbolic domination (Dezalay 1994).

By definition, the field of economic regulation is a site of confrontation between different groups or categories of producers, each continually attempting to redefine the rules of the game, or to modify the conditions of their application, in their own interests. In this unstable and changing universe, these regulatory bodies provide a semblance of order and continuity. Even if it is only an illusion, this pseudo-regulation may turn out to be all the more durable to the extent that the different social partners are sometimes reluctant to reopen a fragile compromise. In these conditions, rather than modify arrangements embodied in custom, it may seem easier to think up new ones, which could be operated in parallel or in competition with the previous provisions. Far from being homogenous and rational, regulatory space is on the contrary characterized by the coexistence of highly typified systems, each of which bears the marks of the social context and the political compromises by—and for—which it was devised.

If this rather incoherent system nevertheless manages to work relatively smoothly, this is very likely due to a certain number of acts of professional 'betrayal' which permit a minimal degree of communication between all these 'regulatory régimes' which conflict and compete with each other. Furthermore, by moving between these different symbolic and institutional universes, these mediators in the field of power acquire diversified skills and multiple contacts which they can invest in one régime or another, according to the opportunities arising from the political or economic conjuncture. These strategies of adaptation accelerate—as well as facilitating—the restructuring of the 'market' in regulation around 'new' symbolic and institutional apparatuses, which are often less novel than they would seem.

Although there is some merit in this analogy with a market, it should not be pushed too far. These symbolic apparatuses are indeed in competition, as much to attract potential producers of expertise as to convince a public of potential consumers as to their credibility, since it is the latter which is the condition of their economic efficiency. Yet this market for symbols is highly segmented. It is particularly hard for producers to circulate since this space is partitioned up between institutions and rationalities each of which jealously defend its territory. Furthermore, many of these producers are far from interchangeable, since they are 'marked' by their social origin and/or their career trajectory.

The credibility of these experts in regulation depends on their believing in what they practise or preach. As Bourdieu (1991) suggests, since they are

understood how to acquire the social capital and sufficiently diverse networks of alliances to allow them to take best advantage of the new tactical opportunities offered to them by the unceasing battles waged in the field of power.

condemned to be taken seriously, these dealers in illusions are the first victims of the beliefs they propagate. If, as has just been shown, ideological
affinities or disciplinary and institutional affiliations are largely the result of
the positional system in the field of expertise, they also tend to introduce
into it divisions which can turn out to be particularly rigid when they are
combined with an *esprit de corps*. Indeed, their influence will be all the more
strong since such affiliations often do no more than reinforce choices and
orientations which owe much to 'habitus' and to social trajectories.

In some cases, for reasons often related to migration phenomena, the
division of labour in the field of power follows quasi-ethnic lines: the more
traditional elite retaining a monopoly of public sector careers while the
newcomers—such as Jews in central Europe (Karady 1993) or the Chinese
in south-east Asia (Siu-Lun 1988)—mainly investing in the private sector.
Although this extreme situation is not always reached, it is not rare for the
field of expertise to be structured around this antagonism between the public and private poles, each targetting its own preferred clientele based on
social origin and professional trajectory.[27]

Between these two poles the relative dominance and distance of which
may vary according to the place and period, the field of expertise offers a
wide spectrum of situations among which entrants are distributed more or
less according to their ambitions and to the type of capital they command.
Despite everything, whatever room for manoeuvre there may be (and in any
case it is relative) there is a far from exact correspondence between social
position and institutional function. This relative lack of correspondence is
perhaps indeed one of the keys of the transformation of the machinery for
governing the economy. As we have seen above in relation to the New Deal
lawyers, this type of shift can stimulate new entrants into the market for
expertise to invest their capital of specialist competence into new institutions
more appropriate to their convictions or their ambitions.

This same logic can also be found in the process of construction of an
international market of expertise in matters of regulation. The increase in
trade—symbolic as well as economic—provides opportunities for a greater
number of producers of expertise to try to export their techniques to new
territories. 'Globalization' offers an excuse or a banner for strategies of
symbolic imperialism which are supported by many learned or institutional
networks. Very often, beyond the politico-academic objectives which they
proclaim, these 'epistemic communities' are above all aiming to create an
international market for techniques, in which national producers can

---

[27] Such divisions are also found even within a professional group. Thus, Siegrist (1993)
shows that, depending on the region, the legal professions have structured themselves around
either the pole of the state or that of economic power. The same applies to the professions concerned with calculation. The result is therefore a mosaic of professions with significant differences between countries, since they are produced by specific social histories (Dezalay 1993*a*).

exchange 'localized' social capital for a cosmopolitan competence. In the absence of a world State, the latter is guaranteed collectively by this small elite of traders in 'universal' expertise which substitutes its pseudo-learned authority for political legitimacy (Dezalay 1993*b*). As a corollary, the spread of these 'borderless' jurisdictions tends to downgrade purely national techniques as second class competences; this is especially so in the dominated countries which thus find themselves 'provincialized' by the new symbolic imperialisms. Hence, international competition in the market for regulation, both by its causes and its effects, refers back into the positional systems which are constituted around nation states.

In sum, to understand how—and by whom—the continual recomposition of the mosaic of regulatory mechanisms is carried out, it is therefore impossible to avoid developing an analysis which can try to describe, at least in schematic terms, the main characteristics around which this social space comes to be organized; and in particular the terms of trade between the different forms of capital—economic, academic, or cultural—which circulate there and which determine the hierarchy of techniques in the field of the State.[28] For it is these objective positions which, in the last analysis, determine professional strategies, and hence the institutions or the forms of representation which circulate in the field of power.

3.2 The Internationalization of the 'Palace Wars'

Clearly, these 'palace wars' both nourish and feed off the political battles provoked by a process of internationalization which upsets the revenue redistribution processes established by the welfare state to guarantee social peace. Thus, international competition provides a convenient excuse to justify the elimination of a wide range of regulations or of bureaucratic interventions, which the adherents of free trade denounce as fetters on the spirit of free enterprise, or handicaps in relation to heightened international competition. Indeed, the effects of these neo-liberal policies were very soon felt. Since the early 1980s, with the rise in real interest rates, the gulf has again widened between the small minority which has benefited handsomely from the extraordinary revival of the international capital market and the mass of wage-earners (or of unemployed) who have lost the protections or advantages which they previously enjoyed.

At the same time, however, this desire for retaliation on the part of the property-owning classes is also a settlement of accounts within 'professional society' (Perkin 1989). The more intellectual—or idealistic—fractions of the urban bourgeoisie had linked their fate to that of state institutions which

---

[28] Thus, the lengthy period during which lawyers in Latin America enjoyed a quasi monopoly in the field of state power was doubtless due much more to their social (or economic) capital than to their technical competence (Perdomo 1981, 1988; Falcao 1979, 1988).

allowed them to promote an educational meritocracy and at the same time
to play the privileged role of mediator in class conflicts. International economic restructuring not only challenges this system of social pacification
built around the welfare state, it also weakens the positions of those who
embodied and managed that search for consensus and introduces a new
power relationship into the field of the state, as well as that of professional
knowledge.

With the help of the economic crisis—and of the intensification of educational competition[29]—the business bourgeoisie is rediscovering the advantages of educational qualifications which are easily exported and can earn a
good return. By the same stroke, it joins the ranks of a 'professional society' which had partly defined itself to the exclusion of, if not in opposition
to, that bourgeoisie.[30] The rise of professional expertise makes it from now
on one of the privileged spaces for the reproduction of social capital. The
heirs of the business bourgeoisie from now on make massive investments in
the field of expertise and learning. From this strategic base they launch their
attempts to regain ground against the social victories symbolized by the welfare state and to reconquer the places and institutions where economic
power is—legitimately—exercised. The internationalization of economies
thus helps to accelerate a process of recomposition of ruling elites—and
especially of those linked to the state apparatus.

It is true that this offensive benefits from the objective weakening of the
positions of their rivals following the decline of the Fordist model of accumulation to which the oil crises finally dealt the death-blow. Centralism and
state planning had been efficient enough to organise the economic take-off
of the economies of the third world[31] or European post-war reconstruction.
On the other hand, it seems clear that these state or party technocracies find
it much more difficult to manage complex economies, especially those which

[29] As Bourdieu (1987a) has shown, the increasingly universal recognition of educational
qualifications has forced the families of the industrial or financial bourgeoisie to join in this
pursuit of this brand of legitimacy of academic learning which they had previously generally
neglected. This has caused an increase in competition which combines with the attempts at
autonomization of the producers in the field of learning to increase educational rivalry. These
pressures have facilitated the development of what he has called 'refuge schools'. The schools
of business or management, which have proliferated in the past twenty years, are the classic
example of such institutions: by providing the endorsement of an educational diploma for
qualifications transmitted essentially by the social milieu, they provide these family strategies
the means of escaping from a judgment which could be far too strictly educational. Through
them, the business bourgeoisie can arrive directly in the middle of the field of learning and of
expertise. In doing so, it brings its economic rationality into the world of learning which had
till then more or less successfully managed to protect its relative autonomy from those with
economic power.
[30] As I have argued in more detail elsewhere (Dezalay 1995a) this, it seems to me, is what
explains the paradox noted by Perkin, of a professional society whose victory shortly precedes
its fracture and dramatic change of direction compared to the ideals of its founding fathers.
[31] See in particular the analysis by Castells (1992) of the role of arrangements for subsidised
housing in the socio-economic regulation of city-states such as Hong Kong or Singapore.

are closely tied into international exchange. Their business partners—who are also rivals—are quick to complain about dumping, as soon as public subsidies become too large or too visible. Further, the instruments of planning or incentives lose their efficacy since the economic actors can easily find alternative solutions by using external markets to find capital, clients or suppliers. Finally, as Hall emphasizes (Hall 1986), this state technocracy loses much of its political legitimacy once the rise of unemployment reveals its powerlessness to resolve an economic and social crisis which has been continually worsening. Hence it is not only a regulatory model which is in crisis, it is also the credibility of those who embody it.

In such a position of weakness, these holders of state power can only be especially sensitive to the pressures from this new cosmopolitan technocracy of economists, lawyers, and consultants which accompanies the expansion of the multinational firms and the penetration of a financial capitalism with global ambitions. Hence, almost unanimously, all these experts fight for the flexibility of work, against wage 'rigidities', for a reduction of social protection and of the tax burden, and more generally in favour of privatization and of a weakening of the role of the state.[32] In the eyes of these masters of free-trade, state intervention not only hinders the free play of competition, it has above all the great defect of limiting their room for manoeuvre. These zealous apostles of the market economy have the means of making themselves heard, either by punishing the recalcitrant, or by rewarding those who share or become converts to their neo-liberal beliefs. To accompany the integration of their country into the world economy, while themselves joining the nascent international elite, the national economic managers thus have strong incentives to distance themselves from the interventionist bureaucracies which are losing momentum.

The clothing of the lawyer is perfectly suited for the new role being adopted by these state technocrats or party cadres. It is perfectly adapted to the deployment of skills of a generalist sort where personal relations have a predominant role. Above all, as we have seen in relation to the United States of America, this ambiguous position, poised between the public and the private, permits the mobilization of state or political resources, while claiming complete independence from the state. In contrast, in the European model of legal practice, this double game is harder to play, since the gap which has been created there between the social state and legal institutions made it more difficult until now to lead simultaneously this double career of legal practitioner and statesman. Now, it is precisely these two types of skills and experience which are essential for an international competition played out on the borders of law and the state, since it concerns the

---

[32] Thus, in its latest report on employment (June 1994) the OECD's experts write that 'it is necessary to rethink the whole range of economic and social policies to facilitate the adaptation to the emerging modes of production and exchange'.

construction of quasi-state arrangements to ensure the regulation of a market economy encircling the planet.

The opposition between the market and the state is not, actually, as clear—or as schematic—as some militant—or scientistic—discourses would have us believe. As Hall emphasizes, 'Markets are themselves institutions (. . .) depend(ing) on an ancillary network of social institutions, often generated and sustained by state action' (1986: 282). The conversion of the defenders of the state and the public sector into dealers in regulatory expertise thus cannot be reduced to the sacrifice of the general interest in favour of private profits. The credibility of these experts rests not only on their skills but also on their claims to incarnate universal values. This is even more true for lawyers. As we have seen, these dealers in law are in a certain manner condemned to be 'dealers in virtue'. To sell legal services, they are indeed forced to invest in the legitimacy of the law. Rivalry in the market for regulation and economic management thus can't be reduced simply to a 'race to the bottom'. In its own way, it can also produce law, and even forms of state.

3.3 Competing for 'Universals'

An example can be given from recent research in which I have been involved.[33] Although it does not directly concern regulation, but rather the management of economic disputes through international commercial arbitration, the same public-private dialectic is to be found there: the privatization of the state engenders a market for the universal (which means, in this case, a market for justice). And this international competition produces the state (in this case, the embryo of a transnational law and jurisdiction). Certainly, for this specific example as well as more generally, it is far too early to forecast the outcome of this process of restructuring of state processes. One must settle for an analysis of the internal struggles which delineate the first main outlines of this field of international juridical practices. But already, at this preliminary stage, one can only be struck by encountering themes already familiar from the 'regulatory competition' debate: the creation of rivalries between national legal systems which might provoke a sort of anticipatory deregulation, that this 'race to the bottom' would result in the dismantling of the powers of the state, and finally the privatization of public service functions.

Hence, during the 1980s there was a successive series of reforms of the laws of arbitration in many countries. These reforms all displayed the same aim: to try to attract a larger portion of the market in international

[33] See, Yves Dezalay and Bryant Garth, *Dealing in Virtue: International Commercial Aribitration and the Emergence of a New International Legal Order* , to be published by University of Chicago Press.

arbitration by reducing as much as possible the constraints involved in the governance by the state's jurisdiction over this private justice. And each of the promoters of these reforms vaunted the special facilities offered by his country compared to its neighbours—and rivals—in the creation of a sort of 'legal free-port', where the parties were perfectly free to administer their litigation in their own way, choosing their judges and their law, without any interference by the state's courts.

The competition between the great arbitration centres—or those that seek to offer themselves on this new market, which is as prestigious as it is potentially rewarding—acts as a justification for these strategies of bidding up deregulation and the abandonment by national courts of their prerogatives. Indeed, the latter are all the more reluctant to abandon a long tradition of mistrust of this private justice, often considered to be an 'inferior justice', since the right of oversight is also the best protection of the monopoly of national practitioners of law over the market for managing disputes. Strong arguments are therefore needed to persuade them to give it up, and by the same action to open the door to foreign competitors.[34] That is the value of a rivalry that is above all at the level of rhetoric.

In fact, contrary to the media image of these arbitration centres engaged in a no-holds-barred struggle for this rapidly growing market, this field of practices can rather be compared to a club of insiders where personal ambitions must give way to a collective logic. Indeed, all the members of this community are perfectly conscious that the credibility of this private justice is too new, and too fragile, to tolerate strategies of marketing which might be too daring or aggressive. In any case, the rate of growth of this market is probably far from being as miraculous as it is made out to be.[35]

Furthermore, in this small world where personal relations are very close, there is extensive interpenetration between the networks which cluster around the different arbitration centres or institutions. To gain credibility, each of these centres subtly gilds its list of arbitrators by including representatives of other arbitration circles. This relative openness to 'outsiders' is the price to be paid to justify the pretensions to universality of what is

---

[34] In Great Britain, the advocates of a reform of arbitration had thus estimated at several hundred million pounds the lost potential gains to the British balance of payments—and to the London practitioners — resulting from proposed legislation which was perceived by their foreign colleagues as too restrictive and too expensive. These same people today admit quite freely that these figures, which were widely quoted in the press, were pure whimsy. This does not stop them from again brandishing these alarmist threats when the House of Lords is about to give its decision on the question of its right to adjudicate on 'security for costs' in an arbitration (D. Egan 'Splendid Isolation', *Legal Business*, May 1994).

[35] The few published statistics must be treated with caution: they aggregate many small and a few major cases. The latter are often used as promotional samples to attract new clients by displaying the wonders of past successes. We have described this in a forthcoming article as 'making it by faking it' (Yves Dezalay and Bryant Garth 'Grand Old Men vs. Multinationals: the Routinization of Charismatic Arbitration into Off-Shore Litigation', forthcoming in *Law & Society Review*).

often no more than an international marketing drive launched by a few local practitioners. It translates at the level of the management of arbitral cases into a complex system—but one which is also closely codified and monitored—of favours and counter-favours, which ensures more effectively than any rules of procedure the smooth functioning of this extra-normal justice.

In short, this field of practices is quite the opposite of the image of an open and very competitive market which is implied by the rhetoric of international competition. On the contrary, it resembles a closed market where the producers are closely hemmed in, as much by their mentors as by their peers. Personal relations at the heart of networks operating on the basis of complicity and reciprocity reinforce the stability of this market. Since, above all, access is still very tightly controlled by the small core of founding fathers who select the aspirants according to the deference that they show to the values of arbitration, this private justice for traders is therefore, in many ways, further removed from the market—and perhaps better protected from its temptations—than is state justice. It is true that the importance of the financial or political stakes in this type of international dispute requires a certain vigilance, especially taking into account the fragility of this institution which does not have the benefit of a guarantee from the state.

In spite of what has just been said, reference to international competition in the market for arbitration is nevertheless not merely mystification. Behind the tactical argument lies hidden in fact a whole strategy of promotion and of autonomization of arbitration. The legislative auction between the different countries helps to open up new territories for this private justice. It is blazoned in an entire public relations campaign aimed at publicizing and achieving recognition for this method of managing commercial disputes.[36]

The recognition which is sought is in two senses. The national legal authorities in fact do not give up their statutory prerogatives without a quid pro quo. Often, it is noticeable, to facilitate this mutual recognition, one or other of the members of this local legal élite is co-opted and enthroned in this closed circle of arbitrators which is one of the keys for access to an international legal field which is being constructed. In return, this new recruit acts as an intermediary between these two worlds which until now were alien to each other. In one, s/he puts forward the specific merits of his/her national legal culture; in the other s/he acts as guarantor for the legitimacy of this international private justice.

Since it lies at the intersection of different legal cultures, this field of practices creates a breach in the national legal monopolies based largely on their mutual ignorance. Narrow though it may be, this foot-bridge creates the possibility of a confrontation. The result may be, if not the creation of

[36] A campaign waged notably by the organization of conferences or seminars at which the great figures of arbitration are received by the local legal notables.

effective competition, at least a sort of mutual evaluation. The different local élites learn to take the measure of each other: the barrister compares himself to the continental professor or the senior partner of a large North American law firm.

More generally, this market for arbitration creates comparisons which were formerly mere academic exercises. For the learned treatises of comparativists evaluating the merits of different legal practices, it substitutes a real and substantial test: the effectiveness of each when confronted with a specific problem, or when they compete in an actual case.

This evaluation is based on a system of trading between the different fields of practices. It allows a small group of eminent figures in national law to convert into cosmopolitan fame the authority which they possess within the local courts. It also facilitates many other trading transactions: academic lawyers can use it to acquire familiarity with and contacts in the business world; conversely, the business lawyers can use it to acquire the legitimacy and patina of learning.

In short, the market for arbitration operates like a trading floor where the transactions concern the different forms of legal authority and legitimacy. In this way it helps to establish their relative values, and to continually readjust them. From this perspective, there really is a process of competition between national legal systems. But this does not amount necessarily to a 'race to the bottom'. It is rather the opportunity for a redefinition of the rules of the game—and of the resources which the players can mobilize. In the case of international commercial arbitration, this new deal has facilitated the autonomization of arbitration which has become a sort of 'off-shore justice' which is both decentralized and delocalized. But, as we have tried to show elsewhere (Dezalay & Garth, forthcoming), this outcome was far from predetermined. It is the outcome of a paradoxical encounter between a small European coterie of learned lawyers and some multinational law firms of North American origin. It owes as much to the idealism and proselytizing ardour of the founding fathers as to the opportunism of legal entrepreneurs, quick to seize the opportunity offered by the growth in north-south disputes sparked off by the flood of petro-dollars.

Clearly, this particular example cannot claim to have a general applicability. It claims only to be an incentive for further analysis of a phenomenon in which not only are there massive stakes for the future both of the law and of our societies, but which also casts a revealing light on the diversity and specificity of legal cultures. The danger lies in confusing these inquiries. It is probably unavoidable, since it is hard to ask researchers to abstract from their preoccupations or their political commitments. Yet they should bear in mind that they too are playing a double game in the game of law. Without taking a 'reflexive stance' (Bourdieu & Wacquant 1992) they run great risks of fooling themselves.

3

The Regulatory Criss-Cross: Interaction between Jurisdictions and The Construction of Global Regulatory Networks

SOL PICCIOTTO*

Concern with international regulatory competition, or at least its explicit theorization, is relatively recent, although the issues it raises have a much longer history. This is partly because discussion of the regulation of economic relations has also been recently renewed, as privatization and the reduction of direct state intervention in economic activity have brought more sharply into focus the many other ways in which economic transactions and relations are socially ordered, whether by formal or informal, public or private means. The second main factor is that regulatory régimes have been brought into greater interaction, as the removal of direct barriers to the flows of goods and money between states (tariffs/quotas and exchange controls) has shifted attention towards regulatory difference as a barrier to entry of commodities or capital.

Earlier, from the 1950s, the articulated concern was about regulatory conflicts, identified as being caused by 'extraterritoriality' in the application mainly of USA regulatory requirements (ILA 1970; Lange & Born 1987; Picciotto 1983). This led to legal debates about limitations on jurisdictional reach (Bowett 1982; Maier 1982; Brilmayer 1987), intersecting with political debate about the desirability of USA 'unilateralism' (Strange 1986). Attempts were made to develop principles and procedures to accommodate overlaps and conflicts of jurisdiction (OECD 1987), but since the mid-1980s, with changing patterns of international trade and investment, the underlying problem began to change form.

* This chapter is based on research carried out with generous assistance from The Nuffield Foundation. It also benefited from a year I spent as a Jean Monnet Fellow at the European University Institute , and in particular from stimulating discussions on themes relating to this paper with residents of the Institute, both temporary (in particular Daniel Drache, Stephen Castles, Verena Stolcke, Ellie Vasta, and Pedro Ybarra), and longer-term (in particular Renaud Dehousse, Christian Joerges, Giandomenico Majone, Francis Snyder, Susan Strange, and Gunther Teubner). I am also grateful to David Trubek and Heinz Klug for the opportunity to present the paper at seminars at the University of Madison-Wisconsin and for comments from their participants; also to participants in the research seminar at the American Bar Foundation; and to Joe McCahery and Joel Trachtman.

In this recent period, USA analysts have become increasingly concerned with regulatory competition, as the fear was raised that the more stringent regulatory requirements and more developed systems of enforcement in the USA, especially of banking and corporate finance, might damage USA business and its financial markets (e.g. Cox 1992). These new concerns seem due to two main factors: first, the USA becoming a much greater recipient of inward direct investment; and secondly, the creation of strong rivalries between financial marketplaces due to Japan's increasing financial dominance as well as the international liberalization of financial flows. In economists' terms, from having been concerned with capital-export equity (that USA firms should be subject to as high a level of regulation abroad as they are at home, to avoid incentives to capital export), the concern of much of the USA regulatory community has shifted to capital-import equity (that USA firms should not be hampered in home or foreign markets by the higher level of USA regulation). From the different perspective of Europe, what has been highlighted is a conflict between the American and other models of regulated capitalism (Albert 1992), or a drive to 'export' the USA regulatory model seen as a form of 'symbolic imperialism' (Dezalay 1992, and chapter 2, in this volume).

In parallel with these concerns, the issue of regulatory competition came to the fore as part of the process generally described as European integration, which entered a new phase after 1985. A new strategy for regulatory harmonization was central to the adoption of the European Commission's White Paper and the 1992 Single Market programme. The aim was to break the log-jam of unadopted proposals for harmonized regulation which had built up during the 1970s due to political deadlock between the Member States, by using a powerful lever created by the European Court, the principle of Mutual Recognition (Dehousse 1989). This prohibited a Member State from imposing its own regulatory requirements on imported goods or services, unless such regulations fell within fairly narrow grounds of justification.[1] The obligation to allow into their marketplaces goods and services produced under other regulatory systems was important not only because it created a potential for competition between regulatory régimes, but also because this possibility pressurized the member states to reach agreement to harmonize at least a basic floor of minimum regulatory

[1] The path-breaking court decisions were *Procureur du Roi* v. *Dassonville*, case 8/74 [1974] ECR 837, and the *Cassis de Dijon* case (*Rewe-Zentral AG* v. *Bundesmonopolverwaltung für Branntwein* [1979] ECR 649). In the latter case the European Court of Justice held that German alcohol laws, even though not directly discriminatory, could not be applied so as to block the importation of an alcoholic drink validly produced under French laws; unless the importing state could justify its regulations under any of four heads: 'the effectiveness of fiscal supervision, the protection of public health, the fairness of commercial transactions and the defence of the consumer'. These categories have been somewhat expanded subsequently, but the ECJ has taken a strict view of the justifications, rejecting regulatory requirements which are disproportionate to the justifiable aims (Dehousse 1992: 394).

requirements. It was this dynamic which helped the Community to reach most of its harmonization targets by the end of 1992. Although the 'new strategy' for harmonization enunciated in the 1985 White Paper aimed to establish harmonized rules only to the minimum extent necessary, in many areas—notably the key one of financial markets—a broad and often very detailed European code began to emerge in a series of Directives. This interacted with substantial reformulations or modification of national regulatory arrangements, in areas such as financial services, even in states with highly developed financial markets such as the UK and Germany. At the same time, however, it created a dynamic of regulatory competition which threatened to stimulate a downward deregulatory ratchet, with potentially harmful consequences in areas such as product safety (Joerges 1990). Although the pressures for harmonization have acted as a brake against a deregulatory race to the bottom, it has been argued that the EC remains institutionally constrained from developing effective regulatory structures, by what has been described as the 'dual subsidiarity' of its combined emphasis on market liberalization and the privileging of national policies (Dehousse 1992: 388). Streeck (1995) goes further than Dehousse, in arguing that, having failed to create an authoritative supranational polity, coordination within the EU is characterized by 'voluntarism', both inter-governmental and between nationally-based interest-groups, and that this supranational voluntarism has forced the redesign of national regulatory forms to comply with international monetary and fiscal requirements.

These new concerns with regulatory competition both internationally and within the EU have linked up with discussions among USA scholars, especially in relation to corporate law (Charny 1991). In the USA, debate about the Delaware phenomenon was initially based on rather crude assumptions, for example that state legislatures are mainly motivated by a competition to maximize revenue by attracting a high volume of company incorporations and that a company's decision to relocate is costless. However, the discussion was significantly broadened when it began to take greater consideration of the particular characteristics of 'law as a product': an established legal régime once perceived as advantageous becomes hard to change, both because of the state's reliance on it as an asset which produces revenue, and because of the human capital investment made by the legal advisers who generally originate the recommendation to reincorporate (Romano 1985). From this it is a small but important step to look more broadly at the actual production process of law, and the role of corporate lawyers as entrepreneurial intermediaries of regulation, active in its production as well as selling their services to its consumers (Carney, chapter 5, in this volume).

Concerns about regulatory conflict and competition are generally linked to a consideration of the desirability of coordination, usually by central intervention in a federal system or by regulatory harmonization through regional or international institutions (OECD 1993b). However, the processes of diffusion and coordination of regulation are many and diverse. Furthermore, competition and coordination are not merely alternatives: regulatory competition itself generally requires some equivalence between régimes, or some common rules (Dehousse 1992: 396; Trachtman 1993: 74), and as the experience of the EU has shown, the threat of competition can act as a strong spur for coordination. Finally, the dynamics of interaction of regulatory jurisdictions depend on a complex of social and political factors and are not based only on narrow economic considerations.

At this point, however, it is desirable to take a longer perspective and locate these concerns with regulatory interaction within debates about the broader changes taking place in the global economy and society. The next section will therefore relate the debate about regulatory competition to broader discussions of the changing nature and role of the nation-state, in the context of current concerns about globalization. The chapter then considers how international regulatory interaction has developed historically in relation to business regulation, using examples from several areas. The analysis focuses on the problems of legitimation posed by the growth of informal networks of regulatory coordination, generally in response to jurisdictional conflicts and regulatory crises. These increasingly institutionalized networks are creating a kind of globalized arena formed by the intersection of various regulatory communities, which are partially coordinated through semi-formal arrangements, largely at sub-state level. Competition between national regulators is not replaced by these forms of coordination, however, but in many ways provides much of their dynamic. There is a combined process and a tension between centrifugal and centripetal forces in the global regulatory dynamic in the current transitional phase. My argument is that it is within the context of the problem of legitimation that one should evaluate the various strategies and institutionalized alternatives being developed in response to the issues posed by regulatory interaction.

I. FRAGMENTED STATES

In the current period of political fluidity a major focus of contestation is the character and future of the nation-state in the global political economy. While some commentators proclaim the end of sovereignty and the death of the nation-state, others argue equally vehemently for its continuing relevance and vitality. Amid the divergent trends of political developments and strategies, arguments and evidence can be found for conflicting views and varied prognostications. For some, the continuing or revived strength of nationalism, the break-up of empires and confederations such as the USSR and Yugoslavia, and the loss of political momentum towards the forging of a European federation or super-state, demonstrate the evident need for the political framework of the nation-state, if not its enduring vigour. Others see in the regeneration of ethnicity and localism a break-up of the unifying force of the national sovereignties that have formed the cornerstone of the world system. The formation of NAFTA as a counterweight to the EU and the intensification of Japanese investment and trading links in Asia lead some to posit the emergence of a tri-polar global political economy or Triad, while for others the continuing salience of smaller groupings (e.g. the Cairns group) and cross-cutting alliances (e.g. the Anglo-American 'special relationship') demonstrate that we are only witnessing tactical shifts within an enduring multilateralist system. Some see the world as increasingly a single globalized marketplace not only for the enormous volume of extremely mobile financial flows but also for the opportunistic location of production sites for goods and services within multinational corporate networks (R. Reich 1992). Others emphasize that economic exchange, as well as travel and communications, have increased exponentially as much within as between states, with no clear long-term trend towards proportionately greater transnational links (Thomson and Krasner 1989); and that Transnational Corporations are not footloose world citizens but have a strong identification with their home-countries (Hu 1992).

In large part such differences of view result from different perspectives on the nature and functions of the state. Typically, those who emphasize the continued centrality of the nation-state tend to privilege the state as the prime focus for the generation of social cohesion and consensus, or what might be thought of as its 'political' role. On the other hand, those who prioritize the economic management functions of the state have tended to argue that the increasingly global nature of the world economy has undermined its ability to perform these functions: as far back as 1969 Charles Kindleberger asserted that 'the national state is just about through as an economic unit' (Kindleberger 1969: 207). There are also important divergences of view as to the relationship between the 'political' and 'economic' functions of the state. Those for whom the political or consensus-building role of the state depends on managing the economy in a 'redistributionist' way may seek to emphasize those powers which they consider are still retained by individual states, for instance fiscal powers, despite the transfer of many economic regulatory functions to the international arena or to the EU as a regional super-state.[2] Others

---

[2] Thus, Hirst and Thompson (1992) argue that although national powers of macro-economic management are no longer effective, the political role of government in orchestrating social consensus has been strengthened; while this may be correct, they are on more shaky ground in arguing that this can be successfully fulfilled through national-level fiscal policies within the EC, by devising taxes which are resistant to factor mobility. This leads them to conclude that 'new forms of property taxes' will become an increasingly attractive source of tax revenues for governments (373): given the delocalization potential of the forms of financing

are content to argue that there has been a consolidation of state sovereignty, since they consider that the state's key functions are to ensure the monopolization of legitimate coercion and to establish and maintain stable property rights, rather than 'intervening' in the economy in ways which produce market misallocation (Thomson and Krasner 1989). However, from another perspective, it is precisely this weakening of the powers of economic intervention that creates an increasing disjuncture between the economic power and the political functions of the state, described as the 'hollowing out' of the nation-state, as it becomes harder to deliver political consensus.

More fundamentally, some ask whether in the multiple transformations which are described as the 'postmodern condition' we might also be involved in a transition to the 'postmodern state'. Central to this is the discovery by social theorists of the issue of 'globalization', a term that has been used in different and sometimes contradictory senses, but which at its simplest implies that the qualitative transformations of global economic and cultural links and flows mean that human society must now more than ever before be understood and treated as an interconnected whole (Robertson 1990). Within a postmodernist perspective, however, this is far from suggesting the creation of a global unity—on the contrary, globalization may be said to foster differentiation, or at least creates an increased awareness of diversity. The virtually instantaneous availability worldwide of commodities, artefacts, and cultural signs creates some pressures towards cultural homogenization, but also and equally powerfully a potential for the reinforcement of local particularities and cultural difference. As Appadurai puts it: 'The central problem of today's global interactions is the tension between cultural homogenization and cultural heterogenization' (Appadurai 1990: 295). Manifold styles and cultures jostle and compete around the world on supermarket shelves, disc-players and TV screens; there can be a simultaneous worldwide TV audience of many millions for staged events such as the Olympic Games, the bombing of Bhagdad, reportage of an atrocity in Bosnia or Rwanda, or of the first non-racial elections in South Africa. However, such global simultaneity is confined to exceptional dramatic events. Global diffusion of routine news is much more limited and uneven, and mainly of interest to elite, internationally-mobile groups; most news for most people is local. Hence, the process is perhaps better referred to as 'global localization' (sometimes shortened to the awkward term 'glocalization'), emphasizing that the issue is the changing nature of the global-local nexus (Alger 1988), the immediately global context in which often intensely local events occur, due to the dramatic possibilities of space-

of property ownership (i.e., the use of offshore companies as vehicles for property development), the 'new forms of property taxes' would presumably have to be based on residence, which the British experience with the poll tax has shown to be far from an effective redistributional mechanism.

time compression (Harvey 1984). Thus, the slogan 'Think Global, Act Local' has been adopted by both managers of TNCs (Ohmae 1987) and NGO activists.

In political terms, these debates raise the question of whether such changes in the patterns of social relations remain governable within a political system whose central unit is the sovereign nation-state. For international relations (IR) theory these are not new issues. Indeed, since the (relatively recent) attempts to theorize IR as a discipline, in the post-1945 period of the arrival of the USA as the dominant world power, there has been a broad split between on the one hand the realists and neo-realists who have maintained some continuity with the origins of IR in diplomatic history and focus primarily on inter-state (meaning essentially inter-governmental) relations, and on the other hand a variety of neo-functionalists who have preferred to focus primarily on the 'spider's web' of social relations in 'world society' which cut across the 'billiard-balls' of the territorially-defined nation-states.[3] This latter approach has appeared in successive manifestations as interdependence theory, transnational relations, régime theory, and most recently 'policy networks' (Keck and Sikkink 1994; Greenwood *et al.* 1992), 'epistemic communities' (Haas *et al.* 1992) and 'global civil society' (Lipschutz 1992).

In the sociology or social theory of law, also, there has been an important strand that has stressed the 'pluralism' of legal orders: that law develops within a variety of human communities and is neither simply identifiable nor necessarily coterminous with the state. While, under the modern state, state-law asserts its supremacy, it can nevertheless tolerate an often high degree of autonomy for the legal orders of specific groups, from the family and private law of ethnically-distinct communities to self-regulation by business and professional associations. Historically, international commerce was regulated under a lex mercatoria, or by the commercial rules and customs governing particular trades; and some have argued that the recent trend of globalization of business calls for recognition of a new lex mercatoria, mainly expressed in the increased autonomy from state law of international arbitration (T. Carbonneau 1990). However, it has been strongly argued that there is no free-floating law, worth the name, independent of national law, and that arbitration depends on the framework of agreements between states (Reisman 1992) which provide the backing to compel evidence and execute judgments. Nevertheless, the recent process of fragmentation or restructuring of states has undoubtedly greatly strengthened the attraction of 'pluralist' approaches to law in society (Fitzpatrick 1984; de Sousa Santos 1987, 1992), not least in relation to international business regulation (Braithwaite

---

[3] This distinction was most clearly made by Burton (1972, ch. 4), although he built on earlier work by Deutsch, Herz and others; see also Oran Young (1972).

1993). In decentering the state and arguing that there can be a competitive
struggle between regulatory régimes, pluralist theories of law may be said to
have something in common with public choice theories of the state, since
both see the diversity and conflict between legal conceptions or régimes as
a political and strategic process. However, while legal pluralists tend to
assume the need for some sort of normative order (although many are critical of law), public choice theorists tend to see the state as a fetter on the
free play of market forces. In formal legal terms, the allocation of competence in the settlement of private disputes is dealt with by 'conflicts of law'
rules; and these have certainly been undergoing considerable re-evaluation
(e.g. Paul 1991, Trachtman 1994), as a consequence of developments such
as liability litigation becoming a major cost factor for firms operating in
global markets for products and services.

Many of these strands converge in relation to the analysis of perhaps the
most important project for state transformation of our times, the emergence
of the European Union.[4] This process clearly involves the creation of an
institutional framework which is supra-national rather than merely international, and the transfer or pooling by states of important elements of their
national sovereignty. Beyond this, however, there is little agreement about
the dynamic of the EU either among politicians or academics. Some see it
as a transition towards either a federal super-state or a new form of con-
federation, in which government will no longer be exercised mainly at the
national level, but will be shared with strengthened regional and sub-state
levels as well as supra-state institutions. The 'integrationist' perspective has
been underpinned by the view that the increasingly complex and globally-
interdependent nature of the functions demanded of the state has necessi-
tated the creation of supranational structures to fulfil those functions, and
that these will generate the political basis for a super-state either through
'spill-over' or with the help of a recreation of a pan-European cultural identity.[5] With the growing Euro-pessimism of the 1990s, this has lost some
momentum, aided by the persuasive arguments of a new generation of his-
torians who have argued that the Euro-project has been 'an integral part of

[4] Since the Treaty on European Union of Maastricht, the term European Union (handily
abbreviated to EU) officially designates the entirety covered not only by the central institutional framework and policies of the European Community, but in addition the important
areas of 'inter-governmental co-operation' over Justice and Home Affairs and Foreign and
Security Policies.
[5] The classic neo-functionalist works of Haas (1958, 1964) and Lindberg (1963) provided the
theoretical underpinnings for the 'integrationist' ideologies of Europhile politicans and lawyers,
although strongly challenged especially by Hoffman (1966), and declining in the 1970s as the
European project lost momentum. The new impetus provided by the Single Market programme
could not be explained solely in neo-functionalist terms (Moravcsik 1991), but a modified neo-
functionalism is again on the theoretical agenda (Keohane and Hoffmann, in Wallace (1990)),
and it has been put forward as the basis for a political theory of the role of European law itself
(Burley and Mattli 1993).

the reassertion of the nation-state as an organizational concept' (Milward 1992: 3). This account emphasizes that the European institutional framework was established by national elites,[6] and has been developed around policies on which there was sufficient political consensus among such leaders that an integrated European approach (including the important element of locking Germany into an irreversible commitment) was preferable to seeking a more global solution through international channels (Milward 1992: 437ff). While Milward concedes that this process entails the creation of a 'secondary allegiance' towards the Community, he argues that this has not been at the expense of, but has rather restored, the primary allegiances of citizens to their own nation-state.

The latter analysis links in with a broader argument among international relations scholars which, while conceding that new structures of international co-operation have been created as a result of interdependence, maintains that these have in fact strengthened the nation-state. Going even further, some have argued that it is the changing political demands generated within the national state that have transformed the nature of international political processes, leading to a 'domestication' of international politics and the creation of new forms of interaction of international and domestic political processes, which however have sustained the vitality of the nation-state (Hanrieder 1978). For example, there is no a priori functional necessity to find global solutions for environmental problems such as global warming or acid rain. It is rather the dramatization of these as issues that has projected them onto the international political stage, in turn transforming domestic politics. Although it is true that this may result from political and social processes which are still mainly national, the creation of a global public space by the new information media has undoubtedly brought about major changes in the process of opinion-formation and policy-making, of which the state is nevertheless still the fulcrum.

In the most general terms, all these debates concern the nature of sovereignty and its relationship both to territorial space and to cultural identity. If the current period is one of transition to a postmodern or 'post-international' political economy, it entails the fragmentation of political power with the breakdown of general social consensus and cohesion focused on the nation-state and the growth of a diversity of arenas of power, control, and regulation; while simultaneously the global normative framework for allocation of political power between jurisdictions is transmogrifying. The question to be addressed is whether the 'unbundling of territoriality' is leading to 'a rearticulation of international political space' (Ruggie 1993:

---

[6] Even the famous 'founding fathers' were above all concerned with the restoration of their national political structures and shattered economies, e.g., Jean Monnet, who was not only a Euro-pioneer but also the architect of the foundational French post-war Plan: Milward 1992: ch. 6.

171). The modern territorially-defined state is at the intersection of the distribution of political power: its authority to assert an internal monopoly of
coercion depends upon and interacts with the international normative
framework (Giddens 1985, ch. 10).

However, this calls first for some clarification of the nature of the relationship of state power and legitimacy to territorial space, and how it has
been changing. For the purposes of this paper, I will consider these issues
in relation to the changing patterns of regulation of global business.

2. TRANSNATIONAL REGULATORY INTERACTION

2.1 Sovereignty and Jurisdiction

Much of the confusion about the implications of globalization for the
nation-state is due to the reification of the state, reinforced by the concept
of 'sovereignty'. Statehood, as developed in the form of the modern post-
Napoleonic state, is a particular form of governance, in which the overt elements of coercive power are removed from personal relations and vested in
autonomized institutions with a public character. The scope of the formal
power of these institutions is defined in terms of territory; however, the
foundation of modern states took place through political processes central
to which was the cultural conception of the national community. Thus, the
'nation' of the nation-state is not a natural, pre-defined ethnicity but a
powerful ideological construct, an 'imagined community' (Anderson 1991).
The notion of supreme or untrammelled power embodied in the concept of
sovereignty has two aspects, internal and external. Internally it legitimizes
the assertion of the state's monopoly of coercive force. A key prop in this
legitimation is a particular form of legality, based on abstract and univer-
salist principles, which claims to underpin and guarantee the formal equality and freedom of legal subjects facilitating capitalist economic exchange.
Externally it is the states themselves that are free and equal legal subjects,
interacting in a community of a different order and on a higher plane, with
no overarching authority but God.

Thus, sovereignty functions as a particular way of legitimating the distribution of political power. The exercise of power is legitimated within the
state by the generation of consensus around the national common interest
through the institutions and processes of political participation involving all
citizens on a basis of formal equality. Some restrictions on the apparently
unlimited power to adopt national policies in the common interest are
accepted as resulting from the need to bargain with other formally equal
sovereigns on the basis of the national interest of each for reciprocal benefits
or to secure mutual or common interests. The fiction of unlimited internal

sovereignty is complemented and sustained by its corollary, the sovereign equality of states.

The concept of state sovereignty, the unlimited and exclusive powers of the public authorities within the state's territorial boundaries, appears to be fixed and unchanging. Looked at more closely, however, its content and character are highly flexible, and have changed and developed together with the very form of the state as well as the changing nature of social relations.[7] This can be seen very clearly when one focusses on the functional content of sovereignty, state jurisdiction. Jurisdiction may be defined as the scope within which the power of public or state authorities can effectively and acceptably be exercised. The emphasis on effectiveness and acceptability, usually ignored by formalist perspectives, is essential for an understanding of the limits of jurisdiction and therefore of sovereignty. In the modern state, the scope of sovereignty is said to be territorial: 'the right to exercise (in regard to a portion of the globe) to the exclusion of any other state the functions of a state' (Judge Huber, *Island of Palmas* case 1928: 92).

However, this exclusivity can only be fully effective if the state prohibits all transborder interactions. Since transborder social and economic activities entail multiple geographic contacts, even if states exercise their powers purely territorially there will be considerable overlapping and interaction in states' exercise of jurisdiction. The identification of the state with the 'nation' further transforms the basis of the exercise of state sovereignty into the more flexible and elusive notion of national jurisdiction. While the state has generally imposed obligations on all within its borders, the privileges of citizenship have been bestowed on a more restricted category, its nationals. However, the bonds of allegiance between its nationals and the state have also been considered to carry a nexus of obligation justifying the extension of state jurisdiction, by most states in some degree, to their nationals' activities abroad.

It can be seen, therefore, that far from being circumscribed in precise and mutually exclusive terms, the scope of exercise of states' powers defined by their jurisdiction, which is the substance of 'sovereignty', is flexible, over-lapping, and negotiable. This is especially so in relation to jurisdiction to regulate business activities, since the claim to jurisdiction over nationals has been extended to the fictitious legal personality bestowed on the business unit, in particular the company or corporation. Jurisdiction over a corporation can be based on the fictions either of its nationality or residence, and can vary for different purposes, using as criteria either the law under which

[7] This point is made by Barkin and Cronin (1994), who develop an interesting political analysis of how the basis of international legitimacy of states has changed with new definitions of sovereignty, involving a changing synthesis of the key but potentially contradictory 'statist and nationalist forms of legitimation'. Interestingly, they wrongly assume (although the point is hesitantly made) that the legal content of sovereignty changes little over time (ibid.: 107). See also Camilleri and Falk (1992: 25).

it is formed, the location of its 'seat' or head office, or the place from which central management or control are exercised. A 'control' test may be used to justify a claim to jurisdiction over the worldwide activities of transnational corporate groups or Transnational Corporations (TNCs), on the grounds that foreign subsidiaries are subject to ultimate control by their dominant shareholders or parent company, and states have increasingly asserted such jurisdiction over 'foreign' companies especially to defeat or prevent regulatory avoidance by the use of 'foreign' subsidiaries incorporated in jurisdictions of convenience.

A. *Interaction and Conflicts of Business Regulation*

The consolidation of the modern nation-state in the last part of the 19th century, following the American civil war, the unification of Germany and Italy, and the Meiji restoration in Japan, was also the initial period of emergence of nationally-based forms of regulating business, as part of a general process in the main capitalist countries of concentration of capital institutionalized in the corporate form (Horn and Kocka 1979). Although there was a good deal of emulation and transplantation of legal forms, the specific social and cultural forms, and hence the legal and regulatory modes, within which corporate capitalism developed, varied between the main states. However, the main emphasis in this period was on facilitative regulation based on liberal laws of general application, such as the right to create business corporations by registration, and the protection of monopoly rights over technological innovation and creative works through a liberal system for patents and a general copyright. Thus, provided there was no explicit discriminatory bar, cross-national ownership of assets was generally facilitated. Indeed, national barriers to inter-state commerce, such as high tariffs, stimulated transnational forms of business ownership, and the period 1880-1914 was the initial period of emergence of the TNC (Wilkins 1970). This was quite compatible with, and even stimulated by, the existence of national diversity in regulatory forms, provided the international framework was broadly liberal. Thus, the main conflicts in relation to business regulation were over restrictions on foreign ownership and involved pressures to secure rights of national treatment. For example, the Paris Convention of 1883, which established the International Union for the Protection of Industrial Property, left each state largely free to decide the specific form and extent of industrial property protection, but aimed to ensure for owners of foreign patents the right of national treatment as well as a limited right of priority.[8]

---

[8] The history both of the Paris Union (Plasser and Savignon 1983) and the Berne Copyright Convention provide important examples of the development of an internationally coordinated but nationally based form of regulation central to modern corporate capital, but which has recently come under increasing conflicting pressures (Cornish 1993).

To be sure, the application of national regulation to internationally-operating business was recognized as creating jurisdictional overlap and conflict, especially in the case of more interventionist forms of regulation. Thus, the development of direct taxation of income in the main developed capitalist states as the main source of funding for the welfare-warfare state in the first two decades of this century very quickly sparked demands from internationally-operating business for some jurisdictional restraint or coordination, in order to prevent what was identified as 'international double taxation'. The unilateral adoption of a measure of jurisdictional restraint by some states (notably the foreign tax credit introduced in the USA in 1918) led to pressures on other states for similar action, to equalize the conditions of international competition. However, the drawbacks of unilateral measures quickly became apparent: the foreign tax credit, for example, means that the income from foreign branches or subsidiaries is always taxed at the higher of the home or host country rate, and so creates an incentive for host countries to increase their taxation of foreign-owned business, at least up to the home country rate. For this reason, efforts were made to find an international solution through discussions and negotiations initiated through the League of Nations, culminating in an intergovernmental conference in 1928. Although the outcome of these efforts fell short of the comprehensive multilateral agreement for which some had hoped, they did produce a novel form of coordination, the model tax treaty, which could be used as a basis for bilateral agreements between states according to the particular character of their tax systems and of the investment flows between them (see generally Picciotto 1992: chs. 1 & 2). While few such treaties were negotiated in the recession years of the 1930s, the League models provided the basis for the rapid spread of bilateral tax treaties after 1945, helping to facilitate the postwar growth of international direct investment.

As with the Paris Convention for patents, tax treaties leave each state free to decide the scope and incidence of its taxation of income, and they merely classify and assign between states rights to tax according to types of tax and the relationship of the state to the taxpayer. Thus, formally each state is free to determine by its own internal political processes the incidence of direct taxation, for example in defining the concept of income and its application to different types of revenue received by various kinds of legal persons. States are, in principle, equally free to negotiate whatever bilateral agreements seem suitable with any other state, according to the tax systems of each and the patterns of trade and investment between them. However, treaty negotiation is strongly conditioned by the established policies and expert practices of the participants, as well as by the constraints established by the existence and nature of the treaty network (for example, a new provision requested by a particular partner may be refused mainly for fear that others may request it). On the other hand, a state's power over its own tax system is also constrained not only by the global nature of much economic activity, but also by the established patterns of international tax arrangements. A sovereign legislature is formally free to reform national taxes as it wishes, but it must always take account of the effect on investment flows; although it is possible for legislation to be framed so as to override rights created by pre-existing treaty provisions and embedded in domestic law,[9] this will result in protest and perhaps retaliation from treaty-partners, and will require renegotiation of the treaty arrangements.[10]

Thus, these kinds of international arrangements are deeply embedded into national legal and administrative provisions, establishing what may be described as transnational regulatory régimes.

Problems caused by the interaction of nationally-based forms of business regulation became apparent quite early, as these examples show. While in some cases various arrangements for coordination, such as those I have briefly indicated, were quickly developed, in others this did not occur, perhaps because national diversity was too great, or interaction did not cause significant conflicts, for one reason or another. This was the case for antitrust or restraint-of-trade regulation: although there was a fairly rapid process of corporate concentration in the period 1880–1914 in all the developed capitalist countries, the forms it took were very different. The emergence of big business led in the USA to a populist reaction against the 'trusts', the activation of the common law of restraint of trade and the enactment of the Sherman and Clayton Acts, which helped to form a particular pattern of regulatory corporatism (Weinstein 1988, Sklar 1988), in contrast with the more directly state-corporatist forms in Europe. Although the potential for conflict if USA antitrust regulatory provisions should be applied to international business was apparent from an early date,[11] states

---

[9] Treaty provisions may be incorporated into domestic law by Constitutional stipulation, as in the USA, or by statute, as in the UK; in either case they may be overridden by a later statute, although courts have generally required explicit language to show a legislative intention to do so. Hence, where treaties contain terms considered by the courts to be self-executing so as to create rights directly for individuals, what is established is essentially a transnational regulatory regime. An important example of such a regime is direct taxation, since tax treaties create rights for individual legal persons which must be incorporated into national law (see Picciotto 1992, ch. 10). The European Community legal system, being both more extensive and having a stronger integrationist focus in the European Court of Justice (which can impose its interpretations of EC law on national authorities), is described as supranational.

[10] A notable case in point is the dispute between the USA and its main treaty partners over the effects of the 1986 Tax Reform Act in overriding USA treaties: Picciotto (1992: ch. 11.2.b).

[11] In *American Banana* v. *United Fruit Co.* (1909) 213 US 347 the Supreme Court adopted a strong unilateral limitation on jurisdictional scope: Justice Holmes flatly stated that the application of the USA antitrust laws to acts taking place abroad 'not only would be unjust, but would be an interference with the authority of another sovereign'. However, this was much relaxed in *U.S.A.* v. *Sisal Sales Corp.* (1927) 274 U.S. 268, in which the Court held that a conspiracy between USA companies to monopolize the exports of sisal from Mexico to the USA was formed in the USA and affected imports, and could not be protected from USA law merely

co-operated in or connived with an extensive cartelization of world markets in the period 1890–1939, which was little disturbed until after 1945.

The postwar period saw an international spread of competition laws, as the American antitrust gospel was spread through wartime planning for the postwar international economic order,[12] and then through the partial dismantling by the occupation authorities of the German and Japanese industrial cartels and the implantation of competition and 'fair trade' laws. However, the more stringent and strictly enforced US laws soon led to repeated instances of conflict with other countries' régimes, resulting in the enactment of blocking and retaliatory legislation. Disputes over 'extraterritorial' assertions of jurisdiction originated with the application of US antitrust laws to international business structures,[13] but became more generalized as the same phenomenon was recognized in relation to other types of regulation, notably in the application of USA trade and technology export controls (Picciotto 1983, Rosenthal and Knighton 1982, De Mestral and Gruchalla-Wesierski 1990), and taxation by US states such as California of transnational corporations on a worldwide formula apportionment basis (Picciotto 1992: ch. 9). While the political aspects of such conflicts were discussed at summit meetings of G7 leaders, some attempts were made to avoid them by developing a legal doctrine of 'moderation and restraint' in the exercise of concurrent jurisdiction.[14]

because one element in the conspiracy involved inducements to Mexican officials to discriminate against rival firms. Some dozen Sherman Act cases were brought by the USA authorities before 1940 relating to international commerce; all (except for 3 cases against shipping conferences before 1914) concerned monopolization of foreign sources of raw materials in order to push up USA import prices. It was not until the antitrust laws were revitalized in the second phase of the Roosevelt administration by the 'young Turks' that their application to a wide range of international cartels was begun. Cases involving British firms were suspended during the War after Foreign Office complaints (see PRO file FO 371/44589; and for the background to the chemicals industry cases see Reader 1975, chs 23 and 24), but they eventually led to a large number of consent decrees, and to the well-known landmark judgments, notably in the *Alcoa* case enunciating the 'effects' doctrine of jurisdiction: see Picciotto 1983. Details of all antitrust cases initiated by the Department of Justice (i.e. excluding private and FTC cases) are given in US *Bluebook* (1949), continued in CCH *Trade Regulation Reporter, Transfer Binder*.

[12] See Hearings before the Temporary National Economic Committee of the US Congress, Investigation of Concentration of Economic Power (1941), and the Surveys carried out in 1944 and 1946 by the British Board of Trade of international cartels, eventually published by the Department of Trade and Industry in 1976.

[13] However, similar problems had arisen much earlier; for instance, in the 1920s firms with subsidiaries in France objected to the application of a tax on their dividend distributions by the French Treasury, which took the view that the *impôt sur le revenu des valeurs mobilières* could be applied in respect of dividends distributed by a foreign parent company, proportionate to the value of its holdings in its French branch or subsidiary. This led to the negotiation of a half-dozen tax treaties, which merely finessed the 'extraterritorial' aspects, by preserving the French right to tax a 'deemed dividend' from the subsidiary if profits could be said to have been 'diverted' to the parent: see Picciotto (1992: 175).

[14] Initially developed in US case-law, and then in the American Law Institute's Restatement of the Foreign Relations Law of the United States of America (where the issue caused considerable controversy in the negotiation of the Third Restatement of 1987); the principle then received some international endorsement through the OECD (OECD 1987).

B. The Mediation of Regulatory Interaction and the Role of Business Lawyering

The application of nationally-based regulatory régimes to transnational business activities, and their partial coordination through international arrangements such as those discussed in the previous section, created considerable disjuncture between national and international processes of legitimation. Businesses operating in more than one jurisdiction were exposed to different, often divergent, regulatory standards, criteria of fairness, and enforcement procedures. Inter-state arrangements did not attempt to establish internationally-agreed standards, criteria or procedures. These substantive matters were left to each state to determine, but it could be argued that they were to be applied on a non-discriminatory basis within each state's jurisdiction. The elasticity of the scope of this 'national' jurisdiction left considerable room for manoeuvre and negotiation both among the state regulatory officials and between them and representatives of business.

From the point of view of the TNC, operating in different jurisdictions exposed it to diverse and potentially conflicting regulation, and it was legitimate, even essential, for the firm so to organize its affairs as to minimize the regulatory impact. This was especially the case for regulation which imposed direct costs on business, for example income or profits taxes: as we have seen, each state's attempts to ensure fairness in taxation between all those doing business or resident within its jurisdiction nevertheless created overlapping tax liabilities which business resented as 'double taxation'. It therefore seemed natural for firms to reorganize their corporate and financial structures in ways that minimized their tax exposures. However, this did not necessarily affect substantive aspects of business strategy. While taxation may figure as one of the factors to be considered in a firm's strategic and operational decisions, it is unlikely to be determining, even for locational decisions. On the other hand, purely formal legal means could be devised to achieve the desired business goals. Thus, business activities or relationships can be broken down or packaged according to various components (e.g. transfers of goods, services, money, know-how); these may take different legal transactional forms (e.g. sale, licence, share, bond); and they may be routed between entities(public/private company, branch, trust), with various types of jurisdictional links or presence (place of formation, centre of management, etc). Initially, it was essentially the owners and directors of international business firms themselves who originated these devices and techniques, and they developed as part of the international strategies of the firms. Such firms could employ specialists who had or developed particular expertise, and became in-house strategists developing and managing the complex patterns of formal legal relations. External professional consultants were hired to deal with specific problems or conduct negotiations within a particular jurisdiction, where local contacts and knowledge were important. A notorious example is the Vestey family, who built the biggest private fortune in Britain based on combining cold storage and distribution in Britain with access to cheap sources of food abroad, such as eggs from China and beef from Argentina. The Vestey brothers developed a deep resentment against what they considered to be the unfair double taxation burden created by the British rules of residence, but after failing to secure any exemption through a private approach to Prime Minister Lloyd George, they resorted to an elaborate international family trust and corporate structure mainly devised by William Brown, an accountant who was William Vestey's personal secretary. This minimized the profits of their firm Union Cold Store taxable in the UK, and accumulated most of their global profits in a Paris trust, so that only the payments from the trust for their expenses in Britain need be declared as UK income. The Revenue only discovered the existence of the trust by accident in 1929, and the scheme resulted in protracted legal battles lasting several decades, in which the Vesteys scored two notable victories in the House of Lords (Picciotto 1992: 100–102; Knightley 1993).

Thus, in the first half of this century, differences and disjunctures between national regulatory régimes for business were accommodated primarily by internal arrangements devised by and for internationally-active firms. Indeed, it can be said that such disjunctures helped to mould the dominant type of such firm, the TNC, since these firms gain their competitive advantage from their organizational form, which enables them to internalize the exploitation on an international scale of a combination of diverse assets and locations entailing uncertainty, risk and opportunism (Williamson 1985, ch. 11). Hence, the growth of transnational corporate 'big business' was not prevented but in some ways facilitated by the diversities and disjunctures between national regulatory régimes and the imperfections of the international arrangements for their coordination. Where such firms needed to resort to outside professionals to help to devise appropriate or legitimate forms for their business activities, they chose specialists from the regulatory communities rooted in national cultural and political particularities.

It was only slowly that opportunities were opened up for the development of transnational professional practice by lawyers or other regulatory professionals. One of the earliest such fields was business taxation, in relation to which a key part was played by Mitchell B. Carroll. Having qualified in USA, French and German law in the 1920s, Carroll blazed a career in international business law, using his contacts in Geneva and Washington DC to lobby for USA participation in the technical work of the League of Nations on international taxation. He was involved in negotiations with the French government, following complaints by US firms, which led to the 1931 USA-French tax treaty, and not only served as the USA representative on the

League's Fiscal Committee, but carried out a major 35-nation study of international aspects of business taxation for the Committee, funded by the Rockefeller Foundation. He combined his government work with a private practice based in New York from 1933, acting as lobbyist or advocate for business groups, supporting tax treaties, defending tax relief arrangements such as the foreign tax credit, and helping devise new ones such as the Western Hemisphere Trade Corporation. He was a founder of the International Fiscal Association, serving as first President from 1939 to 1971.[15] This Association helped to build a community of national tax specialists interested in international tax matters, mixing officials, academics and private practitioners, with business interests generally dominant.

The type of transnational legal practice developed by such lawyer-diplomats essentially involved devising legal forms for business which could accommodate the interaction of regulatory jurisdictions, and negotiating the limits of acceptability of such forms with relevant state officials. This included lobbying for and helping to formulate national legislation and international arrangements, as well as advising firms on how best to structure their activities and if necessary arguing for the legitimacy of such structures before relevant officials or tribunals. Thus, among the pressures on the Foreign Office which led to the first UK–USA double tax treaty of 1945 were letters from British firms operating in the USA, pointing out that the absence of such a treaty had obliged them to have recourse to 'unsatisfactory expedients such as invoicing goods at higher prices to the subsidiary or leaving profits to accumulate in the US' because of high USA taxes on profit remittances.[16]

The skill of these 'dealers in law' (Dezalay, chapter 2 in this volume) was to deploy arguments based on the formal legal principles of fairness and equal treatment, whether in public forums to secure favourable legislation or court decisions, in the privacy of their offices where legal forms could be devised, or in the semi-secrecy of bargaining or diplomatic negotiations with national tax officials or government Ministers (Picciotto 1995). Thus, if lawyers are thought of as 'creative ideologists' or 'symbol traders' (Cain 1994), this means that they are actively involved in regulatory communities, with state officials (bureaucrats or judges), arguing and negotiating the legitimacy of business activities, as clothed in the legal forms that they have devised. There are differences between giving a bribe, or extracting a political favour, and deploying a legal argument, although some of the skill of the business lawyer may lie in understanding when to use each and how to combine them. The abstract nature of formal legal principles entails an

---

[15] He also maintained an interest in public international law, and proselytized for the foundation of the United Nations; these details are given in a memoir he published in his 80th year (Carroll 1978, see also Picciotto 1995).

[16] Foreign Office file 371/38588 in the Public Record Office: see Picciotto (1992: 39–40).

indeterminacy which allows often considerable flexibility and scope for negotiating the acceptability of relationships or activities, and it is this process of 'creative lawyering' that provides much of the dynamic behind the evolution of regulatory régimes (McCahery and Picciotto 1995).

Special techniques were developed by lawyers who became involved in transnational practice, devising arrangements for international business to deal with the requirements of different interacting jurisdictions. A good example is the way in which the taxation régime for the international oil industry was constructed. This has its roots in the 'Aramco formula', used as the basis for the immensely lucrative concessions negotiated in 1949–51 with the Arab Gulf states, which replaced the per-barrel royalty of the pre-war concessions with profits taxes based on 'posted prices', allowing a notional 50–50 profit split between the companies and the oil-rich states. With the support of the USA State Department, the scheme aimed to provide substantial increases in revenues for the oil-producing states; but this would be largely at the expense of the oil companies' home states, provided the taxes paid at the production stage could qualify as income taxes and be eligible for credit against the companies' home tax liabilities. To facilitate this, the tax laws of Saudi Arabia, Kuwait and Bahrain were drafted by an oil company adviser (Mr Barthelow, formerly of the USA Treasury). Nevertheless, both the USA and UK Treasuries and Revenue services had considerable reservations about what they considered was essentially a scheme to transfer millions of dollars of revenue to subsidize foreign governments without the necessity of obtaining parliamentary approval; and they attempted to put up a joint objection that the oil state taxes were not 'true' income taxes, and thus not allowable for credit. However, they were defeated by a combination of skilful inter-jurisdictional negotiations by representatives of the oil companies and strong political pressures from the State Department and the Foreign Office, which considered that geopolitical strategic factors should override revenue concerns.[17] The allowability of upstream oil taxes for credit against downstream tax liability became built into the politics and economics of international oil, although the terms and forms of the interactions have been periodically reopened and renegotiated. For example after 1975 with the introduction of new production-sharing arrangements, Indonesia asked the USA IRS to draw up a tax which would be allowable for credit in the USA; although this was refused, the same effect was produced by using USA law firms to submit drafts to the IRS until an acceptable version was found (Kingson 1981: 1265).

The process of tailoring the legal and administrative requirements of a jurisdiction to facilitate its interaction with others so as to stimulate international investment or business activities also produced the phenomenon of

---

[17] The story is documented in files in the Public Records Office, especially T236–4234–9; for a more detailed account see Picciotto (1992: 42–44).

the 'haven', or 'state of convenience'. Tax avoidance by the use of convenient foreign jurisdictions had already emerged in the 1920s and 1930s, mainly to shelter private family fortunes, and after 1950 new locations such as the Netherlands Antilles started to market themselves, particularly for the incorporation of holding companies to channel international direct investment. The phenomenon of the tax haven became linked with that of the offshore financial centre, from the early 1960s, when the leading states moved to full currency convertibility while maintaining monetary controls to regulate 'hot money' flows; this created differentials in the application of regulations such as banking reserve requirements, allowing banks to offer favourable terms through their foreign branches, especially to non-residents. By the 1960s also, the 'flag of convenience' became an increasingly prominent feature of international shipping.

It is important properly to appreciate the role of of regulatory specialists or professionals, notably lawyers, economists, and accountants, in order to understand the process of interaction between regulatory jurisdictions. It is not merely that 'creative' lawyering or accounting can discover 'loopholes', thus rendering the regulatory system ineffective, as is sometimes suggested (e.g. McBarnet 1994: 82). Their creativity means that regulatory professionals play an active part in the operation and development of a regulatory régime, since they negotiate and help to formulate the substantive content of decision-making, within the framework of the legitimating rules or abstract norms, which embody formal criteria for fairness, justice and equality among political subjects or citizens (McCahery and Picciotto 1995). For example, the legitimate role and scope of tax havens have since their inception been subject to intense debates. On the one hand, national tax collectors and taxpayer pressure-groups stigmatize them as providing the means whereby the rich can avoid paying their fair share of taxes in their own country. On the other hand, from the perspective of the rich themselves, it seems fully justified that they should seek to avoid unfair or oppressively burdensome taxation, by removing themselves or their wealth to more congenial locations. Professionals have developed the specialized discourses for arguing these issues, and the techniques for applying those principles to practical cases. Thus, there is a long-standing argument from economists that the competition from haven states puts pressure on others whose taxes are inefficient to make their taxation fairer.[18] Lawyers, for their part, hold themselves out as having developed the skills to understand the tax rules of different jurisdictions so as to be able to devise combinations taking advantage of beneficial interactions. However, they have also gone

---

[18] This argument was made, for example, by Luigi Einaudi, who had been one of the four expert economists who authored a report on international double taxation for the League of Nations in 1923, in later lectures to the Hague Academy of International Law (Einaudi 1928: 35–6; cf Bracewell-Milnes 1980).

further and helped to design the laws of appropriate states to make them attractive as havens. This ability to play on both sides, advising private clients as well as the state (stressed by Dezalay, chapter 2, in this volume), is enhanced when it also has an international dimension: those assisting private clients to avoid the regulatory requirements of one state can collaborate with the authorities of another state to tailor helpful legal arrangements which can provide 'shelter'.

There is, certainly, a form of competition between different groups of professionals, both to attract clients and to gain influence within the various public bodies and institutions through which the regulatory process is played out. It should be borne in mind, however, that the discourses these different groups deploy are each rooted in different epistemological perspectives reflecting different aspects of a fragmented social reality. Thus, they cannot replace or extinguish each other, but it is in their symbiotic interaction that they contribute to the reproduction of social relations. Much of this interaction focuses on the national state, which orchestrates the public institutions of government, and the reconciliation of the diverse discourses substantially takes place through the rhetoric of sovereignty and the national interest.

C. The Tensions of Transnational Regulation

Although jurisdictional interaction had led to the development of transnational regulatory practices already in the first half of this century, this tended to reinforce rather than challenge the dual process of legitimation involved in the concept of 'sovereignty' discussed above. Clearly, state officials with specific regulatory responsibilities were organized within their national state's bureaucratic apparatus, which structured their modes of thought and professional practices as well as their loyalties. Although business firms operating internationally might initially have sought for international or even global solutions to problems of unfairness in the conditions of competition, they quickly realized that their best hope lay in mitigating the worst effects of overlapping regulatory requirements, and further that the solution was very much in their own hands. Much could be done by pressurising or persuading national officials and legislatures to modify national regulatory requirements which could be argued to be a hindrance on competitiveness or a stimulus to capital flight. But this could also be complemented by organizing the conduct and forms of their own business so as to make best use of the flexibility and looseness of regulatory rules and procedures, including the elasticity of the scope of jurisdiction.

To be sure, some of the professional advisers who became involved in devising and negotiating the legitimacy of the forms of international business began to develop what could be described as a transnational practice. These pioneers were still mainly individual specialists, such as Mitchell

Carroll, although they helped to create a new type of international arena of regulation. As professionals, they could move, and act as intermediaries, between associations representing private interests, such as the International Chamber of Commerce, and inter-governmental organizations and specialist committees, such as the Fiscal Committee of the League of Nations (where Carroll sat as a national 'expert', even though the USA government was not a member of the League). The foundation of international professional associations such as the International Fiscal Association helped to create a technical discourse uniting the different elements of the regulatory community.

By the 1960s, however, these arrangements came under increasing pressures, of a dual character. Political pressures with a predominantly national focus led in many cases to a rapid development of national regulation of business, of a new and extensive kind, sometimes referred to as 'juridification' (Teubner 1987). At the same time, the reduction of barriers to the movement of goods and investment capital between states intensified the problems of interaction between these, increasingly juridified, jurisdictions. The mushrooming growth of national regulation brought with it a transformation of professional practice, especially of lawyers and accountants, so that large bureaucratic firms offering a range of specialist services replaced the gentleman professionals with their intimate knowledge of clients' affairs (Nelson 1988).

For transnational regulatory practices, these developments led to a generalization of the devices and techniques which had been developed by TNCs and their advisers in the earlier period. The ad hoc arrangements pioneered by the TNCs, and the legitimacy of which had been negotiated by their representatives, became transformed into routinized, bureaucratized schemes which became much more widely available and publicized. Thus, tailor-made devices such as the Vesteys' trust/corporate structure of the 1920s became transformed into standardized formats such as the off-the-peg offshore corporate 'vehicle' for a Eurobond flotation, involving large-scale production processes for major operations such as an international M&A (merger & acquisition) deal. Access to the special facilities of 'haven' jurisdictions was no longer only for the privileged few, but became available to anyone with the price of a ticket to Geneva or the Cayman Islands. Competition in the provision of such facilities rapidly spread their use, breaking through the carefully-negotiated legitimacy limits established between regulators and the advisers of the major corporations and wealthy families who had previously been their main users. The exploitation of regulatory differences in order to accommodate or take advantage of frictions caused by overlap or conflict between jurisdictions was replaced by systematic regulatory 'arbitrage'—deliberately structuring financial and other deals in order to derive profit from even slight regulatory differences.

Thus, in many fields of regulation a dual tension can be discerned, which has led to a generalized process of de-regulation and re-regulation on an international scale (Majone 1990). Often sparked by dramatic incidents or crises, the 'failures' of existing regulatory arrangements have been exposed, and pressures for more effective regulation have mounted. At the same time, it has been clear that there must be closer international coordination of such regulation, due to the opening up of national markets and the creation of more directly global competition not only for goods but a wide range of activities under the heading of 'services'. It is this pressure that has led to the dismantling of national forms of regulation with a 'closed' character (involving direct state intervention), in favour of more 'open' forms, or those which are more susceptible to international coordination.

It has also triggered a competition in forms of regulation themselves (Dezalay, in this volume), amounting almost to inter-jurisdictional warfare. Jurisdictions offer themselves and their communities of specialists as providing optimal locations for particular business activities. In this competitive warfare the weapons are not only price but also quality. Especially in order to break into the market, a jurisdiction may initially offer easy terms: lax regulation, toleration of bank and business secrecy, low charges. This is likely to lead to retaliation against it by interacting jurisdictions, which may refuse to grant the necessary recognitions in their own rules, and attempt to stigmatize it as lacking 'respectability'.[19] Such accusations may be fed by the uncovering and publicising of scandals, such as the wave of 'insider dealing' revelations that swept the world in the 1980s, from Andorra to Japan, supporting a campaign for the adoption of American-style rules and helping to open up cosy local financial markets to invasion by outsiders.

D. *Functional Regulatory Networks and the Problem of Legitimation*

In this section I focus on one of the striking features of the international process of restructuring of business regulation, the growth of international functional networks or communities of regulation. In the traditional model where inter-state legitimation is based on bargaining between national interests, coordination of national regulation takes place by diplomatic means

[19] Thus, the British Treasury and Foreign Office have tolerated or even facilitated the development of many British overseas territories as offshore financial centres, both in the Caribbean and closer to home such as the Isle of Man and Gibraltar, while using inducements such as designated status under UK financial services legislation, and pressures such as co-operation with other authorities including the USA to unmask scandals, to improve the 'quality' of regulation, usually by sending a trusted official from the Treasury or the Bank of England to head the local regulatory body (see e.g., UK 1990). The USA has been engaged in long-standing tussles with Caribbean tax havens, and in the 1980s the USA Treasury attempted to modify USA tax laws so as to allow each such jurisdiction a specific tolerated status in relation to a particular activity (e.g., re-insurance, property development); but this policy of turning the havens into 'boutiques' rather than 'supermarkets' was resisted by the Congress, which hesitated to legitimize them (Picciotto 1992: 164–170).

through intergovernmental agreements or organizations. As the dual aspects of intra- and inter-state legitimation have been put under pressure, in the ways described in the previous section, there has been an increasing growth of direct contacts between regulators with specific functional responsibilities. Thus, officials whose powers and policies have been developed within the hierarchy of the national state, have developed horizontal cross-border contacts with their counterparts in other states, by-passing the coordination of national levels of government and the mediation of diplomatic channels and Foreign Offices. The growth of these links has also resulted from the strategic interplay among regulators, for example to expand the scope of their jurisdiction by creating a forum they can influence, or to counter unilateral assertions of jurisdiction by establishing international procedures to constrain aggressive regulators. These networks are seen by the technical specialists as a necessary functional response to both the increased complexity of regulatory problems and their international scope; but their creation outside the established institutional structures of the national state involves new problems of legitimacy. Although coordinating rules and standards may, with difficulty, be agreed between functional specialists, they are often hard to reconcile with nationally-developed norms and expectations, growing out of a denser cultural background and the broader framework of accountability supplied by the national state. Hence, they provide at best a loose structure attempting to accommodate the tensions between international regulatory coordination and competition.

These contacts can aptly be described as taking place through networks, in a number of senses.[20] Firstly, they are informal or semi-formal in nature: even where they are publicly visible, they are often not founded on conventional legal instruments such as treaties, but on 'gentlemen's agreements' which may be semi-secret. Where some pressure develops for a degree of formalization, the preferred format is often the MOU (Memorandum of Understanding), often described as an 'administrative arrangement' not intended to be a legally-binding agreement. This applies both to the initial agreement establishing the forum and setting out its procedures, as well as to agreements on more substantive matters which result from such contacts. For example, the Concordat, and the Capital Adequacy principles agreed by the Basle Committee (discussed below) have no formal legal status, but

---

[20] The 'network' metaphor has increasingly been used to describe the fluid and criss-crossing nature of international or global contacts of a wide variety of types. It has been deployed by political scientists to map the interactions of agents or actors involved in 'policy-making' (e.g., Heclo 1978, Knoke 1993; Marsh & Rhodes 1992, Marin and Mayntz 1991). The concept has also been used in the context of international organization, to discuss 'principled issue networks' involving non-governmental organizations and others operating on the basis of shared ideals on global issues, mainly human rights and environmental causes (Sikkink 1993; Keck and Sikkink 1994: see below for discussion). In using the term I am not intending to refer to its conceptualization in any such bodies of work, although my choice of the term is for some of the same reasons that others have found it useful.

are nevertheless regarded as binding, at least in honour. Stronger legal force is attributable to agreements between tax administrators, whether in respect of the liability of a specific business or interpreting a tax treaty provision, since such agreements are provided for under the 'competent authority' procedures of tax treaties; nevertheless, their status in international law is unclear, and under national law they are at best persuasive, not binding.[21] Attempts to establish an arrangement to coordinate antitrust or competition law enforcement between the USA and EC authorities, especially for international mergers, have been hampered by restrictions on the powers to strike international bargains of those authorities, especially the European Commission.[22]

Secondly, such links grow up between power-nodes, creating groupings formed according to perceived need. These may, like spiders' webs, take advantage of existing institutions as points of attachment, but form links

---

[21] USA courts have been more willing to accept 'interpretative' agreements than have UK courts: compare *Xerox Corp.* v. *U.S.* 14 Cl. Ct. 455 (1988) with *IRC* v. *Commerzbank* [1990] STC 285. Business has long fought for a more binding and legally-based procedure for resolving individual cases, and arrangements providing for arbitration of such cases (at least if negotiations between officials fail) have now been established in some bilateral treaties, and in a multilateral treaty agreed among the EU member states (Picciotto 1992: 291–5).

[22] A Press Release of 23rd September 1991 announced the signing and gave the text of what was called an Agreement between the Government of the USA and the Commission of the European Communities regarding the Application of their Antitrust Laws. Interestingly, on the same day Sir Leon Brittan, who was the architect and signatory of this document on the European Commission side, also signed another document, with Richard Breeden of the SEC, which was described only as a Joint Statement on the Establishing of Improved Cooperation between the Commission and the SEC on securities regulation. The difference in format was because the European Commission has no powers of its own in enforcing securities laws, but does have specific powers to enforce EC competition law. Nevertheless, EU member states objected to the Commission's having negotiated an international agreement without the prior authority of the Council of Ministers, and this objection was upheld by the ECJ (Case 327/91, decision of 9th Aug. 1994). Although the Commission was confident that this would be soon overcome by the granting of authority by the Council, the court's decision emphasised the limitations on the Commission's powers, which will greatly restrict the scope of this agreement. In particular, the ECJ has been very strict as to the confidentiality of information divulged to the Commission; furthermore, once the Commission has initiated a proceeding, especially under the Mergers Regulation, it has little discretion but is mandated to take a decision: both these factors make it hard if not impossible for it to coordinate its proceedings with the USA authorities. The difficulties of coordinating competition law enforcement have for some time been clear to the authorities themselves; although the OECD established a procedure for notification and consultation in relation to competition law matters with an international dimension dating back to 1967 (amended in 1979 and 1986), its limitations had become apparent. They were highlighted by the complexities posed by the attempt by Gillette to purchase the Wilkinson Sword wet-shaving business in 1989–1991, which led to proceedings in 14 jurisdictions (OECD 1994: 66–83). Sir Leon Brittan was active at that time, therefore, in arguing for greater formalisation of international cooperation, and the USA-EC 'agreement' was an attempt to do so. Brittan also supported proposals to include this issue within the ambit of the GATT/WTO, and a draft was submitted by a private group of experts for an international antitrust code (Petersmann 1993). This made little progress given the weight of other matters which nearly sank the Uruguay Round agenda. They key problem is not agreement on rules, but coordination of decision-making, and it is unlikely that major trading states will cede to any outside body the power to declare a cartel or a merger illegal.

opportunistically and without strict regard to formal organizational membership. A further consequence of this opportunism is that there is considerable overlapping or intersection among networks, between groupings fulfilling the same or related functions.

As an example, one can take the growth of networks of regulators of banks and financial markets.[23] Although they have used formal institutional points of contact, notably the Bank for International Settlements (BIS), and the EEC's Banking Advisory Committee, the main functional activities have developed through different and more informal groupings. Thus, the BIS has since 1963 'hosted' regular meetings (generally monthly) of representatives of central banks, with various functional responsibilities, from the so-called Group of 10 countries, and it helps to provide the secretariat for meetings of the G10 Ministers and Central Bank Governors. In 1974, following the Herstatt Bank collapse, a new grouping was brought into being,[24] designated the Basle Committee on Banking Regulations and Supervisory Practices, involving senior officials from the central banks and banking supervisory agencies of the G10, plus Luxembourg and Switzerland. The work of the Basle Committee has been secretive, but its output has been more publicized: first the so-called Concordat of Principles for the supervision of banks' foreign establishments, and then the 1988 Capital Adequacy Agreement.[25] However, the accounts which have surfaced of the negotiating tactics which produced this latter agreement are interesting. It is said to have been precipitated by a direct approach by Paul Volcker, Chairman of the USA Federal Reserve Bank, to the Bank of England Governor Leigh-Pemberton, apparently without bringing in Peter Cooke, the Bank of England official who was chairing the Basle Committee. The resulting bilateral agreement had the effect of creating a 'zone of exclusion' which threatened Tokyo, Frankfurt and Paris, and it was this threat that brought first Japan and then the EC into line (Kapstein 1991, 1994).

Policy-makers and specialists who have studied the Basle Committee tend to accept that its informal and voluntarily co-operative character is a source of strength, but that the real test of its efforts depends on practical implementation (USA GAO 1994). Implementation of the Concordat has been

---

[23] There is no space here to compare these in detail to similar networks in other regulatory areas, such as antitrust and restrictive business practice regulation (Boner and Krueger 1991, ch. VIII; OECD 1994), or cooperation in tax matters (see Picciotto 1992, ch. 10).

[24] Accounts differ on whether the parent was the BIS itself (Hackney & Shaifer 1986, p. 488) or the G10 (BIS 1986, p. 1); it is now known as the Basle Committee on Banking Supervision.

[25] The Concordat was first issued in 1975, and then in revised form to include consolidated supervision after the Banco Ambrosiano collapse in 1983; a Supplement on the Ensuring of Adequate Information Flows was added in 1990. The Committee's initial Report on International Convergence of Capital Measurement and Capital Standards, with Annexes providing detailed definitions of the capital base, risk weighting of on-balance-sheet assets and credit conversion factors for off-balance-sheet items, was published in July 1988. The texts are reprinted in Effros 1992.

carried out in liaison with a number of other groupings, notably the Offshore Group of Bank Supervisors,[26] while the wider international dissemination of practices generated by these relatively small groupings has taken place through the International Conference of Bank Supervisors, first held in London in 1979.[27] A more shadowy role has been played by the 'groupe de contact' of officials from EC member states: this has been described as 'informal and autonomous in nature', promoting a close relationship between supervisors which 'in turn facilitate . . . a frank and confidential exchange of information on problem cases' (BIS 1986, 65). It has met since 1971, and has continued to play a more direct and practical role than the high-level Banking Advisory Committee set up under the EEC's First Banking Directive of 1977, which has a more formal position in the development of the EEC's programme of Directives harmonizing bank regulation and facilitating their approval by the Council. The partial overlap of membership between these EEC groupings and the Basle Committee has been a source of tension, although such tension may in some contexts prove productive.

These groupings of bank officials, with all their intricacies and semi-formal character, form only part of the picture, since clustered around them are the more informal and often personalized contacts with senior directors and officials and other notables of the banking world. In some cases these also may become semi-formalized for particular purposes, for instance in bodies such as the Group of 30 which involves personalities from banking and investment institutions, or in various sorts of international financial conferences and meetings. Furthermore, these groupings with specific functional concerns about banking in turn overlap with other regulatory networks. Notably, with the breakdown of barriers between different types of financial intermediation and thus between banks and 'non-banks', the concerns of bank regulators, especially in relation to capital adequacy, have converged with those of financial market regulators. The latter have been more visibly and formally institutionalized in IOSCO (the International Organization of Securities Commissions), which began as an inter-American grouping in 1976 and decided to become global in 1983.

[26] BIS 1986, pp. 50–64. Membership of the Offshore Group appears to include Aruba, Bahamas, Bahrain, Barbados, Cayman Islands, Cyprus, Gibraltar, Guernsey, Hong Kong, Isle of Man, Jersey, Lebanon, Malta, Mauritius, Netherlands Antilles, Panama, Singapore and Vanuatu : USA GAO 1994: 64. The close links of the Bank of England with some of these must ensure that it has some influence in this forum, although it is hard to judge how effective a body this really is.

[27] Thus, nearly one hundred countries responded to a 'wide ranging questionnaire' distributed by the Basle Committee secretariat to collect information on the nature and scope of supervision of foreign banking establishments: BIS 1986, p. 2. Other groupings include the Commission of Latin American and Caribbean Banking Supervisory and Inspection Organizations, and the SEANZA (SE Asia, New Zealand and Australia) Forum of Banking Supervisors: BIS 1986, 73–77, USA GAO 1994: App. I.

Probably as important are the networks of bilateral co-operation agreements and the trilateral discussions between the USA, UK and Japanese authorities (Breeden, in Fingleton & Schoenmaker 1992; Steil 1994: 225–9). Beyond this, the disclosure requirements of securities market regulators are related to accounting standards, which are coordinated internationally mainly through the International Accounting Standards Committee (IASC), consisting of the professional accountancy bodies of over 80 countries. Thus, IOSCO's Technical Committee has been working with the IASC to produce acceptable accounting standards (Steil 1994: 222–4).

The contacts which exist at national level between banking and financial markets regulators have contributed to the parallelism or convergence both of their concerns and the regulatory 'solutions' they develop. Nevertheless, there were a number of conflicts among the various parties who attempted to negotiate, through the interaction of IOSCO, the various EU bodies, and the Basle Committee, to try to achieve compatible capital-adequacy rules for banks and securities firms, although the failure to reach agreement in 1992 was as much due to disagreements between the SEC and other securities market regulators, as to divergence between IOSCO and the Basle Committee (Underhill 1995; Steil 1994: 201–6). Joint papers issued by the two groups in July 1994 and May 1995 have attempted to establish a common supervisory information and control framework for banks and other financial firms (*FINANCIAL TIMES*, 16 May 1995), although it seems that differences between their substantive regulatory requirements, especially as to capital, are accepted as inevitable due to different regulatory aims. Negotiations between IOSCO and the International Accounting Standards Committee (IASC) have aimed at IOSCO endorsement of IASC standards to mediate the competitive tension created between USA and other capital markets by the high SEC disclosure requirements (Steil 1994: 224).

Further interlinkages occur through the OECD, which plays a role in monitoring international capital markets, although the specialists tend to prefer the more non-political forums such as IOSCO and the Basle Committee (Goodhart, in Fingleton and Schoenmaker 1992: 104). The OECD is itself an important focus for coordination of international taxation; and although taxation is generally separated by administrative 'Chinese walls' from other regulatory arenas at both national and international levels, there have been issues of intersecting concern, notably bank confidentiality. More recently an entirely new point of attachment has been created which has resulted in a new network relating to bank regulation: the Financial Action Task Force set up by the Group of 7 to combat money-laundering. This has developed a set of requirements, including a 'know-your-customer' obligation for banks, which have been propagated well beyond the G7 countries by seeking endorsements especially from 'offshore' centres, backed by a monitoring system (Gilmore 1992; Park 1991–2).

These developments are commonly explained as resulting from the national regulators' increasing awareness of the need to develop an international coordination of their established national systems of supervision, in response to the internationalization of banking and financial markets. A closer examination reveals a more complex picture, in which international trends in financial markets have been brought home to national regulators by spectacular events (in this context, a bank crash such as Herstatt, or Ambrosiano), which reveal the inadequacies of their national arrangements as well as the need for an internationally coordinated response.[28] Similarly, the greater headway that has been made in creating an obligation on banks to monitor their customers to combat 'money-laundering', through the Financial Action Task Force mentioned above, owes much to its having been attached to the high-profile G7 meetings and the linkage to the 'global panic' about narcotic drugs.

Two points must be stressed to dissipate any functionalist perspectives which might remain about the nature of the growth of these networks. First is the important role of what may be called global dramas: spectacular events which highlight or dramatize a threat which might be systemic and which appears to call for a regulatory response. In the field of bank regulation as already mentioned, these have been bank collapses often identified as caused by dubious practices or fraud, from the Banco Ambrosiano to BCCI. In the international taxation field the issue of transfer pricing was dramatized by the cause célèbre of Hoffmann-LaRoche sparked off by the 1973 report of the UK Monopolies Commission (Picciotto 1992: 188–9). Problems of financial market regulation have been highlighted by the spectacular market-manipulation and insider-dealing scandals involving Guinness, Levine-Boesky-Millken, and many others, most recently, the Barings collapse. A rather different example would be the mythologising of George Soros and his role in the destabilization of the ERM, spotlighting the problem of 'hedge funds'. Although these dramas seem to erupt purely exogenously, they can sometimes be seen to have been either sparked off or their impact heightened by deliberate moves of particular actors, such as

---

[28] Kapstein identifies three major trends resulting from the era of floating exchange rates, high inflation, and volatile interest rates of the 1970s: the globalization of both assets and liabilities which meant that problems originating from international operations directly affected domestic markets; innovations in the forms of financing, especially securitization and the development of instruments buffering financial risk (e.g., interest rate caps and swaps) which led to a rapid rise of contingent off-balance-sheet liabilities; and the growth of essentially speculative intermediation e.g., on foreign exchange markets. As these problems were dramatized for national regulators (for the Bank of England by the secondary banking crisis of the mid-1970s, for the USA by the Continental Illinois crash of 1984) they moved to reform national systems, but the banks quickly pointed out that a unilateral move to tighten national regulation, notably by changing from a simplistic fixed capital-asset ratio to a risk-weighted calculation, would affect their international competitiveness, thus domestic reforms had to be negotiated within an international agenda: Kapstein (1991).

national regulators, in order to put their own concerns onto the international agenda. The importance of the cause célèbre is nothing new, and is a feature also of national arenas (e.g. the effect of Maxwell on UK pensions regulation). However, the global inter-connectedness both of markets and of news media could be said to have created a new kind of global stage for such dramas.

Secondly, the increasing complexity of the problems posed by the dynamics of global markets has created radical uncertainty about the desirability or effectiveness of regulation. This has been seen most starkly in the recent debate over derivatives (Group of Thirty, 1993). This creates powerful arguments, not least by regulators themselves, for regulatory requirements to be minimized, and to concentrate on establishing transparency and accountability so as to improve private monitoring rather than rely on direct oversight or intervention by public officials. It also contributes to a scepticism, especially from an economic standpoint, as to the desirability of international regulatory harmonization, and a tendency to prefer diversity and even competition unless harmonization can be shown to be cost-reducing and effective.

The important part played in the emergence of new patterns of international regulation by global dramas also reflects, I believe, the interacting national/international legitimation problems which I have highlighted. Although there is often reference to the 'democratic deficit' of international institutions, this has been far too inadequately conceptualized. There is no space here to do more than give some indications of aspects of the matter. Most clearly identifiable is the problem that substantial decisions are frequently taken by unaccountable officials operating in arcane and secretive international forums, which exert strong pressure on, even if they do not formally bind, national decision-making processes. These range from major policy matters, such as the bank capital requirements discussed above, to decisions affecting, or having important repercussions for, individuals or firms, such as the resolution of individual claims of international double taxation through the mutual agreement procedures in tax treaties by the 'competent authorities' (Picciotto 1992: 287–295). Specialists and experts feel justified in preferring to deal discreetly behind closed doors with contentious and complex questions, away from the public glare of 'sound-bite' politics; but secrecy can make it very difficult to reach acceptable and effective regulatory solutions. A further major aspect of the legitimacy problem is the fragmented nature of these functional networks. This makes it very difficult to forge consensus around universalizing concepts such as the global 'public good', or even to reach agreement based on instrumental bargaining, since the single-issue focus precludes trade-offs. A few of the responses to the legitimation problems may also be briefly sketched. Firstly, despite their intrinsically secretive character, there has been some movement towards publicising some of the activities of international regulation I have described. Indeed, the formulation and publication of rules and guidelines such as the Basle Concordat is itself an attempt to generate ideological momentum. Tied to this is a process of legalization, both at the international and national levels. Contacts and co-operation between regulators have been 'regularized' through MOUs laying down modalities for exchange of information and consultation, and powers to participate in such arrangements have been embodied in national laws. These have raised a number of issues, treated as technical, but which also reflect the interacting legitimation problems, usually expressed as problems of national sovereignty. Notably, a recurring issue has been the extent of investigative powers of officials, and in particular whether a national official may use the compulsory powers available under national laws in support of a foreign investigation.[29] There have also been pressures for the 'legalization' of international decision-making procedures, especially if they affect individuals or firms, such as transfer-pricing adjudications in taxation (discussed above), or the development of the GATT dispute-settlement procedures and their application to a wider range of trade-related issues now under the WTO.

These two responses, the move towards publicising and the trend to legalization, have provided opportunities for (and been driven by) a variety of intermediaries. In some arenas the nature of the issues or their dramatization have quickly led to a widespread popular concern and the involvement of activist groups. This has been so, for example, in relation to issues such as world poverty, or the environment, and the important meetings of bodies concerned with these topics, such as the annual IMF/IBRD meeting, or the Rio conference on the environment (see Susskind 1992, Palmer 1992) have generated a massive involvement of a wide diversity of activist and pressure groups. On some matters, of which the development and enforcement of the Code on Marketing of Breast-Milk Substitutes is the best-known, pressure-groups have played a key role (Chetley 1986). For others, what has developed has been something like 'policy communities' of a corporatist character, which may have a limited role in ensuring acceptability among those more closely affected but cannot provide a wider democratic

---

[29] USA regulators have generally taken the view that a state should allow its officials to use their national enforcement powers also for the enforcement of another state's laws, under appropriate agreements and safeguards. While this has been accepted by the UK and other countries for financial and corporate market regulation, there has been a reluctance to accept such an extensive obligation for tax cooperation (Picciotto 1992: 274–8). However, arrangements for coordinated or cooperative enforcement have been developed, even for taxation, such as simultaneous examination of related firms in an international corporate group. Here again the initiative has been taken by the USA IRS, which has also been pressing other state tax authorities since 1990 to join it in arrangements for giving suitable TNCs advance approval for their internal transfer pricing methodologies (Picciotto 1992: 291). Perhaps unsurprisingly, these efforts have been supported by the USA-based professionals who can offer business firms their special expertise in complying with such American-style regulatory arrangements.

resonance. Legalization, on the other hand, is the province of professionals, not only lawyers but also their immediate competitors such as accountants (Dezalay & Sugarman 1994).

Finally, there has been a certain movement also towards the institutionalization or institutional regrouping of functional networks. This has, significantly, taken place mainly around trade blocs or trade agreements. The most developed of these, the EU, demonstrates not only the possibilities but also the limits of this strategy, which has evidently fallen short of resolving the 'democratic deficit'. By comparison, the NAFTA has an underdeveloped institutional framework, but it should not be forgotten that at least in a number of areas of business regulation between the USA and Canada, substantial coordination already exists. The most spectacular development has been the achievement of the Uruguay Round in linking trade and market access bargains to other areas of protective regulation, such as intellectual property rights and (to a lesser extent) labour and environmental protection. The evident purpose of this linkage is to provide the backing of a trade sanction to overcome the lack of reciprocity and other limitations of single-issue functional coordination. The motivation for bringing such matters under the umbrella of the WTO was to provide important incentives which could overcome some of the problems in reaching political agreement at international level on matters such as copyright protection for computer software. However, it also introduces a strong element of competition which heightens problems of inequality in international economic power. Thus, initiatives to require WTO members to ratify international labour conventions are resented by both governments and even labour representatives of low-wage countries as attempts to take away their international competitive advantages.

3. CONCLUSION: INTERSECTING JURISDICTIONS AND INTERACTING ELITES

The development of an increasingly dense network of transnational regulatory arrangements has begun to create a global arena in which regulatory issues are debated, principles and guidelines are formulated, and enforcement is negotiated. Although the kaleidoscopic and opportunistic nature of these links, as well as their essentially administrative and technical character, have in many ways provided the very impetus for their growth, they have also posed limits to their effectiveness, which have become increasingly apparent.

Firstly, the core of the networks consists of officials whose powers and authority derive from the national state. Equally, the various groups of professionals and business advisers, who also form part of such transnational regulatory arrangements, generally have their roots in, and derive their own influence from, their national regulatory systems. Thus, proposals for international principles or procedures to coordinate national regulation inevitably take the form of battles between essentially national interest groups and alliances. Where such arrangements have been internationally agreed, they provide a new process or arena for competitive struggles, which once again may be between national champions and alliances. For example, the Basle Committee's Capital Adequacy standards are by no means precise rules which can automatically be applied to the diverse circumstances of all banks, but rather provide a new framework of broadly defined common rules within which regulatory competition takes place.[30] Thus, as pointed out at the beginning of this chapter, regulatory competition and coordination are not mutually opposed or exclusive, but symbiotic.

Secondly, the ad hoc and essentially technical nature of these networks, although initially facilitating their emergence in an unobtrusive and functional fashion, has made it difficult for them to deal with the increasingly acute disjuncture between national and international legitimation processes, discussed above. Regulatory specialists are often very aware that the specialised issues with which they deal, and therefore the rules that they lay down, have broader social and political implications: for example, the calculation of risk in banking is rooted in patterns of savings and investment. The initial growth of functional networks was indeed to a great extent motivated by the view of experts that these social and political ramifications were too complex for international regulatory matters to be dealt with by politicians, who would simply fail to reach effective agreements. This has become harder to maintain, and transnational regulatory issues have been brought out more into the open and even politicized. However, this has generally meant broadening the involvement within the relevant regulatory community of representatives of interest-groups, professionals, and other experts or interested parties. If statesmen or politicians are involved, it is to give a particular issue a serious imprimatur, for example by taking the money-laundering issue through the G7. Thus, rather than politicize a matter by formalizing a network into a 'proper' inter-state organization, issues are referred to an appropriate institution with the requisite political resonance. This also helps to overcome the problems of reaching agreement between nationally-oriented specialists in single-issue forums. It is often difficult, if not impossible, to overcome the resistance of vested interests to a proposed regulatory solution that would put them at a competitive

---

[30] In particular, the 1988 Accord was highly ambiguous on whether and to what extent loan loss provisions (deducted from profit) can be included in capital for regulatory purposes, and different interpretations can make big differences to bank competitiveness (Dale, in Steil 1994: 173–5). In particular, the Japanese authorities are thought to have adopted a lax interpretation of loan default, without which many Japanese banks would suffer significant balance-sheet asset depletion.

disadvantage. By referring the issue to a body with a broader political remit, such partial objections might be overcome by rhetorical appeals to common interests, or by packaging together several otherwise unrelated issues.

The ad hoc nature of the functional forums and networks also greatly adds to the difficulties of achieving coherent approaches to international coordination across related areas of regulation. That said, the specialists involved have shown a surprising ability to develop fruitful liaison between networks. For example, as mentioned above, IOSCO has worked on accounting standards with the IASC, and its failure to reach a decision on capital requirements for securities firms compatible with the Basle Committee's rules for banks was apparently due mainly to disagreement among securities market regulators, and perhaps to underlying differences between the markets involved.

More broadly, the emergence of these transnational regulatory processes can be seen to be related to the issues of international governance, discussed in the second section of this paper. The increasing social diversity and conflicts which have shaken the political foundations of the most stable states while leading to total breakdown in others, combined with the identification as 'global' of a wide range of problems, from world poverty to AIDS and drug trafficking, have led to calls for new approaches to global governance. These have been recently articulated in particular by a Commission composed of international notables (Global Governance Commission 1995). Its Report combines wide-ranging and detailed propos-als for reform of intergovernmental organizations (including greater involvement of NGOs—non-governmental organizations of all kinds) with an appeal for a commitment to common 'neighbourhood values' (respect for life, liberty, justice and equity, mutual respect, caring, and integrity), and for the articulation of a 'global civic ethic'.

Underpinning many of the proposals and much of the rhetoric is the con-cept of the emergence of a 'global civil society', mainly expressed in the growth of NGOs, and their increasing involvement in decision-making by international organizations, especially within the UN system (ibid. 253–5). The Report provides an intriguing combination of practical proposals which are often modest or 'realistic', with idealistic rhetoric and ambitious institutional reforms. In particular, a key proposal it puts forward is for the creation of an Economic Security Council (ESC), to provide overall strategic policy guidance as well as ensure consistency between the goals of the main organizations. However, the emphasis is very much on non-interference with the role of specialised bodies, and although the Basle Committee and IOSCO are mentioned as falling within the overall purvieu of the ESC, it is made clear that their technical functioning and indepen-dence should not be questioned but rather assured (ibid.: 184). Yet even the apparently idealistic rhetoric of a body such as this Commission does no more than articulate in practised diplomatic language concerns held much more generally, not only by ordinary people but even by bankers, financiers and lawyers,[31] that the abstruse problems of international regulation of global economic and financial relations are also fundamental to the prospects for dealing with the immense socio-economic problems of poverty, ignorance and disease facing the world today.

---

[31] For instance, a chapter in a recent book by professionals about international finance (Sechrest, in Norton and Auerback 1993) is entitled 'Six Global Business and Financial Trends: A Lesson about Interconnectedness'. The first five trends identified are currency cycles, the separation of hard and soft currencies, the emergence of the international corporation, the shrinking world, and nuclear power. The sixth trend, to which the author argues the previous five have led, is the 'existing plague upon the globe' including hunger and starvation, homelessness, drugs and crime. The solution advocated is global planning based on the rule of law.

PART II

Regulatory Competition:
Lessons from the USA Federal System

4

Explaining American Exceptionalism in Corporate Law[1]

ROBERTA ROMANO

State competition for corporate charters is unique to the United States of America (USA). This chapter examines American exceptionalism in corporate law by contrasting the legal rules, institutions, and corporate ownership patterns of other federal systems, Canada and the European Community (EC), that impede a state or nation-state's ability to exercise effective jurisdiction over firms, thereby preventing corporate charter competition. Although Canada has a federal system—firms can incorporate in one of ten provinces or under the Canada Business Corporations Act (CBCA) as a national corporation—an active market for corporate charters has not developed. Similarly, the Treaty of Rome envisions a federal system for the EC, with its integrated economic market, but it has not fostered corporate charter competition among EC members, despite concerns by corporate law commentators that it would.

The chapter concludes by considering a theme in the popular press with implications for corporate law, the declining rate of growth of USA productivity relative to other nations. The best available evidence on productivity growth rates indicates that the concern is, in fact, misconceived. More important, the relative decline in the growth rate of USA productivity over the past several decades cannot readily be ascribed to differences in corporate governance régimes.

I. INTRODUCTION: THE PRODUCTION OF AMERICAN CORPORATE LAW

In the USA, corporate law, which concerns the relation between a firm's shareholders and managers, is largely a matter for the states. Firms choose their state of incorporation, a statutory domicile that is independent of physical presence, and can be changed with shareholder approval. One state, Delaware, has dominated firms' domicile choice for the past seventy-five years. Approximately one-half of the largest industrial firms are

[1] This essay is adapted from Romano (1993).

incorporated in Delaware, and the vast majority of firms that change their incorporation state move to Delaware. As a consequence, a substantial proportion of Delaware's revenues comes from incorporations (averaging over 15 percent from 1960–90; see Romano 1993: 6–8).

Delaware's success in the incorporation business is the source of a recurrent debate among corporate law scholars and practitioners concerning the efficacy of corporation codes. In the classic papers, William Cary (1974) contended that Delaware's reliance on incorporation fees led it to engage in a 'race for the bottom' with other states to adopt laws that favour managers over shareholders, and Ralph Winter (1977) countered that the race was instead to the top, as the many markets in which firms operate (capital, product, and corporate control markets) constrain managers to choose the régime most beneficial to shareholders. Otherwise, the firms choosing states whose laws were detrimental to shareholder interests would be outperformed by firms incorporated in share value-maximizing régimes, which would lower their stock prices. Lower stock prices would subject managers to the threat of job loss, either through a takeover or eventual bankruptcy. Winter's critique of Cary's thesis identified a crucial flaw, and changed the parameters of the debate, to whether markets were sufficiently imperfect constraints on managers such that states could enact non-share-value-maximizing corporate law régimes.

Since the publication of the Cary and Winter articles, empirical studies have sought to arbitrate the debate over who benefits from state competition, shareholders or managers, by measuring the economic impact (share price reactions) of management choices of incorporation state and of newly enacted state laws, and where optional, management's choice to be included under such laws. The empirical evidence, which I have reviewed in detail elsewhere, supports the conclusion, contrary to Cary's view, that overall, state competition benefits shareholders.[2]

There is also evidence that states compete for chartering business. For example, corporate law innovations that reincorporating firms emphasize as influential in their domicile choice spread rapidly across the states (see Romano 1985); Carney (chapter 5, this volume). In addition, states that are more responsive to code innovations gain more and lose fewer corporations through the reincorporation process than do less responsive states.[3] Finally, there is a significant positive correlation between a state's corporate law responsiveness and the proportion of its revenues derived from incorporation (franchise) taxes. Delaware, the most responsive state, is not always the

[2] For example, the five studies of reincorporation find that firms experience either significant positive stock price effects or no price effects upon reincorporation and none find negative price effects. See Romano (1993: 16–24).

[3] In my earlier work I constructed a measure of corporate law responsiveness that was a linear function of four corporate law reforms that reincorporating firms indicated as a reason for their choice of new domicile. See Romano (1985).

pioneer in corporate law reform: it excels in responsiveness because when it is not the first to innovate, it is among the first to imitate.

The evidence on competition raises an important question, why has Delaware been able to dominate the market since the 1920s? The key to Delaware's sustained success has to do with its ability to meet the needs of its customers, which are twofold. Reincorporating firms seek a legal régime that reduces the cost of business, and a régime provider who will not renege after the firm relocates and repeal, or fail to continually update, its desirable régime (or require large bribes to maintain a responsive régime). Delaware's preeminence in the corporate charter market results from its ability to resolve credibly the commitment problem. This ability depends on its investment in assets, referred to as transaction-specific assets, whose value is highest when used in a specific relation rather than any other use (Williamson 1985). Such assets cannot be profitably redeployed should that relation be discontinued. In the chartering context, a state must not be able to earn a return on such an asset unless it is used in the chartering business. Delaware has invested in several such assets, the most important of which is an intangible one, its reputation for responsiveness to corporate concerns. It is derived from the substantial revenues earned from incorporations: with a high ratio of franchise taxes to total revenues, it would be difficult, if not impossible, for Delaware to maintain its level of services should it not be able to maintain its incorporation business. This makes Delaware as vulnerable to loss from reneging on maintaining a responsive corporation code as reincorporating firms are, and thus serves to precommit it to continuing on a responsive path.

Delaware has also invested in real assets with little use outside of corporate chartering: a comprehensive body of case law, judicial expertise in corporate law (including a specific court, the chancery court, that hears all corporation cases, unlike the situation in other states where such cases are heard in any court of general jurisdiction), and administrative expertise in the rapid processing of corporate filings. In addition to aiding Delaware's precommitment to firms, this legal capital is a valuable asset to firms, for it provides them with greater certainty concerning corporate law issues, enabling them to plan better complex business transactions.

A final device furthering Delaware's advantage in the chartering market is a constitutional provision requiring a supermajority vote of 2/3 of both houses of the state legislature to revise its corporation code. This makes it difficult for Delaware to renege on its course of a responsive corporation code; while it may slow the enactment of reforms, it increases the likelihood that the legal régime can be no worse than it was at the time of incorporation, which is a desirable feature if firms are risk averse concerning the domicile decision.

Some analogous factors involving human capital tie firms to Delaware, creating a reciprocal hostagelike transaction-specific asset on the corporation's side, just as Delaware has such assets. Delaware's legal capital provides benefits to corporate lawyers for it reduces the cost of specialization; their cost of doing business is reduced and the value of their human capital depreciates less rapidly if attorneys' expertise can be centered on one jurisdiction. They thus have incentives to advise clients to choose and retain Delaware as a domicile. Delaware also aids the bar in maintaining its human capital by circulating unpublished court opinions and by consulting prominent members of the bar, in and outside the state, on all corporate law revisions.

Delaware and firms are therefore joined in a long-term relationship because of reciprocal vulnerability—the loss of their investments in legal and human capital—that cements Delaware's market position. Offering Delaware's code at a lower price will not enable another state to attract firms away from Delaware, as it cannot credibly precommit to maintaining superior service. A challenger starts from a lower franchise tax ratio and incurs start-up costs of developing legal capital. Delaware has, in other words, a first-mover advantage in the chartering business. Once it established a dominant position, it became cheaper for Delaware to maintain a commanding lead over any rival state because there is value in numbers. The more firms in a state, the more franchise revenues it receives and the more it will rely on its charter business, making it ever more important to be responsive to firms. In addition, the more firms there are, the more legal precedents will be produced, which provides firms with a sounder basis for business planning, and thereby attracts still more firms. Finally, the more cases brought, the greater will be the expertise of Delaware judges, enhancing the state's legal capital and preserving its competitive advantage.

None of the important transaction-specific assets that guarantee Delaware's interest will match those of incorporating firms would be present in a national chartering system. Given the size of the federal government budget, franchise revenue incentives will not constrain the national government from behaving opportunistically toward firms. Moreover, there would be no competition prodding the national government to improve its service to firms (the dynamics of state competition would be lost). Finally, while a special corporate law court, analogous to the federal tax and patent courts, could be established to develop some of the expertise crucial to Delaware's success, it would not eliminate the disadvantages of a national régime. It is more difficult to reverse judicial mistakes at the federal than state level (assuming an equal legislative will to be responsive). The support of more legislators is needed,[4] and empirical evidence indicates that Congress moves more slowly than state legislatures in reversing judicial

---

[4] The USA House of Representatives is itself larger than the combined houses of the largest state legislature.

decisions (Romano 1993: 48–9). Moreover, it is unlikely that members of Congress would face reelection difficulties due to positions taken on corporate law matters, as these are low salience issues to the vast majority of voters; to the extent that interest groups therefore will influence their votes, the reason for moving to the national arena (more efficacious laws from the shareholders' perspective) is seriously undermined, for there is no evidence that the balance across interest groups would differ at the national, compared to state, level, and indeed, my own research found the same interests were at play at both levels in the takeover context (Romano 1988).

This is not to say that state competition is a fail-proof system. State takeover statutes have been shown to have harmful effects on shareholder wealth, although even here it should be noted that Delaware has been a laggard rather than a leader on takeover regulation, adopting less restrictive laws than other states, which have not had a negative stock price impact (see Romano 1993: 52–75). Rather, it is to say that state competition offers shareholders better safeguards than a national chartering system, that the provisions in corporation codes will, more often than not, redound to their benefit.

2. PRODUCTION OF CORPORATE LAW IN CANADA

There are two interesting studies of corporate charter competition in Canada, a pioneering study by Ronald Daniels (1991) and a careful critique of it by Jeffrey MacIntosh (1993). Daniels (1991: 151–5) contends that enactment of the CBCA provoked a competitive reaction by provinces, creating uniform code provisions, similar to the situation in the USA.[5] MacIntosh disagrees, maintaining that the diffusion of the CBCA across the provinces is a function of the preferences of the administrators who initiate corporate law reform, rather than charter competition: administrators either strongly prefer uniform laws or develop a consensus view on what constitutes a good law.

Daniels develops his thesis by showing that the role of the Canadian national government in charter competition has been analogous to Delaware's: besides the rapid diffusion of CBCA reform provisions across the provinces, the predominant choice of reincorporating firms is national (ibid. 152, 157, 165 n. 69).[6] Many firms also initially incorporate under the CBCA, with the bulk coming from businesses located in one province,

---

[5] The national corporation statue was introduced in 1975. Daniels does not indicate the reason for this enactment (that is, whether firms or regulators were dissatisfied with provincial regimes). He does note that the national government sought provincial input into the drafting process but because the provinces were reluctant to participate, it acted unilaterally (ibid. 151 n. 49).

[6] Moreover, like the development of Delaware's code, some of the Canadian government's reforms in the CBCA had previously been enacted by provinces (ibid. 154).

Quebec. Daniels suggests that this phenomenon is a function of special political concerns and incorporation fee structure. Changes in incorporation levels across the two régimes (Quebec and Canadian) are related to the growing political success of the separatist party in Quebec and to changes in franchise fees. Quebec's fees are calculated on a scale graduated according to a firm's capital, which imposes a higher charge than other provinces and the CBCA, which assess a small flat fee (ibid. 167–9).[7] In 1985, national incorporation fees were increased from $200 to $500 (Canadian); thereafter national incorporations by Quebec firms slowed, and the total number of national incorporations decreased. Presumably, by 1985, with the union still intact, the Quebec business community was less concerned over the separatist movement, so that price became the determinative factor in an incorporation decision. Recent events reviving the issue of separation (the rejection in 1992 of a proposed constitutional provision concerning Quebec's distinctive status and the close rejection of the independence referendum in 1995) may induce a reversion to national incorporation.

Canada's 1985 fee increase, Daniels suggests, had a political source: Quebec politicians lobbied for a national fee increase to improve their market share of incorporations (ibid. 168–9).[8] He does not, however, address why the national government acceded to such a request. If the national government was competing for corporate charters, then it is difficult to explain why it acquiesced to Quebec's lobbying for higher national incorporation fees. In fact, this datum seems to provide evidence that the national government was not seriously attempting to compete with the provinces, consistent with MacIntosh's view of Canadian corporate law reform, which treats the innovative features of the CBCA as either a random event or a function of bureaucratic preferences rather than a response to corporate demands.

Alteratively, the national government might have been competing for charters, but administrators thought that they offered a sufficiently superior product that firms would be willing to pay a premium for a national domicile, just as USA firms are willing to pay higher franchise fees for a Delaware address. Such an explanation—miscalculation of the price sensitivity of firms—is not compelling, however, because the government did not respond to the significant decline in incorporations after the rate change with a rate reduction to recoup its market position. Another explanation that partially reconciles Daniels's and MacIntosh's competing views of the Canadian charter market is that, whatever its motivation when it adopted the innovative CBCA, the national government simply decided to stop competing for charters when it decided to raise incorporation fees; presumably Quebec was willing to provide the national government with

---

[7] Other provinces abandoned graduated fee systems by the beginning of the 1980s.
[8] None of the provinces raised their fees in response to the national fee increase.

greater benefits than it received from charter revenues, such as support on policy issues unrelated to corporate law, in compensation for the franchise fee revision.

Whether or not spurred by Quebec's lobbying, the national government's fee increase underscores the feebleness of a national government's incentive to compete for charters. A national government's ability to commit itself credibly to a responsive corporation code is limited, despite pioneering efforts at corporate law reform, because firms understand that such a government faces a minimal financial penalty from failure to continue to innovate. Franchise fee revenues are an insignificant percentage of a national government's budget.[9] Hence, such a government is far less motivated than a small state, such as Delaware, to be responsive to firms. The decrease in national incorporations after the fee increase is, then, not simply a function of the sensitivity of firms to charter prices. Rather, it is a function of price and an additional factor, the government's reputation for responsiveness. Action with an adverse effect on the government's reputation will reduce the number of new incorporations, as will an increase in price. In this scenario, firms perceived the national government's fee increase as an indication that it would also capitulate to provincial pressure concerning substantive code content. As a consequence, national incorporations declined as firms realized that it was too costly to run the risk of a national domicile.

To bolster this explanation for the decrease in national incorporations, it would be useful to know whether there were contemporaneously important national issues on which Quebec's support was key and which led to the increase in the national government's incorporation fee. Quebec's desire for separation may have been one such issue: if raising the CBCA incorporation fee disproportionately subsidized Quebec because it was the only province losing corporate revenues under the old rate structure, then the change could route additional national funds to Quebec and mollify separatist impulses. It certainly would be plausible for a national government to place priority on preserving the union over maintaining a reputation as a reliable sovereign for corporations, especially given the infinitesimal revenues that it obtained from corporate chartering.

Daniels concludes that state competition is far less effective in Canada than

---

[9] A crude estimate, providing an order of magnitude, can be extrapolated from Daniels's data on new incorporations under the CBCA and Canada's gross domestic product (ibid. 158, 160 (tables 2 and 3)). In 1988, the national government earned approximately $6 million in fees from new incorporations, compared to approximately $4 million in 1984; these amounts are less than 0.5 percent of Canada's gross domestic product. MacIntosh (1993: 11) indicated that at the current fee level the national government obtains $6 million from franchise fees, an amount equal to 1/25,000 of the national budget. He further suggested that were the national government to recruit an incorporation business more actively, the additional revenues would still be insignificant, amounting to approximately 1/10,000 of the national budget.

in the USA, and MacIntosh contends that it does not exist, because several factors important to Delaware's success are lacking, in particular the development of a comprehensive and specialized corporate law jurisprudence, as well as a significant dependence on franchise revenues. The best explanation for the more limited Canadian competition for charters, which both Daniels and MacIntosh emphasize, is that provinces do not control their corporation codes: authority is shared with independent provincial regulators and national judges. In particular, securities law administrators, whose jurisdiction is based on the residence of the investor rather than on the domicile of the issuing firm, are able to regulate corporate governance and thereby override provincial corporate law régimes (Daniels 1992: 182–4). The Ontario Securities Commission, for example, imposes fiduciary obligations on majority shareholders under its public interest powers (ibid. 183 n. 119). Securities commissions also regulate shareholder communications, going-private transactions, attendance at shareholder meetings, and receipt of financial statements (MacIntosh 1993: 30). As long as a firm has a shareholder in Ontario (a probable event, as it is the most populous province), its corporate law can be dictated by the Ontario Securities Commission rather than the legislature or court of its province of incorporation. This authority has even been exercised over stock transactions involving solely non-Ontario investors (Daniels and MacIntosh 1991: 37). In the USA, by contrast, the Supreme Court has refused to expand the reach of the national securities laws to include traditional fiduciary duties, and it has preserved the states' jurisdiction over corporate governance even in the one area of overlapping jurisdiction, takeover regulation.[10] The Securities and Exchange Commission has also been prevented by the courts from forays into corporate governance.[11]

In addition, the Supreme Court of Canada reviews all provincial appellate courts (Daniels 1992: 186–7). This feature of jurisdictional spillover may be less important than the activities of securities law administrators, however, for Daniels states that in recent years the Supreme Court of Canada has reviewed few provincial decisions involving corporate or commercial matters (ibid. 187 n. 32).[12] Business appeals became discretionary in 1974, when the automatic appeal right for cases whose amount in controversy exceeded $10,000 was eliminated and the court's docket changed considerably, as constitutional cases increased throughout the 1980s with the adoption of the Canadian Charter of Rights and Freedoms (ibid. 187). Still, in the USA there is little if any basis for the USA Supreme Court to review a Delaware court's corporate law decision.

---

[10] *Santa Fe Industries* v. *Green*, (430 U.S. 462 (1977)); *CTS Corp.* v. *Dynamics Corp. of America*, (481 U.S. 69 (1987)).

[11] *Business Roundtable* v. *SEC*, (905 F.2d 406 (1990)) (striking down SEC regulation of shareholder voting) (D.C. Circuit).

[12] From 1986 to 1989, only 14 of 304 cases heard by the Canadian Supreme Court could be classified as corporate or commercial.

A further difference between the USA and Canada affecting corporate law jurisdiction is that all Canadian judges are federal appointees with life tenure (Delaware judges have term appointments). As MacIntosh (1993: 37) notes, even a province that sought to create a special corporate law court along the lines of Delaware cannot do so as effectively as Delaware: the provincial judicial nominees must be appointed through a national process, which is not conditioned on the provincial government's approval. In addition, life tenure diminishes the judge's incentive, provided by the need for reappointment, to be responsive to changing business conditions. Thus, the ability of Canadian provinces to deliver a predictable and stable corporation code like Delaware is attenuated further, because they do not exercise complete control over judicial appointments.

A province's control over what is ostensibly its substantive law and the judges who interpret that law is, then, highly circumscribed. This weakens the incentive to invest in assets that maintain a responsive corporate law régime because the value of such assets can be dramatically impaired by the actions of securities regulators in other provinces or by the Canadian judiciary.[13] The inability of provinces to commit credibly to a responsive corporate law régime, given overlapping jurisdiction, also renders firms less willing to invest in optimizing incorporation decisions, which has a feedback effect, further reducing provincial incentives to compete.

A second important distinguishing institutional feature, besides control of the code, contributes to the difference in competition for charters between the USA and Canada. Large Canadian corporations have greater concentration of stock ownership than their USA counterparts. Daniels and MacIntosh (1990: 80–1) note that more than half the firms in the Toronto Stock Exchange 300 Composite Index are owned by a single shareholder with holdings exceeding 50 percent of the votes, whereas only 12 percent of the (USA) Fortune 500 firms are controlled by a 50 percent shareholder group. As ownership concentration increases, the choice of legal régime declines in importance: management with voting control does not need statutory discretion to operate a firm because it has the votes to change statutory default rules as it pleases. A firm with a concentrated ownership structure is therefore not likely to pay a premium willingly for a corporate

---

[13] I have no explanation for why Canadians tolerate such interference in corporate governance by securities administrators; neither Daniels nor MacIntosh provides one. To the extent that provincial securities administrators cannot discriminate against foreign-incorporated firms, the overlapping jurisdiction problem may be mitigated if all provinces are interested in charter revenue maximization: top provincial authorities could rein in their securities administrators from rendering decisions that undercut the province's corporations laws, and other provinces' laws would, derivatively, be protected. Overlapping oversight still adds unnecessary friction to a competitive system, which may slow the introduction and diffusion of corporate law reforms, as one province's innovation may run into difficulty with administrators in another province that has yet to adopt the provision.

law régime that is superior on several Delaware dimensions, such as organizational flexibility and managerial discretion.

Self-dealing issues are, however, more important from the public shareholders' perspective when ownership is concentrated than when it is diffuse.
If insiders need outside equity capital, they then have an incentive—a lower
cost of capital—to incorporate in a province whose régime best protects
minority interests against self-dealing. But this involves a far more limited
area of corporation laws on which provinces could compete in comparison
with USA law, and thus even vigorous Canadian charter competition would
be more circumscribed than that of the USA.

Jurisdictions such as Canadian provinces that are populated by firms with
concentrated stock ownership, then, have less to gain from corporate charter
competition than those whose firms are more widely held, such as USA states.
Hence, any economic return from provincial competition for chartering would
be far lower than the return in the USA. Causality, however, could run in the
opposite direction: in the absence of vigorous competition for corporate charters, equity investments of public firms could more optimally be concentrated,
as investors compensate for less responsive legal régimes with more immediate monitoring of management. We do not have data to test the direction of
causality in the relation between corporate ownership and charter competition, and I am uncertain whether an adequate test could be constructed.

Differentiation of which shareholder issues matter when ownership composition varies is borne out in a comparison of the two countries' shareholder
litigation rules. Shareholder litigation has been more easily undertaken in the
USA than Canada. Canada follows the British cost rule, in which a losing
party pays the other's costs (costs follow the event), although the losing plain-
tiff-shareholder in a derivative suit can petition the court for indemnification
from the corporation (Buckley and Connelly·1988: 615; MacIntosh 1991: 56).
Furthermore, contingent fees are not as prevalent in Canada; they have only
recently been permitted in Ontario, require local bar society approval in many
provinces, and are legislatively capped, typically at 25 percent.[14] In addition,
class action rules, historically following British procedure, have been more
restrictive than in the United States of America.[15] These Canadian cost and

---

[14] I would like to thank Jeffrey MacIntosh for explaining to me how contingency fees are
used in Canada.

[15] Unlike USA class actions, the British rules require that an amount in liquidated damages
be specified and that class members have identical claims. These requirements discourage suits.
Consequently, most shareholder suits that are not brought under the derivative statutes are
individual (personal) actions. However, Ontario recently reformed its class action rules and
Quebec has also departed from the British practice. The greater historical difficulty in pursuing a class action may not be as consequential as it appears. Canadian securities administrators have much greater discretion than the SEC in affecting firms' governance, so shareholder
claims that in the USA are pursued as class actions may be undertaken, at the government's
expense, by securities regulators in Canada. I would like to thank Jeffrey MacIntosh for
explaining these differences to me.

class action rules severely restricted the incentive for a shareholder to bring a lawsuit against management, an incentive that is weak to begin with because litigation costs typically exceed the plaintiff's pro rata benefit. The USA solution to the collective action problem of shareholder litigation is to create an incentive for attorneys, who are paid on a contingent fee basis, to bring shareholder suits by offering the prospect of recovery of a substantial legal fee from the defendant corporation (Coffee 1985).[16] The old Canadian rules eliminated the USA solution.

Why don't Canadian provinces seek to compete in the dimension of lawsuit accessibility, as USA states do? One explanation is that greater concentration of ownership affects litigation patterns and reduces the need for more accommodating access rules. In particular, controlling shareholders have superior incentives to monitor managers for breach of the duty of care[17] compared with dispersed shareholders with small holdings, and their managers rarely engage in unilateral action to thwart a takeover because firms with controlling owners are not subject to hostile bids. Two common categories of USA shareholder suits are therefore of little concern to the vast majority of Canadian firms (Romano 1991: 60). This reduces the need for increased access to the courts.

A non-efficiency-centered explanation of Canadian shareholder litigation rules is that controlling shareholders and their counsel have exerted influence on Canadian corporation codes to obtain laws that make shareholder litigation difficult in order to enrich themselves at the minority's expense. This, however, is not a persuasive explanation because, in contrast to USA corporation codes, Canadian codes have statutory oppression remedies, which entail simplified filing procedures compared with derivative and individual (personal) shareholder actions in the USA. These provisions are aimed at providing relief against corporate action detrimental to the minority.[18] Moreover, if provinces are not competing for charters in the first place, this would also answer the question why they do not compete on the dimension of lawsuit accessibility, without need of recourse to a controlling shareholder-political conspiracy explanation.

The Canadian experience is not clearly analogous to the close corporation context in the USA, where charter competition is arguably anemic; Canadian firms differ significantly from USA close corporations. In

---

[16] As Coffee and others have detailed, there are serious problems with such an incentive scheme, including conflict of interest between shareholders and attorney and the possibility of frivolous litigation.

[17] USA firms with lower management stock ownership are sued more frequently for breach of duty of care, whereas those with high management stock ownership are more frequently sued for breach of duty of loyalty (Romano 1991: 81–2).

[18] For a discussion of the oppression remedy, and the extent to which courts have interpreted it to cover derivative claims, see MacIntosh (1991). MacIntosh is skeptical of the efficacy of the remedy.

contrast to close corporations, Canadian corporations with concentrated ownership are publicly traded, and thus stock market signals are available to price the legal régime for the minority shareholders. In addition, Canadian firms with controlling owners are typically much larger than USA close corporations. They are consequently more likely to engage in repetitive transactions for which the product of charter competition—standard form contracts—is of value.

There is, however, a simpler answer to the claim that there is little competition for corporate charters in Canada compared with the USA than the story developed thus far. Such an explanation involves numbers: there are far fewer provinces than states, and industrial organization theorists conventionally link competition to market structure (that is, number of producers as well as barriers to entry).[19] Although there are five times as many states as provinces, the credible commitment explanation of Delaware's success, built on transaction-specific assets that create a reputation for responsiveness, suggests that competition is viable only for a subset of states, those small enough for franchise revenues to make a budgetary difference. Accordingly, it is questionable whether the smaller number of provinces accounts for the absence of vigorous competition, as opposed to the barrier created by overlapping jurisdictional authority and the more limited demands placed on corporation codes because of the concentration of equity ownership of publicly traded Canadian firms.

3. PRODUCTION OF CORPORATE LAW IN THE EUROPEAN COMMUNITY

The EC federal system provides an important comparison with the USA and Canadian régimes. The Treaty of Rome established as a goal a common European economic market.[20] Coordination of economic policies was essential to achieve this goal, but a strong central government was eschewed. The treaty established instead the aim of harmonizing corporate laws across the EC.[21]

Although EC economic integration aims have been analogized to the commerce among USA states in an American common market (see Kitch 1981: 9; Buxbaum and Hopt 1988: 7; Stein 1971: 59), the USA approach to

---

[19] The earliest work along these lines is associated with Joe Bain (see Tirole: 1988:1).

[20] This goal has since been reformulated to achieve an even broader economic and political union among a larger group of European nations than the original signatories.

[21] Treaty of Rome, March 25, 1957, Rome, 298 U.N.T.S. 11, art. 54 3(g). Harmonization is achieved by means of directives, which are issued by the institutions of the EC (Commission and Council of Ministers) and are addressed to, and binding on, the member states, although each nation is free to choose, through its own implementing legislation, how to achieve the directive's required results (Slaughter and May 1990: 9–10).

corporate law has not been emulated. To the contrary, European commentators frequently justify corporate law harmonization as a mechanism for ensuring that a European Delaware will not emerge (see, e.g., Timmermans 1991: 129; de Bruycker: 1991: 191, 193; Charny 1991: 423).[22] These commentators either concur in Cary's characterization of Delaware as a pariah state or recognize that some European nations pursue, through their corporation codes, objectives other than shareholder wealth maximization and that such policies can be sustained only if there is no charter competition.

Most European nations take what is referred to as an enterprise approach to the corporation, which requires the representation of employees as well as shareholders in corporate decision making. The German code, for instance, establishes a system of two-tiered corporate boards, termed code-termination, in which workers are represented on the firm's supervisory board, which appoints the managing board handling day-to-day operations; other nations, such as the Netherlands, mandate different forms of worker participation including rights to receive information, to nominate board members, and to be consulted on important decisions (see Stith 1991: 1588–89 n. 25; Buxbaum and Hopt 1988: 180).[23] As the interests of employees and shareholders differ—workers' claims are fixed, while shareholders are the residual claimants on a firm's cash flow, who are paid after all fixed claims are met—maximization of share value is unlikely to be the objective of corporations operating under enterprise-oriented legal régimes. Some commentators, for example, attribute Volkswagen's financial difficulties to labour's alliance on the supervisory board with the largest shareholder, the state government, which fostered a 'politics of jobs' that prevented the firm from cutting costs compared with its international rivals.[24]

It is questionable whether such worker representation provisions enhance shareholder value. If they did, one would expect USA states and firms to opt for such arrangements: the powerful dynamic of state competition

[22] For consistency, I continue to use the term 'corporate law' although the conventional terminology is 'company law,' following UK usage.

[23] Worker participation entered into European codes in the mid-1970s (Buxbaum and Hopt 1988: 260–61). Its German roots are, however, far more ancient. Because worker participation is not a feature of UK corporate law, the fifth directive on corporate governance (comprising minimum standards on corporate board composition and employee participation) has produced the greatest controversy in the harmonization of corporation laws; it was first drafted over twenty years ago and is not likely to be adopted in the near future (Wooldridge 1991: 80). Indeed, the latest draft seems to give up on attaining a consensus and permits member states to choose from various models of governance to retain their diverse solutions (Buxbaum and Hopt 1988: 203). Buxbaum (1987: 75–6) suggests that the difference in corporation law objectives is related to the difference in choice of law rule: the common law or Anglo-American tradition that narrowly defines corporate internal affairs as relations between managers and shareholders 'leads more readily than does the broader [European] enterprise law concept to the use of the contractually fixable state of incorporation, rather than to the more objectively set siège social as the reference point for a corporate conflicts of laws rule'.

[24] See Protzman, F., 'Volkswagen Sees Need for Shake-up', *New York Times,* March 15, 1993, pp. D1, D8.

ensures that provisions perceived to increase share value are enacted over time. Interestingly enough, although the German model of a two-tiered board is available to French firms, almost none have adopted it (Hopt 1992: 115–6). Some USA states and firms have adopted other-constituency statutes and charter provisions, takeover provisions that have a surface resemblance to the European rules, but are distinctive in practice. These USA provisions permit directors to consider employee interests in decisions regarding control changes but do not require such consideration, and employees have no right to enforce a provision, let alone any specific representation or participation rights (see Hansen 1991; Romano 1990: 1164–5).

A further institutional difference complicates the analysis of the objectives of German firms. German corporations do not independently fund their pension commitments through investments in securities, as USA firms do. Rather they, accumulate balance sheet reserves, retaining earnings and investing internally. Some scholars view this practice as justification for codetermination: workers have a long-term claim on the firm, their pensions, which warrants representation on the board (see Kübler 1994: 565). Such pensions are still fixed claims, however, and not residual claims analogous to an equity interest in the firm. Not only must pension commitments be insured under German law, but shareholders, not workers, bear the risk of poor management because pensions are debts that must be paid whether or not internal reserves are adequate. Other commentators suggest a different connection between codetermination and German pension practice. In their view, the unfunded pension arrangement is necessary to safeguard the balance in board membership created by codetermination: if German pension funds were invested in stock, then the supervisory board's balance would be tilted even more toward labour than at present because employees could appoint directors beyond their statutory allotment as a group, through the votes of their pension fund shares (see Hauck 1994: 555). Recalibration of statutory requirements of codetermination boards on implementation of a pension policy funded similarly to USA firms through stock investments is not perceived by these commentators to be a viable political option. These competing explanations of the relation between pension fund investments and codetermination indicate that the objective of German corporations is difficult to characterize and may well not be maximization of equity share prices.

Nations pursuing mixed objectives in corporation codes cannot compete effectively for corporate charters (at least not in a race to the top) against states whose codes focus on shareholders: stock values of firms incorporated in the former nations will be lower than those in the latter, where firms will prefer to locate. Financial capital is far more mobile than labour, and the higher capital costs of a non-share-value-maximizing régime will therefore not be sufficiently offset by lower labour costs in a firm's decision calculus. To preserve multiple objective codes, nations will therefore seek to prevent the emergence of an active charter competition: the absence of competition ensures the viability of their corporation laws. The EC's harmonization process achieves such a goal. Harmonization need not eliminate competition entirely,[25] but, by mandating a floor, it severely reduces the returns from innovation and, correspondingly, from competition.

Quite apart from normative concerns over state competition and the harmonization effort, there are a number of legal and institutional barriers to an active European market for corporate charters. The most important barrier is the prevailing choice-of-law rule: except for the UK and the Netherlands, European nations follow the law of a company's real or effective seat (*siège réel*) rather than of statutory domicile (registered office) (Timmermans 1991: 133). Reincorporation is far more, if not prohibitively, expensive under a real seat rule than under a statutory domicile rule, because physical assets (a firm's headquarters) must be relocated to change legal régimes. The greatest expense of such a move is probably not the cost of new facilities but rather that of relocation of human capital. Despite the goals of integration, cultural differences across EC member states are still pronounced, and it is consequently problematic whether top management would be willing to move or commute to another country.[26]

Moreover, under both the real seat rule and the British statutory domicile rule, reincorporation is far more expensive than in the USA because a transfer of the registered office is treated as a liquidation and the firm is taxed on hidden reserves (that is, asset appreciation) (Wooldrige 1991: 8).[27] Reincorporations are not taxable events under USA tax laws.

Changing legal régime is therefore quite difficult, if not prohibitive, for European firms. The incentives to be responsive to innovations in corporate law in order to increase the number of domestic incorporations are, correspondingly, weak, if not nil. In fact, Richard Buxbaum (1987: 215–7) suggests that the real seat rule originated in efforts to prevent competition: in the nineteenth century, when the UK became what he terms a European Delaware, French corporations were prevented from taking advantage of the UK law by changes in doctrine regarding corporate seat.

There are several additional roadblocks to competition for corporate charters, but, in contrast to the real seat rule, these can be more easily

---

[25] See Stith (1991); Timmermans (1991: 140)(the Netherlands 'legislator has sometimes refused to go further than the minimum level required by company law directives arguing that otherwise Dutch business would be disadvantaged in its competition with companies from other Member States').

[26] Europeans are generally less mobile than USA citizens. See 'U.S. Regions Offer Lessons for the EC', *Wall Street Journal*, August 3, 1992, p. 1.

[27] The tax can be avoided if the government approves the transfer of the company's headquarters (Reindl 1990: 1278). Such transactions are also taxed in real seat regimes.

overcome by a nation that desires to improve its charter business, whether or not other nations choose to compete. First, European nations do not impose annual franchise taxes (see Commerce Clearing House 1993; Diamond and Diamond 1991). Virtually all European countries, however, tax stock transactions and the issuance of shares and impose filing fees on initial incorporations (see ibid.).[28] If incorporations do not generate an annual source of revenue, then there is little incentive for a nation to compete to obtain such business. In contrast to the real seat rule, this is not a true barrier to charter competition. The real seat rule's obstacle to competition cannot be eliminated by one nation adopting a statutory domicile rule because it requires mutual recognition across nations to be effective. One nation could, however, offer a superior code in exchange for payment of an annual incorporation fee and, like Delaware, attract firms by offering a superior product that reduces the cost of doing business, making payment of an annual fee worthwhile, even if other nations do not impose such fees. Moreover, because all nations impose initial incorporation fees, there is a source of revenue that will increase on offering a responsive code, even without adopting an annual charge.

Second, it is far more difficult for shareholders to sue directors and officers in Europe than in the USA or Canada. Representative actions, derivative or class, are not generally permitted under European corporate laws, and contingent fees are prohibited in most European countries (Buxbaum and Hopt 1988: 215–7).[29] Institutions essential to shareholder litigation in the USA are therefore missing from the European legal landscape. In addition, fiduciary doctrines are not as well developed in Europe as in the USA. Continental legal systems, for example, do not appear to have the concept of the trust on which such duties rely: France, for instance, does not have a corporate opportunity doctrine, which prevents managers from taking, for personal profit, business opportunities that are offered to the corporation, and the duty of loyalty is generally less well-developed in France and Germany than in the USA (Tunc 1991: 199, 211–2; Buxbaum and Hopt 1988: 184; Hopt 1992: 127). Given such circumstances, shareholder litigation is an event of extremely low probability, and differences in legal régimes will correspondingly be less important to both managers and investors.[30] Accordingly, nations' incentives to compete for incorporations on many crucial corporate law dimensions are attenu-

---

[28] Since 1990, three European countries, Germany, the Netherlands, and the UK, have abolished stock transfer taxes (Jamieson 1991: 318). Although a directive eliminating this tax was proposed in 1976 and revived in 1987, there was no concern when these nations acted that the EC would adopt the directive; rather, the source of the reform was competition for stock exchange business (ibid.).

[29] Buxbaum and Hopt indicate that the EC Commission has proposed articles, in the draft fifth directive, that would require member nations to permit shareholder derivative suits.

[30] See Romano (1985) for a discussion of the importance of litigation in state competition.

ated. This phenomenon does not explain why one nation does not enact rules more accommodating to shareholder litigation, as current EC harmonization efforts do not appear to block such a strategy, although the conflicts of law and tax burden discussed earlier severely curtail a nation's ability to capture, and profit from, a substantial market share of EC incorporations.

Shareholders without a lawsuit option for disciplining management will demand other mechanisms to protect their interests or else will pay less for their investment. European nations could presumably compete on such alternative dimensions. Compared with USA corporation codes, however, shareholders' rights are more attenuated in other dimensions as well. Rights of inspection of company books and records are not universal (see Davis 1989; Stith 1991: 1587–8 n. 24, 1593–4). In addition, shareholder voting rights are more frequently restricted in Europe than in the USA (ibid.). A common strategy employed by German corporations, for instance, is to limit the number of shares that a shareholder can vote.[31] Absence of competition in these other governance dimensions, however, may be related to the dearth of litigation. Delaware's success is due not simply to a superior corporation code but also to the development of a rich body of case law that assists firms' corporate planning. Without a steady stream of lawsuits creating precedents to interpret code provisions, the attractiveness of a jurisdiction as a corporate domicile is diminished. This problem would be compounded by a jurisdiction's concomitant lack of judicial expertise, as the dearth of cases would not make it worthwhile for judges to become knowledgeable in corporate law. It may therefore not be worthwhile to engage in a vigorous corporate charter competition when shareholder litigation is not a viable option. A nation could expend effort at improving its code but still not attract a substantial number of incorporations: a poorly developed case law, without any prospect for improvement, would make corporate planning difficult, as the boundaries of permissible action are unknown.

Differences regarding shareholder rights aid in explaining why there is no European competition for corporate charters, but such an explanation begs the question of why this is the situation. Why don't European nations adopt USA litigation, shareholder rights, and other governance procedures and thereby profitably compete for incorporations? To repeat a tired refrain, difficulties of attracting businesses because of the real seat rule is surely part of the answer. But another institutional factor helps to explain the absence of competition, involving a feature that also distinguishes Canada from the USA, differences in corporate ownership patterns. A striking characteristic of European capital markets is their undercapitalization when compared

---

[31] See 'In Defense of Voting Restrictions', *Financial Times,* June 12, 1992; Baums (1993).

Roberta Romano

with USA markets: market capitalizations are a far smaller percentage of European nations' economies (Solnik 1991: 99–101, 120; Hawawini 1984: 21–4). USA stock market capitalization is approximately 50 percent of gross national product, whereas the corresponding European figures are far lower (Solnik 1991: 99): it is approximately 20 percent for Germany and 24 percent for France. (Table 1 provides comparative market data.)

Table 1. Comparative Data for Capital Markets, Selected Countries, 1988

Country	Value[a]	Volume[b]	Concentration[c]	GDP[d]
United States	2,481	1,356[e]	.14	4,840.2
United Kingdom	718	166	.22	845.5
West Germany	241	174	.42	1,176.7
France	224	69	.25	939.5
Canada	221	68	.24	505.9
Switzerland	148	n.a[f]	.49	178.5
Italy	135	31	.45	836.1
Spain	87	28	.47	354.0
Netherlands	86	30	.72	224.8
Belgium	58	11	.53	152.2

[a] Market capitalization value in billions of USA dollars.
[b] Total value of share turnover in billions of USA dollars on major exchanges.
[c] Concentration (percent of market capitalization) of ten largest firms.
[d] Gross domestic product in billions of USA dollars
[e] New York Stock Exchange volume only.
[f] Data not available.

Sources: Solnik, B. (1991), International Monetary Fund (1991).

In many European nations, such as Germany and France, corporate capital is raised privately through banks and not in the capital market (Solnik 1991: 101), a process that helps to explain the thinness of their equity markets. Whether control is held by families or banks, stock ownership of European corporations is more concentrated than that of USA or UK firms (see, e.g., Wright, *et al.* 1991). Ninety percent of European takeovers, contested or otherwise, occur in the UK, for example, because of differences in capital markets: other European capital markets are less developed, require less corporate disclosure, and are dominated by banks and insurance companies as shareholders (Fitchew 1991: 375).

As noted in the Canadian context, it is difficult to test empirically whether charter competition has contributed to the great depth of USA capital markets compared with European nations or whether the depth of the capital market fosters charter competition.[32] The interrelation is important because governance needs differ across firms with concentrated or diffuse equity ownership. Competition for charters is less important for privately held than public corporations, because differences in corporate law régimes are not as significant to such firms: owners are few in number and have voting control and hence can run a firm without serious constraint. Agency problems between managers and shareholders are therefore less likely in such firms than in publicly traded companies with diffuse stock ownership. More important, in contrast to the Canadian setting where most large corporations have concentrated equity ownership, there is no comparable market discipline for many European firms, because they are not publicly traded. Hence, a key feedback mechanism that provides information to investors and drives state competition—share prices—is missing in the European context.

The relatively small number of publicly traded European corporations, compared with the USA and Canada, is balanced by a substantial number of large privately held firms. This distinctive pattern in choice of business form is a function of the search for more flexible organizational forms by European firms that appears to be analogous to the search for more advantageous corporation codes by USA corporations. That is, there appears to be a European genus of state competition, which involves choice of business form rather than choice of incorporation state. The number of limited liability or private companies in Germany (Buxbaum and Hopt 1988: 171–3) and Belgium (Wymeersch 1991: 227–8), for instance, has grown much more rapidly in recent years than publicly traded corporations.[33] Limited liability companies are corporations that cannot issue stock that is publicly traded; they are distinct legal entities subject to different and less restrictive codes than public corporations. Competition over choice of business form is more limited in scope than American-style charter competition, for the choice of form entails forgoing access to capital markets. But this may not be too costly a trade-off for European firms, given the thinness of European capital markets.

---

[32] The distinctive practice concerning German pensions noted earlier may also affect the liquidity of German capital markets: pension funds, which are the largest players in many other nations' equity markets, have no demand for German equity (Hauck 1994). If pension assets are used for internal projects because capital markets are less developed, then charter competition might lead to a redirection of pension assets outside the firm. It is, however, probable that many German managers would continue to engage in internal project financing through pension assets to avoid the discipline imposed by external capital markets.

[33] Although the significance of an increasing use of the private corporation form by European firms can be overstated—new incorporations of closely held corporations also outpace that of public corporations in the USA, because most new businesses are small-scale enterprises—it is an important phenomenon because most such USA firms do not opt into the special close corporation statutes and instead choose the same corporate law régime as public firms.

Commentators contend that businesses choose the limited liability corporation to avoid the more onerous regulation imposed on public corporations, such as higher taxes, more extensive worker participation régimes, and more rigid legal requirements (Buxbaum and Hopt 1988: 171; Wymeersch 1991: 228; Rojo 1991: 44–5).[34] The most important regulatory restraint for comparative purposes is the rigidity of corporate law rules for public corporations. The bulk of worker participation rules typically cannot be avoided by choice of business form: they apply to all enterprises with a specified number of employees.[35] Some of Germany's largest corporations are, in fact, limited liability companies. In contrast, in the USA privately held corporations that choose to obtain different default rules by opting into a state's close corporation statute must meet statutory limits on the number of shareholders and are therefore small businesses. No large USA firms are incorporated under a close corporation stature, and only a few are privately held. The best explanation for this difference, again, is the powerful motivation of participants in business to select the wealth-maximizing legal régime from among the menu of alternatives, however sparse the menu.

4. IS THERE A RELATION BETWEEN PRODUCTIVITY AND CORPORATE GOVERNANCE?

The legal and institutional differences across the USA, Canada, and Europe make it difficult to ascertain whether one approach to corporate law is superior to another. But a repeated theme of commentators is that European, as well as Japanese, corporate governance arrangements with more concentrated stock ownership, particularly by financial institutions, compared with USA firms, are superior because in certain sectors those nations' firms have been more successful competitors than their USA counterparts. Some commentators locate the failure not in the federal system of state competition but rather in national legislation restricting the stock ownership of financial institutions (e.g., Roe 1991; Porter 1990). The implication, regardless of the

---

[34] According to Rojo, German public companies are diminishing in numbers because of tax law and rigidity in legal form, which, unlike private company rules, cannot be tailored to firm needs.

[35] This is not true in all cases. To attract the business of international holding companies, the Netherlands exempts such corporations from its worker participation regime. The exemption is not inconsistent with domestic labour's being the principal influence on the régime: holding companies and small-scale businesses have few production employees, and, hence, as their internal organization is not of concern to labour unions, their exemption from the regulatory régime is acceptable to the unions. This suggests that the transposition of charter competition over choice of domicile into competition over choice of corporate form may be caused by the mixed objectives of European corporation codes (that is, they do not take maximization of share value as the goal of the firm).

statutory source of concern, is that the predominant corporate governance arrangements of foreign firms are preferable to those of USA firms and that the USA ought to adjust its corporation laws and other laws shaping corporate governance such as the Glass-Steagall Act, which prohibits stock ownership by banks, to match those of other nations. Because there are no comparative empirical studies showing that corporate governance arrangements affect productivity, the position hinges on the significance attributed to other nations surpassing the USA on a variety of productivity growth measures in recent years. For instance, growth in productivity measured by GDP per capita from 1870 to 1979 was 691 percent for the USA but 1,396 percent for Germany, and 1,653 percent for Japan; as measured by the growth rate in GDP per work-hour from 1970 to 1979, it was 1.92 for the United States of America, 4.5 for Germany, and 5.03 for Japan (Baumol, *et al.* 1989: 13,88). The debate focuses on relative growth rates because in absolute productivity the USA has retained its lead.

The most comprehensive study of productivity to date, by William Baumol, Sue Anne Batey Blackman, and Edward Wolff (1989), shows that the significance of differences in short-term productivity growth rates has been vastly overblown.[36] They make several important points about productivity measures that are critical to understanding their significance. First, productivity growth rates are extremely volatile in the short run and hence are best estimated over long periods. Second, the lag in the rate of USA productivity growth compared with other nations is a long-standing phenomenon, going back a century, and is not of recent vintage, as critics suggest. Third, the decline in USA productivity in recent years is only a comparative decline: it is a decrease compared with the phenomenal spurt in USA productivity following World War II. The current growth rate is, in fact, similar to the historic USA normal growth rate. The extraordinary increase in postwar USA productivity growth equals (and thus can be seen to compensate for) the steep decrease in productivity growth during the Great Depression. When a growth trendline is computed, USA productivity has remained constant from 1880 through 1980. Moreover, *all* industrial nations have experienced the same temporal pattern of productivity growth rates, an unusual postwar increase and a slowdown during the 1970s. Fourth, and most important, short-run productivity differences are not indicia of economic decline because of the phenomenon of international convergence. When one nation's productivity is superior to that of many other economies, those nations that are not too far behind can catch up, as they learn from the leader through technology transfer. Performance levels thus

---

[36] The data and analysis in the following paragraphs are taken entirely from the Baumol, *et al.* (1989) study, especially from pages 14, 65, 68–71, 89–90, 258–60. This study is particularly interesting because it is a reversal of one of the authors' earlier critical assessment of USA productivity performance in Baumol and McLennan (1985).

converge. The laggard countries have more to learn from the leader than the leader from them, and consequently 'those who were initially behind *must* advance more rapidly than those who were ahead. Otherwise the distance between them could not possibly narrow.' (Baumol, *et al.* 1989: 90 (italics in original)). Baumol, Blackman, and Wolff exhaustively detail the evidence supporting the international convergence thesis.

More recent work, including a productivity measure update through 1990 by Baumol and Wolff (1992) and a study of service sector productivity by McKinsey and Company (1992), reinforces the Baumol, Blackman, and Wolff (1989) study's assessment of the significance of productivity growth rates and indicates that absolute USA productivity has continued to exceed that of Europe and Japan.[37] Baumol and Wolff's latest data on manufacturing performance, for example, indicate that the rate of productivity growth in Germany has, in fact, been slower than that of the USA for more than a decade (a decline predating economic difficulties brought on by reunification) and that Japan's productivity growth rate has slowed down considerably and is now not much greater than that of the USA, while the Japanese level of productivity is still far lower than the USA level.

After reviewing findings of other studies of superior USA productivity in the manufacturing sector, the McKinsey study provides five case studies in the service sector (airlines, retail banking, restaurants, general merchandise retailing, and telecommunications). Because it is difficult to measure the performance of a service industry (the value of output is not always quantifiable), the study examines a variety of labour productivity measures. It finds that, in each sector, labour productivity is higher in the USA than in Europe or Japan. The superior performance of USA firms is attributed to the greater domestic competition these firms face.

The lower productivity growth rate of the USA compared with that of Europe and Japan in the postwar period is therefore best understood as a manifestation of the inevitable catch-up entailed by international convergence. We do not have to introduce differences in corporate governance régimes to explain differences in performance. This explanation of changing relative rates of productivity growth does not imply that low relative productivity growth is not a public policy concern. The hard question for public policy is whether another nation will eventually surpass the USA because the long-term historic USA growth rate is not sufficient to retain world economic leadership. While we have no way of predicting whether the USA will be surpassed as the economic leader, the answer will not be found in mimicking other nations' corporate governance arrangements. The key factors that economists believe affect absolute productivity performance are the national savings rate (investment), the education of the labour force,

[37] The McKinsey study received assistance from several distinguished economists: Martin Baily, Francis Bator, and Robert Solow.

and the magnitude of efforts devoted to basic and applied research (Baumol, *et al.* 1989: 258–60). There is no evidence of a relation between any of these three factors and corporate governance rules. Commentators concerned about the effect of corporate governance on comparative economic performance do not emphasize and sometimes do not even mention these key factors. The omission is probably not as odd as it appears: there is no theory, as well as no evidence, relating these fundamental factors to corporate governance patterns.

Moreover, the disparate corporate governance systems that commentators treat as significantly related to performance—USA firms have dispersed stock ownership; European firms have concentrated ownership and, in Germany, heavy bank involvement; and Japanese firms have extensive corporate cross-holdings of equity, forming corporate groups—were all in place before World War II, well before the postwar years in which the steep relative decline in USA productivity has been identified.[38] In conjunction with the Baumol, Blackman, and Wolff (1989) data, this institutional detail indicates that changes in the rate of growth in productivity cannot be directly attributed to differences in corporate governance structure.

The point of this review of the comparative productivity literature is not to endorse existing USA restrictions on active equity investment by financial institutions. Indeed, such regulation ought to be repealed to permit greater experimentation with corporate governance and ownership structures; repeal is the policy most consistent with the enabling structure of competitive state corporation codes, which enhances firm value, as this chapter has emphasized. The point is rather that the desirability of such reform does not, and should not, stem from preoccupation with USA competitiveness, and that the common belief of the comparative failure of USA business is a canard. If improved relative performance is the goal, it is inappropriate to try to force USA corporations to adopt the internal organization of other nations' firms. USA firms are, in fact, more productive than their competitors in nearly all sectors, and we ought to approach reform efforts with that central fact as the point of reference.

A variety of anecdotes from USA history and other nations is relevant to a reconsideration of USA rules restricting corporate ownership by financial institutions, although this evidence does not make the effect on corporate governance of such ownership reform easy to predict. A fascinating study by J. Bradford De Long (1991: 205) indicates that, at the turn of the century, adding a Morgan banker to a corporate board increased stock value

---

[38] In the prewar years from 1870 to 1929, there is no discernible pattern between corporate governance form and productivity growth rate. The USA rate surpassed that of Japan in all years but 1890–1900 and 1913–1929 and that of Germany in all years but 1880–1900 (Baumol, *et al.* 1989: 88). Stockholdings had already become diffuse compared with German and Japanese firms in this period.

by 30 percent. De Long (ibid. 223–4) finds no evidence that public investors were exploited by Morgan: companies with a Morgan director sold at higher multiples of book value than other companies, and stock offering prices and subsequent rates of return were comparable to non-Morgan companies. Although Morgan was engaged in both commercial and investment banking at the time, De Long's data do not indicate what positions, if any, as owner or creditor Morgan had in the companies on whose boards its partners served. In addition, De Long cannot determine whether the source of the value added by a Morgan banker is that of effective corporate governance (that is, that the market viewed a Morgan appointment as a screen for corporate quality, as an active monitor who would protect firm value) or of monopoly rents (that the market perceived the appointment as an indicium that the firm would be able to create a monopoly through business interconnections that now would be established with other Morgan firms). Thus, De Long's data are suggestive, rather than conclusive, that repeal of the Glass-Steagall Act would improve corporate governance and thereby enhance share value.

Alfred Chandler's (1990) recent comprehensive study of the modern industrial corporation provides a contrary example concerning the impact of financial institutions' involvement in corporate governance. Chandler (1990) chronicles the development of the largest industrial corporations across the most dynamic industries in the USA, Germany, and the UK: the corporations that invested in production, distribution, and management capabilities established first-mover advantages that led to their domestic as well as international dominance in industry share. As Chandler (ibid. 139) notes, one of the initially successful firms in its industry, United States Steel, is 'one of the very few examples of banker control in American industry'. Yet, unlike the other first movers in his study, US Steel lost its early leading position because of poor management. As one reviewer states, 'Chandler leaves little doubt that he believes that the financiers and lawyers running US Steel made serious mistakes'. (Teece 1993: 205 n. 12)

One would be hard pressed to make predictions from these two contradictory anecdotes concerning the effect of repealing the Glass-Steagall Act on share value. Another interesting study of early American banking by Naomi Lamoreaux (1991) further muddies the water. Lamoreaux's research suggests that USA banks might not adopt the active investor role of German and Japanese banks even if the option were made available. Nineteenth-century New England banks voluntarily exited from arrangements similar to those of German and Japanese bankers—ones in which banks lend to insiders with interlocking bank and corporate managerial positions and actively monitor and influence borrowers' behaviour—and instead engaged in financial intermediation; the new arrangements were undertaken for efficient risk-reduction reasons (Lamoreaux 1991: 161).

Thus, at least in one region of the USA, the divorce of private bankers and industrialists began long before it was required by federal statute.

This pattern of banks not exercising control over industrial corporations is reinforced by contemporary comparisons. As Jack Coffee (1991: 1277) has noted, UK firms are not subject to USA-type ownership restrictions, yet they have dispersed stock ownership rather than a bank-dominated governance structure. This difference may be a historical accident, that is, it may be due to disparate industrial development in the UK and Germany in the late eighteenth and early nineteenth centuries that led to the establishment of different financial institutions (see Tilly 1966: 134–5; Gerschenkron 1962). But whatever the reason for the difference, it makes plan that regulatory barriers are not a sufficient explanation for USA governance structures. Indeed, in contrast to the USA legal régime, Japanese regulation prohibited the development of capital markets, forcing corporations to rely on bank financing. When the restrictions were loosened in the 1980s, there was a dramatic shift away from bank debt to public debt.[39]

These examples suggest that it would be a mistake to maintain that USA corporate governance institutions are best understood as political and not economic (that is, efficient). A more useful way to characterize the connection between politics and economic organizational form, particularly in the contractual context of business organization, is to recognize that private parties are persistent in devising institutions that circumvent or minimize the effect of political constraints on economic development.[40] The genius of American corporate law in this regard is that the dynamics of state competition reduces the number of extraneous regulations that must be bypassed.

5. CONCLUSION

The making of American corporate law is unique among federal political systems: state competition has produced innovative corporation codes that quickly respond to changing market conditions and firm demands. Corporate law commentators have long debated whether this responsiveness is for the better. The best available evidence indicates that, for the most part, the race is for the top and not the bottom in the production of corporate laws. But the direction of American corporate law reform is not linear. The adoption of state takeover statutes, which have adverse effects

---

[39] Bank debt of public corporations declined from 90 percent in 1975 to less than 50 percent in 1992 (Hoshi, *et al.* 1993).

[40] See, for example, Tilly (1962)(detailing how Rhenish bankers and entrepreneurs created financial mechanisms that circumvented the Prussian government's restrictions on their economic development).

on shareholder wealth, demonstrates that state competition is far from perfect. Perfection is not, however, the appropriate yardstick for measuring the output of state competition: the time frame of analysis matters. In the short run, there will inevitably be deviations from the optimum in a federal system. But in the long run, competitive pressures are exerted where states make mistakes, as in the example of the majority of firms opting out from coverage of Pennsylvania's draconic takeover statute, a statute which other states have not copied (Romano 1993: 68–9). Such self-correcting forces are absent in a centralized national system of corporate law, where firms have no alternative incorporation choices.

Some commentators have maintained that national differences in corporate governance indicate that USA corporate institutions are a response to political rather than economic forces, with the (often unstated) corollary that they are organizationally inferior. There is scant evidence supporting this contention, especially when comparative productivity data are examined. The effect of politics on business organization is far more subtle and interactive: private parties will design institutions to circumvent political constraints on profitable economic activity. Although corporate managers may lobby for laws ensuring a quiet life and succeed in some instances, USA capital markets are remarkably resilient in devising mechanisms for disciplining them, such as the leveraged acquisitions of the 1980s. More important, the genius of American corporate law—the dynamics of state competition—limits the number of wealth-decreasing regulations that need to be finessed, thereby reducing the cost of doing business.

5

Federalism and Corporate Law: A Non-Delaware View of the Results of Competition

WILLIAM J. CARNEY*

INTRODUCTION

The United States of America (USA) has witnessed a lengthy debate over the virtues and vices of corporate federalism. For a long time the debate consisted of assertions based on differing characterizations of judicial decisions and statutory changes. This phase was followed by a debate based on a model of behaviour, drawn from theory about the behaviour of capital markets. Both sides assumed that a competition for corporate chartering business existed, in which Delaware was the clear winner. Both sides also assumed, without systematic examination, that a competition existed, in which states other than Delaware sought to modernize their statutes to retain this chartering business. The result, according to either view, was a profound effect on the shape of American corporate law. That law was both more uniform and more 'liberal' than would otherwise be the case. But these claims have remained assertions, essentially unexamined by scholars, with the single exception of Romano's path-breaking work (Romano 1985; 1993). The focus of most of the literature has been on the dominant producer of corporate law, Delaware. This chapter attempts to fill these gaps by focusing on production by the other 49 states.

Part I provides an interest group theory to explain why states would attempt to compete with Delaware. Delaware possesses certain 'first-mover' advantages that have kept it the dominant producer of corporate law for nearly a century. The process of reincorporation to Delaware has been a steady one. If writing corporate laws is costly, what would explain the attempt of states to keep pace with Delaware, or perhaps even to provide innovations before it? This chapter suggests that at least two interest groups benefit from modern local corporate laws—local corporate lawyers and managers of firms incorporated within the state. It examines the collective action problems facing these groups, and suggests they will specialize in the

* I wish to thank Barry Adler, Paul David, Fred McChesney, Geoffrey Miller, Robert Rasmussen, and Warren Schwartz for their helpful comments on an earlier draft of this paper. Particular thanks are due to Susan Dignam for her exemplary research assistance.

types of law changes they will sponsor. Their differing collective action problems also suggest different rates of adoption for innovations sponsored by each group.

Part II provides evidence about the degree of uniformity, the rate of innovation, and the ultimate character of American corporate law. It finds that American corporate law is relatively uniform across most states. Further, it finds that a principal source of differences in these laws is the pace of innovation. In this respect it provides additional support for Romano's earlier study of the rate of dissemination of innovations in corporate law. It also examines several important recent changes in corporate law—provisions authorizing exculpation of directors from negligence liability and anti-takeover laws. These changes have occurred rapidly, at least during the 1980s, until the takeover boom cooled down.

The findings also provide support for the hypothesis that American corporate law is more enabling, and provides greater managerial flexibility than would be the case if it were not influenced by competition. While it is impossible to test this hypothesis directly, indirect tests can be attempted. In this case, the findings compare American corporate laws with a European model—the EC's directives on company law. While not a direct analog of the Model Business Corporation Act in the USA, they provide significant evidence about the general shape of European company laws, and what the EC considered either best practice or most common practice in the member states. These directives are significantly more regulatory than most USA laws. Further, in some respects they bear a strong resemblance to earlier generations of USA laws.

Part III examines evidence about the rate of change and the sources of change. It suggests that the rate at which corporate law changes may be a function of the interest group sponsoring the change. Corporate lawyers appear to face more collective action hurdles than corporate managers, leading to the prediction that management-sponsored changes will be disseminated among the states more rapidly. Evidence from the 1980s supports this hypothesis.

I. THE ROLE OF INTEREST GROUPS IN CORPORATE LAW CHANGE

Any explanation of the production of corporate law involves the presence of interest groups with sufficient cohesion and interest to motivate legislation. Macey and Miller (1987) have provided an interest group theory of Delaware corporate law. This section attempts a more general description of how interest groups influence the production of corporate law in other states. Two interest groups have been responsible for most corporate legislation in the USA: the organized bar and corporate management. These groups seem to specialize in their functions. The organized bar has an interest in having local corporation laws that are generally efficient and flexible, and which will attract and hold chartering business. Corporate managers' interests seem more parochial—to preserve their own positions and power, free from accountability, to the extent possible within the constraints of competitive markets.

1.1 Delaware's Unique Incentives to Create Corporate Law

If there is a competition for chartering business, it is a competition with a dominant firm.[1] Delaware is the legal home of more than half of all Fortune 500 companies and more than 45% of all companies listed on the New York Stock Exchange (Macey & Miller 1987: 483; Alva 1990: 887). Further, Delaware is the leading target state for reincorporations, with between 82% and 90% of firms that are relocating selecting Delaware as their state of incorporation (Romano 1985: 244; Dodd & Leftwich 1980: 263).

Much has been written about the incentives of Delaware and the Delaware bar to provide attractive corporate laws and to maximize the fees earned by Delaware corporate lawyers (Macey & Miller 1987; Cary 1974). Because of its small size, chartering revenues constitute a significant part of Delaware's annual budget—between 15% and 20% (Romano 1985: 242). These revenues are sufficient to provide Delaware with an incentive to supply corporate laws that are attractive to managers of large publicly held corporations—the kind that would generate large annual franchise fees. Macey and Miller (1987: 491–3) have suggested that this dominance allows the Delaware corporate bar to capture part of the rents from Delaware's dominant position, but such rent creation and capture would not explain the development of corporate law in other jurisdictions.

1.2 Why Do Other States Compete?

Because of Delaware's dominance, Romano (1985: 226) describes the efforts of other states as defensive—to prevent further losses of corporations to Delaware. Little has been written about the incentives of other states to conform their laws to those of Delaware or to innovate, as Romano (ibid. 240) demonstrates that they do. Revenues from chartering corporations do not represent a significant income source for most large welfare states sufficient

---

[1] One definition of a dominant firm is one that controls not only the current supply, but also the source of potential expansion in the near future. (Alchian & Allen, 1972: 267). Delaware fits this model because it would be extremely difficult, if not impossible, for any other jurisdiction to replicate all of the advantages Delaware now possesses.

to motivate them to write laws to attract chartering business.[2] Reincorporation in Delaware does not mean a significant loss of local employment, because, unlike Europe, it is not necessary to move the principal office of the corporation. Local lawyers may experience some loss of work to Delaware lawyers, but because many local corporate lawyers in large firms practice Delaware corporate law as advisers, this loss is likely to be minimal.

As monopolists over laws within their boundaries, governments frequently lack incentives to modernize local laws if neither significant revenues nor interest groups are involved. Shareholders are too widely dispersed, and in many cases reside in other jurisdictions, and thus do not constitute an effective interest group for changing corporate law. There are disincentives to innovate if revenue considerations are minimal. Free rider problems face legislators and even legislatures that innovate. Legislators who are not corporate law specialists must rely on assistance from interest groups to draft and promote legislation. Individual members of bar associations and corporate management face similar collective action problems in proposing legislative change.

Because of this, and because of Delaware's first mover advantage in corporate law,[3] other states have weak incentives to lead with corporate law innovations, and only somewhat stronger incentives to follow promptly. The principal concern of corporate lawyers in states other than Delaware is only that their law not become so antiquated that corporations are tempted to incur the substantial transaction costs of moving.[4] Yet the evidence is that innovations do occur outside Delaware, and are widely followed by the states (Romano 1985). The puzzle is why such activity occurs outside of Delaware.

---

[2] While corporate franchise taxes accounted for 17.7% of Delaware's total tax revenues in 1990, in only one other state (Louisiana) did they account for as much as 5% (6.3%). In three other states they accounted for more than 4% (Pennsylvania, Tennessee, and Texas). In 38 states they accounted for less than 1% (Romano 1993: 10–11).

[3] See Romano (1985: 240); Macey & Miller (1987: 472, n. 5). Macey and Miller describe this advantage as assuring favourable behaviour because of the large number of corporations already in the state. This is really more a description of bonding than a first-mover advantage. The presence of large numbers of corporations in Delaware has allowed the building of expertise in the courts and a large body of decisions interpreting Delaware law, in addition to providing a bond about future behaviour. It would be possible for other states to post bonds assuring favourable future behaviour, either by adopting Delaware's supermajority vote requirement for amendments to its corporate laws, or by providing compensation to firms that felt compelled to reincorporate elsewhere. But there is no good substitute for experienced and specialised judges interpreting a large body of prior decisions.

[4] For a discussion of these costs see Romano (1985: 246–48). Bernard Black (1990) contends these costs are trivial. Romano has expanded her arguments that these costs are substantial in Romano (1993: 34–35).

1.3 The Role of Lawyers as an Interest Group Outside Delaware

This section offers an interest group explanation of why other states try to keep pace with Delaware in corporate law innovations. The role of Delaware lawyers in changing corporate laws is well documented by Macey and Miller (1987). Delaware lawyers have an interest in a modern, flexible corporate statute that continues to attract public corporations to Delaware. At the same time, one can predict that Delaware law will allow an opportunity for Delaware lawyers to collect some of the rents created by this process. This can be accomplished by encouraging litigation in Delaware's courts, through the provision of an efficient court system (paid for at public expense) that gives priority to corporate litigation and requires participation of Delaware lawyers. Rents can also be created for the bar by increasing the amount of such litigation (within limits) through the adoption of open legal standards rather than bright-line property rules, and liberal rules about standing to bring and maintain derivative litigation (Branson 1990). The Delaware Bar Association has served as an efficient agent to lobby for the changes needed to achieve these goals.

The role of local lawyers in other jurisdictions is less well understood. Romano (1985: 226) has described the charter market as characterized by bilateral investments in assets that are specific to the chartering transaction, involving human capital on the firm side and the corporate legal system on the state side. But local corporate lawyers have invested human capital on the state side as well. By specializing in the law of their own state, local lawyers can generally limit competition for services for their locally incorporated clients to members of the local bar. Importantly, in many states this excludes the potential competition from Delaware lawyers and from those Wall Street lawyers who specialize in Delaware law. In addition to specializing in local law, local corporate lawyers have a general interest in a local corporate law that is modern and flexible, and thus likely to retain local businesses as local corporations. If a corporate client is a Delaware corporation, a local lawyer providing general representation may find that fees from corporate litigation must be shared with or lost to Delaware lawyers, to the extent that plaintiffs now have the option of litigating in the Delaware courts. On the other hand, local lawyers seem generally comfortable advising on Delaware law, even to the extent of giving opinions when required.

Because the losses for local lawyers from reincorporation in Delaware are relatively small, their interest is not likely to be as intense as that of Delaware lawyers.[5] Further, when local lawyers propose corporate law

---

[5] This should be contrasted with the interest of lawyers in litigation, from which they benefit much more directly (see Macey & Miller 493–97, 503–05 (1987); cf., Barry E. Adler (1993) (bankruptcy lawyers benefit directly from costly bankruptcy proceedings).

reforms, those active in the proposal face a free rider problem—of producing a good that will produce a positive externality—benefitting other corporate lawyers and their clients generally. Typically bar associations do not compensate committee members who serve on these committees. Yet such service demands a considerable investment of a lawyer's valuable time. Because writing corporate laws is costly and involves a public good, modern corporation laws are likely to be underproduced. Local lawyers are likely to undertake this activity only infrequently—when local law has become so obsolete that loss of corporations to Delaware has become significantly more probable.

A. Collective Action Problems of Lawyers in Producing Corporate Statutes

The high personal costs borne by lawyers in writing corporate laws suggest that the rate of modernization will be a function of the extent to which lawyers can reduce the costs of writing statutes and can internalize the benefits. Bar associations can and do serve as the organizing force to lobby for corporate law changes, through committees of their members. In this way the work can be divided among specialists, reducing the cost of production, and spreading it over a number of lawyers. Members of bar association committees may obtain some modest side benefits from such activity, of being seen as first movers in terms of expertise in local corporate law, or meeting other lawyers who may serve as a source of referrals. But my own experience serving on such a committee suggests a large amount of altruism, in terms of creating a public good for the state, also plays a significant role. Law creation may involve a consumption good as well—the chance to reflect and consult with peers about ideal statutory solutions to various problems—the counterpart of academic conferences.

In order to reduce the costs of writing a complex corporate law, many states rely on the Model Business Corporation Act as a source of law reform. The Model Act is the product of a national bar committee, the Committee on Corporate Laws of the American Bar Association, which meets regularly to consider developments in corporate law that might call for a legislative reaction. Members of that committee suffer, of course, from the same collective action problems, but the payoffs from committee membership may be greater. Since this is a national committee, it provides national visibility to its members. Members work with prominent corporate lawyers from other states, who may prove a fertile source of referred legal work on local matters. Since many committee members are partners in large corporate law firms that provide a wide range of services, the possibility of some such referrals seems substantial. Again, altruism and enjoyment of a consumption good may also play roles.

The Committee on Corporate Laws has produced three major reforms of corporation law in the past forty years—in 1960, 1969, and 1984, with incremental changes in between. After publication of these versions of the Model Act, local bar committees have used the Model Act to propose modernization of local corporation laws to their legislatures. The result has been a flurry of corporate law reforms following each version of the Model Act. Each local bar can be seen as free riding on the efforts of the ABA's Committee on Corporate Laws. This model predicts that local law reform will be sporadic, and will generally follow production of a new version of the Model Act, or at least some significant alteration in the Model Act's provisions.

The benefits of a modern corporate law are most likely to be internalized by lawyers representing publicly held corporations that are locally chartered but are likely to consider the option of a Delaware reincorporation at some time. These lawyers, as specialists, are likely to be able to collect some form of rents from their local expertise.[6] Furthermore, these rents would be the subject of increased competition if their clients were to reincorporate in Delaware, since there is a much larger body of lawyers, both within and without Delaware, with Delaware corporate law expertise. Because most litigation involving Delaware corporate law issues takes place in Delaware, fees from such litigation would be lost if clients were to reincorporate there. Accordingly, corporate law changes to remain competitive with Delaware should come most rapidly to large industrial states. For similar reasons, lawyers in large industrial states will be the most likely to invest the additional resources required to deviate significantly from Model Act language.

B. Rent Collection or Competitive Returns to Lawyers?

If the market for corporate law were not competitive, Delaware would have attracted all corporate chartering business, or at least that of all large publicly held corporations. That has not occurred. While Delaware is dominant, it is not a monopolist. As the dominant producer of corporate law, it faces a downward sloping demand curve for its corporate charters, and can charge a higher 'price' than can other states (Macey & Miller: 1987: 491); Indeed, Macey and Miller (1987: 492–3) point out that in addition to charging relatively high franchise fees, Delaware extracts additional charges in the form of higher fees for local professionals. Many of these fees are likely to come in the context of corporate litigation. By providing a specialized court that gives priority to corporate litigation, Delaware encourages the bringing of such suits in the Delaware court system.[7] There are several reasons to believe that Delaware makes litigation more costly than elsewhere, thus

[6] Even if these lawyers do not earn true economic rents, their investment in local law expertise produces quasi-rents that are subject to dissipation if their corporate clients reincorporate in Delaware.

[7] Because a Delaware corporation has its situs in Delaware for purposes of jurisdiction, a plaintiff can always choose Delaware courts, although it may also choose the courts of another jurisdiction where the corporation is doing business (see Macey & Miller (1987: 495–98)).

imposing a higher litigation charge on Delaware corporations for the benefit of Delaware lawyers. First, Delaware law concerning derivative litigation remains sufficiently unclear that large legal fees are generated at the procedural stage over such questions as whether demand is excused or required (Branson 1990). Second, fees for successful plaintiffs in derivative litigation in Delaware are based on the results obtained rather than hours spent, opening up the possibility of premium billing for plaintiffs' lawyers.[8] One commentator has concluded that it is a general pattern of Delaware decisions that staying in court is relatively easy for plaintiffs, and that Delaware law has eroded bright line property rules in favor of multiple factor tests that can only be applied through litigation (ibid).

Lawyers in states without market power, seeking to retain clients as local corporations should be willing to forego generating legal fees in some or all of these areas. Rules on legal fees for successful plaintiffs' lawyers in derivative litigation should provide for fewer premiums; procedural questions about derivative actions should provide more bright line rules, and statutes should eschew multiple factor tests in favour of bright line tests whenever possible. Thus, for example, rules might require demand in all derivative suits, as the Revised Model Business Corporation Act (sect. 7.42) does. Where Delaware provides subjective standards for determining the requirement for a shareholder vote on asset sales, a competing state might attempt to create bright line safe harbors.[9] Similarly, one might expect statutes in such states to provide that appraisal is the exclusive remedy for dissenting shareholders, eliminating the possibility of more open-ended equitable claims. Delaware law in one of the most active areas for litigation, involving hostile takeovers and the duties of incumbent target company directors, has remained in flux for the past decade, creating increased opportunities for both advisory work and litigation.[10]

C. The Role of Anticompetitive Corporate Laws

States that expect to lose chartering business to Delaware might be expected

---

[8] See Macey & Miller (1987: 497, n. 103) citing *Dann* v. *Chrysler Corp.*, 42 Del. Ch. 508, 215 A.2d 709 (1965, *aff'd*, 43 Del. Ch. 252, 223 A.2d 384 (Del. 1966); *Thomas* v. *Kempner*, 398 A.2d 320 (Del. 1979)).

[9] Compare, e.g., Del. Laws, Tit. 8, §271(a), as interpreted in *Gimbel* v. *Signal Cos.*, 316 A.2d 599 (Del. Ch.) *aff'd* 316 A.2d 619 (Del. 1974) (holding that the sale of historic lines of business of a conglomerate did not require a shareholder vote) and *Katz* v. *Bregman*, 431 A.2d 1274 (Del. Ch. 1981) (holding that sale of a steel drum manufacturing subsidiary in order to shift to plastic drums required a shareholder vote) with Off.Code Ga. §14–2–1202 (providing a bright line safe harbour where no shareholder vote is required if the assets do not represent more than two-thirds of the value of all corporate assets, and do not generate more than two-thirds of gross revenues).

[10] See, e.g., *Revlon, inc* v. *MacAndrews & Forbes Holdings, Inc.*, 506 A.2d 173 (Del. 1986); *Paramount Communications, Inc.* v. *Time, Inc.*, 571 A.2d 1140 (Del. 1990); *Cede & Co.* v. *Technicolor, Inc.*, 134 A.2d 345 (Del. 1993).

to erect barriers to Delaware's competition. One such barrier would be to decline to recognize legal entities created elsewhere, especially if they maintained their principal place of business within the state. This has been the response of European nations to chartering competition—first of France when it appeared French entrepreneurs were taking advantage of more liberal British company laws to incorporate. France led the way in rejecting the Anglo-American choice of law rule—the 'internal affairs' rule—and chose instead to refuse to recognize entities incorporated under foreign law but with a local (French) base of operations. Indeed, the anticompetitive nature of the doctrine is best demonstrated by the French reaction when French entrepreneurs, seeking to take advantage of more favourable English laws, incorporated in England and named London as their 'statutory' seat of business. France simply required that as to foreign corporations doing business in France, 'the nominal seat be real—i.e., French' (Buxbaum & Hopt 1988: 69; Rabel 1962: 38 & n. 20G). But USA states have declined to do this, apparently out of fear of a flight to nearby jurisdictions (Carney 1995). A milder form of response might call for a partial repeal of the internal affairs rule, by applying certain provisions of domestic law to locally headquartered foreign corporations. Lawyers in states with the most corporate business to lose—large industrial states—are the most likely to incur the additional costs of writing such anticompetitive statutes.

While a state might opportunistically adopt such laws to prevent local corporations from reincorporating elsewhere, creating high costs of exit might discourage new businesses from incorporating or even locating within the state. Such laws might lead to reincorporations, and even relocations, just prior to going public, to avoid the more restrictive effects of local law. On the other hand, a state with a dominant advantage in attracting chartering business would be unlikely to make exit costly, as part of its bond with contracting corporations to preserve the value of their decision to reincorporate in such a state.

1.4 The Role of Other Interest Groups

A. The Role of Shareholders

For the same reasons that shareholders play a relatively small role in corporate governance, they can be expected to play an even smaller, insignificant role in developing corporate law. If widely dispersed shareholders face collective action problems in corporate voting that counsel rational apathy about corporate elections, they face even larger problems in lobbying for changes in corporate laws. If shareholders are able to organize, we would expect them to do so where it would be most effective—at the corporate level. Thus activism by United Shareholders of America and by various institutional investors has been directed almost exclusively at the corporate level.

This does not mean, however, that corporate law changes necessarily operate to the disadvantage of shareholders. For the reasons that Winter (1977) and others have previously suggested, corporate managers have incentives to choose legal régimes that are most conducive to shareholder welfare in most instances. All of the evidence that rejects the 'race to the bottom' hypothesis and is consistent with the 'race to the top' hypothesis suggests that to a large extent corporate law changes benefit shareholders, and that managers function as loyal agents (Hyman 1979; Dodd & Leftwich 1980; Romano 1985: 272; Bradley & Schipani 1989; Netter & Poulsen 1989).

B. The Role of Managers

One role of managers is to select the body of corporate law that they deem most appropriate for their corporations. The evidence about the price effects of reincorporation is consistent with the hypothesis that they select jurisdictions with the goal of maximizing shareholder welfare.

Collective action problems are significantly reduced for corporate managers who have access to corporate funds for lobbying activities. Like lawyers, they can organize through previously existing trade associations when necessary. The interests of corporate management will be more limited but at the same time more intense than those of the bar. In general, management will prefer flexible statutes to more regulatory ones, but when local laws are inflexible, management, unlike the bar, has access to both voice and exit options, since it can either lobby for local law reforms or reincorporate in a more favorable jurisdiction (Hirschman 1980). Accordingly, its interest in general matters of state corporate law will be less intense than that of the bar.

Management's legislative interests will become more intense when they are threatened with personal losses as a result of corporate law, either from liability rules or from loss of their positions through contests for corporate control. When these issues arise, we can expect prompt lobbying by management groups, and more rapid legislative responses. Because of the increased speed of legal change, it is likely that there will be a greater diversity of state laws adopted under such circumstances, because competitive markets have not had an opportunity to sort out superior and inferior solutions to problems. As with lawyers, we can expect greater variance from standard forms in large industrial states where corporate managers are more numerous, better organized and funded.

2. COMPETITION AND UNIFORMITY

In this section I will develop and test three hypotheses about corporate laws in a competitive system. The first hypothesis is that competition will lead toward uniformity of corporate laws. The second hypothesis is that innovation will play a role in assuring that corporate laws within a competitive system are never uniform; that is, corporate law is dynamic, and not static. The third hypothesis is those laws will be less regulatory and more enabling than laws developed by states not engaged in such a competition.

2.1 The Hypotheses

The prediction of uniform state laws in a competitive market is not original with this chapter (Romano 1985: 229 & n. 4) (citing Manne (1967) and Easterbrook & Fischel (1983)). Indeed, this is one area where both critics and defenders of the American corporate system seem to agree, although they may differently characterize it as a 'race to the bottom' or a 'race to the top' (Cary 1974: 66; Fischel 1982; Winter 1977). Anyone who has reviewed the annotations to the Model Act to learn about important variations will come away with a subjective sense that the similarities vastly outweigh the differences. There are, of course, notable exceptions to this similarity, notably in such states as California and New York.[11] The literature suggests nothing about the degree of uniformity, nor the areas in which corporate law will be more or less uniform.

Romano (1985) has already documented the process of diffusion of innovations in corporate law. The gradual dissemination of innovations assures that many provisions of corporate law will not be entirely uniform at any one time. Second, default rules, or 'opt-out' provisions, are less important to public corporations, because contracting in the absence of default rules is relatively less costly for larger firms. For that reason, there will be less competitive pressure for these rules to be uniform.

The hypothesis that a competition among the states will be less regulatory and more enabling also stems from the 'race for the bottom' literature, which characterizes corporate laws as increasingly permissive, and affording corporate managers greater powers and flexibility, and perhaps less accountability. That literature suggests the following features of American

---

[11] Baysinger & Butler, (1985), explain this as a process of specialization by the states between those writing laws helpful to publicly held firms with widely dispersed ownership and those with more concentrated ownership. The difficulty with their analysis is that their more restrictive states, California, Illinois, New York, and Texas are all states with a significant number of large publicly held corporations (albeit with somewhat more concentrated ownership). Romano (1985: 247) shows that these states were the largest losers of corporations when reincorporations in other jurisdictions occurred.

corporate law would be different from those of laws developed in the absence of competitive pressures. First, fewer reports to shareholders would be required. Second, fewer shareholder votes would be required to authorize transactions. Third, corporate powers to engage in any business would be granted as a matter of course. Fourth, corporations would be less accountable to stakeholders other than shareholders.

2.2 The Methodology

This study utilizes the Revised Model Business Corporation Act (RMBCA) as its standard against which to test corporate law uniformity. The RMBCA is the dominant single model of corporate law, and attempts to incorporate important innovations, while offering a statute that would appeal to a large number of states.

I have focused on what I regard at the more important provisions of USA corporate law to examine this claim. What follows is based on John MacKerron's (1993) recent classification of provisions of the RMBCA. It does not include all of the provisions that MacKerron has included. I have omitted provisions that appear to duplicate other provisions of general laws, codifications of common law rules, as well as duplicative rules and trivial rules, such as the right of shareholders to use agents to inspect records, or to make photocopies. I have included opt-out provisions, which allow firms to contract out of otherwise mandatory rules in the sample. These rules are less important, particularly for public corporations where the cost of tailoring contracts is not high. Reflecting the relative unimportance of these rules to such enterprises, some of them are simply not addressed by the laws of many states. In this area in particular, my search techniques may not have identified all such rules. Because they are less important than other categories, the statutory comparisons in the Model Act do not always address their existence in state laws. Finally, my LEXIS searches were based primarily on word patterns found in either the 1984 or 1968 versions of the Model Act. States employing different word patterns could easily have been missed. 'Pure' enabling rules are included as important because the entity treatment of the corporation requires recognition by the state, which is frequently preceded by a filing with state officials. Thus, changes in articles of incorporation, mergers, and dissolution are conditioned upon filings.

Comparing the results of USA law with those of nations not subject to competitive pressures presented a more formidable task. The laws of other English-speaking nations were not used, because they may be subject to some competitive pressures, as a result of having the same choice of law rule—the internal affairs rule—that permits forum-shopping in the United States of America. European laws are not available on LEXIS, and language barriers exist which make such a direct comparison impossible for this author. As a result I chose to employ the Directives adopted by the European Community for the harmonization of company laws as a model.[12] While these laws require changes in the law of many member states, they serve something of the same purpose as the RMBCA—to reflect the best current practice of the member states, in the view of the authors.

2.3 The Uniformity of State Corporation Laws

The basic results of the survey of the uniformity of state laws are depicted in Figure 1. It covers 142 provisions of the RMBCA, and show that they have been adopted by an average of 35.76 states. The degree of uniformity is probably somewhat higher, because my search techniques probably did not find all provisions that were essentially the same.

Not all provisions are of equal importance, so I have attempted to isolate those provisions described as important by other writers. This leads to a higher level of uniformity. I examined the adoption rate of the purely mandatory provisions of the RMBCA. These 25 provisions are adopted in an average of 41.6 states. Three of the provisions were innovations in the 1984 revision, and thus have notably lower adoption rates—requirements that some shares must have unlimited voting rights and residual economic rights; limits on the extent to which boards can change the size of a board previously approved by shareholders, and statutory statements of officers' duties of good faith and care.[13] If these three provisions are eliminated, the adoption rate for the remaining 22 provisions rises to 45 states. Eight provisions, or roughly one-third, are in effect in all jurisdictions.

I also examined six mandatory provisions that MacKerron (1993) describes as having been characterized as important by the reporters for the RMBCA, Hamilton and Macey. These provisions were adopted by an average of 42.5 jurisdictions. This understates the degree of uniformity in state law, because the RMBCA's formulation of prohibitions of indemnification of directors is new. All states prohibit indemnification where the director is held liable to the corporation, with exceptions, and it is safe to assume that receipt of an improper personal benefit would lead to liability to the corporation in most if not all instances. If this provision is treated as substantially uniform across the states, the adoption rate rises to 46 states. MacKerron has added 18 other mandatory provisions to the reporters' list that he believes are important. These provisions have been adopted in an

---

[12] See Commission of the European Communities, *Harmonization of Company Law in the European Community: Measures Adopted and Proposed: Situation as at 1 March 1992* (Office of Official Publications of the European Communities, 1992) (cited hereinafter as 'Harmonization').

[13] The provision on directors' duties can also be characterized as trivial, because it simply restates the duty of care generally enforced by the courts in the absence of statute.

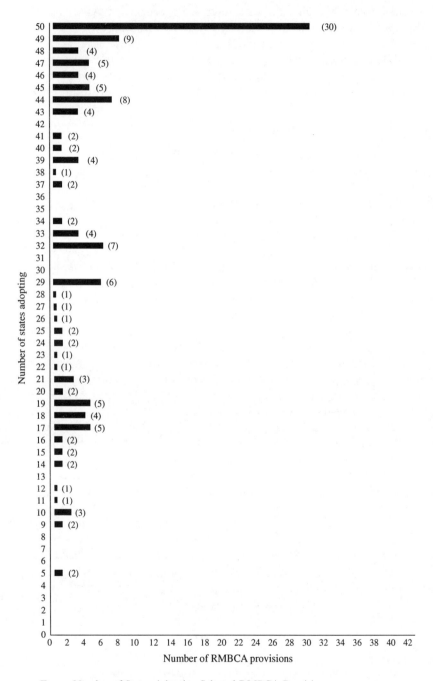

FIG. I. Number of States Adopting Selected RMBCA Provisions

average of 37.8 states. If these provisions are combined with those identified by the RMBCA reporters, the total rises to 24 important provisions that have been adopted in an average of 40 states.

Roberta Romano has offered a transaction cost explanation for reincorporations, in which she explains that reincorporations are driven by the prospect of certain types of transactions, which corporate officials presumably believe can be accomplished or defended at lower cost in a new jurisdiction, typically Delaware. She identifies public offerings, mergers and acquisitions, and takeover defenses as the most frequent causes of reincorporation. The 31 mandatory provisions I have identified as being relevant to these transactions have been adopted by an average of 37.38 states.

MacKerron's (1993) study did not separately identify provisions authorizing exculpation of directors from liability as a separate provision. Nevertheless, this provision, added to the Model Act in 1990, represented an important change in the Model Act (ABA, Committee on Corporate Laws (1990)). With the remarkable decision of the Delaware Supreme Court holding directors liable for a breach of their duty of care in the *Trans Union* case, corporate directors became aware that they might be liable for their decisions under circumstances where they had previously thought they were protected (*Smith* v. *Van Gorkom* 1985). The legislative response to this crisis was immediate and overwhelming. With Delaware's legislature in the lead in 1986, 38 states passed virtually identical legislation within five years, permitting corporate charters to elect to exculpate directors from all liability for negligence, while six others either placed ceilings on liability or simply removed such liability by statute. In all, 44 states acted within five years. This demonstrates that the process of adopting corporate innovations can be both widespread and rapid where the change is perceived to be an important one.

2.4 The Role of Innovation

I then tested the hypothesis that uniformity is significantly lessened by the process of innovation. I examined the date of the original innovation for all RMBCA rules that were adopted by 20 or fewer states. The date of the introduction of the innovation into the Model Act, rather than its first adoption by a state, is used for this purpose. The average age of these RMBCA provisions is 11.32 years. Twenty-six of these provisions were introduced in the 1984 revision of the Model Act, while two were added in 1990. If these 31 statutes were removed from the set, the adoption rate for the remaining laws would increase to 41.58 states.

The effects of innovation on uniformity of state laws can be seen most dramatically in the area of antitakeover laws. Anti-takeover statutes of the 'first generation,' which focused primarily on disclosure and administrative approval of proposed bids, were adopted by 37 states in the 13 years following this innovation in 1968 (Romano 1985: 234 Fig.1). With the decision of the Supreme Court in *Edgar* v. *Mite*, declaring the Illinois statute invalid, these statutes were either repealed or held invalid by lower courts, so the adoption process was halted, to be replaced by a variety of other antitakeover statutes, described hereinafter. The speed of adoption of this second generation of statutes was far more rapid than the first—(37 states in 8 years vs. 37 states in 13 years) (compare Romano ibid).

Three basic forms of statutes were adopted in response to the Supreme Court's ruling in *Edgar* v. *Mite* (the 'second generation' of these statutes). The earliest to be widely adopted was the so-called 'fair price' statute, which required mergers with 'interested shareholders' (bidders who had not received prior approval of the target's board) to secure exceedingly high shareholder votes to approve mergers between bidder and target. This type of statute was adopted by 25 states in eight years. Romano (1987) has described the role of corporate management in lobbying for the Connecticut version of this statute.

The second two forms of statutes could be seen as substitutes for each other, although many states chose to adopt both. In the 'control share' statutes, a bidder was stripped of voting rights upon reaching certain ownership thresholds, unless voting power was restored by the remaining shareholders. This form of statute was held constitutional in *CTS Corporation* v. *Dynamics Corp. of America* in 1987. It was adopted by 25 states in eight years, and 15 of these states adopted such a statute in the three years after the Supreme Court's decision. In 'business combination' statutes, the alternative form, mergers between bidder and target were forbidden for a period of time, usually three years from the bidder's acquisition of a significant ownership position, with certain exceptions. These statutes were adopted by 18 states in four years. If these two statutes are taken together, one or both of them were adopted by 34 states in eight years. No further adoptions occurred after 1991, largely because a recession in the United States of America and the collapse of the junk bond market that provided financing for some hostile takeovers eliminated the major sources of financing for takeovers.

As the Delaware courts confined management with new rules of judicial review, managers searched for new justifications for self-serving tactics. As a result, between 1983 and 1992, 26 states passed statutes that either permitted management to consider other constituencies or, in the milder form, authorized charter amendments to this effect (Orts 1992: 27; Matheson & Olson 1991: 1540–5; Mitchell 1992: 579, n. 1). Again, the speed of adoption was impressive: all of these adoptions occurred within six years.

The variety of statutes adopted during the 1980s in response to takeovers detracted to some extent from the essential uniformity of corporate laws. This can be attributed to the speed with which such laws were passed. No single statute was tested first and found to provide a superior solution to the 'problem' faced by incumbent managers. Accordingly, there was no process by which one form competed over time and survived. Second, there was some uncertainty during much of the period about the constitutionality of various proposed laws.

2.5 The Character of USA Law

The European Community's directives on company law were designed to provide essential uniformity, or at least compliance with minimum standards, of company laws throughout the community. This process of 'harmonization' was designed to facilitate a common market, although in my view the directives go very far beyond what the American experience suggests is necessary for that purpose (Buxbaum & Hopt 1988: 194–95)[14] They were seen as standardizing the protection of shareholders and creditors throughout the community (ibid. 201). They are distinctly European, and were not drawn from the Anglo-American corporate law tradition. As a result, they provide a useful basis for comparison with USA law.

The continental nations stopped any competition for charters with the adoption of the 'real seat' rule of conflicts of law, which required local businesses to incorporate where they were headquartered if they were to receive the benefits of corporate status (Carney 1995). To the extent that the EC pattern deviates from the USA pattern, we can infer that a lack of competition among the member states would be a contributing cause to such differentiation. I examined the rate of adoption by USA states of the principal provisions of the company law directives thus far adopted by the European Community that are of general application to European companies. Figure 2 sets out the adoption rates. The most striking result is the bipolar nature of the distribution: either virtually all USA states have similar provisions, or none do. Of 131 EC provisions, 95 were in effect in no USA jurisdiction. On the other hand, 14 were in effect in all 50 states. The remaining 22 provisions were adopted by what appears to be a random number of states.

An American corporate lawyer reading the Directives is struck by how mandatory they are. Publication plays a much larger role in Europe than in the USA (I have treated filing with the Secretary of State as the equivalent of publication, but in Europe publication appears to mean publication in a national gazette.) More details are required in articles of incorporation, and minimum capital is required before business can begin, an anachronism still present in a few USA state laws. Par value appears to be taken as seriously in Europe as it was in the USA in the late 19th and early 20th centuries. Provisions requiring all shares to be subscribed at the time of incorporation harken back to the days of special chartering in the USA, when legislative

[14] The characterization of the reach of the directives is mine.

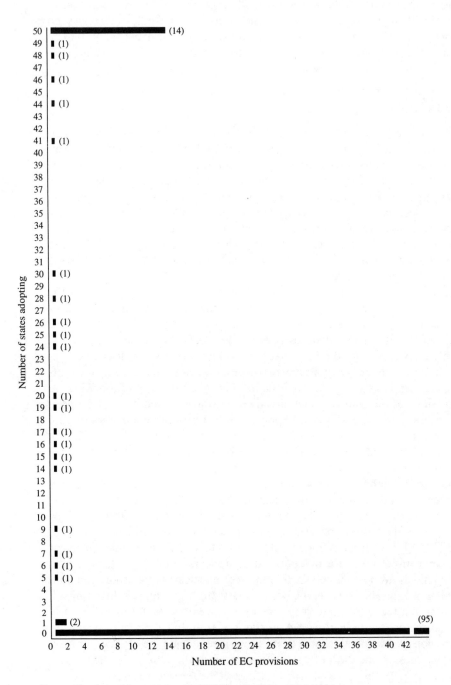

FIG. 2. Number of States Adopting EC Directives' Provisions

issuance of a special charter was on condition that funds were committed for the project. These provisions preclude the kind of financing flexibility made possible by the concept of authorized but unissued shares and blank preferred shares, both of which delegate to the board of directors total discretion over new financings. Distributions to shareholders are strictly regulated using concepts similar to the old legal capital rules of the Model Act, which were eliminated as useless in 1980. Preemptive rights are mandatory unless shareholders waive them at the time of a new issue. Laws regulating mergers require an outside expert's opinion to be delivered to the shareholders, a practice that has become widespread, if not legally required, in the USA. Merger provisions, such as those requiring that shareholders in constituent corporations receive shares in the surviving corporation, are more restrictive than USA laws, which permit the use of any kind of consideration in mergers. Provisions covering 'divisions,' which apparently involve the sale of all of the assets of a corporation to two or more corporations, are simply unknown to USA law, where all sales of substantially all assets not in the ordinary course of business are treated alike, regardless of the number of buyers. This impression of a striking difference between USA and European law in terms of the extent of mandatory rules is shared by at least one European observer (Tunc 1982).

To the extent that these requirements focus on capital structure they have implications for the flexibility of a corporation to seek new financing. And to the extent that they provide additional regulation of mergers, they add to the cost (in time as well as funds) of business acquisitions. Romano (1985: 250, 252–3) has identified flexibility of financing and acquisitions as two of the major reasons why firms migrate. To the extent that restrictions on these activities dominate the contents of some of the directives, they strongly suggest that competitive pressures in the USA explain the vast differences in approach in these areas. The other major difference, that of the extent of disclosures required by company law, is largely the result of the separation of securities laws from corporation laws in the USA. State blue sky laws, which antedate the federal securities laws in the USA, require disclosures from issuers seeking capital within each state's borders, and thus obviate the need for similar provisions in corporation codes. Thus a strict comparison of the directives with USA corporate laws, excluding securities laws, may overstate the dissimilarities slightly.

Ronald Daniels' (1991) work on the effects of competition for charters in the Canadian system provides further support for the hypothesis that competition produces less rather than more regulation. Until enactment of the Canada Business Corporations Act (CBCA) in 1975 by the federal government, which provided an alternative to provincial chartering, little innovation had occurred in Canadian corporate law (ibid. 150–51). Daniels (1991: 152) describes ten core reforms introduced by the CBCA. Included among them were at least five that were less regulatory: (i) the ability to operate one-director corporations; (ii) specific provision for the adoption of pre-incorporation contracts; (iii) eradication of the *ultra vires* doctrine by endowing the corporation with the power of natural persons; (iv) the ability of the corporation to repurchase its issued and outstanding shares; and (v) the capacity of directors to convene meetings by telephone. The result was the rapid adoption of these reforms by provincial governments, in response to the competitive threat posed by a more flexible statute (ibid. 152–55). The result was greater uniformity of corporate law.

3. THE ROLE OF INTEREST GROUPS IN THE DIFFUSION OF INNOVATIONS

3.1 Collective Action Problems and the Rate of Change

I propose to begin the examination of the rate at which uniformity of corporate laws is achieved by comparing four corporate law provisions identified by Romano as representing stated reasons for reincorporation and major improvements in Delaware's 1967 revision of its corporate law. In Romano's (1985: 233) words, they are '(1) the explicit elaboration of a standard for director and officer indemnification; (2) the exemption from stockholder vote of mergers involving a specific percentage of the corporation's stock, (3) the elimination of appraisal rights in corporations whose shares trade on a national exchange, [and] (4) anti-takeover statutes . . .' I have replaced Romano's set of anti-takeover laws, most of which were held to be invalid by the Supreme Court, with a second generation of anti-takeover statutes.[15]

The literature on the diffusion of innovations suggests that the rate of adoption over time can be graphed by an S-shaped curve which is initially concave and later becomes convex (Jensen 1983). One explanation for this pattern is the 'demonstration effect', which states that as the proportion of users adopting the innovation increases, the competitive pressure on holdouts to adopt increases. The evidence suggests that this is only a partial explanation for changes in corporate laws, where the rate of diffusion of change appears to be a function of the interest groups driving the change, and of the intensity of their interests.

Figure 3 examines the diffusion of change in the statutes examined by Romano (1985: 234). It differs from Romano's account both in the extent

---

[15] *Edgar* v. *MITE Corp.*, 457 U.S. 624 (1982). While this decision declared only the Illinois anti-takeover statute invalid, the similarity of most other state and anti-takeover statutes made it clear that they would not withstand constitutional scrutiny. Some were declared invalid by lower courts; other were repealed when second generation anti-takeover statutes were enacted; a few still remain, but presumably are neither enforced nor relied upon.

Number of Adopting States

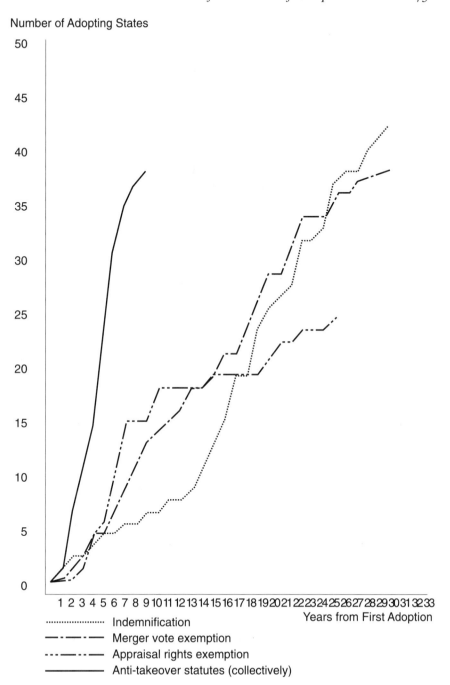

FIG. 3. Romano's Legal Diffusion Process (extended)

of the periods examined, and in the dates of adoption for specific statutes. The differences are minor, except with respect to anti-takeover statutes, where I examined a second generation of such laws. This replication of Romano's path-breaking work is provided because it provides a base line for comparison with other changes set forth herein after.

3.2 Indemnification Provisions

Romano's (1993: 234 fig. 1) study shows that indemnification provisions were adopted by 43 states in the 22 years following the innovation in this area in 1961. By 1992 all 50 states had provided for indemnification of directors. The chart covers only 42 states, due to space limitations. The rate of change was relatively leisurely, given the doubts cast upon corporate power to indemnify directors by a 1939 New York decision.[16] Today these statutes differ primarily in the specificity with which various aspects of the power are addressed, including procedural requirements and standards for permissive indemnification. Because these statutes addressed questions of directors' liability, one would have expected a more rapid legislative response, given what should have been the intense interest of corporate managers in this subject. My best guess is that managers attached less importance to this issue in the years preceding the hostile takeover movement of the 1970s and 1980s, because there were so few instances where directors were held liable for negligence.[17]

3.3 Elimination of Shareholder Voting on Short Form Mergers

Romano's (1985: 234, fig. 1) study shows that provisions eliminating shareholder votes on mergers of parent corporations and subsidiaries in which they owned the overwhelming majority of the stock (usually 90% or more) were adopted by 22 states in the 18 years following this innovation in 1963. By 1992 at least 48 states authorized such mergers.[18] The rate of diffusion of this change is approximately equal to that of indemnification statutes, although the initial rate of adoption for these statutes was higher than for indemnification (14 states in 10 years vs. 7 states in 10 years). Nevertheless, forty years were required for adoption by all 48 states, which is about the same as for indemnification statutes.

[16] *New York Dock Co.* v. *McCollom*, 16 N.Y. S.2d 844 (Sup. Ct. 1939).
[17] The most famous study of this question found only four cases where directors were arguably held liable for breach of the duty of care of making decisions, and even these cases carried a distinct aroma of fraud or self-dealing (see e.g., Bishop (1968); see also Carney (1988)).
[18] This research is currently incomplete; all 50 states may have authorised short form mergers.

3.4 Elimination of Appraisal Rights for Listed Corporations

Romano (1985: 234, fig. 1) showed that provisions exempting corporations from appraisal if their shares were listed on a national stock exchange were adopted by 26 states in the 14 years following this innovation in 1967. This trend was halted by the reversal of the position of the drafters of the Model Act in 1978.[19] Nevertheless, the reform was adopted by 29 states before the trend reversed. The initial rate of adoption (18 states in the 10 years from the first adoption) is more rapid than for other changes. Because this change was included in the 1968 revision of the Model Act that formed the basis for corporate law modernization in many jurisdictions, I suspect that the Model Act had much to do with the rapidity of the change.

3.5 Anti-takeover Statutes

While I will later describe antitakeover statutes as management-sponsored, I include the rate of adoption of so-called 'first generation' statutes here primarily because this was part of Romano's original study, but also because it provides evidence of the more rapid rate of change observed with management-sponsored statutes.

4. SOLVING COLLECTIVE ACTION PROBLEMS

Macey and Miller (1987) have documented the role of the organized bar in Delaware in promoting corporate legislation. A similar role appears to be played by the bar in many other, if not all, jurisdictions. The collective action problems described in Part I suggest that bar associations will avoid costly legislative reform proposals until production costs are reduced, and they can avail themselves of economies of scale. The ABA's Committee on Corporate Laws produces the Model Business Corporation Act, which can serve as a model for wholesale revision of a state's corporate law, thus reducing collective action costs for state bar associations. The 1984 revision of the Model Act was a complete one, providing an entirely new structure for the act. Because it was drafted in a 'code' format, it was relatively more accessible than earlier versions, and inspired a quick revision of corporate statutes. Eighteen states adopted new corporate statutes based on the Revised Model Act between 1985 and 1992. Indeed, it appears this wholesale revision was responsible for the relative speed of adoption of many of the legal reforms shown below in figure 4. Further, nineteen states continue to have statutes based on the 1969 version of the Model

---

[19] 38 *Bus. Law.* 2587 (1978).

Number of Adopting States

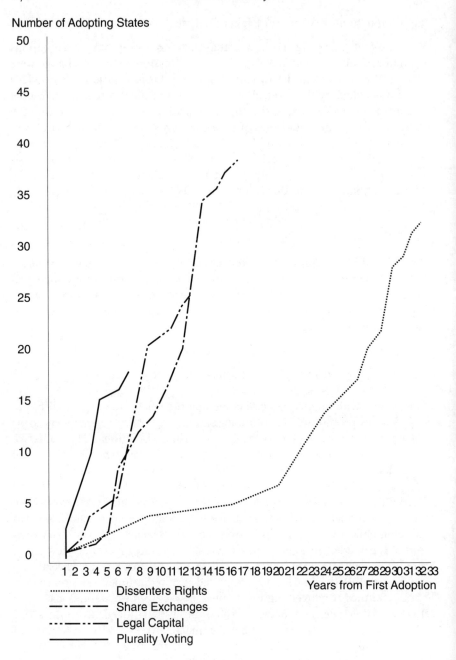

FIG. 4. Diffusion of Model Act Changes

Act, indicating the lag that occurs because of the high cost of wholesale law revision.[20]

The influence of the Model Act on the rate of diffusion is impressive. Of the four substantive changes listed, only two were new to the Model Act with the 1984 revision—the exclusivity of dissenters' rights and plurality voting. Yet in 14 states all four of these reforms were first adopted with revisions based on the Revised Model Act. They are highlighted in table 1. No states had adopted a provision authorizing share exchanges prior to the Model Act's introduction of this concept in 1976. No state had adopted provisions eliminating the old legal capital rules prior to the Model Act's elimination of these provisions in 1980. Similarly, there were no states that allowed shareholder action by plurality voting prior to introduction of this concept in the 1984 Model Act.[21] It is also noteworthy that Delaware has not adopted any of the reforms listed here, although, to be fair, it never adopted the Model Act's approach to legal capital.[22] This raises at least a question of whether Delaware remains as active in corporate law reform as Romano's (1985) article suggested, or whether the Delaware bar and legislature determined that these provisions would not be advantageous to publicly held corporations of the type Delaware seeks to attract. Since these reforms increase corporate flexibility, the latter explanation seems implausible.

4.1 The Role of Corporate Managers in Legal Change

A. The Rate of Management-Favoured Changes

At this point I turn to a group of statutes where the rate of diffusion is far higher than those previously discussed. They include anti-takeover statutes and statutes limiting directors' liability, both of which are of intense interest to corporate managers. The statutes I have studied here were all adopted after 1980, so that I cannot exclude the possibility that the rate of diffusion of changes in corporate law has accelerated generally. This could be because interest groups have become better organized, or because of technological changes, such as improved access to changes in laws of other jurisdiction through loose-leaf services, corporate law newsletters, or access to on-line data bases. It could also be because corporate lawyers have become more

---

[20] 1 *Rev. Model Bus. Corp. Act Ann* (1992 Supp. xxxiv.vii). The Model Act reports 20 states with the 1969 version in its 1992 Supplement, but does not reflect Utah's 1992 adoption of the Revised Model Act.

[21] Delaware, however, did expressly provide what was implicit in other states—that directors were to be elected by plurality voting (see Del. Code Ann. tit. 8, §216(3)).

[22] See Del.Code Ann. tit. 8, §§154 & 170. While these provisions do not track the 1969 version of the Model Act, they do contain their own complexities, and can be criticized on many of the same grounds as the former Model Act provisions.

Table I. Dates of Adoption of Statutes

State	Dissenters Rights	Share Exchanges	Legal Capital	Plurality Voting	Model Act
Alabama	1983				
Alaska	1988				
Arizona					
Arkansas	1987	1987	1987	1987	1987
California	1975	1989			
Colorado	1977	1981	1993		
Connecticut	1959				
Delaware					
Florida	1989	1989	1989	1989	1989
Georgia	1988	1988	1988	1988	1988
Hawaii	1983	1983	1983		
Idaho	1979	1979			
Illinois	1983	1983			
Indiana	1984	1986	1986	1986	
Iowa	1989	1989	1989	1989	1989
Kansas					
Kentucky	1988	1988	1988	1988	1988
Louisiana	1990				
Maine					
Maryland	1976	1988			
Massachusetts	1964				
Michigan	1981	1989	1989		
Minnesota	1981	1981			
Mississippi	1987	1987	1987	1987	1987
Missouri	1990				
Montana	1991	1991	1991	1991	1991
Nebraska	1981	1981			
Nevada	1991	1991	1991		
New Hampshire	1981	1981	1992	1992	
New Jersey	1988				
New Mexico	1983	1983	1983		
New York	1961	1986			
North Carolina	1989	1989	1989	1989	1989
North Dakota	1985	1985			
Ohio					
Oklahoma					
Oregon	1987	1987	1987	1987	1987
Pennsylvania	1988	1988			
Rhode Island	1982				
South Carolina	1981	1981	1981	1988	
South Dakota	1985				

State	Dissenters Rights	Share Exchanges	Legal Capital	Plurality Voting	Model Act
Tennessee	1986	1986	1986	1986	1986
Texas	1967	1989			
Utah	1992	1992	1992	1992	1992
Vermont					
Virginia	1985	1980	1985	1986	1986
Washington	1989	1989	1989	1989	1989
West Virginia					
Wisconsin	1989	1989	1989	1989	1989
Wyoming	1989	1989	1989	1989	1989

specialized, and are willing to devote more time to changing corporate law because their payoffs from such activity have increased. Nevertheless, in the absence of compelling evidence of such changes, the explanation that appears to dominate is the interest group theory—that these subjects were of intense interest to corporate managers, who organized to lobby for them.

Anti-takeover statutes of the 'first generation,' which focused primarily on disclosure and administrative approval of proposed bids, were adopted by 37 states in the 13 years following this innovation in 1968 (Romano 1985: 234, fig. 1). After the 1982 decision of the Supreme Court in *Edgar* v. *Mite*, declaring the Illinois statute invalid, these statutes were either repealed or held invalid by lower courts, so the adoption process was halted, to be replaced by a variety of other anti-takeover statutes, described hereinafter. The speed of adoption of this second generation of statutes was far more rapid than the first—(37 states in 8 years vs. 37 states in 13 years).[23] The speed of adoption of this group of statutes with other, more 'general interest' laws, is compared in Figure 3, above.

Figure 5 focuses on the changes in the 1980s, both in anti-takeover statutes, so-called 'other constituency' statutes, and in statutes limiting directors' liability. In part, it disaggregates the 'anti-takeover' statutes in figure 3. It includes, in addition to the traditional antitakeover statutes, so-called 'other constituency' statutes that permitted boards facing hostile bids to abandon their undivided loyalty to shareholders in favor of a broader, amorphous rule that allowed them to consider the welfare of other 'stakeholders' in the firm, such as customers, suppliers, and employees. Between 1983 and 1992, 26 states passed statutes that either permitted management to consider other constituencies or, in the milder form, authorized charter amendments to this effect (see Orts 1992; Matheson & Olson 1991; Mitchell

[23] Compare Romano (1985: 234, fig. 1).

Number of Adopting States

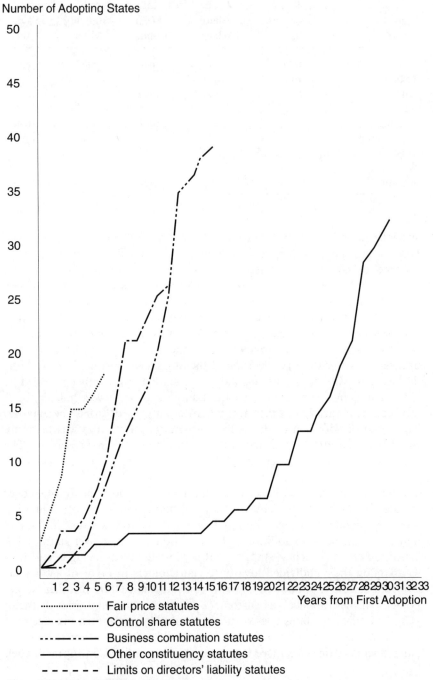

FIG. 5. Recent Legal Diffusion Processes

1992). Again, the speed of adoption was impressive: all of these adoptions occurred within six years. Finally, figure 5 includes the adoption of statutes that permitted corporations to contract out of directors' liability for breach of their duty of care—the legislative reaction to the misguided decision of the Delaware Supreme Court in *Smith* v. *Van Gorkom*. Thirty-eight states passed virtually identical legislation within five years, permitting corporate charters to elect to exculpate directors from all liability for negligence, while six others either placed ceilings on liability or simply removed such liability by statute. In all, 44 states acted within five years. The enormous increase in the rate of diffusion of these changes is the most notable feature of the changes of the 1980s.

These statutes were generally adopted at the instance of management teams that either were already under attack or anticipated such attacks. Romano has detailed the special interests that led to adoption of the Connecticut law, and similar stories can be told about other states—the adoption of antitakeover statutes inspired by attempted takeovers of local firms, e.g., Burlington Industries in North Carolina, Dayton-Hudson in Minnesota, Greyhound in Arizona, and so on. I can personally attest that Georgia's 'constituencies' statute was adopted at the instance of attorneys for the former C&S Bank, when it anticipated a bid from North Carolina National Bank (which subsequently acquired C&S notwithstanding these statutes). In general, these are stories of well-organized local management teams with a great deal at stake, who were able to use corporate resources and promises of future political support to obtain favourable legislation, at the expense of dispersed and often non-resident shareholder interests.

This demonstrates that the process of adopting corporate innovations is both widespread, and increasingly rapid. The only study contrary to this conclusion is that of Baysinger and Butler (1985), who argue that various states have specialized in providing efficient and distinctive statutes for publicly held and closely held firms. They identified 'strict' jurisdictions, those that provide relatively more regulation, on the basis of departures of public corporations for other states of incorporation (Baysinger & Butler 1985: 184–5). They identified as 'strict' jurisdictions California, Illinois, New York, and Texas (ibid. 185). Two of those states, New York and California, have made notable departures from the necessary conditions for competition in corporate law, by partially rejecting the American 'internal affairs' rule of conflicts of law in favour of their own versions of the 'real seat' rule, so that departing corporations remain governed by local law with respect to some aspects of their internal affairs, unless they incur the considerable expense of physical relocation.[24] Despite this

---

[24] Cal. Corp. Code §2115 provides that certain sections of the California Corporation Code apply to foreign corporations meeting certain tests. The statute provides that if a corporation

attempt to restrict departures, these states are among the largest losers of corporate charters.[25]

B. Evidence of Market Constraints on Management's Power to Change Corporate Laws

As previously mentioned, there will be constraints on the adoption of anti-takeover laws. New firms offering suboptimal contracts when going public are likely to feel the disapproval of the investing public most keenly. Firms with large institutional ownership may also feel pressures to opt out of these laws, as well as from other takeover defenses such as poison pills. For these companies, the choice of jurisdiction remains important. Indeed, it will remain important even for insulated managements, because there are tools for displacement of management other than hostile tender offers, such as proxy fights (Manne 1964). Thus many firms will continue to attach importance to the background legal conditions when deciding where to incorporate. And to the extent that some states remain in the competition for these charters, their legislators will be constrained in adopting suboptimal laws. For a company that has made the decision to reincorporate but has not selected a jurisdiction, as well as for new companies anticipating public offerings, transaction costs do not interfere with selection of the optimal jurisdiction. Thus, at the margin, the presence of inefficient anti-takeover laws can cost a state important chartering revenues. Under this theory, it would not be surprising to find that Delaware has been reluctant to adopt anti-takeover laws. It has neither a fair price statute nor a control shares acquisition statute. Its business combination statute[26] was only adopted in 1988, after at least five other states had adopted such statutes, and at least ten had adopted control share acquisition statutes. Indeed, in 1988 twelve states adopted one or the other of these provisions. As important, Delaware's business combination statute was not mandatory, as were many,

has an average of more than 50% of its (1) property located in California, (2) payroll payable in California, and (3) its sales in California, and if more than 50% of its securities are held by California residents, it must comply with the specified provisions of the California Corporation Code (see the discussion of this section in *Wilson* v. *Louisiana-Pacific Resources, Inc.*, 138 Cal. App. 3d 216, 187 Cal. Rptr. 852 (1982)). New York regulates certain foreign corporations transacting a local business with respect to dividends, share purchases, loans to directors, access of local residents to shareholder lists, mergers, derivative actions and indemnification of officers and directors (see N.Y. Bus. Corp. L. §§1315–19). These statutes withstood constitutional challenge under the dormant commerce clause in *Sadler* v. *NCR Corp.* d 928 F. 2d 48 (1991).

[25] Baysinger & Butler (1985: 184–85); Romano, (1985: 247). Nevertheless, these alterations in conflict rules may have prevented some losses. Of the four states mentioned by Baysinger & Butler as 'strict' states, New York and California retain a higher percentage of locally head-quartered firms (44% and 59%, respectively) than the other two strict states, Illinois and Texas (17% and 39%, respectively).

[26] Del. Code Ann. tit. 8, §203.

but was an opt-out provision.[27] The required threshold for a successful tender offer was not 90%, as in some jurisdictions, but 85%,[28] apparently in response to criticism that 90% would create an insurmountable barrier to hostile tender offers.[29] Finally, where the restrictions in most of these statutes apply for five years, Delaware provided only a three-year restriction on take-out mergers (Matheson & Olson 1991: 1440–1).

These features of Delaware's response suggest that its legislature was indeed constrained by its concern over investor reactions to these statutes, and the effect that would have on the choice of chartering jurisdiction. The adoption of any statute at all can be seen as a concession to incumbent managers seeking protection and threatening to move to more protective jurisdictions, but the relative moderation exercised must surely be explained by the effects of a competitive market for charters.

5. CONCLUSION

American corporate law reveals a pattern of substantial uniformity, apparently resulting from a competition among the states for chartering business, despite Delaware's dominant position. That pattern is less than complete because of a constant process of innovation, driven by interest groups with discrete interests in corporate law. The speed with which innovative legislation is dispersed among the states appears to be a product of the identity of the sponsoring interest group and the collective action problems it faces. Indeed, rather than refer to a competition among the states, we might more accurately refer to a competition among localized interest groups. That competition is constrained by the availability of alternative legal régimes and efficient capital markets, which has led to a more flexible régime than that faced by European companies.

---

[27] According to Matheson & Olson, (1991: 1525–29), at least five of the business combination statutes provided for no opt out.

[28] Compare, e.g., Off. Code Ga. Ann. §14–2–1132 with Del. Code Ann., tit. 8, §203.

[29] *See RP Acquisition Corp.* v. *Staley Continental, Inc.*, 686 F.Supp. 476, 488 (D.Del. 1988) (detailing the legislative history of section 203).

6

European Capitalism: Between Freedom and Social Justice

PROF. DR. H.W. DE JONG

I. INTRODUCTION: A PLURALISTIC SYSTEM

Capitalism is the economic system in which firms, privately owned, produce goods and services for markets where consumers spend their incomes in accordance with their own free choices. The goal of the system is, to quote Marx (1890: 138, 149, 295), the generation of surplus value: 'The production of surplus value, . . ., is the specific end and aim, the sum and substance, of capitalist production'. The quotation, as given above,[1] is, I think, one which deserves general acclaim, for it denotes the essential features of capitalism to bring forth goods and services valued in and by markets and to do so on a progressive basis. Capitalism—or the free market economy, if one prefers a less ideologically oriented term—is not a system which is static or stagnant, but something which grows and develops, be it with ups and downs. Its fluctuations manifest leaps forward and crises of adaptation, but always and in the long run, like the Echternach procession: two steps forward and one backwards.

Both features also indicate the limitations of capitalism. The market economy produces only market values, and thus does not bring forth the values from outside the market system without which no society can be sustained. Justice, social companionship, sympathy and love, honesty, and other values which make society worthwhile and desirable are not produced by the market system itself. There is a lively debate whether capitalism contributes to or distracts from these extra-market values or just relates to them in a neutral way. It is a debate which is as old as capitalism itself.[2] In my view, the extra-market values derive from religion, human ideals as

---

[1] The sentence quoted omits a part which does not command widespread agreement, viz. 'The production of surplus value, or the extraction of surplus labour, is the specific end and aim, . . .'. In Socialist theory surplus value results form the exploitation of labour; other theories may ascribe the surplus value to entrepreneurial innovations or to the conversion of lower valued goods and services into higher ones as a result of the combined activities of firms or to the (efficient) organizational structures and decisions which meet the fundamental uncertainties prevailing in market economies.

[2] Some of the recent discussions about the 'ethics of capitalism' can be found in Strain (1989), Puel (1989), and Biskup (1990).

formulated and expressed by philosophy and literature and, not the least, from the human condition itself: the majority of people, in every part of the world, just want to live in social groups, which need some sense of justice, mutual trust and sympathy and basic honesties to be sustainable. Thus, the first limitation of capitalism is its inability to produce the extra-market values mentioned, alongside the surplus (market) values, the generation of which is its 'specific end'.

The second limit follows from the dynamic nature of the market economy. Dynamic developments are applauded by some people, but abhorred by others. Everyone will agree with the inscription above the porch of a cloister in the Eifel-hills which says: 'Let us keep the old when it is good, but build upon old ground the new you brood'; the difficulty is, obviously, that people differ in their valuations of the 'good' and the attractiveness of the 'broods'. Thus, both limitations of capitalism, inherent in the market values it produces in myriad dynamic ways, require institutionalized political decisions reflecting the views of a majority of the population or at least of its leading groups. This leads up to the admittedly vague idea of a culture, formed by history, law, customs, geography, and morals, peculiar to a national or regional entity and to which capitalism adapts itself.

Nowhere is this more visible than in Europe with its pluralistic society. Basically there is no such thing as European capitalism; the system divides itself into many varieties and one could easily find different types even within small countries, let alone large ones. However, in order not to end up in agnosticism, I will schematize and distinguish three main types of European capitalism, according to its dominant features, especially with respect to corporate organization. First, there is the Anglo-Saxon type of free market capitalism, in which the business corporation is organized by its owners on a public basis; that is, comparatively speaking many companies are listed on stock exchanges, which fulfil the functions of capital supplier and risk distributor, and bring about the separation of ownership and control. The latter is in the hands of managers, who are supposed to serve the interest of the owners. If they do not do so, but instead pursue their own interests, public bids for control and management of the firm by some other firm can be accepted by the owners, who also have some representation on the board of directors to look after their interests. Employees are a hired production factor and have no say in the management of the corporation.

Likewise, banks, who do provide many services to non-financial business, normally have no participations in corporations which are of a long-standing nature. The separation between equity ownership and managerial control is therefore seconded by the separation between the suppliers of equity capital and debt capital. Thus, there is a double agency problem, viz. between shareholders and managers, and between shareholders and debtholders.

Lastly, government has only a restricted role to play in the Anglo-Saxon free market economy: it is supposed to order the functioning of the market by means of honouring the contracts concluded between the various parties and to keep them free from monopolistic influences. The Anglo-Saxon system therefore gives priority to the freedom of action of the individual to pursue his own course and relies on the outcome as being an optimal one in the social context.

Second, one may distinguish the Germanic type of social market capitalism. The adjective 'social' here denotes a double aspect of the system. On the one hand, it means that the various groups concerned—management, shareholders, employees, and banks—have a stake in the control of the corporation, although this is not uniformly organized; the relative share of the stakes depends on various circumstances. Banks and insurance companies often possess smaller or larger blocks of shares, receive deposited shares of owners, who transfer voting power to them which they may exercise, are represented in the supervisory boards (sometimes as chairman) and lend credit to the affiliated companies as 'house-bankers'.

Employees likewise have representation on the supervisory boards, especially of the larger corporations and, moreover, by law have rights and obligations vis à vis the corporation (e.g., in the Netherlands with respect to closure of plants, liquidation or the merger of the firm). Labour is no mere hired production factor, but shares social and corporate responsibilities. Family ownership is relatively widespread, not only in small and medium-sized types of firms, and the public capital market much less important than in Anglo-Saxon countries; contested take-over bids can hardly be realized.

On the other hand, the system can also be dubbed a social one because of the role of government which is supposed to fulfil a mediating and coordinating role, even if only in the last resort. In particular, it is supposed to contribute and inject, through law and institutions, some of the extra-market values, such as solidarity and social justice, which are considered to shore the market system. In sum, social market capitalism is a less clear-cut type of capitalism, where rights and responsibilities with respect to control are more widely distributed over the various participant groups in firms, mirroring, as it were the original democracy of Germanic tribes, where the leadership had to take account in its decisions of the diverse interests. The system nevertheless is oriented towards free and open markets in products and production factors, prevailing over the firms concerned through competitive régimes. Competitive forces may be exerted on a more long-term basis than in the Anglo-Saxon system, accounting for a relatively slower working through of important changes as well as a preponderance of decisionmaking by the leadership prevailing over the interest of shareholders.

The third type is the Latinic type of capitalism, where ownership is, like in the Germanic type, strongly vested in family control, though in addition and peculiar to this type, state enterprise and financial groupings are also important structures. Therefore, ownership and control do not deviate as much as in Anglo-Saxon enterprises and hostile take-overs occur infrequently. State enterprise and government interference in the economy are important phenomena, although radical changes have quite recently been announced in both Italy and France. For these reasons, which boil down to a preponderance of internal control mechanisms with unexpected developments and effects, I have dubbed this type of capitalism a pragmatic system.

Finally, two additional features should be added. They relate to monetary stability and the independence of the Central Bank, which are an explicit goal of economic policy only in the social market economy and the striving for more equality in incomes and opportunities. The latter feature differs between countries, but those belonging to the social market type have a tendency to pay more attention to this goal of policy. Tables 1 and 2 summarize these features with respect to the overall types of economic systems and the corporate system. A comparison of those tables shows the remarkable parallelism between both systems, although France seems to be moving into the direction of the social market economy (privatization, mon-

Table 1. Main types of economic systems

	Free Market Economy	Social Market Economy	Pragmatic System
Private property	+	+	+
Free market/protected interests	+	+/–	–/+
Monetary stability (independent CB)	–	+	–
Public policy interference	–	–/+	+
Social protection	–	+	–/+
Co-operation between social partners	–	+	–
Equality of incomes & opportunities	–	+	–
Examples:	United States United Kingdom Ireland	Germay Benelux Denmark France (since 1985)	Italy Greece Spain Portugal

Table 2. Differences and resemblances between the three groups of countries with respect to specific criteria (++ stands for 'very important', + for 'important' and – for 'less important' or absent)

	Anglo-Saxon	Germanic	Latinic
Shareholder sovereignty	++	–	+
Bank-oriented	–	++	+
Employee influence	–	+	–
Industrial grouping	–	–	++
Market for corporate control	++	–	–

Source: Moerland (1995)

etary stability, and an independent Central Bank). The latter observation, by establishing a growing resemblance of the main features of the economic system among the core economies of the EU, prompts one to think that a monetary union will some day be instituted among them instead of throughout the EU as a whole as the Maastricht Treaty proposed. For monetary union between countries requires a minimum of agreement between the workings of the system and the financial and economic policies necessary to accommodate these.

In the second part of this paper I will sketch a statistical profile of European big business, and, in the third part, we will derive the effects on corporate behaviour and performance of the diverging structures. In the fourth part, I will conclude the paper by drawing attention to the relative decline of the Anglo-Saxon type of corporation in a long-run perspective. Despite its higher profitability, the lower value productivity of the Anglo-Saxon firm, in comparison with the Continental corporation seems to account for this.

2. A PROFILE OF EUROPEAN CORPORATE ENTERPRISE

2.1 The value-added data base

Because of the plurality of European corporate structures, the different structures might influence the behaviour and performance of firms and this is indeed what follows from the distribution of the hundred largest corporations according to some well-known criteria (Table 8). An initial appreciation of the use of various standards of measurement confirms the structural diversity outlined in part 1. Anglo-Saxon corporations are profitable to the capital suppliers (owners)—that is why their stock market values and return on capital employed (ROCE) are so high—whereas the Continental firms, and especially the Germanic corporations have size and added value. Because sales and net added value correspond rather closely throughout the various types of corporations, both criteria could be used as the basic ingredient for a statistical profile of large-scale European business.

However, two reasons induce one to prefer added value: first, added value or surplus value is the theoretically better criterion to use, as every corporation, whatever its structure or professed goal, must generate this result; also, (net) added value can be divided among the main participant groups to establish their shares. And, by dividing total added value through total employees, one gets a clear idea of the productivity the corporation achieves irrespective of its sales or degree of vertical integration. Finally, net added value reduces sectoral distortions with respect to the use of capital-, labour-, or raw material intensive processes of production and gives a better view of the importance of sectors or firms for the economy, with respect to size and productivity.

Second, good and internationally comparable figures for added value were unavailable up till recently. Now, there is a data base, started by the (Dutch) Financial Economic Magazine and the Accountancy Section of the University of Amsterdam, which presents refined figures derived from the annual reports of the hundred largest European companies. An effort was made to achieve a standardized annual account in accordance with the international accounting rules. This related (if necessary) to goodwill (immaterial assets) which was written off over a 10-year period, the application of historical cost valuation instead of replacement or actual value, the correction of book values and depreciation (which in some countries, by means of the annual report, serve as a basis for taxation, in other countries not, and thus distort the comparative valuations) while provisions were added to property (except for pension purposes). In many cases these provisions are used to manipulate the financial statements for fiscal or managerial reasons (for example, oil companies practise profit equalization, other companies manipulate restructuring provisions to influence profit and loss statements, etc.).

By restating the annual accounts in accordance with internationally accepted good practice (such as contained in the USA GAAP, EC Fourth Guideline, and International Accounting Standards Committee procedures, which, however, are not obligatory in European countries, or offer choices) the authors were able to eliminate or reduce the most glaring discrepancies. Still, some prominent European firms, especially state-owned firms, could not be incorporated in the list because of insufficient transparency in their accounts. This was also true of Italian state owned firms. The result is a data base which is better for comparative purposes than anything we have so far, even though still not perfect. The data base relates to the years 1991 and

1992 and gives gross and net added value and the distribution of the latter into labour (wages and social charges), capital suppliers (interest, dividend, third party shares, reserve dotations, and the specific corrections) as well as the profit tax. Developments through time cannot as yet be investigated, but the base offers a picture of European large business from a structural point of view.

Table 3. The distribution of Added Value of Europe's 100 largest companies (in '000 million ECU; 1991)

		%
Total Net Added Value:	363 billion ECU	100
Distributed to:		
– employees	288.4	79.5
– capitalists,	45.1	12.4
of which to owners	24.9	6.9
– government	29.5	8.1
Capital suppliers:	45.1 billion ECU	100
– net interest	9.9	22.0
– dividends to owners	21.8	48.3
– share of third parties	3.1	6.9
	—	—
Distributed to capital suppliers	34.8	77.2
Retained in Corporations	10.3	22.8

2.2 The formation and distribution of surplus value

The gross output of an economy is achieved by the combined efforts of entrepreneurs or managers, labour, and capital suppliers and the effect, after accounting for deliveries of firms to each other, is the gross added value. If replacements for the wear and tear of assets are deducted, a net added value (NAV) results which measures the real economic contribution of those efforts. It divides into wages and social charges, interest, taxation, and profits. In 1990/91, the European gross domestic output (measuring EC countries plus some important outsiders such as Sweden, Norway, Switzerland, and Austria, who have intensive relationships with the EC) was some 5000 billion ECU. As will be seen from table 3, the total NAV of the hundred largest corporations was 363 bn ECU, or slightly over 7% of the European GDP. Table 3 also gives the distribution between the suppliers of labour, capital and governmental services, the proportions of which are some 80, 12, and 8 percent. Table 3 is also instructive with respect to the shares of the various capital suppliers.

In the second part, it shows that owners get 21.8 bn ECU in dividends out of the corporations (or 48.3% of the 45.1 bn ECU), third parties 3.1 bn ECU and lenders 9.9 bn ECU. Corporations retain nearly 23% or 10.3 bn ECU. Table 3 is as it were the reference table for tables 4 and 5 where the formation and distribution of net added value across the various national-ities of the hundred largest firms are exhibited. From table 4 one can see, that the German corporations outweigh the others, providing for 31.5% (114.5 bn ECU) of the NAV of the hundred largest. In 1992 this share rose to nearly 33%.

Although their share in the number of corporations is less than the British one, both their mass and their average size (5.0 bn ECU) surpass those of other national groups. Italian, Swiss, Benelux, and French corporations also have at least average size, the others less. Figures for 1992, which have become available in the meantime and which were derived according to the same method, do not change the results more than marginally. In total, NAV remained largely the same as in 1991. Whereas the British and Scandinavian parts slightly declined the number of French corporations rose from 20 to 24, and their average NAV fell from $3.8 bn to $3.5 bn as some smaller French firms made their way into the one hundred leading firms. The reverse applied to some of the lower classified Benelux corpora-tions.

Table 5 compares the distribution of net added value. In this table Shell and Unilever have been kept separately and not, as in table 4 been divided

Table 4. Net Added Value of European Corporations (1991 first columns; 1992 second columns).

	Number		NAV in bn. ECU		Average NAV bn. ECU	
	1991	1992	1991	1992	1991	1992
German Corporations	23	23	114.5	121.9	5.0	5.3
British Corporations	28	29	81.4	79.9	2.9	2.8
French Corporations	20	24	75.3	84.0	3.8	3.5
Swedish/Norwegian Corporations	11½	9½	26.5	23.8	2.3	2.5
Benelux Corporations	8	5	26.4	25.9	3.3	5.2
Swiss/Austrian Corporations	5½	5½	21.8	24.2	4.0	4.4
Italian Corporations	4	4	17.1	14.8	4.3	3.7
Total 100 largest European	100	100	363.0	374.5	3.6	3.7

* Shell, Unilever, Asea-Brown Boveri have been equally divided between countries.

equally between the UK and the Netherlands. The separation underlines their Anglo-Saxon character, being different from the structure of Benelux or Continental corporations. The striking feature of this table is indeed this difference. Anglo-Saxon firms pay out a much lower share of the NAV to labour (less than 70%) in contrast to Continental firms (over 80%), whereas the shares going to capital suppliers (20%) and government (over 10%) are much higher. In particular, German and Italian firms have high labour shares and low capital shares. Thus, from an overall point of view, represented by the last row of table 5, Anglo-Saxon firms stand out at one extreme, and German and Italian firms at another, whereas French, Benelux, Scandinavian, and Swiss firms (there was only one Austrian corporation in the hundred largest) occupy a middle-ground in the distributional proportions.

The picture gained from these tables sustains the view developed in the introduction where it was stated that the Anglo-Saxon type of firm is struc-

Table 5. Distribution of Added Value in European countries (1991) (100 largest corporations)

		Shares in Total Value Added (%)		
	N	Labour	Capital	Government
Germany	23	88.6	4.7	6.7
Benelux	7	81.1	14.1	4.8
France	20	80.2	14.3	5.5
United Kingdom	27	68.0	20.6	11.4
Shell-Unilever	2	57.4	20.3	22.3
Italy	4	92.2	4.0	3.8
Sweden/Norway*	11½	82.0	12.6	5.4
Switzerland/Austria	5½	81.0	12.2	6.8
Europe	100	79.5	12.4	8.1

* Asea-Brown Boveri equally divided
Source: Database Financial Economic Magazine/University of Amsterdam.

tured in such a way that it reflects the dominance of the owners (capital suppliers) and gives less weight to labour, whereas Continental firms have, to a more or lesser degree, the reverse structure. This agrees with an earlier study, using other variables, namely profit margins, rate of return on capital, employees, and market values, which came to the conclusion that Anglo-Saxon type of firms are profit oriented, whereas Continental firms are sales or growth oriented, and that the distribution derives from the structural régimes, characterizing the various types (see H.W. de Jong 1991: 13–15).

3. PERFORMANCE OF LARGE CORPORATE TYPES

An interesting question now is whether the various types of European capitalist enterprise show performance differences, and, if so, whether these differences are related to the corporate structures. This is not an easy question
to answer because various factors may influence performance, and, moreover, the availability of data for NAV of only two years, restricts the elo-
quence of the outcome. Nevertheless, we can proceed some distance on the
road and we can find some remarkable results, which may prompt further
investigations.

3.1 A few reservations

The first thing to note is that productivity per firm is best measured by
dividing net value added through the total number of employees. That standard, though good in theory is not a perfect one in practice: two sources of
distortion are the world-wide character of many of these corporations and
the varying use of part-time labour. The first problem cannot in practice be
taken care off, for many corporations do not publish the number of their
European employees. If productivity per employee in and outside of Europe
would be on the same level, this would not be problematic, but we know
that in some sectors and even between countries there are discrepancies,
especially if firms are strongly represented in third-world areas.

The use of part-time labour also differs between countries and sectors.
Retailing is one example, but to some extent this can be taken into account
by working with full-time labour units. A check on both possible distortions
can be provided by looking into sectors where they are largely absent, for
example steel and aircraft production, which are wholly European in their
locations. These checks support the outcomes of the general statistical comparison made below.

A second point which merits some consideration is the fact that the business cycle develops unevenly throughout Europe. In 1991, the UK and
Sweden were already feeling the downturn, whereas Germany and The
Netherlands, and to a lesser extent France and Italy were still in booming
conditions. This difference might influence the numerator of the quotient,
though the effect is possibly mitigated by (a) the extent of multinationality
of the corporation concerned, and (b) the flexibility of its response, for
example by reducing its labour force. A clear view on the importance of the
effects of cyclicality on the Net Value Added per Employee (NVA/E) could
only be gained by comparing the quotient for various years of good and bad
economic conditions. We do not have as yet the NAV figures for successive
years on a European level, but Dutch figures, which are available for a suc-

cession of years do suggest that the distortion is modest and confined to a few sectors only.

3.2 The result and some explanations

Table 6.1 gives the productivity of European large firms, as measured by the NVA/E, distributed as between their countries of origin. Shell and Unilever have been allotted to the UK (which makes no difference to the division, however, as Shell is much above, and Unilever below the average or median). The average large company had a value added productivity of 39,700 ECU and the median company a productivity of 37,400 ECU. Determination of the percentages of large companies per country which are above average and above median gives a striking result: both the UK and Italy have a large share of firms performing below the European standard, whereas German, Swiss, French, and Benelux firms have clear above (average and median) productivity. Both findings are too pronounced to be accounted for by the reservations voiced above with respect to the quality of the statistical base data (see also below, last section Postscript). Moreover, the 1992 figures on average and medium company performance

Table 6.1. Net Added Value per Employee of European large firms (100 largest firms, measured in ECU's)

	Total	Germany	France	Benelux	Sweden/ Norway	Switzerland/ Austria	UK	Italy
					1991 Average company : ECU 39,700 NVA/E Median company : ECU 37,400 NVA/E			
Above Median	51	15	12	4	6.5	3.5	7	1
Below Median	49	8	8	3	5	2	22	3
Total number of firms	100	23	20	7	11.5	5.5	29	4
% above median		65	60	57	59	64	24	25
above average	46	14	11	4	5.5	3.5	8	1
below average	54	9	9	3	6	2	21	3
% above average		61	55	57	48	64	27	25

support the 1991 finding that corporations from the Continental core economies are more productive in the high performance range as those from an Anglo-Saxon origin (Table 6.2). Their average net value added per employee in both years was 20% higher than that of Anglo-Saxon firms.

The conclusions from this table are:

1. Anglo-Saxon corporations contribute some 25% to the net added value of the 100 largest European firms; Continental corporations contribute some 66%.

2. The average size of the largest continental firms is at least one-third higher than of Anglo-Saxon corp.

3. The performance ratio is clearly in favour of the continental firms: 60% versus 30%.

What is the explanation for these marked differences in the performance of large European firms?

We could advance some reasons which, a priori, have some plausibility. Size of business might be one. Scale economies, of whatever nature, might

Table 6.2. A Comparison of Anglo-Saxon and Continental large firms

Size	Number		NAV (bn ECU)		Average NAV (bn ECU)	
	1991	1992	1991	1992	1991	1992
Anglo-Saxon Corp.[1]	29	30	91.4	89.8	3.2	3.0
Continental Corp.[2]	56	57	232.4	250.1	4.2	4.4
100 largest European Corp.	100	100	363.0	374.5	3.6	3.7

| Performance | Net added value per employee | | | | | |
| | Number | | % above median | | % above average | |
	1991	1992	1991	1992	1991	1992
Anglo-Saxon Corp.	29	30	24	30	27	27
Continental Corp.	56	57	63	59	65	55

[1] UK and Irish firms plus Royal Dutch-Shell and Unilever.
[2] German, French, Benelux and Swiss/Austrian firms.

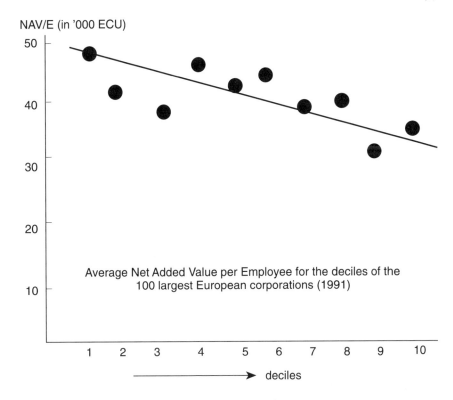

NAV/E (in '000 ECU)

Average Net Added Value per Employee for the deciles of the 100 largest European corporations (1991)

deciles

FIG. 1: Net Added Value per Employee and Corporate size

be responsible for productivity differences; the figures as presented in figure 1 induce one to think of this factor, but, more probably, they reflect the increasing earnings and social charges which accompany larger size of firms, because of the fact that these firms have more mechanized output operated by a higher educated and professionalised staff. Also, unionization and union pressure may be stronger in larger firms. The rise of earnings per employee with an increasing size of plant and firm is a time-honoured and general experience (Sargant Florence, 85/86). Of course, scale economies might, to some extent, contribute to this phenomenon.

The sectoral composition of firms from various countries might deviate, such that some sectors with high or low productivity are more strongly represented in particular countries and thus might influence the results of table 6. Table 7 does indeed point towards such differences in sectoral representation: motorcar and components production is strong in Germany, France and Italy, but not in the UK or Benelux; large chemical firms are of relative importance in Germany and France, while food and drinks firms and retailing corporations figure prominently in Britain. However, the sectoral

Henk de Jong

explanation of the productivity differentials between Britain and Italy on the one hand and the other continental firms on the other hand has to be largely discounted. This follows from the second column of table 7, which gives the level and spread of NAV/E per sector. Countries have prominence in both highly and lowly productive sectors, e.g., Germany in chemicals (high), motorcars (medium), steel (low); France in chemicals, the UK and Switzerland in pharmaceuticals (all highly productive). In general the table conveys a strong impression of the broad distribution of sectoral occupations by large companies throughout the countries, with only two exceptions: Germany has eleven out of 23 firms in only two sectors, and Italy is, given the size of its economy, seriously underrepresented in most sectors (partly due to insufficient data).

One feature which table 7 also brings out, is the wide spread in productivity per sector (column 3). That means that large firms in the same broad sectors of industry show great differences in value productivity per employee: in electrical industry this may differ from 24,200 ECU to 70,000 ECU, in food industry between 13,700 ECU to 66,800 ECU, etc. An interesting question now is: do these differences in value productivity show a sys-

Table 7. Value productivity and sectoral distribution per country.

Sector	N	NAV/E	D	F	UK	NL/B	S/N	Swi/A	I
Auto's & comp.	13	23.0–56.9	5	3	1		2		2
Electricals	7	24.2–70.0	1	2	2	1	0.5	0.5	
Oil & gas	7	36.4–88.6		2	2.5	1.5	1		
Chemicals	13	38.4–58.7	6	3	1	2	1		
Foods	7	13.7–66.8		1	2.5	0.5	1	1	1
Drinks	3	19.5–94.7			3				
Retailing	9	14.8–32.9	2	1	5	1			
Pharma & Cosm.	5	52.6–76.1		1	2			2	
Transport	1	25.2			1				
Steel	4	23.3–33.8	3	1					
Mining; non–ferr.	4	27.7–60.2	2	1	1				
Machinery,comp.	4	20.7–47.0	1	1			1		1
Aircraft	3	23.6–60.2		1	2				
Publishing	1	50.5	1						
Paper	2	37.2–40.8					2		
Public Utilities	3	21.5–36.1		2				1	
Construction	3	24.6–59.5		1	1		1		
Airlines	5	42.4–65.9	1		1	1	1	1	
Telecom	3	36.1–46.2			2		1		
Conglomerates	3	26.7–49.3	1		1	1			
Total	100	13.7–94.7	23	20	28	8	11.5	5.5	4

N = number firms; Shell, Unilever and ABB equally divided between countries; NAV/E = Net added value per employee in thousand ECU. Highest and lowest for the sector

tematic relationship with the nationality of the corporations? Comparing the sectors in which there are five or more corporations represented one arrives at the following results:

– in motorcars and components, all five German firms achieve a value productivity which is above that of the median company of the sector; for French and Italian corporations the picture is mixed, some are above, some below the median; the Swedish and British firms are below that benchmark;
– in electrical industry and electronics, all French and German firms have an above median productivity, whereas the other firms are below; in oil and gas all Continental firms, except one have an above median productivity, but the British firms (except for Shell) are below median;
– in chemicals, nine German and French firms (except for two) are above median; in contrast British, Benelux, and Swedish corporations have a productivity score below the median;
– in foods all Anglo-Saxon firms have a value productivity below the median, whereas the Continental firms are above the standard;
– in retailing, where British firms are strongly represented, their value productivity is below the median, like that of Continental firms; however, even the best British firm, Marks & Spencer, is still way below the firms of Karstadt, Kaufhof, and Carrefour.
– in the pharmaceutical, aircraft and airline sectors, the outcome is mixed, with both Anglo-Saxon firms and Continental firms having a value productivity above and below the median.

Thus, the conclusion is that Anglo-Saxon firms, except for a few (Shell, Glaxo, British Airways) do show a performance which is below that of the European median company, whereas Continental firms, and especially the German and Swiss firms, perform better than the median corporation. It is not the sector orientation which is responsible for the value productivity differences, but rather individual company performance. This conclusion is the more remarkable because it is so general, i.e., it cuts through cyclical and non-cyclical sectors, and through more nationally and multi-nationally oriented firms. Should we then accept that British management is less good than continental leadership? That is hard to believe; most probably the explanation has to be sought elsewhere.

3.3 The theory: performance as a result of corporate structure

The fact that average value productivity of Anglo-Saxon firms is lower than that of Continental corporations does not mean that their profitability is also lower. Table 5 did show already that the share of capital in Anglo-Saxon firms is markedly higher; table 9 clearly demonstrates that

Anglo-Saxon corporations are profit-makers, in contrast to Germanic type
of firms. That table derives from another data base and is constructed as
follows: in the *Financial Times* list of the largest 500 European corporations
for 1991 (January 13, 1992) one assembles the 100 largest firms according
to sales, stock market value and a return on capital employed (ROCE) of
over 25% and allots them to nationalities. For comparative purposes the
100 largest according to the value added derived from the earlier mentioned
source (Financial-Economic Magazine of November 25, 1992) were added.
The results are clearly impressive. Whereas the classifications according to
sales and net value added hardly differ, the other two show that the Anglo-
Saxon firms are profit makers, in contrast to the Germanic corporations
who have size. The Latinic firm shows a more balanced picture than the
other two groups.

Table 8. The 100 largest European corporations.

	Sales	Net Added Value	Market Value	ROCE >25%
Anglo-Saxon Corporations	29	29	44	67
Germanic Corporations	43	45	33	9
Latinic Corporations	28	26	23	24

Note: Shell and Unilever included in the Anglo-Saxon group

By way of explanation, consider the following theory. In figure 2, both types
of corporations are schematically exhibited. The Anglo- Saxon firm is supposed to pursue maximum profits and to limit its expansion to OA, denot-
ing size. Thus its total net added value will be area OACD. In contrast, the
Germanic corporation tries to achieve maximum output, having a net value
added sum of OBEF, at zero profits. In both cases the necessary minimum
dividends and interest payments (at equal rates but proportional to size) are
covered by the distance between the dotted line and GE. In this picture,
depending on the shape of the profit curve, the Germanic corporation will
have a higher mass of net value added (area OBEF) than the Anglo-Saxon
corporation, whereas the latter will earn excess profits. Moreover, its profit
margin (excess profits divided by total net value added) will be positive, as
against a zero margin for the Germanic corporation. In addition, the share
of wages and social charges, as a percentage of total net value added will
be lower for the Anglo-Saxon corporation than for the Germanic corpora-

tion, assuming a labour force proportional to size of resp. OA and OB. But now, starting from this situation, the Germanic corporation will find that its profits are zero and that its bill of wages and social charges is a higher proportion of net value added than that of its international competitors; the management may well decide to rationalise on labour, rather than loose market share. In this way it will improve, comparatively speaking, on its net value added per employee. This rationalization—directly and indirectly—increases unemployment in the European economy, unless small and medium-sized business expands strongly and is able to pick up the labour supply.[3] Note that the Anglo-Saxon corporation pays more government taxes as well, assuming equal rates of profit tax between countries.

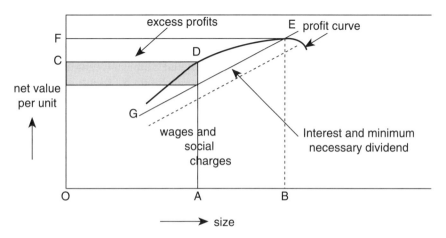

FIG. 2

Thus, the exhibit of figure 2 explains all the relevant features noted earlier, provided we accept the basic assumption that the Anglo-Saxon firm, because of the ownership structure is a profit maximiser and the Germanic or Continental type of firm may strive for sales growth or relatively high market shares. In the latter case, it is not necessary for the corporation to seek sales growth or market share in preference for profits; a strong leadership in the Continental corporation setting high profit goals and sticking to these may well achieve the same outcome as the Anglo-Saxon corporation. Thus, it has—at least in principle—both options, unlike the Anglo-Saxon firm. But more likely is the pursuit of the other goals, because the stakeholders influencing the decisionmaking in a Continental type of firm are

[3] For various reasons this has not been the case (H. W. de Jong 1989: 283–305; Acs and Audretsch 1990: 1–25).

more numerous and more varied in their purposes. Consequently, compromise solutions are found, reflecting the pressures of employees, unions, banks, governments, municipalities, etc. and saving the appearances by keeping the size of the corporation or its market share at the cost of profitability. If shareholders then start to complain, the leadership will feel prompted to seek ways to improve profitability and for both reasons labour and other stakeholders have no excuse not to cooperate. A concerted effort to improve productivity will restore the balance. This is the virtuous productivity cycle, based on the cooperative model of the firm. In a recent USA publication, various authors arrive at a similar conclusion (Mishel and Voos 1992).

Another feature explained by this theory is the sectoral distribution of the respective types of corporations (Table 7). In mass-production types of industries like motorcars, chemicals, steel, mining and non-ferrous metals, and (to a lesser extent) electrical industry, the Anglo-Saxon corporation is underrepresented and the Continental firm is over-represented (oil and paper are exceptions for obvious locational and historical reasons). In contrast, Anglo-Saxon corporations are overpresented in the sectors where markets are differentiatible and/or nationally circumscribed (foods and drinks, pharmaceuticals, retailing, business services). Such markets allow firms to continually seek the maximum profitability of point D in figure 1, for example by means of brands and advertising. Thus, they suit the performance goals flowing from the structural type of the Anglo-Saxon firm. The shape of the profit curve is of importance. A strong decline after point D favours an Anglo-Saxon type of strategy, whereas a gradual sloping of the curve over a long stretch towards E spurs the firm's leadership to pursue a Continental strategy. It would seem that these shapes of the profitability curve correspond to the sectors of industry in which both types of corporations excel. Again, if we would compare the hundred largest firms in the service industries not included in the previous tables, the finding would be that Anglo-Saxon corporations are strongly represented in business services whereas in financial services the distribution corresponds more closely to the size of the economies concerned (M. W. de Jong 1991: 342–345; Elfring 1993: 385–392).

4. CORPORATE STRUCTURE AND LONG-RUN GROWTH

The explanation given in part 3 has clear implications as to developments in the corporate landscape. One might derive the following tendencies:

First, the Anglo-Saxon type of corporation has generally lost out to Continental and Japanese firms between 1960 and 1990. Table 10 is based on Franko's (1991) selection of the 180 largest corporations in the world

Table 9. Distribution of corporate types, 1960–1990.

Corporate Type	1960	1970	1980	1990
Anglo-Saxon	140	125	106	76
Continental	30	34	47	56
Japanese	4	18	23	37
Other	—	—	3	3
Total	174	177	179	172

Note: Not all industry columns added up to 12 firms. Firms from the US, UK, Canada, Australia, and New Zealand were included as Anglo-Saxon type of firms.

Source: Franko, 1991. Table 1.

Table 10. The 500 largest firms in the world.

	1967	1992	Difference	Distribution of the rest in 1992
United States	280	142	−138	19
Canada	10	8	−2	—
Europe	114	141	+27	19
Japan	29	115	+86	13
Other Countries	5	32	+27	11
Total	438	438		62
Of which in Europe:				
United Kingdom	46	37	−9	4
Germany	24	29	+5	3
France	18	27	+9	3
Benelux	8	11	+3	1
Italy	7	6	−1	—
Portugal/Spain	—	5	+5	—
EFTA	11	26	+15	8
Total	114	141	+27	19

Sources: Rowthorn (1971) and Fortune 1993

throughout three decades. If available, the 12 largest firms were listed per sector and distributed to corporate types for each of the successive years. The 15 large industrial sectors, including banking, were derived from the *Fortune* lists.

Another approach, also based on the *Fortune* 500 gives the same tendency. In table 10, I have compared Rowthorn's (1971) distribution of the

438 largest companies in the world for 1967 with the distribution of those largest companies for 1992, and, again, there is a substantial increase in the share of the Japanese and Continental European firms and a marked decline of the Anglo-Saxon type of corporation.

Table 11. Multinational firms in advanced sectors

1992	Total Sales (bn$)	US	Europe	Japan
Motor Cars & comp.	940.4	298.0	321.4	296.6
Petroleum Ind.	902.5	354.9	334.6	82.1
Electronics & app.	736.4	163.7	210.4	270.9
Chemicals	405.2	116.1	210.0	76.0
Pharmaceuticals	164.4	83.6	60.9	15.8
Computers	232.7	125.1	12.2	95.3
Machinery	231.0	47.4	107.5	69.4
Aerospace	169.4	124.2	41.5	—
Total	3782.0	1313.0	1298.5	906.1
Firms Total	500	161	160	128
of which in advanced sectors		90	87	72
% share in sales		55.9	54.4	56.3

Source: *Fortune*, The Global 500, 1993

Table 11 gives the distribution of the 500 largest corporations between the three main economic regions in terms of advanced sectors. The 500 largest corporations had in 1992 combined sales of nearly $5500 billion, which were a share of 40% of the total GDP of the US, Europe, and Japan. Of the 27 sectors of industry distinguished by Fortune, eight have been selected as advanced sectors. Their sales were $3780 billion, being two-thirds of the total. It will be seen that:

– the shares of European and American firms are now about equal; the Japanese share is 80% (in numbers) and 70% (in sales) of the USA/European share;
– the shares in advanced sectors are about equal;
– there is specialization in sectors according to economic regions; and
– In service sectors there is likewise specialization between the main economic areas, though the Japanese share is much less prominent.

Second, the decline was a general one, though in varying proportions as between sectors. The decline was modest in aerospace, foods and drinks, business services, pharmaceuticals, computers and office equipment; it was severe in chemicals, steel, non-ferrous metals, banking, textiles, electrical equipment and electronics, motorcars and tires. The Continental firm lost out in textiles only, and stabilized in aerospace, machinery and tyres. In all other sectors it had a growing share in the number of the largest firms, as the Japanese corporation also had. But large Japanese firms were practically not represented at all in sectors like paper, petroleum, chemicals, pharmaceuticals, aerospace, foods and drinks; in contrast they manifested themselves strongly in textiles, banks, motorcars and tires, computers and electronics. Thus, the tremendous shift in the distribution of the largest companies over the various types, was accompanied by an increasing specialization over the sectors of industry. Similar tendencies are visible if one looks at market shares instead of number of firms (Franko: 1991, Table 1).

Third, within Europe there was a strong growth of German, French, Benelux, and Swiss firms, in accordance with their high value productivity, whereas the (modest) Italian share was stable and the UK share declined. In 1970, the Anglo-Saxon type of corporation (UK firms plus Shell and Unilever) had over one-third, in 1990 less than one-fifth as a share of the 180 largest firms. (Table 9); according to the approach used in table 10, the UK share declined from 40% in 1967 to 26% in 1992.

5. CONCLUSION

We therefore end up with the general conclusion that the Anglo-Saxon type of corporation, even though it achieves a remarkably better profitability than the Continental firm, has a lesser degree of value productivity and also a lower growth rate. Consequently, its average size in terms of total net value added is now less than that of the Continental firm and it is losing out in all sectors of industry. The latter tendency is quite marked in mass production types of industry and in banking, but less so where product differentiation by means of reputation, of advertising and R&D spendings are important such as is the case in business-services, foods and drinks, pharmaceuticals, and aerospace. The strong merger intensity and the free market for corporate control which exist in Anglo-Saxon corporate capitalism are obviously not a sufficient counterweight to the high value productivity based on the social coherence which is the distinguishing characteristic of the Continental (and Japanese) type of capitalist enterprise. Clearly, corporate structure guides performance into different directions and, in the long run, changes the corporate landscape.

Finally, the reader should note that the achievement of maximum profits is not a necessary condition for a well-functioning capitalist system. Profits are an ex post, distributional category of uncertain magnitude, of which firms must have a satisfactory level to attract capital suppliers. The justification for a (large) firm's existence is, however, its generation of increasing surplus value through time.

POSTSCRIPT

Since this article was written data on Net Added Value for the years 1993 and 1994 have become available and were published in the Financial Economic Magazine of November 1994 and 1995. These data and their processing according to the procedures described in the article, confirm the main points, viz. the differences in value productivity and profitability of the respective types of corporations. Average net value added per employee for the years 1991–1994 were 48,000 ECU for Germanic corporations, 46,000 ECU for Latinic corporations and 41,700 for Anglo-Saxon firms. The percentages of the firms having an above-median NAV/employee were resp. 56.8, 53.2 and 35.3. On the other hand, the share of capital suppliers in the total net value added for those years was remarkably higher for the Anglo-Saxon firms (23.5%) than for Germanic (8.8%) and Latinic firms (14.4%).

The currency troubles which occurred in 1992/3 did not substantially influence the results, partly because the three regions included countries, the currencies of which depreciated against the ECU. It is true that the British firms which already had an above-average productivity in 1991 further improved their performance, and a few which were not so good in 1991 recovered remarkably. But several of the weaker ones dropped out of the lists altogether, so that the number of Anglo-Saxon firms receded further, in tune with the tendency outlined in tables 9 and 10. In sum, the conclusions drawn in section 5 can be vindicated also with respect to the extended period 1991–1994.

7

Regulatory Competition as Regulatory Capture: The Case of Corporate Law in the United States of America

WILLIAM W. BRATTON AND JOSEPH A. McCAHERY*

I. INTRODUCTION: GOVERNANCE BY INSTITUTIONAL
SHAREHOLDERS AND CORPORATE FEDERALISM

America has a standing agenda of corporate governance reform items. All the items pursue a common, but elusive goal—the institutionalization of effective contractual regulation of corporate managers. The goal appeared to be within easy reach twenty years ago. It was then thought that transactions in markets for corporate control, corporate products, and corporate employment imported sufficient discipline. But intervening business cycles and regulatory barriers have reduced prospects for corporate control through the indirect means of discrete market contracts. Accordingly, the focus of reform initiatives has shifted to the field of relational contracts. There strategies have been mapped out to establish a shareholder role in the ongoing negotiation and monitoring of corporate contracts as the means to the end of reducing the costs of management influence[1] within the firm. The strategists look to activist agents of shareholding investment institutions to execute these plans. The plans thereby confront, and purport to surmount, longstanding economic and legal barriers to collective action by shareholders.

This shareholder participation movement has had modest successes. Activist institutions have challenged the authority of managers of unsuccessful firms by making use of a federally-mandated privilege to have shareholder governance proposals included in management's annual proxy statement and submitted for a vote.[2] The institutions submit proposals for

---

* This chapter is a condensation of the authors' 'Regulatory Competition, Regulatory Capture, and Corporate Self-Regulation', 73 North Carolina Law Review 1861 (1995), which holds the copyright.

[1] See Milgrom and Roberts (1988: 156).

[2] Management must include in the annual proxy statement precatory shareholder proposals that meet process and suitability guidelines set down in the Securities Exchange Commission's Rule 14a–8, 17 C.F.R. sect. 240.14a–8 (1994).

contract terms designed either to alleviate problems of informational asymmetry between managers and monitors or to help to realign incentives to reduce the costs of management influence (cf. Milgrom and Roberts 1990: 82). These interventions are dialogic in character because the governing federal rules provide that the proposals lead only to nonbinding votes. But they can precipitate reforms nevertheless. The proposing institution signals its dissatisfaction with the target firm's performance, and thereby impugns the reputational interests of its managers. The managers as a result often negotiate contractual concessions with the proponent as a way of securing the proposal's withdrawal. Sustained institutional pressure of this sort can have more significant consequences, prompting the board to replace the chief executive officer or even to restructure the firm's line of business.

These discrete, issue-based institutional interventions stand in contrast to two other possible modes of shareholder participation—coalition-based voting for institutional representation on the board of directors and relational investment in large blocks of shares. These are fuller relational models that hold out a prospect of larger governance payoffs through sustained, high-intensity monitoring. They loom large in the commentary but have not yet shown up in the practice because they present unsolved collective action problems. The discrete voting contests seen in practice entail low out-of-pocket costs and serve as vehicles for reputational gain by a narrow segment of institutional agents. In contrast, proxy solicitations for institutional board representatives and institutional block-holding entail substantial investments without a clear-cut financial or reputational payoff. Existing federal regulations add to the costs.

Law reform commentary on shareholder participation directs itself to the removal of these federal regulatory barriers. But, significantly, the commentary also leaves open a question as to whether, even given the barriers' removal, institutional volunteers would have financial incentives sufficient to justify investment in full-scale participation. This open incentive question makes it plausible to project that the contractual renegotiation of governance terms instanced by issue-based voting challenges will dominate over direct monitoring of investment decisionmaking as the means to the end of value creation through shareholder participation.

We note an imbalance in the commentary. The law reform movement tends to press against the federal side of a two-sided system, foregoing consideration of the state law (and federalism) implications of the shareholder participation strategies that have succeeded. Today's activists would play with stronger hands if they could propose binding contractual amendments in addition to the nonbinding resolutions provided for in the present federal procedure. But state law effectively blocks such proposals by granting management complete control over the voting agenda respecting the charter, the central corporate contract. No one questions that this state-mandated agenda control restricts shareholder enforcement opportunities (see, e.g., Black 1992: 825–26). Even so, state law tends to be overlooked in the legal confrontation with impediments to shareholder collective action. The commentary's imbalance is surprising given the general view that the state system operated during the 1980s to impose excessive constraints on the operation of the market deterrent.

In this chapter, we carry the confrontation with legal impediments to shareholder participation to state corporate law and the system of competitive incentives that shape it. We survey the legal landscape that channels discrete institutional interventions and explore possibilities for expanding the menu of contractual reforms attainable through shareholder initiative. In so doing we make a new theoretical case for a reform proposal made in passing many times in the past:[3] Federal preemption of state law's allocation to management of an exclusive privilege to initiate corporate charter amendments. We argue that this reform would ameliorate some of the cost and incentive barriers that impede institutional shareholder action.

This recommendation requires us to confront the theory of regulatory competition that legitimates the state system. American corporations are free to chose their state of incorporation, and the states compete for their legal business. In the view of the system's proponents, this market mechanism results in a relational contract between the state and the chartering firm and thereby assures state responsiveness to the preferences of those who stake capital in corporations. We counter that the political and process characteristics of this relational contract are not fully explored in the proponents' market-based model of regulatory competition. This causes their model to understate distortions resulting from the interplay of multiple sovereigns and interest groups in the resolution of corporate commitment, information, and enforcement problems. In our counter story, competition facilitates and entrenches the capture of the mandating sovereign by one of two contracting parties, the managers. This arrangement effectively prevents the other party, the shareholders, both from registering any demands at the law's formation stage and from participating in the negotiation of corporate contracts. Corporate law, as a result, evolves with neither optimal mandatory terms nor effective process rules for opting out of default terms.[4]

The system, thus described, presents a mixed problem of economics and politics. Such a problem, in our view, calls for a mixed political and economic solution. We look for guidance to learning from the field of public

---

[3] See, e.g., Cary (1974: 702); Black (1990a: 582); Coffee (1987: 744–76); cf. Romano (1993: 83–84); Macey (1994: 944).

[4] The proponents also offer too simple a picture of the incentives that determine the behavior of Delaware, the leading chartering state. In the capture model presented here, state-federal political instability emerges as a positive force that occasionally causes Delaware to confront conflicting demands of managers and shareholders and effect a somewhat more even-handed mediation between them.

regulation, learning that highlights the formative role that process and structure rules play in capture's amelioration. We show that these theories of public regulation can be adapted to the private governance situation of the corporation, providing a basis for central government intervention that refrains from displacing the states' role in corporate law creation but removes some of their mandatory process rules. Preemptive intervention, thus narrowly targeted, would open opportunities both for shareholder participation in contract negotiation and shareholder influence on the formation of state law. It would thereby leave the ultimate solution of the corporate agency problems to the economic actors themselves, and provide the states with incentives to make balanced responses when their preferences conflict.

2. REGULATORY CAPTURE AND THE SUPPLY AND DEMAND DYNAMIC OF THE CHARTER COMPETITION SYSTEM

2.1 The corrupt sovereign versus the responsive sovereign

The original case for federal intervention against state charter competition combined a public interest theory of regulation with a fiduciary strategy for improving corporate law. William L. Cary's leading article denounced Delaware, the leading corporate domicile,[5] as a corrupt sovereign (Cary 1974). In his view, there appeared to be 'no public policy left in Delaware corporate law other than the objective of raising revenue.' The 'public policy' at stake was the integrity of corporate managers; the revenue objective had led a single state to 'grant management unilateral control untrammeled by other interests,' thereby sacrificing the national interest (Cary 1974: 684, 697–98). Cary looked to federal intervention to eliminate the firms' incentives to incorporate in Delaware.

Cary assumed that regulation could and should pursue a notion of the general good. By the time he wrote in 1974, however, that theory of regulation had already fallen from favour in the social sciences, to be replaced by capture theories of regulation (Levine & Forrence 1990: 168–69; Olson 1965: 14–22). These described regulation as an arena in which special interests compete to use government power for advantage. They also debunked the public interest story of regulatory motivation—now regulators should be expected to behave no differently than actors in private economic relations. This shift in political theory, coupled with the emerging market deterrent view of corporate law, permitted Cary's race to the bottom to be reversed into a race to the top (Winter 1977: 254–62).

---

[5] Delaware is home to one half of the largest American corporations, and the new domicile of 80 percent of reincorporating firms (Romano 1985: 244).

The race to the top story drew on the central assertion of regulatory competition theory—that jurisdictional competition ameliorates the distortions that result as interest groups compete for, and win, political favours. Under this theory, competition for domiciliaries causes government policies to be matched with diverse citizen preferences and thus fosters innovation (Romano 1993: 4–5). Citizens signal their preferences respecting legal goods and services when they migrate from régime to régime. Their ability to exit disempowers government actors, whose welfare diminishes as citizens depart, taking along votes and revenues (Daniels 1991: 142–43). Given competition, law production goes forward without time consumed on the task of reconciling competing preferences. The theory also implies a preference for state over national lawmaking. Since the revenue enhancement constraint on the national government is less intense, the national lawmaking process will be slower, less responsive to productive concerns, and more susceptible to the influence of organized interest groups (Romano 1993: 4–5, 48).

Regulatory competition theory applies to corporate law on the assumption that state corporation codes may be viewed as products consumed by corporations. In the resulting description, competition for the legal business of firms forces the states to adapt the law on a trial and error basis to the dynamic conditions in which the firms operate (Romano 1993: 6, 9). Reincorporating firms are the marginal consumers of this legal product. They seek a predictable legal régime that reduces their costs. Delaware provides this with comprehensive case law, well-specified indemnification rules, and an expert judiciary (ibid. 32–34, 39). The firms also seek a guaranty that the new state of domicile will maintain the desirability of its code—the reincorporating firm and the target jurisdiction enter into a relational contract that entails a risk of opportunistic breach. Even as the firm invests to gain access to the target's favorable legal régime, the target remains free to change its politics and transform itself into an unresponsive jurisdiction. The competitive jurisdiction has to reduce this possibility by offering a credible commitment. Delaware's commitment stems from its dependence on franchise tax revenues—the coupling of a small population and a large number of incorporations has caused these to amount to between ten and twenty percent of its total tax revenues in recent decades (Romano 1993: 36–37). Delaware also invests in assets specific to its incorporation business—its caselaw, and judicial and administrative expertise. The commitment and the assets together constitute a reputational capital that Delaware protects with internal process and structure rules that deter political disruption.[6] The store of capital bolsters its market position. Other

---

[6] These include its direction of corporate matters to a specialized chancery court, its practice of appointing rather than electing its judges and limiting them to twelve year terms, and its requirement of two-thirds majorities of both houses of its legislature for the approval of corporation code amendments (Romano 1993: 38–42).

states cannot credibly precommit to offer superior service, and thus are deterred from incurring the necessary start-up costs. A first-mover advantage in Delaware results (ibid. 40–41, 43–44).

As originally articulated, this market-based race to the top validation of state law bypassed the problem of the shareholders' lack of influence over state lawmaking with a reference to the control market deterrent. The assertion, in effect, was that the managers' option of exit adequately disciplined the states, while the possibility of shareholder exit by tender to a hostile offeror adequately disciplined the managers. This story lost its persuasiveness as managers and state politicians collaborated to hamper the market deterrent with the antitakeover legislation of the 1980s. This manifest case of charter market failure reinforced the opponents' assertion that the system leads to suboptimal lawmaking. Following the lead of Roberta Romano (1985), the market deterrent school moved to a middle ground position on charter competition (see also Winter 1989: 1528; Easterbrook and Fischel 1991: 222). There they defend the state system, except to the extent that it inhibits the control market.

Others returned to the attack. Lucian Bebchuk (1992), taking the lead,[7] argued that the middle ground result stems from a structural defect in the competitive system that disables the production of a maximizing legal régime. The market leads the competing states to focus on the variables that influence reincorporation decisions. From this there follows a concern for management preferences rather than shareholder value itself. Accordingly, nothing deters the states from pursuing policies of management accommodation respecting the fiduciary and market deterrents (ibid. 1452–75). Bebchuk concluded that much state takeover regulation should be preempted and federal fiduciary standards should be imposed (ibid. 1495).

Debate on the desirability of federal intervention continues among those occupying different middle ground views of charter competition. At the debate's bottom line lies the allocation of the theoretical burden of proof for or against intervention, the assumption being that the side bearing the burden loses the game. Several points have been sharply controverted. Opponents of intervention point to a body of event studies showing that reincorporation in Delaware does not reduce shareholder value; proponents argue that convergence among the states on the basic points of corporate law denude the results of persuasiveness (compare Romano 1985; Romano 1993: 18, with Bebchuk 1992: 1449–50; Eisenberg 1989: 1508; Coffee 1987: 767–78). Opponents draw on a contractual theory of the firm and point out that new federally-mandated fiduciary deterrents would retard the evolution of contractual corporate arrangements; proponents respond that the consensus view on contracting out continues to favour fiduciary mandates in

[7] See also Bratton (1994: 437–40); Charny (1992: 441–43); Seligman (1993: 60–63); Karmel, (1991: 91–96).

view of the rational apathy that impedes shareholder choices of governance terms (compare Romano 1993: 90–91, with Bebchuk 1992: 1496–99). Opponents argue that the federal political landscape remains as hostile as that of the states, making perverse effects a likely result of a law reform movement; proponents respond that the federal venue is marginally more hospitable and that centralized politics facilitate shareholder collective action (compare Romano 1993: 75–82, with Bratton 1994: 432).

2.2 Charter competition as regulatory capture

This middle ground discussion of federal intervention takes on the binary quality of the old race to the top/race to the bottom discussion as its participants iterate positions from the historic debate over market and fiduciary deterrent strategies. But, as the replay has proceeded, both sides have recognized possibilities for both market success and market failure. This more open-ended theoretical framework allows more flexibility in the diagnosis of the problem. And, significantly, the stronger assertions of regulatory competition theory have dropped out of the picture for the most part. The 1980s antitakeover alliance between the states and the managers has dispelled the notion that identification of a market phenomenon at a significant stage in the lawmaking process, taken alone, assures the ideal result of legislation based solely on the exogenous preferences of individuals. It has become clear that imbalanced interest group influence in this market-driven lawmaking process prevents that result, divesting regulatory competition theory of a legitimating effect.

Regulatory competition matches individual preferences and legal results because actors have the opportunity to exit cheaply from an unsatisfactory jurisdiction. The charter system, of course, does allow for exit from an unsatisfactory jurisdiction, but, because the exit privilege applies to firms rather than to shareholders, it does nothing to ameliorate the agency problem. Corporate law has evolved under charter competition so as to block shareholder access to the determination of reincorporation decisions. Existing market disciplines offer no way around that barrier because they create no incentives to encourage the development of a shareholder-favourable state. Successful control contests, whether by takeover or proxy fight, displace one group of managers with another. The displacing group, unless it has taken the firm private, remains in an agency relationship with the firm's shareholders and thus has no reason to look for a jurisdiction activated by the shareholder interest.[8] And, due to the peculiarities of

---

[8] The displacing group that plans to make further acquisitions with the target has an interest in the removal of state law antitakeover barriers. But reincorporation to a hypothetical shareholder-favorable jurisdiction would not help with this problem, since the law of the target jurisdiction applies in a takeover. The only solution to the acquiring firm's problem, then,

America's constitutional structure, the competing jurisdictions—which lack a balancing incentive—have national lawmaking power over the shareholders of domiciliary corporations. In this variant of regulatory competition, then, exit from one jurisdiction provides no remedy for the dissatisfactions of the disadvantaged interest group.

A. Capture theories of regulation

The mixed framework invites the retelling of the charter competition story in terms of politics of interest groups and organizations, both economic and governmental. In this story, charter competition becomes the mainspring of a uniquely stable arrangement of regulatory capture.

Under capture theories of regulation, interest groups and political decisionmakers enter into jointly maximizing relationships. The simple demand model of capture asserts that lawmaking follows lawmakers' responses to demand patterns (Tollison 1988: 343; Posner 1982: 265). Particular responses depend on interactions between the lawmaker's risk profiles and the projected benefits of legislative action (Peltzman 1976: 214; Stigler 1971: 10–13). The lawmaker, being risk averse, tries to avoid conflicts—given no demand for legislation, nothing is done; given organized demand, the lawmaker attempts to satisfy the interest group making the demand with beneficial legislation (Becker 1983: 371–99). In addition, interest groups desiring to influence legislation encounter collective action problems. Different groups have variant abilities to overcome them—the smaller the group and the higher the per capita stake of its members, the greater the likelihood that the members will work out a collective arrangement and enjoy the benefits of governmental influence (Olson 1965). This activity results in a social loss from rent-seeking (Higgins, Shugart and Tollison 1988: 127–28; Tullock 1980: 46–47): Legislators create rents for the benefit of successful interest groups, distributing them based on a self-seeking vote calculus (Mitchell 1990: 98–99; Weingast 1984: 148–49).

An additional body of capture theory supplements this demand model with a supply side story. Exclusively demand-based models of law production tend to treat the political process as a black box and, as a result, do not attempt to describe how legislative trades are accomplished and enforced (Weingast and Marshall 1988: 133). This is a problem, since legislative trades, unlike private contracts, can be undone at the subsequent behest of a competing group. For example, an interest group deal, obtained in the legislature through logrolling and other trading mechanisms and then

is interest group pressure to work against antitakeover legislation nationwide. But at this point conflicting interests among acquiring firms enter into the picture. Today's acquirer may be tomorrow's target; the managers of large acquirers can afford to be patient and work around state barriers in making hostile acquisitions, meanwhile enjoying the prerogatives of the state law regime.

embodied in a legislative directive, can be undercut later by an administrative agency responding to a competing interest group. Or, more simply, a piece of legislation later can be amended or repealed because a competing group makes its influence felt on the legislature. Supply side explanations of interest group dealmaking confront this problem of political insecurity by drawing on organizational economics for the point that institutional arrangements have an impact on outcomes. This body of work disaggregates the government into a complex of principal-agent relationships (McCubbins 1987; Weingast 1984). In these models, legislatures develop process and structure machinery to control the opportunistic conduct of both career bureaucrats and legislators[9] (McCubbins 1989: 441). These devices include the legislative committee system, which helps to overcome problems of asymmetric information between legislative principals and bureaucratic agents through ex post monitoring, and process requirements for rulemaking, which provide advance notice of noncomplying conduct.[10] The processes of the legislature also contribute to transactional stability—legislative procedures and committee jurisdictions give the congressional gate-keeper the ability to resist short-term internal pressures (Shepsle 1992: 245).

B. Charter competition as a form of capture

These capture theories of legislation and administration provide a useful basis for explaining the success of the charter competition system and the preeminence of Delaware. Exit through reincorporation provides a potent ex post enforcement device to the managers who purchase legislation from the state, particularly a small state dependent on charter revenues. Ex ante, the code the managers purchase provides them with control of the enforcing exit decision by blocking shareholder access to the charter. The state's incentive to collect rents from new incorporations assures that the process legislation securing the exit route will not be amended during a future period so as to make exit more difficult.

Thus the state's rent incentive joins the deterrent of possible reincorporation to assure the managers that the deal will stick. The combination does more than that, however. It also mitigates any collective action problems the managers might encounter in getting the future legislation. Should

---

[9] A related, and more abstract, line of discourse considers the effects of given modes of voting process on the ordering of preferences among elected representatives, refuting the chaos predicted under early social choice theory. See, e.g., Ordeshook (1986: 267–301); Baron and Ferejohn (1989: 1189–98); Coleman and Ferejohn (1986: 9).

[10] For a formal agency model of information asymmetries and capture relationships between legislatures and agencies, and producer groups and public interest groups, see Laffont and Tirole (1993: 480–500). But cf. Shleifer and Vishny (1994), who claim that an approach turning on information asymmetries is not plausible in cases where the problem of inefficiency is essential to the performance of politicians (for example, state run enterprises), and that, therefore, corruption is central to the operation of the firm.

desired legislation not be obtained, exit can be effected unilaterally, and there will remain up to 49 states from which to choose. Furthermore, the chartering state's rent flow includes fees to practicing lawyers in addition to franchise taxes. This assures an identity of interests between management and key actors on the supply side. In this scheme, the organized bar in the chartering state can be expected to act as an effective advocate for the management interest, without forcing management to organize a trade association to enter into a formal lobbying relationship. Delaware practice confirms this prediction. Delaware delegates both agenda control respecting, and drafting responsibility for, any amendments to its corporate code to its bar association. The bar and legislature have a longstanding 'understanding'— amendments to the corporations code must first be drafted and approved by the bar association's corporate law section and the bar association itself.[11]

Capture by charter competition exacerbates the shareholders' collective action problem even as it ameliorates management's. State law not only blocks shareholder access to the charter, it provides only management with routine compensation for expenses incurred in voting contests.[12] Meanwhile, the bar emerges as the only interest group within the chartering state having an incentive to advance the shareholders' interest in lawmaking processes. Litigating lawyers promote shareholder welfare as an incident to making a living as enforcers of the fiduciary deterrent. Unfortunately, this confluence of interests results in a strictly limited set of shareholder benefits. The lawyers would have an incentive to promote lawmaking that strengthens the market deterrent only if the change holds out a prospect of prompting additional litigable disputes. The same would go for lawmaking that enhances possibilities for shareholder-enforced self-regulation. Such incentives seem unlikely to arise in practice. Fiduciary breaches that bring rents to lawyers stem from excess management influence; any market or self-regulatory governance strategy that has a cognizable chance of working well in practice ultimately threatens to diminish those rents by reducing the incidence of unproductive influence activities. In addition, the bar's interest diverges from the shareholders' even within the sphere of fiduciary enforcement, with the bar favoring a system that trades substantial money judgments to shareholders in exchange for substantial attorneys' fees.

In short, no interest group in the chartering state has a rent incentive reliably tied to the advancement of the shareholders' interest in the minimiza-

---

[11] See Moore (1987: 779–81). Active drafting and discussion is largely limited to the corporate law section, which performs the legislative function of sifting the comments of interested parties. Each of the three largest corporate servicing firms have representatives to the section. The legislature rubber stamps the bar's recommendations (Alva 1990: 888–92, 910).

[12] See *Rosenfeld* v. *Fairchild Engine & Airplane Corp.*, 128 N.E. 2d 291 (N.Y. 1955; Bebchuk and Kahan 1990).

tion of influence costs within the firm. The shareholders, then, must self-organize in order to advance an agenda in state lawmaking processes. Unfortunately, the charter competition system structurally limits prospects for payoffs that would justify the costs of organization. Furthermore, any sustained shareholder effort would have to be pursued in multiple jurisdictions. By default, then, federal law emerges as the preferred venue for organized shareholder efforts to alter legal structures so as to make firms operate more effectively (Bratton 1994: 430–33). Federal lawmakers, unlike their counterparts in the states, have not been captured by the management side pursuant to a deal with sticking power. This is, of course, only a negative qualification that by no means implies probable success for a shareholder influence campaign. Process costs still loom large at the federal level, and management retains both organizational advantages and well-worn paths of influence. But the turf at least is open. Rent incentives tied to chartering decisions are absent, and a large number of players, each making complex and political calculations in a dynamic environment, makes it easier to contest management influence.[13]

2.3 Conflicting demands on the captured state

We draw no race to the bottom conclusions from this capture model of corporate lawmaking. Rather, the model serves to explicate the theoretical implications of the middle ground framework, putting a different gloss on the same practices purveyed as productive relational contracting in the race to the top story. Since many matters of state corporate law find shareholder and management interests in alignment, it complicates but does not displace the relational contract reading.

The capture model does suggest exploration of strategies of federal intervention designed to diminish state law's imbalanced supply side incentives and imbalanced opportunities to make demands. But it does not thereby imply that federal fiduciary standards are the most desirable mode of intervention. Federal fiduciary standards would ameliorate both the supply and demand side problems by imposing shareholder-favorable norms. They also would entail a difficult trade off, because process infirmities could follow from the appointment of the federal judicial system to the shareholder guardian role. The infirmities lie in the possibility that a pre-emptive change in the venue of corporate common lawmaking from the Delaware courts to the federal courts would so materially alter the composition of the product sold in the charter market as to denude Delaware of significant relational capital. The loss of the first-mover role in common lawmaking would leave

---

[13] The SEC embodies this possibility—historically, its actors tend to satisfy the demands of neither the shareholder nor the management side. And, they bring an inherited, albeit limited ideology of shareholder protection to their ongoing mediative activities.

Delaware marketing a product of diminished value and weaken its relational tie with firms. The rents that support Delaware as a center of information on corporate governance disputes would dissipate, possibly leading to corporate lawmaking on a level of diminished sophistication.

Thus one assertion of regulatory competition theory—that national lawmaking processes carry process infirmities avoided when the subject matter is left to the competing states—continues to bear on the debate. The captured state system can enhance economic welfare to the extent that its competitive element causes the lawmaker to weigh regulations' effect on the firm as a whole and take possible harm to it into account. Arguably, then, the preferred solution to the corporate agency problem leaves the subject matter with the states but finds a means to interpose the shareholder interest into state lawmakers' demand picture. This would render the capture benign.

Past practice provides a base point from which to begin this reordering of incentives. Shareholder demands have, in fact, figured into the existing competitive régime in a secondary posture, influencing the shape of Delaware's fiduciary caselaw. This result appears surprising if we view state law under the pure product competition model. To account for it, the model must be expanded to encompass the political instability that results from the national attention that Delaware lawmaking attracts because of its dominant market position.

A. Delaware lawmaking and the threat of federal intervention

The deal struck between the chartering state and management can never be entirely secure because the possibility of removal of corporate lawmaking to the federal level inheres in the constitutional structure of the United States of America. Delaware, as the entity most dependent on corporate law revenues, is the contracting state most prone to view that possibility as a threat. This structural constant suggests that Delaware lawmakers may have secondary incentives to respond to shareholder interests (see Bebchuk 1992: 1455; Eisenberg 1989: 1512; Cary 1974: 688).

It plausibly can be hypothesized that Delaware actors remain averse to possible destructive exercises of federal preemptive power and have incentives to avoid exciting its application. Federal law reform discussions of the past two decades have given Delaware actors cause for concern because the often-proposed remedy of federal fiduciary standards would have an adverse impact on their interests. This vulnerability stems from the competitive evolution of corporate statutory law. Competition has caused state corporate codes to converge in their broad outlines. The result is that Delaware's case law, judges, and speedy process figure prominently in its substantive law product line (Ayres 1992: 1414–15; Manning 1987: 784–85).

Federal assumption of the large fiduciary component of this product might deprive Delaware of the principal justification for its premium price, resulting in an outbreak of price competition in the market and the erosion of Delaware's position as an informational center.

Recognition of a perceived federal threat implies a model in which Delaware faces conflicting demands, each threatening potential negative consequences. First, the management interest must be satisfied to prevent corporate migration out of the state and entry into competition by competing states. Second, federal actors, as proxies for the shareholders, must be satisfied to avoid destructive intervention. The conflicting demands complicate the business of response: The conflict leaves Delaware with an incentive to avoid taking the lead in adopting rules favouring managers at the shareholders' expense. Other states have a different incentive. If they offer innovative management side payments they may siphon business from Delaware; if the federal government intervenes to stop them, they lose little. So long as a given state has a small market share, its actions attract little attention. Delaware, in contrast, cannot take any significant steps without close scrutiny nationwide (Eisenberg 1989: 1512–13). It remains under pressure to follow new developments elsewhere, but emerges in a mediative role.

A question arises as to how Delaware, alone in this competing demand situation, can structure a mediative response without losing business, given a market still keyed to management preferences.[14] Two factors make this picture plausible. First, no full service alternative domicile exists, and only a handful of other jurisdictions have strong incentives to incur the start up costs to market a full service operation. But a potential competitor has no assurance that a third jurisdiction will not duplicate its efforts (Daniels 1991: 182), and given the low cost of reincorporation (Black 1990: 586–90), no assurance that its new customers will remain. Second, the shareholders' newly discovered capability of self-protective collective action may effectively deter management reincorporation proposals. Beginning in the late 1980s, incidents of shareholder resistance caused managers to drop the assumption of automatic shareholder approval of antitakeover proposals requiring charter amendment (Rock 1991: 484; Black 1990b: 571). Thus, departure from Delaware may not be the open option it used to be.

Evidence of the dual demand model's robustness can be found in the recent pattern of Delaware lawmaking. Given statutory convergence among the states

---

[14] Delaware's mediative output can be explained in terms of the interests of managers as a group—well-timed interventions to protect shareholders serve to defuse the federal threat and to make Delaware a buffer state that protects corporations from federal intervention. But the benefits of a mediative jurisprudence are more questionable from the point of view of individual managers seeking an optimal environment. They have an apparent incentive to cause their firms to migrate to states adopting less equivocal antitakeover policies, free riding on the firms that stay. Of course, if a large number of firms surmounted this collective action barrier and successfully shopped for a more responsive jurisdiction, federal intervention becomes more likely. The same thing might happen if a large number of firms left Delaware, starting a new race to the bottom.

and the dominance of the management interest, the problems of conflicting demand show up only intermittently in the corporate legislative process. Antitakeover legislation is the principal recent instance, and Delaware's corporate bar moved late and with caution in putting an antitakeover statute before its legislature (Alva 1990: 906–08). The conflict becomes more apparent in the adjudication of fiduciary cases, particularly those dealing with corporate control transfers.[15] Here the shareholder interest has found Delaware intermittently responsive. The Delaware judiciary abruptly changed a long-standing habit of monolithic fidelity to management interests in 1977,[16] and Cary's 1974 article has been accorded a role in the break (Eisenberg 1989: 1511–13; Coffee 1987: 764–66). The federal threat, thus crystallized, impressed upon the Delaware courts the practical importance of solicitude to shareholder interests. This post-Cary behaviour pattern has persisted and still yields headlines as highly publicized cases articulate surprising new shareholder-protective applications of basic fiduciary rules.[17] The pattern has been volatile,[18] however, and shareholder protective intervention has been a more intermittent than constant theme. That the Delaware courts indulge in this back-and-forth at apparent cost to a reputation for certainty, predictability, and management responsiveness, confirms the presence of competing demands.

[15] There is an analogy here to the allocation of responsibility between legislatures and agencies. Legislators faced with a conflicting demand problem can avoid confrontation with the competing interest groups and resort to the expedient of delegating lawmaking authority to an agency; with state corporate law, the judiciary tends to assume this function. Delaware, as it responded to sensitive developments in the corporate control market of the 1980s, kept open its options by employing equivocal judicial rules in preference to clear cut legislation.

[16] The case was *Singer* v. *Magnavox Co.*, 380 A.2d 969, 980 (Del. 1977), which imposed strict fiduciary standards on parent firms in cash out mergers. The *Singer* rule was in turn rejected for a looser, process based approach in *Weinberger* v. *UOP, Inc.*, 457 A.2d 701, 704, 715 (Del. 1983). Oddly, *Singer* came down after the immediate threat of federal preemption of state fiduciary rules under the antifraud rules of the securities laws had been removed by the Supreme Court in *Santa Fe Industries* v. *Green*, 430 U.S. 462, 479–80 (1977). The story told at the time was that the brush with preemption at the hands of the federal judiciary and the wider critical atmosphere provoked by Cary and others had prompted the Delaware Supreme Court to reverse its direction and become more accommodating of the interests of investors so as to diminish the threat of intervention.

[17] *See Unocal Corp.* v. *Mesa Petroleum Co.*, 493 A.2d 946, 954–55 (Del. 1985) (applying an expanded review of tender offer defensive tactics under proportionality test); *Revlon, Inc.* v. *MacAndrews & Forbes Holdings, Inc.*, 506 A.2d 173, 182 (Del. 1986) (inventing a duty of management defending tender offer to auction company in limited circumstances); *Smith* v. *Van Gorkum*, 488 A.2d 858, 873–81 (Del. 1985) (suddenly expanding the duty of care to cover board approval of arm's length merger); *Cede & Co.* v. *Technicolor, Inc.*, 634 A.2d 345, 366–71 (Del. 1993) (applying a heightened duty of care scrutiny of boardroom merger decision and suggesting expanded remedial concept inclusive of post-merger gain); *Paramount Communications, Inc.* v. *QVC Network, Inc.*, 637 A.2d 34 (Del. 1994) (holding that management has an obligation to achieve best value reasonably available for shareholders).

[18] Equally famous cases often appear to restrict the application of the new rules. *See Weinberger* v. *UOP, Inc.*, 457 A.2d 701, 703–4 (Del. 1983) (overruling *Singer* in favour of less restrictive process scrutiny of cash out mergers); *Moran* v. *Household International*, 500 A.2d 1346, 1356–57 (Del. 1985) (sustaining poison pill defense under *Unocal*); *Paramount Communications, Inc.* v. *Time Inc.*, 637 A.2d 50–4 (Del. 1989) (limiting application of *Unocal* and *Revlon*).

Two caveats must be noted. First, the federal threat does not play an exclusive causative role in this conflicting demand model. Courts and judges sell reputations for speed, dependability, and predictability, but they also stake reputational capital in their working roles. This gives the judges an independent incentive to protect the legitimacy of the system by balancing the satisfaction of interest group demands with public-regarding results (Rasmussen 1994: 72–80; Miceli and Cosgel 1994: 44–49). Delaware judges, responding to Cary's well-publicized allegations of corruption, have represented a commitment to this role integrity. They describe themselves as mediators between management and shareholders—protectors of market risk-taking who nevertheless impose ethical constraints (Quillen 1993: 129; Moore 1987: 779–800).

Second, the identification of competing demands should not be taken to predict a pattern of even-handed mediation. Although the federal threat holds out the potential of substantial injury, it remains a low probability event. Potential impairment of competitive position and loss of incorporations is a more immediate problem for Delaware, and also amounts to a competing reputational concern for Delaware judges, given limitations on their tenure. If we look at the pattern the Delaware courts took during the 1980s in charting a course between competing demands on sensitive corporate control matters, we can infer that the Delaware courts took advantage of informational slack[19] to develop a body of caselaw that gave an appearance of greater weight to shareholder interests than is justified on close inspection of actual payoffs. In highly publicized cases the courts announced vague standards that held out the prospect of enhancement of shareholder value. But in the less well-publicized cases that followed, they took the opportunity held out by complex facts to refrain from applying the standards in management-constraining ways (Brudney and Bratton 1993: 1087–95, 1129–30). The full set of results tallied by the lawyers who make reincorporation decisions signalled considerably more room for management manoeuver than did the public profile signalled by the leading cases.

B. *The litigation anomaly*

Full description of the complex of incentives that shape Delaware law requires further consideration of conflicting interests on the supply side. We have already suggested that managers implicitly rely on the Delaware bar to represent their interests in the state. But the bar's interests are far from perfectly aligned with management's, since litigation against managers also provides a source of income. Delaware has a unique collection of process

---

[19] Slack results from monitoring costs that prevent interested parties from observing all actions taken by a regulator. To the extent slack is present, a regulator is more likely to be captured by an interest group; a self-interested regulator pursues public regarding policies only when little or no slack is present. See Levine & Forrence (1990: 183).

rules that advance this local interest. These encourage derivative litigation,[20] making sure that the local bar gets a share of the action by requiring that Delaware lawyers make appearances and filings.[21] Competing demands also result in some systemic concessions to managers,[22] but the concessions by no means counter Delaware's reputation as a fee-generating center for corporate lawyers. The litigation rules thus stand as the great anomaly in the charter competition discussion, synchronizing with neither the race to the top nor the race to the bottom description.

Jonathan Macey and Geoffrey Miller (1987: 471–72) have explained the litigation rules with a supply side account that highlights the impact of internal interest group politics on the production of Delaware law. In their account, all groups within the state have a common interest in producing a marketable legal régime, but the groups differ on the relative proportions of costs imposed and revenues earned. The taxpayers have an interest in higher direct costs (franchise tax revenues) and lower indirect costs (legal fees). The lawyers' interest in fees would be served by lower direct costs leading to a greater number of incorporations, and by higher indirect legal costs even at the sacrifice of some incorporations to the extent that the legal fees paid exceed those lost. Macey and Miller (ibid. 472–73, 503–04) assert that, unlike Delaware, a state acting as a pure profit maximizer would limit indirect costs so as to maximize direct costs. Delaware fails to conform to the product model's predictions because the bar acts as a small, cohesive interest group that extracts special concessions from the legislature at the expense of the general public (ibid. 504–08).

Macey and Miller rightly emphasize the organized bar's political power. But two factors that align the interests of the bar with those of the rest of the state need to be added to their description. First, the federal threat may temper the incentive of Delaware's lawyers to lobby for a reduction in direct charges to customers. Increasing Delaware's market share substantially above the level of one half of public incorporations would make Delaware even more of a 'national' lawmaking center, enhancing its visibility and vulnerability to challenge at the national level. Given a state with a monopoly position, traditional federalism objections to intervention carry less weight. Second, rules that encourage litigation in Delaware play a secondary role in

[20] It differs from many jurisdictions in not requiring plaintiffs in shareholder derivative actions to post security for expenses. See Del. R. Civ. Proc. 23.1 (1991). It facilitates service of process on nonresident directors with a broad consent to service statute. See Del. Code Ann., tit. 10, sect. 3114 (1993). It also is liberal in its fee awards to derivative plaintiffs' lawyers: Under its nonpecuniary settlement practice, defending managers can trade a high fee for a small overall recovery (Coffee 1987: 761–62).

[21] See Del. Sup. Ct. Rule 12, Del. Ch. Ct. Rule 170.

[22] Delaware ameliorates the litigation rules' immediate impact on managers by allowing for liberal indemnification. Its courts also have been inventive in recent years in placing procedural barriers in the way of a trial on the merits of derivative claims. See *Aronson* v. *Lewis*, 473 A.2d 805, 813–14 (Del. 1984); *Zapata Corp.* v. *Maldonado*, 430 A.2d 779, 781–86 (Del. 1981).

production. Delaware's case law and judges figure prominently in its substantive law product line. Its code's advantages are less distinct than those of its cases, given statutory convergence among the states. But Delaware does not completely control the production of caselaw. The first option on the choice of the forum for new disputes tends to lie with the plaintiff, and in many instances Delaware law questions can be litigated in other states or in federal courts. This gives Delaware a reason to offer incentives to plaintiffs. Their co-operation gives Delaware the opportunity to apply its own law, preserving the first mover advantage and generating a flow of cases. These, in turn, are products sold in the charter market.

The need to satisfy the demands of the national plaintiff's bar reinforces the internal bargaining position of Delaware's bar, further explaining the state's delegation to the bar of the corporate legislative function. But the delegation to the bar also helps to stabilize the capture arrangement with management.

3. FROM THREATENED FEDERAL INTERVENTION TO SHAREHOLDER INTERVENTION—A STRATEGY OF COUNTERVAILING INTEREST EMPOWERMENT

The foregoing survey of the charter competition system highlights three points. First, although the system can be described as one of voluntary exchanges, that description does not by itself justify the system because these exchanges entail the capture of public authority. The states here effectively sell the coercive exercise of their authority on behalf of a purchasing group. The system thereby lacks not only the exit possibilities presupposed by regulatory competition theory, but the exit possibilities present when actors freely make contracts. Although the system affords relational benefits, it also channels distributions within the firms that enter into contracts with the states, making losers of the principals and winners of the agents. Second, the relative stability of the charter market cannot be completely accounted for with a relational contract model that recognizes only one possible route of defection by the state—defection to anticorporate interests opposed to the interests of both shareholders and managers. Contracts in the charter market are also structured to guard against state defection to the shareholder interest. In addition, in a federal system, state public authority, once captured, can be recaptured by a competing interest that manages to invoke federal authority (Moe 1991: 124). Potential federal intervention makes this recapture a constant possibility in corporate law. Third, federal-state political instability can have wealth-enhancing properties. Under a conflicting demand model of Delaware law, the federal threat reinforces the shareholder voice, moving Delaware in the direction of shareholder value enhancement. The stronger the threat, the more pronounced the move.

Taken alone, however, the federal threat does not provide a workable basis for solving the corporate agency problem. Substantial political barriers to shareholder capture of federal authority keep the threat distant and make it possible for Delaware to defuse it with minimal concessions to the shareholders, while providing management with maximum feasible protection of its own prerogatives. Nor does the threat lend itself to institutionalization as a component of a federal intervention strategy designed to intensify the conflicting demands on the states. Institutionalization implies the congressional mandate of a prospective and graduated scheme that ripens into preemptive mandates only to the extent that some background normative standard remains unsatisfied.[23] Such a carrot-and-stick approach also implies a fully articulated federal corporate law policy. It is hard to imagine how such a scheme, once implemented on a national basis, would amount to anything short of blanket preemption that sacrifices the relational benefits of the state system.

Federal intervention nonetheless could help to place a stronger quantum of shareholder demand before state lawmakers. In regulatory theory, one expedient for the problem of agency capture by a producer group is consumer empowerment through the grant of standing in regulatory processes to public interest groups (Ayres and Braithwaite 1991: 57–58). This tripartite strategy follows from the insight that the structuring of conflicts between agents, including third parties, can assist in the collection of information and the reordering of incentives in a desired direction (Laffont and Tirole 1993: 611). Empowerment brings the representatives of the countervailing interest inside the system. Once inside, they assist legislative principals in overcoming the problem of asymmetric information in agency control. The countervailing interest generates information about the agency, supplementing the costly process of direct supervision.[24] Empowerment also reorders the incentives of the agents of the countervailing interest. Their inside position holds out an incentive to abandon obstructionist strategies and develop co-operative relationships with both regulators and producers. Ideally, they assist the evolution of win-win outcomes in the ongoing regu-

---

[23] Under this 'big stick state' theory of regulation, the regulatory authority makes self-regulation generally available, but holds out a graduated threat of command and control regulation and punishment for uncooperative parties, thereby building in an incentive to comply (Ayres and Braithwaite 1992: 39–40).

[24] Cf. McCubbins and Schwartz (1984:166), distinguishing between 'police patrol' oversight, direct monitoring of the agent by the principal, and 'fire alarm' protection, a passive form of oversight in which third parties bear the bulk of the cost of providing information. This model is extended in Lupia and McCubbins (1994), with a model of a multistage, single-shot two person game involving a principal and an agent, showing how the principal learns from fire-alarm oversight.

latory bargaining game. Finally, since these public interest figures attain their status as agents in the world of grassroots politics, they are relatively unsusceptible to capture. Since their guardianship positions are contestable, reputational incentives make defection to competing interests unlikely (Ayres and Braithwaite 1991: 71–73).

The strategy of countervailing interest empowerment shares objectives with the strategy of regulatory competition. Both seek regulatory flexibility and balanced control of regulatory structures that deter capture of regulators (ibid. 59, 71, 84). The choice between the two may depend in part on the situation. Regulatory competition theory assumes that competition provoked by exit frees the regulator from interest group control. Interest group empowerment addresses the capture problem where competition either has been blocked by regulatory coordination, or, as has occurred in the case of corporate law, has served as a mechanism to enforce the capture arrangement.

The corporate law reform that we suggest here—shareholder initiative to amend the charter and effect reincorporation—is the corporate law equivalents of an interest group empowerment strategy. The avenue of shareholder initiative makes it possible for the shareholders to make competing demands on the states themselves, and thereby gain a seat at the table when state laws are formulated. The problem with this strategy, of course, is the problem of shareholder collective action. But, as the next part shows, the gravity of that problem has diminished.

4. INSTITUTIONAL SHAREHOLDER PARTICIPATION AND FEDERALLY-MANDATED ACCESS TO THE CORPORATE CHARTER

4.1 Institutional shareholder participation: theory and practice

Historically, shareholders of public companies are an Olsonian latent group (Rock 1991: 452–59). That is, a collective good—active monitoring of management—would make them better off given proportionate distribution of its costs, but the law provides no cost sharing mechanism, and the free rider problem prevents the emergence of a volunteer or group of volunteers with an incentive to provide the good. Given dispersed shareholdings, the nontrivial costs of active monitoring, and the alternative of exit through sale, the benefits obtainable without investment in monitoring exceed the benefits obtainable from investment (ibid. 455–56). In addition, rational apathy prevails when the system mandates that matters be presented for shareholder approval. The rational small shareholder does not invest in information respecting governance matters, given the likelihood that the collective action problem prevents an effective group response (Grundfest 1993: 910).

Collective action theory allows for the possibility that a subgroup of a latent group will organize and provide the public good if the benefits from action to each member of the subgroup exceed the costs incurred (Hardin 1982: 41). Increased concentration of shareholdings in institutional hands makes it conceivable that investment in monitoring might be cost beneficial for institutional subgroups (Black 1990b: 525). Concentration also promises to mitigate the rational apathy problem. The decision whether to become informed about the governance issue depends on the costs and expected benefits of the effort and the initiative's probabilities of success. The cost is independent of the number of shares held. With individual shareholders holding larger proportionate stakes, the expected returns from a given information investment go up, as does the proponent's probability of success (ibid. 585–89).

Subgroup formation depends on the size of the group, the cost of action, and the magnitude of the benefit to be obtained. Proponents of law reform to facilitate shareholder participation direct most of their attention to the first two factors. Since the number of members needed to form a subgroup declines as ownership concentration goes up, the proponents argue for relaxation of regulatory barriers that impede the accumulation of large holdings in given firms by single investors or organized groups of investors (ibid. 579–80). The proponents also circulate blueprints for cheap strategies, since, as the costs of a given initiative go down, subgroup formation can go forward with a lower level of concentration and a lower projected probability of success.[25]

In sum, the proponents assert that, given certain legal adjustments, prospects for financial gain by themselves will induce governance initiatives by institutional investors. They project sustained relationships between managers and institutional monitors, looking to the use of institutional votes to nominate and elect expert outside monitors, and the placement of substantial blocks of shares with public-regarding[26] institutional owners. And they promise a payoff for this costly action in improved investment policy and day to day management.

But there is a counter story. This asserts that, even given legal adjustments, governance initiatives realizing the full promise of co-operative gain through enforced self-regulation cannot be expected. Two points are emphasized. First, agency relationships within investment institutions create disincentives that prevent subgroup formation, even assuming a projection of a positive return to the subgroup from an investment in governance.

---

[25] See Grundfest (1993:868) (minimum cost strategy of 'just vote no' campaign). They also stress that scale economies lie in the application of a single governance device to multiple companies, and argue for rules that transfer the cost of shareholder initiatives to the firm (Black 1990b: 579–80, 584).

[26] That is, activated by the interests of the shareholders as a group.

Since the individual manager's performance is measured against the performance of the market as a whole and subgroup investment benefits the market as a whole, successful governance investments do not necessarily improve the individual manager's performance profile (Rock 1991: 473–74; Garten 1992: 630–32). Second, the benefits of cost-intensive relational investment remain underspecified. In theory, these lie in informational access and ongoing constructive criticism by the institutional monitor. In practice, underperforming companies are publicly identified in the ordinary course, and standard remedies respecting investment policies, incentive schemes, and governance structures are part of the conventional wisdom. To the extent that institutions cheaply can tie the communication of these points to credible threats against target managers, the available set of governance benefits can be secured through discrete engagement. Incentives for more substantial investments in ongoing relationships remain speculative, absent a special technical capability on the part of the particular monitor. As a result, risks of perverse incentives and commitment problems come to the fore of the relational picture. A strategically placed institutional holder could opt for side payments from management in preference to public-regarding informational development, or, given a hostile tender offer, the institutions in the subgroup could defect from an implicit undertaking to management to be patient (see generally Ayres and Crampton 1994; Rock 1994).

The practice has tended to bear out the counter story's predictions. Ambitious proposals for institutional board membership (Gordon 1994; Gilson and Kraakman 1991), and block-holding (Gilson and Kraakman 1993; Ayres and Crampton 1994) have not yet been extensively tested in practice (Coffee 1994). Instead, institutional initiatives against badly-managed firms tend to take the form of discrete, issue-based voting contests that focus on short term results (Pozen 1994; Grundfest 1993). Such exercises have low out-of-pocket costs. And, in contrast to the proponents' prediction that financial incentives by themselves will induce subgroup formation, they appear to be driven by the selective incentive of reputation. The leadership role has been taken by a narrow segment of institutional agents—public pension fund managers whose indexed portfolios reduce their share of immediate financial returns, but whose independence from management influence creates a possibility for reputational enhancement through constructive antimanagerial political activity.

They have been surprisingly successful. Action is communicative: The shareholders as a group are invited to join in a nonbinding governance proposal;[27] their doing so is taken to indicate dissatisfaction with the firm's

---

[27] The means of access is the precatory shareholder proposal, a medium for nonbinding, shareholder-initiated voting proposals made available by preemptive mandate under federal proxy rule 14a–8. Institutions began making these proposals in the late 1980s in reaction to

performance. In the alternative, the proponent announces performance dissatisfaction directly and invites others to concur by voting no on management proposals (Grundfest 1993).[28] None of these initiatives entails a takeover threat in the present climate. Yet they nevertheless result in preemptive negotiations and concessions by managers, and, in some cases prompt the termination of the chief executive by the outside directors.[29]

The shareholder threats appear to be credible because they impact on the reputational interests of chief executives and independent board members. The campaign declares that the target executives possess undesirable characteristics (Grundfest 1993: 927–28), detracting from their standing in the business community (cf. March and Schapira: 1413), and in some cases, their marketability. Extraordinary risk aversion to such reputational impairment can be expected on the managers' part, if, as seems reasonable, we can assume that employment contracts are incomplete and do not fully compensate for tenure insecurity and the costs of changing jobs (Milgrom and Roberts 1988: 158–59). Preemption by negotiation serves the managers' interest by defusing the threat and providing them with some control over the settlement process (Gilson, *et al.* 1991: 45).

More broadly, the appearance of a vocal shareholder interest group changes the manager's institutional environment. The institutions articulate a normative challenge of manager's conduct of the business.[30] Their challenge has a more destabilizing effect than ordinary external criticism, due to their equity investments, long term presence, and ability to marshal votes respecting both present and future matters for shareholder action. They represent an unstable sector in the larger domain of institutional relationships with which the manager deals.[31] By negotiating, the risk averse manager

expanding legal constraints on takeovers. The first generation of proposals concerned poison pills. In subsequent years the subject broadened to cover the shareholder voting process (Gilson and Kraakman 1990: 868), and process and structure rules designed to make boards more effective in monitoring and designing incentive arrangements (Grundfest 1993: 931). Shareholder voting patterns changed also. Historically, shareholder proposals were largely vehicles for expression by social activists and garnered only trivial percentages of the shares voted. Institutional governance proposals, in contrast, garner significant votes — in 1990, nineteen institutional proposals received more than 50 percent, a larger number of successful proposals than in the history of the device (Barnard 1991: 1156).

[28] The leading activist institution, the California Public Employees Retirement System (CalPERS), has for a number of years published an annual list of underperforming companies and urged shareholders to vote no for management's candidates in the year's board election.

[29] Chief executives were terminated at two of CalPERS' 1992 targets, IBM and Westinghouse. Another target, Sears, took the institutions' advice about concentrating on the core business and dismembered itself. Heads also have rolled at Goodyear, Allied Signal, Tenneco, Shearson, Kodak, and K Mart.

[30] Firms are, from a sociological perspective, normative environments. Institutional norms are rationalized prescriptions that identify social purposes as technical ones and specify rule-like means to pursue these technical rationalities (Meyer and Rowan 1977: 343–44).

[31] See Powell and DiMaggio (1991: 30)(looking to extrainstitutional sources of institutional change as a complement to the internal interest group story of the firm).

(March and Schapira 1987: 1414) seeks to stabilize, and, hopefully, influence the relationship.[32]

4.2 Federally-mandated shareholder initiative

The law reform agenda surrounding the institutional investor movement tends to look in the federal direction. This is partly because the proxy process is heavily federally regulated. Reform initiatives already have prompted the SEC to remove barriers to shareholder initiative.[33] But the reformers would like to see additional changes that would shift more of the costs of shareholder initiative from proponents to firms. The primary agenda item here is mandatory inclusion of shareholder board nominees in the firm's proxy statement.[34]

There is also a broader federal law reform agenda that follows from the financial theory of shareholder participation. This asserts that present levels of institutional concentration could give rise to financial incentives sufficient to induce subgroup formation if ancillary federal legal constraints that increase the costs and risks of collective action were removed.[35] We have no basis for controverting this prediction, but, looking to the counter story and the practice, we note a substantial possibility that the present economic structure of the industry may by itself deter the appearance of the requisite financial incentives. In the latter event, institutional shareholder participation can be expected to persist only in the discrete form, with reputational incentives figuring in significantly as inducements. The possibility that the future framework for action will be thus limited implies expansion

[32] The threat also can destabilize the relationships of inside managers and outside directors by reorienting the outsiders' incentives. Ordinarily, the outside directors, being corporate players themselves, see that their interests lie in cooperation with management. But shareholder intervention gives rise to a public question about the outsiders' effectiveness, creating a dual demand that has an impact on different components of the same reputation. If the conflict becomes severe, the outsiders resolve it by forming a coalition and exercising their board voting power to oust the chief executive. Thus publicity and reputational interests combine to effect a transfer of control.

[33] The change permits shareholders to publish their views in the media without prior agency approval. (17 C.F.R. sect.240.14a–2(b)(1)(1995)).

[34] Without such a reform, the proponent must invest in its own proxy solicitation, a prohibitively expensive process absent a control acquisition objective.

[35] The targets are (1) disclosure requirements imposed on holders of more than 5 percent of a class of securities under section 13(d) of the Williams Act, 15 U.S.C. sect. 78m(d) (1988); (2) liability of controlling persons for securities law violations of controlled persons under section 15 of the Securities Act, 15 U.S.C. sect. 77o (1988), and section 20(a) of the Exchange Act, 15 U.S.C. sect. 78(a)(1988); (3) short-swing liability for trading profits of 10 percent holders under section 16(b) of the Exchange Act, 15 U.S.C. sect. 78p(b) (1988); (4) restrictions on capital structures and incentive compensation for advisors of investment companies under sections 18(d) and 23 of the Investment Company Act, *see* 15 U.S.C. sect. 80a–18(D), 23(a), 23(b) (1988); and (5) portfolio diversification requirements under the Employee Income Security Act (ERISA).

for the law reform agenda—to increase the benefits attainable through discrete action in addition to reducing the costs of relational shareholder participation. Toward this end, we state the following case for an incremental levelling of the field that state law provides for shareholder initiative.

A. The State Law Agenda System

State law agenda-setting procedures for shareholder voting in public corporations have easily-described outcome implications. Control of the proxy machinery gives management working control over the mandatory shareholder board vote.[36] Shareholder votes also are mandated for fundamental changes—charter amendments, dissolution, and certain mergers and significant asset sales. But, under the process rules of most state codes, these matters may not be put before the shareholders until a resolution has first been approved by the board.[37] The condition of board approval amounts to a management veto—to control the agenda one must control the board. The shareholders have a veto in turn, but no access to the agenda.[38]

These process rules came into corporate law with the turn of the century shift toward an entity conception of the corporation—a shift that had the incidental effect of affording freedom of action to the managers of new, mass-producing firms (Bratton 1989: 1489). Previously, an agency theory of board authority had prevailed and shareholder access had been the rule (Gordon 1991: 349). New Jersey, the early leader in the chartering of large firms,[39] conditioned amendment on board approval before 1895.[40] Delaware followed in its corporations code of 1899,[41] a piece of legislation that manifested its determination to enter into charter competition with neighboring New Jersey. Access limitation provisions diffused into the

---

[36] As the foregoing discussion of barriers to shareholder voting coalitions implies, management's practical control is vulnerable only to a challenger willing to invest in a takeover or full-blown proxy contest.

[37] See Delaware Code Annotated, tit. 8, sects. 242(b)(1)(charter amendments), 251 (b),(c)(mergers), 271(a)(sales of substantially all assets), 275(a)(dissolution).

[38] This absolute control over the corporation's contractual agenda is subject to two exceptions. One is the section 14(a) precatory shareholder proposal, pursuant to which a shareholder who meets suitability requirements can set an agenda item, but only for a nonbinding vote. The other is a state law shareholder access privilege respecting by-law amendments (see, e.g., Delaware Code Annotated, tit. 8, sect. 109(a) (1991)), the utility of which is limited. By-laws may contain any provision relating to the business or its conduct, not inconsistent with the rest of state law or the charter. This means that coverage of subject matter in the charter preempts contrary treatment in the by-laws, opening possibilities for strategic tiering of provisions. The exploitation of this possibility is a basic corporate lawyering skill. Where the charter does not cover the subject matter and foreclose a shareholder by-law amendment, a shareholder by-law still as a practical matter must qualify as a shareholder proposal under Rule 14a-8. Unfortunately, the SEC has been notably restrictive in its treatment of by-law initiatives.

[39] New Jersey began to liberalize its code after 1890, with considerable financial success (Grandy 1993: 43–45).

[40] Dill (1899: 42–43) (New Jersey General Corporation Act sect. 27).

[41] *See* Section 135 of the Act of 1899, 21 Del. Laws, 1899, ch. 273, sec. 135.

codes of other states during the subsequent decades.[42] This historical sequence can be read as further confirmation of the capture of state codes by the management interest: It is no accident that this component of management agenda control dates to the first instances of the purchase and sale of corporate codes.

B. A Proposal for the System's Modification

We propose a federally-mandated privilege of direct shareholder access to amend the corporate charter at the annual meeting of shareholders, with cost-shifting to be effectuated through access to the proxy statement for the making of proposals.[43] We would limit this access privilege to matters of process and structure and exclude most business matters allocated to the board by state codes.[44] The boundary dividing process and business would have to be drawn in the preempting legislation. In drawing it, we would place contract terms relating to management's incentives on the 'process' side. Thus, whatever the state law status, access would be granted respecting poison pill redemption and opting out of any state legislation with an opt out permission, in addition to traditional process matters such as the structure and composition of boards and committees. More tentatively, we also propose access for substantive proposals respecting executive compensation.[45] But we would exclude access to formulation of the business plan,

---

[42] By 1960, 25 state codes conditioned charter amendment on board approval (2 Model Business Corporation Act Annotated 230–31 (1960)); by 1970, 28 state codes did so (2 Model Business Corporation Act Annotated 2d 260–61 (1971)); by 1993, 40 state codes did so (2 Model Business Corporation Act Annotated 3d 1172–73 (Supp. 1993)). Today, only ten state codes leave a door open to shareholder access.

[43] There will be ancillary problems respecting the proposal's preemptive reach. States could nullify a narrow access mandate in numerous ways. For example, a code's system of process and structure default rules could be reconstituted as a system of mandates. Or, a state could amend the process provision governing charter amendments to differentiate amendments by source and require a supermajority for shareholder-initiated proposals. We think that the proposal's inclusion of access for reincorporation decisions provides a circumstantial guaranty against the former possibility. As to the latter possibility, two drafting solutions suggest themselves. The preempting legislation could either provide that a simple majority always suffices, or provide that the required percentage for a shareholder initiated proposal be no lower than that provided in respect of a management proposal. The latter, less intrusive, approach should suffice, on the assumption that no state would respond by amending its code to require supermajorities across the board.

[44] See Delaware Code Annotated, tit. 8, sect. 141(a)(1991) (business of corporation to be managed by or under direction of board).

[45] These carry a deterrent impact that could give the proponent useful manoeuvering room in the right case. But they also create special risks of abuse. The very manoeuvering room they could create increases the risk that a proponent might exchange the withdrawal of the proposal for private rents. In addition, substantive compensation proposals would be particularly attractive to actors with political agendas unrelated to shareholder value. Such a hostile, politically-motivated proposal, if directed to an extraordinarily well-compensated but effective manager, could destabilize a valuable working relationship; that deleterious effect need not depend on a high probability of passage. We put this component of our proposal on the table for

in particular matters of investment and disinvestment. Finally, we would include a share ownership qualification—one low enough to permit a small number of players in the activist network to qualify a proposal, and high enough to exclude the gadflies.[46]

Gordon (1991: 361) has warned that shareholder initiative could have two perverse effects—rent-seeking and vote cycling. As to the first, Gordon argued that, given concentrated shareholding and unlimited shareholder access to the charter, there would be a risk of logrolling effected through shareholder side agreements that direct the firm to suboptimal projects benefitting the shareholders' businesses. We think this risk is cognizable, and accordingly, leave matters of investment and disinvestment out of our proposal so as to delimit its utility to actors engaging in governance activity in pursuit of short-term financial gain.[47]

As to the second, Gordon hypothesized that, given diverse shareholder preferences, shareholder access could lead to corporate versions of a standard Arrovian voting cycle (see Arrow 1951; McKelvey 1976). Voting cycles, however, can be contained by process institutions (Shepsle and Weingast 1985: 69; Shepsle 1989: 135),[48] and we would include such a

discussion based on an appraisal that a big stick, placed in the hands of serious proponents, has a value that outweighs the risks.

[46] On the technical point as to whether this proposal requires new congressional legislation or could be promulgated as a rule by the SEC, we look to legislation as a practical matter. The legislative history of section 14(a) of the Exchange Act provides a basis for a strong argument that the SEC does have the authority to impose shareholder initiative on the states by rule (Ryan 1988: 146; Fisch 1993: 1170–74). That result depends, however, on the theory of statutory interpretation the observer brings to bear (Bainbridge 1992: 1112), and a recent, notably restrictive judicial ruling of section 14(a) has left the SEC with cause to be risk averse in experimenting with new rules. See *Business Roundtable* v. *SEC*, 905 F.2d 406, 411–15 (D.C. Cir. 1990). We also note that part of what our proposal seeks to achieve could be achieved by rule on a relatively secure statutory basis. Specifically, the SEC could (and we think should) amend rule 14a–8 to include by-law amendments.

[47] It must be noted that the process and structure limitation diminishes incentives for side-deals without assuring their absence. Return to the above example of a proponent who threatens management with a new, rent-reducing, incentive compensation scheme. Although defined as process and structure, the proposal remains susceptible to withdrawal in exchange for a side-payment. The guarantee against such a transaction lies not in the subject matter limitation but in the proponent's projected incentive profile. So long as the proponent comes to the role seeking reputational rather than financial capital, trade-offs will be structured with a view to reputational gain. Thus a pension fund entrepreneur concerned with vote-getting credibility can be expected to structure trades that entail a concrete shareholder-beneficial component. Any additional consideration sought by this actor seems more likely take the form of influence within the firm than the form of rent. Influence within the firm, unlike money, gives this actor opportunities for further reputational enhancement, and at least holds out a prospect of shareholder benefit. At the same time, even an undisclosed rent deal creates a risk of reputational injury for the proponent.

[48] Shepsle and Weingast point out that cycling becomes a problem only in the simplest of majority rule institutions—without agenda controls, without strategic voting, and with an agenda constructed on an ongoing basis; in practice agenda-setting institutions and agent sophistication constrain majority outcomes. So long as actors in voting institutions take full advantage of strategic opportunities available to them under those institutional rules, majority-vote cycles are unlikely. See also Skog (1994: 282–84). For a survey of the anti-cycling literature, see Green and Shapiro (1994: 114–20).

process rule: Proposals only may be considered at the annual meeting, and under the proxy voting system, proposals are submitted for a one round majority vote. The problem stemming from unlimited access would not be cycling but inconsistency of result—for example, both the status quo based and the new compensation scheme could be approved. A breaker rule could be included to deal with this problem. If management deems two proposals to be inconsistent, it refers the matter to a third party adjudicator. If the proposals are inconsistent, the first in time reaches the agenda.[49] Two candidates are available for this adjudicatory role—the SEC staff and the independent directors' committee. We prefer the latter in theory; but, since any disputed matter would find its way to the SEC staff in any event, the former amounts to the practical choice. In either case, a result is reached and there is no cycling. One problem remains: The possibility of inconsistency over time[50] and attendant costs.

We think the consistency problem is minimal, even absent a breaker rule. We envision a percentage ownership requirement keyed to institutional holding patterns and set high enough so that two or three institutions must coordinate on the proposal. The idea is to rely on the practice pattern to assure process coherence. The leading players in the shareholder participation movement have been motivated by reputational gain. Process and structure initiatives that lead to conflicts with other institutional players hold out little prospect of reputational enhancement (cf. Brams 1994: 118–19). Furthermore, in a case where a proposal responds to a bargaining impasse with a long-term target or complete nonco-operation from a new target, one would anticipate coordination and information sharing among the institutions involved in the campaign. Finally, since reputational gain here ultimately depends on vote getting ability, we would expect proponents to select their proposals and targets with care.

C. Projected Benefits

We direct our access proposal to the pattern of discrete shareholder participation led by agents of public pension funds. We make a projection of beneficial consequences on the following model of engagement, abstracted from the practice pattern.

---

[49] Here a possibility for management manipulation opens up. If management hears of a proposal, it arranges with a friendly shareholder to propose an inconsistent proposal first. Assume that management wants to block a proposal for a compensation committee. The management nominee would propose that the charter, which says nothing about compensation committees, be amended to say the corporation shall not have a compensation committee. The result is the status quo on either a yes or a no vote. To get around this problem, proposals that have a status quo effect would have to be excepted from the first in time rule.

[50] This problem easily could be treated with a provision that bars for a period of years any subsequent shareholder initiative on the subject matter covered by a successful initiative.

Let us start with a proponent who publicly selects a corporate target and either launches a negative voting campaign or makes a precatory proposal. Public targeting indicates the proponent's judgment that the influence costs at the firm are unnecessarily high. If the proponent's determination has credibility, the targeting injures the reputations of the firm's managers and makes it more likely that the shareholders will obstruct future management proposals. The managers have three choices as to their response. First, they can take action amounting to a counter-signal showing that the proponent has selected incorrectly and thereby rehabilitate their reputations. Second, if no such response is available, and they are sufficiently risk averse with respect to reputation and shareholder relations, they can indicate responsiveness by starting a dialogue with the proponent. Third, they can do nothing and let the campaign take its course.

Access to the charter gives the proponent more room to manoeuver in the second and third cases. In the second case, the proponent gets a significant payoff only if the campaign's reputational effects are severe enough to cause realignment of the firm's internal coalitions and termination of the chief executive. Otherwise, dialogue leads to a payoff in the form of contract concessions. At the negotiations, the proponent has cost and reputational incentives to make a quick deal and take home some sort of contract modification. Management presumably will want to give up as little as possible in the way of concrete terms, consistent with an appearance of responsiveness. Management, in addition, at all times retains the option of nonco-operation. The proponent, armed only with a precatory proposal in addition to reputational threats, thus is not in a particularly strong position to extract meaningful concessions (cf. Grundfest 1993: 932 n. 354). If management has a pending proposal of its own, a credible negative voting campaign could mean a stronger bargaining position. Charter access lets the proponent go past the negative, which depends on management's agenda, and take its own mandatory agenda to the table. Armed with a mandate, the proponent with credible vote-getting ability can close off management's option of nonco-operation. Furthermore, the mandatory stick can be wielded directly against the managers' influence within the firm as well as against their reputations: The proponent, for example, could go to the table with a new incentive compensation scheme that reduces the manager's rents. In the trade-off surrounding the proposal's withdrawal, the proponent can select from the whole agenda of process reforms.

Charter access also could be useful in the case of a completely unresponsive firm. Precatory proposals have no governance consequences for managers willing to suffer the reputational consequences of nonco-operation and to risk the long-term consequences of poor shareholder relationships. Such a refusal to co-operate puts the proponent in a repeat play situation. Charter access lets the proponent step up the stakes in a second round, proposing an incentive compensation scheme, or an amendment that redeems a poison pill and calls for a shareholder vote as a condition to the promulgation of a replacement. Such a punishment campaign would, we suspect, have to be carefully targeted, with the proponents concentrating resources on a selected firm for a demonstration of enforcement power. A successful demonstration would reinforce the importance of shareholder relations and enhance cooperative incentives among the group of targets as a whole.

Charter access also holds out the possibility of short-term financial gain in some circumstances: Poison pill redemption can make the stock price go up if a takeover is a near likelihood. The chance of gain might favorably alter the economics of subgroup formation, inducing private institutional players into the game on occasion.

The utility of a bigger stick that holds out an intermittent financial incentive could increase over time. The current pattern of discrete intervention turns on reputational incentives on both sides. Reputational incentives can change with circumstances from period to period. Pension fund entrepreneurship could diminish in intensity if, as the roster of players changes, the replacements discover that most of the available reputational gain has attached to the departed players of the first generation. Management reputational concerns also could change over time. The activists already have targeted the largest, worst-managed firms. New targets will represent less obvious cases of high influence costs, making nonco-operative responses a more likely possibility. Old targets, meanwhile, become repeat play situations over time; as dialogue with institutions becomes an ongoing fact of life for these firms, reputational threats may loom less large and management's long-term concern about shareholder relations matter more. A power to expand the mandatory agenda puts the proponent in a more proactive position.

Federally-mandated charter access would ride atop the state system, giving the shareholders access to the corporate contract but not otherwise interfering with the production of state law. Taken alone, it would not impair the responsive benefits of the state system. Nor, taken alone, would it ameliorate the system's management bias. Accordingly, our definition of appropriate shareholder 'process' amendments would include reincorporation proposals. We would set up the following two-step process for shareholder-initiated reincorporation. The proponent's resolution would mandate the convening of a committee of independent directors that would, after consultation with an outside consultant, recommend a best alternative domicile. The following year, the shareholders would vote on a resolution to approve or reject a move to the new jurisdiction. We employ the independent director intermediary to solve the problem of selection. Two proponents could suggest different states; a given proponent's choice could be uninformed or, conceivably, could result from a side-deal with actors in the jurisdiction chosen. In any event, public pension fund agents, being state employees, do not seem well-suited to this particular gatekeeper function. Of course, there remain possibilities for management influence over the independent directors. But, since we make this proposal more with a view to deterrent effects in states sensitive to incorporation business than with expectations of frequent utilization, we think the compromise workable.

The point of the shareholder reincorporation initiative, as stated above, is to provide state lawmakers with a long-term incentive to respond to shareholder interests. We doubt that it would result in any short-term disruption of today's charter market. No state presently stands out as a candidate for the role of shareholder-sensitive charter mongerer. Indeed, Delaware's laggard role as an antitakeover jurisdiction during the 1980s makes it a possible shareholder-directed destination for firms located elsewhere. As a practical matter, then, the deterrent of shareholder-directed reincorporation would complement the federal threat, reinforcing Delaware's moderate legislative pattern and encouraging its judges in their attempts to mediate between the conflicting interests.

The burden to make use of initiative to invigorate the charter market would be on the shareholder proponents. To make active competition work here, they would have to expand their entrepreneurship so as to locate a jurisdiction, persuade it to go into competition and invest in an informed judiciary, draft an attractive code for it, and bring it some business. If all of that happened, Delaware would be pressed by a dual demand that could make for difficult choices. Moves in the direction of the shareholder interest to counter the threat of exit by established firms could cause it lose new business from entrepreneurial firms on the move to maturity, but such conflicts are the ordinary incidents of active competition.

5. CONCLUSION

The benefits we project are modest. An experiment with process and structure access very well might result in no significant changes, either due to sporadic utilization of the access privilege, or a co-operatively-based response by the larger group of shareholders against the forcing of governance terms on managers, except in extreme, end period situations. In the alternative, extensive and underinformed utilization could conceivably cause incentive or other contractual problems in given firms. But we think management has sufficient resources and enough of an informational advantage to protect firms from this problem. On our most sanguine projection, charter access, used responsibly and occasionally, would bring process rules that lower management influence costs to a small group of mature firms. Our hope is that competitive evolution would then take its course, so that the rules that work best are voluntarily adopted by other firms. From there, we would hope that responsible and occasional use of charter access encourages ongoing contractual innovation, with all players contributing, institutional agents, managers, and lawyers.

Some years ago, a corporate law debate over the desirability of mandatory and enabling rules came down to simple difference of opinion. The enabling side emphasized the importance of innovation and flexibility, the defenders of mandates emphasized process infirmities. The discussion here goes back to that point of difference. State law has done an excellent job of assuring that firms can draft contracts that accord managers freedom of action to invest and disinvest, but it has not evolved to open up all possibilities for productive firm contracting. State law remains the best vehicle for realizing those possibilities, but a demand-side barrier prevents state law experimentation. An incidental federal intervention taken in order to facilitate the experiment will not hurt the state system, and might do it some good.

8

Supply-Side Inefficiencies and Competitive Federalism: Lessons from Patents, Yachting, and Bluebooks

IAN AYRES*

INTRODUCTION

The ongoing debate about whether Delaware's dominance in the market for corporate charters is a race to the top or a race to the bottom often turns on whether one believes corporate managers are driven to incorporate (or reincorporate) in the state that provides the most efficient law. William Cary (1974) and his followers have argued that managers abuse their discretion to incorporate in states that benefit managerial interests at the expense of shareholder interests; Ralph Winter (1977) and his followers (*see, e.g.*, Easterbrook & Fischel 1991) have argued that, because managers' discretion is constrained by promoters or by the threat of a potential takeover, managers will tend to incorporate in states that provide laws which maximize the value of corporate equity.[1] Thus, in the end much of the debate about corporate competitive federalism turns out to be a question of agency costs and whether these agency costs are constrained by various forms of market discipline.

This chapter explores different types of inefficiencies that may be generated even if the managers faithfully try to maximize shareholders' interests. Thus, this chapter examines inefficiencies that might persist even if firms were wholly owned by managers—so that there were no separation of ownership from control.[2]

Extending the image of Roberta Romano (1985; 1993) that corporate statutory law is a 'product' supplied by the franchising state and purchased (as an input) by the firm, this chapter focuses on supply-side inefficiencies, whereas the race to the bottom theorists of Cary's ilk focused on the

---

* William K. Townsend Professor of Law, Yale Law School, Jennifer Brown, William Bratton, Jeremy Bulow, Paul David, and Roberta Romano provided helpful comments.

[1] Winter himself (1989) has recently been careful to temper his earlier race to the top thesis.

[2] In an earlier article, I suggested that state legislatures would not compete to supply efficient close corporation law (Ayres, 1992a). It is important to see that this was at heart a demand side theory because it argued that close corporations were unwilling for various structural reasons to incorporate in foreign jurisdictions offering value-maximizing law.

demand-side failure of self-serving managers to seek corporate franchises in states which maximized firm value.

As Romano (1985: 228 n. 8) observed, both traditional race to the top and race to the bottom theorists shared a belief that racing states tried to supply the legal product demanded in the marketplace. And Romano (1985: 228 n. 9) was the first to provide some evidence that speed of responsiveness was associated with success in attracting corporate charters. The widely-held belief that the states respond quickly to changing demand is part of a general belief in competitive federalism as a laboratory for democracy. But this chapter suggests that state competition may not efficiently respond to changes in demand—even if we make the extreme assumption that managers demand value-maximizing corporate law.[3]

This chapter tells three different stories about why states might not supply value-maximizing statutes. Besides focusing on supply-side market failure, each of these stories is evolutionary in character in that each focuses on the possible failure of competitive federalism to respond to changing demands over time. It should also be stressed that my goal is to merely explore the theoretical *possibility* of supply-side inefficiency: while I relate two of my stories to the development of antitakover legislation in the USA, I do not (for now) wish to assess the extent to which these stories can be used to explain the actual evolution of corporate governance.

Although this article focuses on the possibility of market failure in the supply of corporate charters, none of the stories amounts to a 'race to the bottom'—especially if that term takes on its original sense of systematically selling out shareholder interest to further the interests of management. Instead, the inefficiencies uncovered here suggest that, within the broad incentives that states have to supply the most desired product, there can be impediments along the way that forestall first-best efficiency (or, in Winter's original parlance, a race to the top). These models thus complement William Bratton's theory (1994) of corporate law's race 'to nowhere in particular.'

For convenience, I refer to these stories as patent, yachting, and bluebook models. The 'patent' model suggests that individual states may have insufficient incentives to innovate because statutory innovations are not accorded intellectual property protection. The 'yachting' model suggests that a dominant state (such as Delaware) may have strategic incentives to mimic (or, in the terms of yachting, 'cover') the inefficient statutory innovations of other states. And finally, the 'bluebook' model suggests that a dominant state such as Delaware may have an incentive to promulgate innocuous updates of its corporate statute both to create additional litigation for its attorneys and to increase the difficulty of replication by competitor states.

---

[3] While Romano was the first to show a positive correlation between responsiveness and competitive success (Romano, 1985: 228 n. 9), her evidence is not sufficient to establish that the states efficiently supply whatever is demanded.

This chapter's focus on supply-side market failure is inspired in part by the seminal work of Jonathan Macey and Geoffrey Miller (1987).[4] While previous analysis of competitive federalism stressed states' desire to maximize charter revenues, Macey and Miller argued that states might decide to indirectly extract some of the rents (for supplying desirable corporate law) to benefit private interest groups within the state—chiefly local bar members. This interest-group distortion represents one type of supply-side inefficiency that would obtain even without any demand-side agency costs. This chapter explores three other types.

I. THE PATENT STORY

The simplest (but theoretically strongest) reason to believe that innovations in corporate law will not occur at the efficient rate is that innovations are not accorded the same kinds of protection that are accorded to patents and other types of intellectual property.[5] Individual states have a reduced incentive to solve problems of corporate governance because successful statutory solutions may be quickly copied by rival jurisdictions. Thus, even if state legislatures are engaged in a race to the top with respect to the creation of corporate law, there are strong theoretical reasons to expect that the race will not proceed at an efficiently fast pace.

A vivid example of the absence of patent protection can be seen in the state competition for antitakeover statutes. In the 1980s there was clearly a demand by at least some corporations for protection from hostile takeovers. States encountered great difficulty trying to find a statutory formulation that would pass constitutional muster.[6] Attempts to formulate a constitutional statute were fraught with costs because any antitakeover statute was sure to produce legal uncertainty as the constitutionality of the statute was litigated. A state deciding whether to pass a second- or third-generation antitakeover statute had to weigh these costs against very limited competitive benefits. Even if a state succeeded in articulating constitutional restrictions, other states could immediately copy the sum and substance of their statute.

---

[4] Lucian Bebchuk's (1992) 'externality' theory of inefficient competitive federalism also represents a supply side theory in that inefficient law would be produced even if corporations demand value-maximizing law.

[5] This idea was originally formulated by Susan Rose-Ackerman (1980). Ron Daniels (1991: 149) has applied this insight to the competition for corporate charters: 'Lacking a robust intellectual property regime, successful legal innovation can be costlessly and quickly adopted by 'free-riding' jurisdictions. As a consequence, many of the expected gains from successful legal products in terms of enhanced market share are denied to innovating states.'

[6] The Supreme Court created the doubt about the constitutionality of state antitakeover legislation with its 1982 decision in Edgar v. Mite, 457 U.S. 624 (1982), where it held that the Illinois Business Takeover Act violated the commerce clause.

Indeed, this imitation occurred with lightening speed. Within one year and a half of the Supreme Court decision holding the Indiana antitakeover statute constitutional,[7] 26 other states had passed similar statutes (Carney, chapter 5, this volume). Indiana and a few other innovating states bore substantial costs in creating legal uncertainty and gained virtually no advantage in attempting to compete for corporate charters.

Indiana's incentive to pass the statute ultimately did not turn on an attempt to win more incorporations; rather, Indiana was merely trying to protect an incumbent corporation from a hostile bid (Romano 1987; Butler 1988). The fact that this incentive was sufficient in this case provides no assurance that there are sufficient incentives to experiment with other legal innovations. Legal innovation is neither costless nor riskless. Because any state can free-ride on the successful innovations of another state, there are reduced incentives to bear the cost of innovation. Put simply, a strong-form belief in competitive efficiency cannot coexist with the widely-held belief that free-riding undermines efficient investment.[8]

This free-riding argument can do more than impede the speed of innovation. As a theoretical matter, free-riding may prevent a socially valuable innovation from ever occurring. For example, Jennifer Brown (chapter 9, this volume) has recently argued that there may be a considerable legislative incentive to be the first state to legalize same-sex marriages. As a practical matter, the first state that legalized same-sex marriage would probably not fear free-riding by other states because the political opposition to same-sex marriage in other states would preclude imitation. But it is possible to construct a counterfactual hypothetical in which no state would legalize same-sex marriage even though all agreed it was socially valuable:

Assume that legislatures believe it is equally likely that legalization of same-sex marriages would produce a total of either $4 or $22 billion in tourism; but legislatures believe that moral repugnance of some of their constituency to legalization is equivalent to a loss of $5 billion in tourism.[9]

---

[7] The United States Supreme Court upheld the constitutionality of Indiana's 'control share' statute in *CTS Corp. v. Dynamics Corp. of Am.*, 481 U.S. 69 (1987).

[8] This line of argument uses one cherished efficiency theory to undermine another cherished theory. For similar arguments, see Ayres (1992*a*: n. 2) (common law efficiency theory and race to the top theory cannot both be true if we observe persistent disagreements between court and legislative corporate law making) and Ayres (1992*b*) (quota theory is inconsistent with theory that employers will avoid disparate treatment claims for layoffs by failing to hire protected classes of workers initially).

[9] Brown (chapter 9, this volume) estimates that the present value of enhanced tourism might exceed 4 billion dollars. The idea is that single-sex couples would travel to marry and honeymoon in the first state that legalized same-sex unions. If more than one state legalized these unions, the total spent on marriages and honeymoons might be reduced, but for the purposes of this hypothetical, I assume that the potential tourism from same-sex marriage is a fixed amount (but it is initially uncertain what the size of this amount is).

This example also crucially assumes that a state is not harmed if its residents enter into same-sex marriages under the law of another state. If this assumption fails, the legalization of same-sex marriage might be viewed by other (non-legalizing) states as a negative externality.

Even though legalization (under a patent régime) would produce an expected gain of $8 billion,[10] without patent protection no state may want to be the first to legalize. If the tourism generated from legislation turns out to be low, the state will lose the equivalent of $1 billion in tourism, and if the tourism generated is high, three other states might quickly imitate by passing similar statutes.[11] This ex post imitation could drive the initial state's share of tourism down to $5.5 billion. As a result of this free-riding, any state would expect to lose $1 billion if the tourism demand was low, and to only earn on net one-half billion if the tourist demand turned out to be high: thus any state would expect to lose if it were the first to innovate.

The effect of this secondary competition is exacerbated if subsequent states bear lower political costs in being the second, third or *n*th state to recognize same-sex unions (This might describe the political costs associated with the subsequent state legalization of gambling). Thus, if subsequent states had to bear political costs equivalent to only a $2 billion loss in tourism, no state would legalize even if it was clear that there would be a high tourist demand for this new legal 'product'. If tourism demand for same-sex marriages is known with certainty to be $22 billion, a state considering whether to be the first to legalize would expect 10 additional states to legalize (so that each state—including the initial state—would earn only $2 billion in tourism). Realizing that this shared revenue would not cover the higher first-mover costs (assumed to be $5 billion), each state would refuse to move first.

While this example reductively has monetized the political opposition to single-sex marriage (Sunstein 1994), it illustrates how the absence of patent protection can destroy a state's incentive to be the first to engage in socially valuable innovation. In many competitive federalism contexts there may only be an incentive to be a 'second-mover': racing states will want another state to bear the first-mover costs, but will want to be the second (or subsequent) state to innovate to garner a larger portion of increased consumer demand.[12]

A crucial assumption in this marriage example is that second movers can react quickly and capture a pro-rata share of any tourism. Professor Brown

[10] The expected revenue from legalization in a single state would be $13 billion [(22+4)/2], so the net expected revenue would be $8 billion (13–5).

[11] The fourth state to legalize same-sex marriages would expect to earn one half billion dollars [(22/4)–5], but a fifth state would expect to lose $600 million from legalization [(22/5)–5].

[12] Joseph Farrell and Garth Saloner (1985) have formalized the perverse consequences of such 'second-mover' incentives. Besides providing an explicit mathematical formulation, these authors have also illustrated this phenomenon with the now-famous example of penguins: Apparently penguins like to eat fish, but fear being eaten by walruses. As penguins crowd near the water's edge it is optimal to be the second penguin to jump in. The first penguin discovers whether or not a walrus is lurking beneath the surface, and the third (and subsequent) penguins have a lower chance of finding fish. The second penguin has the highest expected payoff in trading off the probabilities of finding fish and finding walruses.

(chapter 9, this volume) has shown, however, that in the context of same-sex marriage there will likely be an initial 'pent-up' demand that will confer disproportionate benefits on the first state to permit this category of marriage. Moreover, in many other contexts the first-mover state will develop expertise (via a learning curve) or a reputation that will give it a competitive advantage over subsequent entrants.[13] In the same-sex marriage context, the first-mover state may garner disproportionate patronage if the targeted class of tourists remains grateful for the long awaited innovation (Brown, chapter 9, this volume).[14]

The possibility of free-riding does not therefore necessarily destroy the incentive to innovate. After all, the same type of free-riding has not chilled Marty Lipton's firm, the drafter of newfangled poison pill provisions, from innovating. But, at least as a theoretical matter, the same lack of intellectual property protection might also dampen private incentives to devise valuable contractual innovations. As Roberta Romano (1989: 1599) has noted: '[F]irms may not want to customize their charters, but to free ride on the innovative efforts of others. There would then be a "suboptimal" rather than "superoptimal" level of charter deviations.' The open marketing of poison pills suggests that an important part of Wachtell, Lipton's service may have been not the ex ante drafting but the ex post defense of the pill's validity. Just as Delaware's advantage may stem more from its judicial servicing of its statute, Wachtell, Lipton's advantage may have come from its being able to brag that none of its pills had ever been struck down.[15] The lesson of this patent story is therefore not that statutory innovation is impossible, but merely that *some* innovations will not occur. Other

[13] For example, Richard Schmalensee has shown that a 'pioneering brand' may establish a reputation that acts as a barrier to entry to others considering subsequent competition (Schmalensee 1982) (detailing the role of brand loyalty in the market success of innovators). This is particularly true if the product is an 'experience good' that consumers cannot judge except through experience. For example, if a first-mover brand for a new type of razors or bleach succeeds in demonstrating to consumers that their product works, consumers may be reluctant to risk damaging their body or their clothes with relatively untested products. In the corporate context, a state's treatment of fiduciary duty litigation (or other areas governed by 'standards' instead of 'rules') may be just such an experience good that prevents subsequent competitors from easily capturing a pro-rata share. Thus, we should expect the patentability problem to be greatest with regard to innovative legal 'rules' that might be easily replicated by other states. Many aspects of the antitakeover statutes were rule-like—so that any competitive advantage that Indiana gained by passing the first constitutional anti-takeover statute was probably quickly dissipated by the subsequent passage by other states.
[14] Professor Brown points to the product loyalty that gay consumers have shown toward Absolut Vodka because it was the first national advertiser to advertise in a gay publication. Professor Brown also discusses the possibility that legalizing same-sex marriage might induce long-lived enmity. Moreover, telephone consumers do not seem to have shown any particular loyalty to MCI or Sprint for introducing discount telephone prices in the USA.

innovations will occur, but not at the socially efficient speed. And as seen with the antitakeover statutes, some innovations will be prompted by intrastate interest-group lobbying (and not by interstate competition).

This patent story raises the possibility of a role for additional, but limited federal intervention. The patent story underscores a fact that is often obscured in race to the top rhetoric: federal law must play a crucial role in creating the conditions for competitive federalism. In the corporate context, there could be no statutory competition if the USA Supreme Court did not prohibit (or limit) the ability of non-franchising states to regulate the internal affairs of corporations incorporated in other states.[16] The patent story suggests that even adherents of the race to top theory might want the federal government to go further in creating the preconditions for efficient competition.

Specifically, Congress might be called upon to preempt other states from imitating (free-riding on) the statutory innovations of a competing state for a limited number of years. Preempting states from imitating the statutory innovations of sibling states would not discriminate among the individual states from an ex ante perspective. Even though that preemption would restrain some states' legislative freedom once an innovation had occurred, ex ante there is no discrimination by this form of patent protection, because each state has an equal legal opportunity to engage in the innovation.[17]

In the end, it might certainly be true that the costs of implementing this new type of preemption might not be worth the candle: federal legislators or an administrative agency might abuse this quasi-patenting power to constrain competition. But before we dismiss this form of federal intervention out-of-hand as an example of the nirvana fallacy,[18] it is useful to compare

[15] However, savvy rivals may have been able to free-ride on even this reputational capital. Law firms that plagiarized the Wachtell, Lipton pill might expect that Wachtell, Lipton would be willing to donate its services to defend the pill's validity—so that an unfavourable precedent would not be created.

[16] If non-franchising states could impose their local regulations concerning internal governance, there would be no incentive for a corporation headquartered in Missouri to incorporate in Delaware. *See* Hovenkamp (1991: 298–301).

[17] The same-sex marriage example poses a much harder constitutional issue, because patent-like preemption would foreclose competing states from extending this basic civil right to its citizenry for a limited number of years. The crucial constitutional issue, however, is whether same-sex marriage is a basic civil right. Currently, no court has accorded this civil right a constitutional status, *but see* Baehr v. Lewin, 852 P.2d 44 (1993), so preempting some states from legalizing same-sex unions would likely be constitutional if one concluded that Congress could preclude all states from legalizing these unions.

Indeed, besides this targeted preemption, it might be appropriate for federal intervention to boost the value of the patent. Just as non-franchising states are required to recognize the incorporations of other states, it might be useful to force non-solemnizing states to recognize the validity of same-sex unions under either constitutional full-faith-and-credit analysis or by preempting the individual states from promulgating choice of law rules in derogation of such recognition. *See* Brown (this volume) (discussing choice of law rules).

[18] For a description of the nirvana fallacy, see Tauke (1989) ('existence of costs is taken as sufficient grounds for branding an arrangement suboptimal without considering the feasibility of alternative arrangements').

the generally accepted success of the patent office.[19] This patent story is useful because it probes the limits of the 'law as product' image of corporate statutes. If corporate statutes are really like products, the idea of giving patent protection to true innovations should not provoke such a visceral gag reflex. Arguments against giving states intellectual property protection quickly run the risk of proving too much.

2. THE YACHTING STORY

The last section argued that patent inefficiencies might lead to too little legal innovation, but other supply-side inefficiencies may lead to too much legal change. In this section, I explore a yachting model which generates inefficient innovation and argue that it might capture some elements of corporate charter competition.

The essence of this competitive inefficiency can be gleaned from a two-yacht race (such as the America's Cup) by analysing the optimal strategies of the yachts in the middle of the race at a point where one boat has gained a lead over the other. Before proceeding to specifics of this story, let me caution the reader that I was born and raised as far inland as possible in the USA and my knowledge of yachting is less than rudimentary. The following should be interpreted as a fable that might illuminate other contexts even if it does not accurately describe yachting.

The efficient direction to steer the boat (the efficient 'tack') is determined by the direction of the prevailing winds (in conjunction with the direction of the destination). One might expect both boats to choose the efficient tack—but in many race contexts neither boat chooses this tack in a competitive equilibrium. Even if the leading boat is taking the efficient tack, the trailing boat may choose to steer in another direction hoping that the wind will change to favour this new direction. The trailing boat reasons that if it takes the same tack as the lead boat, it will have no chance of gaining on the lead boat (because, assuming both boats are sailed equally well, both will take advantage of the same wind). Even though an inefficient tack increases the expected time it will take to finish the race, the inefficient tack can increase the trailing yacht's chance of victory because, if the wind changes in its favour, the trailing yacht will gain ground on the lead yacht.

The leading yacht often does not ignore this perverse strategy of the trailing yacht. Indeed, lead yachts often choose to 'cover' the trailing yacht by mimicking its tack. *See, e.g.,* Fisher (1995) (first-place boat 'tacked to cover' second-place boat). As long as the lead yacht efficiently covers the trailing

---

[19] At the very least, economic scholars have difficulty pointing to clear errors with the broad outlines of the patent system. *See, e.g.,* David (1993) *and* Priest (1986).

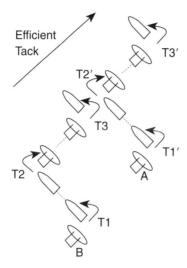

Fɪɢ. ɪ The perverse yachting incentives for inefficient tacking and cover

yacht so that both boats uniformly present themselves to the wind, the trailing yacht will not have an opportunity to gain ground. Of course, once the lead yacht covers the trailing yacht's inefficient tack, the trailing yacht will have an incentive to 'come about'—changing directions again possibly back to the efficient tack.[20] A Cartesian example of the yachts' vectors is depicted in Figure ɪ. At time ɪ (T_1), the trailing yacht (yacht B) commences an inefficient tack (tack right) and the leading yacht (yacht A) tacks immediately (at time $T_{1'}$) to cover. At time T_2, yacht B returns to the efficient tack (tack left) and yacht A again moves as soon as it can (at time $T_{2'}$) to cover. The inefficient tacking and covering produces the figure's zigzag course.

---

[20] Inefficient tacking by the trailing boat and inefficient cover by the leading yacht can also be induced when the wind is coming from behind two yachts so that the trailing yacht (yacht B) can create a 'wind blanket' which slows the speed of the leading yacht (yacht A).

By changing course to windward, yacht A could gain speed and sail out of yacht B's wind blanket, although, of course, yacht A might no longer be sailing the rhumb line to the next mark. . . . If B also jibes, A may have to sail even higher, or perhaps jibe again and sail away from B in order to keep her wind clear. This manoeuvre may have to be repeated a number of times. Take care, however, that a third competitor, sailing a straight line course to the next mark, does not pass or gain significantly while yachts A and B are duelling. . . . [T]he yacht astern, or behind, becomes the attacking yacht and determines to a great extent the tactics the leading yacht must employ—and the course she must sail . . . .Cox & Muhlfeld (1963: 283).

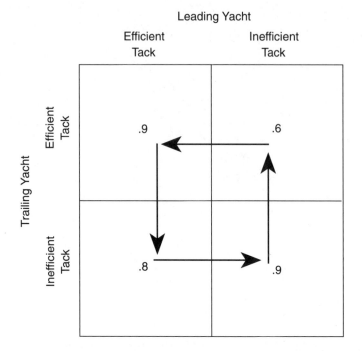

Number in each quadrant equals probability of lead yacht victory
Horizontal arrows represent strategic incentive of leading yacht
Vertical arrows represent strategic incentive of trailing yacht

FIG. 2

This rivalry is depicted in a more traditional game-theoretic fashion in
Figure 2. If we start in the upper left-hand quadrant, in which both yachts
are taking the efficient (fast) tack, then the trailing yacht has a strong incentive to change directions to the inefficient tack: in this example, changing
directions hoping that the wind will shift doubles the trailing yacht's probability of victory (from ten to twenty percent). The figure also depicts the
leading yacht's incentive to 'cover' even inefficient tacks: as can be seen in
the leading yacht's incentive to move from the lower-left to the lower-right
quadrant. Even though taking an inefficient tack increases its expected time,
it perversely increases the leading yacht's probability of victory because it
reduces the probability that the trailing yacht will benefit from a shift in the
wind. Once the lead yacht covers the inefficient tack, the trailing boat now
has a particularly strong incentive to switch directions back to the efficient
tack (because this will give it an advantage given the prevailing winds): this
incentive is depicted in the figure by the reduction in the leading boat's
probability of victory to 60 percent. Of course, the upper right-hand corner

is not an equilibrium as the leading yacht will once again strive to cover (moving us back to the upper left-hand quadrant). The yachts are likely to cycle (counterclockwise) through the strategies represented in the four quadrants.

Because of the lead boat's strong incentive to cover even inefficient tacks, in many yacht races the second boat controls the direction of both boats. This yachting rivalry is a classic example of a discoordination game which has no equilibrium in pure strategies: Just as in the child's game of matching pennies, one player (the lead yacht) wants to match the other's strategy and the other player (the trailing yacht) wants to choose a non-matching strategy (Rasmusen & Ayres 1993). Moreover, the strategic interaction leads to excessive changes in direction (zigzagging) and significantly slower times.

While I would like to apply this yachting fable to the competition for corporate charters, the differences between these contexts are so vast that I readily admit that the entire enterprise is fraught with danger.[21] Most importantly, the leading yacht's incentive for inefficient cover quickly breaks down if more than two yachts are racing. With two trailing yachts, it may become impossible to cover both—so it is more likely for the leading yacht to cleave to the efficient tack. However, even here the leading yacht will often cover the most threatening competitor (or at least partially cover by tacking somewhere in between this competitor's tack and the efficient tack).

It is also important to see that, unlike the patent story, the yachting story generates a first-mover advantage for innovation. For the story to make strategic sense, the trailing yacht must be able to benefit from already being pointed in the correct direction relative to the changing wind (possibly because it takes time for the leading yacht to come about). But the first-mover incentive is to innovate inefficiently—tacking induced by the trailing yacht slows the speed of both yachts.

This yachting story has two important predictions for corporate law: (1) inefficient innovation by trailing states; and (2) inefficient cover by Delaware (the prototypical leading yacht). It is important to stress again, however, that the first half of the story will only occur if the trailing state can benefit from being the first to adopt an innovation that may become valuable. In the corporate context, even without patentability there might be a first-mover advantage with regard to legal innovations that are more valuable after judges have experience in their application. A judicial 'learning curve' explanation or reputational advantage may create the necessary type of first-mover advantage.

A trailing state trying to attract some of Delaware's corporate clientele to reincorporate might choose to adopt innovations that only might become

---

[21] For example, yacht races produce all-or-nothing payoffs for the participants while competitive federalism admits many degrees of success.

necessary in the future. Some of Pennsylvania's vaunted efforts to compete might be seen as trying to innovate ahead of the corporate demand. The first important lesson of the yachting model is that, absent competition, some states may have chosen to wait until more information about demand had developed. Of course, absent competition, states might generally be lackadaisical about providing the laws that their chartered corporations demand. However, the yachting story suggests that competition may cause some states to inefficiently 'jump the gun' in search of a potentially valuable future innovation. Moreover, the story suggests that this premature innovation should not come from Delaware but from those trailing states that are trying to vie with Delaware for charter revenues.

Ultimately, the ease of copying statutory innovations may undermine the yachting incentive for introducing changes too quickly and, as argued above, lead to inefficiently slow statutory innovation. However, the second implication of the yachting story—predicting 'inefficient cover'—may have vitality even if yachting-like incentives do not explain the legislative behaviour of the trailing states. Specifically, I would argue that inefficient cover may help explain one of the central conundrums for race to the top adherents: Delaware's passage of antitakeover legislation.

Because the antitakeover legislation was so clearly inefficient, Easterbrook and Fischel (1991) have openly been at pains to explain its passage (Ayres 1992c). The private-interest-group theory explains the passage of antitakeover legislation in other states,[22] but is not as plausible in Delaware with more diffuse and non-resident corporate constituents.

But Delaware's passage of the antitakeover legislation is consistent with the yachting model (even in its multi-boat incarnation). After 26 other states (including all of its closest rivals) had passed antitakeover legislation, Delaware had a strong incentive to cover (Carney, chapter 5, this volume). As long as some corporations demand antitakeover legislation, Delaware can eliminate (or reduce) a reason for these corporations to emigrate from Delaware. By covering, Delaware may be moving in an inefficient direction, but, because so many of its rivals have already moved in this direction, it reduces the chance of giving up part of its dominance by following suit. Indeed, the fact that Delaware's covering was only partial is also consistent with the model because, as argued earlier, in multi-yacht races the leading yacht often compromises between the efficient tack and the covering tack.[23]

[22] In the trailing states, antitakeover statutes were passed to aid particular incumbent takeover targets. *See* Romano (1987: n. 16) *and* Butler (1988: n. 16).

[23] This inefficient cover story represents an alternative to Professor Eisenberg's theory (1989: 1512) that Delaware was responding to a threat of federal intervention. The federal preemption story, like the yachting story, suggests that Delaware would 'avoid taking the lead in the adoption of rules favouring managers at the shareholder's expense' (Bratton 1994: 30). Under both theories, Delaware is a follower (not necessarily the last to innovate, but) not the leader. But while Eisenberg's theory suggests that Delaware would fear preemption, the inefficient cover theory suggests that Delaware might have welcomed federal preemption that reifies its lead.

The inefficient-cover prediction certainly cannot explain all of Delaware's behaviour. Roberta Romano (1993: 885) has found: 'With regard to most major corporate law reforms, . . . Delaware was the first or second state to act.' However, more work can be done to examine the cases where Delaware has chosen to follow instead of lead.[24] Indeed, the analysis of this section suggests that the decision to follow itself may constitute prima facie evidence that the innovation was premature.

3. THE BLUEBOOK STORY

While the yachting story predicted excessive innovation by trailing states, we now explore the possibility of excessive innovation by the dominant competitor. The metaphor for this model is *A Uniform System of Citation*—commonly known in the United States of America as the 'bluebook'.[25] The bluebook sets out a number of rules for legal citations in law reviews and other types of legal writing. The bluebook is published by a consortium of four elite law reviews who then require that its rules be observed in their publications. Possibly because of the dominant position of these law reviews in the academy, the vast majority of law reviews across the USA require that all published citations conform to the bluebook's rules.[26] Most first-year law students must buy the bluebook and study its mandates.[27]

I would like to suggest that the law reviews that publish the bluebook have an incentive to engage in excessive innovation. This is not a prediction of a race to the bottom, but a prediction of excessive innocuous change—where the inefficiency comes in the need to learn arbitrary new rules, not in the quality of the rules themselves. The bluebook publishers have this perverse incentive because every new edition of the bluebook generates a large one-time demand as lawyers and legal libraries are driven to buy the

[24] For example, it should be possible to use the data of Bill Carney (this volume) to analyze how quickly Delaware acted in passing a broad variety of reforms that have had widespread market penetration.

[25] THE BLUEBOOK: A UNIFORM SYSTEM OF CITATION (15th ed. 1991). To non-legal scholars in the USA, the term 'bluebook' is often used to refer to a listing of used car prices. See, *e.g.*, KELLY BLUE BOOK (1994). This used-car 'bluebook' is updated periodically to reflect possible changes in whole sale and retail prices for used cars. The same excessive innovation strategy described in this section may surprisingly affect this publication as well. The used-car blue book may earn additional revenues when it publishes a new edition, because many market participants want to trade based on authoritative information. The authors of this dominant series thus may have a perverse incentive to have too many updates: even if it would be socially optimal to have updates only annually or semi-annually, they may make more money if they update quarterly.

[26] For example, Kansas Law Review requires that its authors comply.

[27] The bluebook has one rival in the legal marketplace of ideas—the 'maroon book' which springs from the University of Chicago. THE UNIVERSITY OF CHICAGO MANUAL OF LEGAL CITATION (1989). *See* Posner (1986). However, to date the market penetration of the late comer is relatively slight.

authoritative source. It is not surprising that the bluebook is now in its 15th edition. Of course there may be pressing aesthetic reasons why a certain reference needs to be put in 'large and small capital letters' instead of 'italics,'[28] but along with these aesthetics is the knowledge that each new edition will reap an economic windfall.[29]

Lest law students be singled out for abuse, let me stress that the same kind of incentive leads to excessive innovation with regard to law professors' revision of textbooks. Producing a new edition with only superficial changes can increase sales because students can no longer rely on outdated 'used' books.[30] This incentive for excessive innocuous innovation can succeed even in the face of competition from other casebooks. Even though each arbitrary new edition requires adopting professors to engage in additional teaching preparation—in part to find out what has been changed— teachers will often stay with the textbook that has been modified rather than switch to an entirely new casebook. A dominant producer is most likely to engage in excessive innocuous innovation when incumbent users will face higher 'switching costs' in switching to another manufacturer than in merely switching to an innocuously 'new and improved' edition of the same manufacturer. *See generally* Klemperer (1987) (describing use of switching costs to increase future profits) *and* Klemperer (1992) (providing examples of switching costs and describing their effects in the market).

Another example of excessive innocuous change might be found in the computer software industry. Even though there are often competitive types of software, incumbent users often find it easier to learn the new rules governing an upgrade rather than to switch to an entirely new type of software. And incumbent users may be forced to buy an innocuous upgrade to maintain compatibility with other users. Hence, even though upgrade competition in this dynamic industry seems to be primarily driven by legitimate technological innovation, manufacturers may have an additional incentive to innovate to generate the additional revenues from selling upgrades.

Moreover, the process of upgrading may itself enhance consumers' switching cost. If software competitors are trying to develop compatible software which can be used in conjunction with a dominant brand, then the dominant brand may have incentives to introduce arbitrary innovations that make it more difficult for rivals to achieve compatibility. Put simply, it

[28] Some changes in new editions legitimately seem to be prompted by changes in technology (viz. rules regarding citation of computer databases) or changes in social norms (viz. increased references to first names responding in part to patriarchal determination of last names).
[29] The bluebook story points more generally to the fact that arbiters of fashion have incentives for excessive innocuous intervention. This might be exemplified not only by the annual fall fashions, but also by Dr. Seuss's fable of the star-bellied sneeches (Geisel & Geisel 1961). Unfortunately, I do not have a well-developed theory of how one becomes an arbiter of fashion.
[30] To make this strategy effective it is important that the early materials be changed sufficiently so that the new edition has different page references.

is harder to imitate a moving target. For example, it would not be surprising if one of the motivating factors behind a Lotus upgrade would be a desire to make it more difficult for incumbent users to switch to Quattro Pro. Or it is rumoured that the mantra for the Windows development team at Microsoft was: 'It's not done until Lotus won't run.'—meaning that Lotus incompatibility was one of the goals to give Microsoft's Excel spreadsheet a competitive advantage.[31]

Among many legitimate motivations, Delaware may similarly be moved to enact innocuous and arbitrary amendments to its corporate law to generate additional rents and to make its code more difficult to copy. Extending the thesis of Miller and Macey (1987: n. 12), the Delaware bar may prefer seemingly innocuous change that gives rise to additional litigation. New statutes often give rise to an initial wave of clarifying litigation—so that the Delaware bar (much like the bluebook editors) may have an additional incentive to lobby for statutory change.

Statutory modification may also make it more difficult for other states to develop copycat legislation. For example, even though Nevada has explicitly attempted to incorporate Delaware standards into its corporate governance, amendments to the Delaware code force other states to continually try to catch up. Even innocuous differences between Delaware's code and that of other states may be sufficient to deter migration from the dominant state—if corporate counsel have difficulty evaluating (or pricing) individual statutory components. As a result, Delaware may have an incentive to differentiate its product for differentiation's sake itself. Innovating to increase the difficulty of imitation might even be one of the consequences of non-patentability. Because Delaware cannot patent its legitimate innovations to prevent imitation, it may be driven to engage in other inefficient statutory changes to help protect its intellectual property.

This bluebook story is more ephemeral than the patent or yachting stories. I have not tied the analysis to any particular statutory amendment in Delaware. But the plausibility of the phenomenon in the publishing of other authoritative standards—whether they be bluebooks, textbooks, or software—suggests that the phenomenon may play an analogous role in 'publishing' new editions of the Delaware corporate code. This is particularly true because, unlike private publishers, Delaware does not have to worry that users will continue to use the prior edition. For example, users of WordPerfect software were at least initially reluctant to switch to version 6.0. Private publishers face an additional constraint in producing innocuous innovations in that the user base may stick with the prior standard. Delaware as a publisher of law does not face this constraint because its amendments invalidate the prior law. While WordPerfect users can continue

---

[31] I thank Peter Cramton for telling me this rumour.

to use version 5.0 (eschewing the bug-laden improvements of version 6.0), Delaware corporate users cannot (easily) continue to use version 1987 once version 1994 becomes authoritative.[32]

The bluebook story thus predicts that Delaware will innovate first. And while this seems to accord with facts, the bluebook story does not by itself explain why trailing states would want to imitate the innocuous innovations. This is a serious weakness of the model. It is possible that states might copy even needless innovations for fear that divergence from Delaware on innocuous provisions would make it more difficult for them to compete with Delaware to retain their current base of incorporations. The idea here is that even counsel of corporations domestically incorporated would need to stay abreast of the intricacies of Delaware law in order to engage in transactions with the great number of Delaware corporations. Compatibility with Delaware is so important that corporate codes that differ may become disfavoured. While this provides a possible explanation for why trailing states would mimic the innocuous innovations of Delaware, I have not been able to conjure striking statutory examples of Delaware innovations that seem to be motivated by a desire to spur the additional revenues of unsettled law. In the end, the bluebook story is presented here more as an additional example of how strategic inefficiencies in the supply of real products can illuminate our understanding of competive federalism.

4. CONCLUSION

This paper has argued that, even if corporations demand value-maximizing law, supply-side inefficiencies may prevent a strong-form version of the race to the top. The supply-side incentives depend crucially upon whether a state may benefit from being first to promulgate an innovation (and even more particularly upon whether Delaware has the same incentive to innovate as competitor states).

Federal law plays an important role in establishing the parameters for state competition. The federal rules controlling statutory patentability in particular will affect whether there is a first-mover advantage to value-maximizing innovation. A distressing implication of these models is that it is not clear whether or how the federal rules should promote such an advantage. The patent story showed that the absence of a first-mover advantage could give rise to one type of inefficiencies, while the yachting and bluebook

---

[32] If the amendments merely establish a new default with regard to some aspect of corporate governance, then corporations could reestablish the prior governance by contracting around the amendment. Elsewhere I have argued that even a change between two default rules may produce non-trivial corporate effects, because private parties may have difficulty privately establishing standard-like governance as easily as the state (Ayres 1992c: n. 36).

stories suggest that first-mover advantages could give rise to other types of inefficiency. As in other areas, policy-makers and scholars need to judiciously choose among competing models on the basis of the models' falsifiable predictions. *See* Schmalensee (1979: 995).

The supply-side inefficiencies described in these models are at odds with the simplest models of industrial organization. Our first economic intuition is that competitors should supply the kind of good that is demanded in the marketplace. Even monopolists usually have an incentive to supply the efficient *quality*: monopolists price inefficiently, but they want to produce efficiently (i.e., supply the qualities that consumers demand) so that they can maximize their markup.

However, these intuitions are qualified when a firm must produce a single type of product for heterogeneous types of competitors. A seminal article by Michael Spence (1975: 417) pointed out that a monopolist choosing a single quality would have an incentive to choose a quality that was preferred by 'marginal' consumers who are indifferent between purchasing or not (given the monopoly overcharge). Tying product quality to the preferences of marginal consumers can be inefficient if the average (or 'inframarginal') consumer prefers a different type of product.

The Spence model is instructive because it illustrates as a general matter that producers may have incentives to supply products with a socially inefficient quality. But Spence's result only holds if producers are constrained to produce a limited number of products[33]—because otherwise the savvy producer would supply different types of products to satisfy the different types of demand. The Spencian model is thus consistent with the specialization thesis of Richard Posner and Kenneth Scott (1980) (*see also* Basinger & Butler 1985)—that different states might specialize in providing corporate statutes for different types of corporations—because states would only need to specialize in providing a particular type of corporate franchise if providing multiple types of governance were infeasible.

As applied to corporate law, this Spencian logic suggests that: 'Reincorporating firms are this market's marginal consumers. . . . The market causes the states to focus on the variables that influence reincorporation decisions' (Bratton & McCahery, chapter 7, this volume). Roberta Romano's empiricism suggests a way to test this theory. Romano identified particular types of firms that are most likely to reincorporate. Delaware may not have incentives to supply the demands of its many infra-marginal consumers (who are sufficiently satisfied with Delaware corporate governance that they are unlikely to change—even if several parts of the code fail to provide efficient law). In future work, I hope to identify the parts of the

---

[33] In Spence's original model (1975), fixed costs of producing different product types constrained the number of products.

code and the types of corporations that theory predicts would be neglected in Delaware's attempt to choose the product quality that will maximize its rents.[34]

Roberta Romano's insight that law can be thought of as a product invites a broader application of the industrial organization theory about the determinants of product quality. To date corporate scholars have only scratched the surface of this rich literature—detailing the possibility of subtle strategic inefficiencies. Arbitrage between these two academic markets seems particularly appropriate.

---

[34] An initial part of this research argued that close corporations were infra-marginal consumers—in the sense that their choice of jurisdiction was not sensitive to differences in substantive corporate rules (Ayres 1992a: n. 7). As a result, I suggested that Delaware and other states had diluted incentives to provide value-maximizing law for these firms. This future research would extend the insights of Lucian Bebchuk (1992: 1452 n. 12, 1454).

9

Competitive Federalism and Legislative Incentives to Recognize Same-Sex Marriage in the USA

JENNIFER GERARDA BROWN*

I. INTRODUCTION

In *Baehr* v. *Lewin*, 1993, the Supreme Court of Hawaii held that Hawaii's marriage statute discriminates on the basis of gender and may therefore violate the state constitution's equal protection clause. The statute allows marriage only between a man and a woman; same-sex couples are excluded.[1] The trial court in *Baehr* (1993: 68) must now decide whether the law serves a compelling state interest. Some predict that the state will be unable to justify the law and that Hawaii will become the first state to solemnize marriages between people of the same sex.

Same-sex marriage clearly raises serious questions about discrimination, tradition, and morality. But economic concerns are also at stake. Because certain states could reap substantial economic benefits by being the first to solemnize same-sex marriage, the debates about the issue to date have been incomplete. While *Baehr* and cases like it permit state courts to legalize same-sex marriage on constitutional grounds, the thesis of this chapter is that certain states might have an independent rent incentive to be the first to legalize same-sex marriage. The first state to solemnize same-sex marriages could draw visitors from every state in the union, and the present value of increased tourism revenue could exceed $4 billion. This estimate is based on conservative assumptions about (a) the number of same-sex couples who would travel to a first-mover state for weddings and honeymoons, and (b) the spending that the average wedding would generate.

This increased tourism revenue could in turn redound to the benefit of all the state's citizens. Tourism does not just increase retail spending in a state. It also creates jobs, increases the average household income, and benefits the state directly through taxes and license fees. Hawaii's Department of

* A longer version of this article appears at 68 So.Cal.L.Rev. 745 (1995), and portions of that article are reprinted here with permission from the Southern California Law Review.
[1] Haw. Rev. Stat. sects. 572–1.

Business, Economic Development, and Tourism estimates that $4 billion in direct spending by tourists generates $440 million in state and county tax revenues, thousands of jobs, and $2.4 billion in household income for the state's residents. This increased revenue could have a particularly dramatic effect in a small state like Hawaii, where it could raise the present value of household wealth by more than $6,700.

Just as competitive federalism leads states to compete for charter revenues and other types of interest-group rents, it could also lead states to compete for the tourism revenue from solemnizing same-sex marriages. As Connecticut is to insurance; Delaware is to corporate law; and Nevada is to gambling, marriage, and divorce; so Hawaii (or some similarly situated state) could become to same-sex marriage. States have competed for the sorts of individual and collective benefits sketched here, and same-sex marriage could provide another opportunity for such competition.

This chapter examines the economic incentives to recognize same-sex marriage, detailing the 'first-mover' advantage that might inure to a state that breaks ground in this area. Based upon three assumptions about the number of gay men and lesbian women in the USA, the probability that they would marry if permitted, and the amount of money they might spend on their weddings and honeymoons, I present both quantitative estimations of potential benefits and qualitative analysis of some offsetting risks, such as boycotts, tipping, or competition from other states. The chapter also identifies the factors that might make a state more or less likely to enter the race to recognize same-sex marriage.

2. THE ECONOMIC INCENTIVES TO RECOGNIZE SAME-SEX MARRIAGE

2.1 Estimating the potential for enhanced tourism

This section estimates the enhanced tourism that could be enjoyed by the first state to solemnize same-sex marriage. These estimates rest on three crucial assumptions:

1. Same-sex marriages on average will generate $6,000 of in-state spending.
2. The number of gay men and lesbians in the United States of America is somewhere between 1% and 3% of the general population.
3. Gay men and lesbians will marry at a rate that is at least 1/3 the rate for the general population.

The next section explicitly defends these assumptions and argues that they produce conservative estimates of expected revenues. The goal of the present section is to show the potentially dramatic impact that same-sex marriage could have on a state's tourism.

Using these assumptions I construct a 'pent-up demand' model—which assumes that even though same-sex marriage is not legally recognized, some gay men and lesbians have already formed enduring unions and would be ready to solemnize them shortly after legalization—to estimate the revenue to be generated by legalizing same-sex marriage. This initial flood of demand should be followed by a continuing demand (or 'flow') as additional same-sex unions are formed.

A. The 'Pent-Up Demand' model

By assuming that substantial pre-legalization matching has taken place, we find a 'stock' of couples with an immediate, pent-up demand for same-sex marriage. In the USA, approximately 45% of the total population is currently married (Bureau of the Census 1993: 53). If we assume that same-sex couples would marry at roughly 1/3 the rate of different-sex couples, we assume that 15% of gay men and lesbians would be married at any given time if legally permitted. This number might be arbitrarily high or low, since we are trying to predict behaviour under conditions (the legality of same-sex marriage) that have never existed before.

Table 1 illustrates one approach to estimating the demand for same-sex marriages and the revenue they would generate. First, if 3% of Americans are gay or lesbian, then the gay population in this country is 7.65 million. Second, if 15% of gay men and lesbians currently want to marry, we find a pent-up demand for 573,750 same-sex marriages. Third, if each same-sex couple would spend $6,000 in the state where the wedding occurs, Table 1 presents a 'stock' or pent-up demand for same-sex marriage that could yield $3.4 billion in revenue.

This stock of same-sex marriages would probably not be released immediately upon legalization. The pent-up demand would probably clear over a number of years—perhaps five to ten. Because same-sex marriage has not been legal and gay and lesbian couples have not been able to wed, however, some initial swell would be likely, tapering off to a smaller but steady flow as the pent-up demand is satisfied.

In addition to this pent-up demand, we can expect a continuing stream of same-sex marriages in the future. Table 1 estimates this additional *annual* demand for same-sex marriage by assuming that gay men and lesbians would marry at one-third the rate of the general population—approximately 10 marriages per thousand people (O'Connell 1993). Accordingly, Table 1 assumes 3.33 marriages per 1,000 gay people per year. Applying this annual rate to the total number of gay men and lesbians in the United States of America, we find in Table 1 an ongoing demand for approximately 25,500 same-sex marriages per year. Again, if each same-sex union generates $6,000 in revenue, the 'flow' of tourist revenue from same-sex marriage reaches $153 million per year.

Table 1. Estimates of Tourist Revenue from Same-sex Marriage

	Stock Analysis	Flow Analysis
Number of Gay People in USA[a]	7.65 million	
Number of Same-sex Marriages[b]	573,750 marriages	25,500 marriages
Tourist Revenue from Same-sex Marriages[c]	$3.4 billion	$153 million
Present Value of Tourist Revenue[d]	$4.3 billion	

[a] Calculated assuming that 3 percent of the 255 million people in the USA are gay.
[b] Calculated assuming that 15% of gay people have a current demand for marriage and that an additional 3.33 marriages per thousand gay people would occur each year.
[c] Calculated by multiplying the number of marriages by $6,000 per wedding.
[d] Calculated assuming a ten percent interest rate, the stock of pent-up demand is cleared evenly over 5 years, and additional annual demand flows for 20 years.

These estimates of the stock and flow of marriage demand can be used to calculate the present value of legalizing same-sex marriage to the first state that moves in this direction. The 'stock' of demand will take some time to clear. The present value estimate in Table 1 is calculated assuming: 1) all of the couples who were ready to marry before legalization (the pent-up demand) will get married in the first-mover state in the five years immediately following legalization; 2) the flow demand will begin to form in the first year following legalization and continue for 20 years; and 3) the appropriate annual discount rate is 10%.[2] A state cannot expect to reap all of the benefits of this legal change immediately. But even if we discount the expected stock and flow revenue from same-sex marriage to its present value, we find that legalizing same-sex marriage could yield a benefit of $4.3 billion. Even varying the assumptions, it is difficult not to generate many millions of dollars of enhanced revenue: for example, even if we had assumed that only 1% of the population is gay and same-sex couples wish to marry at only 1/10 the rate of the general population, we find that a state could generate over 430 million dollars in revenue.

The pent-up demand model has the advantage of capturing the reality that many gay unions already exist and would immediately seek recognition from the first possible state. Indeed, shortly after the Hawaii Supreme Court's decision was announced in *Baehr* v. *Lewin*, gay marriage activists reported, '[w]e're already getting a lot of calls and letters from the mainland with people who want to come here to get married. We have to tell them, "no, not just yet." ' (Gray 1994).

[2] A valid discount rate based solely on the cost of capital would no doubt be lower than 10%, but the 10% interest rate and the 20-year limit on the flow demand also reflect the risk that the state will lose its first-mover advantage.

B. *The benefits of enhanced tourism*

For states that rely upon tourism as an important industry, it may seem obvious that increased tourism will produce benefits. The various ways in which tourism benefits a state are not so obvious, however, and require some discussion. When people travel to a state they spend money on transportation, lodging, food, and retail goods. Citizens of the state who own or work at businesses in these sectors will enjoy increased revenue. Direct spending by tourists also generates a second round of spending as hotels, restaurants, and retail stores make purchases with the money the tourists brought to the state. This indirect or induced output is one byproduct of tourist revenue which often keeps the increased revenue circulating in the state (*See* Lundberg 1989: 148). In addition, the state directly benefits as it taxes some of the direct and indirect spending generated by the tourism. Sales tax, license fees, and special taxes (on hotels or alcohol, for example) increase the state's revenue. All of this economic activity creates jobs, and states with high unemployment rates benefit when less demand is placed on their unemployment or welfare budgets.

The analysis of tourism's effect on a state economy has its own vocabulary. The consequential benefits of tourism are commonly measured by the use of 'multipliers,' or ratios that measure 'multiple spending within an economy' (Lundberg 1989: 147). Multipliers are highest when tourist dollars can circulate within a state's economy, stimulating additional transactions. Trading relationships within an economy are called 'linkages' (McIntosh 1992: 92). Donald Lundberg (1989: 148) explains:

the various sectors of an economy are linked together, each part affecting the others. When the links increase in number and strength, the impact of the tourist dollar on the economy also increases and less money leaves the area. In other words, the more money that remains in the economy, the fewer the leaks and the higher the multiplier effect. . . . The greater the percentage of the tourist dollar that remains in the economy and the faster it is respent, the greater its effect in 'heating' the economy of an area.

The multiplier measures the effect of an additional dollar entering an economy, tracking the 'turnover' from the additional income and its impact on various sectors of the economy (Lundberg 1989: 147). For example, tourism qualifies as an export that brings new money into an economy. The portion of that new money that remains in the economy, being spent and respent, determines the impact that tourism revenue has on underlying measures of social welfare: indirect spending, state revenue (primarily from taxes), household income, and job creation (Lundberg 1989: 147).

The multiplier effect can be dramatic in some state economies. Consider, for example, Hawaii's calculations of the economic activity generated by 'visitor-related expenditure' (II.D.B.E.D.T. 1992: 203). I determined above that the present value of new tourism from legalizing same-sex marriage could most likely exceed four billion dollars. For the sake of simplicity, let us adopt $4 billion as the present value of revenue to be generated. Using Hawaii's own calculation of the multiplier effect within its borders, Table 2 shows that this $4 billion in direct spending by tourists will in turn generate an additional $3.2 billion in indirect sales. Perhaps most importantly to the citizens of Hawaii and their representatives, this additional $4 billion would increase the present value of household wealth by $2.4 billion ($6,700 per household) and create 19,000 jobs in the earlier years following legalization—dropping to 3,500 jobs once the 'pent-up demand' is satisfied.[3] In addition to these private benefits, a $4 billion increase in tourism would, according to the state's estimates, generate $440 million in additional state and county tax revenues. Enhanced tourism from legalization of same-sex marriages can thus contribute to core elements of social welfare: jobs, household wealth, and state tax revenue.

Table 2. Income, Employment and Tax Benefits Generated By Marriage Tourism Revenue

Estimated Additional Tourism Revenue[a]	Total Additional Sales Generated[b]	Household Income[c]	Jobs[d]	State and County Tax Revenues[e]
$4 billion	$7.2 billion	$2.4 billion	19,000 short term 3,500 long term	$440 mill.

[a] Present value estimate of additional tourist revenue that might be generated from lifting prohibition against same-sex marriage.

[b] Present value estimate assuming 1.8 tourism multiplier. H.D.B.E.D.T. (1992: Table 211)

[c] Present value estimate assuming .6 income multiplier. H.D.B.E.D.T. (1992: Table 211).

[d] Assuming (short-term) revenue for first 5 years of $833 million and subsequent (long-term) annual revenue of 153 million. See supra Table 1. Also assumes .0023% job multiplier. H.D.B.E.D.T. (1992: Table 211)

[e] Present value estimate assuming .11 tax revenue multiplier. See H.D.B.E.D.T. (1992: Table 211)

These estimates, however, turn crucially on whether the dollars recirculate within the state. If 40% of each dollar spent on lodging goes to local employees of the hotel, for example, that dollar may benefit the local economy more than a dollar spent in a bar, because the bar may have had to

---

[3] The number of jobs cannot be discounted to present value the way monetary figures can be. In the 'pent-up demand' model, legalizing same-sex marriage creates $833 million of additional tourism in each of the first five years following legalization and $153 million per year in subsequent years. We can use Hawaii's multiplier to calculate the number of jobs created during each phase of the post-legalization period.

import the alcohol, causing most of the dollar to 'leak' to recipients outside the relevant community (such as a winemaker in California). The benefits of legislation will differ from state to state because tourism dollars leak out of some states more quickly than others.

2.2. Defending the assumptions

The estimates produced by the 'pent-up demand' model are the fairly straightforward result of multiplying the number of gays, the proportion of them who would wed if permitted, and the amount each couple would spend. Because the method for deriving estimates is so straightforward, it should be simple for any reader who is unpersuaded by my assumptions to substitute larger or smaller numbers.

A. The average amount spent on weddings

It is reasonable to assume that each same-sex wedding will generate average spending of $6,000 in the first-mover state. This estimate is less than half the average amount spent by different-sex couples on weddings and honeymoons in the USA—$13,000 to $19,000 (PR Newswire 1993a; Leckey 1993; Giordano 1993). Some surveys have shown that the average annual household income is $49,525 among respondents who identify themselves as gay or lesbian, while the national average for the USA is $36,620 (Greenberg 1993; Flinn 1993a; Morris 1993; *But see* Elliott 1994: C17). While 4% of the general public has an income above $100,000, 15% of gay households have incomes that high (Greenberg 1993).

Not only do many same-sex couples have the sorts of disposable income that could support expensive weddings, they may also be more likely than the general population to spend money on travel. 'They represent a travel marketer's dream,' says Sharon Rooney, who works for the San Francisco Convention and Visitor's Bureau (Flinn 1993a). Some studies show that gay men and lesbians took an average of 4.61 trips within the USA in the last three years, and in 1992 41% of gay men and lesbians travelled internationally (Greenberg 1993). In 1993, Overlooked Opinions studied travel in the gay community and found that gay men and lesbians are seven times more likely to travel abroad than the average American (*SEATTLE TIMES* 1993). Even if same-sex couples were accompanied by only two guests (on average), the guests' additional food and lodging in the first-mover state would bring total expenditures related to the wedding well above $6,000:

Ceremony & Reception	$1,100
Honeymoon	$2,800
Expenses for Guests/Entourage	$2,300

Effective Airfare[4] $1,000
Total $7,200

When these expenses for ceremony and reception, food and lodging, and transportation are totaled, we find a sum of $7,200, well above our conservative $6,000 estimate.

If the $6,000 assumption seems inflated, the impact of an even more conservative assumption can be easily calculated. Assuming that same-sex weddings would generate only half as much tourism revenue ($3,000 per wedding) simply halves the impact on the state economy: legalizing same-sex marriage would still generate about two billion dollars in tourism and increase household wealth in a state like Hawaii by more than $3,000. Few legislative initiatives could match this impact.

B. *The number of gay men and lesbians in the USA*

Since 1948, when Alfred C. Kinsey and his associates released their path-breaking study, *Sexual Behavior in the Human Male*, the oft-cited statistic is that 10% of the population is gay (Kinsey 1948: 650–51). This number has come under fire, however, as more recent studies have found smaller percentages of the population reporting predominantly or exclusively homosexual activity (Gephard 1976: 27–28). Problems with methodology may cause these studies to under-estimate the number of gay men and lesbians in the USA. Arguably, however, studies that underreport the number of gay people due to cultural bias might be helpful in our attempt to determine how many gay and lesbian couples would opt for marriage if given the chance. Because the marriage would necessarily be a public act, it is likely that only couples who are 'out'—and therefore more likely to respond truthfully to surveys that ask about their homosexuality—would choose to marry.

Richard Posner (1992), in his book *Sex and Reason*, estimates that 3% is probably an accurate measure of the portion of the population that is gay and lesbian. One could argue for higher estimates, and indeed, some studies have reported them (Dietrich 1993; Jacobs 1993). For the sake of conservative argument, I adopt the very lowest estimates, and assume that 1 to 3% of the USA population is gay or lesbian. The total population of the USA is 255 million (Bureau of the Census 1993: 8). Thus I assume that the total number of gay men and lesbian women in this country is somewhere between 2.55 and 7.65 million people, as shown in Table 1.

---

[4] In Hawaii, tourist expenditures on air travel have only 57% of the impact on private income that general tourist expenditures have (H.D.B.E.D.T. 1992). If same-sex couples and their entourage (again, assuming an average of only two guests) spent $400 on airfare per person, their travel expenses could generate an additional $1033 of effective spending in the first-mover state (once discounted to account for leakage).

C. *The proportion of gay men and lesbians who will wed*

The estimates of additional tourist revenue presented above turn in part upon the likely demand for same-sex marriage if a state were to legalize it. This section argues that gay and lesbian couples would travel to marry in a foreign state to secure both symbolic and legal benefits. The limited empirical work that has been done in this area has revealed high levels of commitment among many gay couples and a strong desire for marriage (*PARTNERS NEWSLETTER FOR GAY & LESBIAN COUPLES* 1991; Demion and Bryant 1990; *PARTNERS NEWSLETTER FOR GAY AND LESBIAN COUPLES* 1990; Bell & Weinberg 1978: 91, 97).

The desire is reasonable: tremendous legal and symbolic benefits inure to couples who formalize their relationships in marriage. Both state and federal tax liability can be affected by marital status, though it must be noted that for some couples, marriage increases rather than decreases their aggregate income tax liability (Robinson & Wenig 1989: 842–43; Price 1993*b*). Employment benefits often turn upon a couple's marital status.[5] Many health plans allow only married couples to enjoy coverage under one spouse's health plan.[6] If one member of a same-sex couple is incarcerated, his or her partner may have restricted visiting privileges.[7] Immigration law gives preferences to USA citizens' family members, spouses, and fiances when they seek to emigrate from another country.[8] When one partner dies, a surviving spouse retains certain powers, including the right to inherit under a state's intestacy laws;[9] the right to make decisions about cremation, burial, and funeral arrangements;[10] and the ability to remain in a rent-controlled apartment.[11] Hospital visitation rights are typically granted only to traditional family members (Cox 1986: 46–50). Ability to authorize emergency medical treatment is also usually limited to traditional families (Cox 1986: 50). Same-sex partners have had to litigate in order to serve as guardians of injured or ailing partners.[12] These are privileges that would be granted as a matter of course to married people.

[5] *Rovira* v. *AT&T*, 760 F. Supp. 376 (S.D.N.Y. 1991); *But see In re Michael D.*, S 24774, Cal. Unempl. Ins. App. Bd. (Sept. 13, 1985).
[6] *Hinman* v. *Department of Personnel Administration*, 213 Cal. Rptr. 410, 415–19 (Ct. App. 1985).
[7] *Doe* v. *Sparks*, 733 F. Supp. 227 (W.D. Pa. 1990).
[8] 8 U.S.C. sect. 1186(d)(1)(A); *Adams* v. *Howerton*, 673 F.2d 1036 (9th Cir. 1982), *cert. denied*, 458 U.S. 1111 (1982).
[9] *Matter of Estate of Cooper*, 564 N.Y.S.2d 684 (1990).
[10] *Stewart* v. *Schwartz Brothers Jefferson Memorial Chapel, Inc.*, 606 N.Y.S.2d 965, 966 (1993).
[11] *Braschi* v. *Stahl Associates Company*, 543 N.E.2d 49 (N.Y. 1989).
[12] In *re Guardianship of Sharon Kowalski*, 478 N.W.2d 790 (Minn. Ct. App. 1991); Stoddard (1989).

In *Baehr*, the Hawaii Supreme Court referred to a list of 150 'rights and benefits' under Hawaii law that are contingent on marital status.[13] Hawaii is typical of many states that allocate certain benefits and rights only to legally recognized spouses.

A final category of marriage benefits become effective if the relationship ends. The state can reduce the transaction costs of negotiating the dissolution of marriage. With marriage comes a state-sponsored dispute resolution service providing adjudication or, often, mediation. The substantive default rules governing division of property could also help same-sex couples to allocate resources at the end of their relationships, but the legal system does not currently lend them this aid.[14]

Granted, some of these benefits could be secured through contract (Lopez 1993: 360; Bullock 1992: 1054; Maltz 1992: 955; 1991: 504). Gay and lesbian couples could draft wills to insure that their partners would be provided for upon their deaths, and they could execute powers of attorney assuring that their partners would have some say in health care decisions. Couples could also contract ex ante for division of property if their relationships should end, and thus gain some of the benefits of the rules that pertain to divorce. But such agreements create transaction costs, which in some cases might be substantial, and enforcement is uncertain in some contexts. Giving same-sex couples access to the same default rules that govern different-sex marriage contracts would confer a significant benefit. Moreover, many benefits of marriage—such as tax deductions or prison visitation rights—can be granted only by the government, and are not susceptible to creation by private contract (Bonhall 1994).

Thus, gay men and lesbians have legal and economic reasons to seek the right to marry. A desire for these tangible benefits could fuel substantial demand if a state were to solemnize same-sex marriage. The demand might be dampened, however, if couples marrying in the first-mover state were unable to secure recognition of the marriage upon returning to their home states. The Full Faith and Credit clause of the USA Constitution generally requires states to give effect to the statutes and other legal acts of sibling states, but this constitutional mandate adheres only when choice of law rules dictate that the law of one state applies to a dispute being adjudicated in another state. This issue of interstate recognition thus raises important questions about choice of law.

Some commentators have boldly declared or tacitly assumed that the Full Faith and Credit clause would require sibling states to recognize same-sex marriages if any state decided to celebrate them (Damslet 1993: 591; Cameli

[13] (1990: 49); Plaintiffs' Memorandum in Opposition to Defendant's Motion for Judgment on the Pleadings Filed on July 9, 1991 at 20, *Baehr* v. *Lewin*, No. 91–1394–05 (August 29, 1991).
[14] *De Santo* v. *Barnsley*, 476 A.2d 952 (Pa. Super. Ct. 1984).

1992: 477; Gray 1994). Article IV (Sec. 1) of the United States of America Constitution requires that 'Full Faith and Credit shall be given in each State to the public Acts, Records, and judicial Proceedings of every other State.' 'Public Acts' include statutes, and thus would appear to include the licensing of same-sex marriages pursuant to an inclusive marriage law.[15]

Despite its apparently sweeping effect, however, the Full Faith and Credit clause might not require sibling states to recognize same-sex marriages celebrated in the first-mover state. Granted, the clause does place some constitutional constraints on the ability of the several states to ignore the acts of sibling states. But those constraints are ill-defined, leading to the 'dominant view' that 'the phrase cannot be taken literally, and therefore, it need not be taken seriously at all' (Laycock 1992: 294).

The dictates of the Full Faith and Credit clause apply only against a backdrop of well-established choice of law rules (see Regan 1987). These rules determine as a threshold matter that the law of a particular state is applicable; only then does the Full Faith and Credit clause require other states to apply that law (Laycock 1992: 290). If choice of law principles allow a state to ignore a same-sex marriage solemnized in the first-mover state, there is nothing in the Full Faith and Credit clause to trump that decision. Thus choice of law rules will determine the legal effect of same-sex marriages celebrated in the first-mover state.

The general choice of law rule applied to marriages is that a marriage valid where contracted is valid everywhere (Restatement 1971: sect. 283; Scoles & Hay 1992: 438 n. 6). The Uniform Marriage and Divorce Act (N.C.C.U.S.L. 1973: sect. 210) codifies this rule:

All marriages contracted . . . outside this State, that were valid at the time of the contract or subsequently validated by the laws of the place in which they were contracted . . . are valid in this state.

This provision—or something substantially similar—is the law in at least 17 states, including several populous states that could produce many of the same-sex couples who wish to marry. Because the general choice of law rule seems to refer back to the laws of the state that celebrates the marriage, one might conclude, as several commentators have, that the Full Faith and Credit clause would require other states to recognize a same-sex marriage celebrated in the first-mover state. In the absence of any competing choice of law rules, states that have adopted the Uniform Marriage and Divorce Act probably would recognize same-sex marriages celebrated in the first-mover state.

This analysis could lead one to ask: if a state were willing to recognize same-sex marriages contracted in the first-mover state, why wouldn't the

---

[15] *Hughes* v. *Fetter*, 341 U.S. 609, 611 (1951); *John Hancock Mutual Life Ins. Col.* v. *Yates*, 299 U.S. 178, 183 (1936); *Bradford Elec. Light Co.* v. *Clapper*, 286 US. 145, 154–55 (1932).

state also be willing to amend its own marriage statute to permit same-sex marriage? The recognition of same-sex marriages celebrated elsewhere will come to a state's courts on a case-by-case basis. Courts could thus grant limited recognition, reserving the state's ability to ignore the marriages for some purposes. Legislative legalization of same-sex marriage, on the other hand, would commit the state to a more general policy of permitting same-sex marriage. Thus the political vulnerability of elected representatives might deter them from acts that judges (many appointed or with life tenure) could perform both more gradually and with greater insulation from public disapproval.

Two competing choice of law rules—a 'strong public policy' rule and the Uniform Marriage Evasion Act—could provide a means to avoid the general rule of recognition. When a couple returns home and seeks recognition of their same-sex marriage contracted in the first-mover state, the home state might refuse on the ground that recognizing same-sex marriage would violate the 'strong public policy' of the home state. The 'strong public policy' principle as a choice of law rule is found in the Restatement (Second) of Conflicts. According to the Restatement (1971: sect. 283(2)), '[a] marriage which satisfied the requirements of the state where the marriage was contracted will everywhere be recognized as valid unless it violates the strong public policy of another state which had the most significant relationship' to the marriage. As Scoles and Hay (1992: 433) explain, [i]t is only where there is rather violent conflict between the enjoyment of an incident (of marriage) and the assumed social order where enjoyment is sought that an otherwise valid marriage will be denied recognition.

Before invoking the 'strong public policy' rule, a court would probably identify the *purpose* for which the couple seeks recognition of the marriage, or the 'incident of marriage' at issue. If a couple sought to claim tax deductions or health benefits, for example, recognizing the marriage would require the court to acknowledge the marriage as a valid, ongoing entity (Scoles & Hay 1992: 462). If, on the other hand, one of the spouses had died and the surviving spouse sought bereavement benefits or an intestacy share of the decedent's estate, a court might recognize the marriage, but solely as a status enjoyed in the past—there would be no ongoing relationship to be affirmed (Scoles & Hay 1992: 450).

In addition, the source of the attack on the marriage might make a difference. In many of the cases invalidating marriage because of incest or age limitations, the challenge to the marriage is internal: one 'spouse' seeks to have the marriage annulled or otherwise declared invalid.[16] If, on the other hand, the marriage has continued for some time or the attack is external—by someone other than a party to the marriage—according to Scoles and

---

[16] *Wilkins v. Zelichowski*, 140 A.2d 65 (N.J. 1958).

Hay (1992: 452) 'this greatly strengthens the validation policies of sustaining expectations and protecting those relying on the marriage.' Some same-sex couples might marry in the hope that the validity of their marriage will not be tested for many years (when one of them dies in old age, for example), and that the passage of time will solidify the marriage in the eyes of a court.

Many states would no doubt rule that same-sex marriage is inconsistent with their 'strong public policy.' In *Loucks* v. *Standard Oil*, (1918: 198, 202), however, Justice Cardozo articulated a rather exacting standard for measuring the strength of the public policy at issue:

The courts are not free to refuse to enforce a foreign right at the pleasure of the judges, to suit the individual notion of expediency or fairness. They do not close their doors unless help would violate some fundamental principle of justice, some prevalent conception of good morals, some deep-rooted tradition of the common weal.

In the marriage context, courts have stated that a marriage which is valid where celebrated should be invalidated in another state only if it is 'odious by the common consent of nations, or if its influence is thought dangerous to the fabric of society.'[17] The 'strong public policy' exception is thus in theory very narrow; in the context of marriage it is invoked to deny recognition of marriage only rarely, and almost always at the request of one of the putative spouses. Moreover, the Commissioners on Uniform Laws expressly stated that the Uniform Marriage and Divorce Act does *not* incorporate the 'public policy' exception (N.C.C.U.S.L. 1973: sect. 210, official comment).

The invocation of public policy might be undercut or reinforced by other laws in these states. For example, if the state or large metropolitan areas within it have domestic partnership laws, those laws could demonstrate that the public policy of the state already allows some recognition for same-sex unions. Currently, dozens of municipal or county governments have promulgated policies granting benefits and other protections to domestic partnerships, and the states where they are located might acknowledge these statements of local public policy. In addition to laws protecting domestic partnerships, some state governments have enacted laws protecting gay rights generally. Repeal of a state sodomy statute might reveal a strong movement among the state's citizens to protect the privacy of gay men and lesbians. Laws that generally protect gay rights in this way might estop a state from asserting that recognizing gay marriage would 'violate some

---

[17] *Re Chace*, 58 A. 978 (R.I. 1904). In 1912, the National Conference of Commissioners on Uniform laws recognized a broader set of marriages that might violate public policy: 'e.g. marriage with *particeps criminis*, or with a minor without parental consent, or within a specified time after entry of final decree of divorce, or between a white and a colored person' (N.C.C.U.S.L. 1912: 125–30).

fundamental principle of justice, some prevalent conception of good morals, some deep-rooted tradition of the common weal'.[18]

If a facial difference between the law of a couple's home state and that of the first-mover state is not enough to support a 'strong public policy' exception, then some stronger showing of public policy in the home state will be required. Because the state would have to justify its refusal to recognize the marriage in the face of the Full Faith and Credit clause, constitutional values would be at stake. The Full Faith and Credit clause may therefore give the gay or lesbian couple a constitutional hook on which to hang their marriage, even though other constitutional theories have been generally unavailing.

In addition to the 'strong public policy' exception, states might invoke Marriage Evasion statutes to support their refusal to recognize same-sex marriages celebrated in the first-mover state (N.C.C.U.S.L. 1912: 127–28). The Marriage Evasion Act allows a home state to nullify a marriage celebrated in another state if the couple are actually domiciliaries of the home state and were wed out of state for the purpose of evading the laws of their own state. The National Conference of Commissioners on Uniform State Laws withdrew the Marriage Evasion Act in 1943, because it had not gained 'widespread adoption' and 'merely tend[ed] to confuse the law' (N.C.C.U.S.L. 1943: 64). Nonetheless, many states have retained some evasion provisions in their marriage laws.

Courts might invoke these marriage evasion provisions to invalidate same-sex marriages celebrated in the first-mover state if they found that same-sex couples traveled to the first-mover state specifically to evade the laws of their home state. Because this chapter discusses incentives for a first-mover, it assumes that most couples marrying in the first-mover state *would* be evading their own states' prohibitions on same-sex marriage. Scoles and Hay (1992: 444) have asserted that states are most likely to deny recognition to marriages validly celebrated in sibling states if 'the legislative prohibition in the common domicile . . . is explicit in declaring the marriage void, or if the violation of the domiciliary notion of good morals as to the incident in question is flagrant.' Although none of the several states have legalized same-sex marriage, only four states have explicitly prohibited it.[19] Therefore, although the existence of a Marriage Evasion statute in a couple's home state might create some risk that a marriage contracted in the first-mover state would be invalidated, it is not certain that a court would invoke the statute. And couples who live in states without evasion

---

[18] *Loucks* v. *Standard Oil Co.*, 120 N.E. 198, 202 (N.Y. 1918).

[19] Ind. Code Ann. 31.7.1.2 (1993); Tex. Family Code Ann. sect. 1.01 (West 1993); Utah Code Ann. 30–1–2 (1987); Va. Code Ann. 20–45.2 (1990). *See also* Md. Fam. Law Code Ann. 2.201 (Supp. 1989) ('Marriage between a man and a woman is valid'); Ohio Rev. Code Ann. 3101.01 (1989) (same).

provisions can marry in the first-mover state knowing that their marriage will not be invalidated based solely upon their 'evasive' motivation (Applebaum 1993: 21).

If one state began to recognize same-sex marriage, of course, we could expect to see some legislative backlash in other states. Those without marriage evasion statutes might enact them specifically to discourage their residents from contracting same-sex marriages out of state. In addition to this reactive legislation related to choice of law, some states might amend substantive statutes and regulations to confer benefits on married couples *other than* same-sex couples married out of state. Because the demand for same-sex marriage exists in a dynamic world, legal changes following the first-mover's decision to recognize same-sex marriage could amplify or subdue that demand as time passes.

Even if a marriage between people of the same sex were to receive only limited recognition in the couple's home state upon their return, many couples would nonetheless travel to another state to have their marriages solemnized. This is because marriage carries great symbolic weight.[20] Many different-sex couples marry in order to declare and confirm their commitment to each other, and they value a state's certification of that commitment (Sherman 1992; Butler 1990). Same-sex couples could value marriage for the same reason, particularly because the current state of the law excluding them from marriage marginalizes their relationships and contributes to a sense of 'second class citizenship' (Leonard 1993; Salholz 1993). Even if a marriage celebrated in one state were to receive only limited recognition in other states, same-sex couples might derive some comfort and encouragement from the knowledge that—at least in one state—their union has been given the fullest endorsement the law can impart. Many same-sex couples might choose to marry for the symbolic benefits alone.

2.3. Other influences on a state's expected revenue

Earlier I estimated the tourism revenue that a first-mover state might capture by recognizing same-sex marriage. The state might enjoy additional benefits more difficult to quantify. These include slight increases in tourism by same-sex couples wishing to gain advantages in immigration, increased tourism by people who are not visiting the state in order to marry but wish to show support for the legal change, and increased visits by couples whose marriages need 'servicing' through divorce proceedings. These additional

---

[20] The symbolism could have concrete effects for private employers who want to grant benefits to partners of gay and lesbian employees but lack a good test for deserving relationships. Even if the home state refused recognition of the marriages for public purposes, the first mover's celebration of the marriage could serve as a proxy for the quality of commitment that merits the award of employee benefits in the private sector.

benefits are not the only potential influences on a state's expected revenue, however; the state must also consider some downside risks in the form of boycotts and tipping. Finally, a state might worry that revenue could dramatically decrease if other states were to compete by legalizing same-sex marriage.

A. Enhanced revenue: sympathy tourism and divorce

Recognition of same-sex marriage could draw additional categories of tourists besides same-sex couples who live in other states. For example, a first-mover stands to gain increased revenue from what we might call 'sympathy tourism.' Some people may travel to the state not specifically to get married, but rather to support the first state that legalizes same-sex marriage.

In recent years, gay rights advocates have taken stock of the community's economic clout. The 'gay dollars' phenomenon, in which dollar bills have the words 'gay dollars' stamped or written on their face, is meant to demonstrate the spending power of the gay community.[21] The gay community and its supporters have sought to exercise that spending power positively. For example, when voters in Tampa, Florida enacted an anti-gay rights ordinance, the Human Rights Task Force of Florida responded by instituting a '*buy*cott' rather than a boycott. The group published a directory of businesses that have 'policies in support of gays and lesbians' (Wright 1993: 48). In the first 5 months of the directory's publication, the list grew from 105 to 430 entries (ibid.). Todd Simmons, spokesperson for the Human Rights Task Force of Florida, explained: 'We decided on an approach that would empower us economically and politically. The buycott has improved our standing in the community. Businesses and other institutions have changed their policies to get in our book' (ibid.).

Recently, several large companies have launched advertising campaigns targeted to gay consumers, including AT&T, Anheuser-Busch, Apple Computer, Bennetton, Philip Morris, Seagram, and Sony (Elliott 1994: C1). The story of Absolut vodka illustrates the way gay and lesbian consumers demonstrate loyalty to sympathetic manufacturers and other businesses. Absolut was one of the first major labels to advertize in gay publications. According to Rick Dean, Vice President of Overlooked Opinions (a Chicago-based market research company), 'the gay community tied it back—Absolut was there on the back cover of gay publications before the others, and Absolut vodka is poured at gay bars' (Gottschalk 1993: 7H). George Slowik, publisher of *Out* magazine, notes that gay men and lesbians are 'an audience not accustomed to being courted, so they're more apt to

---

[21] For example, Shocking Gray (1993: 5), a catalog of books, clothing, and other merchandise targeted to gay men and lesbians, sells 'gay dollars' and 'queer $' stamps.

notice who's supportive and who's not, particularly at this point. The first ones in will reap extra benefits in each category' (ibid.). The same sort of loyalty that allows Absolut to 'reap extra benefits' as the 'first one in' could allow the first state that legalizes same-sex marriage to reap extra revenue from tourists wishing to show their support for the legal change.

This brand loyalty is also evident in the travel industry. According to one marketing executive, '[a]ll a mainstream company has to do is show up at a gay travel expo and because of brand loyalty, gay and gay-friendly travelers will use them and their business will increase' (Glauberman 1994*a*). In Hawaii, where the same-sex marriage debate is most active, the Chair of the Hawaii Visitor's Bureau received a letter from the operations manager of a travel/tour agency stating, 'I personally know of a number of wholesale travel companies . . . who have already been in the process of preparing major campaigns to promote Hawaii to the Gay/Lesbian travel market' (Zdanow 1994). When mainstream companies appeal to the gay travel market, they tap into a potentially vast revenue source. Not only do gay households generally have higher incomes than the average American household, but they also appear to travel more. Because many gay men and lesbians are childless, they enjoy greater flexibility to travel than many American families do (Morris 1993 [quoting David Alport, publisher of *Out and About*]).

One of the greatest advantages of sympathy tourism is that its benefits would probably outlast the first-mover monopoly. Even after other states start celebrating same-sex marriages, gay people and their friends would remember that the first-mover state was the groundbreaker. Loyalty to that state could continue to generate substantial tourism revenue even after same-sex couples start to celebrate their marriages in other states. Sympathy tourism, moreover, would extend beyond gay consumers, as many heterosexual tourists would register their support for gay rights by travelling to the first-mover state.

The first-mover state might generate additional revenue if same-sex couples were to return to the state for divorce proceedings. Although the general rule is that jurisdiction to grant a divorce lies in the state where the parties are domiciled (Scoles & Hay 1992: 497), at least one state—New York—has 'exercised jurisdiction on the basis that it was the state of the celebration of the marriage.'[22] If the first-mover state were to make clear to couples that by marrying in the state they were submitting to the jurisdiction of the state for any divorce proceedings, then one spouse in a same-sex marriage could return to the first-mover state for ex parte proceedings to obtain a divorce decree. The parties would be on notice that the state might exercise this jurisdiction, and the divorces could generate additional revenue.

---

[22] *David-Zieseniss v. Zieseniss*, 129 N.Y.S. 2d 649 (1954); *See also* Scoles & Hay (1992: 499).

Moreover, some same-sex couples might return to the state together to obtain divorce decrees. If a couple's home state would not recognize their marriage even to assist them in dissolving it, the couple might prefer to 'fight it out' in the courts of the first-mover than to be left entirely without judicial guidance. According to Scoles and Hay (1992: 503), if both parties to the marriage appear in the first-mover state (i.e., if the divorce is *inter partes*), the determination of jurisdiction in the divorcing court and the adjudication of the divorce will be conclusive, and 'entitled to the same effect under the Full Faith and Credit Clause as they enjoy in the state of rendition.' This return of same-sex couples seeking divorces would again generate revenue for hotels and other travel-related businesses. The first-mover state's dedication to servicing the marriages it celebrates could also benefit another interest group: the local bar.[23]

These additional positive influences on a state's revenue are difficult to quantify. The additional tourism attributable to couples seeking divorces could be quite small. Sympathy tourism, on the other hand, could have a major influence on revenue in the first-mover state for years, and the impact could outlast the period during which the first-mover has a monopoly on same-sex marriage.

B. Diminished revenue: tipping and boycotts

Although solemnizing same-sex marriages could confer significant benefits, it could also impose costs on the first-mover state. This section will consider the sorts and severity of the costs a state is most likely to bear if it were to legalize same-sex marriage. Significant increases in tourism might require improvements in the state's services and infrastructure, including additional police, road services, etc. To the extent a state has developed such services and infrastructure and currently suffers excess capacity in its tourism industry, however, it may already be absorbing these costs without the corresponding benefits of expanded tourism. Moreover, if additional demand were to exceed the state's existing capacity, the resulting expansion would likely create jobs for state residents in a variety of industries. Therefore, while expanding tourism is not costless, benefits are likely to outweigh the costs. More important risks a state is likely to face are tipping and boycotts.

1. Tipping

'Tipping' refers to the tendency of 'majority consumers' to exit a market when a certain proportion of minority consumers have entered (Gewirtz 1983: 630; Frey 1979; Goering 1978; Schelling 1972). When a market 'tips,' the presence of some critical mass of the minority consumers causes majority consumers

---

[23] The local bar similarly benefits in the corporate context, where Delaware has dominated other states in providing corporate law and services. This has created an extremely stable interest group that consistently takes an interest in state law relating to their area of expertise (Macey & Miller 1987).

to avoid the market altogether, so that the minority consumers become the only ones in that market (Smolla 1981: 893). As Gewirtz (1983: 630) explains, '[a] tipping point and flight therefore put a limit on achievable integration.' The term 'tipping' most often describes the dynamic of racial segregation in education or housing markets. An historically white neighbourhood may start to become integrated when one or two black families move in. If the proportion of black households grows larger than some white residents are willing to tolerate, however, this increased presence may touch off 'white flight' from the neighbourhood. After the initial white flight, the proportion of black households becomes even higher—touching off successive rounds of white flight. The area may 'tip' from an integrated neighbourhood to one that is predominantly or exclusively black. Tipping often drives down the overall demand in the market and consequently market prices fall.

Tipping could operate similarly in tourism markets. If many heterosexual tourists prefer not to be with gay men or lesbians, they might avoid tourist destinations that acquire a reputation for being 'gay friendly' or supportive of gay rights. Some straight tourists might even avoid 'gay friendly' destinations because they fear others might mistake them as gay. Some resort destinations do indeed seem to be perceived as particularly popular with gay men and lesbians. Fire Island, New York; Provincetown, Massachusetts, and Key West, Florida are popular vacation spots for the gay community (Flinn 1993a: A11). Even heterosexuals who actively support gay rights may avoid predominantly gay vacation spots.

State governments could fear that they would lose more tourist revenue than they gain if heterosexual tourists simply avoid destinations with a high proportion of gay tourists. The experiences of cities that have attracted many gay and lesbian tourists, however, might allay these fears. San Francisco, for example, continues to draw tourists from many demographic groups, despite (perhaps due to) the fact that many gay men and lesbians populate the city and have been politically active there (Flinn 1993b).

Moreover, tourists who would avoid gay resort spots such as Fire Island, Key West, or Provincetown might be less disturbed by same-sex couples on honeymoon. Couples on honeymoon tend to keep to themselves, and are less likely to socialize with large groups. Thus, 'the scene' that develops at other gay-friendly tourist spots may be less likely to form in a first-mover state that caters specifically to couples who are marrying.

The geography of the state could help to mitigate tipping. The ability to distribute honeymooners over several different areas and cities could prevent the state as a whole from tipping, even if discreet areas were to become more popular with same-sex couples. Indeed, Fire Island does not prevent Long Island from attracting tourists, Key West is only one of the many popular islands along the Florida Keys, and Provincetown has not caused the entirety of Cape Cod to 'tip' to a gay vacation spot.

2. Boycotts

In some ways, boycotts appear similar to tipping. In boycotts, as in tipping, some segment of the market avoids a product or destination. In tipping, the avoidance occurs because the higher percentage of homosexual tourists lowers the value of tourism for some *individual* heterosexuals, so that they stop buying (*See* Smolla 1981: 894; Schelling 1972: 165–67). In boycotts, on the other hand, consumers act *concertedly* to avoid a product (that they would otherwise buy) in order to protest some action (Smith 1990: 135–36). The consumers may still value the product (e.g., a week of skiing in Colorado or a baseball game in Cincinnati, Ohio), but some higher principle (such as gay rights) trumps the consumers' other preferences (ibid. 172).

A tourism boycott would harm a first-mover state only if tourists who would have visited the state chose not to because of the boycott. If particular groups of people have not been frequent visitors to the first-mover state, a threatened 'boycott' by these groups would really amount to nothing more than a protest, with no impact on purchasing decisions. If, on the other hand, the first-mover state has relied heavily upon these groups of people for tourism, a boycott by them could inflict some damage.

If the legislative and policy debates regarding gay rights are any indication, the groups most likely to disfavor same-sex marriage (and therefore to organize a boycott) are radically right-wing organizations (that often present themselves as politically and religiously conservative Christian organizations). Prior boycotts by conservative Christians have not been particularly successful, however (Sidey 1989). Christian boycotts appear to succeed only when Christians are the primary consumers of the product. For example, when Christian organizations launched a boycott against Time Warner to protest the company's publication of allegedly offensive books and rap music, the only division of the company that suffered was Warner Alliance Records, a Christian music company (*CHRISTIANITY TODAY* 1992). As one activist noted, '[t]he American Family Association has a list of places they are boycotting as wide as a New York City phone book. The effectiveness of these boycotts has been minimal' (Rosegg 1994).

It is difficult to quantify the risk of a potential boycott against the first-mover state. One way to approach such an estimate, however, is to consider how many USA visitors would have to stay away from a first mover state in order to offset the increased revenue from same-sex couples. For example, in 1992 Hawaii received 3.7 million USA visitors who spent an average of 8.4 days in the state (Waters 1993: 110). Thus, USA visitors represent 31.08 million visitor days. At ten days per couple and with an entourage of two guests spending the average 8.4 days in the state, each same-sex wedding would represent 36.8 visitor days. With a stock of same-sex weddings releasing at a rate of 114,750 annually for the first five years, same-sex marriage represents a total of 4,222,800 visitor days, or 13.6% of the total for the United States of America. One could argue, then, that to merely offset the increased revenue from same-sex marriage (and not taking into account increased revenue from sympathy tourism), 13.6% of the USA visitors to Hawaii would have to *sustain a 5-year* boycott of the state.

Moreover, a state like Hawaii may face a boycott whether it decides against or in favor of same-sex marriage. Some of the most visible boycotts in recent years were those protesting anti-gay-rights legislation in the state of Colorado and the city of Cincinnati. Hawaii, too, has now been mentioned as a state that might feel the chill of rejection from gay travellers if the state's legislature attempts to amend the constitution in order to outlaw same-sex marriage (Glauberman 1994*b*: C1). The president of Hilton Hotels is evidently anxious to prevent such a boycott. Nine days after Dieter Huckstein submitted letters protesting same-sex marriage to the state's Judiciary Committee, the president of Hilton Hotels Corporation, Carl Mottek (1994), explained that 'Hilton hotels have and always will provide service to people from all walks of life regardless of race, color or sexual orientation.' He protested: 'We are and have been ardent supporters of civil rights.' The hotel chain has taken no official position on same-sex marriage in Hawaii, but it seems to fear loss of business from the gay and lesbian community.

In sum, a state that seriously considers legalizing same-sex marriage may face the threat of boycott no matter what the result. Conservative groups may boycott the state if the legal change occurs. Gay and lesbian travellers may boycott if, having raised the issue, the state fails to change the law. Because boycotts generally have limited impact, however—and it is not clear whether a boycott from the right or left would inflict more damage—this seems to be a weak ground for denying same-sex marriage.

C. *Losing the first-mover advantage: competition from other states*

At first glance it might seem that the estimate of 4 billion dollars in enhanced revenue proves too much. If there is this much money to be made, more than one state might be tempted to compete for the bounty and the first-mover advantage would be short lived. Even though other states will compete for same-sex tourism, it does not necessarily follow that the *prospect* of subsequent competition will deter a state from wanting to be the first mover. It is theoretically possible that a state would not want to incur the costs of moving first if it perceived that subsequent movers would compete away many of the benefits. But the prospect of competition ought to cause a state to move more quickly. The history of competitive federalism suggests that first movers often generate disproportionate and long-lived benefits, as demonstrated by the ongoing dominance of Delaware in the provision of corporate law (Romano 1985: 265–73).

Under the 'pent-up demand' model, demand for same-sex marriage will be highest in the first few years following legalization. This declining demand for same-sex marriage means that the greatest benefits from legalization will be captured in the early years, when the first-mover still has the monopoly on servicing the stock of pent-up demand. Because the estimations of enhanced revenue are discounted to present value assuming a 10% discount rate, the revenue generated in later years following legalization represents a much smaller portion of the total estimates than revenue in the early years. This relatively high discount rate was used in part to capture the risk that other states might compete to recognize same-sex marriages in later years. The estimations of enhanced tourism revenue presented above, therefore, already account for the risk of competition from other states.

Finally, some benefits of first-mover status may persist even when other states begin to compete. Travel companies might specialize in same-sex marriage packages. Many of these firms would develop state-specific expertise. To protect their capital, they might encourage clients to go to the first-mover even after competing states enter the market. In addition, some couples might prefer to marry and honeymoon in a place where they are assured many other people have been and are doing the same thing (on the safety-in-numbers theory). This would strengthen the first-mover's advantage even after additional states begin to celebrate same-sex marriages. Sympathy tourism, or loyalty to the first-mover state because it was the first to make the legal change, could lead many travellers—both same-sex couples and other tourists who support gay rights—to prefer the first-mover state even when other states present alternative wedding venues.

Therefore, it is theoretically coherent to argue that a decision maker would decline to be the *first* because it fears others would follow, but if so then same-sex marriage would seem to be the only example of this theory in practice. At the very least, any concern about competition from other states could come only from those who were persuaded that legalizing same-sex marriage would produce substantial tourism. Not all states are equally likely to compete. Political, economic, and social conditions will determine whether legalizing same-sex marriage would be attractive to the various states. A first-mover state might determine that it is unlikely to face any competition from other states in its region, and so can capture greater revenue for a longer period of time. The next section analyzes whether particular states would be likely to legalize same-sex marriage.

3. POTENTIAL FIRST-MOVER STATES

Same-sex marriage would benefit some states more than others. Ideally, the first-mover state should have a relatively small population, to maximize the benefit of the legal change to each citizen of the state. Legislators are most likely to vote in favor of recognizing same-sex marriage if they can persuade skeptical constituents that the legal change means money in their pockets. An additional $4 billion in tourism revenue obviously has greater per capita impact in a state with 3 million residents than it has in one with 23 million. Therefore, a small population is one factor that will weigh in favor of a state moving first to legalize same-sex marriage. This is consistent with the pattern of competitive federalism, in which smaller states have been the leaders in other areas of the law (e.g., Delaware with corporate law, South Dakota with banking, and Nevada with gambling) (Macey & Miller 1987: 471; Wilson 1983: 165).

These factors suggest that Hawaii is well situated to benefit from legalizing same-sex marriage. Hawaii's population of only 1.1 million people makes it one of the smallest states in the Union. Because of this small size, increases in state revenue can have a greater impact on each resident of the state than the same revenue would have in a larger state (Bureau of the Census 1991: Table 'Population and Housing Counts by Region, Division, and State: 1990 Census'). Table 2 estimated how $4 billion in enhanced tourism revenue would affect a state's *total* income, taxes, and employment. Table 3 shows the *per capita* impact of these effects on three small states (Hawaii, Nevada, and Vermont) and one large state (California).[24]

Dividing the $2.4 billion in additional household income among Hawaii's 1.1 million people produces a per capita income increase of $2,166, as shown in Table 3. In a larger state, such as California, the same amount of money produces a much smaller benefit for each resident—only $80. The per capita impact is thus 25 times larger in Hawaii than in California. Similarly, the present value of increases in income are much greater per household in Hawaii ($6,742) than in California ($231). Hawaii's state tax revenue could grow by .96% as a result of the increased tourism, and unemployment in the state could decrease by almost 13.5%. In California, the increased tourism revenue would affect state tax revenues and unemployment rates much less dramatically. Table 3 thus illustrates the importance of small size, and suggests the benefits available to individual state residents.

Since it is highly unlikely that increased household income would be evenly divided among residents of Hawaii, some have even more to gain from legalizing same-sex marriage (Macey & Miller 1987: 472). People who own or work in certain businesses might receive even more than $2,166 in increased personal income. Wedding consultants, florists, musicians, restaurateurs, hoteliers, and tour guides would benefit most from the legal change

---

[24] The 'multipliers' for other states could raise or lower these numbers; Table 3 combines Hawaii's multipliers with population figures from other states. Other states might garner even greater benefits than Table 3 suggests if their economies are less 'leaky' than Hawaii's. Hawaii must import most goods its uses—from furniture to food—and its remoteness can add substantial shipping costs (see Reinhold 1993).

Table 3. Per Capita Impact of Single-Sex Marriage Tourism in Particular States

State	Present Value of Income Per Capita[a]	Present Value of Income Per Household[a]	% Increase In State Tax Revenues[b]	% Decrease In State Unemployment[c]
Hawaii	$2,166	$6,742	.96%	13.5%
Nevada	$1,998	$5,150	1.6%	8.0%
Vermont	$4,263	$11,429	2.6%	16.7%
California	$80	$231	.04%	.3%

[a] Calculated assuming that present value of private income from legalization of same-sex marriage equals $2.4 billion. See supra at Table 2. State population and household figures are taken from Bureau of the Census (1991).

[b] Calculated assuming the present value of state tax revenues from legalization of same-sex marriage equals $440 million. See supra at Table 2. The present value of prelegalization revenues is calculated by capitalizing the 1992 general revenues at a 10% rate (Dept. of Commerce 1992: Table 2).

[c] Calculated assuming that legalization creates 3,500 permanent jobs. See supra at Table 2. Unemployment statistics were taken from Dept. of Labor (1993).

as their business would increase. Basic public choice theory suggests that these groups would lobby enthusiastically for the change if they had complete information and were behaving rationally.

Some potential for increased tourism will help to create incentives to legalize same-sex marriage. Tourism potential is important both in generating demand for travel to the state and in supplying the increased demand. The first-mover state should have the sorts of scenery, activities, and attractions that would lead same-sex couples to stay in the state for their honeymoons, spending the money that the first-mover hopes to secure. The first-mover state should also have the capacity to satisfy the increased demand that same-sex marriage is likely to create. If the state has some excess capacity in its tourism industry (e.g., vacant hotel rooms, empty airline seats, tourist attractions that could accommodate more visitors), the promise of additional visitors will be especially appealing. Even if the state enjoys generally high hotel occupancy rates, same-sex marriage could nonetheless be attractive if it would supply greater numbers of 'high end' tourists who might support increases in hotel room rates.

Hawaii is ideally situated to take advantage of an influx of marrying and honeymooning couples. It is an attractive tourist destination that could easily generate same-sex honeymoon demand. So great is the state's tourism potential that Hawaii has staked most of its fortunes on this single industry. In 1988, in-state and out-of-state visitors spent $9.2 billion in Hawaii. No other industry provides more jobs within the state (USA Travel Data Center 1991: 74). With very little manufacturing in the state, approximately one-third of Hawaii's annual gross product can be attributed directly to tourism (Reinhold 1993).

Hawaii also has the excess capacity to supply the demand for same-sex honeymoons. Travel to the state has decreased as both Japan and the United States have faced sluggish economies and competing locales have begun to draw travelers to other tourist destinations. For example, more American travelers are vacationing in Mexico or the Caribbean, and Japanese tourists are exploring other destinations in the Pacific Rim (Block 1994; Pelline & Evenson 1993: D4). Other, external forces may create additional problems. Military base closings will hurt the hotel industry generally. According to Mark Woodworth, Director of Hospitality Industry Consulting at Coopers & Lybrand, Hawaii will be among the three states hardest hit by the change. Thus, Hawaii has excess capacity in an industry that is absolutely critical to its economic health, at a time when its tourism prospects are diminishing.

Average daily room rates have not kept pace with inflation in Hawaii, rising only 3% between 1990 and 1993. (Pelline & Evenson 1993: D4). The state's hotel occupancy rate peaked at 86.3% in 1990, but has declined precipitously since then (*TRAVEL WEEKLY* 1994). For the first eleven months of 1993, the statewide hotel occupancy rate was down almost 2% (to 72.1%) from the same period in 1992 (ibid.).[25] Hawaii suffers a tremendous glut in luxury hotel rooms (Waters 1993: 111). The occupancy rate for luxury rooms is even lower—about 60% (Barlett 1993)—even though a typical hotel needs an occupancy rate of about 70% to turn an operating profit (Pelline & Evenson 1993: D4). And when luxury hotels start to lower their rates, it affects the entire market, as Somerset Waters explains: 'As these new top-grade hotels reduce rates or offer special deals to capture tourists, pressure is exerted on the next level of first-class hotels to lower their rates' (Waters 1993: 111).

When tourism declines in Hawaii, hotels are not the only businesses to suffer. Tourism affects other segments of Hawaii's economy dramatically. For example, retail sales are closely tied to tourism. A report published by the Bank of Hawaii concludes that 'the impact of visitors on retail sales is so strong that tourism, almost by itself, determines the direction and level of retail sales' (Waters 1993: 111). For example, a 10% drop in visitor arrivals, according to the Bank of Hawaii, would cause a $570 million decline in retail sales.

---

[25] The numbers are compiled by PKF-Hawaii, a hotel consulting firm. Average room rates had also fallen for that period. For the first 11 months of 1993, the average room rate was $103.21, down from $104.24 for the same period in 1992.

Not all visitors have such an impact on retail and other sales within the state. First-time visitors appear to spend more money than repeat visitors, who have already seen many of the state's attractions on earlier visits (Waters 1993: 112). Thus, the challenge for Hawaii is to attract 'first-timers' (Barlett 1993). By legalizing same-sex marriage, Hawaii could draw many travellers who have never visited the state before, and might not have opted to do so absent the opportunity to marry there.[26] The chance to marry legally could lure couples from eastern and midwestern states, areas that Hawaii has targeted for some of its marketing efforts (Waters 1993: 112).

Thus, Hawaii's strong reliance on tourism, combined with excess capacity in the industry, make clear that the state must increase the number of visitors from the mainland. Legalizing same-sex marriage would attract precisely the travellers Hawaii needs most: first-time visitors from all over the USA (central and eastern states as well as the west coast), honeymooners who are ready and able to splurge on a once-in-a-lifetime trip, experienced travellers who are willing, perhaps, to stay in luxury accommodations. Hawaii's remoteness, moreover, could work to its advantage. In a more centralized state (e.g., Wisconsin) many couples might stop for their wedding, but only briefly, on the way to another state (such as Hawaii) for their honeymoon. Couples who travel to Hawaii for their weddings, on the other hand, will have spent sufficient time and money reaching the state that they will be less likely to choose yet another spot for the honeymoon. And Hawaii is attractive enough that once same-sex couples reach the state for the wedding, many will prefer to stay for their honeymoons.

The political climate within a state will also help to determine whether it is likely to legalize same-sex marriage. If a state tends to be more 'liberal' or 'progressive' on social issues, same-sex marriage is more likely to get serious consideration. For indicia of such a 'liberal' tradition, we could look to the people in power or the laws currently in place. A governor or attorney general who is a left-leaning democrat might bring greater enthusiasm to the job of proposing or defending same-sex marriage legislation. A state may be more likely to embrace same-sex marriage legislation if it already has any of the following: 1) an equal rights amendment in the state constitution, 2) a state-wide gay rights statute, 3) major cities with human-rights ordinances covering sexual orientation, or 4) a strong tradition of diversity and tolerance. States that lack sodomy statutes would also be more likely to legalize same-sex marriage, though a sodomy statute in the state would not be an insurmountable barrier. We might consider not only the status of progressive legislation—i.e., whether or not it has been enacted in any given

---

[26] The assumption that same-sex couples might be first-time visitors is supported by studies showing that Hawaii does not rank in the top ten destinations for surveyed gay and lesbian travellers (*MONTREAL GAZETTE* 1992).

state—but also the history of the legislation, noting particularly the speed with which the bills became law.

Simple inertia may prevent a state legislature from legalizing same-sex marriage. But a judicial nudge from the *Baehr* court in Hawaii could reverse the force of this inertia. If the state supreme court rules that Hawaii's ban on same-sex marriage does indeed violate the state's equal protection clause, the legislature could overrule the court only by mustering the energy and the political will to amend the state's constitution. Even if the desire to capture enhanced tourism revenue is too weak to drive affirmative legalization of same-sex marriage, it might serve as a basis for a legislator's refusal to amend the constitution in the wake of a court decision legalizing same-sex marriage. The tourism rationale would give legislators an additional basis (not premised on advocacy for gay rights per se) for refraining from overruling the supreme court. Combined with those who would simply discourage tinkering with the constitution, the tourism boosters might prevent a legislative reversal of the court's decision.

Legislative hearings regarding same-sex marriage have elicited widely divergent views. Some residents of Hawaii have stated their strong opposition to the change, even suggesting that natural disasters will be more likely to hit the islands if same-sex marriage is legalized (Tangonan 1993*a*). Other citizens and organizations have strongly supported the idea of same-sex marriage (ibid.). Hawaii enjoys a strong reputation for diversity and tolerance. No single demographic group forms a clear 'majority' of the citizenry (Kaser 1989), and interracial marriages are common (Price 1994). Legislators could be expected to give greatest attention to the individuals and organizations that most affect their chances of reelection, so that each legislator would have to gauge the views of his or her district. While there has been vague talk of enhanced tourism, legislators and their constituents have never been confronted by quantitative estimates. Thus, an important part of the debate has been missing.

4. CONCLUSION

As same-sex marriage has become the subject of public debate, courts have considered constitutional arguments: same-sex couples have claimed rights to equal protection, free exercise, and freedom of association; states have asserted interests in procreation, morality, and tradition. Legislators will hear similar arguments. But a legislature also can consider the impact of legal change on the fiscal health of the state. This chapter has demonstrated that if a legislature were to consider this factor, it would find that the case for legalizing same sex marriage grows even stronger.

If certain states have so much to gain from legalizing same-sex marriage,

why have they not already made the change?[27] Several answers to this question are possible. The gay and lesbian community has become a vocal political force only in the last 20 years or so, and has understandably focussed
on outlawing discrimination in employment, housing, and banking.
Marriage was viewed with ambivalence by some, or as an unattainable goal
by others. As the community takes stock of the symbolic and legal impact
marriage has on people's lives, however, the right to marry has increasingly
been included in the gay-rights agenda. Most of this advocacy has been
played out in the courts, which are perceived to be more likely than legislatures to protect minority groups. Courts have granted some protections
for gay and lesbian families, and these decisions may be changing public
perceptions of the gay community.[28] As legislatures increasingly acknowledge that gay men and lesbians can and do form family units, the notion
that such unions merit state certification may seem less and less far-fetched.
Moreover, as gay men and lesbians make their sexual identities known, legislatures may see the economic and political power of this group of people
and those who support them. Thus, although the fight for marriage rights
in legislatures is fairly new, gay rights advocates may turn to legislatures
more in coming years.

The gay community is not the only interest group with something at stake
in the debate. The hotel and restaurant industries also stand to gain from
legalization of same-sex marriage. But even those who might benefit from
change do not always choose to lobby for it. Fear of alienating existing customers might keep some businesses from trying to gain new ones. After all,
Hilton Hotels must operate nationally, not just in Hawaii. In the 1950's
when the Jim Crow laws came under attack in the South, many hotels and
restaurants stood to gain if public accommodations were integrated (Posner
1992: 657). Many hoteliers and restaurateurs may have secretly wished for
integration, but dared not make known these secret hopes in fear that they
would lose many of their only—exclusively white—customers (Epstein 1992:
127). Perhaps the situation is similar in Hawaii even now. The Hawaii
Visitors Bureau maintains a neutral stance about same-sex marriage, but
knows that legalization would bring new visitors to the state. When a Hilton
employee speaks publicly against same-sex marriage, the President of the
corporation scrambles to mollify gay travel organizations, insisting that
Hilton supports civil rights. The tourist industry may know that it will
benefit from legalization, but prefer that someone else be held accountable
for the change.

---

[27] Scholars must confront this question whenever they propose an innovation that private
actors could benefit from but have not yet chosen to implement (see Donohue III 1991; Gilson
& Kraakman 1991: 905).

[28] *See, e.g., Braschi* v. *Stahl Assoc.*, 543 N.E.2d 49 (N.Y. 1989); *Stewart* v. *Schwartz Bros.—
Jefferson Memorial Chapel, Inc.*, 606 N.Y.S. 2d 965 (1993).

Meanwhile, tens of thousands of gay and lesbian couples want to marry. They are ready to hold ceremonies, host receptions, and steal away to hotels and resorts for honeymoons. They will spend money—lots of it—in the first state that legalizes same-sex marriage. Four billion dollars may rest on the table, waiting for one of the players to seize the prize.

POSTSCRIPT

Since the time this chapter went to the printers (and revisions within the body of the text became prohibitively expensive), same-sex marriage has become the subject of heated political debate in the USA. Despite the fact that the Hawaii court is not expected to decide *Baehr* until 1997, many states have attempted to preempt the legalization of same-sex marriage by passing statutes that would deny recognition to any same-sex marriage celebrated in another state. As this chapter goes to press, such anti-marriage statutes have passed in twelve states, failed in seventeen, and are pending in five states. Meanwhile, the USA Congress is considering the so-called 'Defense of Marriage Act' (DOMA). These statutes would define marriage for federal purposes as 'between one man and one woman as husband and wife', and would permit the various states to refuse to recognize a marriage between members of the same sex if such unions were to be legalized in the USA. President Bill Clinton has announced that he will sign DOMA if it passes through Congress. For a current summary of the legislative reactions to *Baehr*, consult the Partners Task Force for Gay & Lesbian Couples home page, http://www.eskimo.com/demian/toc.html.

It is difficult to gauge the impact of such legislative activity on the demand for same-sex marriage. On the one hand, increased uncertainty about the extent to which other states would recognize a Hawaii same-sex marriage ought to dampen the zeal of couples who seek to marry for the tangible benefits that accompany the institution. On the other hand, marriage for gay and lesbian couples has become a political question with intense emotional elements. Symbolism takes on additional importance in such a climate, for both advocates and opponents of same-sex marriage. All of the rhetoric and activity to block legal change seems only to deepen many couples' resolve to be wed as soon as they are permitted to do so.

PART III

*Institutions and Regulatory Coordination:
the Case of the EU*

10

Competition among rules in the single European market

STEPHEN WOOLCOCK[1]

1. THE ISSUES AND WHY COMPETITION AMONG RULES IS IMPORTANT

The balance or tension between harmonization and competition among national rules is central to the development of the EC and the Single European Market (SEM). The approach to market regulation within the Single European Market embodied a constructive ambiguity. Some national regulators/governments saw the establishment of a single market as a means of retaining control over markets in the face of increased internationalization of production and economic interdependence which was undermining the viability of national regulatory policies in a number of sectors. National governments and regulators were aware that the global market pressure for change could not be resisted at a national level.

For these regulators European level regulation offered a means of retaining some degree of regulatory control over the forces of international markets without losing the benefits of increased economies of scale and scope of a larger market. On the other hand, some governments and regulators saw the creation of a single market as a means of promoting liberalization and thus working 'with the grain' of the international market pressures. For these, the creation of the single European market was part of the wider process of liberalization and thus a means of removing barriers to trade stemming from different national regulatory policies.

The ambiguity in the single market initiative was constructive in the sense that it enabled governments with very different views of the role of regulation in the market to sign up to the Single European Act and the objectives of creating a genuine single European market. This common support for the objectives of the SEM enabled the legislative programme to be completed. This legislative framework for the establishment of the SEM itself also

[1] This paper draws on work carried out by the European programme of the Royal Institute of International Affairs and funded by the Economic and Social Research Council's Single European Market Initiative. The full results of the research and of the wider initiative can be found in David Mayes (ed.) The evolution of rules in the single European market, 1995.

embodies a balance between harmonization and competition among rules. The question today concerns how the rules of the EC evolve? The balance between harmonization and competition among rules will have an important influence on the whole shape of the EC post 1993. If the scope for competition among national rules is limited, because market failures at a European level require central regulation or harmonization of rules, there will be a need to conduct more regulation from a European level. This will in turn mean that more effective means of carrying out market regulation at a European level will have to be developed. At present the European Commission offers only a partial solution. New instruments such as independent regulatory bodies will have to be developed, if there is a genuine need for European levels of regulation. If, on the other hand, there is considerable scope for competition among national rules, central regulation will be limited and national or sub-national bodies will retain regulatory competence. In other words the scope of competition among rules, the subject of this chapter, will determine the demand for new European regulatory policies.

This relates to the important and sensitive issue of subsidiarity. The greater the scope for competition among rules, the greater the scope for subsidiarity in the sense of the responsibility for decisions being left at the national or sub-national level. The debate about subsidiarity has, to date, been characterized by a lack of any clear understanding of what subsidiarity means and a lack of clear criteria for deciding what should be done at which level. An analysis of competition among rules may therefore contribute to this debate by identify the scope for harmonization and the scope for competition among rules and thus subsidiarity. The areas in which competition among rules can operate effectively without the risk of market or regulatory failure, would be areas in which regulatory competence could be carried out at national or sub-national levels. The same is also true for the reverse case, in other words those who wish to use the concept of subsidiarity in order to ensure that as much regulatory power as possible remains at the national, or sub-national level, will also need to show that competition among rules may be applied without significant problems.

Perhaps the most important question concerning the application of competition among rules in the 'new approach' adopted in the single European market is will it work? The credibility of the single European market initiative and—in so far as the credibility of the SEM is important for the credibility of the European Union itself—the credibility of the EU, depends on the effectiveness of what has come to be known as the 'new approach'. The 'new approach' recognizes that it is not possible to harmonize all regulation and standards at the European level. This approach limits harmonization to measures that are seen to be essential, for reasons of public health and safety, and then provides for mutual recognition of national regulations, which may differ, over and above these minimum essential requirements. The credibility of this approach relies on mutual trust between the national authorities involved. If a national regulatory body today does not trust the regulators in other member states to keep the suppliers of a good or service in that country up to the minimum EC requirements or up to their equivalent national requirements, there will be a reluctance to recognize the goods or services supplied from the country concerned. Pressure for the reintroduction or maintenance of national controls on a host country basis would increase and with it the danger of a reversion to nationally fragmented markets. At the very least, a lack of mutual trust would mean that mutual recognition would not work and the credibility of the new approach and the SEM would be seriously undermined. In other words the 'new approach' relies heavily on the effectiveness of competition among rules.

Another important issue is whether competition among rules will result in a 'race to the bottom,' in which competition between national regulators leads to 'sub-optimal' levels of regulation or provision of public goods. For example, will a 'race to the bottom' in social legislation undermine any attempt to establish a social dimension to the single European market? Will competition for mobile capital investment result in competition among rules in social policy and thus undermine the ability of national policies aimed at maintaining or establishing relatively high levels of social provision? Will competition among rules in the area of environmental regulation result in a 'race to the bottom' and thus undermine the ability of national or regional governments to maintain or attain higher or improved environmental standards? If environmental regulations vary between countries or locations within the EC, will industries migrate to such locations. In competition among rules at the EC level the threat of such a move by a major investor might be enough to affect policy makers. At a time when unemployment remains a central concern of all governments, there could be a tendency to 'compete' for investment by maintaining lower environmental standards than the neighbouring countries or by even lowering standards.

Competition among rules is also important in terms of what it can tell us about whether there is a process of convergence or divergence taking place within the EC. Is competition between the national rules resulting in convergence towards a set of common Euro-rules? Competition between different national rules is seen by some as a means of finding the best rules through a process of learning. Therefore convergence towards a single set of Euro-rules could still result even if there is no ex ante harmonization. Alternatively, will the scope for diversity which competition among rules leaves for national regulators and governments result in a divergence between national rules and thus a looser, less integrated EC? This might happen, for example, if divergences between national rules or enforcement measures undermined the credibility of the SEM initiative in ways suggested above. A third possibility is that differences remain but there is neither divergence or convergence. In other words the pressures resulting from locations or countries competing for investment through deregulation may be balanced by other factors, such as strong national or local preferences for higher environmental protection or social provision. In such cases one might find out that a kind of steady state condition develops in which national policy differences remain and there is neither convergence or divergence.

Finally, the effects of competition between national rules on the evolution of rules in the EC will have important implications for third countries. An EC with a single set of rules resulting from convergence within Europe is a very different kind of trading partner to the looser, more diverse EC that might result from divergence. Regulatory policies are becoming increasingly important elements in international trade so developments in the field will become more rather than less important for international trade relations.

If competition among rules succeeds in Europe it may find a wider application. With growing international economic interdependence, existing GATT principles of national treatment are reaching the limits of their effectiveness. If it works competition among rules could be exported from Europe to the multilateral system.

2. THE EVOLUTION AND PRACTICAL APPLICATION OF COMPETITION AMONG RULES WITHIN THE EC

A key contribution to the development of the concept of competition among rules can be traced in the evolution of rules on technical regulations in the EC. Different national approaches to technical regulation mean that, despite the EEC Treaty and the efforts to harmonize rules during the 1970s, the EC was a very incomplete common market. The harmonization of national technical regulations proved slow and ineffective. If it took 11 years to agree on standards for mineral water it would have taken centuries to complete the job (Sun and Pelkmans 1995). Faced with new challenges in a wide number of different markets, those seeking to make a reality of the common market, have developed a concept of competition among rules as a means imparting momentum into the process of liberalization and removing logjams in EC decision-making. The 'new approach' to technical barriers to trade within the EC is the paradigm case. Rather than struggle to harmonize all national rules, the Council of Ministers would in future only harmonize the minimum essential requirements. Above this floor, the application of mutual recognition would provide for competition between national approaches. The paradigm was then applied in other cases, such as services, and it was this application which really saw the emergence of competition between national rules within the EC. In order to understand the perception of competition among rules in the minds of those involved in the evolution of EC legislation, it is necessary to describe the evolution of the 'new approach' to technical barriers to trade.

The origins of the new approach can be traced back to national legislation on technical regulations and standards. In Germany, the country with the most developed national standards in the shape of the Deutsche Industrie Normen (DIN), an approach was adopted which made use of reference to technical standards as a means of showing compliance with performance or output standards. The German Geratssicherheitsgesetz (law on the safety of equipment) introduced the idea in 1968. Although the standards were voluntary, compliance with the DIN standards was seen as the best means of showing compliance with safety rules. This idea subsequently found application at the European level in the shape of the 1973 Low Voltage Directive (LVD). This was based on performance requirements of a certain level of safety, rather than specify detailed requirements in the Directive. Reference to voluntary standards was seen as one convenient (but not the only) means of showing compliance with the performance requirements. The LVD also introduced the concept of delegating responsibility for common standards to the voluntary standards making bodies, in this case the Committee on European Electro-Technical Standards (CENELEC).

Faced with the log-jam in EC efforts to remove technical barriers to trade, a working party of senior national officials on standardization was set up in March 1979. This identified two main problems: first, there was a lack of transparency in the national regulations in force on technical regulations, and second, a lack of any common approach to conformity assessment. On the first issue, the Commission prepared the so called 'information directive', finally adopted in 1983, which required all new national technical regulations to be notified to the EC, and thus other member states. This was followed by a standstill period during which other national regulators and the Commission could consider whether European technical regulations should be established. The information directive therefore enhanced transparency and provided an opportunity of developing European rules to replace divergent national rules or regulations. The second issue of conformity assessment was more difficult because of differences in national approaches to regulation. The main difference was between Germany and France.

Having developed a comprehensive set of technical standards in the shape of the DIN standards, the Germany regulators had moved away from including detailed specifications in regulations and towards an approach which specified performance requirements. In order to satisfy such requirements the German technical regulations then used the principle of reference to technical standards. So, in testing for conformity with safety regulations the German testing bodies were in effect requiring compliance with German DIN standards. In contrast French regulators continued to rely on the specification of technical requirements in regulations. Both approaches provided considerable scope for maintaining or introducing technical barriers to trade, because foreign suppliers had to comply either with DIN standards or with the detailed French regulations. Legally, however, it was easier to find that the French regulations infringed Articles 30–36 (EEC), which require the removal of all quantitative restrictions and measures having equivalent effect.

In the early 1980s these differences provoked a major trade row between France and Germany in which France accused Germany of blocking access to its market by insisting on the use of DIN standards. The political solution found was to recognize French AFNOR standards as technically equivalent to the DIN standards, and a list of such equivalent standards was published in the *Bundesanzeiger*. Five French test centres were also certified in the German regulations, thus introducing the concept of mutual recognition of conformity assessment. This compromise between the two national approaches cleared the way for the adoption of the 'new approach' at the EC level. It also demonstrated the potential costs, in terms of increased tensions and trade barriers, of not finding some more effective means of dealing with such technical barriers to trade within the EC, which, despite the treaty requirements, had not been removed.

The final, important element of the new approach, that of minimum essential requirements, was provided by the European Court of Justice (ECJ). In its now famous *Casis de Dijon* decision in 1979, the ECJ ruled that a product legally sold and marketed in one member state must be admitted for sale in another member state, subject to the importing state's essential health or safety and consumer protection regulations. The ECJ in fact ruled that mutual recognition was obligatory for all products provided they satisfied the essential requirements. The ECJ is therefore an active participant in European regulatory policy in the sense that it can determine that health and safety measures in one country are 'equivalent' to those of another. If the Council does not set the minimum requirements the ECJ can. This has had the effect of providing the Council with an incentive to regulate. The ECJ has also ruled that if national measures are retained they must be proportional to the objectives sought, and this has been applied quite strongly (Sun and Pelkmans 1995).

It was the combination of these ideas which produced the 'new approach.' Provided that minimum health and safety regulations are satisfied any product sold in one member state can be legally sold in other member states. EC harmonization may determine a common set of such minimum essential requirements. But even when there are no harmonized rules the ECJ may decide that 'equivalent' protection exists. Voluntary technical standards help in this determination but they are only one means of proving compliance. The development of such voluntary technical standards is delegated to the non-governmental standard-making bodies. Finally, conformity assessment is carried out in each member state, by certified bodies, and their tests are recognized by the regulating authorities in other countries.

In other words the 'new approach', evolved as a result of pragmatic decisions by those drafting national and EC regulations, politicians trying to resolve a Franco-German trade row, and lawyers in the ECJ trying to resolve a dispute on the interpretation of a key provision of the Treaty of Rome. The success of this approach in removing log-jams from the path of market integration within the EC led to it being subsequently applied more widely, in efforts to inject momentum into the policy making process and complete the SEM.

The principle was also applied in the service sector. The 1989 Second Banking Coordination Directive (SBCD) set the precedent for the application of the concept. This established the principle of home country control, according to which suppliers of services can provide them in all EC member states provided they comply with the regulations of the home country. Again there are minimum essential requirements. In this case in the shape of prudential safeguards, such as capital adequacy requirements. Provided these were satisfied service providers permitted, by one national regulator, to sell services on one market also had to be allowed to sell on other markets. In other words there was mutual recognition of national regulation of service providers. Having set the precedent of the SBCD the EC then introduced similar directives for insurance and investment services.

The principle of mutual recognition was central to the EC White Paper of 1985 which launched the SEM. By designing a new strategy for regulatory coordination not only of technical regulations and financial services, but also university degrees and professional qualifications, the EC has moved towards facilitating mutual recognition. Where there is mutual recognition, the degree of competition between national rules is particularly intense. For example, one would expect an intense competition among rules if a British bank can sell services on the more regulated German market while complying with relatively liberal British regulations. The pressure would be on the German regulators to deregulate in order to ensure German banks can compete.

Earlier experience in the EC suggests that mutual recognition will only be accepted as the basis for accommodating different national rules when the difference between the national approaches is not too great.

The experience with such efforts over the years has led those who follow European integration to argue that some degree of harmonization or at least rapprochement is needed before mutual recognition will work (Sun and Pelkmans 1995). From the point of view of European integration, mutual recognition is important because it represents a more intense form of competition among rules, which will bring greater pressure for policy approximation or rapprochement and thus complete the job of creating a SEM. Mutual recognition is, in effect, a recognition that national regulatory systems are equivalent (Majone 1993*c*). If there is no confidence that this is the case, national regulators are unlikely to accept products or services approved by other country regulators. One example of how mutual recognition did not develop because of the lack of such an acceptance of equivalence is the failure of the so called 'multi-state' procedure in the approval of pharmaceuticals (see below). Another crucial precondition for mutual recognition is effective enforcement, without which there will be no mutual trust.

This explains why the view among analysts of European integration tends to be that competition among rules and harmonization are complementary rather than alternatives (Sun and Pelkmans 1995). The view that they are alternatives tends to be more strongly held by analysts using public choice approaches. It must be stressed that seeing competition among rules and harmonization as complementary does not mean that everything should be harmonized. Indeed, competition among rules is seen as an alternative to the (failed) policies of complete harmonization that were followed by the EC during the 1960s and 1970s. But some harmonization is required to ensure that the regulatory régimes in different countries are recognized as being broadly equivalent. Over and above such levels of common rules, competition among rules comes into its own. The provision of mutual recognition then provides a means of accommodating the remaining differences between national approaches without them being used as the basis for protectionism. According to this view there is no need to harmonize everything, difference may and should remain. Once the minimum requirements are met, the rest should be left to the 'market for regulation,' in which competition among national rules or regulations provides the benefits attributed to competition among rules, such as dynamism, and experimentation.

If one accepts the view that harmonization and competition (among rules) are complementary, there still remains the question of what happens in those areas still subject to regulatory competition. Will this result in convergence towards a common Euro-norm or will national diversities continue? This is an issue taken up latter in the chapter. Given that the 'new approach' directives are still in the early stages of implementation, there are not yet any clear answers to this question.

Competition among rules can, therefore, be seen as a radical, open-ended, alternative to harmonization, which allows a market for regulation to reflect divergent national (or sub-national) preferences for public goods. According to this view, the effort should not go into harmonizing national regulations but into making sure the market for regulation works effectively, for example by limiting regulatory failures and improving information. An alternative view, is that competition among rules can be seen as a more efficient means of bringing about regulatory convergence than ex ante harmonization. Of course, it is possible to seek a clear distinction between these two approaches to competition among rules in the theoretical writings on the topic, when it comes to application the issues become much less clear-cut.

The debate on competition among rules must also be seen in the context of wider economic and political objectives. After all, competition among rules cannot be seen as an end it itself. It is at most a means of achieving a broader economic objective or efficient resource allocation and thus stable economic growth. But preferences concerning—at least in the short to medium term—the trade-off between growth and redistribution objectives, or other goals such as sustainable economic growth, will also play a part in any discussion of competition among rules. If competition among rules is the best means of pursuing growth and efficiency objectives, it may still be questioned in terms of the other objectives.

General political views on the desirability or otherwise of European integration and the transfer of powers to common institutions will also influence positions on competition among rules. For example, if the objective is to limit the transfer of power to the EC and retain regulatory control in the hands of national bodies, there will be a tendency to use competition among rules as a justification for such a policy. The case made by the integrationists for the need for common policies because of externalities can be countered by arguing that regulatory competition is more efficient. There may also be a tendency to try to extend the scope for competition among rules by correcting imperfections in the market for regulation, such as the lack of information for consumers about different regulatory policies, rather than accepting the need for more common policies. In the debate about subsidiarity, therefore, competition among rules may be used as a justification for retaining regulatory power at the national level. Those favouring integration may well tend to stress the limitations of competition among rules and the need for common approaches to deal with externalities at a European level.

3. REGULATORY COMPETITION, ARBITRAGE, AND EMULATION

It is also important to try and be clear about terminology. Competition among rules can be seen as a general term covering regulatory competition, institutional competition, regulatory arbitrage, and regulatory emulation.

Regulatory Competition is competition between regulators to attract

investment or business activity or to promote the competitiveness of indigenous industries by providing a more favourable regulatory environment.
Such competition need not, of course, mean a reduction in standards of regulation. Some regulators may promote competitiveness by increasing the
standards required of national suppliers. For example, higher standards of
security on financial markets may attract business rather than discourage it
by raising costs. Institutional competition is essentially the same as regulatory competition.

Regulatory Arbitrage is the action taken by market operators in selecting
the best location for investment or economic activity depending on the local
regulatory environment. For example, companies may shift investment or
activity from a country if that country increases taxes.

Regulatory Emulation is the process whereby regulators change their policies as a result of observing that the regulatory policies pursued by other
countries are more effective or more likely to meet the objectives of the regulators.

One of the difficulties in assessing the impact of regulatory competition
is that changes in policy may come about as a result of potential outcomes
rather than real outcomes. For example, in the case of regulatory competition a regulator may change policies in anticipation of the effects of policy.
For example, the (partial) liberalization of the British telecommunications
sector was undertaken, in part, on the expectation that it would help Britain
maintain and strengthen its position as the hub for international telecommunications in Europe. Companies potentially affected by changes in regulation, or the lack or changes, will also lobby regulators and possibly
threaten that unless regulation is appropriate they will invest elsewhere.
Again regulators have to act on the basis of the potential effects of regulatory competition.

4. THE ADVANTAGES AND DISADVANTAGES

Competition among rules offers a number of advantages over other
approaches to dealing with diverse national rules under conditions of international economic interdependence. These include:

choice or diversity in national regulatory systems. This enables national regulation to be tailored to the specific needs of the national economy, rather
than being obliged to adopt a European norm which may not be appropriate to local conditions. This provides, among other things, the advantage of
providing weaker economies with a means of competing with more efficient
economies. Thus lower wage, lower productivity, less regulated economies
are able to compete with higher wage, higher productivity, more regulated

economies. If weaker economies were obliged to accept the same levels of regulation as the stronger economies they would not be able to compete.

simplification of procedures. Competition among rules obviates the need for a significant amount of ex ante harmonization and thus simplifies the task for European and national regulators and politicians.

reducing the danger of regulatory failure. The competition between national regulations or rules reduces the risk of political compromises resulting in 'bad' central harmonization (i.e. regulation which is determined more by political expediency and the need to reach a compromise than by good regulatory practice). Competition between regulators may also reduce the risk of regulatory failure due to regulatory capture by vested interests, for example if they possess superior information to the regulators. With harmonized or central regulation there is a danger that the central regulator becomes captured. When there are a number of national regulators operating within a single market, such as the SEM, this danger is reduced because the rents extracted through regulatory capture would make the industry concerned less competitive. Faced with the risk of loss of market share the national industry concerned would have to approximate the regulatory policies of its neighbours which would result in lower rents for the regulated industry and thus more competitive products. The existence of competition between different national regulatory régimes may also provide 'yardsticks' against which to measure the efficacy of national regulation. (Nicolaides 1991) Competition between national regulators may also check the danger of bureaucratic capture in which the regulators protect their own interests at the expense of consumers.

experimentation. Regulatory competition enables experimentation, flexibility, and innovation in regulatory policy. In a period of rapid changes in technology and markets, regulatory policy must remain flexible if it is to remain in touch with market developments. Competition among rules offers flexibility and thus dynamism. Just as monopolistic markets tend to be inflexible and unresponsive to consumer demands, so, by analogy, a single set of harmonized rules is less responsive than competition among rules and a 'market for regulation.' The scope for this will depend on the scope of competition and the degree of harmonization (i.e. of essential minimum requirements) needed to ensure regulatory competition is effective.

limitation of the loss of national sovereignty. Regulatory competition enables national regulators and/or governments to retain control over a wider range of policy decisions. In reality the degree of national control is constrained by competition from other national regulators. Extensive market liberalization, especially the total freedom of capital within the EC, combined with the intense pressures from mutual recognition, means that the scope for genuine policy choice may be limited.

In assessing the impact of the competition among rules it is also important to be aware of the potential disadvantages and limitations of the
approach. These include:

externalities. Competition among rules cannot, by itself, cope with externalities, such as, for example, cross border environmental pollution, the risk
of market failure such as a collapse in the banking system or the existence
of market dominance. The externalities in, for example, cross border pollution mean that national regulators cannot have full control over levels of
pollution in their jurisdiction unless there is co-operation and, in effect,
some harmonization or approximation of policies with other countries.
Market failure, another form of externality, could arise when lax or inadequate regulation or supervision in one country results in a bank failure.
Where there are high levels of economic interdependence, this could result
in banks within other jurisdictions failing.

transaction costs. The flexibility of competition among rules may have a
down side in the shape of higher transaction costs and uncertainty for business. Flexibility means that regulators have an opportunity for experiment,
but they may be tempted to do so too often. Frequent changes in policy can
result in transaction costs for regulators and the regulated industry.

There is also a strong preference among business interests for clarity and
stability in regulation. There are advantages in bringing about changes in
regulation progressively through a series of small steps, but this may result
in what has been termed 'creeping regulation.' The flexibility provided by
competition among rules may also be abused by governments, to pursue
short term political objectives which would not be possible in a system of
regulation based on a consensus of national policies and interests.

the risk of non-tariff barriers remaining or being introduced. Pure competition among rules enables divergent national policies. As the EC experience
during the 1960s and 1970s clearly showed, divergent national regulations
provide a fertile ground for covert— or not so covert—barriers to trade. In
the case of the EC, harmonization of minimum essential requirements and
mutual recognition is seen as a means of ensuring national differences do
not represent barriers to trade. If the SEM loses credibility as a result of
adverse economic conditions and a lack of mutual trust undermines mutual
recognition, competition among rules could reintroduce barriers to trade.

zero or sub-optimal regulation. As discussed above, there is also a risk that
competition among rules will result in competitive deregulation and ultimately in a 'race to the bottom' and zero or sub-optimal regulation. For
example, if one country introduces a lower corporation tax and succeeds in
attracting more investment as a result, (or if authorities in other countries
at least perceive that there may be a relocation of investment out of their

territory if they maintain higher taxes), other countries would compete, resulting in a competitive reduction in taxes. Reduced taxation reduces the ability of governments to provide public services/goods which then fall below socially optimal levels. The counter argument is that there is an opportunity cost to reducing taxes. For example, investors also want effective infrastructure or training for employees. There could therefore be a limit to any competitive deregulation.

excessive levels of regulation. Competition among rules need not always result in a lowering in the level of regulation. Indeed the example of the German Packaging Ordinance suggests that competition may also result in higher levels of regulation. Legislation in one country can result in pressure for equivalent legislation in other countries as the packing example shows and thus for EC regulation. Such upward pressure may result from individual countries pursuing unilateral policies. If the country concerned is important enough there may be an element of smaller countries being forced to follow.

possible undermining of the welfare state. If competition among rules takes the form of immobile factors of production competing for mobile factors of production, and if capital is mobile in Europe but not labour, one might expect the trend to be towards lower levels of taxation and progressive pressure on redistribution functions of the state. Tax on capital will tend to decline, increasing the burden of taxation on immobile labour. The situation may get worse with enhanced labour mobility within the EC as this is likely to mean a tendency for younger more qualified workers to move. This could then accentuate the problem of funding pensions in coming years.

oligopolistic competition among regulators. If there is a market for regulation or rules, there is no reason to assume that this will be a perfect market. Indeed, with only a limited number of strong national regulators within the EC one could envisage an oligopolistic form of competition among rules. 'Collusion' between national regulators could result in joint efforts to limit competition rather than promote it. Alternatively regulators may find it more comfortable to retain the status quo and thus avoid the uncertainties and risks of regulatory competition.

5. PRECONDITIONS FOR COMPETITION AMONG RULES

For competition among rules to be effective a number of conditions have to be satisfied. This section discusses the well known or conventional conditions as well as suggesting a number of less familiar ones.

The four freedoms

The existence of an open market for trade in goods and services and free movement of the factors of production is needed if competition among rules is to work effectively. If national barriers to trade remain, producers in regulated markets will still be insulated from competition, and will therefore have less need to move to another cheaper location or to press for national regulatory reform. In other words regulatory jurisdictions have to interact for regulatory competition to occur (Nicolaides 1991). This is clearly illustrated in the case of airlines, where the lack of liberalization and the inability to supply air services in other member states has meant that the scope for competition among regulators, for example, in attracting customers, has been limited. In contrast the telecommunications sector has been liberalized to some degree and as a result there has been some regulatory competition. After the lead taken the British in the partial liberalization of telecommunications, continental PTTs came under pressure to liberalize service provision in order to contain regulatory competition from Britain and the USA.

Transparency

If companies are not clear about the nature of regulation in other countries or locations they will be unable to compare the relative merits of each and will not therefore engage in regulatory arbitrage. Consumers would be unable to compare products and voter consumers would be unable to compare locations, should they be mobile enough to consider moving. Without transparency, regulators in one country will be unaware of the policies pursued in other countries and unable to compare these policies with their own. There would therefore be no emulation of other national regulatory policies. For competition among rules to work in a balanced, unbiased fashion it would also require information to be supplied evenly across the EC. Asymmetric information among regulators, suppliers, or consumers will tend to undermine the effectiveness of competition among rules.

Discreetness

For regulatory competition to be effective it is necessary to have transparency not only in relation to the nature of regulation in different countries, but also to the effects of differences in regulatory policies. Regulatory competition is most likely to occur when it is possible to compare directly the effects of different regulatory policies. When a range of factors affect any outcome it is difficult for both the regulators and regulated to be clear on the impact of any given regulatory change. A lack of transparency in the effects of regulatory competition can therefore blunt its impact. This is analogous to diseconomies of scope in which the clustering of policies prevents voters or investors from expressing their preferences. Such clustering also dampens the effectiveness of competition among rules.

Investment decisions provide an example of this. The decision to chose one location over others is based on a wide range of factors including the size and growth of the economy concerned, the general climate of industrial relations as well as factors which can be more directly linked to specific regulatory decisions, such as the level of local taxation or provisions concerning redundancy provisions for workers. When it is difficult to desegregate these different factors, the competition becomes more between different clusters of policies than between rules or regulation. In effect this means competition between different systems rather than between specific rules.

Another way of looking at this is to see regulatory policy in a particular field as being embedded in a wider national regulatory system or style. There are a number of examples of such embedding of regulation into a broader national approach. In the area of company law and arguably financial market regulation, different models of corporate governance or systems of providing corporate finance have proved greater than the sum of their parts over the years. Efforts to reform part of the system, such as to address the 'problem' of short termism in Britain, have foundered on the fact that change in one area can only be brought about by change in the system as a whole.

Environmental regulation may provide another example of how regulatory policy is in the process of becoming more embedded or linked with other policies. For example, the establishment of closer links between environmental policy and energy and transport policies, through the need to address the issue of green house gas emissions, means that it will become increasing necessary to consider the whole platform of policies rather than regulation on any single area (Weale 1993).

Enforcement

The enforcement of regulation is important for two reasons. First, the absence of effective enforcement of regulation is likely to undermine competition among rules, because of the lack of certainty concerning the rules applied. Transparency would be undermined because neither regulators or regulated would be clear of the nature of regulation in countries with ineffective enforcement. This would then run the risk of a 'competition in laxity, which would, in turn, undermine mutual trust. As was pointed out by, among others, the Sutherland Report on the implementation of the European Community's internal market programme, mutual trust is an essential requirement for the effective operation of the 'new approach'

and mutual recognition (Sutherland 1993). Thus, competition in non-
enforcement or laxity would soon undermine the credibility of the SEM.
This conclusion of the Sutherland Report formed the basis of the European
Commission's subsequent strategy paper on the internal market (European
Commission 1993). The view expressed there is that considerable effort has
to go into improving co-operation between national enforcement and regulatory agencies to enhance mutual trust. If co-operation between national
enforcement authorities is to be increased as a means of ensuring effective
enforcement, what impact will such co-operation have on competition
among rules?

It is not yet possible to address this question, as moves to increase co-
operation between the enforcement bodies are only just beginning. But it
may be that closer links will stimulate regulatory emulation, in so far as the
bodies responsible for enforcement are in communication with those determining regulatory policy.

Mutual recognition

A general question arises over whether mutual recognition is a precondition
for competition between national regulators. Mutual recognition will result
in more intense competition between the national regulatory systems. But it
is possible to envisage situations in which competition among rules can still
work without mutual recognition. For example, competition among rules
appears to operate at a global level between the major capital markets without mutual recognition. If the EC were to introduce a transaction tax on
foreign currency transactions in order to punish speculators, the expectation
would be that business would go to 'off shore' centres.

Another example, in which European policies affect policies elsewhere is
the impact that reform in European financial service regulation during the
late 1980s had on similar reform efforts in USA and Japanese banking regulation. Reform proposals in 1989 were, in part, justified in terms of the need
to respond to policy developments in Europe in order to ensure USA banks
remained internationally competitive and Japanese regulation remained in
touch with international developments. When multinational companies can
chose between locations on a global scale, there is a degree of competition
among rules. Another example, is genetic engineering, in which the
European industry argues that relatively tight environmental regulation in
the EC is 'driving' companies out of Europe and into the United States of
America, where regulations are less stringent. While mutual recognition is
not a precondition for competition among rules, experience within the EC
suggests that in many cases the provision of open markets for capital and
labour, the four freedoms within the EC, is not sufficient to ensure that regulatory competition can operate and that mutual recognition is necessary.

Regulatory rapprochement

If mutual recognition is a precondition for regulatory competition, there is also strong evidence from studies of European integration, that regulatory rapprochement or some harmonization of policies is a necessary precondition for mutual recognition. Some observers have argued that it is necessary for states to 'pursue very similar public interest goals' if mutual recognition is to be effective (Majone 1993*c*). Harmonization, possibly far-reaching harmonization of essential health and safety requirements, is seen as a precondition for the effective operation of mutual recognition (Majone 1993*a*; Sun and Pelkmans 1995).

Competition policy

A European level competition policy was included in the Treaty of Rome because of the need to ensure that private restrictions on trade did not replace public restrictions. The need for a strong European competition policy would remain under a system based on mutual recognition and competition among rules. The use or abuse of private sector market power remains a justification for EC competition policy. It is also needed to ensure that competition among rules works. Majone suggests that central control and monitoring should also be extended to the market for regulation. In other words EC competition policy should be applied to prevent collusion between the national regulators.

6. HOW DOES IT WORK

One of the difficulties in developing any general model of the impact of competition among rules, is that the responses of the regulators and regulated vary from case to case and from sector to sector (Sun and Pelkmans 1995; Hosli 1992).

The response of companies and investors will be crucial for the operation of competition among rules, because they are the medium through which competition takes place. But companies will base decisions of practical commercial criteria. Policy factors as a whole will be only one factor among commercial criteria and economic factors such as market size and growth. Companies also seek to assess the balance of policy factors and there may be some factors favouring a particular location and others with negative effects. This makes it difficult to determine what impact policy divergence has in any one area of policy. Company responses will also vary from sector to sector and over time. So assessing the impact of competition among rules will mean filtering out all these other variables.

An assessment of the impact of competition among rules also faces the same difficulties as any assessment of the impact of the single European market. As past studies have shown (Woolcock *et al.* 1991) the SEM went hand in hand with increased international competition, and it is not always easy to determine what actions are due to developments within the EC and what to do with international trends. Interviews with companies have often produced ambiguous answers. Many firms interviewed stated that the SEM was one factor but not the only factor. Others said that the SEM resulted in them bringing forward decisions they would otherwise have made but at a later date. (Woolcock *et. al.* 1991)

The competition among rules will take two general forms. There will be regulatory competition between different locations (countries) for the mobile factors of production, i.e. capital. The medium through which this competition will occur is therefore the exercise of regulatory arbitrage in the locational decisions of investors. Companies will tend to invest in the location which they feel most matches their preferences for public goods. The difficulty with this form of competition in practice is, as noted above, that companies invest in different locations for all sorts of reasons. Even if the environment in a given country is not what a company prefers, it may still invest there if it is confident that it can make a good return on the investment.

The other form of regulatory competition occurs when indigenous companies lobby their national regulators in an effort to improve the national policy mix offered. For example, German employers lobbied the Federal German government for a reduction in German corporation tax, arguing that if this was not forthcoming they would be forced to invest more abroad. In most cases the threat is expressed by a trade association or collection of industrial companies. Trade unions, consumers, and environmentalists will also engage in the lobbying process. Rather than an individual 'market based' process the pressure is more political: more 'voice' than 'exit'. One must therefore not only consider what companies actually do but what they threaten to do.

The third form which competition among rules may take is regulatory emulation, in which regulators observe that other national regulations offer benefits and emulate them. In this they are likely to be encouraged by lobbyists who, for their own reasons, point out the benefits of foreign regulatory policies.

All cases require action, either by regulators or companies (or individuals in cases of movement of labour). There is some evidence to suggest that this condition will only be met if the whole exercise is seen to be credible. This is particularly true with the second form of competition in which companies, either individually or collectively, seek to change national regulations. They will only engage in the effort to do so if there is a reasonable prospect that the government will change its position.

Even when companies have rights, under the treaty, to act against cases of discrimination they may chose not to do so. This is a major problem with the enforcement of rights in the EC. The case of government procurement provides an example. When faced with non-compliance by large important customers, many suppliers are unwilling to initiate court action and risk 'biting the hand' that they hope will feed them with future contracts. This means that the enforcement mechanisms built into the EC legislation, which rely on companies acting, may not always be effective. Companies have also shown a reluctance to initiative cases against regulators, for fear that the regulators will make things hard for them in the future.

Sun and Pelkmans (1995) have developed a model for assessing the actions of regulators and companies under conditions of regulatory competition in the EC. This includes three possible tracks to regulatory competition: (i) a direct track through the existence of mutual recognition and the four freedoms: and two indirect tracks when residual barriers to free movement or mutual recognition exist; (ii) a judicial track in which the ECJ imposes mutual recognition; in other words a case is brought to the ECJ, and the ECJ rules that the standards met by foreign products are equivalent to the local standards; and (iii) a regulatory track in which the Council of Ministers acts under Article 100a (EEC) to set minimum essential requirements. This model also includes an element covering private sector responses. The expectation that emerges from the model is that regulatory competition will be greater when there is mutual recognition than when either of the indirect tracks is taken. The incentive for companies and regulators to respond is also less in the cases of indirect regulatory competition (Sun and Pelkmans 1995).

7. THE IMPACT OF COMPETITION AMONG RULES AT DIFFERENT LEVELS

Competition among rules can operate at different levels. At the national level, it can operate between different national regulatory styles. At the horizontal level, it can operate between different regulatory structures or philosophies. Finally at the sectoral or sub-sectoral level its can operate between different regulations.

The national level

Despite the difficulties making generalizations about the different national regulatory styles, it is possible to identify some general characteristics of regulatory policy which distinguish the national approaches. As Majone (1993*b*) has pointed out, Europeans have generally lagged behind the USA when it comes to developing coherent national regulatory policies. In the USA, regulatory policy has made extensive use of independent regulatory agencies (IRCs) beginning in the 1930s if not before. The stronger direct role of the state in most European economies, meant that state ownership, or more or less direct control by the state, played a much more important role in Europe. As a result independent regulatory bodies in sectors such as telecommunications and power have only recently been set up in Europe and only then in countries, such as Britain, which have moved to privatize their utilities.

At the national level the only broad exception to this has been the Federal Republic of Germany. In the post war reconstruction of Germany, a combination of a desire to limit the central powers of the state, the liberal economic philosophies of the Freiburger School, and a good measure of the USA administrative tradition, resulted in the creation of a number of important independent regulatory bodies. Thus the Bundesbank was established as an independent central bank at a time when the prevailing European model was one of politically controlled central banking. The objectives and operational framework (Ordnung) of the independent regulatory bodies were established in the form of codified rules, which assumed a quasi constitutional nature. These rules were often based on broad cross party consensus.

This contrasted with the more flexible and more discretionary approach of most other European countries in which the government of the day determined the objectives, as well as the operational frameworks and specific decisions of regulatory policies. This is what we shall call the distinction between the codified and discretionary styles of national regulation.

Another distinction that can be made between national styles is the degree to which regulatory policies are based on a broad political consensus of the main political parties, bureaucratic agencies, and interest groups. Here the contrast is primarily between the northern European consensus-based approach of the Germans, Dutch, and Danish and the more adversarial style of the British and French. The telecommunications sector provides an interesting example of the application of these different styles. In Britain liberalization and privatization of the telecommunications sector was determined by the responsible cabinet ministers. There was no effort made to engage in dialogue with other political parties, which opposed privatization, or interest groups such as trade unions and telephone users, with a view to establishing a national consensus. Legislation was simply pushed through Parliament and implemented. To engage in dialogue and to seek a consensus was seen as simply inviting opponents to frustrate reform and thus a recipe for failure.

In contrast the German reform of telecommunications, which ultimately proved to be as radical as the British, was brought about only after a concerted effort to establish a broad national consensus on the need for reform.

Reform proposals were considered by a semi-independent committee and a consensus was sought among the political parties on the implementing legislation. A more general comparison can be made between the British and German approaches to liberalization and deregulation during the 1980s. In the British approach specific detailed decisions were determined by government. In Germany the prospect of deregulation was the subject of a broad debate between interest groups on the basis of a report by an independent commission on deregulation (Deregulierungskommission 1991). Perhaps inevitably this procedure resulted in delays, but in specific areas radical reform was introduced on the basis of a broad policy consensus.

The creation of a genuine single European market results in competition between these two broad approaches to national regulatory policy. In the drafting of EC legislation there will be a competition between the two approaches. But in those areas in which there is as yet no EC legislation, competition between the different national regulatory styles will be played out in the 'market'. The issue is whether there will be a convergence between the two, and in common EC regulation which one will be adopted. Experience to date in the EC suggests that the codified approach is likely to find a greater application in Europe than the discretionary approach. This can be illustrated in the area of competition and industrial policy in which the drafting of EC legislation is progressively introducing a framework of codified rules as the basis for regulatory policy and there are concomitant reductions in the scope for the application of regulatory power by national bodies. This process has not gone very far in some areas and national discretion remains. But there are very few cases in which EC discretion is replacing national discretionary policies. When EC level legislation replaces national legislation it tends, therefore to create a more codified, less discretionary framework or regulation (Wallace and Woolcock 1993).

The picture is much less clear with regard to whether the consensual or non-consensual style will predominate at a European level. To take the example of telecommunications the EC Commission went out of its way to establish a broad consensus among regulators, operators, and consumers in support of its approach to European policy in the sector. At the same time, however, directives have been adopted on a qualified majority basis and the Commission has itself forced through change in the telecoms sector in the face of opposition from national governments by using its own powers under the treaty. In the important area of social policy there have been efforts to promote the Social Dialogue and consensual type agreements between employers and workers, such as in the consultative provisions on labour market policy in the Treaty on European Union. But in this and many other fields one cannot speak of an EC level consensual approach to regulation developing.

Horizontal policy issues

The second level on which competition among rules operates is the horizontal policy level. This covers issues such as social and environmental policies or national policies on technical regulations.

Technical regulation

Perhaps the best example of competition between different regulatory structures can be found in the approaches to technical barriers to trade discussed above.

Different structures can also be found in the field of taxation, where some countries have relied on greater direct taxation and others on indirect taxation. Arguably competition among the tax régimes has brought about a convergence of structures, accompanied by some harmonization, such as the provision of a floor for the levels of indirect taxation. Levels of corporation tax have, for example, converged over the last decade from around 50% to and average of about 35% in the EC. This suggests also some pressure for reductions in tax levels (Begg *et al.* 1993). The reduction more or less coincides with the removal of capital controls and the concomitant increase in capital mobility towards the end of the 1980s. It seems to support the view that competition among rules will lead to downward pressure on the levels of taxation on capital.

Differences in the predominant national philosophy also appear to operate at a horizontal level. The predominant British view of social policy appears to be based on the assumption that increased social or employment rights will necessarily mean a reduction in efficiency. As more rights will tend to lead to lower propensity on the part of employers to take on labour, they will also undermine cohesion within society. In other words increased rights of those currently employed are at the expense of the unemployed. The predominant view held in Germany and the Low countries is that it is still possible to increase the rights of workers at the same time as improving efficiency and cohesion (Gold 1993). There is as yet little evidence of convergence between these broadly different philosophies and the underlying differences seem to limit any competition among rules on specific pieces of social regulation.

The environment may hold other examples of how national philosophies differ, or perhaps that national philosophies on the role of environmental policy have achieved different stages of development. In Germany, the Netherlands, and Denmark environmental economics and the integration of environmental objectives in economic policy-making has reached a developed stage. As a result countries such as The Netherlands have developed clear national targets for the environment which other policies are then geared to help achieve. This is not (yet) the case in countries such as Britain and France nor in some of the 'southern' member states of the EU, where economic policy objectives have not yet been as affected by environmental considerations (Weale 1993). In environmental policy one can see some convergence between policies. The Treaty on European Union included, for example, a requirement to consider environmental policy objectives in all EC policies. But this is still to be operationalized in detailed policy issues as it has been at a national level in the Netherlands and Germany.

There are some signs that competition among rules tends to work on the national and horizontal levels through the pressure for convergence from below. This was the case in the convergence between national approaches to technical regulation. It also appears to be the case in the environmental sector (Weale 1993). This may be because national regulatory structures or styles are so entrenched that no country is prepared to change to adopt another style. As the technical regulations (paradigm) case showed, however, experts working on practical issues may soon find ways of getting around differences in structure or style. Competition policy also illustrates how the collection of many detailed decisions in the EC and the ECJ developing and interpreting Articles 85 and 86 (EEC).

Regulatory emulation seems to have been important in some cases. For example, the general move towards independent central banks is in part due to the observation, over many years, of the effectiveness of the German model in terms of maintaining price stability and sustained economic growth. But the political weight of a country or countries has also clearly affected discussions. In the case of monetary policy, Germany's economic strength meant that it was able to shape the agenda. In environmental policy the importance of Germany has also played a role. But consider, by way of contrast, the Danish unilateral move to raise the level of environmental regulation in the case of bottles.

Sectoral level competition among rules

At a sectoral level the degree to which individual regulations are embedded with others is less, so that one would expect a higher degree of competition among rules. But even here there are factors which limit the impact of competition among rules.

Capital markets

The EC Directive on Free Movement of Capital of 1988 required the removal of all capital controls by 1990, with transitionary periods for certain countries. This does not mean automatic free capital movement, because regulation of certain activities and sectors still limits investment and capital flows. For example, regulation of financial services markets designed to limit investor and systemic risk differ from country to country and these differences can limit market access and capital flows. It was therefore necessary for the EC to adopt legislation to open financial markets. Equally, the existence of national public or private monopolies, such as in the energy, transport, or telecommunications sectors can limit investment.

In the EC the efforts to establish a single financial market have included provisions on banking, investment services, and proposals for the creation of a single currency. The banking provisions were implemented at the beginning of 1993. While these provided for a single passport and home country control for banking, the need for local market presence in order to gain effective access, at least in retail banking, has meant that the degree of competition between the major national banks has been fairly muted to date (Woolcock *et al.* 1991). In securities, where transactions concern a more limited number of market operators, one would expect that the free movement of capital would result in more intense competition among rules. But the evidence to date suggests that in this sector also, the amount of regulatory competition has been limited.

It is true that some markets for securities have come under pressure from the increased growth in turnover in foreign equities, especially in the London market. The London market now accounts for no less than 95% of all the foreign equity traded within the EC. The fact that this business is important for London, accounting for some 44% of its turnover, has also led to efforts by London to retain this leading position. Thus the development of trading systems, such as the SEAQ, were designed to attract foreign equity trading. This has had a significant impact on some markets. For example, Amsterdam, where much of the equity trading involves institutional shareholders, has lost an important share of dutch share trading to the London market. Even 30% of German shares are traded in London, but as this mainly affects the larger companies it is less of a threat to the German stock exchanges. Nevertheless the competitive pressure has led to regulatory changes in Germany as well as the Netherlands in an effort to retain market share (Steil 1993).

Another example of how regulatory competition is more intense in a clearly defined sector, in which trade is essentially in capital, is that of the withholding tax on investment income. In 1989 Germany introduced a 10% withholding tax on investment income, but within about six months some DM 100 bn in capital flowed out of Germany into other countries (Begg *et al*, 1993). The German tax authorities tried to persuade their EC partners to introduce a similar tax, but when this attempt failed, the German authorities were obliged to drop the tax. Such intense competition between tax levels is what might be expected in an area so immediately affected by the free flow of capital, but so far it has been the exception more than the rule.

In the area of securities there have been efforts to limit competition by national legislation, such as the Italian law introduced in January 1992 which requires securities firms to be separately capitalized if they are to conduct business in the Italian market. This makes it more expensive for non-Italian firms to participate. The so-called Club-Med Group of countries including France, Italy and Belgium have also sought to prevent their nationals trading on 'un-regulated' markets. The British have seen this as an attempt to prevent the growth of trading on the SEAQ system. These countries have also succeeded in getting a transitionary period until 1996 during which they will be able to retain their dualist structures, so that banks will not be able to operate on securities markets in these countries until 1996 (Steil 1993).

As in other areas, EC level legislation has set out to establish common minimum regulatory requirements, such as the inclusion of securities firms in the capital adequacy provisions. Such legislation will therefore limit the degree of regulatory competition and regulatory arbitrage in a sector in which one would expect competition to be at it most intense. There is also some doubt that there will be a 'competition in laxity' in the sector. There seems to be a broad expectation among analysts of the sector that regulators will want to provide investors with security for their investment. This means providing a well regulated and secure market rather than participating in a 'race to the bottom' (Steil 1993).

Pharmaceuticals

The pharmaceuticals sector in Europe provides an example of how divergent national regulatory structures have ensured divergent policies. It also illustrates how the absence of mutual trust in the national certification or enforcement of controls, in this case on the registration of drugs, can undermine mutual recognition.

The efforts to phase-in mutual recognition in the pharmaceutical sector began in 1977, in an effort to reduce the costs of duplication in national registration procedures for new drugs. The European Commission proposed what was called the multi-state procedure whereby when a new drug was approved by one national registration authority, the company applying for registration could also apply to another four countries with the expectation that these would also approve the drug. However, companies did not use this procedure because national registration authorities were not prepared to accept registration by other national authorities. Consequently, the drug companies continued to apply to the individual national bodies. Between 1977 and 1985 the multi-state procedure was only used forty times and in many of these cases the national authorities used the safeguard measures under which they could question the registration decision taken by other national drug registration authorities.

Despite efforts to strengthen the multi-state procedure in the early 1980s, little progress was made until 1990 when the European Commission proposed the introduction of a two level approach. According to the proposals, which were finally adopted in 1993, new sophisticated products will be registered by a new centralized European Medicines Agency (EMA). This will draw on national expertise, but is in effect one of the first independent regulatory bodies to be established in the EC. In order to limit the risks of regulatory capture, the legislation setting up the agency seeks to ensure that decisions are based on scientific judgement. Ultimately decisions will be taken by the European Commission, following the expert opinion of the scientists. The Commission has some flexibility to take account of Community interests, but in order to safeguard against the abuse of such powers, decisions to approve or disapprove registration are subject to review by the ECJ.

The pharmaceutical sector in Europe is also characterised by different national pricing policies. Some countries, such as France and Italy, have traditionally controlled prices of drugs in order to reduce the costs of drugs for their health care services. Germany has had no price controls, except voluntary measures, in part because of the interests in helping to ensure the strong German pharmaceutical industry remained able to fund research and development into new drugs by charging higher prices on innovative products. The British have followed an intermediate path. It is interesting that these different pricing policies have continued despite the ability to sell drugs across borders. The ability to sustain such different pricing policies within the common market can be explained by the close links between drug prices and health care policy on the one hand, and the link between drug prices and industrial policy objectives on the other.

In one respect the pharmaceutical sector illustrates convergence. This is the question of the length of the patent life of new drugs. A longer effective patent life, in other words the number of years a patented drug can be sold on the market before it faces competition from generic drugs offering the same effects, is of central importance to the pharmaceutical industry. The longer the effective patent life the greater the chances of sustaining an industry that can develop new profitable drugs. In the case of patent life, the regulatory competition has come from the United States of America, which introduced longer patent life for drugs in order to compensate for the time it now takes to test new drugs. Japan followed suit and the EC was ultimately forced, by its industry, to fall into line, despite the costs in higher expenditure on drugs for the national health schemes. Competition from the United States of America has also affected the EC's regulation in the field of bio-technology. Efforts in Europe, especially in the European Parliament, to place strict controls on the release of genetically engineered products into the environment have been affected by the risk of investment in research and development in genetic engineering flowing out of the EC and into the USA where the controls are less strict.

A further interesting international dimension to the pharmaceutical story is the recent development of trilateral co-operation between the EC, Japan, and USA on testing procedures for drugs. Led by the industry, which is concerned about the ever rising costs of duplicative testing of drugs, there have been extensive efforts in the framework of the International Conference on Harmonization of Technical Requirements for the Registration of Pharmaceuticals for Human Use (ICH). In other words the kind of pressure that led to more central regulation of registration in Europe is also to be seen at an international level (Braithwaite 1993).

To sum up therefore the pharmaceutical sector illustrates that mutual trust is essential for mutual recognition to work. It also shows how the linking of a regulatory policy, price controls on drugs, to other policy areas, can help ensure that divergent national regulations continue to exist within the common market. In fact the divergent pricing policies created divergent industrial structures, which in turn helped to perpetuate the national policies. Finally, the sector shows that regulatory competition is not restricted to Europe, it can also operate globally.

8. THE SCOPE FOR COMPETITION AMONG RULES

The general conclusion that appears from a very complex picture, is that the scope for competition among rules is fairly limited. Those who see it as an panacea for problems of deciding between national and EC level regulation, or as a means of avoiding having to decide on the form of European level regulatory policies, seem likely to be disappointed.

The main reason for this is that some of the main preconditions for the effective operation of competition among rules are unlikely to be fulfilled, at least, at present. The completion of the single market does provide for the four freedoms. But even here there is a need to make some qualifications. For the foreseeable future local market characteristics, or the legacies of past national policies and practices, mean that there will not be a homogenous market. The degree to which national regulators are exposed to competition from other régimes is therefore moderated to some degree, even when there is mutual recognition.

The transparency condition is also only partially satisfied. Many of the EC's internal market measures have contained provisions for increasing the transparency of national policy. There must, however, remain some question about the availability of information for individual consumers. The main limitation with regard to transparency is, however, the absence of any transparency on the effects of different national regulations. This point has tended to be passed over by the more theoretical discussions of competition among rules. What is meant is what was described above as the need for 'discreetness.' In other words regulatory policies tend to be bundled together and interdependent so that it is difficult if not impossible, in many cases, to identify the impact of differences in regulation in one specific area. This means that there is no transparency with regards to the effects of competition among rules.

Regulators and economic operators can seldom say with any certainty what impact any change in policy will have. Under such circumstances regulators are unlikely to change policies as a result of regulatory competition and market operators will be unable to quantify the impact of policy differences in any arbitrage. Any impact of differences will therefore tend to be diluted. This is not to say that differences will have no effect. They will be stressed in lobbying aimed at reducing business costs, but the absence of any real measures of their impact means that they may not figure more than any other subjective factor.

A great imponderable concerning competition among rules and the SEM in general, is whether the existing rules will be effectively enforced. Competition among rules will not operate unless the national rules are enforced. A 'competition in laxity' can hardly be said to be an efficient or desirable development and would have serious implications for the credibility of the whole SEM. This remains an imponderable because the job of enforcing the SEM legislation has only just begun. The legislative programme set out in the Cockfield White Paper has been more or less completed. Implementation of the directives in national legislation has also made considerable strides. But the EC and member states have only recently turned their attentions to enforcement. Proposals have been made in the Sutherland Committee report on enforcement (Sutherland 1993). These include suggestions for closer co-operation between national regulatory bodies responsible for enforcing EC directives, and measures to enhance awareness of European law and the remedies available under European law in cases of unfair competition or non-compliance. While the Commission of the EC has picked up on these proposals in its Strategy Paper on the reinforcement of the internal market, these measures are still to be fully acted upon.

Until an effective system of enforcement can be established and national authorities can be reassured that regulators in other countries are enforcing EC and national rules, there is still a tendency to seek high degrees of regulatory rapprochement in order to be sure that mutual recognition does, in fact, mean a recognition that regulation is equivalent in other countries.

9. THE RISK OF ZERO OR SUB-OPTIMAL REGULATION

Much of the concern expressed about the neo-liberal bias in the competition among rules approach is based on the fear that there will be a process of competitive deregulation which leads to a 'race to the bottom' or sub-optimal regulation. On the basis of existing research, this fear does not seem to be justified.

There are various reasons for this. First, the preference within the EC approach to market integration is based a fairly high degree of harmonization. This effectively sets minimum standards or levels for regulation. This is the case in the tax field, where there a floor has been set for value added tax of 15% (although there has been no harmonization of corporation tax), it is only above this that competition between tax régimes operates. In technical regulation for health and safety the harmonization of minimum essential requirements (performance standards) sets a lower limit. The same is true for many areas of environmental policy and even in the field of social policy, outside the areas of wage determination and social security. With the implementation of the Social Chapter of the Treaty on European Union by the eleven there is also likely to be an adoption of the Directive on European Works Councils.

The existence of a blocking minority of certain key member states has also helped ensure that the levels of minimum regulation established within the Community have not been sub-optimal. In the field of social policy Germany has consistently refused to accept EC level legislation which might undercut the levels of provision established in Germany. For example, the fact that no agreement could be reached on a range of company law directives was because Germany resisted any legislation which might undermine German codetermination laws. In environmental policy Germany, The Netherlands, and Denmark represent a blocking minority on any EC directive which threatens to open the way to low levels of EC regulation.

There is also clear evidence of the ability of national regulators to maintain standards above those of the common EC level. This is possible when, for example, there exists a broad national consensus on the need for such higher standards. This would suggest that the kind of pressure that would otherwise be forthcoming from companies that face higher costs, either does not materialize, because the companies themselves are a part of the consensus, or is neutralized by the political desire on the part of governments not to risk undermining the national consensus between parties or within interest groups. This kind of a consensus has been important in the social policy field in Germany and in the environmental policy field in Germany, the Netherlands, and Denmark.

A related point to that of national consensus is the limits placed on dereg-ulation when a particular policy is enmeshed or embedded within a broad national policy objective or practice. Again environment provides an exam-ple of how this prevents deregulation and, as we shall see later, results in pressure for higher standards.

Apart from these more political checks on any race to the bottom, there are also economic rationales for maintaining levels of regulation. First, there is the case that market imperfections or externalities exist which require regulation. Second, the case can be made and is made that higher levels of regulation can bring benefits in terms of enhanced competitiveness. In environmental policy, for example, the case has been made that industry will benefit from higher national standards in that it will develop more sophisticated environmental technologies, which will enable it to compete more easily. This case has been made in Germany and has, by and large, been accepted by German industry.

A similar case for 'trading up' is made in the field of social policy. This case argues that if European industry is to compete with low cost countries in the developing world or with middle income countries that have consid-erably lower wages, it must trade up and produce higher value-added prod-ucts. The case is made that European industries will never be able to compete head-to-head with the NICs on wage costs, so that attempts to trade down and produce goods more cheaply through lower wages will weaken rather than strengthen the competitive position of European indus-try. A sectoral level example of the case for trading up can be found in the regulation of financial markets. While a case might be made for deregula-tion as a means of attracting more international investment and business, the experience of the early deregulation initiatives in the 1980s was that investors are also concerned about the protection of their investment and are reluctant to place funds in a capital market which cannot provide sufficient protection. Therefore regulation to ensure the prudential security of financial institutions becomes a means of attracting investment.

In any given case a number of such factors may be brought to bear and thus limit the downward pressure that might otherwise result in a race to the bottom. The evidence so far therefore suggests that a race to the bot-tom is an unlikely scenario, although it cannot be excluded in all cases. In many cases the new directives have only just been introduced and it may be some time before it is possible to conclude with any certainty what the long term effects may be. While arguing that there is no major risk of a 'race to the bottom;' Begg and others have suggested that possible future trends in taxation may result in continuous pressure on the ability to fund the wel-fare state. Corporation taxes, as noted above have already converged towards a lower level. It is not clear whether there will be further downward pressure on corporation taxation. On the one hand, it is possible to argue that most of the impact will have come with the introduction of full free-dom of movement of capital in 1990 (1992 for some member states). But capital mobility could further increase if there is an erosion of some of the still quite important local market characteristics which at present limit mobility.

At present labour mobility is also low and the indications are that it will remain relatively low. Marginal increases in labour mobility among high wage earning groups could, however, create downward pressure on higher levels of income tax and thus exacerbate the problem (Begg *et al* 1993).

10. CONCLUSIONS: CONVERGENCE OR DIVERGENCE

The question of convergence may be addressed on the three different levels considered earlier: the national, horizontal, and sectoral levels.

At a national level there does appear to be a convergence towards what has above been called the framework approach in which the EC regulatory approach is to establish, by means of directives and regulations, a frame-work within which markets are to operate. In order for such an approach to operate effectively and for there to be effective monitoring and day to day enforcement of regulation at the European level, it is arguably neces-sary to establish independent regulatory bodies. But there would appear to be considerable doubt about the willingness of national governments to accept such independent regulatory bodies. In high profile cases, such as monetary policy or the environment, there is a strong resistance to estab-lishing such bodies. Only when the agencies are buried in technocratic nego-tiations such as on the European Medical Agency, was it possible for an agreement to be reached on the establishment of an independent body. Even more unclear is whether there is convergence on the issue of consensual or non-consensus-based regulation.

The discussion of the horizontal level of policies, such as social and envi-ronmental policy, illustrates the limitations of competition among rules due to the policy linkages or 'embeddedness' of individual policies. While regu-latory policy addresses specific issues of social, environmental, or company regulation, these specific measures are embedded in a set of established national philosophies and practices. Some cases, such as that of environ-mental policy, suggested that this bundling or linkage of policies, i.e. envi-ronment with energy, transport, or other policies, is also increasing. If true this will tend to strengthen rather than weaken such bundling and thus dilute the impact of competition among rules in any part of the bundle.

If there is convergence it appears to come from technical discussion between experts rather than from free competition between national poli-cies. That is, technical consultations between experts tends to bring about a convergence on the specifics of the directive or regulation at hand. The collective impact of these changes may then bring about a convergence in the national approaches to the policy area.

If it is true that policy issues are becoming more rather than less interlinked, the question remains as to the longer term effects of such linkages. Two scenarios might be envisaged.

Policy linkages increase and consolidate national policy approaches and the differences between them. This means that competition exists but it is more in the shape of conventional competition between national approaches or national systems. The alternative scenario is that linkages lead to increased policy integration through approximation or rapprochement until more and more areas of policy are integrated. This latter scenario is the traditional integration scenario in which integration in one area leads to spill-over effects in others. During the 1980s there was clearly evidence of integrative spill-over taking place. Since then the issue has become more questionable, and as suggested above much will depend on enforcement as to whether the trend is reversed.

The main issues from the point of view of competition among rules is that neither scenario suggests the kind of stable, steady state competition between different national regulations or policies which is favoured by the advocates of competition among rules in preference to harmonization.

The external implications

Given the uncertainties surrounding the ultimate course of events in Europe it is impossible to come to conclusions on whether the EC will in future have common policies as a result of convergence, or significantly diverging policies. In the short to medium term the most important implication of the application of competition among rules in Europe is that this approach itself differs in some quite fundamental ways from the approaches adopted in other regional and multilateral agreements. The new approach to integration based on some regulatory rapprochement, mutual recognition and home country control is fundamentally different from the traditional approach (to trade) used by most other trading entities. For example, GATT still relies on national treatment and non-discrimination, even if these are finding it more and more difficult to serve as the basis for policy in what is becoming a more and more interdependent world economy. NAFTA also uses national treatment, host country control and eschews mutual recognition and common policies.

In multilateral negotiations it will become increasingly important to ensure that these different approaches can be accommodated. The potential for trade frictions can be illlustrated by the EC–USA dispute over reciprocity in 1988–1989. Having introduced mutual recognition and home state control in the regulation of European banking, the EC suggested that reciprocity could only be achieved if the USA followed suit. The USA position was that its international policy on banking was based on national treatment and this was what it offered to the EC and other trading partners. Although the issue was defused in the late 1980s, the fundamental differences in approach remain.

Is competition among rules applicable at the global level?

The answer to this question would seem to be negative. Other major trading entities, such as the USA and Japan, have shown, through their approaches to recent trade agreements that they are unwilling to cede the degree of sovereignty that would have to be ceded to adopt an approach based on mutual recognition. This means that a formal agreement based on the kind of competition among rules which exists within Europe is not possible at a global level. But this does not mean that de facto competition among rules cannot and does not exist at a global level. As we have seen in the examples of capital and financial markets, there are indeed already elements of competition among rules, both in terms of regulatory competition and regulatory emulation.

11

European Integration and a Pensions Problem: Coping with a Chameleon

GRAHAM MOFFAT

I. INTRODUCTION

A central issue for the EU in the 1990s is how far it can develop on the basis of liberalization of the free movement of economic factors, while allowing or retaining a significant degree of national diversity in social and welfare provision. A related question, central to the concerns of this book, is the extent to which there needs to be integration or coordination between the differing national regulatory frameworks, or whether differences and competition between them can provide important incentives to produce an optimal regulatory scheme, whether by deregulation or reregulation.

The issue discussed in detail in this chapter, the regulation of non-state or supplementary pension provision, provides a pivotal case-study. In principle, pension arrangements appear to be very much a matter for the different national welfare states rather than European policy-making, and it is not surprising that for many decades the whole issue of retirement provision was seen by EC policy-makers as a Pandora's box (not to say a can of worms) which it would be preferable to keep tight shut (Mortensen 1992: 5). Yet, for a variety of reasons, a number of initiatives were undertaken as part of the development of the Single European Market (SEM), to develop EU law on non-state pensions. In this context, the initiatives came from within the European Commission (CEC) itself, unlike the impetus for equal treatment in pensions, where European-wide political pressure from the women's movement (and later the trade unions) created stronger direct political pressure (Ellison, 1994). It is not easy to disentangle either the socio-economic policy motivations, or the institutional logic, which lay behind the CEC actions. Equally, at least at the time of writing, the proposals resulting from the initiatives had made little, if any, progress, and the outcome seems to justify the view that such social policy arrangements are so deeply embedded in specific national structures that their coordination through the EU presents intractable difficulties. Nevertheless, a closer examination seems to show that the EU institutional process has provided an important framework for the identification and shaping of policy issues, helping to create the orientation within which the policy debate proceeds. While, in this instance and at this stage, the harmonization proposals have been put on a back burner, they will have influenced the shape of the national reforms under way in several states, and these new national arrangements may well in their turn take strong account of the European trends which have been identified. Each state will consider how to position its national system in relation to the emerging international policy trends.

2. SUPPLEMENTARY PENSIONS AND THE EUROPEAN UNION: AN AGENDA FOR CHANGE?

2.1 A constitutional impetus.

The constitutional justifications, if not the policy motivations, for EU action on pensions policy are easy to find. As an economic union, the central provisions of the Treaty of Rome in Title 3 are directed towards securing the 'Free movement of persons, services and capital'. Recent EU pensions initiatives have attempted to build on this constitutional foundation.

A. Freedom of movement for persons

In an economic union it comes as no surprise that freedom of movement of persons is mainly directed at freedom of movement for workers. Thus Article 48 of the Treaty aspirationally states that '(1) Freedom of movement of workers shall be secured within the Community . . .' and goes on to say that such freedom includes the right to accept offers of employment throughout the EU and the right to free movement within the Member States for this purpose. It can certainly be argued that this freedom might be impaired if movement were to involve the loss of pension entitlement. In relation to social security, and this includes benefits available under the headings of old age and survivorship, EU regulations exist (directly applicable in every Member State) which seek to coordinate aspects of the highly diverse systems of the Member States and thereby minimize any disadvantages regarding benefit entitlement that might result from moving between states during one's working life (Article 51 and Regulations (EEC) 1408/71 and 574/72). However, this coordinating jurisdiction does not apply to the private supplementary pension schemes which constitute the second tier of pension provision. Hence the understandable concern that the absence of any formal coordination arrangements may, in the words of the Social Charter action programme 'cause workers to lose rights and may form an obstacle to the development of the occupational mobility of workers between different member states: . . .' (CEC 1989: 25). In similar though more assertive vein, the 1993 social policy Green Paper argues that it would be unacceptable if fear of losing benefits were to discourage workers from exercising their right of free movement (CEC 1993*a*: 61). Thus one of the questions posed for discussion in that Green Paper was what type of action should be taken at community level to provide for a better protection of mobile workers 'in particular by facilitating the acquisition, preservation and transfer of occupational pension rights'.

It certainly seems plausible that the absence of appropriate protection of supplementary pension rights acts as a barrier to labour mobility.[1] However, it is surprisingly hard to establish that in practice labour mobility is indeed affected in the manner suggested. At the very least the scale of the problem should not be exaggerated. As Marsden (1992) amongst others has pointed out, most workers have tended to be tied to fairly small, spatially limited and local labour markets, a trend reinforced by social and linguistic considerations. More particularly, even among the active EU migrant worker population, estimated in 1991 at rather less than 3 million (Jolliffe 1991),[2] the number of instances where pensions issues could even conceivably be a factor in influencing individual decisions on mobility was believed then to be less than 200,000. This is simply because most migrant workers are reliant on state pension rather than any supplementary pension provision.

Nevertheless, it is still very possible that the creation of the Single European Market (SEM) will involve a higher level of labour mobility. Two dimensions in particular are of immediate relevance. First, it is not difficult to see that further increase in the rate of cross-border mergers and/or acquisitions within the EU could lead to more extensive *corporate internal labour markets* extending across national borders, especially for professional and managerial staff. Perhaps more importantly, with the implementation of mutual recognition of professional and other qualifications, there may emerge an inter-firm or occupational-based labour market so that highly-qualified groups come to see their careers as spanning national borders. This is not to overlook, at the other end of the occupational spectrum, the long-standing community wide labour market in unqualified labour but, as previously indicated, supplementary pension provision has rarely been relevant for this group.

The empirical question that this speculation about the consequences of extended labour markets does not address is whether there is any evidence that distinctive and divergent national systems of pension provision do act

---

[1] It should not be overlooked that the complexities of the coordination of state social security provisions via regulations has itself generated considerable criticism: see e.g., Laske (1993); Luckhaus (1995); Steiner (1992); and generally Pieters (ed.) (1991).

[2] See Salt *et al.* (1994) for a comprehensive statistical analysis of European migration flows in general.

as a barrier to labour mobility. It is quite conceivable that concern about pension provision is viewed as a peripheral consideration in individual or corporate decisions about mobility. For individuals the most fundamental obstacle to labour mobility is a lack of available jobs, but even where vacancies may exist there are other obstacles, such as the previously mentioned problems of language and accommodation, that are more potent than a lack of transferability of pension rights (see Kleinman and Piachaud 1993: 9–10). Ermisch (1991), for instance, argues on the basis of admittedly limited evidence that workers' mobility shows a lack of responsiveness even to favourable differences in social benefits or take-home pay.[3] It also appears that decisions about mobility in a corporate context are largely unaffected, although rendered administratively more cumbersome, by the pensions problem (see Maier 1991 and Harrison 1991). Scepticism about the present relative importance of possible loss of pensions entitlement to questions of labour mobility does not detract from a conclusion that some degree of harmonization, or at least coordination, may become increasingly attractive. This will particularly be the case if, as seems probable, reliance on supplementary pension provision as an element of financial provision for old age becomes quantitatively more important across the countries of the EU.

B. Freedom of services and capital movement

Facilitating labour mobility does not provide the sole justification for the involvement of EU institutions in seeking to influence pensions policy. An equally firm ground for involvement is to be found in the two other freedoms mentioned above: freedom of establishment and to provide services, and free movement of capital. Certainly, the sheer size of pension funds within some Member States has constituted a source of pressure for intervention at EU level. Since these funds in 1992 held over 900 bn ecus in assets,[4] the conviction unsurprisingly grew that the internal market in financial services would be incomplete unless these funds were brought within the liberalizing régime for financial services being introduced and erected on the three principles of home country control, mutual recognition, and minimum harmonization (Kollias 1992). In particular the CEC view, most clearly evident in the approach of the Directorate General for Financial Institutions and Company Law (DG XV), was that there should be both full freedom for cross-border investment of pension fund assets and freedom to employ the services of fund managers from any Member State. This perception was based partly on the proposition—reflecting the views of some Member

[3] See also Marsden (1992) who suggests that the limited real wage differences among Member States (+/– 15% of the Community mean) are insufficient to 'cause major migrations in search of higher incomes' (at 26).
[4] This figure is drawn from estimates provided by the European Federation for Retirement Provision (EFRP).

States—that liberalizing measures should be adopted for pension funds so as to achieve symmetry with directives, such as the Third Life Assurance Directive (92/96/EEC), being introduced for life assurance undertakings and other comparable institutions. Symmetry was thought to be warranted on the basis that insurance undertakings themselves (both life and non-life) play a highly significant role in overall pension provision within the EU, and both complement and compete with[5] pension funds. Thus insurance undertakings offer their services to employers and others who operate or wish to establish pension arrangements as an alternative means either of ensuring the funding of the full pension promise, or of providing death and ill-health benefits, or by providing insurance against the insolvency of the pension fund itself or of the employer. (The competitive role of life insurance undertakings in relation to pension funds as pensions providers is, however, offset by their role as managers of the assets of the pension funds against which they effectively compete.) The EEC Commission was also strongly influenced by the consideration that the Freedom of Capital Movements Directive—agreed in 1988 and operative with effect from 1 July 1990 (88/361/EEC)—would lose a good deal of its force unless full freedom for cross-border investment of pension fund assets were achieved (Brittan 1990).

It would be misconceived, however, to conclude that the sole inspiration behind Commission initiatives was simply a concern to achieve full freedom of movement of labour and capital, and freedom of services, all in pursuit of the completion of an integrated SEM. Important though these considerations are, there are also far-reaching demographic and economic influences at work which are simultaneously bolstering the case for EU-wide intervention while weakening the hitherto sceptical stance of both EU and national authorities towards such intervention.

2.2 The demographic impetus

Most European states are experiencing a combination of a reduction in average fertility rates (see Appendix A Table 1) and increasing life expectancy through a reduction in mortality rates. These trends are increasingly influencing attitudes towards the financing of pensions and

---

[5] Pension funds, being established to provide pensions for employees of a specific employer, industry or group, do not compete with insurance undertakings or other pension funds to provide pensions for individuals not within the specified client group. Nevertheless to the extent that pensions are provided through a pension fund, rather than through insurance policies or annuity contracts, there is a loss of business for insurance undertakings. Whether those establishing a pension arrangement choose to operate by means of a pension fund or an insurance undertaking may depend upon the cost and nature of the insurance product, as may a decision whether a pension fund's trustees or administrators choose to employ the services of an insurance undertaking for management of fund assets. It is in this context that the Commission sought the adoption of symmetry with the life assurance directives.

consequently towards the appropriate structure of provision for retirement. One commonly articulated implication is that the projected ageing in population will be accompanied by a decrease in labour force participation rates, the combined effect of which will be to increase the old-age dependency ratio (see Appendix A Table 2). The CEC's Green Paper, using data covering all OECD countries rather than just the Member States of the EU, suggests (1993: 24) that by the year 2020 'the ratio of people of age 65 or older to those in working age, i.e., between 15 and 64, *may* have increased by about 50%' (emphasis added). One potential consequence of such a development is said to be an increase in the cost of public financing of retirement pension payments, in the order of an additional 5% of GDP (see Appendix A Table 3, and generally on this issue Heller 1989; Schmahl 1991; Sturm 1992). This leads to the argument that increases of this order of magnitude would be financially and politically unacceptable, and that those Member States placing greatest reliance on state pay-as-you-go pensions will be compelled to shift the balance of retirement provision more towards reliance on supplementary pensions. Proponents of this view might point, in particular, to contemporary developments in Italy (see Franco and Frasca 1992) and the 1991 *Livre Blanc sur les Retraites* published by the French Government which critically reviewed the French system of pensions provision.[6]

However, the inferences to be drawn from the anticipated demographic changes are not clear-cut. The extent of any consequential financial burden depends critically on the relationship between the numerator (public expenditure) and the denominator (GDP) in the equation. As regards the latter the proportionate costs of ageing, although admittedly not their incidence on the population, are plainly sensitive to shifts in the GDP of member states. Of greater significance is the number of variables—imponderables may be an equally apt description—that influence the numerator. Changes in pension age, in rates of accrual of pension entitlement, in qualifying contribution requirements, and in labour force participation rates (particularly among the 55–64 age cohort) can all be highly significant in modifying the perceived costs associated with demographic ageing (Hills 1993; DSS 1993; Besseling and Zeeuw 1993). Moreover, there are formidable difficulties, at least in the short to medium term, in shifting from a pay-as-you-go system to a funded basis, since current workers can hardly be expected to fund both their own future pensions and those of the now and soon to be retired. It might be argued, more radically, that the perceived problems associated with population ageing could be modified by active immigration policies to compensate for the prospective demographic imbalance. However, a com-

---

[6] Subsequent reform proposals from the government, the National Assembly, and the Patronat (the French employers' association) appear to have been deferred on political and economic grounds: *Financial Times* 28 July 1994 and 14 November 1994.

pensatory strategy such as this would require large and sustained immigration levels whose political and social acceptability is highly questionable (Salt *et al.* 1994: ch. 6; Sturm 1992: 33–34).

It is therefore apparent that responding to the costs of providing pensions for an ageing population presents difficult policy challenges to national social policy mechanisms. But this policy problem also potentially provides an added impetus to EU involvement. Emerson has suggested (1991: 13) that the problems posed by these demographic pressures and the difficulties associated with their solution, provide an entry point for EU activity: 'at the very least Member States will surely want to consult and concert their responses to the ageing problem, and to seek solidarity in numbers in promoting difficult policy changes, and to avoid possible beggar-thy-neighbor effects'. Thus, for example, the Italian Government in 1992 emphasized to its electorate that the changes to its generous state scheme represented an attempt to bring Italy more into line with European Community practices.[7]

2.3 Economic considerations.

These demographic-driven pressures could be categorised as constituting negative reasons for contemplating a change in the balance between public/private pensions provision. However, the perceived demographic crisis provides in addition a departure point for more positive reasons for changing the public/private mix. Leaving to one side any ideologically based preference for private over public provision, it may nevertheless be claimed that placing greater emphasis on pre-funded private or occupational provision will have beneficial capital formation and capital market effects. In so far as this claim rests on a conviction that such a shift could produce a net increase in the private individual saving ratio rather than merely changing its composition, it can only be said that the economic debate on this issue remains unresolved (Feldstein 1974; Duskin 1992; Pesondo 1992; Barr 1992). Wherever the balance lies in this debate, and indeed in comparable debates on the effects of institutional investment generally, there appears to be a perception in the CEC, perhaps almost an axiom, that the EU needs to encourage the development of pension funds in the interests of economic growth (Brittan 1990).

Thus there exists a complex mix of socio-economic considerations that could justify pensions initiatives at an EU level. Some of these considerations imply a CEC central role in stimulating an expansion of and ultimately convergence in supplementary pension provision and its regulation,

---

[7] *Financial Times* 11/12 July 1992 p. 2. The radical pension reform proposals of the Berlusconi government encountered fierce opposition and were deferred. (The caretaker government of Lamberto Dini subsequently negotiated a compromise agreement with the main trade union confederations, by which significant changes to Italian state pensions were introduced on 1 January 1996. (See *Employment Europe*, no. 407, November 1995, p. 23.))

whereas others might be met by simply securing a more modest measure of coordination between national systems.

Certainly, for whatever mix of their motivations, initiatives were initiated by the Social Affairs Directorate (DGV) and DGXV, although in the initial phase at least progress was at best patchy, at worst barely discernible. The policy process by which the attempts to foster an EU legal competence have occurred is examined in detail below, but the outcome to date seems to show that there remain formidable obstacles to any substantial convergence or even coordination in this area.

2.4 The countervailing constraints

One major obstacle can be traced to the pre-emptive role of national welfare states. This presents difficulties because almost all supplementary pension schemes are designed to mesh with the national state social security schemes. The same is true of their relationship to national fiscal laws. Consequently, Member States have different fiscal and administrative régimes for supplementary pension schemes (Watsons 1994; House of Lords 1992). The financing of supplementary pension schemes also differs widely, varying, for instance, from a pay-as-you-go system in France, to predominantly pre-funding in the UK, with Germany by contrast relying in large part on yet another system based on corporate book-reserve provision. When it comes to rights concerning vesting and transfer of entitlements these also vary between Member States; the difference between the UK with its two year vesting period for members' rights and the much longer vesting periods of ten or twelve years under the German system is particularly striking (Jolliffe 1991). To the extent that these problems are primarily technical in nature, or at least do not produce significant fiscal difficulties, they may prove to be surmountable, for instance, if necessary for particular groups of mobile workers by means of bilateral agreements between Member States. Yet of itself this resort to bilateral resolution of the problem by Member States merely acknowledges the reality that matters of taxation and social security still represent bastions of sovereignty for Member States. That sovereignty presents the most formidable constraint of all on EU competence.

The distinctive fiscal, social security and indeed regulatory régimes in the Member States may, however, be only the surface manifestation of deeper differences. Comparative theories of the welfare state suggest that various 'models' or 'régimes' of social policy structure can be identified within the EU (Abrahamson 1992; Esping-Andersen 1990; Leibfried 1992). Although there is considerable debate both about the concept of 'régimes' and the particular elements contained within them (Castles and Mitchell 1992; Langan and Ostner 1991; Manning 1993), there is some consensus on a typology distinguishing a Nordic universal welfare model, a more occupationally-based support system derived from and associated with Bismarckian principles, and an Anglo-Saxon or Beveridge residual model. Some have also identified a fourth and more rudimentary régime associated with the southern 'latin rim' European states (Abrahamson 1992; Leibfried 1992). The significant lesson to be drawn from these various analyses is that the pronounced institutional differences between Member States with respect to régimes of retirement provision did not emerge accidentally. They reflect elements of political compromise and policy choices derived from different ideological, cultural, and historical antecedents. Hence these different régimes of retirement provision may be said to reflect the distinctive social policy traditions identified above. Even so the typology described above is historically derived, and it is hard to predict how far contemporary developments in pensions policy will continue to be determined by the factors that shaped these different systems. Nevertheless, the extent to which it is possible to attain some convergence in the structure of pension systems within the EU, or even coordination of the standards of protection provided, will depend not just on the capacity to surmount technical hurdles but also on how deeply entrenched are the political and social cultures that underlie the different pension régimes.

These are potentially formidable obstacles. Nevertheless the CEC has felt obliged to abandon its previous abstentionist stance on supplementary pension issues. There is no monocausal explanation for this new stance. For DG V, an important motive is the need to prevent increased reliance on supplementary pension provision developing into a substantial deterrent to labour mobility. The possible implications of a perceived 'demographic crisis' leading to a 'financial crisis' for state social security is an additional contributory consideration. There is evidence that the CEC is concerned to ensure that any consequential shift within Member States to a greater reliance on supplementary pensions remains consistent with the stated objectives of securing adequacy of and convergence in social protection standards (CEC 1992a). For DG XV the imperatives of completing the SEM in financial services and the more long-term concern for the competitive position of European industry constitute the principal driving forces.

The common thread linking the various initiatives is an underlying perception that the role of supplementary pensions in retirement provision will and should increase. In this connection the CEC can be portrayed as a facilitator: compiling an information base here, transmitting knowledge and ideas there, and all the while stimulating debate within Member States. Yet might this be to understate the full role of the Commission? Portraying the CEC as a facilitator or neutral bureaucracy may not fully explain the nature of its involvement in the present context. Cram's notion (1993) of the CEC as a 'purposeful opportunist' seeking to expand the frontier of the possible provides a useful insight for interpreting the policy initiatives in the pensions area. From this perspective CEC initiatives can be interpreted as attempts to steer pensions policy towards an increased role for supplementary pensions, with the ultimate objectives of securing a formal convergence of pension systems and coincidentally an extension of community regulatory competence.

Whatever may have been the reasons for the more activist role adopted by the CEC, what remains to be explained is its apparent lack of success.

3. SUPPLEMENTARY PENSIONS AND THE EUROPEAN COMMISSION INITIATIVES: WHITHER LIBERALIZATION?

Before considering why the outcome of the CEC forays into the pensions arena has been, as suggested above, 'at best patchy at worst barely discernible', it is necessary to address two key interlocking issues concerning the division of legal competence between EU law and that of Member States. First, creating the SEM as fundamentally a construct of a system of rules prompts the question: precisely what regulatory space is available to the institutions of the EU to restrict the capacity of individual Member States to regulate the conditions under which supplementary pension schemes are to be provided and to operate? Secondly, where any such intervention does occur or is postulated what is its regulatory nature?

Any analysis of the nature of EU competence which proceeds from the assumption that the creation and completion of a 'common market' is the pre-eminent goal, is likely to conclude that EU institutions are fundamentally concerned with the removal of obstacles to free movement of capital, persons, and services. What might then flow from such an analysis? One possible consequence, if the development of intervention in product market regulation is taken as a benchmark, would be an extension of EU jurisdiction accompanied by an equal and opposite constraint, possibly quite severe, on the regulatory competence of individual Member States. The influence of the interpretative approach of the ECJ to Article 30 of the Treaty of Rome provides a tempting analogy here. Under this approach, particularly evident in the *Dassonville* [1974] ECR 837 and *Cassis de Dijon* [1979] ECR 649 cases, restrictions were imposed on those domestic rules of Member States having the effect, even if not the intention, of hampering free movement of goods (Gormley 1985; Dehousse 1992). The impetus for this court-centred initiative appeared to be a felt need to respond to the perceived shortcomings of the more conventional process of seeking to harmonize national laws (McGee and Weatherill 1990; Rasmussen 1986). The well known difficulties associated with harmonization—achieving consensus and ensuring effective implementation of and compliance with community

instruments—led to the emphasis on mutual recognition of national regulations and standards. In essence, in a product market context, this policy
means that a product lawfully manufactured in one Member State is taken
in principle to be of a quality suitable to be sold in any other Member State.
The transposing of this approach from the market for manufactured products to that concerned with the provision of financial services, which might
include supplementary pensions, is reflected in the adoption of the three
principles of the single 'licence' or 'passport', mutual recognition, and home
country control (see Kollias 1992; CEC 1987). The central tenet of mutual
recognition is not, however, an end in itself. The underlying assumption, as
Majone has pointed out, is that it will foster competition between the regulatory approaches of individual Member States, a competition which will
ultimately result in a market-driven convergence around one or perhaps a
few regulatory models (Majone 1991: 100–102; Dehousse 1992: 392–393;
and see generally Reich 1992).

It is possible to view the process just described—'harmonization by other
means'—as a further stimulus to deregulatory pressures within the EU,
leading to an outcome which is often termed 'negative integration', i.e., the
removal of obstacles to the full operation of a free market in the EU
(Tinbergen 1954; Pinder 1968; Liebfried & Pierson 1992). Yet any portrayal
of the process as constituting a picture of 'universal deregulation' or 'economic liberalism unconfined' would be misleading, indeed simplistic, on several counts. First, EU law continues to recognize the possibility of rules
acting as lawful barriers to trade. This is perfectly consistent even with the
tenets of a liberal economic order as long as such regulation is designed to
correct the effects of market and information failures (Majone 1993). Thus,
in the context of financial services, the incorporation within CEC initiatives
of basic definitions and rules concerned with solvency and prudential standards could be justifiable on the basis of their being designed to underpin
important objectives of investor and consumer protection. However, a
corollary of the mutual recognition process is that, both for Member States
and interest groups, the focus for securing the adoption of regulatory standards and influencing their content potentially shifts to the EU rather than
the Member State level.

The second reason for qualifying any analysis couched exclusively in
terms of 'negative integration' is to be found, albeit somewhat tangentially,
in the social policy and labour market dimensions of supplementary pension provision within the EU. As indicated previously, such provision is
closely tied to the systems of state pensions, the first tier of pension provision, in each Member State. Respect for the sovereignty of Member States,
allied to the limits of community legal competence in this area, has resulted
in a strategy of 'coordination' of entitlements provided under national systems rather than their harmonization. For certain social security rights

national rules governing entitlement have been coordinated aiming to ensure that social security rights of migrants are not lost through the operation of national rules. The emphasis is very much on coordination: this preserves the independent domestic systems and simply attempts to modify those aspects hindering mobility.[8] There is emphatically no attempt at harmonization in the sense of creating common standards or common forms of entitlement. This respect for national systems of social security therefore throws a doubt on whether notions of a 'deregulatory dynamic' derived from analysis of EU intervention in the regulation of product market sectors can usefully be applied in seeking to interpret initiatives in the area of supplementary pensions.

Lastly, the possible impact of a 'spillover effect' cannot be ignored (Lange 1993; Leibfried and Pierson 1992). By this is meant not the coincidental by-product of policy in one area on another, but rather 'spillover in its classical policy sense of increased regulation in a secondary area [being] functionally necessary to accomplish regulatory goals in a primary policy area' (Lange 1993: 27). The primary regulatory goals may, of course, include the achievement of a deregulated framework. In the present context this perspective would lead us to consider whether problems associated with completion of the internal market for freedom of movement of capital or services can be resolved without necessitating the invasion by EU institutions and EU law of the domain of social policy with regard to pensions. Put more directly, can a common market for cross-border investment and for pensions management be achieved without a corresponding intervention at EU level to recognise and to protect the interests of members of supplementary pension schemes. In short, will 'deregulation spur demands for reregulation' (Liebfried and Pierson 1992: 353).

The above analysis suggests that fitting developments on supplementary pension provision into any one analytical framework of social policy regulation can be problematic. The complicating factor is that the pensions problem, if such it may be called, potentially straddles the borderlines of three distinct freedoms, viz. freedom of capital movement, freedom to provide services and freedom of movement of persons. In other words, initiatives in this context may need to respond to and respect the capital market, product market and labour market dimensions of supplementary pensions. This multi-faceted character potentially creates a number of tensions in any attempt to assert an EU competence. These tensions in turn provide a clue as to why the prognosis for a successful outcome to CEC-driven intervention is so problematic.

---

[8] Coordination has three basic principles of operation: non-discrimination, aggregation of insurance/employment records, with consequentially either liability to pay benefit imposed solely upon the competent State or apportionment of entitlement ('proratization'), and exportability of benefit. See generally sources in fn. 1.

4. CONTEMPORARY DEVELOPMENTS

The multi-dimensional nature of the regulatory issues associated with pension provision not only renders the adoption of any one distinct analytical framework difficult but also presents more prosaic problems of categorization. These are amply illustrated at the institutional level within the CEC itself where there appears to be a lack of clarity as to where responsibility for handling pensions matters should lie. Two Directorates-General, V and XV, are directly and actively involved in developing separate initiatives to reduce obstacles to labour mobility arising out of supplementary pension provisions, whilst DG II has also sought more indirectly to influence development of CEC policy in this area. The potential for confusion that can spring from conflicting objectives and competing interests amongst these parties—sectional interests and ambitions are interwoven with jurisdictional issues here—is apparent enough and there is evidence that to some extent the Directorates operate oblivious to what each other is doing.

Notwithstanding this overlapping of conceptual themes and jurisdictional questions, it is convenient for both descriptive and analytical purposes to consider the various initiatives under the separate rubrics of (i) Financial Services and (ii) Labour Mobility.

4.1 Financial Services

Whereas responsibility for those aspects of pension provision concerned with the internal market for financial services clearly lies with DG XV, its initial forays into the area also encompassed an aspect of labour mobility closely linked to the concerns of multinational corporations, that of cross-border membership of pension schemes—i.e., the facility for a single firm to establish a pension scheme in one country for its employees in several countries. This first became apparent when the public phase of Commission involvement commenced with a speech in November 1989 by Sir Leon Brittan, then responsible for financial services in the Commission, proposing three objectives for pension funds, all within the broader context of completing the internal market for financial services. This initiative was developed further in a paper (Brittan (1990)) emphasizing the need for EU legislation to achieve the three objectives which are: first, to facilitate full freedom of cross-border membership of pension schemes within the EU and thus open up the possibility of pan-European funds; second, to counter restrictive national legislation on cross-border investment of pension funds; and third, to ensure full freedom to provide the service of managing pension funds. A working paper followed which was circulated to Member States in October 1990 (CEC 1990).

Consultation with Member States' experts soon revealed that the objective of freedom of cross-border membership would present formidable practical difficulties of implementation. Foremost amongst these were the fiscal implications: different tax treatment of contributions and benefits in the different Member States allied to a degree of mistrust both between Member States themselves[9] and by them of CEC motives—would its involvement in the direct tax treatment of pensions be the thin end of a very large wedge?—all combined to suggest that progress would prove at best slow, at worst unattainable.[10] The CEC was also sensitive to the likelihood that for any proposal on cross-border membership to be acceptable to sufficient Member States, some formal element of membership participation in pension scheme administration would be necessary. Although no longer anathema to the UK pensions industry (Pensions Law Review Committee 1993), and the British government has been moving towards accepting such participation, a CEC inspired initiative in this direction would have been unlikely as there could still be UK government hostility to a requirement being imposed from Brussels.[11] The decision was therefore taken to shelve that part of the proposal relating to cross-border membership of pension schemes. The problems relating to labour mobility posed by this decision are discussed further below but it is worth noting here that there may be another more profound obstacle to progress on this front. The CEC subsequently indicated that freedom to provide cross-border membership of pension schemes 'needs to be balanced . . . against the need to ensure that any future proposals do not call into question compulsory supplementary pension schemes operating on a pay-as-you-go basis fulfilling a "social solidarity" function' (CEC 1991*b*: 6). This is a tolerably accurate description of the French 'répartition' supplementary pension schemes. One inference to be drawn is that the French Government would be likely to have strongly opposed cross-border membership as it could potentially threaten the stability and financial viability of its own pension structure or, perhaps more pertinently, threaten to pre-empt any decision to reform that system.

The proposal for a Directive based on the other two freedoms that was eventually adopted by the Commission in October 1991 (the Pensions Directive) was concise—six brief articles—and viewed, certainly within DG XV, as representing no more than clarification of fundamental Treaty pro-

---

[9] Concern seems to centre both on administrative matters and on questions of enforcement and the opening up of possibilities for corporate tax avoidance.

[10] See generally the evidence of Dr U. Jurgens to the House of Lords Select Committee on the European Communities, 4th Report, Session 1992–93 (HL Paper 15) *Pension Funds*.

[11] But note proposals in the White Paper *Security, Equality, Choice: The Future for Pensions* (Cm. 2594) for pension scheme members to be given the right to nominate one third of scheme trustees. Although the UK Government has now to accepted (Pensions Act 1995, s. 16) the principle of a mandatory requirement for member trustees of pension schemes, albeit in a minority, it is by no means certain that it would accept the inclusion in an EU instrument of a provision laying down that principle as a prerequisite for cross-border membership.

visions.[12] The key provisions were contained in Article 3, which required the removal of any national barriers to a pension scheme in one Member State having its assets managed by any 'duly authorised' institution from another Member State,[13] and Article 4, which sought to replace any national restrictions on investment with general principles of 'prudent investment'. Thus Member States were to be required to establish general principles by which investment policy of a 'retirement institution' would have to comply with requirements of 'security, quality, liquidity and profitability of the institution's portfolio as a whole ' and also to diversify assets so as to avoid major accumulations of risk (CEC 1991*b*: article 4(1)(*a*) and (*b*)). Weight is lent to these unexceptionable, indeed innocuous, criteria by the explicit prohibition in Article 4(2) against Member States requiring institutions 'to invest in particular categories of assets or to localize their assets in a particular Member State'. As drafted this article did not appear, however, to prevent a Member State imposing a maximum limit on the amounts that might be invested, for instance, in equities. The imposition of a low maximum limit by a Member State could therefore have the effect of forcing retirement institutions to retain a high level of investment in government securities, an outcome that would run counter to the liberalizing intentions of the directive. The directive also contained a 'currency matching' provision (CEC 1991*b*: Article 4(3)), derived from the insurance directives, permitting Member States to require institutions to hold up to a given percentage of their assets in currencies matching their liabilities. It was this provision that was to prove a focal point for disagreement.

Any hopes that the dropping of the cross-border membership element of the package would lead to a rapid and straightforward passage through the legislative machinery were sadly misconceived. Despite continued negotiation under five Council presidencies agreement could not be reached, and on 16 June 1994 the Council decided to recommend that the CEC withdraw the draft directive. How is it that what was initially viewed as a largely unproblematic attempt to complete the internal market for financial services could fail so comprehensively to command support?

Tactical miscalculations in the drafting of the directive and a lack of familiarity with pensions investment issues amongst the representatives of some Member States[14] may both have played a part in the outcome, but

[12] See in particular Articles 52, 59 and 67 of the Treaty of Rome now reinforced by Article 73(b) inserted by the Treaty of European Union.

[13] Article 3(1) and (3). Duly authorised refers in relation to fund management to the holding of a 'passport' under one of Directives 92/96/EEC (The Third Life Assurance Directive), 89/646/EEC (Second Banking Directive) and 93/22/EEC (Investment Services Directive) and to custodianship under Directives 89/646/EEC and 93/22/EEC or as a depositary for Directive 85/611/EEC (UCITS Directive).

[14] The three Member States potentially most directly affected by the Directive, UK Netherlands and the Republic of Ireland together account for 83% of pension fund assets in the EU.

more fundamental stumbling blocks were to emerge during discussions in Council. Paramount among these difficulties were (i) the scope of the Pensions Directive, (ii) technical difficulties concerned with the supervision, and in particular freezing, by one Member State of assets held in another Member State, and (iii) the requirements for currency matching.[15]

As regards questions of material scope, it was intended that the directive should not extend to include 'statutory social security bodies'. The apparent simplicity of this point proved deceptive since in some Member States there are institutions which, although considered as part of the basic state social security scheme, replace for particular categories of worker, e.g., miners or professionals, the general state social security institution and operate on a basis which to some extent mirrors that of supplementary schemes. In addition certain Member States had raised the possibility of the replacement of their pay-as-you-go statutory scheme by a pre-funded arrangement.[16] The problem of definition was eventually resolved by adopting an approach which combined a non-exhaustive list of excluded institutions, as defined by each Member State, together with designated criteria in Article 2 by which such lists could be both monitored and kept up to date (CEC 1993*b*: Article 2 and annex).

The second source of difficulty stemmed from the principle of a 'single licence' for investment institutions. As applied to management of pension funds, this would involve a 'custodian' and an 'investment manager' being subject to the supervisory régime of the home state, whereas the custodianship and investment of the assets would have to be in accordance with the

---

[15] A fourth issue which caused some disagreement concerned a derogation from restrictions on self-investment by small self administered schemes (SSASs) (see paras 58 and 66 of the House of Lords Select Committee 4th Report *Pension Funds* (1992–93, HL Paper 15) and the Dutch equivalent. SSASs and the Dutch arrangements are established for up to 12 employees who are at the same time share holders and managers of the company, but not other employees, and permit a higher level of self-investment as a form of venture capital, with the members agreeing to the self-investment while consciously recognising the risk of so doing. The UK and Netherlands maintained that absence of a derogation could put small companies out of business; other states opposed any derogation on the ground that a derogation could put at risk the pensions of members, including those who were not share holders or directors.

[16] A particular problem concerned the status of the statutory Dutch pre-funded public service pension scheme the Algemeen Burgerlijke Pensioenfonds (ABP) which operated the largest pension fund in the EU. The Netherlands Government wished to achieve its exclusion from the scope of the Directive because of its budget guarantee, but also because, as the ABP was due to be entirely privatised within 5 years, the Dutch Government did not want to have its hands tied in negotiation. By claiming that as a statutory scheme it was outside the scope of the Directive, the Dutch were potentially setting a precedent for other states to exclude their statutory public sector schemes, e.g., the UK funded local government superannuation schemes. Other States were unhappy at the prospect of freedom of fund management and investment not applying to the largest pension fund in Europe. The problem was circumvented on the basis that the Directive would not become operative until after the Dutch privatisation problem had been resolved. The ECJ has subsequently confirmed (Case C-7/93 *Bestuur van de ABP* v. *Beune* 28 September 1994) that for the purposes of Article 119 the ABP is a supplementary, not a state social security, pension scheme.

laws on financial services of the host state. The technical problem related to questions of supervision and control. In the event of doubts about the solvency or bona fides of a custodian or investment manager, could assets outside the home state be adequately protected by the home supervisor? Could, for instance, assets in the host state be frozen by the home state supervisor, or indeed vice versa? The very existence of the 'problem' springs in part from the lack of harmonization of regulatory systems in Member States, some exercising very close supervisory control through a single agency, others, the UK being the prime example, relying on a flexible interplay of professional standards and law with no one regulator having overall responsibility. Moreover, it should occasion no surprise that during 1992 the Maxwell affair lent added emphasis to consideration of this issue in the Council and by the European Parliament. In the event, although the basis for a compromise solution did appear to exist,[17] the issue remained unresolved because of a more intractable supervisory problem, that of currency matching.

Seemingly in pursuit of the objective that adequate assets should always be available to meet fund liabilities, the directive contained a currency matching requirement. Indeed Article 4(3) incorporated two standards for currency matching: Member States could require pension funds to hold up to 80% of their assets in matching currencies in the case of 'fixed liability' schemes, whereas a lower margin of 60% was stipulated for schemes which did not have a fixed liability, such as 'defined contribution' schemes and 'defined benefit' schemes where entitlement was dependent on final salary. The origin of the 80% figure appears to lie in an analogy drawn with the insurance directives which permit only a 20% non-matching investment (Directive 92/96/EEC: annex 1), whereas the 60% figure was thought by the CEC broadly to reflect the effective maximum external investment practices in the defined benefit schemes common in UK, Netherlands, and Republic of Ireland.[18]

The CEC came subsequently to accept that this formulation for a currency matching régime was misconceived for two principal reasons. First, the insurance-based analogy did not provide a wholly convincing basis for the 80% figure.[19] In contrast with the liabilities of insurance companies, those of pension funds tend to be both more long-term and single currency

[17] The Commission proposed that a request to freeze assets should be made to the regulator in the state where the assets were located who would investigate and 'freeze' where there was an unreasonable refusal by the pension fund itself to provide information or to take the action requested by the regulator. A residual problem for the UK was that no such 'equivalent regulator' existed but see now Pensions Act 1995, ss. 13 and 14.

[18] According to the EFRP, in 1992, for instance, the average figure for non currency-matching investments held by UK private pension funds was 24.55%.

[19] It is understood that the 80% figure was itself only adopted as a compromise solution under the insurance directives.

based. The fact that a proportion of the liabilities of insurance companies can by contrast be short-term and can arise in several currencies, provides insurers with greater flexibility in meeting an 80% currency matching requirement. A numerically equal requirement would in practice therefore be more restrictive of investment freedom for pension funds, which led them to claim that they could be placed at a competitive disadvantage vis-à-vis insurance companies, although some Member States apparently remained unpersuaded of the need for separate standards for insurance and for pensions.[20] The second weakness in the original formulation of the directive was the prescription of the two percentages (80% and 60%) which were to be applicable to the different forms of pension liability. By the time of the Belgian presidency of the Council in 1993, Member States and the CEC had become convinced that this arrangement would be too complicated to apply, most conspicuously to hybrid schemes.[21] The obvious solution was to opt for a common figure, as the preferred UK solution of simply relying on a general standard of prudence rather than any specific currency matching formula received inadequate support.[22] On this point it proved impossible during some eighteen months of negotiation to obtain a satisfactory level of agreement.[23] Attempts to achieve a compromise of 70% proved unacceptable, being too lax for some and negating the point of principle for those who wanted the removal of any currency matching requirement. Following further unsuccessful attempts at compromise under the Belgian and Greek Presidencies, in December 1993 and March 1994 respectively, the Commission, decided to withdraw the proposal.

The question remains: how could a proposal so fail to command support when it was supposedly merely clarifying fundamental Treaty principles and was ostensibly supported by all Member States, by ECOSOC, by the European Parliament and by the pensions industry?

Several factors contributed to this outcome. One such factor was an incident with no immediate or direct connection to the different interests and perspectives of the Member States. To the extent that either the approach of the CEC or elements of the Directive itself came to be seen as associated

[20] In certain Member States, insurance undertakings and pension funds are currently subject to identical investment requirements and a single regulatory and supervisory regime. An uncoupling of the two by reason of different EU obligations would have created implementation difficulties, as well as internal objections by insurance undertakings of unfair competition.

[21] As the name implies, a hybrid scheme contains elements of both defined benefit and defined contribution schemes.

[22] With masterly understatement a Department of Social Security (DSS) consultation paper noted that 'support for the UK position is limited (DSS Information Paper on the Draft Pension Funds Directive, August 1992, para. 8.2). In sporting parlance it was UK, Netherlands, and Republic of Ireland v. The Rest.

[23] Although negotiations may have been conducted 'in the shadow of' QMV, the Commission would have been reluctant to support an outcome dependant on Member States with relatively small pension fund sectors (a majority) outvoting those Member States with correspondingly large pension fund sectors.

with a UK model of pension management and investment practices, which could after all lay convincing claim to be a well tried and tested system, the Maxwell affair cast a cloud over the proceedings. At the very least, the depletion of the pension funds of the various companies controlled by the late Robert Maxwell raised doubts about whether an appropriate regulatory balance had been struck in the UK, in particular whether an approach to investment regulation which placed reliance on a somewhat nebulous notion of prudence provided adequate safeguards. Indeed, the Maxwell factor contributed significantly to the decision to delete the innovative Article 3(2). This provision, which would have allowed the pension funds of multinational groups to consolidate their management, was anathema to all Member States post-Maxwell—the sole point of unanimity on the draft directive. Many of the amendments to the directive proposed by the European Parliament at First Reading, and rejected by the Commission, were also Maxwell-inspired.[24] However, it is improbable in the extreme that Member States or the pensions industry would have allowed this one example of malpractice to dictate an outcome contrary to their broader interests. Therefore, tempting though it may be to attribute responsibility for the failure to adopt the directive to the Maxwell affair, the complete answer must be sought elsewhere.

Here a distinction must be drawn between the contemporary circumstances that triggered the final decision to recommend the withdrawal of the directive, traceable in part to the procedural consequences of the Treaty of European Union, and the more fundamental concerns within some Member States about the medium to long-term consequences of adopting the directive. As regards the former, with effect from 1 January 1994 the European Parliament has been able to invoke the co-decision procedure under Article 189b in respect of measures already in the legislative pipeline. One of the four selected by the Parliament out of the array of 40–50 available measures was the draft Pensions Directive. It is conceivable, given its strongly expressed objections to the Parliament's original amendments, that the CEC would not wish the directive to become embroiled in the new extensive co-decision procedure with the enhanced powers it bestows upon the Parliament. However, this essentially procedural explanation still begs the key question as to why Member States could not reach agreement on issues such as currency matching. The possibility cannot be ruled out that seemingly arcane debates about 'percentages' and some other technical points act as a screen for more profound objections. Consider, for instance, the

---

[24] The Commission view as expressed by Sir Leon Brittan was that most of the proposed amendments, including those concerning investment in depressed areas of the EU, eastern Europe and the Third World and one proposing 50% membership participation in scheme administration, were outside the scope of the Directive and therefore unacceptable; see European Parliament Debates No. 3-424/24, 16 November 1992 and generally Zavvos (1994).

implications of the proposition that the Member State with a financial services sector arguably most equipped to benefit from any liberalization of regulatory régimes for the provision of pension management services would be the UK, with its large fund management companies and well-established system of fund management (see House of Lords 1992–93: para. 16). At present the market for such services in the EU is limited but could expand significantly if, in response to the demographic and cost considerations mentioned earlier in this chapter, an increase in funded supplementary schemes were to occur.

Such an outcome would be a source of concern amongst some Member States if it were to lead to UK managed investment being disproportionately concentrated in the large and highly-developed Northern European, particularly UK, primary and secondary capital markets. This possibility has far-reaching implications for those Member States seeking to strengthen savings and investment in their domestic economies and to develop their local financial markets goals which would be endangered by any substantial expatriation of domestic 'pension saving' to financially stronger markets (CEC 1994). Moreover and more fundamentally, this outcome could have detrimental consequences for the cost of capital in some Member States, and thereby exacerbate the difficulties in achieving the timetable for economic convergence and monetary union. The economic validity of these propositions is immaterial for the purposes of this chapter. What is evident is that there exists a latent conflict of interest between those Member States that favour full freedom of capital movement and those that do not *yet* do so. Thus, at one level requirements for currency matching of assets to liabilities could be argued as being concerned with safeguarding a scheme's assets in the interests of members. At another level those same requirements can be interpreted as being designed covertly to protect national markets in securities. The self-interest of a Member State can therefore provide a plausible though not openly advocated reason for seeking to defeat or defer the Pensions Directive. From this standpoint it would be wholly rational for any Member State not wishing to incur the odium of opposing a measure which, it will be recalled, purports merely to be clarification of fundamental Treaty principles, to support a position that renders the measure unacceptable to other Member States and to the CEC.

The probability that Member States will find it necessary to expand their reliance on non-state supplementary schemes provides a further clue to possible underlying hostility to the directive. Aside from the financial services and capital market implications, some Member States may be concerned that the directive could, in effect if not in intent, pre-empt decisions yet to be taken at national level about the direction of any change. To bowdlerise a rather tired footballing cliche: 'the Pensions Directive is an instrument five years ahead of its time'.

4.2 Freedom of movement

The side-stepping of the problems associated with full cross-border membership of pension schemes did not mean a complete abdication of CEC interest in pensions matters relating to labour mobility and to the concerns of migrant workers and employers. Indeed DGs V and XV both sought independently to develop initiatives in this area. However, although these initiatives almost inevitably entailed overlapping policy implications—both having to contend with the fiscal autonomy of Member States—, a relevant distinction is that whereas the DG V initiatives addressed the wider problems of the acquisition, preservation, and transferability of pension rights in general, the DG XV initiative was restricted to a narrower range of issues affecting only seconded workers.

Somewhat confusingly to the onlooker, even if not to all CEC officials, while DG XV was consulting with representatives of Member States on the proposals in its discussion paper on, inter alia, cross border membership, DG V was simultaneously preparing its own contribution to the debate about freedom of movement and the role of supplementary pension schemes. In its 1989 Social Action Programme (CEC 1989) the CEC drew attention to the lack of Community provisions protecting migrant workers against the loss of supplementary (i.e., non-State) social security rights. Having picked up the baton, the CEC, in the shape of DG V, published in July 1991 a Communication to the Council of Ministers 'to stimulate a Community-wide debate' (CEC 1991a). The CEC probably wisely had opted to proceed along a gradualist path, recognising that the practical problems, both fiscal and technical,[25] required close examination if any substantive progress was to be made.[26] Moreover the CEC recognised that the seemingly obvious route of extending the application of the coordinating Regulation (1408/71/EEC) to cover, not solely statutory social security schemes, but also supplementary schemes, in their application to migrant workers, would be untenable, not least because of the differences in the funding arrangements of supplementary schemes in the various Member States.[27] The system of 'aggregation and apportionment' under 1408/71 could apply to state social security schemes, all of which operate on a pay-as-you-go basis. The almost universal consensus of Member State

[25] The CEC pointed in particular to the difficulties associated with Member States' different requirements with regard to vesting periods, calculation of transfer values and protection of 'dormant' or 'deferred' rights: SEC (91) 1332, para. 3.2.6.

[26] In keeping with developing a function as an 'observatory' and central repository of knowledge, the CEC appointed a Committee of Experts to monitor developments at national level and to assess the actual or potential impact of Community measures that may affect supplementary pension schemes (see CEC 1994).

[27] The Commission's views were influenced by the consensus that emerged from a conference of pensions specialists at Bremen in early 1990 as to the impracticability of attempting to pursue a coordination strategy akin to that under Regulations 1408/71 and 574/72; see Schmahl (1991)

governments, employers and pensions administrators is that such a system would be unworkable in a funded non-state pensions context.

The perception by the CEC of the limited possibilities of progress appeared to be vindicated by events in the latter part of 1992, under the UK presidency. The UK sought to persuade the Council of Ministers to agree to a draft resolution—a non-binding instrument, albeit one requiring unanimity—requesting Member States to implement or promote measures which would 'recognise that each member should be able to move to a job in another Member State without having to fear any undue loss of rights to future supplementary retirement benefits'. As formulated, the draft resolution would have covered the status of all migrant workers, but here again progress proved difficult to achieve. The resolution itself was less stringent than the CEC and some Member States would have liked. It was recognized that French pay-as-you-go schemes would find it impossible for financing reasons to comply with a requirement to make transfer payments for former members to funded schemes in other Member States, and that any such commitment would be opposed by France. The resolution therefore provided alternative methods of safeguarding members' acquired rights, firstly by preservation and partial revaluation and secondly by transferability.

One particularly intractable problem, which led to the specific inclusion of the reference to *acquired* rights, and one which highlights the profound difficulty in achieving even limited coordination, concerns variations in vesting rights in different Member States. In contrast to most other Member States, where pension rights vest after one or two years' service, non-state pension rights in Germany, for instance, do not vest until age 35 and a minimum of 10 years pensionable service. It would scarcely have been feasible for German employers to allow migrant workers, but not German workers changing employment within Germany, to acquire and have preserved pension rights after one or two years' service. But to grant full rights to all workers would both run contrary to the perception held by German employers of supplementary pensions as a reward for long-service and, more importantly in a state where the vast majority of pension schemes are non-contributory, add substantially to the labour costs of German employers. Even with watered-down proposals[28] limiting the rights to preservation and transfer of acquired rights, unanimity could not be not achieved and the draft resolution was therefore not adopted.[29]

[28] Certain Member States were unwilling to agree to watered down proposals on the ground that these would work to the detriment of their own nationals many of whom were migrant workers who would hope to benefit on retirement and return to their home state from the proposals in the resolution.

[29] In June 1995 DGV issued a proposal for a draft directive to safeguard 'supplementary pension rights acquired by workers in one Member State when changing employment to another Member State'. Agreement on the proposal, which requires unanimity, has not been obtained and the matter was referred back to a working group in February 1996.

Before assessing the role that the CEC attempted to fulfil in this area, brief mention must be made of yet a further initiative undertaken by DG XV. The shelving of the plan to include cross-border membership of supplementary schemes within the scope of the Pensions Directive does not mean that the whole of that aspect of the enterprise was abandoned by DG XV. Contemporaneously with the UK initiative at the Council of Ministers, DG XV published, in September 1992, a Working Paper on cross-border membership of supplementary pension schemes, but with a yet narrower focus on migrant workers (CEC 1992*b*). The Working Paper concentrated solely on the pension position of migrant workers who move across national frontiers while still remaining with the same employer or group of employers, and who wish to remain in the pension scheme of their home country employer. The intention was that the fiscal treatment of both the employee and employer contributions to the scheme should be the same as they would receive were they to be made to an approved arrangement in the host state. The change of emphasis to concentrate only on posted workers does not remove the technical difficulties that have beset all the initiatives, but it did reduce the size of the practical problem, if only because the numbers of workers involved are relatively small. The hope, if not expectation, was that the smaller scale of the problem would encourage a pragmatic response from Member States. Thus, in the style of a tentative suitor, the Working Paper invited a positive response to a distinctly minimalist approach, based on a combination of the principles of coordination and mutual recognition, albeit limited, of fiscal treatment. A process of consultation about the proposal was initiated in 1993, but it still remains at an exploratory and information-gathering stage.

4.3 Pensions and the CEC: strategies undermined or mission impossible?

It is evident from the above account that the immediate *direct* impact of the various EU initiatives on pensions policy and practice in Member States has been limited in the extreme. From one perspective any other outcome would have been surprising. After all, under Article 51 unanimity is required for any specific EU measure on social security, aimed at facilitating freedom of movement of persons. Moreover, this legal prerequisite simply reflects a political principle giving pre-eminence to national sovereignty, an approach unequivocally acknowledged in the area of social protection generally in the 1992 Recommendation: 'because of the diversity of the schemes and their roots in national culture, it is for Member States to determine how their social protection schemes should be framed and the arrangements for financing and organizing them' (CEC 1992*a*).

On the other hand, it might equally be claimed that the various initiatives of the CEC deserve to be judged in terms of their indirect impact. Thus, apart from the obvious motive of encouraging Member States to coordinate their fiscal approaches in this area, the Communication, and indeed the continuing activities of DGs V and XV, may stimulate some Member States to incorporate broadly comparable proposals, for example, on vesting and transferability, when seeking to expand supplementary pension provision. The consequence would be to render future coordination more feasible. This depends on an expansion occurring in supplementary pension provision, and here even the now withdrawn Pensions Directive may at a general level have had a catalytic effect.[30] A CEC formal view has certainly been that one purpose of the Directive would have been to establish a framework of rules for those Member States wishing to encourage a growth of funded supplementary pension schemes.[31] How far this almost facilitative role tips over into agenda-setting and then ultimately to an expansion of policy competence for the CEC remains an open question in the pensions context. For the moment, however, the locus of debate about the future direction of pensions policy has shifted back to Member State level, a point we return to in the Conclusion to this chapter.

The emphasis on the persuasive and informational dimensions of the various initiatives leaves us with a legal conundrum, at least as far as the original rationale for the Directive is concerned. The CEC has a legal role as guardian of the Treaties, and the Pensions Directive was claimed to be merely clarificatory of the way in which the Treaty provisions relating to free movement of persons, services and capital apply to institutions for retirement provision. Could not the CEC therefore initiate infringement proceedings under Article 169 if it considers a Member State is imposing, for instance, national restrictions on fund management or 'excessive' currency matching requirements?[32] This is certainly possible, but such an action would face considerable difficulties. The decision of the ECJ in *Keck & Mithouard* (C-267 and 268/91, 24 November 1993) significantly nuancing the earlier judgment in *Dassonville* [1974] ECR 837, reinforced the air of uncertainty post-*Bachman*[33] about the fate of infringement proceedings against rules purportedly regulating national socio-economic conditions (Gormley 1994). There is also uncertainty as to whether or not the activi-

---

[30] One representative of a prominent pensions industry organisation suggested to the writer that the Directive 'has concentrated minds' and stimulated some liberalization of the rules within Member States.

[31] See evidence of Dr U. Jurgens to the House of Lords Select Committee on the European Communities, 4th Report Session 1992–93 (HL Paper 15) *Pension Funds* para. 175.

[32] 'Excessive' in the sense of not being objectively necessary for the 'prudential supervision of financial institutions' (Capital Movements Directive 88/361/EEC article 4).

[33] *Bachman* v. *Belgium* (Case C-204/90) and *EC Commission* v. *Belgium* (Case C-300/90) [1993] 1 CMLR 785 where the ECJ held that certain restrictions on tax deductibility which in practice constituted a restriction on the freedom to provide services could nevertheless be justified 'if necessary in order to ensure the cohesion of the relevant fiscal system'.

ties of institutions for retirement provision, most of which it must be emphasized are non-profit bodies, would escape jurisdiction by virtue of Article 58.[34] Lastly, one consequence of a strategy of litigation would be to allow the ECJ in effect to determine what constitutes e.g., 'prudence' and 'proportionality' in a pensions context. For this very reason alone there may be a pragmatic reluctance to initiate proceedings potentially involving highly technical questions on pensions issues about which the ECJ may not be fully conversant and without the benefit of any clarificatory measure being in place.[35] It is in this context that the decision by DG XV on 17 December 1994 to publish a Communication (94/C 360/08) to replace the withdrawn Pensions Directive is best viewed. As well as constituting the CEC's interpretation of the applicability of the relevant EU Treaty rules, the Communication has the attractive attribute for the CEC of providing a framework within which future litigation can take place (see generally Louis 1990).[36]

5. FORMULAE FOR FAILURE

The failure to make significant progress on the pensions front at EU level can be interpreted as just one minor setback on the road to a fully-integrated single market. Moreover, technical arguments can certainly be adduced to explain the lack of progress. But there is also evidence to support a conclusion that the liberalizing measures have fallen victim to 'vested interests' determined to prevent or at least delay progress. McGee and Weatherill, in their study of the range of responses that can be deployed by various social actors to achieve that type of outcome, conclude that 'not surprisingly, national governments appear to be the most effective at controlling developments' (1990: 595).[37] Doubtless, an element of naked national self-interest was present in the responses of Member States to the pensions agenda. Plainly a Member State could perceive its national economic interest to lie in impeding the adoption of a regulatory framework incorporating the principle of mutual recognition, if to do otherwise would facilitate the domination of an embryonic pan-European pensions industry by those Member States with established management and investment

[34] Under Article 58 non-profit making 'companies or firms' are excluded from the requirements concerning right of establishment and freedom to provide services.

[35] There is a hint of this in CEC evidence to the House of Lords Select Committee, *op cit.* fn. 31, para. 166.

[36] 'France and Spain have initiated proceedings before the European Court of Justice seeking annulment of the Communication (Case C-57/95).

[37] In the immediate context, the otherwise highly effective lobbying by the EFRP in helping to inform and to influence opinion on the Pensions Directive, could not prevail against the interests of those Member States hostile to the proposal.

expertise. But it would be misleading to attribute the apparent stalemate in policy initiatives at EU level solely to such fine calculations. The outcome also seems to reflect a determination on the part of some Member States to defer the adoption of a pan-European regulatory framework until they have decided domestically how to allow supplementary pension provision to develop. A complementary interpretation therefore is that the national 'vested interest' here revolves around questions of sovereignty and determination of policy at a Member State level.

These considerations bring us closer to the heart of the problems of analysis and policy prescription presented by the pensions issues discussed in this chapter. We have seen (i) that the CEC and Member States alike are becoming increasingly familiar with the potential costs of maintaining adequate financial provision for the elderly, and (ii) that first and second tier pension provision is commonly closely linked to both the fiscal and welfare systems of Member States. Yet it is these two domains which now constitute the principal repositories of ever-diminishing national sovereignty. National governments are therefore understandably reluctant to accept a further diminution of their sovereignty by ceding any major transfer of social policy authority to the EU (see Leibfried and Pierson 1992). One hypothesis that flows from these observations is that a strategic objective of the CEC—to influence Member States to reduce reliance on first tier state pension provision—may paradoxically be attainable only at the cost of sacrificing, at least for an interim period, the ambition to attain full freedom to provide services and freedom of movement for capital and labour. Secondly, in terms of the analytical frameworks outlined earlier in the paper, the reasons for the failure of the various pensions initiatives lends support to the proposition that harmonization and mutual recognition should be understood as complementary rather than alternative approaches (see e.g., Majone 1991). Thus, it was an inadequate degree of approximation between supervisory régimes and an absence of trust between regulatory and fiscal authorities that posed important obstacles to adoption of a mutual recognition approach. However, it is also the case that these considerations conveniently coincided with national competitive self-interest. Consequently one cannot categorically say that a mutual recognition approach will not be adopted nor that such an approach would not lead to competition between regulatory systems. What the evidence from this study does suggest is that, in some contexts, a degree of formal convergence—e.g., in fiscal and regulatory systems—must precede mutual recognition and its companion, competition through rules, if the latter methods are to be adopted as routes to substantive convergence.

These propositions point towards a set of still more fundamental questions to be addressed, primarily at Member State level. It is here that the potentially conflicting policy agendas surrounding labour market and welfare state dimensions of pensions policy become more overt.[38] It is also here that prediction and prescription become uncomfortably entangled, in part because debates in some Member States are still very much at an embryonic stage. Nevertheless three particular focal points of debate can briefly be identified here, all of which have implications for the nature of any EU regulatory role that might eventually emerge.

The first and most fundamental point concerns the balance between state and private provision. Decisions about changing the public/private mix have implications broader than simply reducing the financial cost of state involvement in pension provision. State pension provision, particularly of the first tier variety, has historically incorporated an element of income redistribution between rich and poor and also has tended to be associated with a philosophy emphasizing social solidarity, both inter-generational and between cohorts of the same generation. These dimensions are commonly and not surprisingly absent from private pensions which, as Aaron has emphasized, are 'an instrument of market capitalism' (1992: 136). A reflection of these contrasting perceptions can be discerned within the CEC: on the one hand DG XV seems concerned to create a climate whereby Member States will look to rely increasingly on private provision, while on the other hand DG V has continued to emphasize the importance of social cohesion.[39] Although these objectives are not wholly incompatible, finessing their attainment will require that the policy implications be addressed.

A second and associated point concerns the relationship between supplementary pensions and labour markets, with particular reference to questions of coverage and adequacy of replacement income in retirement. Coverage of supplementary pension schemes has rarely exceeded 50% of the active labour force (apart from in France where membership is compulsory for everyone subject to the state social security régime), partly because such schemes have commonly excluded many part-time, temporary, and low-paid workers—exclusions which have affected women more than men. The resulting structure of entitlement seems likely to be accentuated by contemporary changes in work patterns with the emphasis on numerical flexibility (see Atkinson 1986 but cf., Pollert 1991; Department of Employment 1994). It seems probable that for increasing numbers of workers, periods in work will be interspersed with regular spells of inactivity in the labour market. Patently these trends could ultimately have a significant constraining effect on the acquisition and value of supplementary pension entitlement.

---

[38] The academic literature is rapidly expanding. Excellent introductions to the issues are OECD (1988a), (1988b), (1992) and Mortensen (1992). See also Falkingham and Johnson (1992) and Dilnot *et al.* (1994) for a more specific UK focus.

[39] See e.g., Council recommendation on the convergence of social protection objectives and policies (92/442/EEC): 'whereas social protection is an essential instrument of solidarity . . .'

The third focal point for debate returns us to a bone of contention—membership participation in scheme management—between the European parliament and the CEC during the ill-fated attempt to have the Pensions Directive adopted. The price of progress, were any attempt made to resurrect the initiative, would probably be an element of membership participation. In other words, it may prove difficult to disentangle the financial services dimension from an employment agenda in which notions of 'social partnership' or, more fundamentally, 'members' property rights' potentially clash with a competing philosophy which perceives supplementary pensions in terms of employer autonomy or prerogative. In a sense this employment agenda is implicit in the view expressed by the CEC in its Communication on Supplementary Social Security Schemes to the effect that (1991*a*: para. 2.5.5):

[w]hat seems to be important for the development of voluntary occupation schemes is the quality and stability of [the] legal framework which directly affects the cost of running a benefit programme. . . . Legislation, while improving the social protection of workers, can also provide guidance for employers who want to set up occupational pension schemes and who have a large choice of possible pension scheme designs.

It is considerations of cost and autonomy of employer decision-making which raise questions about the scope for a regulatory framework incorporating any significant role for employee participation. Employers are unlikely *voluntarily* to provide or contribute to supplementary pension provision unless it remains in their interests to do so.[40] Here the Spanish and UK experience is instructive, since under neither system are employers under any legal obligation to make supplementary pension schemes available to their workers. According to some sources the response from employers in Spain to the qualified plan status offered under the terms of Law 8/87 governing Pension Plans and Pension Funds (Ellis 1989; Noble Lowndes 1995), has been lukewarm, partly because of the requirement for employee representation in scheme management. In the UK also, concern has been expressed by employers about any increase in regulatory burdens arising from the fall-out from the Maxwell affair.[41]

---

[40] See DSS (1993*b*) for the result of a small-scale survey of employers' reasons for voluntarily establishing and maintaining supplementary pension provision.

[41] Note in this context the approach of the Pension Law Review Committee (*Pension Law Reform* (CM 2342-1, 1993) para. 1.1.16): 'we have had regard both to the level of concern expressed about the security of pension funds, the rights and interests of members in those funds, and *to the need to avoid measures which will discourage employers from continuing to provide good pension schemes*' (emphasis added).

6. CONCLUSION

One premise of this chapter is that EU initiatives in the area of pensions policy are underpinned by a particular strategy or, if not a strategy, at least by a tacit acceptance of a conventional wisdom. This sees an extension of supplementary pension provision as a necessary feature of any resolution of a perceived crisis in the public financing of an ageing population. But remedies for complicated problems are rarely simple, and another premise of this chapter is that pensions provision constitutes a complicated problem in part because it can present a variety of features—the chameleon. On the one hand, from the financial market perspective of one influential economist 'an optimal system [of pension provision] would probably include only a minimal pay-as-you-go sector catering for basic needs and for alleviation of poverty, with the bulk of earnings replacement being provided by private externally-funded plans' (Davis 1994: 27). On the other hand, the solution of placing reliance in voluntary private provision within a liberalized financial services regulatory framework will not necessarily result in labour market and social protection issues—e.g., questions of coverage, portability, security of entitlement, and social cohesion—being adequately addressed. Not all of these difficulties are insurmountable. To some extent gaps in coverage and security can be minimized respectively by requiring employers to offer and pay for pensions and by the state acting as ultimate guarantor.[41] Yet this would serve only to reintroduce the basic financing problems in another guise. There remain intractable tensions between the application of economic orthodoxy to the investment process, and the claims of solidarity and social cohesion. For those Member States faced for the first time with the need to develop a national pensions strategy covering all tiers of pension provision, a fundamental challenge will be to accommodate the tensions. One trite prescriptive conclusion of this chapter, therefore, is that a series of policy choices about supplementary pension provision need to be resolved at Member State level before any substantial progress at EU level, be it via mutual recognition or otherwise, can be anticipated.

A conclusion that ascribes a formulative pre-eminence to Member State as against EU regulatory competence adds one final dimension to the analysis. This bears upon the characteristics of integration within the Single Market. Without stretching the analogy unduly, analysis of the extent and nature of EU competence in the realm of pensions policy has echoes of broader debates about the scope for creating a social dimension in the Single European Market (SEM). It is a commonplace that in completing the SEM project, emphasis

---

[42] But as Duskin (1992: 20) has pointed out 'If, by this means, the flaws inherent in private systems are resolved . . . a public system will have been re-created off-budget, but perhaps at an increased cost'.

has been placed upon 'negative integration', in the sense of removal of barriers to a free market. On this view harmonization of the product markets for goods and services is driven by a deregulatory dynamic, an ethos evident enough in the Pensions Directive. It can be argued, by way of contrast, that any process of labour market integration which seeks to incorporate elements of social protection requires a positive programme of regulation.[43] Liebfried and Pierson (1992) take this analysis a stage further by invoking the concept of 'positive integration'. This is interpreted as synthesizing concepts of social justice and welfare with a process of negative integration so as to create an appropriate social dimension.[44] Both the analysis and the prescription seem as apposite to the development of an EU competence over pensions policy as they do to any element of the social dimension more narrowly defined. Indeed, the very failure to develop a pensions strategy based on positive integration, allied to the behaviour of the CEC as a 'facilitator' of economic orthodoxy (Kleinman and Piachaud 1993: 14), in part explains the policy outcomes described in this chapter. However, the fact that the role of positive integration has been at best a marginal influence in shaping EU regulation is not necessarily an augury for the shape of future pensions policy. That shape will be predominantly determined by the outcome of national policy debates, and it is significant that these debates have to some extent been initiated and shaped by the negotiations, analysed here, within the European institutions.

POSTSCRIPT

Recent activities at EU level indicate that the CEC is developing a twofold response to the set-backs administered to the several liberalization proposals discussed in this chapter. One response seeks to find a way forward through a process of dialogue between the CEC and Member States. A Communication from the CEC (*The Future of Social Protection* [COM(95) 466]) proposes that 'a process of common reflection', to be initiated and orientated by DG V, should take place between Member States and EU institutions within a framework which emphasizes the need to make social protection systems more employment-friendly and efficient. The future of supplementary pensions is one issue on that agenda.

The second response at EU level is a CEC internal initiative. An inter-directorate working group, consisting of representatives from DGs V, XV, II, IV and XXI, has been established to work towards a common strategy on supplementary pensions encompassing all the issues of social responsibility, financial security, capital freedom, competition, and taxation. A report from the group is expected in February 1997. If a common strategy is realisable, its principal initial aim is likely to be to influence debates within Member States and between those states and EU institutions, rather than to develop a fresh round of regulatory proposals.

---

[43] See e.g., Doogan (1992) Rhodes (1991) on the tensions created for social policy formation by the fact that the integration process is moving in opposite directions in different markets.

[44] Liebfried and Pierson follow Pinder (1968) and Tinbergen (1954) in interpreting positive integration in terms of developing the capacity to modify market distribution of life chances.

APPENDIX A

Table 1. *Fertility rates.*[1]

Country	1950	1960	1965	1970	1980	1985	1990
Belgium	2.3	2.6	2.6	2.2	1.7	1.5	1.6
Denmark	2.6	2.5	2.6	2.0	1.6	1.5	1.7
France	2.9	2.7	2.8	2.5	2.0	1.8	1.8
Germany	2.1	2.4	2.5	2.0	1.5	1.3	1.5
Greece	—	2.3	2.3	2.3	2.2	1.7	1.5
Ireland	—	3.8	4.0	3.9	3.2	2.5	2.2
Italy	2.5	2.4	2.7	2.4	1.7	1.4	1.3
Luxembourg	—	2.3	2.4	2.0	1.5	1.4	1.6
Netherlands	3.1	3.1	3.0	2.6	1.6	1.5	1.6
Portugal	3.2	3.0	3.1	2.8	2.2	1.7	1.4
Spain	2.5	2.9	2.9	2.8	2.2	1.6	1.4
United Kingdom	2.2	2.7	2.9	2.4	1.9	1.8	1.8
EEC average	2.6	2.7	2.8	2.5	1.9	1.6	1.6

[1] Average number of live children born to each female during her lifetime.
Source: OECD/SME health expenditure data base.

Table 2. *Projected old-age dependency ratios.*[1]

	(Per cent)								Per cent change	
	1980	1990	2000	2010	2020	2030	2040	2050	1980–2040	2010–2040
Belgium	21.9	21.1	22.0	23.5	26.9	33.3	36.0	34.0	64	53
Denmark	22.3	22.6	21.5	24.3	30.5	36.4	42.1	39.1	89	73
France	21.9	20.9	23.3	24.5	30.6	35.8	38.2	37.6	74	56
Germany	23.4	22.3	25.4	30.6	33.5	43.6	48.2	41.6	106	58
Greece	20.5	18.2	22.6	25.7	27.4	30.8	34.0	34.2	66	32
Ireland	18.2	18.5	16.9	16.3	18.7	22.7	27.1	30.8	49	66
Italy	20.8	20.1	22.6	25.7	29.3	35.3	41.0	37.9	97	60
Luxembourg	20.0	21.6	25.5	27.5	31.9	37.1	36.4	32.2	82	32
Netherlands	17.4	18.4	19.7	22.1	28.9	37.8	42.0	37.6	141	90
Portugal	16.1	17.9	20.8	21.4	23.7	28.7	33.1	33.4	106	55
Spain	17.2	19.4	21.8	23.0	25.3	31.1	38.2	38.6	122	66
United Kingdom	23.2	23.0	22.3	22.3	25.5	31.1	33.1	30.0	43	48
EEC average	20.2	20.3	22.0	23.9	27.7	33.6	37.5	35.7		

[1] (Population 65 ÷ population 15–64) × 100: 1980 actual ratios: 1990 to 2050 projected ratios.
Source: OECD (1988b), p. 32.

Table 3. *Projections of public pension expenditure*[1]

| | (Per cent of national income) | | | | | | |
	1984	2000	2010	2020	2030	2040	2050
Belgium	14.2[2]	13.8	14.8	17.0	21.0	22.7	21.5
Denmark	10.1	9.5	10.8	13.5	16.2	18.7	17.4
France	14.3	16.5	17.3	21.6	25.3	27.0	26.6
Germany	13.7	16.4	19.7	21.6	28.1	31.1	26.8
Greece	10.8	13.0	14.7	15.7	17.7	19.5	19.6
Ireland	6.7	6.2	6.0	6.8	8.3	9.9	11.2
Italy	16.9	19.7	22.4	25.6	30.8	35.7	33.0
Netherlands	12.1	13.4	15.0	19.6	25.7	28.5	25.5
Portugal	8.2	10.6	10.9	12.1	14.6	16.9	17.0
Spain	10.0	11.7	12.3	13.6	16.6	20.4	20.7
United Kingdom	7.7	7.5	7.6	8.6	10.6	11.2	10.2
EEC average	11.3	12.6	13.8	16.0	19.5	22.0	20.9

[1] Expenditure ratio for 1983.   [2] Arithmetic mean.
Source: OECD (1988a), p. 35.

12

Competitive and Non-Competitive Regulatory Markets: The Regulation of Packaging Waste in the EU

JOEL R. PAUL[1]

I. INTRODUCTION

Opponents of the World Trade Organization, the European Union, and the North American Free Trade Agreement (NAFTA) have popularized the idea that regulatory competition will lead to a race to the bottom. According to the conventional view of regulatory competition represented by these critics, where capital, finished goods, and services are relatively mobile across national borders, regulators will be induced to lower regulatory standards to compete for scarce investment capital (Paul 1991: 70–4; Batra 1993: 215–30; Daly & Cobb 1989: 51–61). This paradigm of the relationship between private capital and state regulators describes a regulatory market in which competing states offer infrastructure, labour, and market access to private capital subject to certain regulatory conditions or costs, and private capital is free to select the state that offers the most favourable regulatory régime. If the production of widgets in the USA is advantaged by better highways, smarter workers, or close proximity to a large market, then private capital may be willing to pay higher regulatory costs than it would pay in a foreign state. The competitiveness of this regulatory market will be increased if states offer truly homogeneous infrastructure, labour, and market access. To the extent that reductions in trade barriers to goods and services allows equal access to all national markets regardless of where a good or service is produced or provided, regulatory competition intensifies.

Several approaches to the phenomenon of regulatory competition suggest themselves. One approach is to show that private capital is only marginally influenced by regulatory conditions in determining where to situate production. In fact, national markets are not homogeneous; differences in

[1] I am grateful to Robert Housman, David Kennedy, Duncan Kennedy, Al Klavoric, Anne-Marie Slaughter, and Joseph Weiler for their comments on earlier drafts and to my research assistant Theresa Swinehart. This chapter is a revised version of the author's article 'Free Trade, Regulatory Competition and the Autonomous Market Fallacy' published by the *Columbia Journal of European Law*.

infrastructure, labour, and market access as well as political stability, culture, and national loyalties may be more significant influences on investment decisions than regulatory costs. Indeed, there is no conclusive empirical evidence that regulatory competition does affect the decision of capital to locate in foreign markets (Woolcock, chapter 10, in this volume).

An alternative approach is to argue that regulatory competition leads to an 'optimal' level of regulation where the marginal costs of regulation precisely equal the marginal gains. National regulators pursuing their own bureaucratic agendas might be inclined to fix the level of regulation so high as to strangle productive investments. The ability of private capital to exit the national market and find a more hospitable investment environment elsewhere disciplines state regulators from excessive regulation.

A third approach is to accept that regulatory competition results as a byproduct of the reduction of trade barriers and to reduce regulatory competition through policy coordination among state regulators, harmonizing national regulatory standards to establish a common position, or delegating regulatory authority to some centralized multilateral or supra-national entity. In the EU, for example, all three strategies are evident. Member states have coordinated some policies like social welfare and labour rights, the EU Council has issued directives to member states requiring them to legislate uniform or harmonized standards in some sectors like banking and conservation of natural resources, and the Council has exercised its regulatory authority to establish common trade policies toward non-member countries.

I will refer to this third approach as the 'harmonization/centralization' strategy for avoiding or reducing regulatory competition. The harmonization/centralization strategy seeks to prevent a diminution of regulatory standards by reducing or eliminating regulatory competition. Non-competitive regulatory markets behave like monopolies in which consumers of regulation cannot influence the cost of regulation. The level of regulation may not be optimal, but it will be 'maximal' in the sense that it is the highest level of regulation desired by the regulatory authorities. In effect, the regulatory authorities, according to this conventional view, can unilaterally set the level of regulation without taking into consideration the implied threat that capital might 'walk' or choose another jurisdiction.

In reality, of course, capital always has options for challenging regulatory policies, even if these policies are coordinated among competing national jurisdictions. First, there are usually states outside the regulatory monopoly that constitute potential or actual competitors for capital. If the NAFTA sets a uniform policy on eliminating pollutants from steel mills, the steel manufacturers can close plants in North America and open mills in Asia. Steel produced in Asia can be imported to North America in the absence of significant trade barriers. Regulatory monopolies are compelled to take competing jurisdictional policies into consideration in ensuring that the cost of regulation is not higher than the advantage gained from producing within the monopoly, (for example, the advantage from market proximity).

Second, capital is never hostage to a single industry. Investment can usually shift from one industry to another or from direct investment to portfolio or government securities. Capital can move to consumption or land speculation. If government regulation raises the cost of steel manufacturing so high that it is no longer as profitable as alternative investments, capital may withdraw from steel manufacturing and shift to plastics, treasury bills, or condominia.

Third, capital is not a passive player in regulation. Regulatory authorities are held accountable to the politicians who seek reelection. Industries provide campaign funds and mobilize their employees and communities to support or oppose politicians who frequently intervene in the decisions of regulatory agencies. Often, the policymakers themselves are selected from the affected industries or solicit the views of industry in formulating policy. Indeed, the notice and comment provisions of administrative law require administrative agencies to take into account the interests of industry.

While acknowledging these countervailing considerations in particular situations, a proponent of the conventional strategy of harmonization/centralization could fairly argue that in general regulatory competition unchecked will tend toward a race to the bottom, while harmonized/centralized regulatory policies will tend to raise regulatory standards for individual states. The harmonized/centralized policy might be sub-optimal in the economic sense, but it will still be maximal, in the sense that it imposes higher costs on capital. This argument requires further explanation as to why maximal regulation would be desirable, even if it were suboptimal. Harmonized/centralized policy can more closely represent national public policy without the interfering influence of private capital. Public policy, even if sub-optimal, is defensible on grounds of democratic accountability. The policies set by national regulators roughly approximates the will of the majority of citizens expressed through their national representatives. At the very least, national regulators are more directly accountable to popular political pressure than market actors maximizing profits by selecting the lowest cost regulatory régime. Admittedly, national regulators are also accountable to the industries they regulate, which may wield far greater influence on regulatory agencies than is wielded by the general public, which is often unaware of regulatory policies and unable to organize effectively to influence regulation.

This chapter questions the conventional strategy of harmonization/centralization and suggests that under some circumstances regulatory competition may lead to a higher level of regulation than would be achieved under harmonization/centralization. It proceeds with a case study of one form of

Joel Paul

environmental regulation in the EU. Two purposes are served by this example. First, it illustrates how regulatory competition may in some circumstances lead to higher levels of national regulation. In focusing on the
disposal of packaging waste, I do not mean to suggest that this example is
typical or even common. I seek to identify those elements that may explain
why national regulators competed for higher levels of regulation rather than
to engage in a race to the bottom, as the conventional view would predict.
Second, it demonstrates how the shift from national regulation to a centralized regulatory régime or a harmonized standard may lead to lower levels of regulation than would otherwise prevail. My purpose is not to argue
that harmonization/centralization are the wrong strategies in every instance,
or that competitive regulatory markets are always preferable to non-
competitive regulatory markets. Rather, I conclude that the complex relationship between regulators and market actors may lead to different outcomes depending on the degree and nature of competition in the regulatory
market.

2. THE REGULATION OF PACKAGING WASTE

One way to compare the effect of a competitive and non-competitive regulatory market is to consider the experience of the EU in regulating packaging waste. Prior to 1995, member states regulated packaging waste through
a variety of national regulatory régimes. In 1995, the EU adopted a directive on packaging waste that was intended to harmonize regulations
throughout the EU. My purpose in focusing on this case study is to test
whether the adoption of a harmonization strategy necessarily raised regulatory standards.

The EU produces more than 108 million tons of solid waste annually.
Solid waste represents two forms of environmental injury. First, it wastes
virgin resources, including trees, metals, and petroleum. Second, waste disposal by dumping or incineration is a continuing source of damage to soil,
air, water and the health of plants, animals, and humans. In the EU, about
one-half of all solid waste, more than 50 million tons annually, is caused by
packaging. Of that amount, the EU recycles less than 20 per cent. The bulk
of all packaging waste, 60 to 80 per cent depending upon member state, is
dumped in landfills. The remainder is incinerated (Reeves 1993: 4–6). Paper
packaging waste alone fills almost 20 per cent of new landfill sites and plastic packaging fills another 12 per cent. If these two sources of waste could
be eliminated, it would be equivalent to saving one-third of all new landfills
(Cooper and Lybrand 1994).

Landfills adversely affect the environment in numerous ways. Landfills
permanently eliminate space from other productive uses, the seepage of the

waste into water tables can contaminate surrounding soil and water supplies, and decaying solid waste produces methane gas that can cause health
hazards, noxious fumes, damage to vegetation, and even explosions.
Throughout Europe, and especially in countries like Germany and the
Netherlands, available landfill sites are growing scarce. Yet, dumping
remains a relatively inexpensive form of disposal for solid waste.[2]

Incineration, the second most common form of disposal, also has adverse
environmental and health effects. Incineration produces toxic gases such as
dioxins and hydrogen chloride, which can damage plant, animal, and
human health. To avoid dioxins, incinerators must operate at very high tem-
peratures, which consume significant amounts of energy, and must be
equipped with scrubbers, which are not always available or economical.
Certain plastics when burned cause hydrochloric acid which can destroy
vegetation and pollute the air and water. Finally, incinerators spew a variety of air-born pollutants, including carcinogens.[3] To avoid this Hobson's
choice between dumping and incineration, some authorities, particularly in
Germany and the Netherlands, have exported solid waste to neighboring
European countries or to developing countries in Africa. Exporting environmental hazards has led to increasing political tensions inside and outside
the EU.[4]

Packaging waste is a classic example of market failure where the price of
packaging does not internalize the social cost of the waste and the cost of
dumping or incinerating packaging waste does not internalize the social cost

[2] Average cost in USA dollars:

Country	Incineration	Landfill
Germany	130	60
Netherlands	120	45
France	60	20
U.K.	55	30
Spain	40	15

By contrast, average recycling costs in the USA in USA dollars:

Plastic	180
Clear glass	75
Steel cans	65
Corrugated boxes	50
Mixed paper	35

Source: National Solid Waste Management Association (1990).

[3] Reeves (1993: 43–46). Serious questions can also be raised about the environmental costs
of recycling in some situations. Recycling often requires large amounts of water for cleaning
and energy for transporting waste long distances and then converting waste to recyclable material. *Single-, Multiple-use Plastic Packaging being Compared in Research on Recycling*, Int'l.
Env. Daily (BNA), Aug. 11, 1993. Nevertheless, it is fair to say that on balance recycling and
re-use of waste packaging is less costly on average to the environment of most industrialized
countries than landfills or incineration.

[4] *See generally*, Basel Convention on the Control of Transboundary Movements of
Hazardous Wastes and their Disposal, *reproduced in* 28 I.L.M. 649 (1989)

to the environment. One way an economist might conceptualize the social cost of environmental damage would be to imagine some measure of the social value that the environment serves. The environment has the capacity to regenerate natural resources over time, including plants, animals, and minerals, which are often required for production. Second, it removes and recycles waste products and impurities generated by human civilization. Third, the environment can influence climate conditions which may affect human health and welfare. Finally, the environment affects and renews the human spirit, influencing social behaviour in a myriad of subtle and overt ways. These four functions can be described as naturally occurring 'services' provided by the environment (Kaufmann, Pauly, and Sweitzer 1993: 130–3).

In the economist's view, the market for waste fails to adequately price the value of this environmental service. The service performed by the environment is a 'pure public good,' meaning it is freely accessible to everyone, and it would be practically impossible to exclude anyone from using these environmental services. The economist argues that the role of government is to internalize the social cost of packaging waste either through a tax or regulation so that the market operates more efficiently. In addition, or in the alternative, the economist might argue that the market value of packaging waste does not adequately reflect the social benefit of recycling waste rather than using virgin materials. Even if the supply of waste for recycling increased, the cost of recycled materials would probably remain high because of the expense of collecting, sorting, and processing packaging waste. So an economist might conclude that a related objective of regulation would be to subsidize the price of the recycled material or mandate demand for it. If either the price of dumping were increased to reflect the fair value of these environmental services or the social benefit of using recycled material was reflected in the lower price of recycled material, the private market would produce the optimal amount of pollution, according to conventional micro-economic analysis.[5]

This economic perspective may be useful to frame the regulatory objectives: taxing the producer of waste for the social cost and subsidizing the recycler for the social benefit they perform. In actual practice, however, the cost-benefit analysis cannot neutrally determine the correct 'price' the market should charge (Kennedy 1981). The varied and powerful critiques of cost-benefit analysis exceed the scope of this paper, but two central problems are the methodology for determining the correct price and the maxi-

---

[5] The optimal amount of pollution constitutes the point at which the marginal loss of value from the diminution in environmental services associated with increased economic activity is equal to the marginal gain in value from the increased economic activity. If the marginal loss of value is greater than the marginal benefit of economic activity, then it is sensible to reduce the level of economic activity to raise welfare. Alternatively, if the marginal benefit is higher that the marginal cost, the economic activity should be expanded to maximize human welfare (Kaufmann *et al.* 1993: 126–128).

mization of social utility or welfare. First, the social cost or benefit may be priced differently depending upon whether one relies on the offering price or the asking price. For example, if the manufacturer has a right to dump waste, a homeowner located adjacent to a landfill site might be able to offer $1,000 to be free from the noxious fumes and eyesore; but if the homeowner has the right to prevent the manufacturer from dumping, she would probably ask for much more than $1,000 from the manufacturer in exchange for giving the manufacturer the right to dump waste near her property line. The price differential may reflect differences in income level; relatively poor parties might offer to pay less than what they would ask for if they were selling the same good. Or the price differential might result from the observed tendency of most individuals to value what they have more than what they might gain. Second, even if it were possible to determine the correct price, it would tell us nothing about the marginal gain in welfare or utility experienced by a consumer when a manufacturer ceases to produce a non-recyclable plastic container. In general, individuals will value a scarce good more than an abundant good. Individuals living in a densely populated area with few landfill sites may experience a greater marginal benefit from each non-recyclable plastic container held off the market than the manufacturer, even if the latter is able to pay a higher price for the right to produce packaging waste. Optimizing income does not necessarily optimize welfare, if losers value their marginal loses more than the winners value their marginal gains.

3. NATIONAL MEASURES TO REGULATE PACKAGING WASTE

EU member states have adopted a variety of strategies in response to the social externalities generated by packaging waste. Most member states have relied upon measures intended to drive down the cost of recyclable waste and to hold manufacturers, and indirectly consumers, responsible for the additional social costs of packaging waste. These national measures have had two consequences. First, the effect of subsidizing recyclable waste in some countries has created competitive pressure on private market actors in other countries to support equivalent national packaging regulation. Second, the threat that national measures could create barriers to the free movement of goods across the EU, has compelled the Commission to react with a proposal of its own to harmonize the national systems at a higher level of packaging regulation than had previously existed in most of the EU.

The Netherlands and Germany have two of Europe's most comprehensive environmental programs, and both are particularly concerned with the problem of waste disposal. Since the problem of packaging waste is associated with consumerism, it may be natural that the concern is greatest in those countries that enjoy the highest standard of living, and which therefore generally consume the greatest volume of packaging per capita.[6] Moreover, these countries enjoy the financial means to ameliorate the situation. Steps to regulate packaging waste were first initiated in the Netherlands, Germany, Denmark, and Italy with the intention of both limiting the production of packaging waste and promoting the recovery of waste material.[7]

3.1 The Netherlands

Beginning in the early 1980s the Dutch Government embraced the concept that manufacturers and distributors should be responsible for the whole lifecycle of a product from cradle-to-grave. The lifecycle concept, derived from the 'polluter pays' principle, was endorsed by the Organization of Economic Co-operation and Development (OECD).[8] This revolutionary concept posited that the producer or distributor should bear at least some responsibility for the waste created by a product. Here we have an example of the state imposing on private producers the obligation to collect and dispose of waste. The lifecycle concept privatized the traditionally public function of waste disposal, while at the same time it imposed public obligations on private actors. In this sense, the lifecycle concept challenged the public/private frontier.

In June 1991, Minister Alders concluded the Covenant on Packaging with the Stichting Verpakking en Milieu (the 'Foundation for Packaging and the Environment'). The Covenant was written as a legally enforceable contract between the government and the Foundation representing the 'packaging chain,' including manufacturers and distributors involved with producing or

[6] Packaging Waste

Country	Tons/Capita	GDP/Capita (USD)
Germany	.14	22,320
France	.14	19,490
Italy	.13	16,830
UK	.11	16,100
Spain	.1	11,020
Netherlands	.15	17,320
Belgium	.17	15,540
Denmark	.18	22,080
Portugal	.08	4,900
Greece	.06	5,990
Ireland	.09	9,550

Sources: 1) Centre Francais du Commerce Extérieur (CFCE) as reported in Reeves (1993: 2); World Bank (1992).

[7] This survey of member states is not intended to be exhaustive.

[8] The polluter pays principle states that polluters should bear the costs of pollution control, which should be reflected in the costs of good and services, and should not benefit from environmental subsidies that would distort trade (Hunter, Summer, and Vaughn 1994: 32).

using packaging or packaged products and recyclers of packaging. The Covenant was intended to eliminate all dumping of packaging waste by the year 2000. The Covenant contained both qualitative and quantitative objectives. The qualitative provisions call on producers to avoid packaging materials that are harmful to the environment, such as dyes containing heavy metals, lead closures on bottles, polyvinyl chloride, and bleaches. These provisions also encouraged manufacturers to use plastics and bottles that could be more easily recycled or re-used. The quantitative provisions set out a schedule to reduce by the year 2000 the weight of packaging by at least ten per cent of the total weight produced in 1986 for each form of packaging material. The packaging chain promised to develop new forms of lighter packaging that require less materials and avoid excess packaging. In addition, the packaging chain agreed to minimize by 2000 the use of materials that damage the environment, such as additives, non-recyclable plastics, lead tops, and paints, to use re-usable packaging to the extent feasible, and to recycle at least 60 per cent of used packaging which cannot otherwise be re-used. The agreement provided that 80 per cent of non-reusable glass, 60 per cent of cardboard packaging and 50 per cent of plastics would be recycled by December, 1995. Moreover, the packaging chain undertook to establish separate collection facilities for glass and paper, to encourage retailers to adopt deposit and return programmes for packaging and to develop additional recycling capacity. In consideration for the industry's commitments, the Dutch Minister of the Environment agreed to issue regulations and to discuss implementation plans working closely with the packaging chain. The Covenant also established a committee of government and industry representatives to monitor compliance with the Covenant's terms and an arbitration procedure to handle disputes. Finally, the annex to the Covenant contained a list of practical visible steps to be taken in one-to-two years to minimize packaging. Examples of these measures include charging customers for shopping bags in supermarkets, packaging detergents in compact containers, eliminating unnecessary wrapping on pet food, reducing the weight of tinplate in cans and of glass in jars, and making labels on glass jars more easily removable.

It is still too early to assess how significantly the Dutch Covenant has reduced packaging at its source. The packaging chain has succeeded in establishing neighborhood collection facilities throughout the country. The close relationship between the environment ministry and representatives of the packaging industry has cultivated trust and a co-operative spirit. Many Greens in the Netherlands are critical of the Covenant's gradual voluntary approach. As a result, there is increased pressure to move faster on recycling packaging waste, and in the EU, the Netherlands has been an insistent voice for tougher packaging regulations. Members of the Dutch Parliament have called for an eco-tax on excessive packaging and on dumping solid waste in landfills. Opponents of the Covenant have argued that this is overly ambitious and that the German packaging ordinance, discussed below, has generated additional recyclable waste that exceeds both the capacity of recyclers and the market demand for recycled material.

3.2 Germany

At the same time that the negotiations over the Packaging Covenant were being concluded in the Netherlands, the German Government approved an ordinance to regulate packaging waste.[9] The Greens had demanded action in response to the disappearance of landfill sites, increased acid rain from the incineration of polyvinyl chloride, litter, dioxins from bleached paper, and wasted petroleum, and timber. The packaging ordinance, often named for the German Environmental Minister Klaus Töpfer, was a response to the political demands of the Greens, who had reached 14 per cent in the polls (Calder 1992: 41). The Töpfer law established a far more comprehensive mandatory system than the Dutch Covenant to restrict the use of environmentally unsafe materials in packaging, to minimize the use of packaging and to provide for recycling facilities through the private sector. The ordinance applied to any manufacturer of packaging, or packaged products, or any distributor of packaging or packaged products.

In essence, the German law imposed a fundamental requirement on all distributors and manufacturers to take back any packaging of the same kind as manufactured or distributed by that party from any consumer, regardless of whether the consumer actually purchased the product from that party. Most significantly, incineration and dumping of packaging waste were prohibited. Manufacturers and distributors were required to provide for the reuse or recycling of any packaging waste. Distributors of non-recyclable packaging for beverages, detergents, spray paints, and cleansers were required at every stage of distribution to charge certain deposits to be reimbursed when the packaging was returned.

Manufacturers and distributors were exempt from this burdensome 'take-back' obligation if they agreed to participate in an alternative private system that provided for regular collection of packaging waste from consumers subject to the regulation of the appropriate authorities of the individual German states. To obtain approval by the state authority, the private system is required to collect and recycle or reuse certain minimum percentages of glass, tin, aluminum, cardboard, paper, plastic, and compound packaging within each state. To facilitate this ambitious parallel private system of

[9] Regulation on the Avoidance of Packaging Waste [Verpackungsverordnung—VerpackV of 12 June 1991] 31 I.L.M. 1135 (1992), effective 1 January 1993, repealing the Regulation on the Taking Back of, and Charging Deposits on, Plastic Drinks Packaging of 20 December 1988 (Federal Law Gazette I p. 2455).

waste collection and recycling, the law allowed manufacturers and distributors collectively to contract with third parties. Violations of the regulation were subject to fines as an administrative offense.

Since January 1993, all of the German state authorities have approved a single private alternative system called the Duales System Deutschland (DSD). Packaging waste from consumer products displaying a green dot can be returned to DSD for recycling, re-use, or disposal. By 1994, more than 80 per cent of all consumer products displayed the green dot. For the right to display the green dot, producers agree to pay a small fee determined by the type and volume of packaging. These fees are passed on to consumers in the form of higher prices. DSD provides weekly home pick-up services throughout the country for green dot packaging waste. Households are expected to sort the waste by material into one of several colored plastic bags provided for that purpose. DSD then delivers the packaging waste to recyclers without charge, or to an increasing extent, DSD provides subsidies to recyclers to defray the high cost of recycling certain material, especially plastics.

DSD began operations in July 1991, with the participation of more than 600 companies. German consumers responded to the recycling program enthusiastically. By 1993, DSD reached virtually all German households and was receiving as much as four times the amount of packaging waste it had anticipated.[10] Over 60 per cent of household waste paper, 50 per cent of glass, 40 per cent of cans, and 20 per cent of plastic packaging were returned to DSD. The unexpected and overwhelming participation by consumers vastly exceeded Germany's capacity to recycle waste. For example, in 1993, DSD collected 409,000 metric tons of plastic containers. Total recycling capacity for plastic waste in Germany was only 124,000 metric tons.[11] The surplus of packaging waste precipitated a series of financial, diplomatic, and legal problems for DSD.

First, overwhelmed by more waste than it had the capacity to recycle within Germany, DSD was compelled to store waste or pay recyclers to take waste off its hands. At the same time, more than one-half of the firms utilizing the green dot had failed to pay their fees to DSD. The unanticipated expenses of transporting, handling, sorting, and subsidizing the huge volume of packaging waste, combined with the shortfall of fees, threatened DSD's financial solvency with a DM500 million (USA $290 million) debt and compelled DSD to raise user fees on its green do.[12] By 1994, fees ranged from one to four pfennings approximately per package depending on weight and type of material.

[10] Int'l. Env. Daily (BNA) (1993).

[11] *Germany's Recycling Overfloweth*, *Chemical Week*, June 16, 1993, at 65.

[12] Nao Nakanishi, *Germany Rescues Ambitious Recycling Scheme from Scrapheap*, *The Reuter Library Serv.*, Oct. 29, 1993; James O. Jackson, *World-class Litterbugs*, *Time*, Oct. 18, 1993, at 80, *Rubbish*, *The Economist*, July 3, 1993, at 46.

Second, the spillover of packaging waste onto other countries hurt other countries' industries and became a source of diplomatic embarrassment with other member states of the EU. On the one hand, the DSD provided German recyclers with an abundant source of free or subsidized waste material. As a result, paper millers and plastic manufacturers elsewhere in Europe complained that the scheme unfairly advantaged German industry. For example, by 1994, about one-half of all paper products in Germany were manufactured from waste paper provided free by the DSD.[13] On the other hand, some German recyclers, paid by DSD for recycling waste, allegedly paid foreign companies to take waste off their hands.[14] DSD and its subcontractors exported huge quantities of packaging waste to France, eastern Europe, and southeast Asia for dumping or for recycling in Britain, France, Ireland, Italy, Luxembourg, the Netherlands, and Spain. The infant recycling industries in these countries were so flooded by subsidized German waste, that domestic waste could no longer be accommodated and was added to domestic dump sites or incinerated.[15]

Third, as DSD became a dominant force in the recycling industry, it became embroiled in a number of legal challenges. The German Cartel Office and the Commission initiated separate investigations of DSD for possible violation of the German and EU competition laws. The German Cartel Office was responding to complaints from paper recyclers that DSD was operating to control the market by offering large subsidies to certain contractors. DSD sought to reassure the Cartel Office that it would make subsidies available to independent firms. Then the Cartel Office raised additional concerns about DSD's plans to handle packaging waste from industrial and commercial businesses. The Cartel Office has issued an order preventing DSD from entering this market, which DSD appealed to a Berlin court.[16] In 1993, the Frankfurt Public Prosecutor's Office opened an investigation into allegations that DSD's subcontractor for plastics, VGK

[13] John Eisenhammer, *German Waste Drives Creates a Stink*, Independent, Feb. 17, 1994, 37; Krolik (1994: 12).

[14] According to some reports, German recyclers paid foreign companies up to DM600 (US$360) per ton (Ariane Genillard, *Recycling has Neighbors Crying Foul-Complaints of Cheap Waste Exports to European Countries*, Fin. Times, Jan. 25, 1994, at 6).

[15] Alison Maitland, *Germany Rebuts Criticism of Its Waste Recycling Laws*, Fin. Times, Oct. 19, 1993, at 3. In France, for example, paper-makers received up to FF300 per ton for accepting German waste paper. Paper-makers were therefore disinclined to purchase French waste paper. The prices of French waste paper fell from FF90 to FF10 from 1992 to 1993. In 1993, DSD exported 450,000 tons of waste paper to France. *Packaging Waste: Recovery Loses out to Eco-Tax Option*, Eur. Rep., June 24, 1993, No. 1869. In October 1993 Germany pledged to cease exporting waste and to open two newrecycling plants for processing paper packaging waste. *Seeing the Light at Last*, 9 Packaging Week, Dec. 3, 1993, No. 25, at 25.

[16] *Company Defends Waste Collection Scheme in Legal Opinion Filed with Cartel Office*, Int'l. Env. Daily (BNA), June 17, 1993; *FCO Bars Trash Hauler from Collecting and Disposing of Transport Packaging*, 65 Antitrust and Trade Reg. Rep. (BNA), July 22, 1993, No. 1624, p. 144; *German Agency Takes Dim View of Monopoly in Garbage Collection*, 65 Antitrust and Trade Reg. Rep. (BNA), Oct. 7, 1993, No. 1634, at 478.

GmbH, had defrauded DSD by simulating recycling it did not perform. Documents indicate that plastic packaging waste which VGK was paid to recycle ended up being dumped in France and eastern Europe.[17] Finally, the EC announced in March 1994, that it was initiating infringement proceedings against Germany for distortions to the internal market resulting from the packaging law.[18]

As a result of these financial, diplomatic, and legal challenges facing the packaging ordinance, the German Government is considering a range of amendments relaxing the recycling targets, imposing an eco-tax to restrict packaging at its source and requiring all packaging be marked to indicate whether it is recyclable or returnable.[19]

3.3 France

The adoption of packaging recycling programs in the Netherlands and Germany affected neighboring member states, especially France, in three respects. First, the Dutch Covenant and the German Packaging Ordinance had a powerful demonstration effect. The Dutch and German commitment to reducing packaging waste appealed to green parties throughout Europe. Producers, retailers, and packagers viewed with concern the potential disruption in free movement from national packaging regulations. These private parties also saw the risk that their own governments might be pressured by green parties to adopt equivalent regulations. Some producers favored packaging regulations as a means of lowering packaging costs.[20] Other firms concluded that if packaging regulations would inevitably follow the Dutch-German example, it was more useful to shape those regulations positively rather than oppose them outright. The experience of firms in Germany showed that the packaging regulations could be advantageous for some businesses, and that consumers responded positively to reducing packaging waste.[21] Second, as DSD exported packaging waste to dumps elsewhere in Europe, it aggravated the waste problems of those countries, adding

[17] *Packaging Waste: Recovery Loses out to Eco-Tax Option Europ Rep.*, June 24, 1993, No. 1869.

[18] *Commission to Take Germany to Court Over Packaging Law, Paleokrassas Says, Int'l. Env. Daily* (BNA), Mar. 1, 1994.

[19] Michael Rose and David Perchard, *When Waste is not Wanted—Germany's Recycling Legislation, Fin. Times*, Jan. 25, 1994, at 18.

[20] Many firms have found that recycled material lowers production costs without compromising quality or dependability of supply. David Biddle (1993: 145).

[21] Gerleen H. Braakman, President of the European Organization for Packaging and the Environment, ('EUROPEN'), an association of large packaging firms, commented that 'reduction of the volume of packaging is no longer anti-marketing but rather pro-marketing.' EUROPEN favors packaging regulations, including the proposed EU Directive on Packaging discussed below. EUROPEN argues that reducing the volume of packaging saves resources, reduces costs and attracts consumers. *See generally, Packaging Waste: Exclusive Interview with Head of European Packaging Lobby*, EUR. REP., Oct. 13, 1993, No. 1893.

urgency to the call for packaging regulation.[22] Green parties gained support
for packaging regulations in response to the perception that Germany was
exporting its waste problems. Third, and most importantly, the large
increase in the supply of recycled waste material drove down the price of
competing materials in other countries and forced some competitors out of
business.[23] This was especially true of French manufacturers and recyclers
of paper and plastics.[24] The French Environment Minister Michel Barnier
called on Germany to prohibit the export of packaging waste to France and
threatened to stop imports of German waste if the Germans did not comply. In the Council, France asked Germany to modify its recycling law, and
Germany responded by offering to open bilateral talks with the countries
that had complained about the disruptive effect of German waste exports
on their own industries, which included France, the United Kingdom, the
Netherlands, Spain, Italy, Ireland, and Luxembourg.[25] Even French recycling firms that benefitted from access to subsidized German waste paper
and plastic found it difficult to compete with German recycling firms that
enjoyed even greater access to subsidized waste material for recycling. The
French recyclers wanted France to adopt a comparable system to remain
competitive with Germany.

Anticipating the disruptive effect that German waste imports would have
on French industry following the enactment of the German packaging ordinance, the French Government adopted a Decree on Packaging Waste on
April 1, 1992, which took effect as of January 1, 1993.[26] The French decree
endorsed the strategy of 'valorization,' meaning the recovery of materials.
Like the German ordinance, the French decree required the producer,
importer or retailer of a product to be responsible to 'take back' all used
packaging. Companies could either act individually or by establishing joint
organizations. The organizations required government approval and were
subject to regulation. The French decree required valorization of at least 50
per cent of all steel, aluminum, plastic, and paper packaging and 60 per cent
of glass packaging by 1997. It did not, however, set any numerical quota

[22] In 1993, Germany exported more than one-half of the 400,000 tons of plastic it collected
to foreign landfills. Ariane Genillard, *German Waste Recycling is Hit by Success, Fin. Times*,
June 18, 1993, at 2.
[23] *E.g.*, Bronwen Maddox, *Waste Mountains Prove Difficult to Conquer: The Lesson of a
German Recycling Scheme that came to Grief Through Overspill, Fin. Times*, July 28, 1993, at
5.
[24] French collectors of waste paper claimed that subsidized German waste paper would
drive them out of business, costing 27,000 jobs in the industry. *French Waste Paper Collectors
Protest at German Imports, The Reuter Eur. Community Rep.*, June 15, 1993.
[25] *France Threatens to Act Over German Packaging Waste Exports, Agence France Presse*,
June 29, 1993.
[26] Decree 92.377, Art. 4, of 1 April 1992, provides in relevant part: 'Any producer, any
importer . . .any person responsible for first placing on the market goods sold in packaging
(. . .) shall be required to contribute to or to provide for the disposal of all his packaging
waste . . .'

for recycling. By 2003, the decree would require the recovery of 75 per cent of all packaging. No more than one-quarter of that amount could be incinerated.[27] The decree differed from the German law in three respects: First, unlike the German law, the French did not require private parties to collect and sort packaging waste, leaving that responsibility to the local sanitation agencies. Second, unlike the German law, the French decree included energy recovery by incineration as an acceptable alternative to disposal. Third, the French law set no specific targets for recycling, reuse, or incineration. Instead, it provided for broad objectives and continuous monitoring of progress.

Pursuant to the decree, the French Government in co-operation with private producers, retailers and importers established a 'blue-dot' programme comparable to DSD's 'green dot' programme. 'Eco-Emballage,' a consortium of private industry was formed to operate the valorization programme. Participants in Eco-Emballage were required to pay an initial fee of FF 50,000 (US$8,600) plus approximately one centime per packaged unit introduced into the French market. The fee collected by the French Government would finance the collection, sorting, and delivery of recyclable packaging waste to French companies for reuse, recycling, or incineration.[28] Approximately one-half of French households participated in pilot waste recovery and sorting programs established by Eco-Emballage by July 1993. Each community establishing a pilot program was funded by Eco-Emballage.[29] Eventually most French companies and foreign importers are expected to join Eco-Emballage, which will be responsible for all packaging waste, except plastics.

French plastic manufacturers have independently established a consortium, 'Valorplast,' to facilitate plastic recycling so as to better compete with the German plastics manufacturers. By 1993, more than 1,200 French firms were participating.[30] Due to the limited capacity to recycle plastics, the amount of plastic to be recycled was initially limited to 40,000 metric tons annually.[31] Valorplast has focused its collection efforts on France's five-billion bottles of mineral water consumed annually, which constitute about 25 per cent of the plastic waste generated annually in France.[32] By 1996,

---

[27] *French Legislation Shakes up Industry*, 46 *Canadian Packaging*, Sept. 1993, No. 9, at 9.

[28] As of August 1993, more than 2,500 firms belonged to Eco-Emballage, paying over FF 250 million ($43 million) in fees. It was expected that more than FF 2.5 billion ($430 million) eventually might be needed annually. *French Legislation Shakes up Industry*, *Canadian Packaging*, Sept. 1993, No. 9, at 9.

[29] *French Packaging Waste Group Will Not Raise Subscription Fees in 1994*, Int'l. Env. Daily (BNA), August 6, 1993.

[30] *Creation of Recovery Organization Announced by French Plastic Manufacturers*, Int'l. Env. Daily (BNA), April 1, 1993.

[31] Ralph Back, *UIC Calls for Halt to Environmental Legislation Program*, Chemical Week, October 13, 1993, at 22.

[32] *French Plastics Recyclers Set Target*, Chemical Week, Jan. 26, 1994, at 8.

Valorplast hopes to recover one-fifth of these, totalling 40,000 tons of plastic. Valorplast's 1994 annual budget is approximately FF 40 million (seven million dollars), raised from industry fees and contributions from Eco-Emballage. Four specialized organizations of Valorplast will recycle different kinds of plastics into polyvinyl chloride bottles, padding for textiles and outdoor furniture, among other things.[33] Lightweight plastics that cannot be recycled, such as plastic bags and plastic wrap, will be incinerated for energy recovery. Valorplast projects that its approach to recovering large quantities of plastics and incinerating the balance will lead to higher recovery levels at one-fifth the cost of the DSD.[34]

In 1994, the French Government proposed additional legislation requiring all industrial and commercial businesses whose weekly production of waste packaging exceeded 1,100 litres to reuse or recycle the materials either on their own, through an approved processor or through a third party engaged in the transport and trade of waste packaging, such as Eco-Emballage.[35]

3.4 Belgium

Even prior to the German and Dutch recycling programs, waste exports to Belgian landfills were a cause of concern to Belgium.[36] Following the adoption of the Töpfer law, political pressure increased for Belgium to act. The Government of Prime Minister Jean-Luc Dehaene needed the support of the French-speaking Ecolo (green) parties to enact the federal constitutional reforms agreed to in February 1993. The price for the green parties' support was the adoption of an eco-tax on packaging and selected disposable consumer items produced from virgin materials, such as disposable cameras and razors. Prime Minister Dehaene agreed to the adoption of the eco-tax,

---

[33] *French Plastics Industry Stars Packaging Recycling Program*, 4 Bus. & Env't, No. 4, Apr. 1993.

[34] Nancy Russotto, *The Environmental Battlefield, Chemistry and Industry*, No. 16, Aug. 16, 1993, at 644.

[35] *Alerts & Updates: France's Packaging Waste Bill, Bus. Eur.*, Apr. 4, 1994.

[36] One response to the influx of foreign waste was the adoption of a ban on all foreign waste by the Walloon regional Executive in 1983. The Wallonia ban was challenged by the Commission as an obstacle to free movement of goods in violation of Articles 30 and 36 of the Treaty and as inconsistent with Directives 75/442 on waste management and 84/631 on the supervision and control of the transfrontier shipment of hazardous waste. The Commission initiated an Article 169 enforcement proceeding. *Commission v. Belgium*, 9 July 1992, Case C-2/90. The European Court held first that waste was a 'good' subject to the free movement provisions of Article 30. The Court, however, upheld the Wallonia ordinance in a narrowly reasoned judgment that the restriction could be justified and was non-discriminating on the basis of the nature of the waste prohibited, even though the ban expressly excluded all foreign waste, regardless of the type of waste. The Court struck down the ban as it applied to hazardous waste products, which were covered by Directive 84/631. *See generally*, von Wilmowsky (1993); Hancher and Sevenster (1993).

which was enacted in August 1993, over the opposition of industry and commercial interests.[37]

The eco-tax, which is intended to take effect in 1995, would range from BFr10 to 20 (27 to 54 cents) per item depending on the type of material and weight.[38] The tax charged to the customer is intended to encourage consumers to use more recycled material. The law establishes minimum targets for the use of recycled goods, and if a seller failed to meet these targets, certain of its goods would be subject to the eco-tax. If, for example, the law requires that 60 per cent of beverage containers in a store's stock must be made from recycled material and only 40 per cent are, all beverage containers sold at that store would be subject to the eco-tax.

Plastic producers in Belgium and France claimed that the tax discriminates against polyvinyl chloride plastics. There was also some doubt expressed by, for example, French water producers like Evian, as to whether it would create a barrier to free movement. As a result of this concern, Belgian retailers, packagers, and producers joined with importers to form an alternative to the eco-tax known as 'Fost Plus'. Fost Plus, an industry consortium modelled on DSD and Eco-Emballage, sought an exemption from the eco-tax for producers that agreed to take back their products for reuse and recycling. Participating companies in Fost Plus pay a fee to the government to establish a privatized system for packaging collection, sorting, and recovery.[39] Fost Plus, which began operating in January 1994, hoped to establish reciprocal treatment for its members' packaging waste with DSD and Eco-Emballage.

3.5 Denmark

Denmark banned non-refillable soft drink containers in 1971 and established the first comprehensive system of recycling in the EC in 1978 providing for the public municipal collection of recyclables from households and businesses.[40] Denmark also established a deposit-and-return system to encourage consumers' participation.[41] In June 1993, Denmark amended its

[37] *Belgium Enacts Experimental 'Eco-Tax' on Disposable Goods*, 19 *World Envt'l. Rep.* Aug. 6, 1993, No. 16.

[38] Special Act of July 16, 1993, Concerning the Achievement of the Federalization of the State, Art. 369 *et seq.*, Belgium Stat. The eco-tax was delayed pending the final approval of the EU Directive.

[39] Hilary Clarke, *Survey of Belgium*, FIN. TIMES, July 12, 1993, p. 10.

[40] Lov om genanvendelse af papir drikkevare-emballager samt begraensning af affald, Lov nr. 297 Lovtidende 851 (1978) [Law on the recycling of paper and beverage containers and the reduction of waste].

[41] A 1981 Danish law imposed a compulsory deposit-and-return system for certain beverage containers. Non-conforming containers were prohibited, including beer cans, which prevented U.K. beer from being sold in Denmark. The Commission objected to the law, and in 1984, the law was amended to allow the distribution of certain kinds of beverage containers that were non-conforming, provided that the quantity did not exceed 3,000 hl annually In its

environmental law by authorizing the minister of the environment to issue regulations requiring consumers to return certain products and packaging to producers or importers and requiring those firms to bear the costs of recycling or disposal.[42] The environment minister was further authorized to impose administrative fines for non-compliance with the regulations.

The Danish Government has set a target for the year 2000 of reducing packaging waste by 15 per cent and increasing recycling to 75 per cent of beverage containers and 80 per cent of all packaging materials. The Government has also reached a voluntary agreement with industry, like the Dutch Covenant, to reach 80 per cent recycling of transport packaging by 1995 (Reeves 1993: 21).

The Danish model places an equal responsibility on both consumers, producers and packagers to recycle, whereas the German law relies on the voluntary participation of consumers. Presently, it is unclear the extent to which Danish producers and packagers will follow the model of the DSD and Eco-Emballage. In the politics of the EU, Denmark has been a leading voice for establishing a strict standard for recycling packaging and for allowing member states to exceed those standards. Denmark opposed the EU Directive on Packaging as adopted, fearing that it would lower Danish national standards. In conjunction with the Netherlands and Germany, Denmark has established an important alliance for packaging regulation within the Council.

3.6 United Kingdom

The UK has been relatively slow in responding to the packaging waste problem. The Conservative government has looked to private industry for direction in this area, and industry has been divided over the appropriate strategies for reducing packaging at its source, recovering waste, and financing the transport, sorting, and handling of packaging waste. As early as 1990, a Government White Paper called for a national target of recovering 50 per cent of all waste by 2000. Following the adoption of the German law, the flood of subsidized packaging waste and recycled material from Germany threatened the British paper, plastics, and recycling industries. Beginning in 1991, the British Government set up an Ad Hoc Group on Packaging to formulate an action plan with the participation of industry. Industry was at least partly motivated by concern the government might

Danish Bottle judgment, the European Court held that the protection of the environment was a mandatory requirement which may limit the application of Article 30, and that a deposit-and-return scheme was not disproportionate. However, the Court found that by restricting the quantity of beverages sold in non-conforming containers, Denmark had violated Article 30. *See* 302/86 *Commission v. Denmark*, E.C.R. 4607, 1 C.M.L.R. 619 (1989).

[42] Lov om aendring af love om miljobeskyttelse, Lov nr. 477, Lovtidende 2523 (1993) [amendment of environmental protection law].

otherwise impose a mandatory scheme as other member states and the Commission began drafting and implementing their own systems for recovering packaging waste.[43] Industry and government tried repeatedly and failed to reach consensus on a plan of action. As discussions dragged on, industry and political leaders sounded the alarm: British manufacturers were threatened; the fledgling recycling industry could collapse under the weight of subsidized recycled material from Germany. Environmental concerns were overshadowed by the threat of foreign economic competitors.

In 1993, the British Government requested proposals from the Producer Responsibility Industry Group on a staged plan to recover at least 50 per cent of packaging waste by 2000. The report, delivered in February 1994, provided for a comprehensive system of recycling modelled on the French Eco-Emballage. The primary responsibility for collecting and sorting household packaging waste would remain with local authorities, but industry would establish a consortium, 'VALPAK', to finance and implement the recovery of waste materials. The plan would rely upon the government to require all private producers, packagers, and retailers to participate. Government would collect a fee from packagers and/or producers and importers or a tax on all packaged goods. The plan would cost about 200 million pounds annually, which is less than a tenth of the cost of operating the DSD in 1993. Industry leaders remain divided over the plan, and the government has not yet introduced legislation.[44] The uncertain direction of the British recycling program has also been reflected in a somewhat ambivalent attitude toward the proposed EU packaging directive, as discussed below.

3.7 Italy

Unlike other European governments that have concentrated their legislative efforts on increasing the supply of recycled material, Italy created both demand for, and supply of, recycled material. Legislation requiring that packaging be made from recycled materials was introduced in the early 1980's. Industry opposition successfully stopped numerous legislative programs from taking effect. In 1988, the Italian Parliament mandated recycling and required producers and packagers to join a consortium to facilitate recycling.[45] Four private recycling consortia have been formed,

[43] Ron Goddard, *Tight Schedule for Action Plan on Waste; British Government's Plan to Reduce Packaging Waste, Packaging Week,* Feb. 12, 1992.

[44] Producer Responsibility Industry Group, *Real Value from Packaging Waste: A Way Forward.* (A report for public consultation presented to the Secretary of State of the Environment and the President of the Board of Trade) 7 Feb. 1994; Charles Clover, *Shoppers' Levy Planned to Fund Recycling, The Daily Telegraph,* Feb. 8, 1994, p. 2.

[45] Conversione in legge, con modificazioni, del decreto-legge 9 settembre 1988, No. 397, recante disposizioni urgenti in materia di smahimento dei rifluti industiali, Gazzette Officale Della Republica Italiana Nov. 10, 1988, [Law 475 of November 9, 1988]; (Reeves 1993: 16–17).

each responsible for recycling different packaging materials. The consortia are financed by a levy on packaging and co-operate with local authorities in the collection and sorting of material. For example, Replastic, which is the consortium responsible for all plastic resins, pays subsidies per household to the local authorities for collecting plastic containers separately.[46] About 40 per cent of plastics and 50 per cent of glass and metals were recycled by 1993. Since January 1, 1991, Italy has required that all paper materials used for packaging must be made from recycled fibers. By 1993, almost 90 per cent of all paper packaging was derived from recycled material. Partly in response to the market disruptions caused by DSD, broad political support has emerged in Italy for the basic framework of the Italian recycling program. Numerous reforms have been proposed to widen its scope or to make it more flexible.[47] Italy's packaging scheme conforms closely to the proposed EU packaging directive, and Italy has been a consistent supporter of the directive.

3.8 Conclusion

Denmark, Germany, and the Netherlands adopted packaging regulations to manage their national solid waste problem. Public power was exercised over private producers and consumers engaged in producing and disposing of packaging waste. According to the regulatory competition model, we might expect private parties subject to regulation to shift their consumption and production to other jurisdictions without such regulation. Instead, consumers and producers in unregulated jurisdictions, including France, the UK, Belgium, and Italy, lobbied for the adoption of equivalent national laws. Indeed, competition among private packaging companies and recyclers of waste forced foreign competitors to support regulation. Rather than behaving autonomously, market actors constructively engaged state authorities to raise regulatory standards.

There is an irony to the interaction of market and state actors raising national measures: these national measures are themselves seen as potentially distorting the EU market. Some market actors, non-member states and the Commission have viewed national regulations to minimize packaging and require recycling of packaging waste as disruptions to the single market. Must a Portuguese company redesign its packaging for the Dutch market? Must a USA firm join DSD or take-back its own packaging in the German market? Must a company redesign its packages for 15 different national markets? Industry groups, member states, foreign firms, and the

---

[46] *Replastic Agrees to Pay Part of Costs for Local Authorities to Collect Plastics, Int'l Env. Daily* (BNA), Feb. 25, 1993.
[47] *Parliament to Consider Major Overhaul of Waste Disposal, Treatment Provisions, Int'l Env. Daily* (BNA), Nov. 24, 1992.

Commission have all expressed concern about the need to harmonize national packaging regulations to avoid such distortions.[48] These concerns led to proposals in 1991 for an EU directive on packaging.

4. EU DIRECTIVE ON PACKAGING

The Council and Parliament adopted the directive on packaging and packaging waste on December 20, 1994.[49] The directive aims to harmonize national measures under Article 100a. The directive requires the recovery of 50–65 per cent, by weight, of all packaging waste within five years.[50] Recovery includes the reuse of packaging, recycling of waste materials and recovery of energy through incineration. Within this general recovery target, the directive requires recycling 25–45 per cent of packaging waste, including at least 15 per cent of each type of packaging material.[51] The directive prohibits national requirements for recycling more than 45 per cent of packaging waste, which conflicts with existing laws in Germany, Denmark, and the Netherlands. The directive permits member states to maintain higher standards if the EC confirms that these higher standards are consistent with environmental protection, avoid distortions to the internal market, do not hinder compliance by other member states and do not constitute an arbitrary means of discrimination or a disguised restriction on trade within the EU. Recognizing the difficulty of transportation and the low level of packaging waste per capita in Greece, Ireland, and Portugal, the directive provides that these member states are only required to recover 25 per cent of their packaging waste within five years and are not expected to meet the full requirements of the directive until 2005.[52]

---

[48] For example, the European Plastic Association called on the Community to adopt a Community-wide program of mandatory recycling to create a level playing field for plastic manufacturers outside Germany. Mary Murphy and Ron Goddard, *Concessions Hope for EC Packaging Directive*, 7 PACKAGING WEEK, No. 38, March 11, 1992, at 1; David Gardner, Quentin Peel and John Hunt, *Green Germany Drags Brussels into Environmental Arena, Fin. Times*, Jan. 24, 1992, at 2; *Packaging: Community Regulation in the Pipeline, Eur. Rep.*, July 3, 1991, No. 1690, p. 1; John Thornhill, *Repackaged, Recycled, Restricted, Fin. Times*, Dec. 6, 1991, p. 17.

[49] European Parliament and Council Directive of 20 December 1994 on packaging and packaging waste. *94/62/EC*, [hereinafter Directive]. Under the co-decision procedure, the European Parliament adopted the Council's common position on May 4, 1994, with relatively minor amendments after rejecting a large number of green amendments to strengthen the directive. The Commission adopted all the Parliament's amendments on May 25. The Council of Environment Ministers failed to reach agreement on June 9 over the objections of Belgium, Denmark, Germany, and the Netherlands. Under the Maastricht Treaty's conciliation procedure, representatives of Parliament and the Council reached agreement in December 1994, and the Directive was adopted both by Parliament and a meeting of the Council on December 20.

[50] Directive, Article 6(1)(a).   [51] Directive, Article 6(1)(b).

[52] Directive, Article 6.

After the initial stage, the Commission would review the waste situation and recommend appropriate levels of recovery and recycling, and within ten years the Council will substantially increase targets for recovery and recycling. The directive requires member states to ensure that systems are set up to provide for the return of all used packaging, including all imported products under nondiscriminatory conditions and to ensure that packaging waste is effectively recovered.[53] Such systems are required to provide for industry participation. To facilitate recovery, the directive requires member states to institute within five years a system of marking on all packaging indicating whether the packaging is reusable or recoverable.[54] In addition, the directive requires member states to provide information on packaging waste to enable the Commission to adopt effective waste management policies[55] and consumer education on the advantages of reusable and recoverable packaging.[56] The directive leaves to member states the choice of instrument for the attainment of the recovery targets and it allows member states to adopt economic instruments, including eco-taxes, subject to the adoption of an eco-tax by the Council.[57] It prohibits member states from impeding the marketing of any packaging that satisfies the directive.[58] Finally, the directive requires all member states to implement preventative measures to minimize packaging waste[59] and to ensure that within three years all packaging complies with certain essential requirements on composition and design specified in Annex II of the directive.[60]

The directive has been criticized by some member states, environmentalists, and consumer groups as inadequate and preferential to industry in numerous respects. First, Denmark, Germany, and the Netherlands favoured the adoption of a strict hierarchy of recovery methods that would restrict incineration as a method of last resort. Other countries preferred incineration as more cost effective than recycling.[61] Second, Belgium objected to the Parliament's amendment calling for the adoption of economic instruments, including eco-taxes, by the Council. Belgium was concerned that the EU eco-

---

[53] Directive, Article 7.   [54] Directive, Article 8.   [55] Directive, Article 12.
[56] Directive, Article 9.
[57] Directive, Article 15. The original text of the directive would have authorized member states to use 'economic instruments' (such as eco-taxes or fees) so long as they did not conflict with Council measures, distort competition, create obstacles to trade, impose disproportionate burdens, or discriminate against particular products. During the second reading, the Parliament amended the proposed directive to call on the adoption of uniform economic instruments by the Council. This amendment became a principle point of contention in the Council and required a conciliation procedure.
[58] Directive, Article 18.   [59] Directive, Article 4.   [60] Directive, Article 9.
[61] The Commission argued that the appropriateness of requiring refillable containers or recycling or heat generation depends upon the availability of water and alternative energy sources and the cost of transporting refillable containers back to the place of manufacture. For example, France has invested heavily in incineration for energy generation. *Environment Official Denounces Calls for Environmental Rule Moratorium*, INT'L ENV. DAILY (BNA), Oct. 18, 1993.

taxes would displace the national eco-taxes to be levied on non-recyclable packaging and products in Belgium.[62] This provision was changed during the conciliation procedure to permit Belgium to levy eco-taxes. Third, Greens and Denmark, Germany, and the Netherlands expressed concern that the Commission could compel them to lower existing standards to comply with the harmonized standard.[63] It is unclear whether the Commission will in fact require member states to reduce higher standards.[64] Fourth, the Benelux countries, Germany, and the Greens generally complain that the directive would give countries too much discretion in certain respects.[65]

Though the directive was adopted by a qualified majority of the Council, it remains controversial. Some Greens bitterly criticize the directive as a sell-out to industry.[66] It is true that industry aggressively lobbied the Parliament to stop the efforts of the Greens to tighten the directive and has responded positively to the directive's adoption.[67] There is a risk that Germany's

[62] As Council President, Belgium had strongly supported the proposed directive, but following the European Parliament's amendments, domestic political opposition forced the Belgian Government to withhold its support in the Council. *Belgian Ministers to Consider Compromise Text, The Reuter Eur. Community Rep.*, June 9, 1994; *Belgium Forces Conciliation for Packaging Directive, The Reuter Eur. Community Rep.*, June 8, 1994.

[63] Germany, Denmark, and the Netherlands argued unsuccessfully that under the Maastricht Treaty, environmental concerns take priority over harmonization. The Dutch Environment Minister Hans Alders described the maximum limits on recovery of packaging waste as 'ridiculous' and argued that if it takes effect 'We'll have to drop 35–40 per cent of recycled glass in landfill.' *Divided EU Agrees on Packaging Directive, Int'l Env. Daily* (BNA), Jan. 11, 1994. The proposed directive had imposed uniform targets for the first five years for recovery and recycling of 60 per cent and 40 per cent, respectively, and for ten years, 90 per cent and 60 per cent, respectively. Under the Belgian presidency, the Council decided to amend these uniform targets with a range that would allow member states to take into consideration their special circumstances. However, Denmark, Germany, and the Netherlands already have legislated standards in excess of the high range permitted by the directive. This led to the adoption of Article 6, allowing higher standards subject to the Commission's approval.

[64] Article 100a(4) of the Treaty provides that if a member state deems it necessary to apply national measures to protect the environment which do not conform to a harmonization measure, the member state must inform the Commission which 'shall confirm the provisions involved after having verified that they are not a means of arbitrary discrimination or a disguised restriction on trade between Member States.' Arguably, the Commission would have no discretion to refuse to confirm the packaging regulations adopted by Germany or Denmark merely because they deviate from the proposed directive. The Court has recently ruled that in applying Article 100a(4) the Commission must give a clear statement of its reasons as to why a derogation should be permitted. France v. Commission, C–41/93, May 17, 1994, (annulling a Commission decision allowing Germany to impose tighter restrictions on pentachlorophenol in certain products than were permitted by EU Directive 76/769/EEC on the harmonization of laws concerning certain dangerous substances).

[65] For example, some wanted the directive to require producers to be responsible for collecting and recovering waste either by charging a deposit or arranging for collection at the point of sale or establishing a consortium of European producers to collect and recover waste. Others wanted the directive to provide for minimum levels of reuse of packaging.

[66] *See, e.g., Packaging Waste: Parliament Backs Council Position with a 'Disappointing' Vote, Eur. Env't*, No. 432, May 17, 1994; *Greenpeace Accuses Belgium of Sabotaging 'Packaging' Directive, Eur. Env't*, No. 422, Dec. 14, 1993; *Greenpeace Criticizes Belgian Push on Packaging Directive, The Reuter Eur. Community Rep.*, Nov. 30, 1993.

packaging regulations in Germany, the Netherlands, and Denmark may be weakened by the Commission if it determines that their requirements distort competition or obstruct the internal market. One could also point out that paradoxically while market competition led to higher regulatory standards among EU members, the intervention of the EU may ultimately lower requirements for recycling. It is tempting to describe the outcome of this debate as one more example in which the regulatory authority was captured by industry. It is equally true that for at least Ireland, Greece, Portugal, Spain, and the UK, the adoption of a directive will raise regulatory standards significantly, and that the assertion of a legitimate EU interest in the waste problem generally opens the way for future regulation. Moreover, the adoption of an EU packaging directive will have a powerful demonstration effect on countries outside the EU, including the USA, that must adapt their exports to meet EU packaging and marketing standards.

The interaction of member states, EU technocrats, Greens, and industry led to a different outcome than the conventional paradigm of a race to the bottom would anticipate. The movement of capital from high-regulatory jurisdictions to low-regulatory jurisdictions was not the decisive force in the outcome of this debate. In actuality, the relationships of public and private, municipal and international, consumers and producers, workers and investors, technocrats and politicians, were more complex and less predictable than regulatory competition theory takes into account.

Several factors might explain why packaging waste regulations expanded throughout the EU. Certainly, one factor was that the regulations were implemented at the point of consumption rather than at the point of production, so that all producers selling in the same market were subject to the same requirements and could not opt out of them. Another factor, was that the regulation conferred certain benefits on some producers, namely recyclers and some packagers, who then had an interest in supporting such regulation. A third factor was that the packaging and recycling industries were able to pass the costs of regulation on to consumers without fear of foreign competition, and fourth, consumers were willing to pay the costs of such regulation because of a high level of green consciousness. Finally, the opportunity of green parties and organizations to participate in the democratic process created a powerful voice in favor of increased regulation.

5. CONCLUSION

This description of the interaction of public and private parties in the legislative processes in the member states boldly contradicts the conventional

---

[67] *E.g., ACE Applauds EU Packaging Directive Position, Eur. Env't,* March 31, 1994, No. 429.

assumptions that market actors engaged in free trade drive down regulatory standards. The Dutch and German packaging programmes triggered a reaction in other EU member states based on both political and economic considerations. In every case where packaging regulations have been proposed, the state has relied upon industry in their formulation and implementation. In France, the UK, and Belgium, industry has been crucial in lobbying for the packaging laws. Industry on the whole has been generally supportive of packaging regulations where they have been enacted. Contrary to the conventional paradigm of a race to the bottom, private actors engaged in a competitive regulatory market were integral to raising national regulatory standards.

The reaction of the EU to the competitive regulatory process contradicted the assumption that harmonization/centralization would secure a higher level of regulation overall. The EU Commission viewed the national competitive regulatory process as threatening to the free flow of goods within the EU. Though the Commission and the Parliament shared at least in part the environmental concerns of the Dutch and Germans, their influence on the Council proved inadequate to secure a higher level of regulation. Instead, member states with lower living standards or less sensitivity toward the solid waste problem were able to adopt a Council directive that could have the effect of lowering existing regulatory standards in the Netherlands and Germany. The establishment of a non-competitive regulatory market through the EU harmonization process, contrary to the conventional paradigm, resulted in lower regulatory standards than the standards prevailing in a competitive regulatory régime.

The example of packaging waste regulation in the EU should not lead us to a benign view of regulatory competition. Regulatory competition raised standards in this case because the regulation was implemented at the point of consumption rather than at the point of production, the regulation conferred economic benefits on some producers who were able to pass on higher costs to willing consumers, and the national governments were responsive to green parties and economic interests that favoured regulation. Such conditions may not exist in every case. The point is that the conventional model of regulatory competition and the harmonization/centralization strategy are too simplistic to be predictive. A better theory of regulatory competition would take account of the multi-dimentional interaction of public regulators and market actors in designing strategies to preserve regulatory standards in a global market.

13

Institutional Competition and Coordination in the Process of Telecommunications Liberalization

COLIN SCOTT*

I. INTRODUCTION

The United States of America (USA) and the European Union (EU) face the same set of basic issues in telecommunications policy. Both must respond to and support technological and economic changes affecting the telecommunications industry, in particular the convergence of telecommunications, computing and broadcasting, so as to assure the greatest possible yield of benefits to the widest possible distribution. Yet, despite this common objective, the telecommunications policies of the USA and the EU differ in significant respects. Some of these differences can be explained without reference to regulatory institutions—disparate demographic, geographical, and socio-economic factors ordinarily lead to disparate policy choices. But the magnitude of these differences is not sufficiently great to provide the basis for a complete account of the dissimilarities in the paths taken by the telecommunications policies of the USA and the EU. Reference also must be made to the institutional environments, for institutional factors operate in conjunction with decisions about optimal policy choices to shape the development of regulatory policy (Bulmer 1994*b*; Levy and Spiller 1994: 205; Thatcher 1992).

This chapter juxtaposes the experience of the USA and the EU in telecommunications regulation to show how distinctive constitutional and institutional arrangements have led to contrasting policy outcomes (see also Cappelletti and others 1986: 5–12). More particularly, this chapter explores how tensions between actors in the regulatory environment (Irwin 1988) shape their use of regulatory institutions. It thus concerns itself with

* Some of the Research for this paper was carried out while I was a British Telecom Academic Fellow in Law. Other parts of the paper were initially presented at the Centre for the Study of Regulated Industries conference 'Regulating Telecommunications—an International Assessment of Prospects and Strategy', London, March 1994. I am grateful to Imelda Maher, Peter Muchlinski and Wolf Sauter for comments on earlier drafts and to Bill Bratton for extensive editorial assistance.

regulatory competition, but as an institutional rather than economic phenomenon. The tensions it describes can arise horizontally, for example
where both executive agencies and courts have a role in a particular sphere
but work at cross purposes. Tensions can also arise in vertical regulatory
relationships, as where state and federal governments use their powers in
contradictory ways in a sphere of shared jurisdiction (Jacobs and Karst
1986: 225–238). Sometimes these tensions persist, with the regulatory régime
subsuming and reflecting ongoing conflict between the governing institutions. At other times they are resolved through institutional coordination or
legislative intervention. The tensions and the problems of institutional competition and coordination to which they lead, can be identified at three
levels: (i) at the level of constitutional structure, in particular from the operation of rules governing the allocation of powers; (ii) at the level of institutional arrangements, as the result of the practices of and relations between
executives, legislatures, regulatory agencies and courts sharing jurisdiction
in some degree, whether horizontally or vertically; and (iii) at the level of
policy articulation, as discourse among actors both inside and outside of
government determines the dominant values and objectives lying behind
policies.[1]

At the broadest constitutional and institutional levels, the structural outlines of state activity in the telecommunications sector in the EU and the
USA parallel one another. First, there is shared jurisdiction horizontally in
the USA at the Federal level and in the EU at the Union level, and vertical shared jurisdiction between Federal/Union institutions and those of the
States/Member States. Second, policy objectives have been substantially
institutionalized through constitutional or legislative arrangements in both
the USA and the EU. Third, both jurisdictions have created separate regulatory arrangements for the telecommunications sector while simultaneously
applying distinctive sets of antitrust/competition rules. These parallel regulatory institutions can, however, diverge in their treatment of telecommunications policy due to some fundamental differences between their
institutional agendas and operations. First, telecommunications policy
objectives tend to reflect difference in the relative maturity of the federal
institutions of the USA and the EU. The EU continues to direct itself
towards market integration and the completion of the Single European
Market (SEM), seeking to institutionalize a dynamic of further integration
together with the development of institutions for whom this objective is
their *raison d'etre*. These concerns no longer bear on the evolution of policy under the mature constitutional arrangements of the USA. Second,
juridical and political authorities play different roles in the resolution of

---

[1] The broadest form of institutional perspectives would characterise each of these constitutional, institutional and policy factors as 'institutional in character'. See Powell and di Maggio
(1991).

constitutional tensions in the two jurisdictions. In the constitutional arrangements of the USA the federal courts have played a key role in defining and shaping jurisdictions. In the EU constitutional tensions are more usually, though not always, resolved by political means. Third, although the interplay between a specific telecommunications régime and general antitrust principles has been a central and dynamic factor in shaping policy in both the USA and the EU, these overlapping regulatory institutions have different relative influences and characteristics in each jurisdiction. In the USA the liberalization of the sector was accompanied by a shift from administrative to judicial control as jurisdiction was gradually removed from the telecommunications regulatory agency and relocated in the distinct antitrust system. In the EU telecommunications and competition regulation overlap significantly, with the European Commission playing a key role as to both. Finally, interest group influence comes to bear more forcefully on the USA régime. Lobbyists have a more entrenched role in the USA telecommunications policy,[2] although EU policy making does appear to be more open to those lobbyists who secure entry to the inner policy circle (Mazey and Richardson 1994).

A broad parallel can also be drawn between the USA and the EU telecommunications régimes at the level of policy. Both régimes have been shaped by tensions between the liberalization movement and countervailing economic, political and social constraints. A remarkably stable model of protected monopoly shaped the USA scheme of regulated private ownership and the predominant European scheme of public ownership from the 1920s to the 1970s (Davies 1994; Mayer 1989). This model followed from a 'public service paradigm' (Dyson and Humphreys 1990: 6–7) of the economics of telecommunications. This assumed that any service based around a capital intensive network is likely to be subject to economies of scale (Foreman-Peck and Millward 1994: chapter 1), and that a natural monopoly results where such economies increase up to the point at which demand is satisfied. State protection of the natural monopoly from entry by other, cream-skimming service providers is required because of the social importance of the service provided. State protection in turn calls for regulation of the dominant incumbent to prevent abuse of monopoly position. These economic assumptions, correct or not, shaped political perceptions that telecommunications was rightly a monopolistic sector (cf., Davies 1994), until changes in the political climate and technological conditions brought the assumptions under attack in the 1970s. Today the natural monopoly characteristic is no longer thought to hold true for telecommunications.

---

[2] Trebing (1989: 93–94 has identified three major groups who have been involved in pressing the logic of liberalization: large volume users wanting new suppliers and monopsonistic deals; new market entrants; and incumbent carriers seeking to diversify.

Regulators look for competitive benefits in the provision of services and in substantial parts (and possibly all) of the provision of infrastructure.

On both sides of the Atlantic the shift of the underlying economic paradigm caused the former policy model based on coordination of networks through public ownership and regulated private monopoly to give way to a mixed pattern of competition and coordination (Noam 1994: 454). A number of common policy imperatives can be discerned. Vital conditions of competition, such as interconnection to existing networks, need to be provided through regulation. Standards in relation to equipment and networks have to be sufficiently uniform to permit connection of equipment and interconnection of services without threatening network integrity. Protective regulation is needed to prevent dominant incumbents from abusing their historically derived monopoly advantages. The incumbents' preexisting vertical integration complicates the exercise of articulating the terms of access to their systems by new competitors. Regulation accordingly seeks to achieve transparency in the economics of systems operations. Price controls have been imposed on the incumbents, both to assure competitive access and to assure the continuation of valuable social (and economic) benefits through the maintenance of the universal service obligation which has historically been associated with telecommunications monopolies. Coordination is required to ensure that the infrastructure is paid for through service charges, a relatively simple proposition under conditions of monopoly, but less simple in a competitive régime. Finally, policy makers on both sides of the Atlantic have sought to maintain or develop telecommunications firms able to compete in a global market (Hills 1986: 20). This is reflected partly in support for research and development in telecommunications, information technologies and new broadcasting technologies. But this concern is also evident in competition policies which permit or encourage alliances and mergers which are designed to increase the research capacity of the firms involved, to permit firms to meet the global requirements of their customers, or to combine expertise from more than one sector, for example in telecommunications and computing or telecommunications and broadcasting.[3]

---

[3] A number of factors lie behind the current wave of merger activity and alliance forging in global telecommunications. Increasing domestic competition is forcing threatened dominant incumbents, such as AT&T and BT to seek new markets, typically through alliances with firms already established in the target market. Such alliances exploit both the regulatory position and the market knowledge of the partner. The BT-MCI strategic alliance provides an example of this. Convergence of telecommunications, broadcasting, and computing technologies is fostering alliances and mergers designed to exploit complementary expertise and markets. The Time Warner/Telewest alliance provides an example. Furthermore there are incentives to develop complementary market power in relation to infrastructure, as has been seen in potential telecommunications/cable tv mergers, and the proposed AT&T/McCaw merger which combines fixed and mobile infrastructure. On the demand side multinational enterprises increasingly require global service provision, which is being met through consortia of

2. CONSTITUTIONAL ARRANGEMENTS

In the USA constitutional principles govern the allocation of powers between the various Federal and State institutions. The various treaties governing the establishment and operation of the European Community are strictly speaking conventions. However they create a form of constitutional order and are treated as so doing in this chapter (Harden 1994; Wincott 1994). But, whereas the United States of America has a federal constitution, the EC has hybrid arrangements. Contrary to our expectations of a federal system the Member States play an important part in the political and legislative processes, making its organisation closer to that of an international body such as the United Nations (Cappelletti and others 1986: 29; Dehousse 1992: 388, 390; Majone 1992: 301). At the same time the interpretive activities of the European Court of Justice (ECJ) have resulted in the evolution of a system of constitutional jurisprudence which is closer to that of a federal system (Cappelletti and others 1986: 29; Elazar and Greilsammer 1986: 102). The USA Constitution represents a mature settlement in which established principles govern allocation of powers and protection of property rights. These principles form an important, but now substantially uncontested feature of telecommunications law and policy. Although there is evidence of maturity in the constitutional principles of the European Community (Cappelletti and others 1986: 11) the Community nevertheless continues to evolve and experience significant shifts in processes and doctrines, both through Treaty amendments and through the activities of the key institutional players. The concept of 'integration' that encapsulates the evolutionary character of the Community 'has lost much of its relevance for today's mature federal system in the United States' (Jacobs and Karst 1986: 170).

With regard to economic regulation in the USA the central power is the interstate commerce clause in article I of section 8 of the Constitution. This gives Congress the power to 'regulate commerce . . . among the several states . . .' and the power to make all necessary legislation to exercise that power has been inferred. The jurisdiction of the states is derived from their general common law powers to police activities within their borders, a power that has long been recognised by the federal courts (10th amendment). The Constitution and federal laws prevail over state laws (Article VI). Historically the courts have developed a theory of activities affected by a public interest which justifies more extensive intervention by the government than would be permitted under the literal terms of the Constitution.

telecommunications firms. Alliances such as those forged between BT and MCI, and Sprint, Deutsche Telekom, and France Telecom raise important policy issues for both the EU and the USA. These policy issues are being mediated through the existing institutions of telecommunications regulation and competition policy.

(Letwin 1965: chapter 2; Phillips 1988). The case law has progressively drawn the doctrine more widely so that potentially all modern business may be subject to regulation, though the most extensive intervention has been developed in the case of the utilities (Phillips 1988: 108). There is also a long tradition of independent regulatory agencies in the United States (Graham and Prosser 1991: 220–231), though the extent of true independence of agencies from the executive has varied over time (Majone 1993: 12, 19). The agency system has its critics: Excessive proceduralization of the regulatory process, together with the extensive scope of judicial review of agency decisions have resulted in slow regulation (Graham and Prosser 1991; Phillips 1988). Regulation in the telecommunications sectors is not only slow but fragmented. This by-product of the liberalization process has created attendant opportunities for regulatees to play one regulator off another (Irwin 1988: 13; for Canada cf., Schultz and Janisch 1993). Regulatory jurisdiction is split between the Federal Communications Commission (FCC), State Public Utilities Commissions (SPUCs), the Department of Justice (DOJ) Antitrust Division, the courts (with both antitrust and administrative law jurisdictions), various other federal departments and both state and federal legislatures. Congress holds frequent hearings concerning the problems of fragmented jurisdiction, and has made many attempts to legislate for consolidation have to date not met with success (Grudus 1993: 121; Irwin 1988: 14; Johnson 1992).[4]

The EC Treaty does not directly refer to telecommunications at all, and consequently any action by the Community in this area must be justified by the more general Treaty objectives relating to the completion of the internal market, competition policy, promotion of research and development, development of trans-European networks, and so on. But the Treaty is not self-interpreting in terms of the direction of integrating measures, and consequently considerable space has been filled by the interplay of the institutions.[5] The EU is substantially dependent on the Member States for revenue and only has very limited resources. The Commission accordingly has sought to develop its influence through low cost measures, in particular through the development of regulation, rather than through expenditure programmes (Dehousse 1992: 389; Majone 1992: 304–5, but cf., Peters 1992). It

---

[4] After the conclusion of the text of this chapter Congress agreed to a new Telecommunications Act in February 1996 which introduces both substantive new regulatory principles based on liberalization policies, together with new institutional arrangements, including more extensive rights of preemption for the FCC, and a Joint Federal-State Board to provide for vertical coordination.

[5] The liberalization of markets anticipated by the internal market objective (Article 3(c)) is not necessarily consistent with objectives relating to 'the strengthening of economic and social cohesion' (art. 3(j) and see arts 130a, 130b, 130c, 130d, 130e), 'the promotion of research and technological development' (art. 3(m) and see art. 130, and Title XV) and the' encouragement for the establishment and development of trans-European networks' (art. 3(n) and see also arts 129b, 129c, 129d).

has had to work past constitutional barriers in so doing. The EU institutions have no direct powers of legislation affecting the firms and citizens in the Union. Although the EC Treaty has some provisions that are directly applicable (notably the Competition Title), and the European Court of Justice has sought to develop principles, such as the doctrine of supremacy of EC law, that ensure the acceptance and effectiveness of EC law more generally, the EU is substantially dependent on the Member States to implement Community legislation (Dehousse 1992: 392; Majone 1992: 301). The European Commission uses its limited powers to the fullest extent possible, to initiate policies, to enforce directives against the Member States (Article 169, EC Treaty) and in interpreting and enforcing the competition rules (Articles 85–92, EC Treaty) (Docksey and Williams 1994). The institutional balance has been further tilted towards the Member States by the inclusion of the subsidiarity principle in Article 3b the Treaty on European Union (1992). This principle seeks to resolve the vertical tension between Community and Member State institutions by requiring that regulatory measures are developed, implemented and enforced at the lowest level consistent with effectiveness. This requires in many fields that standard setting and enforcement be carried out by the Member States or by private bodies, and creates the potential that Member States may compete with each other to provide the most favourable business environment, with the Community institutions having a coordinating role only (McGowan and Seabright 1995). The delegation of extensive policy making, fact finding and enforcement powers to independent regulatory agencies, so common in the USA, is alien to most of the Member States, and has to date played little role in the development of regulatory policy (Dehousse 1992: 389, 391; Majone 1993: 28–29). There are however signs of institutional change both at Community level and in the Member States, which have been required to separate operation of telecommunications services from their regulation as one aspect of liberalization of services. Finally it should be noted that directly effective EC law is enforceable at the suit of nationals of the Member States in domestic courts. This means that it is possible for an actual or potential competitor to enforce the competition rules through litigation in national courts.

In the EU jurisdiction for telecommunications is shared between a number of Directorates-General within the Commission, (notably those responsible for Industrial Policy (DG III), Competition Policy (DG IV) and Telecommunications (DG XIII)), the Council of Ministers (the main legislative body of the Community), the courts (the European Court of Justice and the Court of First Instance (which hears appeals from the Commission on competition matters)), and the European Parliament, (which has greater power in the legislative process since the coming into force of the Treaty on European Union (1992)). The Commission's efforts to secure integration of markets through liberalization have had crucial support from the jurisprudence developed by the Court of Justice (Fuchs 1994: 34), which was for many years perceived as more successful than the Commission in advancing the task of integration. The European Union has only a short history of involvement with the telecommunications sector, and virtually no experience of direct regulation of firms in the sector, because of the fact that its jurisdiction is chiefly exercised through the issue of directives applicable to the Member States. Consequently there is no European regulatory agency for telecommunications equivalent to the USA Federal Communications Commission. Policy tensions between promotion of competition and promotion of coordination in telecommunications regulation are reflected within the EU's institutions. Within the Commission itself some DGs such as DGs III, XV (Internal Market) and DG IV (Competition) may be perceived as pursuing competitive policies which are at odds with the coordinating policies of DG XIII, which is responsible for telecommunications (Collins 1994: 92; Thimm 1992: 151). Even as between DG III and DG IV resolution of tensions between industrial and competition policy required some bridge-building activities by the relevant commissioners in the 1990s (McGowan and Wilks 1994: 30). The coordinating tendencies are sometimes less clear than the competitive policies, but are reflected in aspects of the internal market policy which seek to harmonize or approximate regulatory instruments to create a level playing field, the promotion through funding, and hence direction of research and development of key strategic sectors, the promotion of trans-European networks, in energy, transport and communications, and the pursuit of the benefits of the Community's objectives for all the citizens of the Union through programmes of expenditure directed towards regional policy and social cohesion.

3. DEREGULATION AND THE FEDERAL COMMUNICATIONS COMMISSION

The Communications Act 1934[6] established the Federal Communications Commission and gave it the usual range of regulatory powers in respect of interstate and foreign telecommunications (Association 1992: 1045).[7] Thus the FCC has power to regulate market entry, terms and conditions of service, interconnection, construction, and accounting practices. Liberalization has involved the breaking down of this jurisdiction and gradual shift in the ideology of the FCC away from monopolistic assumptions to a world-view closer to that of the antitrust authorities. The State Public Utility

[6] (as amended) (47 USC sections 151–757 (1988)). See also the amendment introduced by the Telecommunications Act of 1996.
[7] For details of the organisation and rule making and adjudicatory procedures of the FCC see (Hilliard 1991).

Commissions have been much slower to reject the monopolistic assumption, thereby creating considerable tension. Liberalization does not necessarily imply deregulation, and in fact the regulatory environment in the USA is more complex than it was at a time when the private monopoly dominated the USA market. The USA market is still highly regulated, with price regulation extending to AT&T's long distance rates, and local telephone companies interstate access rates, and all aspects of intrastate telephone services. The only fully deregulated and detariffed sector prior to the passage of the 1996 Telecommunications Act was Customer Premises Equipment, although even that is subject to the standardizing influence of the Open Network Architecture Order (Crandall 1991*b*: 71).

Antitrust law has been a principal tool in the USA movement to liberalize telecommunications, and its employment has increased the prominence of judicial enforcement in the overall regulatory framework. The institutional shift may be explained partly by a shift in emphasis of entry control, from a policy of restricting market entry to a policy of encouraging it. Where the entry policy is geared towards restriction, then negotiation between regulatory authorities and the protected monopolists may be the appropriate means to control the market. Where, however, there is a shift in policy from restriction to promotion of entry, as we have seen gradually occurring in the USA over the last thirty years, judicial enforcement may be a more appropriate means to tame a dominant incumbent (Gist 1988: 247–9). The shift from control to promotion of entry also has caused the telecommunications regulators to begin to adopt the procedures and thinking of the competition authorities. This effect has been quite marked at the Federal level (Gist 1988: 248; Peters 1985: 266).

The FCC has used two main techniques to liberalize the sector. First it has progressively used rulemaking powers to remove constraints on market entry in different sectors of the market. Secondly it has progressively removed regulatory requirements from all but the dominant common carriers in those sectors where the effects of competition are not sufficiently strong to justify full deregulation. Thus deregulation has partly been achieved by removing activities from the scope of common carriage, which forms the main subject of regulation under the Communications Act 1934, and partly by developing less-stringent regulatory requirements for non-dominant carriers. The courts have provided support for these strategies, ordering structural separation of the dominant carrier to prevent hidden cross-subsidy between monopolized and competitive parts of the sector. The effects of these strategies have been to allow those whose interests would be promoted by legislation to argue their cases strongly in the hearings which form part of the decision making progress, and increasingly to open the telecommunications sector to the scrutiny of the antitrust authorities in those sectors which are substantially deregulated.

This progressive liberalization began in 1959 with a decision that private companies (i.e., not common carriers) could use microwave frequencies above 890 Mc to carry telecommunication signals.[8] Microwave Communications Inc (MCI) sought to exploit the liberalizing regulatory climate and after much delay was granted permission by the FCC to establish a private point to point service as a specialized common carrier.[9] In 1971 the FCC announced a policy of free market entry for such specialized common carriers, although the scope of permitted interconnection with the nationwide switched network remained unclear (Phillips 1988: 697–9).[10] The FCC made an order clarifying this in 1977 and has increasingly preempted state jurisdiction over terms and conditions of interconnection. When, however, MCI and Southern Pacific sought to offer long distance switched services in 1976, the FCC determined that this exceeded the 1971 authorizations. Furthermore in 1978 the FCC determined that AT&T did not have any obligation to provide interconnection of switched services. Both decisions were reversed by courts which are keener to liberalize than the FCC. As a result the FCC, MCI, and AT&T made new agreements on tariffs in 1979 (Phillips 1988: 703). Further liberalization was achieved in the FCC's Computer II decision in 1980. This separated basic from enhanced services and determined that neither enhanced services nor customer premise equipment (CPE) needed be regulated as common carriage. Basic services were defined as the movement of information, whether voice, data, or video. Common carriers were to be allowed to offer enhanced and CPE services, but in AT&T's case only through separate but unregulated subsidiaries (Phillips 1988: 704–706).[11] Customer Premises Equipment (CPE) was liberalized gradually, starting with the *Carterfone* decision in 1968 which held AT&T's tariff to be unlawful since it prohibited 'the use of interconnecting devices which did not adversely affect the telephone system' (Phillips 1988: 700). Continuing problems with AT&T obstructing deregulation by claiming that there was risk of damage to the network were gradually overcome. CPE was finally unbundled and detariffed in 1982.[12]

The concept of the dominant common carrier has emerged as the focal point of this liberalized régime of telecommunications regulation.This follows from the threat of anticompetitive abuse of inherited market position by the dominant firm. For other common carriers many of the regulatory rules have been waived,[13] and under conditions of progressive deregulation

---

[8] *Above 890*, 27 FCC 359 (1959).

[9] *Microwave Communications Inc*, 18 FCC 2d 953 (1969).

[10] 28 FCC 2d 267 (1971).   [11] *Second Computer Inquiry*, 77 FCC 2d 384 (1980).

[12] (See 47 CFR pt 68).

[13] For example, provision of interstate service as a common carrier generally requires authorization from the FCC (USC 47 section 214 and 47 CFR pt 63). Section 214 requires authorization for construction of all new lines, extension of lines, transmission over lines, etc. The main purpose of this provision is to prevent unnecessary duplication of service. although the economics of the sector no longer seems to justify such a rationale. A further rationale for such close regulation is that the traditional rate of return regulation requires the FCC to be able to

antitrust rules have become the main regulatory control over the dominant carriers, seeking to prevent vertically integrated large players from using profits and other opportunities presented by participation in the regulated market to compete unfairly in the unregulated market. This gives rise to a technical problem since it is difficult for regulators to verify internal transfer prices in integrated enterprises and makes it possible for regulatees to hide monopoly profits in unregulated operations (Stelzer and Schmalensee 1983: 255). Predatory pricing may also occur. The 1982 Modified Final Judgement in the AT&T case (noted below) used structural separation in order to achieve the objective of securing competition in the long distance market. However the FCC has increasingly sought to use accounting separation and interconnection rules to prevent cross-subsidy of unregulated by regulated businesses (Association 1992: 1047). Furthermore, between 1980 and 1985 all interstate carriers except AT&T, the dominant carrier, were deregulated as to entry and price regulation. In 1989 the FCC replaced Rate of Return regulation of AT&T with a UK-style price cap.[14]

Conditions of greater transparency have led to greater intervention respecting the price charged for local access to interexchange services. In many instances provision of access is not profitable. In 1984 the FCC introduced a scheme of rates compensation to be levied by BOCs and local exchange carriers (LECs) to interexchange carriers.[15] This system, known as subscriber line charges, is administered by the National Exchange Carrier Association, which was established for this purpose by the FCC, as a self-regulatory trade association.[16] The scheme envisages both interconnecting long distance carriers and end-users compensating the local exchange carrier or BOC for originating and terminating basic or regulated interstate and international services (Walker and Solomon 1993: 263). These charges are controversial, as they increase the burdens on residential users, thereby damaging the universal service principal, but are defended on the basis that the true costs of the network are reflected in the charges and are therefore economically efficient (Phillips 1988: 218). Measures are included to lessen the impact on residential users in rural and high cost areas.[17]

value the common carriers' assets and any changes to service affect such values (47 USC section 213). In the case of domestic non-dominant carriers (i.e., all domestic carriers except AT&T) a general authorization is now given in respect of domestic interstate services, but such carriers are required to notify the Commission of additional circuits semi-annually (47 CFR section 63.07(a)(b)). It may be noted that foreign carriers have been treated as dominant and regulated accordingly regardless of their market position. Deregulation has taken a similar form in relation filing of rates and the mechanism of hearings to consider filed rates. Regulatory requirements have substantially been removed from all carriers except AT&T.

[14] 47 CFR section 61.41ff; FCC Policy and Rules Concerning Rates for Dominant Carriers, 54 Fed Reg 19836, 8 May 1989) (Black 1993; Ghosh 1988). Rate of return regulation remains for other carriers (for its extent and procedure see 47 CFR part 65).

[15] 48 Fed Reg 10358, Mar 11 1983, as amended 55 Fed Reg 42385, Oct 19 1990; 47 CFR pt 69.

[16] 47 CFR section 69.601 (Phillips 1988: 217-8).   [17] 47 CFR section 69.116.

The FCC's liberalization policies have prompted a series of jurisdictional disputes with state regulatory authorities. These tensions stem from the FCC's view that the policies of most state Public Utilities Commission hinder liberalization by protecting local monopolies and facilitating cross-subsidies. It accordingly has sought to use its authority under the Communications Act 1934 to preempt state regulation.[18] These aggressive exercises of administrative rule making power are subject to judicial review under a set of vague Constitutional standards. Technological changes have added to the difficulties these cases present—the court can no longer rely on a simple historical distinction between intrastate communications, the regulation of which is in the exclusive jurisdiction of the states, and interstate and foreign communications, the regulation of which is in the exclusive jurisdiction of the federal authorities (Huntley 1993: 8). More particularly the FCC has attempted to preempt state jurisdiction where the states have attempted to restrict entry and slow new investment (Galst 1992: 109). The regulation of customer premises equipment (CPE), the only area of full deregulation in the USA, provides an example. CPE is used, of course, for both local and long distance telecommunications services. When the FCC decided to deregulate its provision it successfully preempted state powers of regulation so as to develop Open Network Architecture standards.The FCC has additionally preempted state regulation of rates, though it has of course been unable to do this in respect of local and intrastate rates (Crandall 1991b: 156). The extent of permitted preemption remains contentious. In *Louisiana Public Service Commission* v. *FCC*[19] the Supreme Court held that the FCC could not preempt state set depreciation rates for plant and equipment, even though these were used in both inter and intra-state communications. It was held that the FCC could preempt state jurisdiction only when it directly conflicted with FCC regulation governing the interstate network, thus apparently narrowing the preemption doctrine (Galst 1992: 110).

3.1 Regulation and Antitrust as Mutually Exclusive Régimes

The USA antitrust scheme is based on criminal law, (though with extensive availability of civil remedies under the provisions of the Clayton Act), and enforcement falls to the Federal Department of Justice Antitrust Division, which is dominated by lawyers and litigators. The Antitrust Division has been compared to a specialist law firm taking investigations and prosecutions. It is headed by an Assistant Attorney-General, a political appointment. In contrast with the position of a regulatory agency the Antitrust Division is part of the executive, and may therefore be subject to political influence in

[18] 47 USC sections 152(b), 221(b) (1988).   [19] 476 US 355 (1986).

shaping its priorities and activities (Frazer 1992: 53–54). But political influence activity is not the factor that most sharply distinguishes the application of this regulatory scheme to the telecommunications sector. We must instead look to a unique institutional arrangement. USA telecommunications policy has been shaped and controlled to a significant extent through the exercise of the antitrust jurisdiction of a single judge who sits on the USA District Court for the District of Columbia (Kellogg and others 1992: xxiii). The arrangement stems from a path of historical events. The DOJ has a practice of settling cases by means of judicially approved settlement, the consent decree. The DOJ uses consent decrees because they reduce costs and allow for influence in areas that formally fall outside its jurisdiction. Defending firms have an incentive to consent because the decree avoids a finding of liability in a case where such a finding would provide later civil plaintiffs asserting treble damages claims with a *prima facie* case (Boyer 1983: 905–906). Consent decrees also routinely accord courts the power to retain jurisdiction for possible future modification of the decree's terms. The consent decree in question here was approved by Judge Greene of the District Court of the District of Columbia in 1982 in respect of an antitrust action brought by the DOJ against AT&T in 1974. Judge Greene has employed his continuing jurisdiction under the decree to an unprecedented degree, creating a self-standing regulatory régime based on structural separation. This jurisdiction is only now to be dismantled following the passage of the Telecommunications Act 1996.

As has been noted the operation of antitrust principles has been a factor of considerable importance in the dynamic aspects of USA telecommunications regulation (Baker and Baker 1983: 16–17, 21). The provisions of the Sherman Act and other antitrust legislation operate on the assumption that free and open competition is the goal. The utility sectors have, historically, been based on a regulated natural monopoly model. Where such markets are expressly regulated then that regulation is bound to be in tension with antitrust objectives. Evidence of the way the regulatory scheme shapes the market may be relevant, for example, in assessing whether a defendant wilfully monopolized a market (Phillips 1988: 718–9). In some cases Congress has explicitly exempted the sector from antitrust law (telecommunications mergers, for example, are expressly within the FCC jurisdiction rather than that of the Department of Justice), and in others the courts have held that there is an implied exemption, notably where the sector concerned is subject to express and detailed regulation. In each case exemptions are likely to be a matter of degree and shifts in regulatory policy towards liberalization, as have occurred with federal telecommunications regulation, are likely to lead to a reevaluation of the application of antitrust law. It has been argued that the natural monopoly policy is no longer appropriate to the new competitive era (Phillips 1988: 22–23) and that antitrust law has been a key catalyst for change in the regulatory arrangements (Peters 1985: 275). Indeed, one commentator has argued that the real defendant in the DOJ's action against AT&T was not AT&T but rather a regulatory cartel, of which AT&T was a part, and which included the state public utility commissions and a reluctant FCC (Wenders 1988: 22). The political popularity of the subsidy to local residential users made the break up of this cartel impossible by regular regulatory means, but rather had to be pursued through antitrust (Wenders 1988: 25). The promotion of competition in interstate telecommunications has increasingly shifted the emphasis of regulation away from common carriage regulation by the FCC towards the Department of Justice's antitrust role. In order to invoke the antitrust rules it must be shown that there is competition or an arguable prospect of competition in the area concerned (Baker and Baker 1983: 12–13).

The DOJ has become involved with the telecommunications sector a number of times during the century (Peters 1985). But the critical DOJ intervention occurred in 1974, when the DOJ formally alleged monopolization of the market by AT&T. This action may be seen as part of a wider pattern of DOJ actions challenging vertical integration in both regulated and unregulated markets during this period (Peters 1985: 268): The action, brought under section 2 of the Sherman Act, was based on two key antitrust principles, those of leverage and essential facilities. The leverage allegation claimed that the monopoly of local facilities gave AT&T unfair access to other markets such as intercity service and terminal equipment. The essential facilities (or bottleneck) allegation was based on the refusal of AT&T to grant equal access to competitors of an essential facility, the network (Huntley 1993: 12; Huntley and Pitt 1990: 84–85). The DOJ additionally alleged that AT&T was pricing intercity services without regard to cost, demonstrating that they retained a monopoly and that the FCC was unable to regulate the price effectively. Not only was there a well established cross-subsidy from long-distance to local, but also some predatory pricing in the long distance market, facilitated by a local to long-distance subsidy (Huntley and Pitt 1990: 85). The DOJ sought to find ways to quarantine competitive from monopolistic market to prevent cross-subsidy through structural remedies (Brennan 1987: 756–65; Huntley and Pitt 1990: 86). Four distinct markets were identified: local service (provided by franchised monopolies), long distance (dominated by AT&T, but progressively being deregulated), Customer Premises Equipment (CPE) (deregulated in 1978) and network equipment (in which monopolistic procurement practices favouring Western Electric had allegedly continued). (Huntley 1993: 12–13; Huntley and Pitt 1990: 83–84).

The terms of the Modified Final Judgement (MFJ) approved by Judge Greene were first that AT&T was to divest itself of its local operators. This resulted in the creation in 1984 of seven regional holding companies controlling the Bell Operating Companies (BOCs).[20] Secondly AT&T was to drop the name of Bell. Thirdly the 1956 restrictions on lines of business of AT&T to be dropped, allowing AT&T to enter non-regulated markets (although they were to be prohibited from providing information services for seven years (Huntley 1993: 13)). Fourthly BOCs were to be limited to exchange and exchange access services, customer premises equipment (CPE) and yellow pages, but with ability to apply to District Court for waiver of restrictions in particular services. The concession on CPE and Yellow Pages was provided in order to help the BOCs retain viability at a time when they were loosing the potential for long-distance to local subsidy[21] (Huntley and Pitt 1990: 87). Fifthly BOCs were to provide equal access to all intercity service providers through local loop. In fact only 70% of BOC switches have been converted to provide true equal access to competitors in the long distance market (Huntley 1993: 14; Huntley and Pitt 1990: 91). Unusually the MFJ required the DOJ to report to the District Court every three years, gave the parties power to petition the court for changes to the MFJ, and gave the court the power to act of its own volition, and thereby Judge Greene has retained for the Court continuing jurisdiction over the divestiture and the activities of the new BOCs and the terms of the MFJ generally (Huntley 1993: 13–14; Huntley and Pitt 1990).

William F Baxter, the Assistant Attorney-General who had prosecuted the case and then returned to a law professorship, commented on the MFJ shortly after its approval. According to Baxter, AT&T had the ability to diversify into and distort unregulated markets using its power in the regulated market. The application of 'the AT&T doctrine' which had guided the DOJ was based on four pre-conditions: First that there is a regulated

[20] *U.S.* v. *AT&T*, 552 F. Supp. 131) (DDC 1982), affirmed sub nom *Maryland* v. *U.S.*, 1001 (1983). Assistant Attorney-General Baxter subsequently noted that divestiture was not the only solution to the problems identified, but felt that any other solution, for example accounting separation, would undoubtedly require further regulation (Baxter 1983: 247; Crandall 1991a: 157–8). This would have been against the climate of the times. The effectiveness of the divestiture has been criticised on the basis that Bell system was able to replicate itself, through the creation of the Holding Companies, which created a regional Bell system, and Bell Communications Research (Bellcore) as a national coordinating and research body. Bellcore has no independent companies involved and AT&T is the only interexchange carrier linked to it (Peters 1985: 272).

[21] The issuing of the MFJ was followed by a blizzard of applications from BOCs for waiver of restrictions. Of these application over 160 waivers have been granted, representing 60% of the applications. Following publication in 1987 of The Geodisic Report for the DOJ by Peter Huber the DOJ, to the surprise and consternation of Judge Greene, went back to the District Court and asked for the line of business restrictions to be lifted, on the ground that technological changed had ended the bottleneck (Huntley and Pitt 1990: 93–95). BOCs are still restricted from providing long distance service, but in 1991 the District Court permitted them to provide information services (value added services (VAS)) (Association, 1992: 1045); *U.S.* v. *Western Electric*, 767 F. Supp. 308,332 (DCC, 1991. However the MFJ did give the BOCs some scope for the provision of inter-state services through the creation of 161 Local Access Transport Areas (LATAs). Most state regulators have opposed the creation of competition in the intra-LATA market (Huntley, 1993: 14–15).

monopoly with power in the regulated market through natural monopoly or state entry barriers. Secondly the regulated enterprise must be subject to cost-of-service type rate regulation, constraining its rate of return and costs so as to create an incentive to diversify into unregulated sectors. Thirdly the regulator must have ineffective control over the transactions between the affiliated enterprises. Fourthly the affiliated market must be one that structurally admits of competition (or else nothing is lost if the enterprise takes the whole market) (Baxter 1983: 243–4). Even where all four conditions are present, wrote Baxter, if the benefits of integration in terms of efficiency and coordination exceeded the social costs then the AT&T doctrine would not apply (Baxter 1983: 245). This test is similar to that employed in the EU under Article 90(2) of the EC Treaty (see below).

The USA antitrust régime looks to injured competitors to provide a key mechanism for enforcement of the rules through private actions. The courts have a very wide jurisdiction in granting relief in such actions, and can grant treble damages, injunctive relief or take on more active supervision as Judge Greene did with the MFJ. The availability of treble damages gives incentives to litigants to frame actions in terms of antitrust (Baker and Baker 1983: 36). Fifty such private actions were mounted against AT&T between the 1968 *Carterfone* decision and the MFJ. These resulted in a number of very large jury awards: MCI's action resulted in a jury award of $600m (trebled to $1.8b), though this was reduced on remand to $37.8m (trebled to $113.4m) (Phillips 1988: 714–5). The complaints in these actions bore a familial relationship to the complaint in the DOJ action. One group of plaintiffs was comprised of independent equipment suppliers who claimed that AT&T's interconnection tariffs and procedures prevented them from competing (Peters 1985: 266). There were also actions by competing long distance suppliers who claimed, with less success, that they could not get reasonable access due to the local monopoly (Baker and Baker 1983: 10–11). In each case these actions were grounded on the use by AT&T of its alleged monopoly or dominant position, combined with its deep pockets in one sector of the industry to stifle competition in another as was the DOJ's 1974 action (Baker and Baker 1983: 13).

Recent merger activity has enhanced the role of the Department of Justice. It not only monitors the structure of deals, but also imposes detailed regulations on the merged entity. This occurs at the expense of the jurisdiction of the FCC. The DOJ's power to regulate mergers derives from the Clayton Act.[22] However the exercise of the powers is subject to the same sort of protracted public consultation procedures which come to bear on administrative rule making.[23] Vertical and horizontal mergers are treated by

---

[22] 15 USC 25 .
[23] 15 USC 16(b)–(h) requires a sixty day period in which comments on the proceedings may be made.

application of separate principles. Horizontal mergers may be justified by reference to economies of scope and scale. Vertical mergers are regarded as potentially more threatening, as they are more likely to enhance market power in one part of sector, by exploitation of position in another (Sunshine 1994). In the telecommunications area the DOJ has sought to promote competitive conditions under which the market will reach the most efficient pattern of distribution and marketing of converged voice, data, and video services (Sunshine 1994). This objective is clearly within the classic remit of a competition authority. However, more detailed objectives and instruments are closer in character to those of a telecommunications regulator. These are applied directly to the firms involved in the merger, rather than more universally to all firms in the sector, as would usually be the case with classic industry regulation. These detailed objectives are: (i) avoidance of cross-subsidy (typically from established to new service areas); (ii) prevention of mergers between competing highways (e.g., between cable tv and local telephone companies, at least for the near future); and (iii) monitoring of mergers between highway owners and content owners (in particular to prevent the favouring of programmers by their partners—this may require some form of equal access regulation for programme content in relation to highways (Litan 1994). In the case of the recent AT&T merger with McCaw, the Department of Justice required a significant degree of structural protection for competition. AT&T has a 60 per cent market share of the USA long distance market, and McCaw a 30 per cent share of the cellular market. The consent decree in this case required McCaw subscribers to have equal access to all long distance operators (a restriction which is also placed on the BOCs). Additionally AT&T was prevented from offering local and long distance cellular services as a bundle. They are required to be priced separately (Litan 1994).

4. EC TELECOMMUNICATIONS LAW AND POLICY

Liberalization requires substantial intervention in the Member States' arrangements to protect and regulate their utility sectors. Although the EC Treaty provides the legal basis for such intervention (Articles 37, 90 EC) efforts to realise its potential give rise to considerable political and interpretive difficulties. The establishment of the freedom to provide telecommunications services is likely to permit key industry actors in the technologically more advanced Member States to enter and take a substantial share of business within the markets of the less technologically developed Member States. Thus important national interests are at stake, which may be protected through actions by Member State governments in the Council, through the action of Members of the European Parliament in

modifying or rejecting proposals from the Commission, or through failure
in the Member State governments to properly implement policies. On the
other side of the equation not all Member States continue to pursue
telecommunications policies through state monopolies. Notably the United
Kingdom's policies have demonstrated the possibilities of privatization and
liberalization, and the UK government has vigorously argued for liberalization throughout the Community. Other Member States have also
adopted policies of liberalization, partly in response to the evolving
Community policy.

4.1 The Institutional Framework

The Community jurisdiction over telecommunications has two main legal
sources in the Treaty. These are the instruments of the Community concerned with completion of the internal market (Article 100A EC), which is
exercised by means of Council Directives, which are proposed by the
Commission and agreed by the Council, subject to the negative veto of the
Parliament (Article 189b EC). The other main jurisdiction is in the area of
competition policy. Although there are effectively two jurisdictions over liberalization in telecommunications the dominant actor in each jurisdiction is
the Commission. Within the internal market jurisdiction the Commission
initiates and researches policies prior to presenting them to the Council and
the Parliament. The Commission has no specific regulatory powers in relation to telecommunications. But it does have powers of monitoring, rule-
making and enforcement as part of its competition jurisdiction, and so in
this sense the Commission may be seen to come close to the position of an
independent regulatory agency. Consequently to the extent that the
Commission wishes to pursue policies independently of the Council of
Ministers and the Parliament the competition jurisdiction provides the most
attractive tools, not withstanding the fact that these tools may not be
entirely apt to meet the substantive policy objectives. In addition the use of
the competition jurisdiction is subject to review only by the Court of First
Instance and the European Court of Justice. This factor has resulted in relatively greater power being exercised within the Commission by the competition directorate (DG IV) in relation to telecommunications. Only in the
1980s did the Commission began to develop policies which would employ
its jurisdiction to seek the adjustment of national monopolies to promote
more competitive and open markets with a view to further integration of
the market even in the hitherto protected telecommunication sector. Finally
the Community is dependent on the Member States to properly implement
directives, whether made under the internal market or competition jurisdiction. However the Commission has substantial powers to monitor and
enforce compliance under Article 169 of the Treaty to permit fining of

Member States for failure to follow rulings under Article 169 (Article 171). Community legislation in telecommunications continues to be the subject of actions by the Commission to secure compliance by the Member States (Cullen and Blondeel 1995: 29–39). The problem of non-implementation is as much of a problem in the case of Commission directives, as with the Services Directive, which is the subject matter of proceedings by the Commission against seven countries.[24]

The Bangemann Group recommended in 1994 the development of a Community telecommunications regulatory authority to address the difficulties of coordinating Community telecommunications policy. This new institution might emerge from an existing organisation such as the ONP Committee, which comprises representatives of national regulatory authorities (Sauter 1994*a*). This proposal remains contentious, but it seems possible that a new regulatory institution will emerge at the EU level to monitor and coordinate the implementation of policy, particularly in relation to licensing and interconnection (Sauter 1994*a*). The precise form of any new EU level regulatory institution and the scope of its powers and appropriate instruments remains uncertain (Adonis 1994). Three EU level institutions having some regulatory powers have so far been created to coordinate aspects of telecommunications policy. The 1987 Green Paper resulted in the establishment of a European Telecommunications Standards Institute to speed up and encourage the work of the European Conference on Postal and Telecommunications Administrations (CEPT). ETSI's role has been particularly important in developing the standards of Open Network Provision, which are published by the Commission.[25] Secondly the 1990 ONP directive established the ONP Committee, which comprises representatives from the regulatory authorities of the Member States. Under the 1990 Directive the Committee's tasks are chiefly advisory to the Commission, but has some regulatory powers in relation to adoption of rules for the uniform application of essential requirements, and of cross-frontier standards (Sauter 1994*a*: 142). Additionally the Committee has a conciliatory role in a case where two firms are unable to resolve disputes in relation to application of the ONP directives.[26] However, proposals to extend the regulatory role of the ONP Committee in the draft ONP voice telephony directive contributed to the rejection of the directive by the Parliament on grounds of broader concerns about delegation of regulatory powers to the Commission and committees (Sauter 1994*a*: 143). Third there

[24] See generally the note by the Commission on implementation of Directives OJ C-154/18 6th June 1994, para. 2.2.2.3 Telecommunikations (sic).

[25] See eg OJ 1993 C-219.

[26] In the case of a recent complaint by ESPRIT concerning its request for a leased line between London and Madrid the Committee brought together the complainant the TO (Telefonica) and the regulator and reached a resolution (Cullen and Blondeel 1995: 38–39).

is the Community Telecommunications Committee, which, like the ONP Committee, is made up of representatives of national regulatory authorities and is chiefly advisory to the Commission. These last two committees may form the core of a new European telecommunications agency, but inter-institutional conflicts between the Commission, the Council and the Parliament make it unlikely that this will happen in anything other than an incremental way (Sauter 1994a: 146). It certainly seems unlikely that the Treaty changes necessary to create a new and fully independent regulatory office will be given sufficient priority to succeed at the 1996 Inter-Governmental Conference.

In order to pursue its preference for liberalization the Commission has had to find methods which both leave it with sufficient autonomy to develop policy but which command the support of the other key constituencies, notably the Member State governments and the Parliament. This the Commission has done through the extensive use of thoroughly researched and well-reasoned policy documents, which have given every phase of devel-opment of policy a feel of inevitability, and through the development of its competition jurisdiction. The 1984 Action Plan[27] was followed up by the 1987 Green Paper[28] which proposed a limited liberalization of the sector, setting out plans for a progressive liberalization of the terminal equipment market, progressive liberalization of Valued Added Services (VAS), and separation of regulation from service provision in telecommunications in all the Member States.[29] However, at that time, and crucially to the accept-ability of the policy, the Commission indicated that Member States would be permitted to retain a state monopoly in voice telephony, justified by Article 90(2) EC (see below), a concession which attracted considerable crit-icism (Knieps 1990). Thus terminal equipment and value added services were liberalized while the Member States were permitted, though not required, to continue to protect voice telephony. The Commission also envisaged an increased role for the Competition Title of the EU Treaty in monitoring TOs, in particular for cross-subsidy and abuse of dominant position in relation to manufacturing.

4.2 Internal Market Jurisdiction in the Telecommunications Sector

The key area of policy in telecommunications liberalization which has been pursued through the internal market jurisdiction is in relation to Open Network Provision (ONP). The ONP régime is designed to provide the con-

---

[27] COM(84) 277.
[28] Towards a Dynamic Economy—Green Paper on the Development of the Common Market for Telecommunications Services and Equipment COM 87 290 Final, 30 June 1987.
[29] Ibid.

ditions for liberalization through the definition of principles and standards for access by new competitors to existing telecommunications networks through interconnection (Ungerer 1992). This differs significantly from the USA Open Network Architecture programme, as the former focuses on uniform service requirements on networks, whereas USA policy focuses on technological standardization (Mansell 1993: 72). The form of the EU policy is dictated by the EU's lack of capacity to provide detailed regulation. Rather it provides general principles and leaves standardization issues to more specialized bodies as the CEPT (whose jurisdiction is wider than the EU), to commercial negotiation by service providers, and to emerging national regulatory authorities. A framework directive on Open Network Provision was adopted in 1990.[30] The conditions set out in the Directive include requirements relating to network security and integrity, interoperability and data protection. The target areas identified in the Framework Directive include leased lines, packet- and circuit-switched date services, ISDN, voice telephony, telex, and mobile services.[31] The setting out of general ONP conditions in the 1990 Directive is to be followed by substantive provisions for the various target areas. For the Commission it is imperative that these successive pieces of ONP legislation fit together, the risk being that Council or Parliament amendments to later legislation might render that legislation inconsistent. In these circumstances Commission officials have suggested that the Commission would have to withdraw the proposal (Ravaioli and Sandler 1994: 11).

Legislation covering two of the target areas has been put on the table. The first specific ONP Directive, adopted in 1992, concerned leased lines.[32] It provides, among other things, basic principles of non-discrimination and objective criteria to govern conditions of access and use of leased lines with harmonized technical characteristics in all Member States, basic principles of transparency respecting leased line availability and tariffs, and clear attribution of the task of implementation to national regulatory authorities. It additionally provides a EC level dispute reconciliation procedure (through the ONP Committee) and encouragement to the provision of one-stop ordering and one-stop billing. The Draft Directive on Application of ONP to voice telephony, originally published in August 1992, proposed an interconnection policy guaranteeing access to networks for all providers of voice telephony service on non-discriminatory terms.[33] The provisions respecting the quality demanded of and price charged to licensed service providers accessing the network presented particular difficulties. Here the Commission has had to address the problem created by universal service obligations (USOs) borne by many incumbent operators It recognised that these operators who have such obligations would lose some of the revenue base from which such obligations

---

[30] 90/387/EEC OJ 1990 L192.   [31] Annex 1.
[32] Directive 92/44/EEC, OJ 1992 L165, Corrigendum OJ 1993 L96.
[33] Now adopted Council and Parliament Directive 95/62/EC, L321/6, 30.12.95.

have traditionally been financed, and would therefore need contributions from new competitors who interconnect to the network. The Draft Directive proposed that access charges should be imposed wherever the network operator and the new service provider have different regulatory obligations imposed upon them.[34] Such charges should be cost-oriented, non-discriminatory, fully justified, based on regulatory obligations and approved by a national regulatory authority. The development of such access charges will require radical change in the accounting practices of many telecommunications operators if the necessary degree of transparency is to be achieved to calculate non-discriminatory interconnection and access charges. A common position on the proposal was adopted by the Council in June 1993, but the Directive was rejected by the European Parliament on procedural grounds in June 1994.[35] A new Draft Directive was published in January 1995. Having made its point concerning the procedural issues which rendered the first Draft Directive unacceptable, the European Parliament gave its fullest co-operation to the Commission in securing agreement to the new version.

Following a review in 1992,[36] the Commission made proposals both to consolidate on early legislation under the terms of the 1987 Green Paper outlined above, and to develop new structures to facilitate the completion of a fully liberalized market in all telecommunications services in the Community by 1998.[37] The Commission holds out the development of universal service principles as an incentive to garner the widest possible support for policies of liberalization. Setting standards above current minima in the Member States gives positive incentives to those concerned with the social effects of liberalization, such as the Parliament, to approve the measures. For those Member States which will need to make greatest progress in developing technology, accounting and regulatory structures the means will come in the form of the promise of funding for development of infrastructure from the Community's Structural Funds. In November 1993 the Commission adopted a Communication on universal service in telecommunications, which sets out minimum standards to include the right to have a phone connected, to have clear standards in relation to installation times and repairs, to have clear dispute resolution mechanisms, and to progres-

---

[34] Com(92)247.

[35] This was the first instance of the Parliament rejecting legislation using its new powers under the co-decision or negative assent procedure established by the Treaty on European Union (Sauter 1994b). Article 189b provides that though the Parliament cannot force the Council to accept its changes it can reject a Directive outright (Bradley 1994: 194–6; Macrae 1994: 177). A conciliation procedure establishes a joint committee which has six weeks to attempt to resolve differences between the Parliament and the Council, but if this cannot be achieved the legislation is lost.

[36] SEC(92)1048 Final, 21 October 1992.

[37] Although it was proposed that Member States with smaller and less developed networks were given additional time to meet the liberalization requirements, giving a true date for full liberalization of 2002.

sively gain access to new services.[38] The Commission is now seeking to legislate for USOs with a new Draft Directive on the Application of Open
Network Provision to Voice Telephony, published in January 1995.[39] The
possible methods for financing the USO are canvassed in the second part of
a new Green Paper on Telecommunications Infrastructure. One possible
model is the development of a system of access deficit contributions (ADCs)
which consist of payments from interconnecting TOs to the dominant operator to reflect the dominant operator's losses associated with providing
affordable access to the network for all customers. This approach has been
pioneered in the UK, but the UK Office of Telecommunications has
recently indicated that it may seek to abandon the ADC régime.[40] The alternative possibility, favoured by the Commission, is to create a universal service fund into which all operators must pay and to use this fund to subsidize
those operators who offer to or are required to provide universal service.[41]

The Commission, having secured agreement for the liberalization of voice
telephony, must next address hitherto neglected questions of infrastructure.
Here its strategy is to link it liberalization policy to broader questions of
employment and economic growth. The report of High-Level Group on the
Information Society,[42] established under the White Paper on Growth,
Competitiveness, Employment[43] emphasized the development of new
infrastructure through market mechanisms, and in particular through liberalization of communications. The proposal in the Report that telecommunications and other infrastructures (such as those used by cable television
and by other utilities companies) be liberalized has subsequently been
adopted by the Commission and the Council and will now need legislation.[44]
Article 90(3) has been used as the basis for a General Telecommunications
Liberalization Directive (see footnote 44).

---

[38] Approved by Council Resolution of 7 February 1994 on Universal Service in the
Telecommunications Sector (94/C 48/01). OJ 16.2.94.
[39] Now adopted: European Parliament and Council Directive on the Application of Open
Network Provision (ONP) to Voice Telephony 95/62/EC, L321/6, 30.12.95.
[40] Office of Telecommunications, *A Framework for Effective Competition*, December 1994.
[41] Commission of the European Communities, *Green Paper on the Liberalization of
Telecommunications Infrastructure and Cable Television Networks Part II* COM (94) 682,
January 1995, pp. 85–86. See also the Draft ONP Interconnection Directive, COM (95) 379
Final, OJC 313/7, 24.11.95.
[42] 'The Bangemann Report' available electronically through DG XIII's World Wide Web
server (http: //www.echo.lu/eudocs/en/com-asc.html) and see Commission of the European
Communities *Europe's Way to the Information Society. An Action Plan* COM (94) 347 Final,
July 1994.
[43] COM (94) 700 Final; (Cockbourne 1995: 132).
[44] See Commission of the European Communities, *Green Paper on the Liberalization of
Telecommunications Infrastructure and Cable Television Networks Part I* COM (94)440 Final,
October 1994; *Part II* COM (94) 682 Final, January 1995. See also the General
Telecommunications Liberalization Directive, 96/19/EC, OJL 74/13, 22.3.96.

4.3 Competition Rules in the Telecommunications Sector

The powers of the European Commission come closest to resembling those of a USA federal regulatory agency in the field of competition policy (McGowan and Wilks 1994: 11). The Commission has independently exercisable powers of rule making, investigation and enforcement, subject only to review by the Court of First Instance and/or the European Court of Justice. These powers are governed partly by the EU Treaty directly, and partly by Regulations issued under the Treaty.[45] In practice DG IV carries out investigations and makes recommendations to be agreed by the full Commission. The chief instrument setting out the Commission's procedures and enforcement powers, Regulation 17 of 1962, was originally drafted in such a way that the Advisory Committee (comprised of representatives of the Member States) would have had powers to reject DG IV's proposed course of action prior to its going to the full Commission for agreement. However as finally drafted the Regulation makes that Committee purely advisory and, though its views remain confidential, it is thought the Commission has agreed courses of action in defiance of the Committee's views (Goyder 1992: 44–45). Articles 15 and 16 of the Regulation give the Commission the power to issue fines up to 1 million ECU or 10 per cent of worldwide turnover, whichever is higher, for breach of Articles 85 and 86 (Korah 1994: 127). Furthermore national courts may award damages to individuals and firms affected by breach of the Treaty articles, though this possibility is not widely exploited.[46] In practice the competition jurisdiction is substantially exercised through pre-clearance and exemption mechanisms in relation to co-operative and concentrative agreements. These procedures give the Commission considerable power to shape agreements and mergers (Boyer 1983: 917). Additionally, as is noted above, the Commission has powers under Article 90(3) EC to legislate to clarify the obligations of the Member States in relation to ensuring that any special and exclusive rights given to firms comply with the competition rules (Jacobs and Karst 1986: 188–189; Usher 1994: 53–56).

The competition rules prohibit concerted practices and collusion (Article 85) and the abuse of dominant position (Article 86) by undertakings within

---

[45] Particularly Regulation 17 of 1962 (Goyder 1992: 33–38). The continuing location of such powers with the Commission is being questions by a number of different groups. Proposals for a European Competition Agency, which would take over the investigative powers are likely to be forthcoming(McGowan and Wilks 1994: 31–32).

[46] *Garden Cottage Foods* v. *Milk Marketing Board* [1984] AC 130; (Korah 1994: 131).

the EU which adversely affect competition or trade between the Member States. These provisions are directly effective, and may be enforced by any individual or undertaking in the Community through the domestic courts as well as by the Commission. These provisions, by virtue of their very existence, put pressure on the Commission to choose a strategy for their application to public monopolies in the telecommunications sector. They also give to the Commission an institutional choice as to the means to pursue liberalization. It could proceed either through ad hoc decision making by itself and the ECJ, or by promulgating a distinctive sectoral policy for telecommunications within the Treaty framework (Helm 1993: 6). The Commission chose the latter path. But its hand might eventually have been forced had it done nothing. The dynamic aspects of the Treaty provisions, and in particular the potential for application of the competition rules by private citizens and firms in the courts would possibly have facilitated a substantial degree of liberalization even if the Commission had not developed a sectoral policy. But within DG IV no lack of enthusiasm for liberalization has been evident.

Liberalization of the utilities sectors has been regarded as a key policy in developing the internal market beyond those measures agreed as part of the internal market programme. The Commission first built up its substantive authority under Articles 85 and 86 in ordinary industrial sectors, and then, having built up some institutional confidence, was in a position to expand into the most protected sectors (Gerber 1994; Scott 1996). Furthermore, with the completion of the internal market in other sectors in sight, the Commission needed to broaden its activities to maintain its status. The competition provisions of the EC Treaty may be used both to pursue actions against particular firms, for breach of Articles 85 and 86 (in the manner of a classic competition authority), or to set more general policies either through the grant of exemptions from the effects of Article 85 addressed to firms (under Article 85(3)) or the issue of directives addressed to the Member States (under article 90(3)), for the purpose of clarifying the obligations of the Member States in relation to Articles 85 and 86 (Castellot 1995). The exercise of these latter instruments of more general policy making has been of considerable importance in the telecommunications sector. In using them the Commission has, on more than one occasion, been dependent on the ECJ substantially sharing its view of the interpretation of the Treaty. Such concurrence has been especially important in relation to Article 90, which provides both the key mediating mechanism between the EC competition rules and the protected utilities sectors, and the key jurisdiction for the application of pressure on the protected sectors, without recourse to Council directives (Taylor 1994). Though Article 90 can therefore be as much an instrument of liberalization as of protection, its application today tends to favour liberalization.[47]

A. Application of Competition Rules to Telecommunications Firms

In 1991 the Commission issued a set of guidelines on the application of the competition rules in Articles 85 and 86 to firms in the telecommunications sector.[48] Telecommunications is the only sector in which such guidance has been issued. The guidelines, which address the conduct only of TOs, not of Member States, give specific examples of conduct that amounts to abuse of dominant position by TOs, such as refusal to provide access to the network and cross-subsidization of non-reserved activities. The also indicate that the Commission will welcome joint ventures and may be prepared to grant exemption from the effects of Article 85 (under Article 85(3) where economic benefits outweigh the restriction on competition (Mosteshar 1993: 10).[49] The guidelines thus perform some of the functions of the USA antitrust régime. But there are a number of significant differences, some substantive and others institutional. The guidelines, for example, emphasize the extent to which the Community is prepared to leave public telecommunications operators structurally intact while reducing the scope of their protected monopolies, contrasting with the structural aspects of liberalization in the USA. They also emphasize that the ONP régime is complementary to, and not part of, the competition régime, stressing that competition rules will be interpreted in the light of the developing telecommunications policy. Here they offer a legislative intervention designed to relieve the tension between competition policy and telecommunications policy (for example in relation to agreements on interconnection). They thus put the EU's liberalization process on a path of institutional dualism quite distinct from the present USA division between telecommunications and antitrust régimes. It can be noted, for example, that questions relating to refusal to provide access to essential facilities, dealt with in antitrust law in the USA, are sub-

---

[47] Article 90 provides

1. In the case of public undertakings and undertakings to which Member States grant special or exclusive rights, Member States shall neither enact nor maintain in force any measure contrary to the rules contained in this Treaty, in particular those provided for in Article 7 and Articles 85–94.
2. Undertakings entrusted with the operation of services of general economic interest or having the character of a revenue producing monopoly shall be subject to the rules contained in this Treaty, in particular to the rules on competition, in so far as the application of such rules does not obstruct the performance, in law or in fact, of the particular tasks assigned to them. The development of trade must not be affected to such an extent as would be contrary to the interests of the Community.
3. The Commission shall ensure the application of the provisions of this Article and shall, where necessary, address appropriate directives or decisions to the Member States.'

[48] Guidelines on the application of EEC Competition Rules in the telecommunications sector, 91/C-233/02, OJ C-233/2, 6 September 1991.

[49] Ibid. para. 36.

stantially dealt with in the EU regulatory policies relating to ONP.[50] The guidelines also mark a divergence between the EU and the USA as to the institutional mode of policy implementation. In adopting them the Commission in effect elected to avoid following the USA pattern of pursuing a litigation strategy against individual firms. Instead policy has been set and implemented through guidance and negotiation, combined with the issue of legislation. This appears to be cheaper and more efficient (Gerber 1994: 133) but the efficacy of the policy is dependent on both the quality of administrative activity at Community level and how well legislative provisions are implemented by the Member States.

Some litigation has also gone forward under Articles 85 and 86, but the resultant decisions play only an interstitial role in the liberalization movement. Article 90 figures importantly in this jurisprudence mediating between public service obligations and competition provision in litigation based upon individual infringements of Treaty obligations by public or private firms. Article 90(2) may provide a firm with a defence to such proceedings, but only when it is clear that there is a conflict between the particular task which has been assigned to it and the application of Treaty competition rules (Goyder 1992: 452–9). The Article 90(2) defence gives to courts the extremely difficult task of judging when performance of public obligations justifies breach of the competition rules, a task which might be thought more appropriate to a specialized regulatory agency. The Court has sought to develop a definition of public service obligations in the postal and electricity sectors, the performance of which would justify breach of the competition rules as being necessary to perform those functions.[51] This emerging jurisprudence is one factor which has required the Commission to address the question of universal service obligations in telecommunications directly.

Technological advances and emerging patterns of global competition have caused the regulation of mergers and joint ventures to assume particular importance in telecommunications policy in recent years. Merger control was not provided for in the EEC Treaty, and early attempts by the Commission and the Court to extend the competition jurisdiction to apply to mergers were viewed as artificial and unsatisfactory (Goyder 1992: 386–394). In 1989 the Community responded with the Merger Control

---

[50] This is so notwithstanding the fact that there is a developed jurisprudence in relation to essential facilities in EC competition law (Glasl 1994). See however the Eirpage decision, Commission Decision of 18 October 1992 OJ 1992 L303/22, in which the Commission held that a joint venture between Motorola and Telecom Ireland to create a paging service could be exempted under Article 85(3) provided that Telecom Ireland would provide equal access to new entrants to the market.

[51] Case C 320/91 *Paul Corbeau* [1993] ECR I-2533 (postal services); Case C-393/92 *Almelo* v. *Ijsselmij* [1994] ECR I-1477 (electricity supplies). In the telecommunications sector see *BT: Italy* v. *Commission* Case 41/83 [1985] ECR 873.

Regulation,[52] designed to control the adverse effects on Community trade of concentration through merger. The Merger Control Regulation encourages businesses to structure their affairs either to avoid coming within or to comply with the criteria set down, which are based on control, turnover, and effect on Community trade. The area where jurisdiction is likely to be least certain is joint ventures. If they have concentrative effects they are likely to come under the Merger Regulation, within the jurisdiction of the Merger Task Force, but if they are purely co-operative then they come under Article 85 and the jurisdiction of the operational unit in DG IV which deals with telecommunications. As between these two procedures the merger control procedure is more attractive to firms, as the Commission decision on compatibility lasts indefinitely and the Merger Control Regulation places strict deadlines on the Merger Task Force. Thus firms have an incentive to structure their joint ventures to make them look concentrative. The problem of delay under Article 85(3) has been addressed by the introduction of accelerated procedure for consideration of co-operative joint ventures in 1993, reducing this regulatory distortion to some degree (Castellot 1995: 111). Under either procedure where infringements are found the Commission's practice is to negotiate to find a solution.

The recent strategic alliance between MCI and BT provides an interesting example because it presented competition/antitrust problems to both EU and USA authorities, designed as it was to permit development of global service. The BT-MCI deal entailed (1) the acquisition of BT North America by MCI; (ii) the transfer of a 20 per cent stake in MCI to BT; and (iii) the creation of a joint venture corporation engaging in the provision of value added services to multinational businesses, including the transfer to the joint venture corporation of BT's outsourcing subsidiary, Syncordia, in exchange for a 75 per cent stake. The Commission held that the transaction fell outside the scope of the Merger Regulation on the grounds that the companies involved do not meet the Community-wide thresholds on turnover.[53] However the agreement did fall within the terms of Article 85(1) of the Treaty, in particular because it involved restrictive distribution agreements between the joint ventures corporation and the parties. But these agreements were granted exemption under Article 85(3) on the ground that they would contribute to the improvement of telecommunications services and that the global telecommunications service market was increasingly competitive.[54] For the

---

[52] Reg 4064/89 OJ 1989 L395/1, corrigendum at OJ 1990 L257/14, and see also Merger Policy on Telecommunications, Regulation 4064/89, OJ L 257/13. For an argument relating to the institutional factors shaping the terms of the Regulation see (Bulmer 1994*a*: 433–444).

[53] Decision of 13 September 1993, OJ 1993 C-259.

[54] *BT and MCI* 1994 OJ C-93/3 30 March 1994 [1994] CMLR (Antitrust Cases) 167. The proposed joint venture between Deutsche Telekom and France Telecom has not been so well received the Commission, which apparently perceives it as being designed to exploit the market position of the two national TOs.

DOJ, the dominant position of BT in the UK was seen to present the key antitrust problems, having the potential to reduce competition in the 'seamless global telecommunications' sector and the international correspondence service between the UK and the USA (Sunshine 1994). Potential abuses included vertical price restrictions and non-price restraints such as limiting inter-brand competition, for example between equipment suppliers (Dick 1994). The Department of Justice responded with regulatory requirements relating to transparency. Details of the joint ventures terms and conditions had to be published to allow competitors to identify distortions between costs and prices and complain where such distortions are apparent. Furthermore BT was prevented from sharing with MCI confidential information about MCI's competitors to MCI which had been obtained by BT as dominant national carrier (Litan 1994).

B. Application of Competition Rules to Member States

Article 222's statement that the EC Treaty shall in no way 'prejudice the rules in Member States governing the system of property ownership leaves the Member States free to continue with nationalized industries. However the Member States are required to 'progressively adjust any state monopolies of a commercial character so as to ensure that when the transitional period has ended no discrimination regarding the conditions under which goods are procured and marketed exists between nationals or Member States' (Article 37). Thus, eventually, the competition and procurement régimes are to apply to all sectors which are of a commercial character. The new emphasis of the Commission on regulating the compliance of Member States with competition requirements, particularly in monopolized sectors, has only occurred in 1980s and 1990s (Gerber 1994: 137–8). The most innovative and daring aspect of the Commission's deployment of the competition rules has been the use of the procedure under Article 90(3) providing for Commission directives to clarify the application of the Treaty competition provisions to the Member States. Prior to the issuing of a Commission Directive relating to transparency of public undertakings in 1980[55] Article 90(3) had been regarded as a mechanism for issuing directives to individual Member States in relation to specific incidents of non-compliance with the competition rules, rather than a means whereby directives of general application could be issued (Scott 1996). The Commission used Article 90(3) as the basis for two important telecommunications directives on terminal and services. Both directives designed to clarify the obligations of the Member States in relation to the telecommunications sector in pursuit of the objectives of the 1987 Green Paper without resort to Council Directives and their

[55] Commission Directive on the Transparency of Financial Relations between Member States and Public Undertakings (80/723/EEC) (OJ 1980 L195/35), and see *France, Italy and UK v. Commission* Joined Cases 188–190/80 [1982] ECR 2545.

---

410   *Colin Scott*

associated institutional problems noted above.[56] The use of Article 90(3) 'allowed the Commission to avoid the need for formal Council approval, when the necessary political consensus was lacking' (Ravaioli and Sandler 1994: 5). Both Directives were challenged by Member State governments in the ECJ on the ground that the Commission has no unilateral authority to legislate for substantive policy changes.[57] The ECJ substantially upheld the Commission's view that Article 90(3) entitled it to make rules in the form of Directives clarifying the obligations of the Member States. Despite this success the contention surrounding the use of this jurisdiction has made the Commission reluctant to use Article 90(3) in other areas such as energy. However liberalization of satellite services was achieved through amendment to the 1990 Services Directive[58] and similar amendments are proposed to achieve liberalization in relation to cable tv services. The Commission additionally used Article 90(3) as the basis for a further Commission directive to liberalize telecommunications infrastructure (fn. 44 above).

The 1990 Commission Directive on Services sought to Liberalize the Community market in respect of Valued Added Network Services (VAS)[59] (Long 1990) by requiring Member States to lift exclusive rights and to separate regulatory functions from service provision. This important institutional requirement has required significant changes in the organisation of telecommunications in all the Member States. More specifically the Member States were required to ensure that the grant of operating licenses, the control of type approval and mandatory specifications, the allocation of frequencies and surveillance of usage conditions were carried out by a body independent of TOs. The Services Directive[60] recognized the tension in the TOs role, stating:

This dual regulatory and commercial function of the telecommunications organizations has a direct impact on firms offering telecommunications services in competition with the organizations in question. By this bundling of activities, the organizations determine or, at the very least, substantially influence the supply of services offered by their competitors. The delegation to an undertaking which has a dominant position for the provision and exploitation of the network of the power to regulate access to the market for telecommunications services constitutes a strengthening of that dominant position . . .' (Recital 29).

[56] Commission Directive on Competition in the Markets in Telecommunications Equipment (88/301/EEC) (OJ 1988 L131/73, 27/05/88); and see *France* v. *Commission* Case 202/88 [1990] ECR I-2223; Commission Directive on Competition in the Market for Telecommunications Services (90/388/EEC) (OJ 1990 L192/10, 24/07/90).
[57] *Spain, Belgium and Italy* v. *Commission* Joined cases C-271/90, 281/90, 289/90 [1992] ECR I-5833.*France* v. *Commission* Case 202/88 [1990] ECR I-2223.
[58] Commission Directive on Satellite Services 94/46/EC (OJ 1994 L 268/15, 19/10/94).
[59] Commission Directive on Competition in the Market for Telecommunications Services (90/388/EEC) (OJ 1990 L192/10, 24/07/90).
[60] 90/388/EEC OJ L 192/10, 24 July 1990.

This was an abuse of dominant position under Article 86, and, where the result of a state measure, incompatible with Article 90(1).[61]

In the move towards liberalization the Community has used the concepts of reserved and non-reserved (i.e., competitive) services, requiring the non-reserved services to be liberalized. Telex, mobile, radiotelephony, paging, and satellite services were not covered by the Directive (Article 1). With respect to all other services, except voice telephony, Member States were required to withdraw all special and exclusive rights (Article 2). Any licensing requirements imposed were to be non-discriminatory and transparent. Member States were permitted to retain exclusive and special rights in respect of operation of networks, but access to these was required to be transparent and non-discriminatory. At least for now the Member States may reserve voice telephony still be reserved to a single TO. The definition of voice telephony is thus the key concept for distinguishing reserved from non-reserved services. In the Directive voice telephony is defined as

The commercial provision for the public of direct transport and switching of speech in real-time between public switched network termination points, enabling any user to use equipment connected to such a network termination point in order to communicate with another termination point. (Article 1).

In effect leased lines, closed user groups, based on an activity or an organisation, message forwarding and voice mail are not within the definition, and must be liberalized. The Services Directive does permit the banning of simple resale of leased line capacity, as this poses a problem for policing the exclusive provision of voice telephony and poses a threat of cream skimming. As has been noted above liberalization of voice telephony and infrastructure are the next targets of Community policy.

5. CONCLUSIONS: INTERNATIONAL REGULATORY COMPETITION AND COORDINATION

The structure within which EC makes its telecommunications policy is closely linked to the emerging policy itself. The structure is both a resource and a constraint for the Community, giving legitimacy to otherwise politically uncomfortable policies on the one hand, but restricting the forms and scope of legislation on the other. For the industry and for consumers the Community framework may similarly be regarded as a resource to be used, in lobbying or in litigating to pursue advantage, or as a constraint on what

---

[61] The next stage here is to provide for mutual recognition of licenses to allow those licensed in one Member State to operate in another. See COM(92)254. After a lengthy period of delay new, more limited proposals contained in COM(95) 545 Final, November 1995 seem to have a better prospect for success.

may be achieved. Similarly in the USA the structure of the regulated
environment and the jurisdictional divisions have played a significant role
in the shaping the dynamic of policy. The tension between coordination and
competition which has emerged is a product not merely of these structures
but also of rapid technological change and competitive pressures in the market, balanced against the complex social and economic objectives to be
found in the political sphere. As the Community heads towards full liberalization of services considerable uncertainty remains about the effect of the
new measures on the market, the key question perhaps being whether the
need for regulation will whither away as competition takes hold, or whether
an emerging oligopoly will need renewed regulation. In the USA too regulatory authorities have become more concerned with promotion of competition, and the appropriate balance between the interests of new entrants
and those of dominant incumbents. At the same time regulation has
attracted more political interest and become more contentious.

In the USA it appears that the long distance market has become the relatively stable domain of a number of large competitors and a considerably
larger number of small ones. The key question is whether state regulation
will continue to protect local monopolies or whether in due course Congress
and the courts will succeed in opening up the whole market. The convergence of broadcasting, telecommunications and computing is already driving this agenda. In the United States of America the unwillingness of state
regulatory authorities to permit cable tv carriers to carry telecommunications has been successfully challenged by the courts in some states (Atkin
1994). Meanwhile the European Union has announced that it intends to follow the lead of the UK in permitting cable tv operators to become fully
involved in the telecommunications sector. In both the EU and the USA the
prospect of an 'information superhighway' or 'infobahn' based upon competing infrastructure networks will require attention not just to regulatory
questions of interconnection to infrastructure, but also access for content
providers and further consideration of regulatory and antitrust questions.
Three aspects of an information superhighway may be distinguished, which
are content (films, text, messages, etc.), transmission infrastructure, and
hardware/software. In economic terms each of these areas raises potential
problems of monopoly and restrictive agreements (as well as other issues)
which regulatory authorities may want to address. Content and hard-
ware/software questions raise important questions, as the recent UK MMC
Inquiry into the Financial Times and the unsuccessful DOJ consent decree
in the case of Microsoft's restrictive agreements show.[62] The USA federal
authorities have already responded to these new demands with new institu-

---

[62] (Page 1993); (Rodgers 1995); Monopolies and Mergers Commission *Historical on-line
database services: a report on the supply in the UK of services which provide access to databases
containing archival business and financial information.* (London: HMSO, Cm 2554)

tions associated with the National Information Infrastructure programme. The prospects for 'the information superhighway' have prompted moves towards greater supranational coordination. The G7 group of countries met in February 1995 to attempt to agree common standards and regulatory initiatives to promote development, and proposed the development of a new international coordinating body.

Globalization is beginning to become as important for regulatory authorities on both sides of the Atlantic as it already is for the key industry players. The main issues here involve not just the expansion of dominant national firms into new markets, but also the changes in regulation that will occur to meet the convergence of computing, broadcasting and telecommunications. At present provisions for reciprocal privileges to enter foreign market appear to be just an aspiration. The Commission noted in its 1992 liberalization proposals that '[f]urther liberalization within the Community must be linked to equivalent opportunities in other markets.' Although some degree of liberalization is occurring in non-EU European countries through the adoption of EC principles (Cullen and Blondeel 1995: 41–45), the main focus for securing access for Community telecommunications service providers to other national markets is the multilateral negotiations in the GATT, and in particular the General Agreement on Trade in Services (GATS), developed in the Uruguay round of GATT. The Commission will continue to monitor developments in the WTO and seek to ensure that Community service providers do secure access to other national markets. Without such equivalent access, some Member States of the Community are likely to be extremely doubtful about a policy of liberalization which opens up their markets to competition from, for example, American and Japanese companies. The French government seems to be set on a course which will delay liberalization of parts of voice telephony and infrastructure until the last possible moment. Consequently the principal of equivalence has been extremely important in relation to access to markets, and continues to hold up the entry of USA and UK TOs into each others markets. At the G7 Group meeting in February 1995 the USA Vice President announced that the USA market would be opened up to operators from other countries where reciprocal access was given to USA firms in that other country. So this chapter concludes by noting that tensions between coordination and competition may be found not only as the product of institutional arrangements, but also at the level of policy, and that although new competitive ambitions are reflected in the policy aspirations of the WTO there are already signs of further global coordination to meet the new regulatory and antitrust/competition requirements of convergence.

PART IV

Shifts and Transitions in Global Governance

14

Dreaming Trade or Trading Dreams: The Limits of Trade Blocs

DANIEL DRACHE

I. INTRODUCTION

I.I The seven principles of economic integration

The global trading system post 1945 was founded on the principles of liberal internationalism—multilateralism, non-discrimination, and the economic theory of comparative advantage. At its core, it promised to organize the world's trading system on a non-political basis so that dominant countries could not use political or military power to follow 'beggar-thy-neighbour' policies and gain an advantage over small and medium-sized nations. Instead, the good performance of nations everywhere was thought to depend on unimpeded technology and investment inflows from private investors, converging production costs, an extended hand to developing nations, and a well-managed set of macro-economic policies to ensure that investment flowed to the strategic sectors (Friedman and Lebard 1991).

To be sure, the reality of the postwar system never fully corresponded with this frictionless vision of the international economy. Despite five decades of liberalized trade, few countries accepted the unqualified logic of efficiency as the principal theoretical foundation of postwar economic expansion. A judicious amount of protectionism enhanced rather than hindered many countries in their race to gain new export markets. Furthermore, the General Agreement on Tariff and Trade's (GATT) success in the postwar world was due in no small part to the fact that much of global trade was excluded from its purview. Services, agriculture, textiles, and intra-firm trade were outside its supervisory powers. It is estimated that by the beginning of the 1990s only a quarter of the world's trade was considered to conform to the precepts of trade liberalization (Ruigrok 1991). Intra-corporate trade, barter, and bi-lateral 'preferential' trade understandings of all kinds accounted for most international activity. GATT's authority was partial at best and it was only able to establish enforceable benchmarks that states were supposed to follow. Nonetheless, these shortcomings did not prevent the system from working surprisingly well when USA hegemony was unrivalled. Trade expanded dramatically and tariffs fell to all-time lows even without any powerful sanction mechanism to punish countries which ignored its norms. Conflicts were addressed by GATT panels, but countries had to negotiate their differences rather than be subject to trade retaliation, the ultimate sanction provided by GATT.

Trade agreements in the 1990s are developing on very different grounds. What the North American Free Trade Association (NAFTA) and the European Community (EC) share in common is that both are ambitious attempts to enlist external markets to obtain political ends. Conceptually, they owe much to the Reagan-Thatcher-Mulroney monetary experiment, but they go beyond the previous model of political co-operation in dramatically new ways. The fundamental change is that they are investment-driven initiatives to accelerate regional economic integration around a triad member, and require a high level of state and market coordination to bring this new relationship into existence. They are constructed around seven principles:

1. They are legally intrusive. They are comprehensive agreements that cover almost all areas of public decision-making as well as private sector activity. Public wealth creation is to be subordinate to the private world of investment and commerce;
2. The trade bloc has vast power over highly sensitive areas of public policy of member states including the environment, culture, work and employment, social policy, and the like. This is done to promote convergence often towards the lowest common denominator. A central concern is that governments will find it increasingly difficult to take policy initiatives which are not shared by other members of the trade bloc particularly in the areas of the environment, social policy innovation, and labour market regulation;
3. Each signatory has prescribed rights and responsibilities and there is a mechanism of enforcement to settle trade disputes among members with a range of sanctions available for non-compliance;
4. Power asymmetry is legitimized because of the dominant member of the bloc be it Germany or the USA to control the central levers of fiscal and monetary policy of the other members;
5. Public accountability through an elected legislature is minimal while most crucial decisions are not subject to public review. Many major decisions are made in secret and the public has little access to full-scale disclosure;
6. Only minimal provision is made for redistribution of trade-generated benefits or the sharing of costs of adjustment although the European Union (EU) has made some progress in this area;
7. The entire agreement is subject to legal review and arbitration by non-elected judges and tribunals. Increasingly, democratic institutions are

marginalized by the transfer of public policy-making to an elite-based judiciary (Mandel 1989).

1.2 Dreaming Trade: is it a sustainable policy?

Elites worldwide now wish to adopt these type of trade-enhancing measures to promote interdependence on a scale never before attempted. Their primary objective is to construct a policy-making environment that will accommodate the many structural changes initiated by the global economy. This is problematic because not only are nation-states themselves much weakened by the globalization of markets and the internationalization of their responsibilities, but trade blocs themselves are enormously fragile (Drache 1994*a*). They promise much by way of job-creation, structural change, and enhanced access but so far this not transpired to the degree that its most enthusiastic supporters claim. The reason this is so is that even if the growth of intra-regional trade has been spectacular over the last decade something more is missing with respect to state strategy and corporate response. No contemporary trade régime has yet developed an effective mechanism to neutralize the asymmetry of power between members; secondly, they have failed to put in place comprehensive programmes to pay for the costly adjustment process; and, finally, neither Europe nor in North America has a trade bloc been able to ensure that access is enhanced for all and not diminished for small and medium-sized countries (Drache 1994*b*).

The linked issues of access (how to enhance it), asymmetry (how to neutralize it), and adjustment (how to plan and pay for the resulting job loss and economic restructuring from these arrangements), hold the key to whether the wheels of integration keep turning. If a trade bloc expects to succeed, it requires a strong set of non-market regulatory institutions to counter the market imperfections and market failure. Larger markets operating with less regulation inevitably create even greater problems of adjustment. If the prospects of increased welfare make a trade bloc tick, a commercially-driven arrangement will flourish and endure. But should it fail to satisfy expectations and prove unable to deliver higher levels of work, welfare, and well-being, it will misfire and ultimately decline. Without these non-market regulatory forms in place, trade blocs, such as NAFTA and the EU, are more likely to become victims of current structural crisis than be any kind of alternative to it.

The first part of the chapter scrutinizes the powerful vision behind the formation of a free trade area. NAFTA and the EU are investment-driven projects committed to removing the remaining restrictions and regulations impeding the free movement of capital. This concept of increasing capital mobility is somewhat deceptive since it does not convey just how sweeping an objective this is for the EU and for North America. Both trade blocs

create a framework that goes far beyond the Organization for Economic
Co-operation and Development (OECD) codes on liberalization of capital
movements (United Nations 1992: 38).

Part two examines the convergence position. Economists employ convergence as an important measure to gauge the success of states working
toward the common goal of dismantling barriers (Emerson 1988). Member
states have to impose discipline on themselves and build a level playing field.
The argument advanced by free trade proponents is that when states accept
the discipline of markets the hoped-for result is greater transparency in state
practice (Bhagwati 1988). Empirically, this claim needs to be scrutinized for
its accuracy as well as tested against current trends. The last section examines the manner in which the EU and NAFTA face very different choices.
The question it addresses is, if economic integration is to go forward, what
different scenarios are on offer for each bloc?

2. THE NEW REGIONAL TRADE ARRANGEMENTS

2.1 What is a Trade Bloc?

NAFTA and the EU are prototypical economic projects reflecting the polar
opposite ends of the economic integration process (Hufbauer & Scott 1992:
6–9). This is because the institutional forms, the interests of capital and
labour, the political parties involved, the market actors, and political cultures are strikingly different. Twelve (now fifteen) European countries building a common future with a supra-national authority having a full range of
administrative, legal, and fiscal instruments is radically different from a
hemispheric arrangement between three countries as diverse as Canada, the
USA, and Mexico. Nonetheless, what these large-scale projects have in
common is a vision of markets as the driving force of well-being and wealth-
creation. Each bloc plans to use trade to restructure market-state relations
to promote trade-led development. For this reason, these trade agreements
are no longer about promoting exports and dismantling tariffs. Rather, they
are designed to promote capital flows, foreign investment, the transfer of
technology, and the location of future production facilities. NAFTA will
not create any new political authority nor is any trilateral mechanism of
coordination envisaged, rather the USA is expected to be and, under the
provisions of NAFTA, entitled to be the legal and political authority of last
resort.

Unsurprisingly mainstream thinking tends to present these new trading
arrangements as something hardly threatening at all. In conventional terms
it can be defined as an association of nation-states that is created to reduce
barriers to the movement of people, goods, services, and investment capi-

tal. Its principal attraction is that it gives smaller regional economies access to larger markets so that they can develop economies of scale and hence generate welfare and efficiency gains through an enhanced export performance (Hufbauer & Schott 1992). For large economies, a trade bloc means something quite different. It provides secure and enhanced market access for its mass production industries and corporations. In this regard, a trade bloc is a powerful enabling device that requires small countries to open their economies regardless of the costs. On the financial front, it offers the triad member of the bloc a new investment frontier for its capital-rich financial sector. To balance these competing interests requires a proven institutional capacity to resolve differences between member states, a favourable international climate and much fortuity. If the trade bloc is sufficiently cohesive over time then it should increase the welfare of its members. The probability of its survival depend on six basic characteristics working to sustain it (Schott 1991).

A. *The Institutional Capacity of NAFTA and the EU Compared*

- roughly equivalent levels of per capita GNP. If there are to be welfare gains and a resulting meshing of economies, consumption norms have to be of the same order. If not, blocs with large disparities will face difficulties because the producers in the rich country will be seen as swamping those in the poorer country.
- sharing a common geographic regionally-based economy. Trade blocs rely on pre-existing geographically-linked communication and transportation systems to extend the market. Minimizing information and transportation costs can be an important source of trade-creation. Common borders and short distances stimulate intra-industry specialization and enhance national and transnational economies of scale.
- compatible trading practices and norms. Countries must share a commitment to far-reaching trade liberalization practices that includes suppressing non-tariff barriers and other state-designated policies. In particular, they are required to oppose industrial targeting and to stop subsidizing or protecting their strategic industries and adopt a rules-based rather than a result-oriented approach to commerce.
- a political commitment to the regional organization of trade. Countries are required to make a large commitment to multi-lateralism. This entails adopting norms or practices which frequently go beyond internationally agreed norms established by GATT. The danger is that multi-lateralism entails creating new customs barriers against third countries (de la Torre and Kelly 1992).
- the active support of a world economic power with a leading international currency. The stability of a trade bloc derives its cohesiveness from using

The Institutional Capacity of NAFTA and the EC Compared

	EC Provisions and Policy Instruments	NAFTA Provisions and Instruments
Asymmetry	Structural funds; European Investment Bank; structural adjustment. Adjustment interest-rate driven by Bundesbank. No formal mechanism of control. Modest redistribution policy.	Joint disputes panel low-level judicial review. US able to appeal decisions through its own trade law system. US interest-rate is the reserve standard for Canada and Mexico. No redistribution mechanism.
Adjustment	Competition policy; industrial strategy; science/technology policy; regional funds. The amount of resources is comparatively small for such a large number of States.	Nothing in NAFTA increases discipline on US Congress. USA is free to pay for adjustment programmes as it sees fit. No co-ordinated response to adjustment. Left to individual member states; Canada and Mexico subject to US trade law.
Access	Brussels has responsibility to guarantee access. Main policy instruments: competition directorate; regional directorate; industrial policy; technology and science policy national industrial strategy of member states plus recourse of ECJ.	Low-level tripartite dispute panel; US Congress not limited by any pro-active provisions in NAFTA. Many rulings appealable. Firms and industries pay full cost. Canada and Mexico subject to US trade law.

Source: Drache

a world currency as its own. Monetary and fiscal policy will increasingly be set for all by the central bank of the blocs' dominant member. Countries have to be willing to dilute their sovereignty in favour of broader regional policies. In a world of linked financial markets, losing control over monetary policy is one of the radically new costs of belonging to a trade bloc (Emerson & Huhne 1991).

* a real potential for growth through economic integration. Countries have to have industries and firms which are capable of winning new market share inside a trade bloc. Countries with weak industries and few competitive sized firms will be disadvantaged by a trading bloc. They will lose rather than gain market share.

The trade blocs issue has emerged as the preeminent problem of the 1990s because it touches on the most sensitive economic and political question of the decade, namely, the future of the nation-state as we know it. The formation of a large, integrated market requires countries to create a supranational authority or its equivalent to direct this large undertaking. Harmonizing tax régimes, formulating new social and employment standards, increasing the transparency of state aids, none of these things can happen without clearly agreed and enforceable administrative procedures at the governmental and non-governmental levels. Thus, the stakes are high. Countries have to cede control over many of the key policy instruments of national economic management in return for the benefits of increased specialization.

Both the EC and NAFTA are comprehensive agreements to foster far-reaching interdependency among their members. Social, environmental, and employment policies that were once regarded as being beyond the reach of integration are on the table. Such a radical departure from past practice means that governments have to restrict their domestic control over the economy and over a range of programmes that impinge directly and indirectly on promoting new market opportunities. If trade blocs succeed in this, and if governments can overcome their narrow self-interest in preserving their sovereignty, then these trade alliances will become a major presence in the world economy. These and other initiatives like them will set out the rules of the game nationally and internationally for the considerable future. As countries rush to open their borders, in theory, every country is to be a winner and gain larger market share for its industries. But is the vision of global markets as self-organizing entities and the way national economies function borne out by experience? The answer to this question is anything but simple.

3. TWO OPPOSING MODELS OF INTEGRATION

3.1 European Integration—Initially a state-driven process

If economics were the principal glue of a trade bloc, deep integration would have happened long ago. But is has not. On both sides of the Atlantic, integration has always had a broader purpose than to enhance the efficiency of markets *tout court*. A crude market model of integration was never the single driving force behind greater European co-operation (Wallace 1990).

In the aftermath of World War II, European integration was largely security-driven. The immediate issue was the threat of German re-armament. The countries of Europe had to find the appropriate forum to bring Germany back into the European community and at the same time offset its power. The Schuman Plan of 1950 contained the nucleus of the idea, bringing together the coals and steel industries of the Six member states under common rules: European co-operation had to be broader than an economic deal. The ulterior purpose of this economic arrangement in Robert Schuman's words was to make war between France and Germany not only 'unthinkable, but materially impossible'. The Plan mandated the authorities to develop a wide-angled view of the social side of economic adjustment. It provided broad social criteria to limit the purely market-side of this arrangement to promote trade liberalization. The idea of establishing social norms and rules that were not narrowly market-bound found its way into the Treaty of Rome in 1957. Article 117 called upon member states to improve working conditions and the quality of life for workers that would permit 'leur égalisation dan le progrès'. It was hoped that the upward pressure on national norms and practices would cause diverse legislatures to strengthen rather than weaken the social dimension of integration (Rehfeldt 1994).

Even in the 1970s, integration never was narrowly market-centered. It went forward because the process was gradual, slow, and non-threatening. Since markets were kept within an established framework, this ensured that the removal of customs tariffs proved less of a hardship than many member countries anticipated privately. All governments relied on a mixture of social policy, industrial strategy, and macro-economic planning to ensure that their policies and programmes were not subject to the global business cycle. The Netherlands, Belgium, France, Germany, and Italy were all positioned to benefit from this new era of open markets. Their leading producers in the core smokestack industries had no difficulty embracing the concept of bigger markets. They hoped to realize additional economies of scale via long production runs from dismantling of tariff barriers.

The belief in larger markets became part of the postwar European miracle which struck a balance between deepening domestic demand and gradually opening their economies to each other. For these countries with strongly developed domestically-based mass production industries the aim of economic integration made enormous sense. Member states relied on a variety of industrial policies to address the adjustment costs of greater openness. With rapidly expanding domestic economies, displaced workers from uncompetitive sectors could expect to find alternative employment in the competitive side of the economy. In North America, as in Europe, integration was seen as something compatible with national sovereignty, particularly in those countries with social democratic governments to provide a range of income support programmes for those who lost their jobs.

On balance, what made trade openness acceptable was that integration went forward because core countries with powerful export sectors were well-placed to capture increased market share. Less advantaged members developed industrial strategies to restructure and take advantage of the new export opportunities. Finally, the rapid expansion of commerce was job-friendly, creating employment opportunities while countries with strong domestic industries and Fordist kinds of collective agreements guaranteed that workers shared in the productivity gains and real wages rose for more than two decades (Drache & Glasbeek 1993).

One of the cherished myths of proponents of free trade is that industrial policy is synonymous with creeping protectionism. This does not square with the empirical reality that economic integration received its greatest push from the golden decades of Keynesian state management of the economy. Jeffrey Schott (1991), an ardent supporter of trade liberalism, calculates that the greatest period of intra-European trade was in the heyday of Keynesian practices. In 1963, intra-European trade was less important than exports to the rest of the world. By 1979, trade within the community was 20 per cent higher than to the rest of the world. Intra-European trade grew sharply in the 1980s before many of the measures to complete the internal market were in place. Between 1985 and 1989, internal trade increased by more than 100 percent rising from $337 billion to $678 billion, an acceleration due as much to the recovery from the 1982 economic crisis rather than any single decision to strengthen the EC trade ties.

Despite this evidence, among liberal economists was born the idea that under all conditions integration promoted a virtuous model of development. At best, this was a half truth and at worst a dangerous illusion (Strange 1988). The fact was that economic integration succeeded because markets were kept in check and only partially liberalized. In agriculture, the one area in which integration did not work easily because of the high costs of adjustment, the EC opted for a balanced agricultural policy, a mix of subsidies and a political compromise to stabilize this sector. The public sector was largely kept off the table as well. All countries could use their public sector to provide goods and services to their citizens that accommodated national developmental goals. This permitted public enterprise to remain a critical tool of industrial and social policy throughout the EC during the 1960s through to the 1980s. While potentially the EC suffered many ups and downs because of the constant tension between France, the UK, and Germany, integration went forward nonetheless because the social dimension was never on the table and because countries had developed extensive social programmes and policies (Esping-Anderson 1992). Social democrats felt so positive about managed integration that they convinced their electorates that trade liberalization and integration was not only a positive development but it enhanced the long-term viability of the welfare state and social democracy.

3.2 North American Co-operation: A distinctive integration process

North American co-operation followed a different model and growth trajectory from its European counterpart. Prior to World War II, co-operation between Canada and the USA was security-centered and investment-driven. By the mid-1930s, almost a third of all USA foreign direct investment was in Canadian resources and industries.

During the war, Canada-USA co-operation reached its high point. For the purposes of the war, the two economies and two military command structures were effectively fused into one. In the aftermath of the war, however, free trade was not on the agenda. The idea of free trade had been rejected twice by the Canadian electorates in 1896 and again in 1911. All successive government saw little advantage in formalizing Canadian-USA relations in a trade pact. The principal worry was that Canada would cease to exist in such an unequal arrangement. The north-south pull of markets would overpower the east-west economic union achieved by the National Policy, Canada's developmental strategy of nation-building. Instead, the Pearson-St. Laurent-Trudeau governments opted for a strategy of co-operation rather than formalized integration.

With Canada's open economy and few controls on foreign direct investment, USA direct investment rose dramatically. By the end of the 1960s, over one-half of Canadian manufacturing was foreign-owned. In certain sectors such as automobile, oil and gas, rubber, and the like, USA investment reached over 75 per cent. American business interests dominated a continentally-oriented Canadian domestic elite who did not see any reason to distinguish themselves from their rich and more powerful USA counterparts. Formal integration also occurred through the 1965 Canadian-USA Auto Pact, but it was largely ad hoc and the answer to specific problems rather than part of a grand design. Much integration was driven by Canadian tax policy. USA investors set up operations in Canada to take advantage of the double depreciation allowance offered by Canadian governments, a provision specifically written into Canadian tax law in the late 1940s to encourage USA investment in the Canadian manufacturing sector.

All these measures (and many others as well) turned Canada into a silent and junior partner of the USA at a time when USA hegemony was unchallenged. But North American integration was never as solid or acceptable as it seemed. By the 1970s, the honeymoon came to an abrupt end as Canada-USA relations became increasingly troubled. The rise of Canadian national movements in the 1970s questioned the high levels of foreign ownership. Canadian governments were forced to introduce screening of USA investment. The oil shocks finally induced the Trudeau government to introduce legislation to Canadianize Canada's energy sector which was more than 80 per cent controlled mainly by USA interests (McCall & Clarkson 1994). In the field of culture, the Trudeau government also clashed with Washington as Canadians prodded their government to promote Canada's cultural industries and reduce the influence and power of USA firms and television interests operating in Canada.

The emergence of a more self-consciously nationalist mode of politics met with popular approval. As the Canadian-USA relationship became more troubled, public opinion supported policies that reduced Canada's wholesale reliance on its continental partner. The concern voiced was that, given the asymmetry between the two countries, if the status quo prevailed Canada would lose control over not only the remaining vestiges of its autonomy but, more concretely, the rest of its public policy agenda including social and environmental programmes.

In view of the very large Canadian state sector and many public enterprises, it was accepted by all political parties that continental integration had to be kept within strict limits that excluded many areas of public policy. For instance, the areas of culture, resource management, and the environment as well as the strategic financial sector, these were largely outside of the integration process. USA investors were not allowed to own any of Canada's major banks. In the critical sphere of culture, Ottawa wanted to reduce USA influence by establishing Canadian content rules in television and by promoting Canadian books and magazines. These measures were highly popular as Canadians across the country forced their government to promote Canada's cultural industries and limit the influence and power of USA cultural industries (Clarkson 1985).

While Canadian Keynesian social policy measures always remained at the low end compared to the full-fledged social democratic régimes in Western Europe, Canadian governments had accepted the need for universal social programmes in the field of health insurance, unemployment benefits, and social welfare entitlements. An enlarged public commitment to social policy was sold to Canadians on the grounds that it made them different than their southern neighbour. Canada had a history of supporting a public enterprise culture and with few multinational corporations, the state had a powerful role in organizing economic life. Keynesian social welfare policies were thus seen as being an integral part of Canada's political culture. Because these social programmes functioned as a powerful brake on economic integration, continental drift remained gradual, ad hoc, and limited to only some spheres of public policy (Drache and Ranahan 1995).

3.3 Trade Liberalization The Public-Policy Agenda

Mainstream economists have relatively few constructive ideas to offer about the institutional dimension of trade blocs (Hufbauer & Schott 1992). They have little to say practically about neutralizing asymmetry, enhancing access, or paying for the costs of adjustment. Rather, they tend to be very bullish about the large benefits resulting from these new kinds of regional alliances. In a recent survey of the theory of economic integration produced during the last three decades, Tovias (1991: 20) concludes that the economics profession has few doubts about the welfare-increasing impact that flows inevitably from these kinds of forms of integration. In his celebrated study of *Protectionism*, Bhagwati (1988) regards the formation of regional blocs as one of the most important postwar developments. For him, the beauty of the free trade beast is that 'free trade for all' must be appreciated as a radical step in the right direction. He announces that it is a step up from the original nationalist version of the trade theory that only focused on the prescriptive power of the theory for one country. His (Bhagwati 1988) words are worth quoting because they capture the passion that the economics profession largely feels for this idea:

If one applies the logic of efficiency to the allocation of activity among all trading nations, and not merely within one's own nation-state, it is easy enough to see that it yields the prescription of free trade everywhere—that alone would ensure that goods and services would be produced where it could be done most cheaply. The notion that prices reflect true social costs is crucial to this conclusion, just as it is to the case for free trade for one nation alone.

So far, the leading trade blocs have not found the optimal path to maximize the efficient utilization of every trade opportunity. Rather what they have succeeded in doing is limiting a member state's power to shape national markets. For many countries this has proven to be a chilling experience. In the areas of macro-economic policy, intra-bloc trade, work and employment conditions, interest-rate volatility, and employment enhancement, a trade bloc régime does indeed dramatically limit member states in precisely the way Bhagwati predicted. But in many other ways, the scenario does not fit his vision at all. The reason is that efficient outcomes do not rely on the price mechanism working in an unimpeded way. By giving corporations a bigger playing field in the expectation that efficient outcomes are to be left to chance, NAFTA and the EC are facing more internal problems than ever. The fact is that on both sides of the Atlantic it has proven next to impossible to separate a country's external trade from its national economy and make it independent of its national self-interest (ibid. 25). Why should this be?

3.4 Neutralizing Power Asymmetries: The Core Challenge

Even though trade blocs promote far-reaching co-operation among governments in ways never before contemplated, such agreements do not diminish the asymmetries between member states. In fact the complex rules, regulations, and directives of the EC and NAFTA create a juridical framework; which permanently embeds this inequality in the structure of the agreement. Because these texts are rules-driven rather than result-oriented, they favour the interests of the dominant and the powerful over any substantive concept of the collective.

In the case of NAFTA there is little evidence that being part of this arrangement has levelled power asymmetries among Canada, the USA, or Mexico. In fact there has been a dramatic growth in the unilateral exercise of USA trade power. For instance NAFTA makes it easier for the USA to use trade harassment measures against Mexico and Canada, without any increase in the discipline on USA practice and policy. Because it is a trade agreement, NAFTA has to be interpreted, and in the North American case the interpretation rests in the final analysis with the USA Congress, lobby groups, and USA trade tribunals. In the absence of any supranational authority they, not some impartial authority, are the final arbiters. As a result this gives Washington the right to intervene in Canada's domestic affairs and decision-making processes.

Under its terms, Washington is entitled to review all Canadian legislation to ascertain whether it (a) impinges on NAFTA, and (b) whether any proposed legislation constitutes a real (or imagined) distortion to trade. That is what Clarkson (1993) had aptly called 'the real constitution of Canada' since Canadian practice, norms, and standards, in short, will be subject to its provisions. But, on the other hand, for the USA, NAFTA creates no new significant norms in American practice, policy, or outlook. Even the side deal negotiated with Canada and Mexico with respect to human rights or other kinds of labour violations carries with it no penalty to enforce USA multinationals to adopt any of the tribunal rulings.

The most serious long term implication is with respect to the political decision-making process. Canadian and Mexican government policy can be monitored on an on-going basis by a bevy of USA tribunals thus preserving a non-partisan and neutral air. On the other hand USA tribunals do not

feel restricted by the text. It is hard to find any significant addition which
restricts USA administrative law or practice. This principle underpins the
Canada-USA free trade deal. The USA implementing legislation makes this
perfectly plain. Article 103 states that wherever there is a conflict between
the provisions of the FTA and USA law, USA law will prevail. Under
NAFTA, USA groups are free to harass Canadian exporters or apply direct
and indirect pressure on Mexican authorities.

The bottom line is that administrative groundrules governing trade disputes have not changed with the signing of NAFTA. Since the FTA came
into effect in 1988, there have been more than twenty-five new trade disputes covering an ever-growing list of products including pork, steel rail,
softwood lumber, auto parts, clothing, rolled steel products, wheat, and
bear. Most of the USA complaints allege unfair subsidization by many
Canadian government programmes including farm marketing boards, environmental and public health norms, regional programmes, and the like.
These kinds of conflicts are more than trade disputes. They challenge
Canadian competence to mount programmes that differ significantly from
USA practice.

The dilemma facing Ottawa is that, even when a bi-national panel created to arbitrate disputes under the Canadian-USA deal upholds Canada's
side, it does not mean that Canadian exports have won a victory. An
unfavourable decision provides American producers further grounds to
press for a new investigation as they are entitled to under USA trade law.
While bi-national panels were supposed to deliver binding decisions, clearly
this is not the case. In the recent case involving wheat exporters, USA farm-
ers continued to charge that Canadian wheat subsidies are unfair and
demand another anti-dumping investigation even though three panels ruled
that Canadian wheat is not subsidized according to existing practices.
Canada's trade minister acknowledged that there is little he can do if the
USA trade representative decides to launch an anti-dumping investigation.[1]
Short of retaliation there is no provision with NAFTA to create objective
standards or to rein in the protectionist elements within the USA Congress.

This variety of crude exercise of market power that so obviously favours
the dominant member of the bloc has no parallel in the EC. Large and small
members are bound by the decisions of the European Court of Justice. In
this important way, the EC has developed a capacity to reduce the big
power influence syndrome within its institutional framework. But so far, in
a multitude of other ways, the democratic deficit as well as the de facto
power of Germany to dominate the EC's monetary policy underlines just
how much asymmetry continues to haunt the process of European integration.

---

[1] *See* TORONTO STAR, February 10, 1993.

The EU with a market of over 300 million people, has struggled to come to terms with how to reorganize its ten steel industries, six automotive sectors, a dozen textile clusters, and the dozens of shipbuilding firms which operate in various regions of the EU. To address this problem, Brussels has relied on regional industrial and competitive policies, but so far none of these proved adequate to the task (Hufbauer 1990; Sbragia 1992). The EC does not have the authority nor the resources to build strong European industries or to tackle double digit unemployment. Because of this, the real costs of integration now outweigh the potential benefits derived from larger markets. This is why state aids and other national policies continue to be used by so many European member states.

4. THE TRANSFORMATION OF WORK AND EMPLOYMENT

4.1 Analyzing the Terrain of the New Global Dynamic

In both Europe and North America the process of building larger markets has already dramatically altered employment and wage standards. The spatial reorganization of industries has set the stage for reorientation of wages and working time. The upward pressure on wages characteristic of the Keynesian-Fordist wage compromise has been dramatically and probably irreversibly broken.

Levy and Murname (1992), for example, show that real income per full-time employee was rising by 2.45 per cent per annum between 1945 and 1975, but by only 0.67 per cent in the 1973–88 period. This trend is identical on both sides of the Atlantic. Wages and consumption historically linked for four decades, no longer are. Since 1980 real wages now lag behind productivity growth in most European jurisdictions. In Canada and the USA, this same de-linking explains the dramatic disappearance of middle income earners from the employment pyramid. Proportionately, there are fewer blue collar workers earning a 'family income' and many more single-parent, most often female workers, being paid poor wages. The high turnover rates are explained by the feminization of labour markets in the rapidly growing service side of the economy (Betcherman 1992; Cohen 1992).

The most recent evidence indicates that the Keynesian virtuous growth cycle [see chart] has been replaced by a very different set of macro-economic objectives throughout the industrial world. For more than a decade, wages have again begun to operate as a mechanism of adjustment. Under the gold standard, a country's external financial position governed the nominal wage. Competitive labour markets ensured wage flexibility which in turn curbed production costs. Under Keynesian practice, governments relied on interest rate adjustment and on currency devaluation to ensure a flexible international economic position. Now, with governments committed to a significant degree of wage flexibility, the assumptions underlying macro-economic policy are radically different.

A. *The Three-in-one Virtuous Growth Model*

For members of a trade bloc, a virtuous cycle now depends on subjecting wage levels to global competitive pressures. Under a régime of trade-driven monetarism, inflation and relative price movements are seen directly to determine a country's external position and market share. Competitive labour markets are relied on to adjust employment, and wage levels are expected to reflect international competitive conditions (OECD 1994).

The result of this policy shift is a near standstill in hourly pay in many manufacturing sectors. This has contributed to a dramatic rise in income and employment inequality in Western Europe and North America. With states on both sides of the Atlantic reducing their spending in order to build a favourable investment climate, this too has had long term distribution implications. It has resulted in a shift in income towards the high end and the low end in earnings scale. This growth of social inequality has gone hand-in-hand with the growth of trade oriented economies.

In terms of wages and working conditions, the concept of a single market at best remains a far-off utopia. Manufacturing costs continue to reflect local conditions and the resiliency of collective bargaining practices. These are not indifferent to market forces but often have a degree of independence which surprises most observers. The wide differences in pay and work conditions are dramatic. In the USA for instance, where wages have been flexible downward, the lowest paid workers have seen their wages fall by 30 per cent since 1970. Since 1987, real wages have not fallen in the core European countries anywhere near USA levels.

By contrast, the level of European unionization has dramatically declined. Centralized collective bargaining has come under enormous pressure as countries have become more dependent on international and intra-regional trade. The British trade union movement has lost over 3.5 million members since 1979. The drop in French union membership has been equally dramatic. It now has the lowest level of union membership of any industrial country, though it has to be remembered that more than 80 per cent of French workers are covered by sectorial collective bargaining agreements and/or have workplace representation through *comite' d' enterprise* arrangements.

While the decline of trade unionism in a post-Fordist world is uneven, what is clear is that the deregulation of the workplace and increased competitive pressures from bigger markets have eroded union power at the bargaining table. Trade unions are less of a social partner than in any time since the end of World War II, even where the level of unionization has not

The Three-In-One Virtuous Growth Model

A Comparison of State Intervention Strategies

	Beveridge-Inspired Social Policy	A Fordist Capital/ Labour Compromise	Keynesian Macro-Economic Management
Canada	low to medium benefits and coverage but universal health system; unemployment insurance available to 80% of workforce until recently. Benefits to be dramatically cut post-NAFTA.	decent collective bargaining; fragmented labour markets; 25,000 collective wage agreements in force.	export-led growth rather than Keynesian policies; uncompetitive manufacturing sector that competes on wages; over 70% exports for USA market system.
USA	poor UIC benefits for only 25% of workforce. Health benefits mostly private but public funds for low income earners.	decent collective bargaining; weak capital/labour accord; 15% private sector and 30% of public sector workers unionized.	weak commitment to Keynesian redistributive and stabilizing principles; military R&D expenditures crucial to USA industrial might.
Western Europe	universal social programmes; extensive social security in health, education and welfare; many entitlements are embedded and difficult to change.	sector and centralized collective bargaining system; strong national labour movements external to workplace initially high levels of industrial unionism; still training a major program and commitment.	strong Keynesian commitment to full employment with incomes policy and deepening domestic demand in many countries. Gradual trade liberalization measures that do not imperil industrial policy.

dropped as precipitously. With wages being put back in competition and subject to new global competitive pressures, a free trade zone becomes the chosen instrument to redefine the terms and conditions of the existing capital-labour compromise (Boyer 1994; Albert 1991).

Unions have always understood that global trade wars bid down the price of labour because companies are being forced to produce more with less of everything. This was not a problem so long as a country's exports and imports were only a small part of its gross domestic product. Once they occupy a major share of total output in an open economy, the effect is dramatic. Wages tend to stagnate and the purchasing power of families will only become more unequal across society unless government intervenes to correct growing inequality. This, however, is no longer part of the framework policy of industrial society. The globalization of production methods within a trade bloc is having many direct consequences on employment opportunities.

4.2 Employment Enhancement versus Trade Efficiency

The current environment for trade blocs has not been kind for job creation. In many sectors there has been new job growth but not sufficient to offset the deep job losses that have already occurred. While there is much debate about assessing the net employment effects, total job loss due to trade-related factors has been profound. In the case of Canada and the USA, employment in manufacturing has fallen to precipitously new lows. Over the last thirty years, the number and quality of manufacturing jobs have shrunk in Canada and the USA. Less than 15 per cent of workers find gainful employment in the manufacturing sector. No amount of export-led growth is likely to reverse this long term trend. Capturing foreign markets will generate some employment gains for the fortunate few, but on balance it is more likely to destroy employment opportunities than provide jobs in record numbers.

The fact is that on both sides of the Atlantic, new computer-based technologies now enable employers in the old Fordist industries to become leaner and more productive. Lean production practices pose an irreconcilable dilemma for labour. On the one hand, new competitive pressures generated by free trade zones require industries to shed labour in order to enhance their market share in foreign markets. On the other hand, trade becomes job-destructive particularly in the mass production industries and in new technologically-intensive sectors as well, when high technology and high value-added industries are forced to compete head-to-head. This is so because the rules of the game have changed even for large corporations. Numbers are critical to costs and reducing costs requires in the end smaller payrolls.

Thus, for example, the decision by International Business Machines (IBM) in the early 1990s to reduce its labour force by a hundred thousand is emblematic of the new order. Investment in technology and new products is not sufficient to make firms leaner. More than anything, large-scale business is convinced that the most important measure to implement is downsizing payrolls. IBM's response to trade competitiveness is not an isolated instance. Seimens, Phillips, Olivetti, General Motors, Volkswagen, Mercedes Benz, all of the world's leaders in North America and Europe have been shedding labour for a better part of a decade. Auto, steel, chemicals, textiles, shoes, shipbuilding, mining, and forest industries continue to downsize their workforce. With fewer people employed in the international side of the economy than ever, little wonder that industrial employment remains flat and its outlook poor.

The jobs-through-trade dilemma takes many different forms in the 1990s. In Ontario, the industrial hub of Canada and one of the oldest industrial regions of North America, even without the free trade agreement job creation has been at a premium. But, since the Canada-USA Free Trade Agreement (FTA) has come into effect, the picture has taken a drastic change for the worse. The shrinkage of Canada's manufacturing sector is long term and permanent rather than temporary and cyclical. Roughly 350,000 manufacturing positions have been lost since 1989. But the bad news is that less than 15 per cent of workers find employment in the manufacturing sector compared with closer to 25 per cent in 1970. A recovery due to a highly devalued Canadian dollar is not going to reverse this trend. With rising interest rates, it is only a matter of time before Canada's export-driven recovery is choked off. This is why employers are hesitant in many sectors to create new full-time positions, and factories respond to crises by demanding a longer work week from their employees rather than hiring more people.

What is different in the 1990s is that trade is no longer an employment-creating strategy in the way it once was in the boom times of the 1950s and 1960s. What governments are loath to admit is that the price for joining the trade bloc is that there are real winners and losers. Rather they believe the process to be a neutral and inevitable consequence of opening markets regardless of the costs and consequences. In fact, the number of industries that fail and the magnitude of job losses are beyond any of the estimates made by mainstream economists. The prestigious Cecchini Report (1988) presented to Brussels and the much-praised Royal Commission on the Economic Union and Development Prospects for Canada (1985) recommended that free trade as the framework policy for Canadian governments, both erred massively in assessing the real effect of free trade on employment levels. The welfare gains have been small compared to the soaring adjustment costs.

Even the reputable Washington-based, International Economics Institute continues to play the numbers game with respect to NAFTA. It estimates 'about 130,000 additional USA jobs are to be created under a NAFTA scenario. . . .' (Hufbauer & Schott 1992: 55–6). This prediction also continues to underestimate the magnitude of employment displacement when trade barriers come down. The losers are always the unskilled workers in many low wage occupations and sectors. They will be displaced at USA firms decamp south of the border where wages are only a fifth of USA levels. The USA, however, is not alone in having to address these difficult adjustment concerns.

A. Managing Structural Change: The Real Frontier

One of the explicit aims of a trade bloc, as we have seen, is to accelerate structural change at the industry level and in the labour market. Competitive pressures assume a high degree of mobility on the part of workers and the workforce. Unless policy instruments exist and governments are committed to dealing with the negative side of bigger markets, a regional trade bloc becomes a high risk exercise benefitting the few rather than creating a higher standard of well-being for the majority. Further, it reinforces a pattern of growing wage inequality that has become more pronounced over the past two decades throughout the industrialized world (OECD 1994). The wages of the young, inexperienced, and poorly paid workers are likely to continue to fall despite the fact that the ideology of free trade promises rising wages and better jobs for all. Trade competitiveness depends more and more on a lean model of production for high technology and higher value-added industries and low wage for labour-intensive industries at the bottom end of the manufacturing scale. So far job growth has been predominately in the part time, low-paying work world. By comparison, highly paid work has become scarcer and more difficult to find.

While trade liberalization is allegedly designed to improve labour market conditions, to date labour market flexibility is focused on reducing existing standards such as minimum wage laws and protection against dismissal. Whether one uses employment figures, state expenditures, social transfers, inequality measures, the market-state-citizen relationship has changed qualitatively. The Fordist-Beveridge state is being dramatically altered. Many of its functions have already been privatized, internationalized, or eviscerated. Even the recent decision to establish works councils in larger, trans-European companies will only be consultative and voluntary in design rather than a uniform structure of compulsory consultation. It is only a very modest addition to existing collective bargaining arrangements and moreover, to date, the innovation has been seen as largely unsuccessful in practice.

With the reform of labour market institutions on hold for the foreseeable future, it is by no means clear that the enormous energy and commitment to a deep form of regional integration is likely to take root. In fact, most employers groups oppose any major changes to industrial relations systems on the grounds that they impose unnecessary costs on companies. They do not see how strengthening industrial relations will improve competitiveness. Rather they have a different tack in mind. Employers federations are calling on government to sell off public enterprises as a way to solve the unemployment crisis and to reduce their deficit. Employers want governments to lower their cost of health care contributions, pensions, and unemployment benefits by adopting a USA style system of deregulation. Evidence of similar policy prescriptions can be found in the international policy recommendations put forward for jobs and employment creation, which urge governments to decrease employers costs in order to boost export opportunities (OECD 1994).

5. THE PROSPECTS FOR TRADE

5.1 The Growth of Non-Tariff Barriers

Despite all measures to liberalize trade, intra-regional trade in both blocs has become more concentrated, but markets have not become more open as many believe. More trade disputes than ever are in the offing between the EC, Japan, and the USA. In all cases, the stakes are high. The USA trade deficit continues to balloon despite a recovery and renewed consumer confidence. To be sure, USA trade with Canada and Mexico remains highly advantageous to the USA even if American exporters have failed to narrow the trade gap with Japan. The disputes involve a broad range of industries including steel export, micro-chip products, automobiles, and aeronautical production to name only some of the 'flashpoint' sectors. Trade disputes also occur within trade blocs and are waged through their institutions, such as the continuing conflicts between European steel producers.

The proliferation of trade conflicts contradicts the belief that trade liberalization ushers in a period of commercial transparency. This is not the case. While both blocs have enhanced trade-creation opportunities for a small number of strategically well-placed industries, the economic evidence also suggests that the establishment of these blocs has fragmented international markets by erecting new barriers against imports from third parties. This can be seen by the increase in the number of trade disputes and in the use of rules and regulations such as customs rules of origin to impose new trade barriers against non-members.

These illiberal practices are on the rise despite the commitment of regional trade arrangements to support open trade. Here the contradictions between the theory of trade liberalization and the practice is marked. Since

1990, the number of anti-dumping actions has risen from 96 to 237 by June 1992. GATT reports that more countries than ever are resorting to this measure, including the EC, the USA, Canada, Australia, and Mexico. Governments are using anti-dumping actions as a means to promote certain industries, a kind of industrial policy by stealth. Trade policy is seen as part of a coordinated and integrated economic strategy not least by the USA government, and on this point there is broad agreement between the Clinton White House and the Republican-dominated Congress. Already more than thirty new disputes have been filed against Canada since 1988. Without any increased discipline on the USA, more trade conflicts are in the offing.

5.2 Future Prospects—Getting the State out of the Market

At the same time, trade imbalances within each bloc have become sharper rather than muted by countries continuing to apply trade liberalization policies indiscriminately. The imbalances within NAFTA are sharpest. American exports to Mexico grew by 40 per cent in 1991 while Mexico's manufactured exports to the USA increased by a mere 8 per cent. By the end of 1993, USA exports had continued to flow into Mexico at an unprecedented rate, but Mexico's exports to the USA had barely grown. The result was that Mexico suffered a massive current account deficit triggered by the steady flow of capital into the country to cover this trade deficit with its largest trading partner.

With the peso over-valued and with Mexico spending billions of dollars to defend it, Mexico's experienced a currency crisis in 1994. President Zedillo responded by allowing to peso to float against the dollar. The collapse of the peso forestalled Mexico's planned recovery, and plunged the country into more uncertainty than ever. As a result, Mexicans faced an unprecedented austerity programme. To this end, wages were frozen, new privatizations of companies in leading sectors, such as Pemex, were proposed, and social spending programmes were to be drastically reduced. It is hard to imagine any other single instance that embodies all the unresolved questions of asymmetry, adjustment, and access as this one: an open economy with no exchange controls, an exchange rate designed to bear down on inflation, and monetary policy aiming for a balanced budget at any price. Indeed, in order to resolve the short term currency problem, the Mexican economy became totally dependent on external support by the USA and, after some USA arm-twisting, on the International Monetary Fund.

Canada too faces a rocky future as a member of NAFTA. The same kind of trade imbalance exists in the Canadian case. Key Canadian industries continue to perform poorly. Michael Porter (1991) found that Canada's national competitiveness declined in the 1980s if measured by market share rather than total dollar value of its two way trade. Again, his figures underline the lack of a clear cause and effect relationship between increased economic integration and export capacity. According to Porter, what is more important than market size is the innovative capacity of a country's firms to upgrade. When the private sector has the institutional means to transform a static comparative advantage into a dynamic one, it is able to exploit new opportunities as an advantage. When it not organized to be innovative in its production methods, then operating in larger markets will lead to a weakening of its home base, and with this its ability to compete in the new circumstances. The difference between success and failure often lies in the macro-economic climate which has direct implications at the micro-level in terms of new employment opportunities.

NAFTA inspired efforts to increase labour market competitiveness in the name of flexibility seem misguided at best. A recovery requires governments to invest in people and restructuring. Imposing wage discipline is likely to have the reverse effect of increasing social instability. All these kinds of job-creation schemes underestimate the role of government as a positive factor in managing structural change, and gloss over the need to reinforce the independent decision-making capacity of the modern nation-state. Is there an explanation why so many industrial countries continue to dream trade when it limits their policy management capacity so dramatically?

5.3 The Long Term Viability of Trade Blocs: The Nitty Gritty of Adjustment

The tough question to confront is whether there are so many destabilizing effects from adjustment as to render NAFTA and EU untenable in their present form? Certainly, with its policy arsenal, the EU is better able to grapple with the many faceted dimensions of this crucial issue than Canada, the USA, and Mexico. It has a large regional and structural aid plan. In 1994, the plan has funds of more than ECU 156 billion, and the money spent on addressing structural aid will more than double between 1994–99. But these funds remain inadequate to the task of reducing the growing social inequality between member countries. The EU remains deeply polarized at the regional level. Even after a decade of strong affirmative action policies on the part of Brussels, little progress has been made building a level playing field between the 'north' and 'south'. In this respect, there are striking similarities in the way regional integration is occurring in the EU and NAFTA.

The most important are the changes in the rules with respect to foreign direct investment and these will have a major impact in limiting the role of the state in correcting regional disparities. There are large wage and income differences between Mexico, Canada, and the USA. These are of the same order as between Portugal, Greece, and Spain on the one hand and

Denmark and Germany on the other. Yet, in both enabling frameworks, investment incentives are to be restricted. Tariff and tax concessions are to be policed; and subsidies and investment grants are to be tightly controlled. Performance requirements that countries in the past have imposed on multi-national and national capital are to be eliminated, restricted, or phased out. Here the list of industrial policy-related practices is long and imposing.

Governments will no longer be able to use local-equity requirements, manufacturing limitations, transfer-of-technology requirements, local content rules, or product mandating requirements to discriminate between foreign and local firms. Also, governments will lose control of another set of policies when they decide to enhance their reliance on foreign direct investment flows. In the past governments could impose export limitations on foreign affiliates as well as charge preferential taxes on foreign investment income. In a trade bloc environment, governments will find that these kinds of measures are now out of bounds (United Nations 1992: 73). If all the proposed prohibitions of trade-restricting measures were passed and enforced, the economic impact of these trade-restricting measures would markedly reduce member state controls over the location of new investments, technology transfers, and local content. The new norms are a response to long term changes in the accumulation régime as it adapts to a continental and regional system of production.

The most important watershed development is to target the nation-state itself as a source of discrimination. Tariffs were designed to create openness in an era of mass industrial production. In a service-dominated economy, the obligation of non-discrimination is the equivalent to the most-favoured-nation principle that forced nation-states to dismantle tariff barriers. The aim of the new principle is to generate a downward pressure on national governments everywhere in order to restrict their ability to influence where corporations will select to make their future investments. The reason is that in the new growth model, the private sector is to be the engine of development in the industrialized world. This requires the expansion of property rights and very different kinds of state policies to promote investment-led integration. The most important change will affect the income patterns of highly competitive labour markets in all participating countries. The challenging question remains: Is this kind of trade régime the best vehicle to promote greater co-operation between countries?

NAFTA is virtually bereft of any kind of common policy storehouse for the foreseeable future. There is no definition of a subsidy in the agreement and this crucial omission enables the USA government to use its own rules and procedures to determine which of Canada's many state programmes constitute an 'unfair' subsidy. In the absence of agreement, the USA Congress has a wide orbit of action to target Canadian and Mexican practices that it opposes. Also, there is the chilling affect dimension on new government initiatives. For instance, the Ontario social democratic government in 1992 had contemplated introducing public automobile insurance, but under NAFTA it was required to pay damages to any USA insurance company that it 'nationalized'. While there were other reasons for not proceeding with its public automobile insurance plan, NAFTA and the FTA give USA corporations legal and extra-legal protection from publically-minded governments that are intent upon expanding the public delivery of services.

Adjustment is yet another critical area that requires that Canadian and Mexican authorities to conform to the new standards to be found within the NAFTA text. The process is to be rule-driven instead of being managed by coordinated government programmes. Here too there is legal and political asymmetry evident. Both Mexico and Canada are linked more directly than ever to the political moodswings of the USA Congress, despite the fact that Mexican and Canadian authorities deny that there is any asymmetrical obligation on their part. The reality is quite different. USA commercial policy is expected to have a disciplining affect on any interventionist stance that they might consider.

While NAFTA sets out new binding and non-binding norms to limit government practices that are deemed trade distorting, a major complication is that there is no specification agreed to by all three parties of which programmes fall into this category. Similarly, another obstacle is the lack of agreement on subsidy practice. In the absence, USA practice and trade law prevails. As well, the NAFTA text establishes new norms and practices with respect to national treatment for its financial sector. Mexico and Canada must not discriminate against USA corporations or firms. Both countries are required to reduce barriers to USA investors in key areas of the economy. Neither country will be able to nationalize or regulate foreign firms without conforming to the new rules of the trade game. In all these ways, NAFTA limits the domestic practices of Canada and Mexico to a degree never before possible.

The contrast with the EU approach to access and adjustment is dramatic. Its most important market corrective instrument is the EC's structural funds programme. These are used to support industrial development for disadvantaged regions. The funding is designed to build a level playing field not only in the south but also parts of France, Ireland, the UK, and even Germany. The funds are also used to address the structural problems facing the EU. In the case of steel and textile industries, funds are allocated to pay for closing firms and laying off workers. In addition, EC funds can be used to defray start-up costs in underdeveloped parts of the EU. For example, Portugal has received large-scale support of a joint venture to produce vans.

It remains an open question just how effective EC structural aid is in fact. In certain countries, such as Spain and Portugal, the monies have helped to modernize and build efficient roads and railway infrastructure. On the other hand, this form of aid has had remarkably little effect in closing the income gap within the EU. A recent Brussels report disclosed that close to 40 per cent of the Union's inhabitants live below the average income norm. By North American standards, the EU continues to devote a large per cent of its resources to promote social cohesion. Yet, regional and income inequalities are on the rise in many parts of Europe despite the existence of these programmes. It is not clear that even with the doubling of structural funds that the periphery regions will become more attractive places for investors.

6. CONCLUSION

The contemporary preoccupation with building regional arrangements is a new twist on a well-worn idea. Countries everywhere want association rather than isolation. The current vision behind European and North American regionalism policies is to promote closer ties between nation states is bold in the extreme. Both are comprehensive agreements designed to foster far-reaching interdependency between members. For this reason these trade blocs appear to be benign, but they are not. NAFTA and the EU are unsustainable in their present form. They lead to the weakening of national authority at precisely the time when national governments need more autonomy and resources to rebuild their industries shattered by the world-wide economic crisis. On both sides of the Atlantic, the magnitude of adjustment is far greater and complex an issue than has been previously anticipated. In the 1990s, export-driven growth has become job-destructive. The fact that unemployment has risen dramatically in all industrial countries raises serious questions about social stability and the long term viability of these kinds of initiatives. As important as job-creation is, the essential issue is that fewer countries want their economic future and well-being to be decided by the dominant partner. Finding ways to address the asymmetry issue will either push NAFTA and the EU to the brink of failure or guarantee that they will have a future.

It is striking that NAFTA and the EU have not located a means to neutralize the power of the USA and Germany respectively. The fact remains that trade is being politicized more than ever. NAFTA is rapidly becoming a dollar bloc and the EU is finding itself marching to the policies of the Bundesbank. With markets more globally-oriented than ever, it is wrong to believe that the agent of integration is the market *pur et dur*. It is closer to the truth to realize that these complex trade blocs depend on the reorganization of the multinational enterprise internationally for their vitality. Its decisions determine whether investment will occur, where production facilities will be located, and which friendly governments will receive technological transfers. Compared with NAFTA, the EU has more policy instruments to push the integration process in a different direction and produce the kind of policy counterweights needed to restrict capital mobility.

Brussels has the power to restructure and shape its industries on a national and Community-wide level. If there was sufficient agreement within its ranks, the EC could produce an integrated package designed to promote macro-economic coordination and address the mayhem of the money markets. The Commission has enough resources to support growth-producing infrastructure projects such as road, rail, telecommunications, and energy networks. This sort of macro-economic approach does not however go to the heart of the matter. If integration is to proceed, it has to be based on addressing the social dimension of European integration. Europe must address the fact that it requires an institutional mechanism to redistribute the welfare gains from the highly successful sectors to the least successful regions. If this is not accomplished, there is no incentive for countries to remain part of the block if their industries do not benefit to the degree promised and employment-creation opportunities fail to materialize. Redistribution of benefits has to be the top priority in the coming decade for integration to prosper.

By contrast, NAFTA's future is risk-laden. Canada and Mexico are confronted with the task of finding a mechanism to delimit NAFTA. At present, NAFTA is an economic integration project driven by the strategic investment needs of the three countries. If further progress is to be achieved, it will be necessary for the participants to find ways to take off the table a host of issues such as environment, culture, resource management, and state aids to industry. If this is not possible, it is likely that there will be strong pressure from interest groups and others to abrogate NAFTA. Presently, public support is at an all time low in Canada for it. In Mexico, the uprising of the Zapatistas and the peso crisis crystallized the opposition to the USA-dominated trade project. Many Canadians and Mexicans now understand that economic integration is a poor substitute for hemispheric co-operation. Neither country want to be burned at the stake of international competition. This is why dream merchants of trade face such an uncertain and risky future.

15

Labour in the Global Economy: Four Approaches to Transnational Labour Regulation

KATHERINE VAN WEZEL STONE

I. INTRODUCTION

Twenty-five years ago, Raymond Vernon foresaw that increased international economic activity would create profound political problems. He warned that the imminent growth of multinational enterprises was a 'threat to national politics . . . [because] [m]ultinational enterprises are not easily subjected to national policy'. Further, Vernon said, the threat to national politics would come not only from multinational enterprises, but also from the shrinking of trade barriers, and improvements in transportation and communications technologies. 'These are likely to raise issues of sovereignty that may, in the end, dwarf the multinational enterprise problem' (Vernon 1970: 396–400). Since then, the globalization of the world economy has proceeded at a fast pace. World trade has displaced domestic trade as the engine of economic growth. Direct foreign investment by multinational corporations has increased dramatically in the past decade. The nations of the world are quickly dividing themselves into trading blocs. Telecommunication and computer technologies have made it easier for firms to engage in production, distribution, and marketing all over the world. Trade barriers are falling, foreign exchange restrictions are disappearing, and national borders are becoming permeable.

While the economic dimension of the global economy can be measured, monitored, and described in quantitative terms, there is also a more subtle, and yet equally powerful, *qualitative* change underway. The global economy has diminished the regulatory capability of the nation-state and thus calls into question conventional views of sovereignty. This results from two distinct factors. First, within trading blocs, much domestic regulation is superseded by multilateral treaties and tribunals that have *de facto*, if not *de jure* trumping power. Second, there is a practical limitation on the ability of one nation to regulate its domestic affairs in a world where labour and capital move freely across national borders. In such a world, legislation that is onerous to the business community, such as most social welfare and worker protective legislation, tends to induce capital flight and to trigger a 'race to the bottom'. Thus the nation-state is becoming increasingly powerless to play its historic role of protector of the health, safety, and welfare of its citizens (Barnet and Muller 1974: 302; Picciotto, chapter 3, in this volume).

The inability of the nation-state to regulate effectively in the domestic sphere raises troubling social, distributional, and political concerns. For example, if domestic economies are no longer amenable to governmental regulation, one can expect an increase in inequality in the distribution of income, wealth, and power both within and between nations. Further, in a world where domestic states have limited power to legislate domestically, the political process based on sovereignty becomes problematic. Once economic regulation is made by transnational bodies, what kinds of power are left to the disempowered nation-state? What is the role of domestic politics, of social movements, and interest groups? And, in transnational tribunals and international agencies, who speaks for the nation, whose interests will be represented as the 'national interest'? And, what is the source of political legitimacy of the disempowered and/or reconstructed nation-state?

In no area is the political dimension of the global economy more troubling than in the area of labour regulation. A society's labour standards and labour regulations are a defining aspect of its standard of living. And yet without the capacity of government to intervene, labour standards are everywhere threatened.

This chapter examines the challenge to domestic labour regulation of the increasingly international economic and legal order. I discuss the several respects in which globalization creates problems for labour and I describe the means by which national and transnational bodies are attempting to address those problems. In doing so, I identify four emerging models of transnational labour regulation which differ from each other in important ways. I show that these emerging models of transnational labour regulation embody different normative choices about what the emerging global economy will look like. I then offer criteria to enable us to evaluate the emerging models of transnational labour regulation and select between them.

The next section describes the many ways in which increased global economic integration is problematic for labour. For example, in the global economy, labour is weakened in its bargaining power with individual employers. Firms that do not want to accept union wage demands or maintain working conditions that meet union standards can evade these by moving facilities overseas to an area where the workforce is less advantaged or less well organized. This is the problem of the 'runaway shop'. Unions in domestic firms, aware of that threat, moderate their demands in order to retain union members' jobs. Labour is particularly weakened in the global economy due to the 'race to the bottom' problem. Companies prefer to produce in legal environments which offer the least protections for labour. This places labour in a dilemma: It both wants domestic protective legislation to improve labour standards but is acutely vulnerable to the capital flight that improved labour standards can trigger. This dilemma is intensified as economic life becomes more global. And finally, globalization weakens labour in its role as a political actor. Historically labour movements have organized in the context of a particular regulatory environment. When the locus of labour regulation moves to transnational tribunals, national labour movements lose their political capital, their ability to act as effective pressure groups.

In the third section, I describe four approaches toward transnational labour regulation that have emerged in the Western world in the past twenty years, each of which is a partial solution to these concerns. The four approaches are: (1) pre-emptive legislation; (2) harmonization of domestic legislation; (3) cross-border monitoring and enforcement; and (4) extraterritorial application of domestic law. Briefly, these approaches are as follows.

Preemptive legislation is transnational legislation that is directly applicable to persons, business entities, and states within a transnational bloc. *Harmonization* refers to legal rules of a transnational body, such as the EU, which create incentives for countries to bring their domestic laws into conformity with each other. The European Union has utilized both preemptive legislation and harmonization to address some labour and employment issues. Both of these are integrative approaches, aiming to make disparate regulatory systems congruent and consistent over time.

In North America, two other models of transnational labour regulation have emerged: *cross-border monitoring and enforcement*, and *extraterritorial application of domestic law*. The former is found in the Labour Side Agreement of the North American Free Trade Agreement (NAFTA), which creates a mechanism through which each country can challenge another's application of the other's own, separate, national labour law regulations. The other North American model of transnational labour regulation, *extraterritorial jurisdiction*, involves applying the labour laws of one country to actions and parties in another country. Extraterritorial jurisdiction is becoming an important aspect of domestic labour law in the United States of America. These two North American models differ from the European models in their overall approach. Whereas the European models are both integrative, as described above, the North American models embody what I call an interpenetration approach, the temporary incursion of one legal system into the affairs of another legal system.

In the fourth section, I explore the differences between the models. I discuss the four models in terms of their ability to solve the various problems that globalization causes for labour described in the second section. I also discuss each of the models' ability to achieve other goals that are posited for transnational labour regulation, including the goals of increasing trade and fostering international co-operation.

I conclude that the various models of transnational labour regulation have different capacities for achieving each of the goals posited, and that no one model is optimal on all criteria. Each model involves a particular solution to the problems of labour regulation in a global economy. Each model embodies a particular role for domestic legislation and creates a particular role for domestic interest group politics. Each implements a different political vision and promotes different distributive outcomes. And each one makes a distinct contribution to international co-operation and world peace. No one model can achieve all goals. I conclude that it is necessary to choose between the various models of transnational labour regulation, and in doing so, we must be explicit about our goals and conscious of the normative and distributional ramifications that each choice embodies.

2. THE PROBLEMS FOR LABOUR REGULATION IN THE GLOBAL ECONOMY

Over the past thirty years, USA unions have seen an explosion of overseas runaway shops and multi-national corporations shifting production overseas (Murphy 1977: 620–1). Globalization hurts domestic labour movements in several respects: It diminishes labour's bargaining power vis-a-vis its employer, it creates a disincentive for labour to actively seek labour protective legislation, it leads to organizational fragmentation, and it causes atrophy of labour's political clout. Each of these dynamics will be described.

2.1 The Decline of Union Bargaining Power

Increased globalization of the world economy means increased capital mobility. Corporations prefer to establish production facilities in countries with lower wage rates, lower labour standards and fewer labour rights. The resultant business flight to low wage areas, commonly known is the 'runaway shop', has been a concern of Western labour movements for many decades. Within the United States of America also, USA corporations began moving to the South in search of lower wages and lower unionization rates in the 1920's. Indeed the phrase 'race to the bottom' was coined by Justice Brandeis in 1933 (*Liggett* v. *Lee* 1933: 557) to describe inter-jurisdictional competition for businesses moving to states with the least onerous regulatory requirements (Charny 1991: 430–1). Corporate flight in more recent years has been motivated by the additional factors of avoiding state worker compensation systems, state unemployment insurance programs, and other labour protective programs. Indeed, states that have few labour protective regulations often use that fact in their advertisements to attract businesses from other, more regulated, states (Bluestone and Harrison 1982: 84).

Companies that can freely and costlessly relocate to low-wage areas are able to resist union demands for higher wages or improved working conditions. Furthermore unions, when facing a credible threat of relocation, revise downward their wage demands (McGuiness 1994: 580–2; Ansley 1993: 1763–1782). Thus the level of a union's bargaining power is a function of the ease by which companies can in fact relocate production to low wage areas. As business relocation costs go down and as relocation possibilities increase, union bargaining clout diminishes.

Capital flight poses a problem for unions in labour-management negotiations. American labour law does not at present give unions a right to bargain about strategic-level corporate decisions, such as whether to relocate across the border or whether to merge with a foreign corporation (Stone 1988: 96–119; 1993: 372–3). Furthermore, firms that make such changes do not take their collective bargaining obligations with them. Thus firms that relocate from unionized high-wage areas to nonunion low-wage areas are free to exploit whatever wage differentials exist, and USA unions have few means to resist.

In a frictionless world, companies would exploit whatever wage and benefit differentials exist around the globe, and unions would be forced to compete with nonunion workers all over the globe. While we do not yet have a frictionless world, transnational runaway shops are occurring more frequently than ever before due to advances in communication technology, the increased quantity and velocity of world trade, and the growth of direct foreign investment and multi-national corporations. Further, the advent of trading blocs, free-trading zones, the GATT/WTO agreement and other 'free trade' reforms are removing legal restrictions on the ability of capital to flow to locations which generate the highest returns at the lowest factor costs. Thus transnational trade pacts and other 'free trade' devices which make it easier for business to move across national borders have the effect of diminishing labour's bargaining power.

2.2 The 'Race to the Bottom' Problem

Not only does globalization undermine union bargaining power, it also undermines union efforts in the legislative arena. When corporations are free to relocate wherever they want, then unions are placed in a prisoner's dilemma. The more effective unions are at obtaining legislative protections in the political arena, the more likely businesses are to move to other areas. In that event, the workers lose the very jobs which made the protections desirable in the first place. Without jobs the workers are worse off than they were before the protections were obtained. This is the dilemma of labour regulation that globalization creates.

There are two aspects to the 'race to the bottom' problem confronting labour. First, is the circumstance in which multinational firms, searching for lower production costs, move production from high wage countries to low wage countries by means of capital flight and direct foreign investment. This situation, while not new for American unions, arises more frequently with globalization. In addition, countries now have an incentive to compete for business by altering their domestic regulations in order to create a regulatory environment that business will find attractive. Countries who consider their low-wage status an advantage in attracting mobile capital, resist attempts to equalize labour rights (von Maydell 1993: 1403). This problem has been termed 'regulatory competition' (see Introduction to this volume; Trachtman 1993). Many scholars have discussed the possibility that regulatory competition will lead to the deregulation of banking practices and financial markets (e.g., Cox 1992), the easing of environmental regulations, the weakening of products liability and other tort law rules, as well as the lowering of labour standards.

Both types of races to the bottom weaken labour in the political arena insofar as they create disincentives for labour to lobby for protective legislation. They thus serve to deprive labour of one important tool for worker betterment—legislative action. However, the second race to the bottom, regulatory competition, is even more problematic for labour than the conventional one. While the traditional 'race to the bottom' undermined labour's incentive to seek legislative gains, regulatory competition undermines political support for American labour standards throughout the electorate. The threat of business flight creates interest groups that want to use low levels of regulation to attract business. This could then trigger a deregulatory spiral in which countries compete for business on the basis of their low labour standards. Domestically, this spiral could be deeply divisive within labour groups, setting organized workers against unorganized ones, workers with jobs against the unemployed, and all workers against both the poor and small businesses.

Some commentators have argued that, at least within a single country, the existence of multiple jurisdictions with multiple regulatory frameworks does not necessarily create sub-optimal levels of regulation or otherwise impair the public welfare (e.g., Ravesz 1992; Oates and Schwab 1988; Fischel 1975). They argue that there is no 'race to the bottom' problem, at least in the area of environmental regulation. They point out that when enacting environmental regulations, local governments make a tradeoff between environmental quality and tax revenues from businesses. The resultant level of regulation reflects the locality's preferences between these two incommensurate goals. According to this view, regulatory competition produces a variety of policy mixes that are tailored to a particular locality's preferences. They conclude that the existence of multiple jurisdictions and capital mobility fosters a desirable method of arriving at policy goals rather than a prisoner's dilemma.

This argument might be true in the environmental area, where the pro-environment groups and the pro-business groups are two different constituencies which each contend for their positions in a local policy-making forum. In such a context, the resultant level of regulation is thus a compromise that reflects the relative power of the two contending factions, a compromise that could be reached at a different point in a different locality where the two groups have different relative strengths. However, that argument does not apply to labour regulation; indeed, the theorists of environmental regulation expressly disavow consideration of employment effects from the social choice between levels of environmental regulation. If employment effects are not only considered, but made central, then the analysis comes out quite differently.

Labour regulation differs from environmental regulation in that the group that stands to benefit the most from such regulation is also the group that has the most to lose from any resultant business flight. That is, labour regulation involves a different type of prisoners' dilemma than is present in the environmental area. With labour regulation there are not two opposed parties, each of which is able to articulate and advocate its own separate interest in a policy arena. Rather, with labour regulation, the group that stands to benefit most is also the group that has the most to lose. Thus, in contrast to environmental regulation, the level of a locality's labour regulation is not a tradeoff, or compromise, between conflicting groups, each with its separate constituency, urging alternative policy goals. Rather, the level of labour regulation represents a Hobson's choice that is created, structured, and framed by the possibility of a 'race to the bottom'.

2.3 Organizational Fragmentation

One strategy that USA unions have used to diminish the possibilities of runaway shops and 'races to the bottom', has been to advocate federal legislation that would equalize labour standards for particular labour issues (Weiss 1993: 1439). For example, the rationale for the USA Congress to enact the Occupational Safety and Health Act in 1970 was to prevent firms from moving to states with low levels of occupational health and safety protection by creating national occupational safety and health standards and enforcement mechanisms (Ackerman 1992: 90). Another strategy has been for unions to organize in low wage states and thus attempt to equalize labour standards between states. Operating under a single set of federal labour laws, unions in a single country such as the United States of America are often able to promote wage parity and limit internal capital movement.

However, when corporations move beyond national boundaries, the countervailing pressures present in a single country operate weakly or not at all. There is little prospect for obtaining supervening legislation to equalize labour standards, and very few prospects for cross-union co-operation. With the exception of Canada, USA unions have little experience organizing or jointly bargaining with unions in other countries or operating under foreign legal régimes (Murphy 1977: 626). In addition, other countries have labour laws and collective bargaining systems that are very different from those in the United States of America. Thus it is difficult for USA unions to collaborate with unions in other countries in a way that jointly harnesses their economic weapons and furthers their joint bargaining goals.

American unions know that without co-operation across national lines, they are forced to compete with labour in different countries to keep domestic businesses at home, to attract foreign businesses, and to keep outsider-workers out. Yet they have had difficulty formulating an effective response to the problem of international runaway shops. Thus they have advocated a grab-bag of policies including restrictions on immigration, opposition to trade agreements, changes in tax rules, and legal restrictions on multinational corporations (Murphy 1977: 624–6). At the same time USA unions have sought to establish, or strengthen, co-operative relations with unions overseas, but such efforts are in their early stages (Turner 1993; Murphy 1977: 627; Friedman 1993: 1422). These somewhat contradictory impulses are in fact related—they are efforts to limit global runaway shops, which in the current international and economic climate seems to be endemic.

2.4. The Deterioration of Labour's Political Role

Another problem that globalization causes for labour is that labour's political power is undermined when the locus of labour regulation moves from a national to an international arena. National labour movements operate in the context of a particular regulatory environment. National or local-level rules establish the parameters of labour standards and determine labour-management bargaining arrangements. Until now, these regulations have been determined at the level of national politics. Much labour organizing and mobilization has been directed toward securing those national labour regulations and/or trying to improve them. Because otherwise diverse labour groups within a given nation-state have similar interests and compatible legislative agendas, unions in most Western countries have been able to organize at the national level and have become an effective player in national politics. However, if the locus of labour regulation is moved to transnational tribunals, then it is difficult for national labour movements to mobilize for gains in the political process. If labour regulation is not made at the level of the nation-state, national labour movements lose much of their political clout. And without political clout, labour's ability to maintain a regulatory régime that gives it bargaining power in the economic realm is seriously compromised (Stone 1988).

More significantly, if labour ceases to be a voice in national politics, then the democratic nature of government is also undermined. Social theorists dating back to De Toqueville have recognized that a robust democracy requires that there be a plethora of voluntary organizations in which citizens can participate. Voluntary organizations are the vehicle by which citizens' private concerns can be shared and translated into public issues, issues which can then generate pressure for legislative or electoral action. Without voluntary organizations, it is almost impossible in a modern democracy for groups to articulate shared concerns and bring their interests into the political arena. Labour unions, as voluntary organizations whose purpose is to promote workers' interests, function not merely as economic workplace-based organizations, but also as political lobbying groups and electoral blocks. They articulate the interests and public policy concerns of a large segment of the population, which would otherwise be silenced and the democractic process would be diminished.

3. FOUR MODELS OF TRANSNATIONAL REGULATION.

Given the many respects in which globalization is a threat to domestic labour movements and labour regulatory régimes, most trade unionists and many labour relations professionals have viewed the rapid march of globalization with alarm. The question of whether the organized labour movements in the Western world can protect their gains in a global economy has been discussed, debated, and bemoaned at length over the past ten years. Despite a pervasive sense of gloom, there has been some optimistic speculation about alternative forms of labour regulation that might emerge in the post-trading bloc world.

For example, it is sometimes posited that transnational labour institutions will be developed, and transnational labour standards will be adopted, that will replace a national labour regulatory régime with an international one. This scenario suggests that transnational labour standards will emerge, along with transnational labour movements to implement them and multilateral tribunals to enforce them, which will recreate at the international level the protections labour currently enjoys domestically.

While this view is not wholly fanciful—there are some developments in the EU to support it—it is a bit rosy-eyed. For example, it begs the question of which regulations will prevail at the multilateral level and how they will be enforced (Rozwood and Walker 1993: 342). It also ignores the fact that at present there are no serious cross-border labour organizations which can engage in multi-lateral bargaining. Further, it ignores the problem of how the multilateral agencies—agencies whose relationship to any particular political constituency is attenuated to begin with—will be persuaded to provide labour protections in the first place (Ludlow 1992).

Rather than embark on an imaginary journey into possible forms of labour regulation in a post-trading bloc world, I want to describe four types of transnational labour regulation that are emerging in fact. If we look at developments in the EU and in North America, we see four distinct types, or models, of transnational labour regulation, each one having particular strengths and weaknesses, and each one embodying a unique theory of the role of domestic labour regulation.

A. *Two European Approaches to Transnational Labour Regulation*

Each of the member states of the European Community has its own legal history, customs, norms, and cultures that have shaped its system of labour rights. Each state has developed a large body of legal rules, statutes, regulations and procedures which establish employment standards for individual workers, including statutory minimum wages, unemployment and job training provisions, and so forth. In addition, each EU country has its own distinct legal and institutional structure of collective bargaining. These European national collective bargaining systems differ markedly. For example, German labour laws provide for industry-wide unions which engage in industry-wide collective bargaining at the national-level. At the same time, German unions have a legal rights to participation both on corporate boards of directors and at the workplace (Summers 1980; Zakson 1984: 114–126). In France, there are several competing national unions in each industry, each of which engages in bargaining at both the national and local level, resulting in fragmented bargaining. There are no legally established codetermination rights but there are extensive protections for individual employment and for collective action (Blanc-Jouvan 1984: 1345–7; Despax and Robot 1987). In Great Britain, unions engage in collective bargaining but have no co-determination rights and relatively few legally enforceable rights of any sort (Wedderburn 1986: 343). Other countries have other union structures and legal régimes of collective bargaining, all of which give protection to some form of collective bargaining, but no two of which are the same. In addition, some countries have a system of labour courts to enforce collective labour rights, some rely on specialized administrative tribunals, and some on courts of general jurisdiction.

The EU addresses this plurality of regulation in two ways. One approach is preemptive legislation. Preemptive legislation includes treaty provisions and EU Regulations that are directly applicable to citizens of the member states. These Regulations set uniform rules for certain labour rights, and have priority over conflicting national legislation. Thus they are a form of unified transnational labour legislation. The other approach is known as harmonization. Harmonization involves structured incentives and pressures created by the EU legal rules which induce the member states to bring their separate labour laws into conformity. Harmonization occurs both directly, through EU Directives, and indirectly through collateral agreements or convergence processes. It is a strategy that is based on the short-term acceptance of differences in regulatory régimes, and it embodies the assumption that, over time, differences will fade and there will emerge a unified set of norms, rules and procedures.

3.1 Preemptive Legislation

The European Economic Community Treaty ('EEC Treaty, or the 'Treaty of Rome') sets out specific provisions of supranational law in certain areas, and sets up structures for EU-wide regulation in other areas. There are very few specific provisions in the EEC Treaty that bear directly on labour law. The few labour provisions are found in Title III, the Free Movement of Persons, Services, and Capital. Articles 48–51 lay down provisions to facilitate the freedom of movement of workers, including the treatment of and social benefits for migrant workers. There are also equivalent provisions concerning professionals and self-employed workers (Articles 59–62). Other Treaty articles cover social provisions relating to workers, such as working conditions and social security (Articles 117–122). However, these provisions state general principles and do not create directly applicable law or enforceable rights. The one major exception is article 119, providing for equal pay between women and men, which has had considerable impact on national laws (Bercusson 1992, and Moffatt, chapter 11, in this volume).

The EEC Treaty also established a Social Fund, the goal of which is to provide vocational training and resettlement allowances for workers who are displaced, and to enable workers to be geographically and occupationally mobile. The Social Fund does not give workers employment rights nor regulate labour conditions; it merely cushions transitions.

The EU Council of Ministers has the power to enact specific labour Regulations if they are within the scope of the Treaty provisions, but it has promulgated very few Regulations on labour matters (Weiss 1993: 1435–7). What few there are concern issues of migrant workers, professional workers, and equality between men and women.

In 1989, European lawmakers attempted to enact a Community Charter of Fundamental Social Rights of Workers (known as the 'Social Charter'). The Social Charter contained a list of 'Fundamental Social Rights of Workers,' which included occupational health and safety protections, guarantees for the right to organize and bargain collectively, rights to adequate social welfare benefits, workplace consultation and participation rights, and protection for children, older workers, and the disabled (Friedman 1993:

1423). Due to disagreement among the Member States, especially the hostility of the UK government, this Charter remained as only a statement of policy and not a legally binding agreement.

3.2 Harmonization

In practice, the Council of Ministers has preferred not to create unified employment rights by means of multilateral Regulations, but rather, in most areas, it has attempted to encourage its member nations to harmonize their labour and employment laws. The goal of harmonization is to provide incentives for convergence, or 'approximation,' between collective bargaining systems. Harmonization occurs in two ways: by Directive and by indirect pressures from rules in other areas that have a collateral impact on labour matters.

(i) Direct Harmonization

An EU Directive is a regulation enacted by the Council of Ministers which the Member States must then enact into domestic legislation. Each Directive usually specifies a time period within which the member states are required to 'transpose' it into their own domestic law. Usually the Directives set minimum standards in a particular area which the member states then must enact in ways that are consistent with their own distinctive labour law systems.

There are presently EU Directives in effect in several areas of labour regulation. The 1975 Directive on collective redundancies, also known as dismissals for economic reasons, requires firms who intend to implement a mass layoff to notify workers affected and confer with the worker representatives.[1] In 1977, a Directive on transfer of enterprises was adopted, which was designed to protect workers who were faced with takeovers and other changes in the ownership of the firms that employ them. It provides that employees whose companies are involved in a transfer of ownership of all or part of a company must have their pre-existing contractual rights, including collective bargaining rights, honoured by the new entity.[2] And in 1980, a Directive on insolvencies provided that firms must guarantee payment of workers' outstanding wage claims and benefits prior to the commencement of insolvency proceedings.[3]

---

[1] Council Directive 75/129 O.J. (l48) 29. This directive was interpreted narrowly in a case before the European Court, *Dansk* v. *Metalarbejderforbund*, Case 284/83 (1985) ECR 553. Weiss 1993: 1449–1456 compares this EC directive on mass layoffs with the Workers Adjustment and Retraining Act (WARN) under American labour law.

[2] Council Directive 77/187 O.J. (L 61) 26. See *Foreningen AF Arbejdsledere* v. *Daddy's Dance Hall*, Case 324/86 (1988) ECR 739 (employees' rights under acquired rights directive cannot be waived); and Weiss 1993: 1457–59 (comparing transfer of ownership directive to successorship rights under American labor law).

[3] Council Directive 80/987 O.J. (l 283) 23, October 20, 1980. See Weiss 1993: 1449 (comparing directive on insolvencies to workers rights under USA federal bankruptcy law).

There have also been Directives addressing workplace safety and health and equal treatment for men and men.[4] In addition, the EU is considering several Directives concerning part-time workers, service workers, and temporary workers (Bercusson 1992: 179–80).

In 1992, at Maastricht, the twelve member states agreed to transform the European Communities into the European Union. In the negotiations leading up to the Maastricht agreement, there were considerable pressures to enlarge the EEC Treaty's social policy provisions, but due to the UK government's continued opposition, this could not be unanimously agreed. Instead, provisions based on the previous Social Charter (mentioned above) were annexed as a Social Agreement accepted by all except the UK. These eleven were authorized by the Protocol on Social Policy to utilize the mechanisms of the EC for the purposes of implementing that Social Agreement. This UK 'opt-out' means that social policy proposals which the UK government is unwilling to accept may be agreed among the remaining states, and become binding on all except the UK.

The Social Agreement made a number of changes in the manner of implementation of labour Directives (Blanpain 1992: 31–54). Most significantly, it provided that labour Directives can be implemented through collective bargaining agreements as well as through legislation and administrative regulation. Thus, it increased the role of collective bargaining within the EC, yet it also created the possibility that the protections contained in certain Directives could be bargained away (Bercusson 1992: 181–4). In addition, the Social Agreement extended the legislative capacity of the EU, and expanded the issues on which the EU (or at least, the eleven excluding the UK) could legislate on the basis of majority voting, rather than unanimity as had previously been required (Bercusson 1992: 182–3; Weiss 1993: 1431–2). These areas include health and safety protection, working conditions, workers' information and consultation rights, equality between men and women, employment protection, collective representation and co-determination. Indeed, in September 1994, the first Directive was agreed under it, providing for the establishment of European Works Councils or other consultative procedures by multinational enterprises employing at least 1,000 workers with at least 150 in each of two Member States (Directive 94/45; O.J. L254/64). A number of multinationals have moved to set up such Works Councils, and although it is not legally binding on the UK, some have included their UK workers in the arrangements (*Financial Times*, 10th April 1995).

The Social Agreement retains unanimous voting for the harmonization of most collective labour rights. Article 2(6) excludes from majority voting provisions dealing with 'pay, the right of association, the right to strike or the

---

[4] Council Directive 89/391 O.J. 1989 (L183); Council Directive 76/207 O.J. (L39) and 86/378 O.J. (L 225).

right to impose lockouts'. Thus unanimous voting was retained for Directives in the areas of job security, representation, and collective defense of workers' interests (Blanpain 1992: 39–40). Apart from the Works Council Directive, the EU has not so far attempted to legislative or harmonize in the field of collective bargaining law (von Maydell 1993: 1416), nor has it issued any Regulations or Directives concerning industrial disputes.

EU Directives have force only to the extent that they are implemented by the member states. Thus the actual meaning of the Directives can vary greatly between states. However, in a landmark decision in 1991, *Francovich* v. *Italy*, the European Court of Justice ruled that a member country could be liable to an individual worker for restitution if it failed to enact a labour protection Directive. In that case, two Italian workers sued the Italian government for failing to implement the 1980 Directive concerning worker protection in insolvencies. The Court ruled that it is 'inherent in the Treaty system' that the member states are liable to individuals who are damaged by the state's failure to implement Directives, or to do so inadequately. This decision will give added enforcement power to the Directives, and may lead to a uniform interpretation of the rights and protections they contain. If they become more uniform in application, Directives will come to resemble the preemptive legislation of the Regulations discussed above, rather than mere harmonization.

(ii) Indirect Harmonization

In addition to harmonization by means of EU labour Directives, the EU can harmonize labour regulation indirectly by means of regulations and Directives in other areas of law. For example, labour policy is implicated by regulations and Directives in the area of corporate law. The EU has a major programme of Directives to harmonize corporate law, including a long-standing draft Directive on corporate structure, and a proposal for a European-wide stock corporation. However, these proposals have not yet been enacted, largely due to disagreement about the proper role of labour in the structure of the corporation. Some member states have extensive co-determination rights for workers built into their current laws on corporate structures, others have requirements for consultation through works councils, while some do not. The Member States have not been able to agree about whether to include codetermination rights in the EU Directive on corporate structure, so neither this Directive nor the European Company proposal has yet been adopted (von Maydell 1993: 1414–5; Weiss 1993: 1561–2). However, if any Directive on corporate structure were adopted, it would have a profound effect on labour's participation rights in all EU nations.

Similarly, any EU Directive on insolvency could have a significant impact on labour. For example, French insolvency law has, as one of its primary objectives, the preservation of workers' jobs. Under French bankruptcy law, this objective has a higher priority than the protection of stockholders (Lividas 1983: 281–2). If this principle is carried over into a European-wide bankruptcy code, it could mean giving labour unions substantial participation rights in bankruptcy proceedings and a large role in the structure of their firms.

3.3 Observations about the European Approaches

As we have seen, the EU has utilized Regulations and Directives to set minimum standards in some areas of employment regulation, but it has not made significant attempts to regulate or harmonize collective labour regulation. The different approaches toward individual employment regulation and collective labour regulation is understandable in the context of European labour relations systems. Prior to European integration, each EU country had legislation establishing a bundle of minimal terms for employment contracts—terms such as minimum wage rates, old age assistance, maximum hours, occupational health and safety protection, health insurance, disability provisions, or job security protection. Frequently these employment standards were similar in structure but differed in their quantitative dimension, such as the precise amount of the minimum wage or the particular sum paid for a particular disability. Because the differences between countries' labour standards were quantitative rather than qualitative, it has been possible to devise a single set of minimal terms which all member countries are required to adopt. Once a unified set of minimal terms is mandated, then each country can adjust its own terms upward or downward to comply with the mandate. No vested interests are disrupted, no labour leaders lose their constituencies, no labour lawyers lose the value of their expertise, and no individual workers lose their jobs. Thus it has been feasible to develop transnational labour standards for individual labour rights within the EU, and to make them mandatory by means of EU-level legislation.

However, when it comes to transnational regulation of collective labour relations, neither harmonization nor preemptive legislation is likely to be a simple expedient. In the area of collective bargaining, each country's own institutions, customs, and labour relations practices have given rise to labour organizations, employer organizations, and labour relations professionals who have a vested stake in the continuation of their own national system. Thus each country's incumbent labour relations personnel, whether they be of a management, labour or neutral perspective, can be expected to resist efforts at transformation that threaten their own particular niche, role, or expertise. They will resist any transnational regulation that attempts to supersede those local regulations, even one that will benefit a particular country's labour movement generally. Hence for collective labour rights, both harmonization and preemptive regulation may be slow to develop (Turner 1993; Lange 1992).

B. *Two North American Approaches to Transnational Labour Regulation*

In North America, there has been no attempt either to harmonize collective bargaining systems nor to unify labour standards, but there has nonetheless been an expansion of transnational labour regulation. This has occurred in two ways: (1) through NAFTA's mechanisms for cross-border monitoring and enforcement of labour standards; and (2) by means of extraterritorial application of USA domestic law. Both North American models of transnational labour regulation create mechanisms through which the labour laws of one country are applied to citizens or corporations in another country.

The North American models of transnational labour regulation differ from the European ones in that the cross-border application of labour laws in the North American models is neither cumulative nor on-going. Rather, the two North American models provide a means by which citizens of one country are given rights or obligations under another country's labour laws on a one-time, single-use basis. NAFTA's cross border monitoring and enforcement permits one country to enforce another country's labour laws in a multilateral tribunal. Extraterritorial jurisdiction permits one country to enforce its own labour laws against another country in its own tribunal. Neither model involves changing the labour laws of any country. In contrast to the two European models, the two North American models do not attempt to integrate separate systems of labour regulation. Whereas the two European models are integrative in their approach, the two North American models embody an approach to transnational regulation which can be termed the *interpenetration* of two legal systems—the temporary incursion of one distinct and autonomous system of regulation into a separate one. The North American models do not aim to facilitate convergence and ultimately unification of regulatory systems, as is the goal of the European models of labour regulation. Instead, the North American models permit temporary, limited-purpose, forays of participants from one system into the affairs of another.

1. Cross-border Monitoring and Enforcement The North American Free Trade Agreement (NAFTA) was signed by the heads of state of Mexico, Canada, and the United States of America in 1992, ratified in 1993, and many of its provisions became effective in January 1994. The initial goal of the treaty is to create a North American free trade bloc and eliminate friction in the mobility of capital and goods between Mexico, Canada, and the United States of America (see Preamble, NAFTA 1992). Ultimately its goal is to create an Americas-wide free trade bloc.

In August, 1993, before NAFTA was submitted to the USA Congress for approval, President Clinton negotiated a Side Accord on Labour Cooperation, known as the NAFTA Labour Side Agreement (1993). He did this in an effort to address concerns about NAFTA raised by organized labour, particularly concerns that NAFTA would cause massive job loss (Cowie 1993). The groups that advocated a Labour Side Agreement hoped it would provide equal and/or fair labour standards throughout the trading bloc (Rozwood and Walker 1993: 335; Gunderson 1994: 12–13).

The Labour Side Agreement that was negotiated did not imitate the European models of transnational labour regulation. Unlike the power that the EC Commission has to enact labour-related Regulations and Directives under the EEC Treaty, the agencies established by the NAFTA Side Agreement have no authority over the actual labour standards of the member countries. The Side Agreement does not seek to equalize labour standards nor to establish a minimum floor of labour standards or labour rights (Cowie and French 1993: 5; Langille xxxx: 618). Neither does it harmonize collective bargaining regulation so as to bring labour conditions between countries into parity. To the contrary, the NAFTA Side Agreement (Article 2) says that no country is required to alter its labour standards in any way. The Side Agreement merely addresses the enforcement of each country's existing labour laws.

The only discussion of substantive protections for labour in the Side Agreement is found in Article I, which says that one of the objectives of the Side Agreement is to 'Promote, to the maximum extent possible, the labour principles set out in Annex 1'. Annex 1 sets out guiding principles to the effect that each country should promote *in its own way*, the ideals of (1) protecting the right to organize, bargain and strike; (2) prohibiting the evils of forced labour, child labour, sub-minimal wages, and employment discrimination; and (3) promoting equal pay for equal work, occupational safety and health, and equal treatment for migrant workers. These 'labour principles' are stated in a general way, as aspirations rather than as enforceable obligations.

While the Side Agreement sets no substantive employment standards, it does provide procedures to ensure that the countries enforce some of their labour laws. However, not all labour laws have their enforcement safeguarded. The Side Agreement's procedures only apply to the enforcement of a country's labour laws dealing with occupational health and safety, child labour, and minimum wages. Regardless of whether the laws of each country are weak or strong, the Side Agreement provides that in those three areas, the laws should be enforced. Thus the procedures for labour law enforcement in the Side Agreement do not attempt to create unified labour standards, even in the areas to which they apply.

The NAFTA cross-border enforcement procedures provide that when one country believes that another country is failing to enforce its own labour laws in the three areas covered—safety, child labour, and minimum wages—it can bring a complaint to the Commission for Labour Cooperation ('the Commission'), consisting of the labour minister of each member state, which attempts to resolve the dispute through consultation and co-operation (McGuiness 1994: 582–87; French 1993; Trudeau and Vallee 1995). Each of the three states is required to establish a National Administrative Office (NAO) to provide information to the Commission. If the dispute is not resolved through consultation by the Commission, one of the three states may request that an Evaluation Committee of Experts (ECE) be convened (Article 23). The ECE is comprised of three members selected by the Council. Its task is to consider whether there has been a pattern or practice of non enforcement of a labour standard that is health and safety-related or otherwise within the three covered areas, and whether the labour standard is 'covered by mutually recognizable labour laws'. The ECE has 120 days to issue a preliminary report and another 60 days to make a final report. After the report is issued, the two countries not targeted by the report may request further consultations on the issue of whether there has been a persistent pattern of nonenforcement by the third country (Article 27). If accord is still not reached, any country may request a special session of the Council to resolve the dispute, and if the dispute is still not resolved within another 60 days, it may request arbitration. An arbitration is held if two-thirds of the Council members vote in favor of doing so. The arbitration is carried out through a five-member panel, which has 240 days to submit a final report (Article 36).

The cross-border enforcement procedures are clearly drawn-out and cumbersome. In addition, they are laced with qualifiers and exceptions. For example, the enforcement procedure calls for sanctions when there is a finding that a party has engaged in a *'persistent* pattern of failure . . . to effectively* enforce its occupational safety and health, child labour, or minimum wage technical labour standards . . .'. (Article 35(2)(b), emphasis added). What constitutes a *'persistent'* pattern of failure, or a lack of *'effective'* enforcement is not specified. In addition, Article 49 carves out an enormous exception to the cross-border enforcement procedure. It states that a party does not fail to 'effectively enforce its [labour laws]' if the action or inaction either

(a) reflects a reasonable exercise of the agency's or the official's discretion with respect to investigatory, prosecutorial, regulatory or compliance matters; or
(b) results from bona fide decisions to allocate resources to enforcement in respect of other labour matters determined to have higher priority'.

There is almost no instance, at least under USA labour law, in which government failure to enforce labour standards cannot be characterized so as to fall within one of these exceptions. These exceptions provide a legal excuse for almost all nonenforcement. In fact, in light of these broad exceptions, it is difficult to imagine any situation in which the Side Agreement's procedures for obtaining labour law enforcement would apply.

While the Side Agreement's enforcement procedures appear to be limited to complaints involving non-enforcement of laws regarding occupational health and safety, child labour, and minimum wages, some unions have tried to give them a broader applicability. In February, 1994 two USA unions filed complaints concerning alleged violations of the right to organize. The Teamsters Union and the International Union of Electrical Workers complained that General Electric Corporation and Honeywell, Inc., respectively, violated the Agreement's protection of free association and protection of union organizing contained in Annex I by firing workers for organizing activities in their Mexican subsidiaries. In April, the USA National Administrative Office—the agency in the USA which determines whether to bring complaints under the Side Agreement—agreed to review the charges.[5] However, while the NAO might have used these cases to give a broad interpretation to Annex I of the Side Agreement, in October they found no evidence that Mexico had failed to enforce its own labour laws, and so it dismissed the complaints.[6]

As currently interpreted, the Labour Side Agreement will not equalize labour standards within North America, nor will it harmonize or bring consistency to the vastly different collective bargaining systems that exist within North America (Rozwood and Walker 1993: 345–7). At best it might lead to more vigorous enforcement of each country's own pre-existing labour laws in some limited areas.

2. Extraterritorial Jurisdiction Another model of transnational labour regulation is the application of domestic labour regulation extraterritorially. From an American standpoint, this means applying USA labour law to labour disputes that occur beyond USA boundaries, or to parties who are not USA citizens. Extraterritorial jurisdiction is becoming an increasingly important feature of American labour law. It is a trend that can be seen in all three branches of government. USA courts are beginning to interpret some of the labour relations statutes in ways that give them extraterritorial reach; Congress has recently amended two major labour law statutes so as to make them expressly extraterritorial; and the Executive Branch has begun to condition trading privileges of foreign countries on compliance with American labour standards.

---

[5] See 145 LRR 493 (BNA, April 25, 1994). For a text of the complaints, see 390 Labor Law Reports, 19,395 (March 4, 1994 CCH); see also McGuiness 1994: 587–590.
[6] 197 Daily Labor Reporter (BNA) AA–1 (October 14, 1994).

(a) Case Law on Extraterritorial Jurisdiction It is often stated that American labour law does not apply extraterritorially.[7] The no-extraterritoriality maxim grew out of a non-labour case decided in 1906. In *American Banana Co.* v. *United Fruit Co.(1909)*, the Supreme Court said that courts should presume that the jurisdiction of American statutes was restricted to American territory. In 1925, the Supreme Court applied the no-extraterritorial jurisdiction presumption to a labour case for the first time. The case, *New York Central Ry. Co.* v. *Chisholm*, arose under the Federal Employers' Liability Act, a workers compensation statute for the railroads, and the Court held that it did not apply to USA citizens working for USA railroads who were injured in Canada.

In 1949, in *Foley Bros.* v. *Filardo (1949)*, the United States of America Supreme Court again invoked the no-extraterritoriality presumption and refused to apply the federal 8-hour law to USA construction workers hired by a USA corporation to perform construction work on projects in foreign countries. In *Foley*, the Court explained the presumption against extraterritoriality as a rule of construction. It said that while Congress had the authority to enforce its laws beyond the territorial boundary of the United States of America, if Congress does not express an intention to legislate extraterritorially, the Court will presume that legislation is meant to apply only within the United States of America. This was because, said the Court, Congress ordinarily is concerned only with domestic conditions. Thus the Supreme Court said that in the absence of clear language by Congress to the contrary, it will presume that legislation is not extraterritorial.

In the decades after *Foley*, the Supreme Court and lower federal courts have applied the presumption against extraterritorial jurisdiction to preclude the application of many federal labour laws to workers outside USA territory, including minimum wage laws,[8] collective bargaining laws,[9] the Age Discrimination Act,[10] and the labour protective provisions of the Interstate Commerce Act.[11] In these cases, the courts relied on the *Foley* rationale—that Congress was presumed to have been concerned primarily with domestic problems when it legislated. They treated the no-extraterritoriality presumption as a rule of construction of Congressional intent.

While the presumption against extraterritorial jurisdiction remained firm

---

[7] *EEOC* v. *Arabian American Oil Co.*, 111 S. Ct. 1227, 1230 (1991); *Foley Bros. Inc.* v. *Filardo*, 336 U.S. 281, 285 (1949).

[8] *Cruz* v. *Chesapeake Shipping*, 932 F.2d 218 (3rd Cir. 1991).

[9] *McCulloch* v. *Sociedad Nacional*, 372 U.S. 10 (1963) (NLRA does not apply extraterritoriality); *Benz* v. *Compania Naviera Hidalgo*, 353 U.S. 138 (1957); *Air Line Dispatchers* v. *National Mediation Board*, 189 F.2d 685 (D.C. 1951) (no extraterritorial jurisdiction for the Railway Labor Act.).

[10] *Zahourek* v. *Arthur Young & Co.*, 567 F. Supp. 1453 (D. Colo. 1983); *Cleary* v. *United States Lines, Inc.*, 555 F. Supp. 1251 (D.N.J. 1983).

[11] *Van Blaricom* v. *Burlington Northern RR. Co.*, 17 F.3d 1224 (9th Cir. 1994).

for a long time in labour cases, there were departures from it in commercial law cases almost from the outset. In 1911, barely two years after the *American Banana* decision, the Supreme Court applied the Sherman Act to an agreement made in England to monopolize USA tobacco imports and exports in the *USA* v. *American Tobacco (1911)* case. In 1927, in *U.S.* v. *Sisal Sales Corp. (1927)*, the Court applied the Sherman Act to American companies who conspired to conduct a monopoly wholly inside Mexico. It justified its result by reasoning that the monopoly would have direct effects within the United States of America. In *American Tobacco* and *Sisal Sales*, the Court avoided overruling *American Banana* by adopting a restrictive definition of what constitutes 'extraterritorial'.[12]

In 1945, Judge Learned Hand of the Second Circuit articulated a new principle for extraterritorial jurisdiction. In *U.S.* v. *Alcoa (1945)*, he ruled that the Sherman Act applied to a group of non-USA nationals who allegedly formed a conspiracy to control a product market, even though the acts occurred outside the United States of America and there was no domestic conduct on which to base jurisdiction. Judge Hand said that there is jurisdiction under the Sherman Act when a defendant outside the territorial United States of America has acted with the intent of producing an effect inside the USA or has taken actions which, in fact, produce a domestic effect (ibid. 443). This new principle of jurisdiction based on domestic interest or effect led to vastly expanded use of extraterritorial jurisdiction, particularly in the areas of antitrust, securities, and trade-mark, law.[13]

In 1993 in *Hartford Fire Insurance* v. *California (1993)*, the Supreme Court expanded the extraterritorial reach of the Sherman Antitrust Act still further, The Court applied the Act to conduct which occurred exclusively in England and which was lawful under British law. The defendants, USA and foreign insurers and reinsurers, were accused of agreeing to boycott certain USA insurers in order to force them to change the terms of the coverage they were offering to their customers. The foreign defendants, together with the British government as *amicus curiae*, argued that the conduct alleged was perfectly legal under British law, and that to apply the Sherman Act to such conduct would disrupt a comprehensive regulatory scheme of the insurance and reinsurance market which the British Parliament had established (ibid. 2910). The Supreme Court rejected this argument, finding that there was no actual conflict between USA law and British law. Rather,

---

[12] See *U.S.* v. *Sisal Sales Corp.*, 274 U.S. 268, 276 (1927) 'by their own deliberate acts, here and elsewhere, [the conspirators] brought about forbidden results within the United States'; Beausang 1966: 189; Turley 1990: 608–613.

[13] See, e.g., *Matsushita Elec. Industrial Co.* v. *Zenith Radio Corp.*, 475 U.S. 574 (1986) *Continental Ore Co.* v. *Union Carbide & Carbon Corp.*, 370 U.S. 690 (1962) (extraterritorial application of Sherman Act); *Steele* v. *Bulova Watch Co.* 344 U.S. 280 (1952) (trademark claim under Lanham Act applied extraterritorially); *Schoenbaum* v. *Firstbrook*, 405 F.2d 200 (2d Cir.) 1968) (extraterritorial jurisdiction for 1934 Securities Act cases).

the Court stated that neither the Sherman Act nor the British law required the defendants to engage in conduct that violated the other country's laws, and the defendants could engage in conduct which was lawful under both sets of legal rules. *Hartford Fire* made it clear that the Court will place few, if any, limits on the extraterritorial application of USA antitrust laws.[14]

Despite the expansion of extraterritorial jurisdiction in commercial law cases, courts continued to refuse to find extraterritorial jurisdiction in labour cases for a long time (Turley 1990). However, in recent years, the rationale for finding no extraterritorial jurisdiction has shifted away from the *American Banana* presumption approach toward an international law/comity approach. For example, in *I.L.A.* v. *Ariadne Shipping Co. (1970)*, a 1970 maritime labour case in which the Supreme Court held that the NLRB had jurisdiction over picketing by a USA union of a foreign ship which employed foreign and USA longshore workers. In reaching its result, the Court distinguished a long line of maritime labour cases where the presumption against extraterritorial jurisdiction had been applied, saying that here the picketing was addressed to the wages to be paid to American workers and hence did not seek to interfere with the labour relations of a foreign vessel.[15]

In 1991, in the case of *EEOC* v. *Arabian American Oil Corp. (1991)* ['*Aramco*'], the Supreme Court refused to apply Title VII of the Equal Employment Opportunity Act to a USA citizen working for a USA firm in Saudi Arabia. However, the *Aramco* Court did not speak of the territorial reach of the legislation, either presumed or express. Rather, it justified its result on the basis of international law and comity principles. The Court said that it should not interpret a statute in a way that causes a conflict with the laws of another nation. Thus it found no jurisdiction despite the fact that Title VII contains both statutory language and legislative history which manifest a Congressional intent that the statute be applied to extraterritorial conduct (ibid. 1240).

The National Labor Relations Board ('Labour Board') has also expanded its notion of the territorial reach of its own jurisdiction. In 1975, it applied the NLRA extraterritorially when an American corporation discriminated against an American employee who worked at the company's Canadian facility and was attempting to unionize the Canadian location (*FREEPORT TRANSPORT, INC. (1975)*). It used a center-of-gravity analysis, and found that a number of factors indicated that the employee's job, while physically in Canada, was actually governed by policies set in the United States of America. This approach directly contradicted the Supreme Court's approach

---

[14] After *Hartford Fire*, the only limitation on the extraterritorial reach of the Sherman Act, and other commercial laws by analogy, is Congressional intent. However, Professor Lea Brilmeyer argues that Congressional intent in this area is a legal fiction in which intent is often imputed on the basis of unstated judicial policy preferences: Brilmayer 1987: 35.

[15] Ibid. 189–99, distinguishing *Benz* v. *Compania Naviera Hidalgo* 353 U.S. 138 (1957); *American Radio Ass'n* v. *Mobile S.S. Ass'n, Inc.* 419 U.S. 215 (1974), and others.

in *New York Central* and *Foley*. In 1977, the Board reversed its long-standing policy of declining to assert jurisdiction over commercial activities of foreign governments and their agencies operating within the United States of America (*State Bank of India* 1977). Further, in 1979 the Board ruled that the NLRA applied to a USA ship operating within Brazil.[16] The Board found that because the ship carried a U.S. flag, it was, for legal purposes, USA territory to which the laws of the United States of America apply (ibid. 1265). All of these developments were part of an expansion of Labour Board's view of its statutory and discretionary extraterritorial jurisdiction.

In the past few years, the circumstances in which courts and the Labour Board have applied the NLRB extraterritorially have expanded significantly.[17] In two recent cases, federal Courts of Appeals have applied the NLRA to extraterritorial conduct. In 1992 the Eleventh Circuit applied the secondary boycott prohibitions to an American union that had requested Japanese unions to exert economic pressure against their own, Japanese, employer. The Court rejected the union's argument that there was no extraterritorial application of the NLRA. It said that union conduct that had the 'intent and effect' of gaining an advantage in a labour dispute in the USA was within the reach of the statute (ibid. 788). It went on to reinterpret the presumption against extraterritoriality as a presumption that Congress intended to avoid 'clashes between our laws and those of other nations which could result in international discord' (ibid. 789).

More recently, in 1994, the Fifth Circuit held that the NLRB had jurisdiction for unfair labour practice charges filed by USA nationals who were employed on a USA vessel that was operating indefinitely in Hong Kong. In *N.L.R.B.* v. *Dredge Operators (1994)*, the court enforced an unfair labour practice charge against a shipping corporation that required the shipper-employer to bargain with the union elected to represent the ship's crew. The ship was a USA flag vessel, but it operated exclusively in Hong Kong. The Fifth Circuit affirmed the Board's assertion of jurisdiction. It said it had jurisdiction because the ship was a USA flag ship, and was thus American territory. Therefore, it concluded, the application of the NLRA was thus not extraterritorial (ibid. 3683). The Court rejected the argument that the Board should not exercise discretionary jurisdiction on grounds of international comity, finding that there was no actual conflict between application of the NLRA and the requirements of Hong Kong law.

---

[16] *Alcoa Marine*, 240 NLRB 1265 (1979); but see *North American Soccer League* 236 NLRB 1317, 1322–1325 (1978) (arguing that Board should include Canadian soccer players in bargaining unit of North American Soccer League) (Board Member Murphy dissenting in part).

[17] There are presently two cases pending for review by the full N.L.R.B. which involve the issue of the Board's application to employees working overseas. They are: *Avco Corporation and U.A.W.*, NLRB Case no. 34–RC–1061 (1994), and *Computer Science Raytheon and I.B.E.W.* Case No. 12-RC-7612 (1994). In both cases, the administrative law judge applied the statute extraterritorially and one side has appealed.

Thus, the no-extraterritoriality principle has not evaporated in labour law, but its rationale has changed. The new rationale has led to expanded use of extraterritorial jurisdiction. Even in the recent Second Circuit case of *Labour Union of Pico Products* v. *Pico Products (1992)*, where the court refused to find jurisdiction for a claim arising under Section 301 of the Labour Management Relations Act brought by foreign workers against their employer, a foreign subsidiary of American corporation, the Court relied on an international law/comity rationale. It said that to construe Section 301 to cover claims to 'enforce collective bargaining agreements between foreign workers and foreign corporations doing work in foreign countries,' would lead to 'embarrassment in foreign affairs' (ibid. 195). There have also been recent indications that the Railway Labour Act has some extraterritorial application, at least in cases in which the USA unions bargain with a USA carrier for application to foreign national employees working on foreign soil.[18]

All of these case law developments demonstrate that there has been a change in the attitudes of courts and agencies about the scope of jurisdiction to USA labour laws. These changes are consistent with similar changes occurring in the legislative and executive branches of government.

(b) Extraterritorial Provisions in Labour Legislation On two occasions in the past ten years, Congress expressly provided for extraterritorial application of certain USA labour laws. In 1984, it amended the Age Discrimination in Employment Act, and in 1991 it amended the Civil Rights Act, making both statutes applicable to USA corporations employing USA workers and operating overseas (Cherian 1992: 563–4). Each of these amendments was enacted in response to Supreme Court rulings to the contrary,[19] and both involve anti-discrimination laws. In addition, the Americans with Disabilities Act of 1990 is coextensive in its extraterritorial application with the Civil Rights Act of 1991, so that it too applies to American corporations operating overseas.

In 1992 Congress considered a bill that would make the National Labour Relations Act apply to all 'USA companies and their subsidiaries operating in any country that is a signatory to a Free Trade Agreement'. The provision was attached to the ill-fated Workplace Democracy Act of 1992, which was stalled in the House Education and Labour Committee (Barella 1994: 899–900). However, these legislative developments demonstrate that Congress is willing to apply some USA labour laws extraterritorially.

(c) Extraterritorial Application of USA Labour Law Through Trade Pacts In addition to recent judicial and Congressional efforts to make USA

---

[18] *Local 553* v. *Eastern Airlines*, 695 F.2d 668 (2d Cir. 1983); but see *Flight Attendants* v. *Pan Am.*, 132 LRRM 2520 (N.D. Cal. 1989).

[19] See *Pfeiffer* v. *Wm. Wrigley Jr. Co.*, 755 F.2d 544 (7th Cir. 1984) (Posner opinion); see generally Barella 1994: 899–903; Zimmerman 1988: 115–118.

labour law extraterritorial, there have been similar initiatives by the Executive Branch. Prior to NAFTA, several USA trade laws have contained provisions which permit the Executive Branch to withhold trade privileges from other countries that do not give their workers basic protections, including protection for the right to organize. Of these, the most notable are the 1983 Caribbean Basin Initiative (CBI), the 1984 Amendments to the Generalized System of Preferences (GSP), the Omnibus Trade Act of 1988, and the Overseas Private Investment Corporation Act of 1985 (Charnovitz 1987, 1986; Howard 1992: 518–522; Cowie and French 1993; Ballon 1987). All of these Acts give the USA executive branch the power to give USA labour laws extraterritorial scope by importing their norms into trade decisions.

These provisions have been utilized from time to time by USA Presidents and by other executive agencies that regulate trade. For example, in 1987, President Reagan acted pursuant to the 1984 amendments to the Generalized System of Preferences, to deny trade preferences to Nicaragua, Paraguay, and Romania on the basis of their alleged labour rights violations. Also in 1987, the Overseas Private Investment Corporation withdrew insurance coverage from projects in Nicaragua, Paraguay, Romania, and Ethiopia for their failure to adopt internationally recognized worker rights (Charnovitz 1987: 573–4). While there are as yet few examples of the USA imposing extraterritorial labour standards via trading pacts, it is a type of transnational labour regulation that could be further expanded.

4. COMPARING AND EVALUATING THE FOUR MODELS

In the previous section, I identified and described four models of transnational labour regulation that have emerged in recent years. The four models can be compared along two dimensions. First, as noted above, the two European models of transnational labour regulation are *integrative*, seeking to unify labour norms and labour standards, while the two North American models are *interpenetrative*, seeking to enforce cross-border norms on a one-time situation-specific basis. Second, the models can be distinguished as to whether they can be implemented unilaterally, or whether they require multilateral action for their implementation. Two of the models—preemptive legislation and cross-border enforcement—are *multilateral* in the sense that they rely for their implementation on actions by several countries jointly enforcing a particular labour standard. Neither preemptive legislation nor cross-border enforcement can occur unless more than two nations decide to apply a particular labour regulation. In contrast, the other two models—harmonization and extraterritorial jurisdiction—are *unilateral* in the sense that they can be implemented by unilateral action of one country.

Extraterritorial jurisdiction is the ultimate unilateral form of transnational regulation: It is one country imposing its own, unilaterally-devised domestic labour standards on another country. Harmonization is also unilateral in its implementation—it requires each country to alter its own domestic laws in order to 'approximate' the laws of others.[20]

Using these dimensions of comparison, the four models of transnational labour regulation can thus be arranged in the following four-part box:

Four Models of Transnational Labour Regulation

	multilateral regulation	unilateral regulation
Integrative approaches	preemptive legislation	harmonization
interpenetrative approaches	cross-border enforcement	extraterritorial jurisdiction

Seeing the dimensions of similarity and difference makes it possible to evaluate the four models and to develop criteria for selecting between them. To approach the policy question, however, it is necessary to consider what are the objectives of transnational labour regulation. In section 2, I described the various problems that globalization causes for labour: the weakening of labour's bargaining power; the potential for a labour standards race to the bottom; the potential for organizational fragmentation due to the difficulties for unions attempting to organize on an international basis; and the potential deterioration of labour's role in national and international political life. Here I will explore how these different models of transnational labour regulation addresses each of those problems. In addition, this section addresses several other goals that are often posited for transnational labour regulation, goals such as raising labour standards, increasing trade by eliminating regulatory barriers to trade, and promoting international co-operation. The latter two differ from the other goals in that they aim to benefit non-labour groups— business, consumers, citizens, and so forth. These additional goals must factor into any policy conclusion about desirable modes of labour regulation.

As we shall see, each of the models promotes different of these goals, and some of the models are impediments to the attainment of some of the goals. Indeed, there is no one model that can achieve all the goals of transnational labour regulation.

[20] While harmonization assumes that a country will act unilaterally when it revises its labour laws to conform to another set of legal norms, one could argue that harmonization is multilateral in that a multilateral agency sets the norms and imposes the sanctions and incentives for a country to harmonize in the first place. However, once there is a multilaterally-established harmonization directive, harmonization is unilateral because it requires each member state to act unilaterally in devising, revising, and above all enforcing, its domestic regulations.

4.1 Preemptive Legislation

The model of regulation that is most likely to limit runaway shops, prevent labour standards 'races to the bottom' and discourage regulatory competition is the one that is most effective at setting uniform labour standards across national boundaries. Uniformity in labour standards would prevent the phenomenon of regulation-shopping, in which corporations move to the least restrictive regulatory environment. Uniformity would also eliminate the fear unions have that by advocating protective legislation, they are contributing to capital flight and costing their members their jobs. Where uniformity in labour regulation cannot be achieved for either political or pragmatic reasons, an alternative is to adopt regulations that set a floor of rights, such as a minimum wage or minimum safety standards, above which parties can further negotiate. If the floor of rights is high enough, it will also have a deterrent effect on runaway shops and races to the bottom although not as powerful a deterrent as uniform labour standards would have.

In theory, uniformity can be achieved most effectively through the EU model of preemptive legislation since the very purpose of this model is to set uniform employment standards. To the extent that the EC Commission has the power to set rules and enforce regulations for labour standards in member countries, it minimizes the possibility of a labour standards race to the bottom. In addition, the EU could legislate rules that would encourage the development of transnational unionism which could then bargain for uniform transnational labour standards. In this was, preemptive legislation also holds out the possibility of creating a uniform system for regulating collective bargaining, a system that would make it more feasible for unions to organize and coordinate bargaining strategies on a transnational basis. Thus preemptive legislation is a strategy that could prevent organizational fragmentation and counteract the weakening of labour's bargaining power that globalization initially creates.

A further strength of the preemptive legislation model is that it furthers the goal of encouraging international co-operation. Indeed, both of the European integrative approaches have as their goal not merely integration, but actual unification of regulatory régimes. They hold out the prospect of developing, over time, shared norms and collaborative means to implement those norms. Furthermore, the integrative models are part of an economic strategy that aspires to become a political strategy—to achieve the unification of Europe into a single political, juridical, as well as economic unit. Thus the preemptive legislation model, as well as the harmonization model, is likely to foster international co-operation and interdependency that will make overt international aggression between EU members less likely.

The limitations on the preemptive legislation model are primarily practical ones. The model requires multilateral action for its implementation and thus it is extremely difficult to gain the necessary consensus to actually set labour standards. To date, the European Commission has not utilized its legislative power to set labour standards on more than a few issues, and it has not attempted to set any uniform rules for governing collective bargaining, strikes, and other forms of collective action. Indeed, most observers predict that the EU is unlikely to attempt any preemptive legislative, or even harmonization, in the area of unionism or collective bargaining in the foreseeable future. Thus, while the preemptive legislation model could theoretically eliminate barriers to trade by equalizing labour standards and labour rights, in practice it is not likely to do so in the near future.

In addition, there is presently in Europe a wide variety of collective bargaining regulatory structures. Each one has many people, groups, organizations, and institutions that function within it, and which have powerful vested interests in its continuation. Thus it is unlikely that we shall see a European-wide collective bargaining system emerge in the near future. Without a uniform framework of legal rules to govern collective bargaining, the preemptive legislation model cannot prevent organizational fragmentation or the weakening of labour's bargaining power that globalization entails.

There is a further concern in the preemptive legislation model. While both integrative models are well suited to furthering the goals of international co-operation and world peace and the goals of establishing a floor of labour standards, they are not necessarily the models that will provide the *highest* labour standards or the *best* legal protection for workers. The integrative models rely on consensus between nations, so that there is a tendency for least common denominator regulations to emerge. This is the dynamic of 'harmonization downward' that has been widely discussed amongst EU scholars (see Woolcock, chapter 10, in this volume). The concerns about harmonization downward were realized in 1989 and 1992 when the EU nations could not enact the Social Charter due to the objections of Great Britain. The two integrative models of labour regulation could lead to the triumph of the weakest regulatory régime.

There yet another problem with the model of preemptive legislation. One of the most important goals of transnational labour regulation is to preserve a role for labour in political life and to protect labour's political clout. As discussed above, unions' role in domestic politics is essential to their ability to mobilize supporters, sustain organizational unity, and protect legislative achievements. Also, it is essential to a robust democracy to have unions functioning as organized interest groups to represent employees' interests in the political process.

The preemptive legislation model potentially diminishes the role of labour unions in politics by taking issues of labour relations out of the reach of the national political processes and placing them in multilateral agencies. Preemptive legislation by definition moves labour legislation out of the national political arena and into a multilateral arena. At present, unions exist in nation-specific environments. In the European Council, votes are cast by country, not by political party or constituency-based group. Yet national unions are rarely powerful enough in their home countries to be empowered to speak for the national interest in an international policy-making setting. As a result, under preemptive legislation, the influence of national unions could become diluted and highly mediated.

4.2 Harmonization

The harmonization model of transnational labour regulation is similar to preemptive legislation in most respects. That is, it fosters uniformity in labour standards, thus counteracting labour standards races to the bottom. It also sets a floor of labour standards and fosters international labour co-operation.

However, there are some differences in the ability of the two integrative models to achieve the policy goals discussed above. First, harmonization, unlike preemptive legislation, relies on unilateral action by each member country. This feature makes it unlikely that Directives on labour standards will be implemented in all EU countries in the same way. To the contrary, harmonization permits a wide range of variation as to how Directives are implemented. Thus harmonization is less likely to create uniformity in labour regulations than will the model of preemptive legislation. To the extent that uniformity in regulation is desirable as an antidote to labour standards races to the bottom, harmonization is less effective than preemptive legislation. Harmonization can, however, establish a floor of rights. But in doing so, it shares with preemptive legislation the potential problem of setting a least common denominator floor, and thus of levelling downward.

Harmonization has several advantages over the other models as well. First, harmonization relies on unilateral action for implementation once shared norms are articulated as Directives. From a practical vantage point, this suggests that it may be easier to enact labour Directives at the transnational level than preemptive Regulations, because countries know that they retain autonomy at the implementation stage. Indeed, the fact that the EU has many more Directives than Regulations on labour issues suggests this to be the case.

Second, harmonization is a model of labour regulation that retains a larger role for labour in national politics than does preemptive legislation. As with preemptive legislation, harmonization Directives require that the legal norms are set multilaterally, the role of domestic labour unions in the norm-setting process is diminished. However, unlike preemptive legislation, harmonization requires legislation to be enacted at the domestic level to implement Directives. Thus it presumes that labour regulations will be debated, adopted, and interpreted at the level of the nation-state. Consequently, harmonization will enable, indeed require, unions to continue their efforts to influence lawmakers and other decision-makers at the national level.

Another possible advantage of harmonization over preemptive legislation is that it might be more conducive of international peace and co-operation. Harmonization sets in motion a process by which countries bring their regulatory frameworks into consistency. It does not involve the external imposition of regulations, but it does provide structured incentives for nations to alter regulations in a consistent way. The emphasis on internal change may be a process that engenders less conflict, opposition, and backlash than preemptive legislation.

4.3 Cross-Border Monitoring

As discussed, the NAFTA model of cross-border monitoring and enforcement has little to contribute to the goal of establishing a uniform labour standards or a floor of labour rights. The NAFTA Side Agreement's cross-border enforcement model does not seek to raise or equalize labour standards. To the contrary, it provides disincentives for member countries to legislate labour protections because each country can be sanctioned for not enforcing its protective labour regulations. Furthermore, because NAFTA removes trade barriers without providing uniformity in labour regulation, each country stands to lose business if it imposes a higher level of regulation than the others do. Therefore, cross-border monitoring encourages races to the bottom and regulatory competition, resulting in the lowering of labour standards.

While labour is interested in finding a framework for transnational labour regulation that eliminates or minimizes the possibility of labour standards races to the bottom, there are some who contend that such races to the bottom are not a problem from a policy-making perspective. Many free-traders argue that efforts to limit races to the bottom are disguised protectionism. They argue that permitting firms to relocate in the lowest labour standards environment is desirable because it increases trade, creates more efficient utilization of global resources, and thus creates greater global wealth (Howse and Trebilcock 1995: 54–9; contra, Langille 1995).

If the goal of transnational labour regulation is to increase trade and eliminate labour regulations that act as barriers to trade, then one would select a model of labour regulation that minimizes regulation, lowers labour standards, and discourages regulatory uniformity. Thus, in furtherance of this policy goal, one would choose the NAFTA model of cross-border enforcement and monitoring.

4.4 Extraterritorial Jurisdiction

The other North American model of labour regulation is extraterritorial jurisdiction of national law. This model, in contrast to cross-border monitoring, can promote regulatory uniformity. Extraterritorial jurisdiction is the application of one country's labour laws to other countries. This method of achieving uniform labour standards has the virtue of requiring only unilateral action, making it relatively easy to implement. However, extraterritorial application of domestic law unifies labour standards on a piecemeal basis. It means that some particular USA laws are applied in some other countries, but there is no systematic application or enforcement of an entire regulatory régime. Thus it is a model that cannot create uniformity on all facets of employment regulation and therefore it has only limited ability to deter labour standards races to the bottom or regulatory competition.

Extraterritorial jurisdiction, like cross-bordering monitoring, is not integrative in its aspirations, and thus will not contribute to the formulation of shared norms and uniform standards between nations. In addition, the extraterritorial jurisdiction model is detrimental to the goal of world peace and co-operation. The exercise of extraterritorial jurisdiction by USA courts and Congress is likely to create tensions in the international arena and could potentially destabilize international relations (Barella 1994: 918). The ability of a nation-state to legislate and enforce laws governing its own citizens is seen as an indelible mark of sovereignty. Nations react with intense hostility when foreign nations attempt to impose foreign rules and procedures on their its own citizens acting within their own borders. Extraterritorial jurisdiction is thus a model that is likely to produce international discord (Cherian 1992).

Extraterritorial application of American law in the commercial law area has been a source of great controversy in recent years (Brilmayer 1987; Zimmerman 1988). Some countries have enacted blocking legislation designed to prevent the application of USA law within their territories (Zimmerman 1988: 120–1; Cira 1982: 253). There is no reason to believe that extraterritorial application of USA labour law will not be similarly greeted with hostility by the international community.

Despite its dangers, however, extraterritorial jurisdiction has some powerful virtues to recommend it. If the goal of transnational labour regulation is to provide the best protection for labour, then extraterritorial jurisdiction might well be the most effective approach. Under this model, one country simply imposes its domestic labour laws on others without having to reach multilateral consensus. As a result, extraterritorial jurisdiction is a model that has great potential for raising labour standards in other countries.

However, this can only occur if the country imposing its labour regulations on others has high labour standards and a well developed system of labour rights in the first place. If the labour protections of the country exercising extraterritorial jurisdiction are weak, then it is a model that will not protect workers domestically or transnationally.

There is an even stronger argument in favor of extraterritorial jurisdiction. Both North American interpenetration models retain a central role for domestic governments to set domestic labour standards. Both cross-border monitoring and extraterritorial jurisdiction are models in which labour regulations are enacted domestically and enforced by domestic legal processes. Rather than eradicate the role of domestic legislatures and courts, the interpenetration models reinforce them. Therefore they also retain a much greater role for labour unions to influence labour standards by means of the domestic political process than do either of the integrative approaches. For this reason, the interpenetrative models are less disruptive of existing organizations, constituencies, vested interests, and power relations than are the European ones. With cross-border monitoring, however, the beneficial effect of preserving labour's role in domestic politics is offset by the destructive impact on labour of the transnational race to the bottom that the model encourages. If the goal is to preserve unionism as a vital element in our democracy, one would select extraterritorial jurisdiction.

5. SUMMARY AND CONCLUSION

I have described four models of transnational labour regulation that exist in the Western world today, and assessed the ability of each of the four models to address the various problems that globalization causes for labour. It is evident that each of the four models of transnational labour regulation has different strengths and different weaknesses in relation to each of the possible goals of transnational labour regulation.

To choose between the models, it is necessary to set priorities between goals, as the existing model can achieve them all.

For example, preemptive legislation, has the capacity to create uniformity of labour regulation, eliminate races to the bottom, and promote international co-operation. But the price of adopting this model is to move the locus of labour regulation from a national to a transnational fora, thereby diminishing labour's role in politics. Unless some mechanism is established at the EU level to reintroduce labour as a player with the ability to articulate its interests separately from each nation's own 'national interest,' the preemptive legislation model could lead to the gradual fragmentation, disorganization, and disintegration of organized labour throughout Europe.

At the other extreme, extraterritorial jurisdiction retains a strong role for labour in domestic politics, and has the potential to provide uniform labour standards, at least on some issues. However, the primary price or this model is escalation of international tensions and the potential for international conflict. NAFTA, which imposes no substantive cross-border labour regulations, comes close to the no regulation alternative. Accordingly, this model solves none of the problems of globalization for labour.

Harmonization could be the perfect mid-point—providing some uniformity while retaining some role for labour in domestic politics. However, it could also be an unstable equilibrium, threatening to tip over into preemptive legislation if the Directives become powerful mandates, and to a no-regulation régime if the Directives permit evasion and opting-out.

To conclude, none of the existing models can satisfy all objectives for transnational labour regulation. And, there is no neutral policy-science that will make these hard choices. However, by recognizing the limitations of each model and the trade-offs they pose, it might be possible to imagine a new model of transnational labour regulation, one that draws from the strengths of each and that avoids the problems that inhere in each one. Such a new form of transnational labour regulation would be a first step toward ensuring that the emerging global economy is fair, equitable and inclusive of all its citizens.

16

Competing Conceptions of Regulatory Competition in Debates on Trade Liberalization and Labour Standards

BRIAN A. LANGILLE

There has been much confusion and controversy in the popular press, political debates, and academic journals about the impact of trade liberalizing régimes, such as NAFTA or the WTO, upon domestic policy, particularly environmental and labour market regulation. To take the labour market as an example, there are two sorts of questions which are mooted in these discussions—first, the direct impact of trade liberalization upon the domestic labour market, i.e., jobs; and second, the indirect impact upon domestic labour market policies and laws. This chapter focuses upon the second debate about the impact of trade liberalization, and economic integration more generally, upon domestic labour market policies—that is, on policies regarding collective bargaining, employment standards, occupational health and safety, etc. within any individual jurisdiction. However, this essay is not directly concerned with the substance of those issues, but rather with the basic structure which provides the framework within which this debate is carried on. The great framing dichotomy of that debate is as follows. Critics of trade liberalization allege, among other things, that such liberalization opens Canadian labour standards, for example, to unfair competition from jurisdictions where standards (the United States of America, for example), or at least their enforcement level (Mexico, for example) are much lower. The critics then argue that we need a 'level playing field' brought about by constraining international 'side agreements' (such as the North American Agreement on Labour Cooperation) or else we will face a 'race to the bottom'. These critics seized upon the idea of a 'race to the bottom' as a critically important conceptual insight which plays the role of an intellectual trump card in their hands.

Against this a number of arguments are deployed, some of which deny the significance or existence of any such regulatory competition, fair or otherwise. But more important are arguments which praise the impact of such regulatory competition. It is these arguments which provide the other half of the frame for our debate over the indirect impact of economic integration. The argument is summed up in the following question: if competition

among producers of widgets if a good thing, why not among producers of
regulatory policy? The argument is simply that law can be regarded as a
product which is produced by jurisdictions and the virtues of competition
in this product market are as obvious as elsewhere.

This is the framing dichotomy of our debate—'efficient and beneficial regulatory competition' versus 'the race to the bottom'. This debate is not
confined to debates about international trade agreements such as NAFTA
or the WTO, but includes the politics of regulation within federal jurisdictions such as Canada or the USA. Here, individual states or provinces are
seen to be facing the same sort of predicament as nations competing internationally, and the question is whether regulatory competition among the
various provinces or states is a good thing or whether constraining ('level
playing field') federal legislation is required to avoid destructive state competition. The European Union provides yet another setting for the question
of whether central control or 'harmonization' as opposed to regulatory
competition among the member states is needed to avoid 'social dumping'—
a phrase more current in Europe than 'race to the bottom, and perhaps a
preferable one, since it introduces the idea of externalizing costs (Trachtman
1993: 47).

This essay focusses upon this threshold framing dichotomy which ani-
mates and structures all these ongoing arguments. The ambition is to further our understanding of these familiar yet unsatisfactory discussions and
to make explicit their intractable nature. At present, the intractability seems
to flow from the fact that the proponents of these opposing points of view
continue to insist upon the validity of the insight which is central to their
thesis with a view to convincing the other side of its merits. Each side has
a conceptual trump card which it considers that, surely, with only enough
patience, good will, and effort the other side should be able to understand,
and as a result agree that it seals the fate of the argument. Each side believes
the debate is winnable by the unassailability of the conceptual coherence of
its central argument, unless the other is insufficiently informed, or too wilfully blinded by political self-interest to see the truth. The real political fall-
out of this continued intractability is that important and current political
debates are deeply unsatisfying. The purpose of this essay is to show that
progress can only be made in bridging the conceptual chasm which divides
the two camps, if the participants in these debates (generally trade economists on the one hand and environmental and labour lawyers on the other)
can be brought to see what it is that really divides them.

The thesis of this essay is not that one side of this debate is 'correct' and
the other 'wrong'. Our problem is this—both sides examine the same phenomenon yet see it differently. We have here competing conceptions of the
same reality. *On their own terms* both of these analyses are correct. The
real question is not whether these competing conceptions are internally

conceptually coherent, for they are, but rather which of these two conceptions should we *choose* to deploy? That is not a point solvable *within* either theory. If this point is accepted, then this essay will have served its purpose as a ground clearing exercise, to remove one of the annoying obstacles to progress in our thinking about the virtues or vices of regulatory competition. It will have disabused participants in these debates of the idea that they have a *conceptual* trump to play, and allowed the debate to proceed on its merits without the problem of conceptual one upmanship.

Thus, I seek here to establish two points. First, that the regulatory competition/race to the bottom debate is not winnable on its own terms. Second, that the solution to our real dilemma lies not in deciding which of our competing paradigms is correct, but rather in deciding which to deploy. To make these points this essay uses as its foil and its focus an excellent recent contribution to the literature which explicitly addresses the relationship of the regulatory competition and the race to the bottom paradigms. This essay, by Richard Revesz, adopts the strategy which I suggest is not available—that of attempting to find a winner in the debate as it is currently framed. The great advantage of using this essay as a focus for my purposes is that it explicitly and carefully lays out the race to the bottom argument and then attempts to show that it is not supportable. I suggest, on the contrary, that a careful reading of the literature relied on by Revesz and central to our debate as it has been understood to this point, does not lead to this conclusion. But this does not mean that the race to the bottom analysis is the correct analysis. Rather, as I have said, it leads to another and more interesting conclusion.

The great merits of Revesz's recent article (Revesz 1992) is the analytical clarity and rigour it brings to our seemingly endless debate. Revesz has studied the literature concerning regulatory competition and races to the bottom in a variety of regulatory contexts. He also brings a certain humility to the exercise, in terms of the care with which he frames his conclusions which are, in essence, not that he or others have disproved or discredited the notion of 'races to the bottom' totally, but rather that all the best evidence and 'theoretical' discussion thus far have failed to produce any evidence of a race to the bottom in circumstances of regulatory competition.

Revesz's main example is competition among the various member states of a federation in environmental regulatory policy with the aim of attracting investment and industry. The question is whether federal legislation is required to mitigate the impact of such competition. Revesz notes the contribution of Richard Stewart (see e.g., Stewart 1993) to the popularizing of the race to the bottom idea as a justification for federal environmental legislation. He then sets out as the central thesis of his article:

This article challenges the accepted wisdom on the race to the bottom. It argues that, contrary to prevailing assumptions, competition among states for industry should not be expected to lead to a race that decreases social welfare; indeed, as in other areas, such competition can be expected to produce an efficient allocation of industrial activity among the states. It shows, moreover, that federal regulation aimed at dealing with the asserted race to the bottom, far from correcting evils of interstate competition, is likely to produce results that are undesirable.' (Revesz 1992: 1211–1212).

   This, it will note noted, is a straightforward declaration that the current debate is resolvable, in favour of the regulatory competition argument.

   However, for my purposes, Revesz's chief contribution is his very useful *formulation* of the 'race to the bottom' idea in terms of the well-known notion of a 'prisoner's dilemma' (Revesz 1992: 1217). That is, that rationally motivated, self-interested behaviour, the standard behaviour assumed of traders in the marketplace, can lead to socially suboptimal results, and that these results can be avoided through co-operation instead of competition. A very useful rendition of the 'story' of the dilemma of the prisoner's is presented by Amartya Sen as follows:

The story goes something like this. Two prisoners are known to be guilty of a very serious crime, but there is not enough evidence to convict them. There is, however, sufficient evidence to convict them of a minor crime. The District Attorney—it is an American story—separates the two and tells each that they will be given the option to confess if they wish to. If both of them do confess, they will be convicted of the major crime on each other's evidence, but in view of the good behaviour shown in squealing, the District Attorney will ask for a penalty of 10 years each rather than the full penalty of 20 years. If neither confesses, each will be convicted only of the minor crime and get two years. If one confesses and the other does not, then the one who does confess will go free and the other will go to prison for 20 years. . . . What should the prisoners do? . . . Each prisoner sees that it is definitely in his interest to confess no matter what the other does. If the other confesses, then by confessing himself this prisoner reduces his own sentence from 20 years to 10. If the other does not confess, then by confessing he himself goes free rather than getting a two year sentence. So each prisoner feels that no matter what the other does it is always better for him to confess. So both of them do confess guided by rational self-interest, and each goes to prison for 10 years. If, however, neither had confessed, both would have been in prison for only two years each. Rational choice would seem to cost each person 8 additional years in prison. (Sen 1986: 69).

   Prisoners' dilemmas involve a *strategic* decision in which each agent makes a choice in circumstances where the reward to each depends upon the reward to all and the choice of each depends upon the choice of all (Elster 1986: 8–9). The basic structure of the prisoner's dilemma is that we have two players each faced with a choice—to co-operate (keep silent) or defect (confess) such that, to follow Elster, we generate the following matrix of decision:

	I CHOOSE	THE OTHER CHOOSES
1.	Co-operation (2 years)	Co-operation (2 years)
2.	Co-operation (20)	Defection (0)
3.	Defection (0)	Co-operation (20)
4.	Defection (10)	Defection (10)

The precise defining characteristic of the prisoner's dilemma is that the preference order of choices for both players is 3–1–4–2. As a result, while their choice 'should' be that which results in 2 years each, rationality operates perversely and leads them to a choice of 10 years each.

Revesz translates this prisoner's dilemma to the problem faced by the two states contemplating the appropriate level of environmental regulation as follows. First, Revesz very usefully gives an account of the circumstance the states would face if they were not locked in a prisoner's dilemma—that is, if they were not involved in a *strategic* decision involving the choices of the other. Revesz asks what would be the optimal choice for environmental policy for states if they were not faced with the existence of other states and thus were not faced with the awful truth that their choice and reward will actually depend upon the choice of and reward to the others (the analogy to the situation where only one prisoner was apprehended).

First, consider an 'island' jurisdiction—a single jurisdiction surrounded by ocean, which is unaffected by what occurs beyond its borders. This island jurisdiction has a number of firms engaged in industrial activity that produces air pollution. The citizens of the jurisdiction suffer adverse health effects as a result of the pollution.

In the absence of regulation the firms will choose the level of pollution that maximizes their profits and, as in the case generally with externalities, will ignore the social costs produced by their activities—the cost borne by the citizens who must breath air of poor quality. The firms will be able to produce their goods more cheaply and pollute more than if they were forced to bear these social costs.

Traditional economic theory holds that the socially optimal level of pollution reduction is the level that maximizes the benefits that accrue from such production to the individuals who breath the polluted air, minus the costs of pollution control.' (Revesz 1992: 1213–4).

Then Revesz again helpfully introduces the second state or province to create a situation of competition.

Second, consider instead a 'competitor jurisdiction'. This jurisdiction is affected by the actions taken in other jurisdictions, and, in turn, its own actions have effects beyond its own borders. I have in mind the state within a federal system. . . . Within the national market then, other factors being equal, firms will try to reduce the costs of pollution control by moving to the jurisdiction that imposes the least stringent requirement . . . As in the island situation, competitive jurisdictions will want to set a pollution reduction level that takes account of the benefits to its citizens of such reduction and of the cost to polluters in the jurisdiction of complying with this level

There will be, however, an additional factor to consider: the location of a firm can lead to the creation of jobs, and thus to increases in wages and taxes—important benefits for a state. As a result of this additional factor competitive jurisdictions will consider the potential benefits, in terms of inflows of industrial activity, of setting standards at a less stringent than those of other jurisdictions and, conversely, the potential costs in terms of outflows of industrial activity, of setting more stringent standards (emphasis added). (Revesz 1992: 1214–5)

Finally, Revesz accurately describes the dilemma:

The simplest example of the race to the bottom is one in which there are two identical jurisdictions. Assume that State 1 initially sets its level of pollution reduction at the level that would be optimal if it were an island. State 2 then considers whether setting its standard at the same level is as desirable as setting it at a less stringent level. Depending upon the benefits of pollution reduction, costs on polluters and benefits from the migration of industry, the less stringent standard may be preferable, and the industrial migration from State 1 to State 2 will ensue.

To recover some of its loss of jobs and tax revenues State 1 then considers relaxing its standard, and so on. This process of adjustment and readjustment continues until an equilibrium is reached in which neither state has an incentive to change its standard further.

At the conclusion of this race, both states will end up with equally lax standards, and they will not experience any inflow or outflow of industry. Each of these competitive states will thus have the same level of industrial activity that it would have had as an island jurisdiction. Social welfare in these states, however, would be less than it would be in identical island jurisdictions, because, as a result of the race to the bottom, the states will have adopted some optimally relaxed standards.' (Revesz 1992: 1216)

This *is* a reasonable representation of the problem of state regulatory competition in terms of the basic structure of the prisoner's dilemma. The choice structure faced by the states is as follows:

	I CHOOSE	THE OTHER CHOOSES
1.	Existing optimal legislation (no change in investment)	Existing optimal legislation (no change in investment)
2.	Existing optimal legislation (loss of investment)	Suboptimal legislation (gain in investment)
3.	Suboptimal legislation (gain in investment)	Optimal legislation (loss of investment)
4.	Suboptimal legislation (no change in investment)	Suboptimal legislation (no change of investment)

It is important to see the point of the prisoner's dilemma—that the choices and rewards here in a competitive situation, as opposed to those in the 'island' situation, are interactive and interdependent. The point of the prisoner's dilemma is not that it is not rational for either state to prefer choice 3 to choice 1. States may well think this to be the case and be quite rational in doing so—the trade off of more jobs (and wages and taxes) may be worth the cost of 'suboptimal legislation'. But the problem is, *so will the other state.* The tragedy of the states and the prisoners lies *not* in that they are irrational in ranking choice 3 as their first choice, but in the consequence that they end up with suboptimal legislation and no change in investment rather than with optimal legislation and the same investment pattern (all else being equal). They 'give away' their optimal standards, perversely, for nothing.

Based on this helpful 'race to the bottom prisoner's dilemma' model of regulatory competition, Revesz makes a number of interesting arguments, the most important of which for my purposes are the following. First, Revesz attempts to demonstrate that the race to the bottom will not 'in fact' occur. Although I use the words 'in fact', Revesz does not base his conclusion on empirical studies on capital relocation in response to regulatory change, but rather on an appeal to a well known series of theoretical studies aiming to demonstrate the absence of any effective incentive for the race to the bottom.

Secondly, the main theoretical points of Revesz's essay aim to demonstrate that the beneficial regulatory competition argument is, on the contrary, sound. In fact, after having so carefully set up our problem in terms of a prisoner's dilemma, Revesz himself actually substitutes another formulation of our issue which then assumes great importance. That question is:

If one believes that the competition among sellers of widgets is socially desirable, why is competition among sellers of location rights socially undesirable? If federal regulation mandating a super-competitive price for widgets is socially undesirable, why is federal regulation mandating a super-competitive price for location rights socially desirable? (Revesz 1992: 1234.)

It is the clarity of Revesz's juxtaposition of the prisoner's dilemma analysis alongside the beneficial competition analysis which makes explicit the central problem of the intractability of our debates.

Let me elaborate upon this claim by undertaking to demonstrate two points. First, I will review the argument which Revesz makes to demonstrate that the prisoner's dilemma analysis is not sound because the incentive to engage in a race to the bottom will not be present. I believe that this literature does not support Revesz's claims and that a better reading, which coheres with our knowledge of the real world, is that the incentive to engage in the race to the bottom will be present. Secondly, we will then be in a position to see that in this real world of state competition for capital investment *both* the prisoner's dilemma analysis *and* the beneficial regulatory competition analysis are available. What one analyst sees as suboptimal the other sees as optimal. I now turn to the first of my claims, that the literature Revesz relies upon establishes, contrary to his analysis, that there are real incentives for a 'race to the bottom'.

The burden of Revesz's task here is, upon reflection, of heroic proportions. It will be recalled that the useful formulation of state competition in terms of a prisoner's dilemma led from the initial account of an 'island' jurisdiction to the situation of two competitive jurisdictions. Having established the optimal trade off in environmental regulation in an island state—what is it that changes in the new competitive situation? The change, in Revesz's own words, is that 'there will be an additional factor to consider: the location of a firm can lead to the creation of jobs, and thus to increases in wages and taxes—important benefits for a state.' (Revesz 1992: 1214–5). That is, the value of the increased investment might well outweigh the cost of the new lower environmental regulation. As I have said, the prisoner's dilemma argument depends upon this being the case—that choice 3 be superior to choice 1. What Revesz then does is rather provocative—he denies that states are interested in attracting more investment and creating more jobs.

This is a rather surprising empirical observation to make in the face of a world in which states vigorously compete for investment and jobs, and in which governments rise and fall based upon their success in doing so. But on this view, because they are indifferent to further investment, there is no incentive to enter a race for more investment by lowering environmental or other standards. There can be no benefit from the creation of further jobs which would weigh at all against the cost of lowering environmental standards. Revesz takes this position not based upon an empirical assessment of investment decisions, but rather by relying upon certain theoretical literatures, beginning with the 'Tiebout model', which deals with the problem of a mobile *population* and competition between multiple jurisdictions for them as residents. The Tiebout Hypothesis is that 'the ability of individuals to 'vote with their feet' by moving to the jurisdictions with the most preferred tax-expenditures package leads local governments to efficiently tailor public goods to the preferences of residents' (Wilson 1995). Revesz notes that the model's assumptions 'assume away' the key to the race to the bottom idea—the impact of job creation. Revesz then considers William Fischel's article (Fischel 1975), which deals with the problem of *industrial* location, but again notes that this study too 'assumes away' the vital incentive to engage in a race to the bottom—job creation. However, Revesz states that the 'shortcomings' of the Tiebout and Fischel models are 'addressed' by the Oates and Schwab study (Oates and Schwab 1988), meaning presumably that they do not 'assume away' the cornerstone of the race to the bottom argument as he himself has presented it—the potential benefits of attracting investment and thus creating jobs.

But Revesz appears to misread the Oates and Schwab contribution in several crucial ways. What Oates and Schwab demonstrate is that under a series of strong assumptions and using a highly particular modelling technique, rational states faced with mobile capital and immobile labour (people) will act rationally when faced with two policy choices—the rate of tax on capital and the appropriate level of environmental regulation. In their model, Oates and Schwab explain,

Jurisdictions compete for a mobile stock of capital by lowering taxes and relaxing environmental standards that would otherwise deflect capital elsewhere. In return for an increased capital stock, residents receive higher incomes in the form of higher wages. The community must, however, weigh the benefits of higher wages against the cost of foregone tax revenues and lower environmental quality. (Oates and Schwab 1988: 336).

The conclusion which Oates and Schwab draw, which is central to the argument which Revesz is attempting to make, is that rational competitive jurisdictions will set a tax rate on capital of zero. In the perfectly ordered market that they imagine for their narrowly defined jurisdictions of homogenous workers there will be an indifference to further investment, and environmental policy will be set such that marginal willingness to pay equals the marginal social costs of the cleaner environment.

Now, a series of problems emerge from this account. The idea, you will recall, is to deny the underpinning of the prisoner's dilemma by demonstrating that rational states would be indifferent to choice 3 or 1 so that no race is possible. This, in spite of the fact that we know states do struggle with this preference choice regularly. Unfortunately, what Oates and Schwab really do is give us a partial explanation of why many states are indeed engaged in prisoner-dilemma type behaviour with such regularity. That is, the point of Oates and Schwab is that if states do not tax capital at zero, then there is an incentive to compete by providing, in their example, suboptimal environmental regulation in order to attract capital. This is the first point. The issue for Oates and Schwab then is the factual one as to whether capital is taxed appropriately at a rate of exactly zero. If capital is taxed inappropriately, then there will be a distorting impact on environmental regulation.

Revesz's progress through the theoretical literature brought him to the point where the Oates and Schwab model was presented because it 'addressed' the 'shortcomings' of the Tiebout and Fischel models. The shortcoming which beleaguered those models was that they 'assumed away' the key to the prisoner's dilemma—the idea of the benefits of attracting investments and jobs to the jurisdiction. But the Oates and Schwab model expressly does *not* cure for this shortcoming. In fact, their model calls for and assumes *full employment*. Moreover, when Oates and Schwab introduce non-workers into their model, the conclusion is that the results are 'not socially optimal' (Oates and Schwab 1988: 349). As Oates and Schwab conclude, their model, far from demonstrating no race to the bottom, has important 'explanatory power' in explaining what 'we know'—that 'states and localities often engage in vigorous efforts to attract new business capital' (ibid.). Hence, as a matter *internal* to Revesz's approach, he has failed to demonstrate that states would be irrational in choosing choice 3 prior to choice 1 in the prisoner dilemma choice matrix. Thus the race to the bottom is off and running because of the conceptual implications of the pursuit of self-interest which it is the point of the prisoner's dilemma to reveal and which Revesz himself has so helpfully laid out for us. This conclusion has the added benefit of being congruent with our knowledge of the real world.

But all of this is, in an important sense, not the main point. There is the further *external* point which is implicitly raised by the methodology utilized by Revesz, which I think is the key to the intractability of the prisoner's dilemma and race to the bottom debates and, for that matter, of the 'fair trade/free trade' issue in general (see, e.g., Barry and Goodwin 1992). This can be seen by asking the following question: what would Revesz have to say about the real world in which there *is* unemployment and in which jurisdictions regularly compete for investment and jobs? On the one hand, it seems that Revesz has already indicated what his view would be—there would be a race to the bottom as he so explicitly set out. Because they are locked into a strategic choice they will, perversely, 'give away' their standards for no additional benefit. Despite this, could it be so on Revesz's understanding of the world? This is our important question. The drift of the article is that states would be indifferent between choice 3 or choice 1. But there are many circumstances in which this is not the case. If this is not the case and states *do* compete for mobile capital, why is the result of that market in regulatory competition not just an optimal result—the equivalent of bidding down the price of widgets? All producers of widgets would prefer that they alone reduce their price by a dollar and that all of their competitors do not. The trouble is, their competitors think the same thing. But, in the market for widgets, this is the 'correct' result.

This question here is, what is the relationship between the beneficial competition and the race to the bottom arguments? In the real world of less than full employment, states will engage in regulatory competition (along with competition in loans, grants, land deals) to attract investment. This is the 'price' of investment. But in these circumstances how could Revesz describe the predicament as a 'race to the bottom', as he has done? Would he not be forced to describe it as a race to the optimal level of regulation? But the point of the prisoner's dilemma would remain—that states would all be 'better off' if they did not engage in this competition. The problem is that the resulting competition for investment can be seen in two ways—as a race to the bottom, or as simply the operation of a market for scarce capital, investment, and jobs. We have here a 'double aspect picture.' We look at the same thing and see it two ways.

The problem with Revesz's article, but also its benefit for our purposes, is thus twofold. He wishes to acknowledge the force of the prisoner's dilemma argument, but then argue that as a matter of fact it would not take place. He gets *both* of these points wrong. First, it seems that as a matter of fact (or 'theory'), the race will occur when the key assumptions are relaxed. Second, it is unclear that Revesz can acknowledge, as he wishes to do and does, the force of the prisoner's dilemma analysis. This may explain the introduction of the important question: 'If one believes that competition among sellers of widgets is socially desirable, why is competition among sellers of location rights socially undesirable?' This *is* the prisoner's dilemma problem re-expressed. But then the important issue is, which version of the question *should* we ask—the prisoner's dilemma version, or the virtues of competition version?

Why is it clear that producers of widgets should compete, yet also clear that jurisdiction 'giving away' the optimal regulatory régime for nothing is an unsound move? Structurally, we have the same phenomenon in each case. Competition among producers of widgets is hard on producers of widgets but good for consumers thereof. But competition among producers of regulation can be seen in the same way—it is bad for producers of regulation (and those regulation is designed to protect) but good for consumers of regulation (those who are to be regulated). The prisoner's dilemma analysis of jurisdictions 'giving away' their optimal environmental legislation in order to attract investment is simply another market transfer from the intended beneficiaries of regulation to the regulated. Even in the original prisoner's dilemma of the two prisoners contemplating confession, the force of the example is derived from the assumption that it is 'bad' to spend longer in jail. But from the point of view of the public, this may not be so, and competition among confessing criminals may be 'good'.

In all of these cases the question is simply from whose perspective and by what standard are we to measure the socially desirable. In the real world of unemployment, the desire for investment will result in the net transfer, as Revesz has shown, from the beneficiaries of regulation to the regulated. Our ability to condemn that transfer rests outside the prisoner's dilemma/ efficient competition analysis. We call them as we see them. We declare which argument is trump. And just as in bridge or other card games played with trump suits, the cards do not declare themselves to be trumps. The players of those cards do.

In my view this accounts for a major part of the intractability of race to the bottom discussions. If there is competition for investment—and there is—then we are stuck with two ways of understanding it. The problem them is one of *deciding* which way to understand the problem. This means that we must decide when competitive markets are useful and when they are not. This is not a matter which can be decided solely from within the theory of markets. Is it sensible for states to engage in 'downward' regulatory environmental and labour competition to attract investment or should they compete only on grounds of better schools, a better trained workforce, etc.? This problem is made even more intense because one of the assumptions which made Revesz's project a simple one was to define all issues in terms of economic rationality. But in matters of labour law and policy, for example, this is a highly controversial assumption to make. Democratic values and human rights values complicate our decisions. In this circumstance we can expect as a *matter of principle* to encounter choices between our two methods of analyses.

There is yet another problem which adds another layer of difficulty to the race to the bottom debate. The difficulty is one of democratic theory. Revesz, and all of the theorists he enlists in support, posit a world in which mobility of capital is assumed. One then adjusts in an economically rational way to this fact. In effect one shifts 'tax' from the mobile factor to the immobile factor. There are many things that can be said about this rational assessment of the mobile factors playing off the immobile ones (particularly jurisdictions). For example, it is very significant that the modern world has created conditions for increased mobility of capital—but not people (labour). But perhaps more interestingly, a common instinct and part of the standard political reaction to trade and investment liberalization policies, has been that they limit the ability of people to govern their own affairs. Policies are now set, to some increased extent, in the international marketplace of regulatory competition. This is a change and, on a common view, a loss. More precisely it is a loss of democratic control and accountability. The issues of environmental and labour policy were at one point established more within the nation state—through political processes. They are now being set in international regulatory competition between states. A central role, if not the central role, of our political processes is to establish the ground rules for and the proper domain of, market ordering (should there be a private market in health care?). The problem is that there is no *international* political forum to engage this enterprise. That is why NAFTA has attracted labour and environmental side deals (the equivalent of federal level playing field legislation). The NAFTA negotiations were pressed to take up the democratic slack created by the circumstance of mobile capital and (relatively or absolutely) immobile people.

In the end, the intractability of our debates arises because, (1) on one view there are races to the bottom; and (2) on the other view, the proper analysis is that there is only a properly ordered market which requires no correction. This problem is compounded by the fact that we have lost the institutional space in which to ask the vital question—should we see a prisoner's dilemma here, or simply beneficial competition?

Bibliography

A.P. (1993), Associated Press, 'Boycott of Cincinnati Urged After Los in Gay-Rights Vote', *New York Times*, November 9, 1993.

Aaron, Henry J. (1992), *The Economics and Politics of Pensions: Evaluating the Choices* in OECD (1992), 137–141.

Abbot, A. (1988), *The System of the Professions: An Essay on the Division of Expert Labour*, (Chicago: University of Chicago Press).

Abel-Smith, B., Stevens, R. (1967), *Lawyers and the Courts: a Sociological Study of the English Legal System, 1750–1965*, (London: Heinemann).

Abrahamson, P. (1992), *The Scandinavian Model: Myths and Realities* Paper to ESF Conference at St Martin, Germany, November 22–26.

Acs, Z. J., and Audretsch, D. B., (1990) (eds.), *The Economics of Small Firms. A European Challenge* (Dordrecht: Kluwer Academic Publishers).

Adler, B. E. (1993), 'Financial and Political Theories of American Corporate Bankruptcy', 45 *Stanford Law Review* 311.

Adonis, Andrew (1994), 'Monopoly Walls Breached', *Financial Times*, 15 June 1994.

Albert, M. (1992), *Capitalismes contre capitalismes* (Paris: Seuil).

Alchian, A., and Allen, W. R. (1983), *Exchange and Production: Competition, Coordination and Control* (3rd edn.). (Belmont, California: Wadsworth Publishing Company).

Alger, C. F. (1988), 'Perceiving, Analysing and Coping with the Local-Global Nexus', 117 *International Social Science Journal* 321.

Alt, J. A., and Shepsle, K. A. (1990) (eds.), *Perspectives on Positive Political Economy* (Cambridge: Cambridge University Press).

Alva, C. (1990), 'Delaware and the Market for Corporate Charters: History and Agency', 15 *Delaware Journal of Corporate Law* 885.

American Bar Association, Section of Business Law, Committee on Corporate Laws (1990), 'Changes in the Revised Model Business Corporation Act—Amendment Pertaining to Liability of Directors', 46 *Business Lawyer* 319.

Andenas, M., and Kenyon-Slade, S. (1993), *EC Financial Market Regulation and Company Law* (London: Sweet & Maxwell).

Anderson, Benedict (1991), *Imagined Communities* (2nd edn.), (London: Verso).

Ansley, Fran (1993), 'Standing Rusty and Rolling Empty: Law, Poverty, and America's Eroding Industrial Base', 81 *Georgetown L.J.* 1757.

Appadurai, A. (1990), 'Disjuncture and Difference in the Global Cultural Economy', 7 *Theory, Culture and Society* 295.

Applebaum, M. D. (1993), 'Are Foreign Same-sex Marriages Between California Residents Valid in California?', *San Francisco Barrister*, December 1993, p. 19.

Arrow, K. J. (1963), *Social Choice and Individual Values* (New Haven: Yale University Press) (2nd edn.) (1951).

Arthur, W. Brian, (March 1989), 'Competing Technologies, Increasing Returns, and Lock-In By Historical Events', 99 *The Economic Journal* 116–31.

Association, American Bar (1992), *Antitrust Law Developments* (3rd edn.), Chicago: Section of Antitrust Law, American Bar Association.

Atkin, David J. (1994), 'Cable Exhibition in the USA', 18 *Telecommunications Policy* 331–341.

Atkinson, J., and Meager, N. (1989), *New Forms of Work Organisation* (Brighton: Institute of Manpower Studies).

Auerbach, J. (1976), *Unequal Justice: Lawyers and Social Change in Modern America* (New York: Oxford University Press).

Ayres, I. (1992*a*), 'Judging Close Corporations in the Age of Statutes', 70 *Washington University Law Quarterly* 365–397.

Ayres, I. (1992*b*), 'Price and Prejudice', 6 July, *The New Republic* 30.

Ayres, I. (1992*c*), 'Making a Difference: The Contractual Contributions of Easterbrook and Fischel', 59 *University of Chicago Law Review* 1391–1420.

Ayres, I., and Braithwaite, J. (1991), *Responsive Regulation: Transcending the Deregulation Debate* (New York: Oxford University Press).

Ayres, I., and Crampton, P. (1994), 'Relational Investing and Agency Theory', 15 *Cardozo Law Review* 1033.

Bainbridge, S. M. (1992), 'Redirecting State Takeover Laws at Proxy Contests', 1992 *Wisconsin Law Review* 1071.

Baker, Donald I., and Beverly, G. Baker (1983), 'Antitrust and Communications Deregulation' 28 *Antitrust Bulletin* 1–38.

Ballon, Ian Charles (1987), 'The Implications of Making the Denial of Internationally Recognized Worker Rights Actionable Under Section 301 of the Trade Act of 1974', 28 *Virginia Law Rev.* 73.

Bancaud, A., Boigeol, A. (1995), 'A New Judge for a New System of Economic Justice', in Y. Dezalay, D. Sugarman (eds.) *Professional Competition and Professional Power* (Routledge: London).

Barella, Derek (1994), 'Checking the "Trigger-Happy" Congress: the Extraterritorial Extension of Federal Employment Laws Requires Prudence', 69 *Indiana Law Review* 889.

Barkin, J. S., and Cronin, B. (1994), 'The State and the Nation: Changing Norms and the Rules of Sovereignty in International Relations', 48 *International Organization* 107.

Barlett, T. (1993), 'State Tries to Combat Tourism Woes: Mainland Arrivals Plummeted 19% in 1992 and Continue to Fall', *Travel Weekly*, 9 August 1993, p. H3.

Barnard, J. W. (1991), 'Institutional Investors and the New Corporate Governance', 69 *North Carolina Law Review* 1135.

Barnet, Richard J., and Muller, Ronald E. (1974), *Global Reach: The Power of Multinational Corporations* (New York: Simon & Shuster).

Baron, D. P., and Ferejohn, J. A. (1989), 'Bargaining in Legislatures', 83 *American Political Science Review* 1181.

Barr, N. (1992), 'Economic theory and the welfare state: A survey and reinterpretation' 30 *Journal of Economic Literature* 741–803.

Barry and Goodin (1992) (eds.), *Free Movement: Ethical Issues in the Transnational Migration of People and Money* (Penn State U. Press: University Park, Pennsylvania).

Basinger, B., and Butler, H. (1985), 'The Role of Corporate Law in the Theory of the Firm', 28 *Journal of Law and Economics* 179–91.

Basle: Bank for International Settlements.

Batra, R. (1993), *Myth of Free Trade*.

Baumol, W. J., and McLennan, K. (1985) (eds.), *Productivity Growth and U.S. Competitiveness* (New York: Oxford University Press).

Baumol, W. J., Blackman, S. A. B., and Wolff, E. N. (1989), *Productivity and American Leadership: The Long View* (Cambridge, Mass.: MIT Press).

Baumol, W. J., and Wolff, E. N. (1992), 'Comparative U.S. Productivity Perform-ance and the State of Manufacturing: The Latest Data', 10 *CVStarr Newsletter of New York University Center for Applied Economics* 1.

Baums, T. (1993), 'Banks and Corporate Control in Germany', in McCahery, J., Picciotto, S., and Scott, C. (eds.), *Corporate Control and Accountability: Changing Structures and the Dynamics of Regulation* (Oxford: Clarendon Press) 267–87.

Baums, T., Buxbaum, R. H., and Hopt, K. J. (1994) (eds.), *Institutional Investors and Corporate Governance* (Berlin: de Gruyter).

Baxter, William F. (1983), 'Conditions Creating Antitrust Concern with Vertical Integration by Regulated Industries—"For Whom the Bell Doctrine Tolls" ' 52 *Antitrust Law Journal* 243–247.

Beausang, Michael (1966), 'The Extraterritorial Jurisdiction of the Sherman Act', 70 *Dickinson Law Review* 187.

Bebchuk, L. (1992), 'Federalism and the Corporation: The Desirable Limits on State Competition in Corporate Law', 105 *Harvard Law Review* 1437–1510.

Bebchuk, L. A., and Kahan, M. (1990), 'A Framework for Analyzing Legal Policy Towards Proxy Contests', 78 *California Law Review* 1071.

Bebr, G. (1992), 'Case Law. Courts of Justice. Joined Cases C6/90 and C9/90, Francovich v. Italy, Bonifici v. Italy' 29 *Common Market Law Review* 557–584.

Becker, G. S. (1983), 'A Theory of Competition Among Pressure Groups for Political Influence', 1983 *Quarterly Journal of Economics* 371.

Been, V. (1991), ' "Exit" as a Constraint on Land Use Exactions: Rethinking of Unconstitutional Conditions Doctrine', 91 *Columbia Law Review* 473–545.

Begg, D., and Seabright, P., and Nevern (1993), *Making Sense of Subsidiarity: How Much Centralization for Europe?* (London: Centre for Economic Policy Research).

Bercusson, Brian (1992), 'Maastricht: A Fundamental Change in European Labour Law', 23 *Industrial Relations Law Journal* 177.

Bergalli, R. (1994), 'Judicial Protagonism as a New Element in Legal Culture', paper presented to XLLLieme Congrès International de Sociologie, Bielefeld, 17–18 July 1994.

Berle, A. A., and Means, G. C. (1932), *The Modern Corporation and Private Property* (New York: Harcourt, Brace & World).

Besseling, P. J., and Zeeuw, R. F. (1993), *The Financing of Pensions in Europe: Challenges and Opportunities* CEPS Research Paper No 14 (Brussels: Centre for European Policy Studies).

Betcherman, Gordon (1992), 'The Disappearing Middle', in Drache, D. (ed.), *Getting on Track. Social Democratic Struggles for Ontario* (Montreal: McGill-Queen's University Press).

Bhagwati, Jagdish (1988), *Protectionism* (Cambridge, Mass.: The MIT Press).

Bhagwati, J. (1993), 'Regionalism and Multilateralism: An Overview', in de Meolo, J. and Panagariya, A. (eds.), *New Dimensions in Institutional Integration* (Cambridge: Cambridge University Press) 22–51.

Bhagwati and Hudec (1996) (eds.), *Harmonization and Fair Trade: Pre-requisites for Free Trade?* (MIT Press, Cambridge, Mass, 1996) (forthcoming).

Biddle, D. (1993), 'Recycling for Profit: The New Green Business. Frontier', *Harvard Business Review* 145.

Biersteker, T. (1992) 'The "Triumph" of Liberal Economic Ideas in the Developing World', Working Paper No 6, Global Studies Research Program, University of Wisconsin.

Birnbaum, P. (1977), *Les Sommets de l'Etat* Paris, Seuil. (1988) *La classe dirigeante francaise*, (Paris: PUF).

BIS (1986), 'Report on International Developments in Bank Supervision', Report No. 5 of the Committee on Banking Regulations and Supervisory Practices, Sept. (Basle, Bank for International Settlements).

Bishop, J. W. (1968), 'Sitting Ducks and Decoy Ducks: New Trends in Indemnification of Corporate Directors and Officers', 77 *Yale Law Journal* 1078.

Biskup, R. (1990) (ed.), *Werte in Wirtschaft und Gesellschaft* (Bern: Verlag Paul Haupt).

Black, Alexander, J. (1993), 'Incentive Regulation for Public Utilities' 4 *Utilities Law Review* 93–97.

Black, B. S. (1990*a*), 'Shareholder Passivity Re-examined', 89 *Michigan Law Review* 520.

Black, B. S. (1990*b*), 'Is Corporate Law Trivial? A Political and Economic Analysis', 84 *Northwestern University Law Review* 542.

Black, B. S. (1992), 'Agents Watching Agents: The Promise of Institutional Investor Voice', 39 *UCLA Law Review* 811.

Blanc-Jouvan, Xavier (1984), 'Worker Involvement in Management Decisions in France', 58 *Tulane Law Review* 1332.

Blanpain, Roger (1992), *Labour Law and Industrial Relations of the European Union: Maastricht and Beyond* (Deventer: Kluwer).

Block, V. (1994), 'Escape to a Dream Isle', *The Washington Times*, 16 January 1994, p. E4.

Boner, Roger Alan, and Krueger, Reinald (1991), *The Basics of Antitrust Policy. A Review of Ten Nations and the European Community, World Bank Technical Paper no. 160* (Washington DC: The World Bank).

Bonhall, B. (1994), 'Partners for Life: Gays in O.C. Are Increasingly Confirming Their Unions Before Family and Friends', *Los Angeles Times*, 13 February 1994, p. E1 col. 2.

Bourdieu, P. (1981), 'Décrire et prescrire', *Actes de la Recherche en Sciences Sociales,* No 36–37.

Bourdieu, P. (1982), 'La sainte famille', *Actes de la Recherche en Sciences sociales*, No 44–45.

Bourdieu, P. (1987*a*), 'The Force of Law: Towards a Sociology of the Juridical Field' *Hastings Journal of Law*, No 38.

Bourdieu, P. (1987*b*), 'Variations et invariants: Eléments pour une histoire structurale du champ des grandes écoles', *Actes de la Recherche en Sciences Sociales*, No 70.

Bourdieu, P. (1989), *La noblesse d'Etat, Grandes écoles et esprit de corps* (Paris: Editions de Minuit).

Bourdieu, P. (1991), 'Les juristes, gardiens de l'hypocrisie collective', in F. Chazel, J. Commaille (eds.) *Normes juridiques et régulation sociale* (Paris: LGDJ).

Bourdieu, P. (1993) 'Esprits d'Etat: Genèse et structure du champ bureaucratique', *Actes de la Recherche en Sciences Sociales*, No 96–97.

Bourdieu, P., de St Martin M. (1976), 'Le patronat' *Actes de la Recherche en Sciences Sociales*, No 20–21.

Bourdieu, P., Wacquant, L. (1992), *An Invitation to Reflexive Sociology* (Oxford: Polity Press).

Bowett, D. W. (1982), 'Jurisdiction: Changing Patterns of Authority over Activities and Resources', LIII *British Yearbook of International Law* 1–26.

Boyer, Allen, (1983) 'Form as Substance: A Comparison of Antitrust Regulation by Consent Decree in the USA, Reports of the Monopolies and Mergers Commission in the UK, and Grants of Clearance by the European Commission' 32 *International and Comparative Law Quarterly* 904–930.

Boyer, Robert (1994), *New Directions in Management Practices and Work Organization* (Paris: OECD).

Bracewell-Milnes (1980), *The Economics of International Tax Avoidance. Political Power versus Economic Law* (Deventer: Kluwer).

Bradley, Kieran St C. (1994) ' "Better Rusty Than Missin"?: The Institutional Reforms of the Maastricht Treaty and the European Parliament.' In David O'Keefe and Patrick M. Twomey (eds.) *Legal Issues of the Maastricht Treaty* 193–214 (Chichester: Chancery).

Bradley, M., and Schipani, C. A. (1989), 'The Relevance of the Duty of Care Standard in Corporate Law', 75 *Iowa Law Review* 1.

Braithwaite, John (1993a), Prospects for win-win international rapproachement of regulation, in OECD Regulatory Cooperation in an Interdependent World (Paris: OECD).

Braithwaite, J. (1993b), 'Transnational Regulation of the Pharmaceutical Industry', 525 (Jan.) *Annals of the AAPSS*: 12.

Brams, S. J. (1994), *Theory of Moves* (Cambridge: Cambridge University Press).

Branson, D. (1990), 'Indeterminacy: The Final Ingredient in an Interest Group Analysis', 43 *Vanderbilt Law Review* 85.

Bratton, W. W. (1989), 'The New Economic Theory of the Firm: Critical Perspectives From History', 41 *Standford Law Review* 1471–1527.

Bratton, W. W. (1994), 'Corporate Law's Race to Nowhere in Particular', 44 *University of Toronto Law Journal* 401.

Brennan, G. (1987), 'Why Regulated Firms Should be Kept Out of Unregulated Markets: Understanding the Divestiture in US v. AT&T' 23 *Antitrust Bulletin* 741.

Brennan, G., and Buchanan, J. M. (1980), *The Power to Tax: Analytical Foundations of a Fiscal Constitution* (Cambridge: Cambridge University Press).

Briffault, R. (1990), *Our Localism: Part II—Localism and Legal Theory*, 90 Columbia Law Review 346–454.

Brilmayer, L. (1987), 'The Extraterritorial Application of American Law: A Methodological and Constitutional Appraisal', 50 *Law & Contemporary Problems* 11.

Brittan, L. (1990), *A Single Market for Pension Funds* Paper presented to the International Pensions Conference at Kerkrade on 2 July 1990.

Brudney, V., and Bratton, W. W. (1993), *Brudney & Chirelstein's Cases and Materials on Corporate Finance* (Mineola, N.Y.: Foundation Press).

Buchanan, J. M. (1980), 'Rent-seeking under External Diseconomies', in J. M. Buchanan, R. D. Tollison, and G. Tullock, (eds.) (1980) *Toward a Theory of the Rent-Seeking Society* (College Station: Texas A&M Press).

Buchanan, R. (1994), *Border Crossings: Nafta, Regulatory Restructuring and the Politics of Place*, Paper presented to the Law & Society Annual Meeting, Phoenix.

Buckley, F. H., and Connelly, M. Q. (1988), *Corporations: Principles and Policies* (Toronto: Edmond Montgomery, 2nd edn.).

Bullock, K. (1992), 'Applying *Marvin* v. *Marvin* to Same-Sex Couples: A Preference for a Sex-Preference Neutral Cohabitation Statute', 25 *University of California at Davis Law Review* 1029.

Bulmer, Simon (1994*a*), 'Institutions and Policy Change in the European Communities: The Case of Merger Control' 72 *Public Administration* 423–444.

Bulmer, Simon J. (1994*b*), 'The Governance of the European Union: A New Institutionalist Approach' 13 *Journal of Public Policy* 351–380.

Bureau of the Census (1991), Press Release, '1990 Census Showed Gain of 14 Million Housing Units Since 1980', 30 April 1991.

Bureau of the Census (1993), U.S. Dept. of Commerce, Bureau of the Census, *Statistical Abstract of the United States*: 1993 (113th edn.).

Burley, Anne-Marie and Mattli, Walter (1993), 'Europe Before the Court: A Political Theory of European Integration', 47 *International Organization* 41–77.

Burton, J. (1972), *World Society* (Cambridge: Cambridge University Press).

Butler, B. (1990), *Ceremonies of the Heart: Celebrating Lesbian Unions* (Berkeley: California: Seal Press Feminist).

Butler, H. (1988), 'Corporation-Specific Anti-Takeover Statutes and the Market for Corporate Charters', 1988 *Wisconsin Law Review*, 365–83.

Butler, H. N., and Macey, J. R. (1988), 'The Myth of Competition in the Dual Banking System', 73 *Cornell Law Review* 677–718.

Buxbaum, R.H. (1987), 'The Origins of the American "Internal Affairs" Rule in the Corporate Conflict of Laws', in Musielak and Schurig (1987) 75–94.

Buxbaum, R. M., and Hopt, K. J. (1988), *Legal Harmonization and the Business Enterprise* (Berlin: de Gruyter).

Buxbaum, R. M., Hertig, G., Hirsch, A., and Hopt. K. J. (1991) (eds.), *European Business Law: Legal and Economic Analysis on Integration and Harmonization* (Berlin: de Gruyter).

Cain, Maureen (1994), 'The Symbol Traders', in Cain and Harrington (1994), *Lawyers in a Postmodern World. Translation and Transgression* (Buckingham: Open University Press) 15–48.

Cain, M. and Harrington, C. (1994), *Lawyers in a Postmodern World. Translation and Transgression* (Buckingham: Open University Press).

Calder, R. (1992), 'Avoid, Minimize, Re-use, Recycle: The German Packaging Ethic', 65 Oct (10) *Soap, Perfumery & Cosmetics* 41.

Cameli, M. (1992), 'Extending Family Benefits to Gay Men and Lesbian Women', 68 *Chicago-Kent Law Review* 447.

Cameron, Duncan and Watkins, Mel (1993), *Canada Under Free Trade* (Toronto: Lorimer).

Camilleri, J. A. and Falk, J. (1992), *The End of Sovereignty? The Politics of a Shrinking and Fragmented World* (Aldershot, Hants.: Edward Elgar).

Cappelletti, Mauro, Monica Seccombe, and Joseph Weiler (1986), 'Integration Through Law: Europe and the American Federal Experience—A General Introduction'. In Mauro Cappelletti, Monica Seccombe, and Joseph Weiler (eds.) *Integration Through Law—Volume One—Methods, Tools and Institutions* 3–68. 1. (Berlin: de Gruyter).

Carbonneau, T. (1990) (ed.), *Lex Mercatoria and Arbitration: a Discussion of the New Law Merchant* (Dobbs Ferry N.Y.: Transnational Publications Inc.).

Carney, W. J. (1988), 'Section 4.01 of the American Law Institutes's Corporate Governance Project: Restatement or Misstatement?' 66 *Washington University Law Quarterly* 239.

Carney, W. J. (1995), 'The Political Economy of Competition for Corporate Charters', in Wouters, J., and Schneider, H. (1995), *Current Issues of Cross-Border Estbalishment of Companies in the European Union* (Antwerp, Maklu).

Carroll, Mitchell B. (1978), *Global Perspectives of an International Tax Lawyer* (Hicksville, New York: Exposition Press).

Cary, W. (1974), 'Federalism and Corporate Law: Reflections upon Delaware', 88 *Yale Law Journal* 663–707.

Castellot, Miguel Angel Pena (1995), 'What are the Union Rules and how are they Being Applied?' Paper presented at "Implementing European Telecommunications Law" Conference in Brussels, edited by European Commission, European Commission 103–120.

Castells, M. (1992), 'Four Asian Tigers with a Dragon Head: A Comparative Analysis of the State, Economy and Society in the Asian Pacific Rim', in R. Appelbaum, J. Henderson (eds.) *States and Development in the Asian Pacific Rim* (London, SAGE).

Castles, F., and Mitchell, D. (1992), 'Identifying Welfare State Regimes', 5(1) *Governance* 1–26.

Cecchini Report (1988), *The European Challenge: The Benefits of a Single Market* (Aldershot: Wildwood House).

Chandler, A. D. Jr. (1990), *Scale and Scope: The Dynamics of Industrial Capitalism* (Cambridge, Mass.: Harvard University Press).

Charle, C. (1992), 'Les Grands Corps' in P. Nora (ed.) *Les lieux de mémoire, III, Les France*—Tome 2 (Paris: NRF).

Charnovitz, Steven (1986), 'Fair Labor Standards and International Trade', 20 *Journal of World Trade Law* 61.

Charnovitz, Steven (1987), 'The Influence of International Labour Standards on the World Trading Regime: A Historical Overview', 125 *International Labour Review* 565.

Charnovitz, Steve (1995), 'The World Trade Organization and Social Issues', 29 *Journal of World Trade*, 17–33.

Charny, D. (1991), 'Competition among Jurisdictions in Formulating Corporate Law Rules: An American Perspective on the 'Race to the Bottom' in the European Communities', 32 *Harvard International Law Journal* 423–56.

Cherian, Joy (1992), 'Enforcement of American Workers' Rights Abroad', (1992) 43 *Labor Law Journal* 563.

Chetley, A. (1986), *The Politics of Baby Foods. Successful challenges to an international marketing strategy*, (London: Pinter).

Christianity Today, 'Warner Alliance Cries Foul over Boycott', 14 December 1992, p. 44.

Cira, Carl A. (1982), 'The Challenge of Foreign Laws to Block American Antitrust Actions', 18 *Stanford. Journal of International Law* 247.

Clarkson, Stephen (1985), *Canada and the Reagan Challenge* (Toronto: Lorimer).

Clarkson, Stephen (1993), 'Constitutionalizing the Canadian-American Relationship', in Cameron, Duncan and Watkins, Mel (1993), *Canada Under Free Trade* (Toronto: Lorimer).

Closen, M. L. and Heise, C. R. (1992), 'HIV-AIDS and the Non-Traditional Family: The Argument for State and Federal Recognition of Danish Same-Sex Marriages', 16 *Nova Law Review* 809.

Coates, A. (1981) (ed.) *Economists in Government, An International Comparative Study* (Durham: Duke University Press).

Cockbourne, Jean-Eric de (1995), 'The Pipeline, Plans and Investigations.' Paper presented at 'Implementing European Telecommunications Law' Conference in Brussels, edited by European Commission, European Commission, 132–140.

Coffee, J. C. (1985), 'The Unfaithful Champion: The Plaintiff as Monitor in Shareholder Litigation', 48 *Law and Contemporary Problems* 5–81.

Coffee, J. C., Jr. (1987), 'The Future of Corporate Federalism: State Competition and the New Trend Toward De Facto Federal Minimum Standards', 8 *Cardozo Law Review* 759.

Coffee, J. C. (1991), 'Liquidity versus Control: The Institutional Investor as Corporate Monitor', 91 *Columbia Law Review* 1277–1368.

Coffee, J. C. (1994), 'The SEC and the Institutional Investor: A Half-Time Report', 15 *Cardozo Law Review* 837.

Coffee, J. C. (1995), 'Competition Versus Consolidation: The Significance of Organizational Structure in Financial and Securities Regulation', 50 *Business Lawyer* 447–484.

Cohen, Marcy (1992), 'The feminization of the labour market', in Drache, D. (ed.) (1992) *Getting on Track: Social Democratic Strategies for Ontario* (Montreal: McGill-Queen's University Press).

Coleman J. L., and Ferejohn, J. A. (1986), 'Democracy and Social Choice', 97 *Ethics* 6.

Collins, Richard (1994), 'Unity in Diversity' 32 *Journal of Common Market Studies* 89–102.

Commerce Clearing House (1993), *Doing Business in Europe* (Chicago: CCH).

Commission of the European Communities (1985), *Completing the Internal Market: White Paper from the Commission to the European Council*, COM (85) 310 final (Brussels).

Commission of the European Communities (1987), *Communication from the Commission to the Council on the Creation of a European Financial Area*, COM (87) 550 (Brussels).

Commission of the European Communities (1989), *Communication from the Commission Concerning its Action Programme*, COM (89) 568 final (Brussels).

Commission of the European Communities (1990), *Completing the Internal Market for Private Retirement Provisions*, XV (90) 224 (Brussels).

Commission of the European Communities (1991*a*), *Proposal for a Council Directive*, COM (91) 301 final, 12 November 1991 (Brussels).

Commission of the European Communities (1991*b*), *Communication to the Council on Supplementary Social Security Schemes*, SEC (1991) 1332 (Brussels).

Commission of the European Communities (1992*a*), *Recommendation of the Convergence of Social Protection Objectives and Policies*, 92/442/EEC (Brussels).

Commission of the European Communities (1992*b*), *Harmonization of Company Law in the European Community: Measures Adopted and Proposed: Situation as at 1 March 1992* (Brussels).

Commission of the European Communities (1992*c*), *Cross-border membership of occupational schemes for migrant workers*, Doc XV/2040/92/EN 16 September 1992 (Brussels).

Commission of the European Communities (1993*a*), *Amended Proposal for a Council Directive*, COM (93) 237 final, 26 May 1993 (Brussels).

Commission of the European Communities (1993*b*), *European Social Policy Options for the Union*, COM (93) 551 (Brussels).

Commission of the European Communities (1993*c*), *Growth, Competition and Employment: The Challenge and Ways Forward in the 21st Century* (Brussels: CEC).

Commission of the European Communities (1993*d*), *Reinforcing the Effectiveness of the Internal Market*, COM (93) 256 final (Brussels).

Commission of the European Communities (1994), *Supplementary Pensions in the European Union: Report by the Network of Experts* (Brussels).

Commission on Global Governance (1995), *Our Global Neighbourhood*, (Oxford: Oxford University Press).

Cooper & Lybrand (1994), *EEC Commentaries: Environment.*

Cowie, Jefferson (1993) *The Search for a Transnational Labor Discourse for a North American Economy: A Critical Review of U.S. Labor's Campaign Against NAFTA*, Working Paper, Duke-UNC Working Group of Labor, Free Trade and Economic Integration.

Cowie, Jefferson and French, John D. (1993), 'NAFTA's Labor Side Accord: A Textual Analysis', 9 *Latin American Labor News* 9:5.

Cox, B. J. (1986), 'Alternative Families: Obtaining Traditional Family Benefits Through Litigation, Legislation, and Collective Bargaining', 2 *Wisconsin Women's Law Journal* 1.

Cox, E. and Muhlfeld, E. (1963) (eds.), *Manfred Curry's Racing Tactics* (New York).

Cox, J. D. (1992), 'Rethinking US Securities Laws in the Shadow of International Regulatory Competition', 55(4) *Law & Contemporary Problems* 157.

Cram, L. (1993), 'Calling the Tune Without Paying the Piper', 21(2) *Policy and Politics* 135–146.

Crandall, Robert W. (1991*a*), *After the Breakup – US Telecommunications in a More Competitive Era* (ed.), Brookings Institution (Washington DC: Brookings Institution).

Crandall, Robert W. (1991*b*), 'Liberalization Without Deregulation: US Telecommunications Policy During the 1980s' 9 *Contemporary Policy Issues* 70–81.

Cullen, Bernard and Yves Blondeel (1995), 'Union Measures Taken in the Telecommunications Area and the Results Achieved.' Paper presented at 'Implementing European Telecommunications Law' Conference in Brussels, edited by European Commission, European Commission, 17–47.

Curtin, Deirdre (1990), 'The Province of Government: Delimiting the Scope of the Direct Effect of Directives in the Common Law Context', 15 *European Law Review* 195–223.

Dahrendorf, R. (1969), 'Law faculties and the German upper class', in W. Aubert (ed.) *Sociology of Law* (London: Penguin).

Daly, H. E., and Cobb, J. B. (1990), *For the Common Good: Redirecting the Economy Toward Community, the Environment and a Sustainable Future* (London: Green Print).

Dam, K. W. (1970), *The GATT – Law and Economic Organization* (Chicago: University of Chicago Press).

Damamme, D. (1987), 'Genèse sociale d'une institution scolaire: l'Ecole Libre des Sciences Politiques', *Actes de la Recherche en Sciences Sociales*, No. 70.

Damslet, O. R. (1993), 'Same-Sex Marriage', 10 *New York Law School Journal of Human Rights* 555.

Daniels, R. J. (1991), 'Should Provinces Compete? The Case for a Competitive Corporate Law Market', 36 *McGill Law Journal* 130–190.

Daniels, R. J., and MacIntosh, J. G. (1990), 'Capital Markets and the Law: The Peculiar Case of Canada', 3 *Canadian Investment Review* 77–84.

Daniels, R. J., and MacIntosh, J. G. (1992), 'Toward a Distinctive Canadian Corporate Law Regime', 29 *Osgoode Hall Law Journal* 863–933.

Dashwood, A. (1994), 'Community Legislative Procedures in the Era of the Treaty on European Union', 19(4) *European Law Review* 343–366.

David, Paul A. (1987), 'Some New Standards for the Economics of Standardization in the Information Age', in Dasgupta, P. and Stoneman, P. (eds.), *Economic Policy and Technological Performance* (Cambridge: Cambridge University Press).

David, P. (1993), 'Intellectual Property Institutions and the Panda's Thumb: Patents, Copyrights, and Trade Secrets in Economic Theory and History', in Wallerstein, M., Mogee, M., and Schoen, R. (1993) (eds.), *Global Dimensions of Intellectual Property* (CITY).

Davies, Andrew (1994), *Telecommunications and Politics: The Decentralised Alternative* (London: Pinter).

Davies, E. Philip (1994), *An International Comparison of the Financing of Occupational Pensions*, Special Paper No. 62, LSE Financial Markets Group.

Davis, S. M. (1989), *Shareholder Rights Abroad: A Handbook for the Global Investor* (Washington, DC: Investor Responsibility Research Center).

de Bruycker, J. (1991), 'EC Company Law—The European Company v. The European Economic Interest Grouping and the Harmonization of the National Company Laws', 21 *Georgia Journal of International and Comparative Law* 191–216.

de Jong, H. W. 'Free versus controlled competition', in B. Carlsson (ed.) (1989), *Industrial dynamics. Technological, organizational and structural changes in industries and firms* (Dordrecht: Kluwer Academic Publishers).

de Jong, H. W. (1991), 'The Takeover Market in Europe: Control Structures and the Performance of large Companies compared', in 6(1) *Review of Industrial Organization*.

de Jong, H. W. (1993*a*) (ed.), *The Structure of European Industry* (Dordrecht: Kluwer Academic Publishers) Third Edition.

de Jong, H. W. (1993*b*), 'Service Industries: innovation and internationalisation', in de Jong, H. W. (ed.), *The Structure of European Industry* (Dordrecht: Kluwer Academic Publishers).

de la Torre, Augusto and Kelly, Margaret, R. (1992), *Regional Trade Agreements* (Washington: International Monetary Fund).

De Long, J. B. (1991), 'Did J. P. Morgan's Men Add Value? An Economist's Perspective on Financial Capitalism', in Temin, P. (1991) (ed.), *Inside the Business Enterprise* (Chicago: University of Chicago Press), 205–236.

De Mestral, A. L. C., and Gruchalla-Wesierski, T. (1990), *Extraterritorial Application of Export Control Legislation: Canada and the USA* (Dordrecht: Nijhoff).

Dehousse, R. (1989), '1992 and Beyond: The Institutional Dimension of the Internal Market Programme', 1 *Legal Issues of European Integration*, 109.

Dehousse, R. (1992), 'Integration v. Regulation? On the Dynamics of Regulation in the European Community', 30(4) *Journal of Common Market Studies* 383.

Dehousse, R. (1994), 'Community Competences: Are there Limits to Growth', in Dehousse R. (1994), *Europe After Maastricht, An Ever Closer Union*? (Munich: Law Books in Europe) 103–125.

Demion and Bryant, S. (1993), 'Summary of Results—Partners' National Survey of Lesbian and Gay Couples', Partners Task Force for Gay & Lesbian Couples (Seattle).

Department of Employment (1994), 'The Flexible Workforce and Patterns of Working Hours in the UK', *Employment Gazette* July, 239–247.

Dept. of Commerce (1992), U.S. Dept. of Commerce, *State Government Finances*.

Dept. of Labor (1993): U.S. Dept. of Labor, *Geographic Profile of Employment and Unemployment, 1992*.

Department of Social Security (DSS) (1993*a*), *The Growth of Social Security* (London: HMSO).

Department of Social Security (1993*b*), Research Report No. 17 *Employer Choice of Pension Schemes* (London: HMSO).

Deregulierungskommission (1991), *Marktoffnung und Wettewerb* Bonn, March 1991.

Despax, Michael and Robot, Jacques (1987), *Labour Law and Industrial Relations in France* (Deventer: Klewer Publishers).

Dezalay, Y. (1992), *Marchands de droit: L'expansion du 'modèle américain' et al construction d'un ordre juridique transnational* (Paris: Fayard).

Dezalay, Y. (1993*a*) *Batailles territoriales ou rivalités de cousinage: Juristes et comptables sur le marché européen du conseil aux entreprises*, (sous la direction de) (Paris: Librairie Générale de Droit et de Jurisprudence).

Dezalay, Y. (1993*b*), 'Professional competition and the social construction of transnational regulatory expertise', in *Corporate Control and Accountability* (J. Mc Cahery, S. Picciotto, C. Scott, (eds.)) (Oxford: Clarendon Press).

Dezalay, Y. (1993*c*), 'Des notables aux conglomérats d'expertise: Esquisse d'une sociologie du "big bang" juridico-financier', *Revue d'Economie Financière*, No. 25.

Dezalay, Y. (1993*d*), 'Multinationales de l'expertise et "dépérissement de l'Etat" ', *Actes de la recherche en sciences sociales*, No. 96–97.

Dezalay, Y. (1994), 'The forum should fit the fuss: the Economics and the Politics of Negotiated Justice', in M. Cain et C. Harrington (eds.) *Lawyers in a Postmodern World* (Buckingham, Open University Press).

Dezalay, Y. (1995*a*) ' "Turf battles" or "class struggles": the internationalisation of the market for expertise in the "professional society" ' *Accounting, Organizations and Society*, 1995.

Dezalay, Y. (1995*b*), 'Technological Warfare: The Battle to Control the Mergers and Acquisitions Market in Europe', in Y. Dezalay, D. Sugarman (eds.), *Professional Competition and Professional Power* (London: Routledge).

Dezalay, Y. and Sugarman, D. (1995) (eds.), *Professional Competition and the Social Construction of Markets* (London: Routledge).

Dezalay, Y., Garth, B., (1995), 'Merchants of Law as Moral Entrepreneurs: Constructing International Justice out of the Competition for Transnational Business Disputes', 29(1) *Law & Society Rev.* 27–64.

Dezalay, Y., Garth, B. (forthcoming) *Dealing in Virtue: International Commercial Arbitration and the Emergence of a New International Legal Order* (Chicago: University of Chicago Press).

Diamond, W. H., and Diamond, D. B. (1991), *Capital Formation and Investment Incentives around the World* (New York: Matthew Bender).

Dick, Rebecca P. (1994), 'Antitrust Enforcement and Vertical Restraints.' Paper presented at ABA Section on Antitrust Law and the Corporate Bar Association of Westchester and Fairfield, November 1994, the Plaza Hotel, New York, New York.

Dietrich, B. (1993), 'Honest Answers? Study's Estimate on Gays Probably Right, Say Experts', *The Seattle Times*, 23 April 1993, p. A1.

Dill, J. B. (1899), *The Statutory and Case Law Applicable to Private Corporations under the General Corporation Act of New Jersey and Corporation Precedents*.

Dilnot, A. W., *et al.* (1994), *Pensions Policy in the UK* (London: Institute for Fiscal Studies).

Dixit, A. (1979), 'A Model of Duopoly Suggesting a Theory of Entry Barriers' 10 *Bell Journal of Economics* 20–32.

Dixit, A. (1980), 'The Role of Investment in Entry Deterrence', 90 *Economic Journal* 95–106.

Docksey, Chris and Karen Williams (1994), 'The Commission and the Execution of Community Policy.' In Geoffrey Edwards and David Spence (eds.), *The European Commission* 117–144 (London: Longman).

Dodd, P., and Leftwich, R. (1990), 'The Market for Corporate Charters: "Unhealthy Competition" versus Federal Regulation', 53 *Journal of Business* 259.

Domhoff, G. (1967), *Who Rules America?* (Englewood Cliffs: Prentice Hall).

Donohue III, J. J. (1991), 'Opting for the British Rule, Or If Posner and Shavell Can't Remember the Coase Theorem, Who Will?', 104 *Harvard Law Review* 1093.

Doogan, K. (1992), 'The Social Charter and the Europeanisation of Employment and Social Policy', 20(3) *Policy and Politics*, 167–176.

Dornbusch (1993), 'The Case for Bilateralism', in Salvatore, D. (ed.), *Protectionism and World Trade* (Cambridge: Cambridge University Press, 1993) 180–199.

Dr Seuss (Geisel, T., and Geisel, A.) (1961), *The Sneetches and Other Stories* (New York).

Drache, Daniel (1994*a*), 'Triple "A" Trade: asymmetry, access, and adjustment, the inflexible limits of trade blocs', in Paraskevopoulous, C. *et al.* (eds.) (1994), *Economic Integration between Unequal Partners* (London: Edward Elgar).

Drache, Daniel (1994*b*), 'The post-national state' in Gagnon, Alain and Bickerton, James (eds.), *Canadian Politics* (Peterborough: Broadview Press, 2nd edn.).

Drache, Daniel, and Gertler, M. (1991) (eds.), *The New Era of Global Competition* (Montreal: McGill-Queens University Press).

Drache, Daniel and Glasbeek, H. J. (1993), *The Changing Workplace Reshaping Canada's Industrial Relations System* (Toronto: Lorimer).

Drache, Daniel and Ranachan, A. (1995) (eds.), *Warm Heart, Cold Country: Social and Fiscal Policy Reform in Canada* (Ottawa: Caledon Institute of Social Policy).

Drury, R., and Xuereb, P. (1991) (eds.), *European Company Laws* (Aldershot, Eng.: Dartmouth Publishing Company).

Duskin, E. (1992), 'Changing the Mix of Public and Private Pensions: the Issues' in OECD (1992), 7–20.

Dyson, Kenneth and Peter Humphreys (1990) (eds.), *The Political Economy of Communications.*

Conclusion. Bradford Studies in European Politics (London: Routledge).

Easterbrook, F. H. (1983), 'Antitrust and the Economics of Federalism', 26 *Journal of Law and Economics* 23–50.

Easterbrook, F. H. (1994), 'Federalism and European Business Law', 14 *International Review of Law and Economics* 125–132.

Easterbrook, F., and Fischel, D. (1983), 'Voting in Corporate Law', 26 *Journal of Law and Economics* 395.

Easterbrook, F. H., and Fischel, D. R. (1991), *The Economic Structure of Corporate Law* (Cambridge, Mass.: Harvard University Press).

Edgell, E. (1993), *Urban Power and Social Welfare.*

Effros, R. C. (1992), *Current Legal Issues Affecting Central Banks* (Washington DC: IMF).

Ehlermann (1995), 'Reflections on a European Cartel Office', 32 *Common Market Law Review,* 471–86.

Einaudi, Luigi (1928), 'La Co-opération Internationale en Matière Fiscale', Académie de Droit International, La Haye, 25 *Receuil des Cours,* 1–123.

Eisenberg, M. (1989), 'The Structure of Corporate Law', 89 *Columbia Law Review* 1461–1525.

Eisner, M. (1991) *Antitrust and the Triumph of Economics. Institutions, Expertise and Policy Change* (Chapel Hill: Univ. of N.C. Press).

Eisner, M. A. (1993), *Regulatory Politics in Transition* (Baltimore: The John Hopkins University Press).

Elazar, Daniel J., and Ilan Greilsammer (1986), 'Federal Democracy: The U.S.A. and Europe Compared: A Political Science Perspective.' In Mauro Cappelletti, Monica Seccombe, and Joseph Weiler (eds.), *Integration Through Law—Volume One—Methods, Tools and Institutions* 71–168. 1. (Berlin: de Gruyter).

Elfring, T. (1993), 'Structure and growth of business services in Europe' in de Jong,

Bibliography

H. W. (ed.), *The Structure of European Industry* (Dordrecht: Kluwer Academic Publishers).

Elliott, S. (1994), 'A Sharper View of Gay Consumers', *The New York Times*, 9 June 1994, p. C1.

Ellis, C. (1989), 'Spanish Pensions—Stalled at the Starting Line', *Pensions Management Journal*, November, 19–24.

Ellison, R. (1994), *Pensions: Europe and Equality* (London: Longman Law, Tax and Finance).

Elster, J. (1986), *Rational Choice* (New York: NYU Press).

Emerson, Michael (1988), *What Model for Europe* (Cambridge, Mass.: The MIT Press).

Emerson, M. (1991), 'Europe after 1992: Aspects of Monetary and Economic Integration' in Padoa-Schioppa (ed.), *Europe After 1992; Three Essays* (Princeton, NJ: International Finance Section, Dept. of Economics, Princeton University).

Emerson, M. *et al.* (1988), *The Economics of 1992* (Oxford: Oxford University Press).

Emerson, Michael and Huhne, Chris (1991), *The ECU Report* (London: Pan Books).

Epstein, R. A. (1992), *Forbidden Grounds: The Case Against Employment Discrimination Laws* (Cambridge, Mass.: Harvard University Press).

Ermisch, J. (1991), 'European Integration and External Constraints on Social Policy: Is A Social Charter Necessary?', May *National Institute Economic Review*, 93–107.

Esping-Andersen, G. (1990), *Th Three Worlds of Welfare Capitalism* (Cambridge: Polity Press).

Esping-Anderson, Gosta (1992), *The Three Worlds of Welfare Capitalism* (Princeton: Princeton University Press).

European Communities, Commission of (1992), *Completing the Internal Market: Current Status January 1, 1992, Volume 1, A Common Market for Services* (Luxembourg: Office of Official Publications of the European Communities).

Falcao, J. (1979), 'Lawyers in Brazil: Ideals and Praxis', 7 *International Journal of the Sociology of Law* 355–375.

Falcao, J. (1988), 'Lawyers in Brazil', in R. Abel, P. Lewis (eds.), *Lawyers in Society, t. II The Civil World* (Berkley London: University of California Press).

Falkingham, J., and Johnson, P. (1992), *Ageing and Economic Welfare*, (London: Sage).

Farrell, Joseph and Saloner, Garth (1985), 'Standardization, Compatibility and Innovation', 16 *Rand Journal of Economics* 70–83.

Farrell, J. & Shapiro, C. (1988), 'Dynamic Competition and Switching Costs' 19 *Rand Journal of Economics* 123–37.

Feldstein, M. S. (1974), 'Social Security, Induced Retirement and Aggregate Capital Accumulation', 82 *Journal of Political Economy*, 905–926.

Financieel Economisch Magazine, Amsterdam, November 1992 and 1993.

Fingleton, J., and D. Schoenmaker (1992) (ed.), *The Internationalisation of Capital Markets and the Regulatory Response* (London: Graham & Trotman).

Fische, J. E. (1993), 'From Legitimacy to Logic: Reconstructing Proxy Regulation', 46 *Vanderbilt Law Review* 1129.

Fischel, D. R. (1982), 'The "Race to the Bottom" Revisited: Reflections on Recent Developments in Delaware Corporation law', 76 *Northwestern University Law Review* 913.

Fischel, W. A. (1975), 'Fiscal and Environmental Considerations in the Location of Firms in Suburban Communities', in Mills, E. S., and Oates, W. (eds.), *Fiscal Zoning and Land Use Controls* 119 (Lexington, Mass.: Lexington Books).

Fisher, B. (1995), 'Sailing: All-Woman Crew Routs Connor', *The Guardian*, 14 January.

Fitchewm, G. (1991), 'Comment', in Buxbaum *et al.* (1991), *European Business Law: Legal and Economic Analysis on Integration and Harmonization* (Berlin: de Gruyter), 375–8.

Fitzpatrick, P. (1984), 'Law and Societies', 22 *Osgoode Hall Law Journal*, 115.

Flinn, J. (1993*a*), 'S.F.: Shangri-La for Gay Tourists', *San Francisco Sunday Examiner and Chronicle*, 29 August 1993, p. A1.

Flinn, J. (1993*b*), 'Castro District's Cachet', *Newsday*, 7 November 1993, p. 10.

Florence, P. Sargant (1964), *The Economics and Sociology of Industry: A Realistic Analysis of Development* (London: C. A. Watts).

Foreman-Peck, James, and Robert Millward (1994), *Public and Private Ownership of British Industry 1820–1990* (Oxford: Clarendon Press).

Franco, D., and Frasca, F. (1992), 'Public Pensions in an Ageing Society: the Case of Italy' in Mortensen, J. (ed.) (1992).

Franko, L., 'Global Corporate Competition: Is the large American Firm an endangered species?', in *Business Horizons*, November–December 1991.

Frazer, Tim (1992), *Monopoly, Competition and the Law.* (2nd edn.) (London: Harvester Wheatsheaf).

Frey, W. H. (1979), 'Central City White Flight: Racial and Nonracial Causes', 44 *American Sociology Review* 425.

Friedman, George and Lebard, Meredith (1991), *The Coming War with Japan* (New York: St Martin's Press).

Friedman, Sheldon (1993), 'The EC vs. NAFTA: Levelling Up vs. Social Dumping', 68 *Chicago-Kent University Law Review* 1421.

Fuchs, Gerhard, (1994), 'Policy-Making in a System of Multi-Level Governance—the Commission of the European Community and the Restructuring of the Telecommunications Sector' 1 *Journal of European Public Policy* 27–44.

Fudenberg, D., and Tirole, J. (1986), 'Preemption and Rent Equalization in the Adoption of Technology', 52 *Review of Economic Studies* 383–402.

Galanter, M. (1981), 'Justice in Many Rooms: Private Ordering and Indigenous Law, 19 *Journal of Legal Pluralism*.

Galst, Jonathan, (1992), ' "Phony Intent?": An Examination of Regulatory-Preemption Jurisprudence' 67 *New York University Law Review* 108–153.

Garrett, G., and Weingast, B. (1993), 'Ideas, Interests, and Institutions: Constructing the European Community's Internal market'in J. Goldstein, and R. Keohane (eds.) (1993), *Ideas & Foreign Policy: Beliefs, Institutions & Political Change* (London: Cornell University Press) 173–206.

Garrett, G. (1992), 'International Cooperation and Institutional Choice: The European Community's Internal Market', 46 *International Organization* 533–560.

Garten, H. (1992), 'Institutional Investors and the New Financial Order', 44 *Rutgers Law Review* 585.

Garvey, Jack I. (1995), 'Trade Law and the Quality of Life—Dispute Resolution

Under the NAFTA Side Accords on Labor and the Environment', 89 *American Journal of International Law* 439–453.

Gatsios, Konstantine, and Seabright, Paul (1989), 'Regulation in the European Community', 5 *Oxford Review of Economic Policy* 37–60.

Georges, S., Sabelli, F. (1994) *Faith and Credit, the World Bank Secular Empire* (London: Penguin).

Gephard, P. H. (1976), 'Incidence of Overt Homosexuality in the United States and Western Europe', in National Institute of Mental Health Task Force on Homosexuality, *Final Report and Background Papers*, p. 22 (DHEW Publication No. [ADM] 76–357) (originally published 1972).

Gerber, David J. (1994), 'The Transformation of European Community Competition Law' 35 *Harvard International Law Journal* 97–147.

Gerschenkron, A. (1962), *Economic Backwardness in Historical Perspective: A Book of Essays* (Cambridge: Belknap Press, 1962).

Gewirtz, P. (1983), 'Remedies and Resistance', 92 *Yale Law Journal* 585.

Ghosh, Sutapa, 'The Future of FCC Dominant Carrier Rate Regulation: The Price Caps Scheme' (1988) 41 *Federal Communications Law Journal* 401–431.

Gilbert, R., and Newberyy, D. (1982), 'Preemptive Patenting and the Persistence of Monopoly', 74 *American Economic Review* 238–42.

Gilmore, W. C. (1992), *International Efforts to Combat Money-Laundering* (Cambridge: Grotius).

Gilson, R., and Kraakman, R. (1989), 'Delaware's Intermediate Standard for Defensive Tactics: Is there Substance to Proportionality Review', 44 *Business Lawyer* 247.

Gilson, R. J., and Kraakman, R. (1991), 'Reinventing the Outside Director: An Agenda for Institutional Investors', 43 *Stanford Law Review* 863.

Gilson, R. J., and Kraakman, R. (1993), 'Investment Companies as Guardian Shareholders: The Place of the MSIC in the Corporate Governance Debate', 45 *Standford Law Review* 985.

Gilson, R. J., *et al.* (1991), 'How the Proxy Rules Discourage Constructive Engagement: Regulatory Barriers to Electing a Minority of Directors', 17 *Journal of Corporate Law* 29.

Giordano, R. (1993), 'Getting Married: Cult of the Bride', *Newsday*, 27 April 1993, p. 15.

Gist, Peter 'Control of Entry in the Regulation of Markets: An Analysis of Telecommunications in the USA and UK.' (PhD., London, 1988).

Glasl, Daniel, (1994), 'Essential Facilities in EC Antitrust Law: A Contribution to the Debate' 15 *European Competition Law Review* 306–314.

Glauberman, S. (1994*a*), 'Island Companies Tap a Growing Market', *Honolulu Advertiser*, 14 February 1994, p. C1.

Glauberman, S. (1994*b*), 'Same-sex Marriages, Tourism a Troubling Mix', *Honolulu Advertiser*, 17 February 1994, p. C1.

Global Governance, Commission on (1995), *Our Global Neighbourhood* (Oxford: Oxford University Press).

Goering, J. M. (1978), 'Neighborhood Tipping and Racial Transition: A Review of the Social Science Evidence', 44 *Journal of the American Institute of Planners* 68.

Gold, Michael (1993), *Social rights: continuity or convergence?* unpublished paper for the Royal Institute for International Affairs study group on competition among rules (London).

Gordon, J. N. (1991), 'Shareholder Initiative: A Social Choice and Game Theoretic Approach to Corporate Law', 60 *University of Cincinnati Law Review* 347.

Gordon, J. N. (1994), 'Institutions as Relational Investors: A New Look at Cumulative Voting', 94 *Columbia Law Review* 124.

Gordon, R. (1984), The ideal and the actual in the law: fantasies and practices of New York City lawyers, 1870–1910, in G. Gawalt (ed.), *The New High Priests: Lawyers in Post-civil War America* (Westport: Greenwood Press).

Gormley, L. (1985), *Prohibiting Restrictions on Trade within the EEC* (Amsterdam: Elsevier).

Gormley, L. (1994), 'Reasoning Renounced: The remarkable judgment in *Keck* and *Mithouard*', March *European Business Law Review* 63–67.

Gottschalk, M. (1993), 'Gay Cachet', *San Jose Mercury News,* 19 September 1993, p. 7-H.

Goyder, D. G. (1992), *EC Competition Law* (Oxford: Oxford University Press).

Graham, Cosmo, and Tony Prosser (1991), *Privatising Public Enterprises* (Oxford: Oxford University Press).

Grandy, C. (1993), *New Jersey and the Fiscal Origins of Modern American Corporation Law* (New York: Garland Publishers).

Granovetter, M. (1985), 'Economic Action and Social Structure: The Problem of Embeddedness', *American Journal of Sociology* 91.

Gray, M. (1994), 'Hawaii Could Be First State to OK Same-Sex Marriage', *San Francisco Examiner,* 20 February 1994, p. A22.

Green, D. P., and Shapiro, I. (1994), *Pathologies of Rational Choice Theory, A Critique of Applications in Political Science* (New Haven: Yale University Press).

Greenberg, P. S. (1993), 'Travel Industry Opening Doors to Gays, Lesbians', *The Plain Dealer,* 9 May 1993, p. 91.

Greenwood, J., Grote, J. R., *et al.* (1992) (eds.), *Organized Interests and the European Community* (London: Sage).

Grémion, P. (1974), 'La concertation', in M. Crozier (ed.), *Ou va l'administration français?* (Paris: SEDEIS).

Gröner, H. (1992) (ed.), *Der Markt für Unternehmenskontrollen. Schriften des Vereins für Sozialpolitik, Gesellschaft für Wirtschafts- und Sozialwissenschaften* (Berlin: Neue Folge Band 214).

Group of Thirty (1993), *Derivatives: Practices and Principles* (Washington DC: Group of Thirty).

Grudus, James Walter (1993), 'Local Broadband Networks: A New Regulatory Philosophy' 10 *Yale Journal of Regulation* 89–145.

Grundfest, J. A. (1993), 'Just Vote No: A Minimalist Strategy for Dealing with Barabrians Inside the Gates', 45 *Stanford Law Review* 857.

Grundman (1980), 'The New Imperialism: The Extraterritorial Application of United States Law', 14 *International Lawyer* 257.

Gunderson, Morley (1994), 'Labor Adjustment Under NAFTA: Canadian Issues', 4 *North American Outlook* 3.

Haas, E. B. (1958), *The Uniting of Europe. Political, Social, and Economic Forces 1950–1957* (Stanford: Stanford University Press).

Haas, E. B. (1964), *Beyond the Nation-State: Functionalism and International Organization* (Stanford: Stanford University Press).

Haas, Peter M., *et al* (1992), Knowledge, Power and International Policy Coordination, 46 *Special Issue, International Organization*, 1.

Hackney, J. V., and Shafer, K. L. (1986), 'The Regulation of International Banking: An Assessment of International Institutions', 11 *North Carolina Journal of International Law and Commercial Regulation* 475.

Hall, P. (1986), *Governing the Economy, The Politics of State Intervention in Britain and France* (Cambridge: Polity Press).

Hancher, L., and Sevenster, H. (1993), 'Case C-2/90, Commission v. Belgium', 30 *Common Market Law Review* 351.

Hansen, C. (1991), 'Other Constituency Statutes: A Search for Perspective, 46 *Business Lawyer* 1355–76.

Harden, Ian (1994), 'The Constitution of the European Union' [1994] *Public Law* 609–624.

Hardin, R. (1982), *Collective Action* (Baltimore: Johns Hopkins University Press).

Haring, John R., and Kathleen, B. Levitz, 'The Law and Economics of Federalism in Telecommunications' (1988) 41 *Federal Communications Law Journal* 261–330.

Harrison, D. (1991), *Financial Times* 24 August.

Harvard Law Review (1991), *The Blue Book: A Uniform System of Citation* (Cambridge, MA).

Harvey, D. (1984), *The Conditions of Postmodernity. An Inquiry into the Origins of Cultural Change* (Oxford: Basil Blackwell).

Hauck, M. (1994), 'The Equity Market in Germany and its Dependency on the System of Old Age Provisions', in Baums *et al.* (1994), *Institutional Investors and Corporate Governance* (Berlin: de Gruyter), 555–64.

Hawaii Dept. of Business, Economic Development and Tourism, *1992 State of Hawaii Data Book* (Honolulu, Haw.: State of Hawaii).

Hawawini, G. (1984), *European Equity Markets: Price Behavior and Efficiency, Monograph 1983–4* (New York: Solomon Brothers Center, New York University).

Heclo, H. (1978), Issue Networks and the Executive Establishment. In A. King (ed.), *The New American Political System* (Washington DC: American Enterprise Institute for Public Policy Research).

Heller, P. S. (1989), 'Aging, Savings, and Pensions in the Group of Seven Countries: 1980–2025', 9(2) *Journal of Public Policy* 127–153.

Helm, Dieter (1993), 'The Assessment: The European Internal Market: The Next Steps' 9 *Oxford Review of Economic Policy* 1–14.

Higgins, R. S., Shugart, W. S., and Tollison, R. (1988), 'Free Entry and Efficient Rent-Seeking', in Rowley, C. K., Tollison, R. D., and Tullock, G. (1988), *The Political Economy of Rent-Seeking* (Dordrecht: Kluwer Academic Press).

Hilliard, Robert L. (1991), *The Federal Communications Commission: A Primer*, Electronic Media Guides (Boston: Focal Press).

Hills, Jill (1986), *Deregulating Telecoms* (London: Pinter).

Hills, J. (1993), *The Future of Welfare* (York: Joseph Rowntree Foundation).

Hirschman, A. O. (1970), *Exit, Voice and Loyalty* (Cambridge, Mass.: Harvard University Press).

Hirst, P., and Thompson, G. (1992), 'The Problem of "Globalization": international economic relations, national economic management and the formation of trading blocs', 21(4) *Economy and Society* 357.

Hoffmann, S. (1966), 'Obstinate or Obsolete? The Fate of the Nation-State and the Case of Western Eruope', (Summer) *Daedalus 95*: 862.

Hollingsworth, J., Schmitter, P., Steeck, W. (1994), *Governing Capitalist Economies* (New York: Oxford University Press).

Hopt, K. J. (1992), 'Directors' Duties to Shareholders, Employees and Other Creditors: A View from the Continent', in McKendrick (1992), *Commercial Aspects of Trusts and Fiduciary Obligations* (Oxford: Clarendon Press), 115–32.

Horn, N., and Kocka, J. (1979) (ed.), *Law and the Formation of the Big Enterprises in the 19th Century* (Göttingen: Vandenhoeck & Ruprecht).

Hoshi, T., Koshyap, A., and Scharfstein, D. (1993), *The Choice between Public and Private Debt: An Analysis of Post Deregulation Corporate Financing in Japan*, unpublished manuscript, University of Chicago and MIT.

Hoskyns, C. (1996), *Integrating Gender: Women, Law and Politics in the EU* (London: Verso).

Hosli, Madeleine (1992), 'Harmonization versus regulatory competition in the European Community' mimeo, Centre for Policy Studies (Ann Arbor).

House of Lords (1992–93), *Select Committee on the European Communities 4th Report* (HL Paper (1992–93) No. 15) Pension Funds.

Hovenkamp, H. (1991), *Enterprise and American Law, 1836–1937* (Cambridge, Mass.: Harvard University Press).

Howard, Thomas (1992), 'Free Trade Between the United States and Mexico: Minimizing the Adverse Effects on American Workers', 18 *William Mitchell Law Review* 507.

Howse, Robert and Trebilcock, Michael J. (1991), *The Fair Trade-Free Trade Debate, Trade, Labour and the Environment*, (unpublished manuscript).

Hu, Y.-S. (1992), 'Global or Stateless Corporations are National Firms with International Operations', 34(2) *California Management Review* 107.

Hufbauer, Gary (1990) (ed.), *Europe 1992 An American Perspective* (Washington: The Brookings Institute).

Hufbauer, Gary and Schott, Jeffrey (1992), *North American Free Trade Issues and Recommendations* (Washington: Institute for International Economics).

Hunter, D., Summer, J., and Vaughn, S. (1994), *Concepts and Principles of International Environmental Law: An Introduction*.

Huntington, David S. (1993), 'Settling Disputes under the North American Free Trade Agreement', 34 *Harvard International Law Journal* 407–443.

Huntley, John A. K. (1993), *Competition and the Provision of a Universal Telecommunications Service: The Deregulatory Paradox* (University of Strathcylde), unpublished paper.

Huntley, John A. K., and Douglas, C. Pitt, (1990), 'Judicial Policymaking: The Greeneing of US Telecommunications' 10 *International Review of Law and Economics* 77–100.

Hyman, A. (1979), 'The Delaware Controversy-The Legal Debate', 4 *Delaware Journal of Corporate Law* 368.

International Monetary Fund (1991), *International Financial Statistics* (Yearbook) (Washington, DC: IMF).

Irons, P. (1982), *The New Deal Lawyers* (Princeton: Princeton University Press).

Irons, P. (1993), 'Cadres et classes dirigeantes en Hongrie entre les deux guerres: La "double structure" et ses conséquences scolaires', in M. de Saint Martin, M. Gheorghiu (eds.), *Les institutions de formation des cadres dirigeants: Etude comparée*. Ronéo, Centre de Sociologie de l'Education et de la Culture (Paris: Maison des Sciences de l'Homme).

Irwin, Manley R. (1988), 'US Telecommunications—Searching for the Optimum Policy' 12 *Telecommunications Policy* 23–15.

Isaac, John (1989), 'Corporate Tax Harmonisation', in Malcolm Gammie and Bill Robinson (eds.), *Beyond 1992: A European Tax System, IFS Commentary No. 13* (London: Institute for Fiscal Studies).

Jacobs, Francis G., and Kenneth L. Karst. (1986), 'The "Federal" Legal Order: The U.S.A. and Europe Compared: A Juridical Perspective.' In Mauro Cappelletti, Monica Seccombe, and Joseph Weiler (eds.), *Integration Through Law—Volume One—Methods, Tools and Institutions* 169–243. 1. (Berlin: de Gruyter).

Jacobs, S. (1993), 'Dispute Over Numbers Puts No Damper on Gay Activism', *The Boston Globe*, 21 May 1993, National/Foreign p. 1.

Jamieson, C. (1991), 'Stamp Duties in the European Community: Harmonization by Abolition?', 9 *British Tax Review* 318–23.

Jensen, R. (1983), 'Innovation Adoption and Diffusion When There Are Competing Innovations', 29 *Journal of Economic Theory* 161.

Joerges, C. (1990), Paradoxes of Deregulatory Strategies at Community Level: the Example of Product Safety Policy, in Majone (ed.), *Deregulation or Re-regulation? Regulatory Reform in Europe and the United States* (London: Pinter), 176–197.

Joerges, C. (1994), 'European Economic Law, the Nation-State and the Maastricht Treaty', in Dehousee R. (1994), *Europe After Maastricht, An Ever Closer Union?* (Munich: Law Books in Europe) 29–62.

Johnson, Andrea L. (1992), 'Redefining Diversity in Telecommunications: Uniform Regulatory Framework for mass Communications' 26 *University of California Davis Law Review* 87.

Jolliffe, J. (1991), 'The Portability of Occupational Pensions within Europe' in Schmahl, W. (ed.), *The Future of Basic and Supplementary Pension Schemes in the EEC: 1992 and Beyond* (Baden Baden: Nomos Verlagsgesellschaft).

Kapstein, E. B. (1991), *Supervising International Banks: Origins and Implications of the Basle Accord* (International Finance Section, Dept. of Economics, Princeton University, Princeton, NJ).

Kapstein, E. B. (1994), *Governing the Global Economy. International Finance and the State* (Cambridge, Mass.: Harvard University Press).

Karady, V. (1991), 'Une "nation de juristes": Des usages sociaux de la formation juridique dans la Hongrie d'ancien régime', *Actes de la recherche en sciences sociales*, No. 86–87.

Karmel, R. S. (1991), 'Is it time for a Federal Corporation Law?', 57 *Brooklyn Law Review* 55.

Karpik, L. (1992), 'La profession libérale: Un cas, Le Barreau', in P. Nora (ed.) *Les lieux de mémoire, III, Les France*—Tome 2, (Paris, NRF).

Kaser, T. (1989), 'What's Doing in Honolulu', *New York Times*, 10 December 1989, sec. 5, p. 10.

Katz, M., and Shapiro, C. (1986), 'Technology Adoption in the Presence of Network Externalities', 94 *Journal of Political Economy* 822–841.

Kaufmann, R., Pauly, P., and Sweitzer, J. (1993), 'The Effects of NAFTA on the Environment', *Energy Journal* 124.

Kay, John (1993), *Foundations of Corporate Success, How Business Strategies Add Value* (Oxford: Oxford University Press).

Keck, M., and Sikkink, K. (1994), *Transnational Issue Networks in International Politics*, Unpublished conference paper.

Kellogg, Michael, Thorne, John, and Huber, Peter W. (1992), *Federal Telecommunications Law* (Boston: Little Brown).

Kennedy, D. (1981), 'Cost Benefit Analysis of Entitlement Problems: A Critique', 33 *Stanford Law Review* 387.

Kindleberger, C. (1969), *American Business Abroad. Six Lectures on Direct Investment* (New Haven: Yale University Press).

Kingson, Charles I. (1981), 'The Coherence of International Taxation', 81 *Columbia Law Review*, 1151–1288.

Kinsey, A., Pomeroy, W., and Martin, C. (1948), *Sexual Behavior in the Human Male* (Philadelphia London: Saunders).

Kitch, E. (1981), 'Regulation and the American Common Market', in Tarlock (1981) (ed.), *Regulation, Federalism, and Interstate Commerce* (Cambridge, Mass: Oelgeschlager, Gunn and Hain).

Kitch, Edmund (1991), 'Business Organization Law: State or federal?' in Buxbaum, R., Hertig, G., Hirsch, A., and Hopt, K. (eds.), *European Business Law–Legal and Economic Analyses on Integration and Harmonization* (Berlin: de Gruyter).

Klausner, M. (1995), 'Corporations, Corporate Law, and Networks of Contracts', 81 *Virginia Law Review* 757–852.

Kleinman, M., and Piachaud, D. (1993), 'European Social Policy: Conceptions and Choices', 3(1) *Journal of European Social Policy* 1–19.

Klemperer, P. (1987), 'Markets with Consumer Switching Costs', 102 *Quarterly Journal of Economics* 375–94.

Knieps, Gunter (1990), 'Deregulation in Europe: Telecommunications and Transportation'. In G. Majone (eds.) *Deregulation or Reregulation—Regulatory Reform in Europe and the United States* (London: Pinter).

Knightley, P. (1993), *The Rise and Fall of the House of Vestey* (London: Warner).

Knoke, David (1993), 'Networks of Elite Structure and Decision-Making', 22 *Sociological Methods and Research*, 23–45.

Kohnstamm, Manuel, (1990), 'Conflicts Between International and European Network Regulation: An Analysis of Third Parties' Rights in European Community Law' 1990 *Legal Issues of European Integration* 49–100.

Kollias, S. (1992), 'The liberalisation of capital movements and financial services: implications for pension funds' in Mortensen, J. (ed.) (1992), 171–179.

Korah, Valentine (1994), *EC Competition Law and Practice* (London: Sweet and Maxwell).

Krugman, P. (1994), 'Competitiveness: A Dangerous Obsession', 73 (March/April) *Foreign Affairs* 28–44.

Krugman, P. (1991), 'Is Bilateralism Bad?' in Helpman E., and Razin A. (eds.), *International Trade and Trade Policy* (Cambridge, Mass: MIT Press).

Kübler, F. (1994), 'Institutional Investors and Corporate Governance: A German Perspective', in Baums, *et al.* (1994), *Institutional Investors and Corporate Governance* (Berlin: de Gruyter) 565–79.

Laffont, J., and Tirole, J. (1993), *A Theory of Incentives in Procurement and Regulation* (Cambridge Mass: MIT Press).

Lambda (1994), Lambda Legal Defense and Education Fund, *Negotiating for Equal Employment Benefits: A Resource Packet.*

Lamoreaux, N. (1991), 'Information Problems and Banks' Specialization in Short-Term Commercial Lending: New England in the Nineteenth Century', in Temin (1991) (ed.), *Inside the Business Enterprise* (Chicago: University of Chicago Press) 161–95.

Langan, M., and Ostner, I. (1991), 'Gender and Welfare' in Room, G. (ed.), *Towards a European Welfare State* (Bristol: School of Advanced Urban Studies).

Lange, D. and G. Born, Ed. (1987), *The Extraterritorial Application of National Laws*, (Paris, International Chamber of Commerce).

Lange, Peter (1992), The Politics of the Social Dimension', in Sbragia, Alberta M. (ed.), *Euro-politics: Institutes and Policymaking in the 'New' European Community* (Washington DC: The Brookings Institution).

Lange, P. (1993), 'Maastricht and the Social Protocol: Why did they di it?', 21(1) *Politics and Society*, 5–36.

Langille, Brian (1991), 'Canadian Labor Law Reform and Free Trade', 23 *Ottawa Law Review* 581.

Langille, Brian (1995), *General Reflections on the Relationship of Trade and Labour (Or: Fair Trade is Free Trade's Destiny)*, (unpublished paper).

Laske, C. (1993), 'The Impact of The Single European Market on Social Protection for Migrant Workers', 30 *Common Market Law Review*, 515.

Laycock, D. (1992), 'Equal Citizens of Equal and Territorial States: The Constitutional Foundations of Choice of Law', 92 *Columbia Law Review* 249.

Le Van Lemesle L. (1983), 'L'économie politique à la conquête d'une légitimité, (1896/1937), *Actes de la Recherche en Sciences Sociales* No. 47–48.

Leckey, A. (1993), 'Even Today's "Downsized" Wedding Still Costs a Bundle', *The Phoenix Gazette*, 21 May 1993, p. D5.

Lee, T. (1994) *The Internationalization of Chinese lawyers: Fact or Fiction?*, Paper presented to the Annual Law & Society Meeting, Phoenix.

Leonard, R. (1993), 'Checks and Balances', *10 Percent* Sept/Oct.

Letwin, William (1965), *Law and Economic Policy in America* (New York: Random House).

Levine, M. E., & Forrence, J. L. (1990), 'Regulatory Capture, Public Interest, and the Public Agenda: Toward a Synthesis', 6 *Journal of Law, Economics, and Organizations* 167.

Levy, Brian and Pablo T, Spiller (1994), 'The Institutional Foundations of Regulatory Commitment: A Comparative Analysis of Telecommunications Regulation' 10 *Journal of Law, Economics and Organization* 201–246.

Levy, Frank and Murname, Richard (1992), 'US Earnings Levels and Earnings Inequality: A Review of Recent Trends and Proposed Explanations,' Vol. XXX (September) *Journal of Economic Literature*, 1333–1381.

Liebfried, S. (1992), 'Towards a European Welfare Sate?' in Ferge, Z., and Kolberg,

J. E. (eds.), *Social Policy in a Changing Europe*, 245–79 (Frankfurt am Main: Campus Verlag Boulder, Colo: Westview Press).

Liebfried, S., and Pierson, P. (1992), 'Prospects for Social Europe', 20(3) *Politics and Society*, 333–366.

Lindas, Christopher (1983), *Winding-Up of Insolvent Companies in England and France*, 281 (Deventer: Kluwer).

Lindberg, Leon N. (1963), *The Political Dynamics of European Economic Integration* (Stanford: Stanford University Press).

Lipschutz, R. D. (1992), 'Reconstructing World Politics: The Emergence of Global Civil Society', 21(3) *Millenium*, 389–420.

Litan, Robert E. (1994), 'Antitrust Enforcement and the Telecommunications Revolution: Friends, Not Enemies.' Paper presented at National Academy of Engineering, October 1994, Washington DC.

Lividas, C. (1983), *Winding-up of Insolvent Companies in England and France*, 281–2 (Deventer: Kluwer).

Long, Colin D. (1990), 'Competition in the Markets for Telecommunications Services: The European Commission's Services Directive and its Draft Competition Guidelines' *International Business Lawyer* 511.

Lopez, A. G. (1993), 'Homosexual Marriage, the Changing American Family, and the Heterosexual Right to Privacy', 24 *Seton Hall Law Review* 347.

Louis, Jean-Victor (1990), *The Community Legal Order* (Luxembourg: Office of Official Publications of the European Communities).

Loureiro, M. (1993), 'La Formation des cadres de gestion économique au Brésil', in M. de Saint Martin, M. Gheorghiu (eds.), *Les Institutions de formation des cadres dirigeants: Etude comparée*. Ronéo, Centre de Sociologie de l'Education et de la Culture (Paris: Maison des Sciences de l'Homme).

Luckhaus, L. (1995), 'European Social Security Law' in Ogus, A., Barendt, E., and Wikeley, N. (eds.), *Law of Social Security*, (4th edn.) (London: Butterworths).

Ludlow, Peter (1992), 'The Maastricht Treaty', 15 *Washington Law Quarterly* 119.

Lundberg, D. E. (1989), *The Tourist Business* (5th edn.) (New York: Van Nostrand Reinhold).

Lupia, A., and McCubbins, M. M. (1994), 'Learning from Oversight: Fire Alarms and Police Patrols Reconstructed', 10 *Journal of Law, Economics, and Organization* 96.

Macaulay, S. (1963), 'Non-Contractual Relations in Business', 28 *American Sociological Review* 1.

Macey, J. R. (1992), 'Organizational Design and the Political Control of Administrative Agencies', 8 *Journal of Law, Economics, and Organization* 93–110.

Macey, J. R. (1994), 'Administrative Agency Obsolescence and Interest Group Formation: A Case Study of the SEC at Sixty', 15 *Cardozo Law Review* 909.

Macey, J. R., and Miller, G. P. (1987), 'Toward an Interest-Group Theory of Delaware Corporate Law', 65 *Texas Law Review* 469.

MacIntosh, J. G. (1991), 'The Oppression Remedy: Personal or Derivative?', 70 *Canadian Bar Review* 29–70.

MacIntosh, J. (1993), *The Role of Interjurisdictional Competition in Shaping Canadian Corporate Law: A Second Look* (Toronto: University of Toronto Law and Economics Working Paper).

MacKerron, J. A. (1993), 'A Taxonomy of the Revised Model Business Corporation Act', 61 *University of Missouri, Kansas City Law Review* 663.

Macrae, Donald (1994), 'Institutional and Decision-Making Changes.' in David O'Keefe and Patrick M. Twomey (eds.), *Legal Issues of the Maastricht Treaty* (Chichester: Chancery) 171–178.

Maier, H. G. (1982), 'Extraterritorial Jurisdiction at a Crossroads: an intersection between public and private international law', 76 *American Journal of International Law*, 280–320.

Maier, H. (1991), 'A Comment on Portability from the Point of View of a Multinational Company', in Schmahl, W. (ed.) (1991), *The Future of Basic and Supplementary Schemes in the EC: 1992 and Beyond* (Baden Baden: Nomos Verlagsgesellschaft) 223–226.

Majone, G. (1990) (ed.), *Deregulation or Re-Regulation. Regulatory Reform in Europe and the United States* (London: Pinter).

Majone, G. (1991), 'Cross-National Sources of Regulatory Policymaking in Europe and the United States', 11(1) *Journal of Public Policy*, 79–106.

Majone, G. (1992), 'Regulatory Federalism in the European Community' 10 *Environment and Planning* 299–316.

Majone, G. (1993*a*), 'Mutual recognition in federal type systems' EUI Working Papers: in political and social sciences SPS No. 93/1 European University Institute Florence.

Majone, G. (1993*b*), The European Community: an 'Independent Forth Branch of Government Lecture on 23 April 1993 in Bremen.

Majone, (1993*c*), Comparing strategies for regulatory rapprochment paper for OECD Public Management Service symposium on managing regulatory regimes between different levels of government, October 1993.

Majone, G. (1993*d*), 'Controlling Regulatory Bureaucracies: Lessons from the American Experience' 93/3 *EUI Working Paper*, Florence: EUI.

Majone, G. (1993*e*), 'Controlling Regulatory Bureaucracies: Lessons from the American Experience' 93/3 *EUI Working Paper*, Florence: EUI.

Majone, G. (1993*f*), 'The European Community between Social Policy and Social Regulation', 31 *Journal of Common Market Studies* 153–170.

Majone, G. (1994), 'The Rise of the Regulatory State in Europe', 17:3 (July 1994) *West European Politics* 77–101.

Maltz, E. M. (1991), 'The State, the Family, and the Constitution: A Case Study in Flawed Bipolar Analysis', 1991 *Brigham Young University Law Review* 489.

Maltz, E. M. (1992), 'Constitutional Protection for the Right to Marry: A Dissenting View', 60 *George Washington Law Review* 949.

Mamou, Y. (1987), *Une machine de pouvoir: La Direction du Trésor* (Paris, La Découverte).

Mandel, Michael (1989), *The Charter of Rights and the Legalization of Politics in Canada* (Toronto: Well & Thompson).

Manne, H. G. (1964), 'Some Theoretical Aspects of Share Voting', 64 *Columbia Law Review* 1427.

Manne, H. G. (1967), 'Our Two Corporation Systems: Law and Economics', 53 *Virginia Law Review* 259.

Manning, B. (1987), 'State Competition: Panel Response', 8 *Cardozo Law Review* 779.

Manning, N. (1993), 'The Impact of the EC on Social Policy at the National Level', in Hantrais, L., and Mangen, S. (eds.), *The Policy Making Process and the Social Actors* (Loughborough: The Cross-National Research Group), 15–32.

Mansell, Robin (1993), *The New Telecommunications: A Political Economy of Network Evolution* (London: Sage).

March, J. G., and Shapira, Z. (1987), 'Managerial Perspectives on Risk and Risk Taking', 33 *Management Science* 1404.

Marin, B. and Mayntz, R. (1991) (eds.), *Policy Networks. Empirical Evidence and Theoretical Considerations* (Frankfurt: Campus Verlag).

Markoff, J., Montecinos, V. (1993) 'The Ubiquitous Rise of Economists', 13(1) *Journal of Public Policy*.

Marsden, D. (1992), 'European Integration and the Integration of European Labour Markets', 6(1) *LABOUR* 3–35.

Marsh, D., and Rhodes, R. A. W. (1992) (eds.), *Policy Networks in British Government* (Oxford: Clarendon Press).

Marx, K. (1890), *Das Kapital. Kritik der politischen Oekonomie* (Hamburg: Vierte Auflage).

Matheson, J. H., and Olson, B. A. (1991), 'Shareholder Rights and Legislative Wrongs: Toward Balanced Takeover Legislation', 59 *George Washington Law Review* 1425.

Maydell, Bernd Baron von (1993), 'The Impact of the EEC on Labor Law', 68 *Chicago-Kent Law Review* 1401.

Mayer, Colin (1989), 'Public Ownership: Concepts and Applications.' In Dieter Helm (eds.), *The Economic Borders of the State* 251–274 (Oxford: Oxford University Press).

Mazey, Sonia, and Jeremy Richardson (1994), 'The Commission and the Lobby.' In Geoffrey Edwards and David Spence (eds.), *The European Commission* 169–187 (London: Longman).

McCahery, J., Picciotto, S., and Scott, C. (1993) (eds.), *Corporate Control and Accountability: Changing Structures and the Dynamics of Regulation* (Oxford: Clarendon Press).

McCahery, J., and Picciotto, S. (1995), 'Creative Lawyering and the Dynamics of Business Regulation', in Dezalay, and Sugarman (1995) (eds.), *Professional Competition and the Social Construction of Markets* (London: Routledge) 238–274.

McCall, Christina, and Clarkson, Stephen (1994), *Trudeau and Our Times, Vol. II* (Toronto: McClelland and Stewart).

McConnell, M. W. (1988), 'A Choice-of-Law Approach to Products Liability Reform,' in W. Olson (ed.) *New Directions in Liability Law* (New York: Academy of Political Science).

McCraw, T. (1984), *Prophets of Regulation* (Cambridge Mass: Harvard University Press).

McCubbins, M. D., and Schwartz, T. (1984), 'Police Patrols v. Fire Alarms', 28 *American Journal of Political Science* 165.

McCubbins, M. D., *et al.* (1987), 'Administrative Procedures as Instruments of Political Control', 3 *Journal of Law, Economics, and Organization* 243.

McCubbins, M. D., *et al.* (1989), 'Structure and Process, Politics and Policy: Administrative Arrangements and the Political Control of Agencies', 75 *Virginia Law Review* 431.

McGee, A., and Weatherill, S. (1990), 'The Evolution of the Single Market—
Harmonisation or Liberalisation', 53(5) *Modern Law Review*, 578–596.

McGowan, Lee, and Stephen Wilks (1994), 'Competition Policy in the European
Union.' Paper presented at "The Evolution of Rules for a Single European
Market" Conference, September 1994, Exeter University.

McGowan, Francis and Paul Seabright (1995), 'Regulation in the European
Community and its Impact in the UK' in Matthew Bishop, John Kay and Colin
Mayer (eds.), *The Regulatory Challenge* (Oxford: Oxford University Press).

McGuiness, Michael (1994), 'The Protection of Labor Rights in North America', 30
Stanford Journal of International Law 579.

McIntosh, R. (1990), 6th edition, *Tourism Principles, Practices, Philosophies* (New
York: J. Wiley).

McKelvey, R. D. (1976), 'Intransativities in Multidimensional Voting Models and
Some Implications for Agenda Control', 12 *Journal of Economic Theory* 472.

McKendrick, E. (1992) (ed.), *Commercial Aspects of Trusts and Fiduciary
Obligations* (Oxford: Clarendon Press).

McKinsey Global Institute (October 1992), *Service Sector Productivity* (Washington,
DC: McKinsey & Co.).

Meyer, J. W., and Rowan, B. (1977), 'Institutional Organizations: Formal Structure
as Myth and Ceremony', 83 *American Journal of Sociology* 340.

Miceli, T. J., and Cosgel, M. M. (1994), 'Reputation and Judicial Decisionmaking',
23 *Journal of Economic Behavior and Organizations* 31

Milgrom, P., and Roberts, J. (1988), 'An Economic Approach to Influence Activities
in Organizations', 94 *American Journal of Sociology* 154.

Milgrom, P., and Roberts, J. (1990), 'Bargaining Costs, Influence Costs, and the
Organization of Economic Activity', in Alt, J. A., and Shepsle, K. A., (eds.)
(1990), *Perspectives on Positive Political Economy* (Cambridge: Cambridge
University Press).

Milward, A. S. (1992), *The European Rescue of the Nation-State* (London:
Routledge).

Mishel, L., and Voos, P. B. (1992) (eds.), *Unions and Economic Competitiveness*
(New York/London: M. E. Sharpe).

Mitchell, L. E. (1992), 'A Theoretical and Practical Framework for Enforcing
Corporate Constituency Statutes', 70 *Texas Law Review* 579.

Mitchell, W. C. (1990), 'Interest Groups: Economic Perspectives and Contributions',
2 *Journal of Theoretical Politics* 85.

Moe, T. M., (1991), 'Politics and the Theory of Organization', 7 *Journal of Law,
Economics, and Organization* 106.

Moravcsik, A. (1991), 'Negotiating the Single European Act: national interests and
conventional statecraft in the European Community', 45 *International
Organization*, 19–56.

Moravscik, A. (1993), 'Preferences and Power in the European Community: A
Liberal Intergovernmentalist Approach', 31 *Journal of Common Market Studies*
473–524.

Moreland, P. W., (1991), 'Efficacy and freedom of mergers and acquisitions', in P.
de Wolf (ed.), *Competition in Europe* (Dordrecht: Kluwer Academic
Publishers/Boston).

Moreland, P. W., (1991), 'Efficacy and freedom of mergers and aquisitions', in P. de Wolf (ed.), *Competition in Europe* (Dordrecht: Kluwer Academic Publishers/Boston).

Moreland, P. W., (1995) *Alternative disciplinary systems in different corporate systems*, 26 Journal of Economic Behaviour and Organisation 17–34.

Montreal Gazette (1992), 'Gay Market Facts', 27 September 1992, p. F5.

Moore, A. G. T. (1987), 'State Competition: Panel Response', 8 *Cardozo Law Review* 779.

Morris, J. (1993), 'Vacation Opportunities for Gay and Lesbian Travelers Growing: Globetrotting, *The Boston Globe*, 15 August 1993, p. B18.

Mortensen, J. (1992) (ed.), *The Future of Pensions in the European Community* (London: Brasseys').

Mosteshar, Sa'id (1993), *European Community Telecommunications Regulation*, European Business Law and Practice Series (London: Graham and Trotman).

Mottek, C. (1994), Letter from Carl Mottek to Steve Jackson, Director of Operations, Pride Tours, Inc., 11 February 1994 (copy on file with author).

Mueller, D. C. (1989), *Public Choice II: A Revised Edition of Public Choice* (Cambridge: Cambridge University Press).

Murphy, Betty Southard (1977), 'Multinational Corporations and Free Coordinated Transnational Bargaining: An Alternative to Protectionism?', 28 *Labor Law Journal* 619.

Musielak, J., and Schurig, K. (1987) (eds.), *Festschrift für Gerhard Kegel zum 75. Geburtstag 26 Juni 1987* (Stuttgart: W. Kohlhammer).

NAFTA (1992), North American Free Trade Agreement 17 December 1992, 32 *International Legal Materials* 296 and 605.

National Conference of Commissioners on Uniform State Laws (1912), *Handbook of the National Conference of Commissioners on Uniform State Laws* (Chicago, Illinois).

National Conference of Commissioners on Uniform State Laws (1943), *Handbook of the National Conference of Commissioners on Uniform State Laws* (Chicago, Illinois).

National Conference of Commissioners on Unfirom State Laws (1973), *Uniform Marriage and Divorce Act*, 91 U.L.A. (St Paul, Minn.: West).

Nelson, R. L. (1988), *Partners with Power* (Berkeley, University of California Press).

Netter, J., and Poulsen, A. (1989), 'State Corporation Laws and Shareholders: The Recent Experience', 18 *Financial Management* 29.

Nicholaides, Phedon (1991) *Competition among rules* mimeo (London: EIPA).

Noam, Eli (1994), 'Beyond Liberalization II: The Impending Doom of Common Carriage', 18 *Telecommunications Policy* 435–452.

Noble Lowndes (1995), *The Guide to Pensions in Europe 1995/6* (Croydon: Sedgwick Noble Lowndes).

North American Agreement on Labor Cooperation 14th September 1993, 32 *International Legal Materials* 1502.

Norton, J. J., and Auerback, R. M. (1993) (eds.), *International Finance in the 1990s. Challenges and Opportunities* (Oxford: Blackwell).

Note (1990), 'Constructing the State Extraterritorially: Jurisdictional Discourse, The National Interest, and Transnational Norms', 103 *Harvard Law Review* 1273.

Nugent, N. (1994), *The Government and Politics of the European Union* (London: Macmillan).

O'Connell, L. (1993), 'State of Matrimony Seems Richer—and Poorer', *The Buffalo News*, 30 May 1993, Lifestyles, p. 1.

O'Hop, Paul A. Jr. (1995), 'Hemispheric Integration and the Elimination of Legal Obstacles under a NAFTA-Based System', 36 *Harvard International Law Journal* 127.

O'Keefe (1992), The Free Movement of Persons in the Single Market, 17 *European Law Review* 3.

Oates, W. E. (1972), *Fiscal Federalism* (New York: Harcourt Brace Jananovich).

Oates, and Schwab (1988), 'Economic Competition Among Jurisdictions: Efficiency Enhancing or Distortion Inducing?', 35 *Journal of Public Economics* 333–354.

OECD (1987), *Minimizing Conflicting Requirements. Approaches of 'moderation and restraint'* (Organization for Economic Cooperation and Development, Paris).

OECD (1988*a*), *Ageing Populations: The Social Policy Implications* (Paris: OECD).

OECD (1988*b*), *Reforming Public Pensions*, OECD Social Policy Studies No. 5 (Paris: OECD).

OECD (1992), *Private Pensions and Public Policy* (Paris: OECD).

OECD (1993*a*), *Employment Outlook July* (Paris: OECD).

OECD (1993*b*), *Symposium on Managing Regulatory Relations between Levels of Government, Public Management Service*, OCDE/GD(93)144, Paris, Oct. 1993 (Paris: OECD).

OECD (1994*a*), *Merger Cases in the Real World. A Study of Merger Control Procedures* (Paris: OECD).

OECD (1994*b*), *The OECD Job Strategy: Facts, Analysis, and Strategies* (Paris: OECD).

Ohmae, Kenichi (1987), *Beyond National Borders* (Homewood, Ill.: Dow Jones-Irwin).

Ordeshook, P. C. (1986), *Game Theory and Political Theory: An Introduction* (Cambridge: Cambridge University Press).

Orts, E. W. (1992), 'Beyond Shareholders: Interpreting Corporate Constituency Statutes', 61 George Washington Law Review 14.

Overlooked Opinions (1993), 'Apples and Oranges: A Discussion of Responses to the Article in the New York Times: "Sed Survey of American Men Finds 1% are Gay" ', 15 April 1993.

Padoa-Schioppa, T. *et al.* (1987), *Efficiency, Stability and Equity* (Oxford: Oxford University Press).

Page, Amy, (1994), 'Microsoft: A Case Study in International Competitiveness, High Technology and the Future of Antitrust Law' 47 *Federal Communications Law Journal*.

Palmer, G. (1992), 'New Ways to Make International Environmental Law.' 86 *American Journal of International Law* 259.

Park, W. W. (1991–2), 'Anonymous Bank Accounts, Narco-Dollars, Fiscal Fraud and Lawyers', 15(3) *Fordham International Law Journal* 652.

Parker, D., and Stead, R. (1991), *Profit and Enterprise: The political economy of profit* (Hemel Hempstead: Harvester Wheatsheaf).

Partners Newsletter for Gay & Lesbian Couples (1990), 'Readers Favor Legal Marriage', July/August 1990.

Partners Newsletter for Gay & Lesbian Couples (1991), 'Looking Over Lesbians', November/December 1991.

Paul, J. R. (1991), 'Comity in International Law', 32 *Harvard International Law Journal* 1–79.

Pelline, J., and Evenson, L. (1993), 'Hawaii Finally Feeling the Pinch: Economy, Competition Batter Tourism Industry', *San Francisco Chronicle*, 23 September 1993, p. D1.

Peltman, S. (1976), 'Toward a More General Theory of Regulation.' 19 *Journal of Law and Economics* 211.

Pension Law Review Committee (1993), *Pension Law Reform*, Cm. 2342–1 (London: HMSO).

Perdomo, R. (1981*a*) *Los Abogados en Venezuela: estudio de una élite intelectual y politica 1780–1980* (Caracas: Monte Avila).

Perdomo, R. (1981*b*), 'Jurists in Venezuelan History', in Dias, C. J. *et al* (eds.) (1981), *Lawyers in the Third World: A comparative and developmental perspective* (New York: International Centre for Law in Development).

Perdomo, R. (1988), 'The Venezuelan Legal Profession: Lawyers in an Inegalitarian Society', in R. Abel, P. Lewis (eds.), *Lawyers in Society, Vol. II, The Civil World* (Berkley London: University of California Press).

Perkin, H. (1989), *The Rise of Professional Society, England since 1880* (London: Routledge).

Pesando, James E. (1992), *The Economic Effects of Private Pensions* in OECD (1992).

Peters, B. Guy (1992), 'Bureaucratic Politics and the Institutions of the European Community.' In Alberta, M. Sbragia (ed.) *Euro-Politics* 75–122. (Washington DC: The Brookings Institution).

Peters, Geoffrey M. (1985), 'Is the Third Time the Charm? A Comparison of the Government's Major Antitrust Settlement with AT&T this Century' 15 *Seton Hall Law Review* 252–275.

Petersmann, E.-U. (1993), 'International Competition Rules for the GATT-MTO World Trade and Legal System', 27 *Journal of World Trade* 35–86.

Petersmann, E.-U. (1994), 'The Dispute-Settlement System of the World Trade Organization and the Evolution of the GATT Dispute-Settlement System Sicne 1948', 31 *Common Market Law Review* 1157.

Phillips, Charles F. (1988), *The Regulation of Public Utilities—Theory and Practice.* Arlington, Virginia: Public Utilities Reports, Inc.

Picciotto, S. (1983), 'Jurisdictional Conflicts and the International State System' 11 *International Journal of the Sociology of Law* 11–40.

Picciotto, S. (1992), *International Business Taxation. A Study in the internationalization of business regulation* (London: Butterworths).

Picciotto, S. (1995), 'The Construction of International Taxation', in Dezalay and Sugarman (1995) (eds.), *Professional Competition and the Social Construction of Markets* (London: Routledge) 25–50.

Pieters, D. (1991), *Social Security in Europe* (Antwerp: Maklu Uitgevers).

Pinder, J. (1968), 'Positive and Negative Integration: Some Problems of Economic Union in the EEC.' 24 *The World Today* 88–110.

Plasser, Y., and Savignon, F. (1983), Paris 1883. Genèse du Droit Unioniste des Brevets (Paris: Librairies techniques).

Porter, M. E. (1990), *The Competitive Advantage of Nations* (New York: Free Press).

Porter, Michael (1991), *Canada at the Crossroads* (Ottawa: BCNI).

Posner, R. (1982), 'Economics, Politics, and the Reading of Statutes and the Constitution', 49 *University of Chicago Law Review* 263.

Posner, R. (1986), 'Goodbye to the Bluebook', 53 *University of Chicago Law Review*, 1343–52.

Posner, R. A. (1992a), *Economic Analysis of the Law* (4th edn.) (Boston: Little Brown).

Posner, R. A. (1992b), *Sex and Reason* (Cambridge Mass: Harvard University Press).

Posner, R., and Scott, K. (1980), *Economics of Corporation Law and Securities Regulation* (Boston: Little Brown).

Powell, W. W., and DiMaggio, P. J. (1991), 'Introduction', *The New Institutionalism in Organizational Analysis* (Chicago: University of Chicago Press), 1–38.

Pozen, R. C. (1994), 'Institutional Investors: The Reluctant Activists', Jan.–Feb. *Harvard Business Review*, p. 141.

Price, D. (1993), 'Bring Your Domestic Partner and Pink Slip', *San Jose Mercury News*, 15 April 1993, p. 20.

Price, D. (1994), 'Hawaii Leads Movement for Gay Marriages', *San Francisco Examiner*, 4, January 1994, p. C7.

Priest, G. (1986), 'What Economists Can Tell Lawyers About Intellectual Property: Comment on Cheung', 8 *Resource Law and Economics* 19.

PR Newswire (1993a), 'Money Management Tips to Consider Before Saying "I do": Remember Marriage Finances in Wedding Plans', 27 July 1993.

Puel, H. (1989), *L'économie au défi de l'éthique. Essai d'éthique économique* (Paris: Editions Cu jas).

Quillen, W. T. (1993), 'The Federal-State Corporate Law Relationship—A Response to Professor Seligman's Call for Federal Preemption of State Corporate Fiduciary Law', 59 *Brooklyn Law Review* 107.

Rabel, E. (1962), *The Conflict of Laws—A Comparative Study* (2nd edn.) (Ann Arbor: University of Michigan Press).

Rasmussen, E. (1994), 'Judicial Legitimacy as a Repeated Game', 10 *Journal of Law, Economics, and Organization* 63.

Rasmusen, E., and Ayres, I. (1993), 'Mutual and Unilateral Mistake in Contract Law', 22 *Journal of Legal Studies* 309–43.

Rasmussen, J. (1986), *On Law and Policy in the ECJ* (Dordrecht: Nijhoff).

Ravaioli, Piero, and Peter Sandler, (1994), 'The European Union and Telecommunications: Recent Developments in the Field of Competition (Part I)' 2 *The International Computer Lawyer* 2–24.

Reader, W. J. (1975), *Imperial Chemicals Industries: A History. Vol. I: The First Quarter-Century* (Oxford: Oxford University Press).

Reeves, T. (1993), 'Packaging Waste in Europe: Confrontation or Cooperation?', *The Economist Intelligence Unit, Special Report R553*.

Regan, D. H. (1987), 'Siamese Essays: (I) *CTS Corp.* v. *Dynamics Corp. of America and Dormant Commerce Clause Doctrine*; (II) Extraterritorial State Legislation', 85 *Michigan Law Review* 1865.

Rehfeldt, Udo (1994), *Effritement du modele social europeen*, Le Monde Diplomatique, juillet.

Reich, Norbert (1992), 'Competition Between Legal Orders: A New Paradigm of EC Law' 29 *Common Market Law Review* 861–896.

Reich, R. B. (1992), *The Work of Nations. Preparing Ourselves for 21st-Century Capitalism* (New York: Vintage Books).

Reindl, A. (1990), 'Companies in the European Community: Are the Conflict-of-Law Rules Ready for 1992?', 11 *Michigan Journal of International Law* 1270–93.

Reinhold (1993), 'Hawaii is Rethinking its Dependency on Tourism', *New York Times*, 2 January 1993, p. A6, col. 3.

Reisman, W. M. (1992), *Systems of Control in International Adjudication* (Durham: Duke Univ. Press).

Response (1993), Defendant's Response to Plaintiffs' First Request for Answers to Interrogatories, 17 December 1993, *Baehr* v. *Lewin*, Hawaii 1st Cir. Civil No. 91-1394-05.

Restatement (1971), *Restatement (Second) of Conflict of Laws* (St Paul, Minn.: American Law Institute).

Revesz, R. (1992), 'Rehabilitating Interstate Competition: Rethinking the "Race-to-the-Bottom" Rationale for Federal Environmental Regulation', 67 *New York University Law Review* 1210–1254.

Rhodes, M. (1991), 'The Social Dimension of the Single European Market: national versus transnational regulation', 19 *European Journal of Political Research* 245–280.

Rhodes, Martin (1994), *'Subversive Liberalism': Market Integration, Globalisation, and the European Welfare State*, paper to the 23nd Annual European Consortium for Political Research, Madrid, April 17–22.

Rice, D. A. (1985), 'Product Liability Laws and the Economics of Federalism', 65 *Boston University Law Review* 1–64.

Robinson, T., and Wenig, M. M. (1989), 'Marry in Haste, Repent at Tax Time: Marital Status as a Tax Determinant', 8 *Virginia Tax Review* 773.

Rock, E. B. (1991), 'The Logic and (Uncertain) Significance of Institutional Shareholder Activism', 79 *Georgetown Law Journal* 445.

Rock, E. B. (1994), 'Controlling the Dark Side of Relational Investing', 15 *Cardozo Law Review* 987.

Rodgers, Paul (1995), 'How Microsoft Beat the Regulators?' *Independent on Sunday*, 26 February 1995.

Roe, M. J. (1991), 'A Political Theory of American Corporate Finance', 91 *Columbia Law Review* 10–67.

Rojo, A. (1991), 'The Typology of Companies', in Drury, R., and Xuereb, P. (1991) (eds.), *European Company Laws* (Aldershot, Eng.: Dartmouth Publishing Company) 41–59.

Romano, R. (1985), 'Law as Product: Some Pieces of the Incorporation Puzzle', 1 *Journal of Law, Economics, and Organization*, 225–83.

Romano, R. (1987), 'The Political Economy of Takeover Statutes', 73 *Virginia Law Review*, 111–99.

Romano, R. (1988), 'The Future of Hostile Takeovers: Legislation and Public Opinion', 57 *University of Cincinnati Law Review* 457–505 n. 11.

Romano, R. (1989), 'Answering the Wrong Questions: The Tenuous Case for Mandatory Corporate Law', 89 *Columbia Law Review* 1599–1617.

Romano, R. (1990), 'Corporate Governance in the Aftermath of the Insurance Crisis, 39 *Emory Law Journal* 1164–89.

Romano, R. (1991), 'The Shareholder Suit: Litigation Without Foundation', 7 *Journal of Law, Economics, and Organization* 55–87.

Romano, R. (1993*a*), 'Competition for Corporate Charters and the Lesson of Takeover Statutes', 61 *Fordham Law Review* 843–64.

Romano, R. (1993*b*), *The Genius of American Corporate Law* (Washington, DC: The American Enterprise Institute).

Rose-Ackerman, S. (1980), 'Risk Taking and Reelection: Does Federalism Promote Innovation?', 9 *Journal of Legal Studies* 593–616.

Rose-Ackerman, Susan (1992), *Rethinking the Progressive Agenda* (New York: Free Press),

Rosegg, P. (1994), 'Gay-marriage Furor Intensifies', *Honolulu Advertiser*, 12 February 1994.

Rosenthal, Douglas E., and Knighton, Wm. (1982), *National Laws and International Commerce. The Problem of Extraterritoriality* (London: RKP for the Royal Institute of International Affairs).

Rowley, C. K., Tollison, R. D., and Tullock, G. (1988), *The Political Economy of Rent-Seeking* (Dordrecht: Kluwer Academic Press).

Rowthorn, R. (1971), *International big business 1957–1967* (London: Cambridge University Press).

Rozwood, Benjamin, and Walker, Andrew (1993), 'Side Agreements, Sidesteps, and Sideshows: Protecting Labor from Free Trade in North America', 34 *Harvard International Law Journal* 333.

Ruggie, J. G. (1982), 'International Regimes, Transactions and Change: Embedded Lib-eralism in the Postwar Economic Order', 36(2) *International Organization* 379–415.

Ruigrok, Winfried (1991), *Paradigm Crisis in International Trade Theory. Forecasting and Assessment in Science and Technology* (FAST) Directorate-General Science Research and Development, Brussels: CEE.

Ryan, P. J. (1988), 'Institutional Shareholder Proposals and Corporate Democracy', 23 *Georgia Law Review* 97.

Salholz, E. (1993), 'For Better or for Worse', *Newsweek*, 24 May 1993, p. 69.

Salt, J., Singleton, A., and Hogarth, J. (1994), *Europe's International Migrants* (London: HMSO).

Samuelson, P. (1954), 'The Pure Theory of Public Expenditure', 36 *Review of Economics and Statistics* 387–389.

Santos, B. D. S. (1987), 'Law, a Map of Misreading: Towards a Postmodern Conception of Law', 14 *Journal of Law & Society* 279–302.

Santos, B. de Sousa (1992), 'State, Law and Community: An Introduction'; Special Issue on State Transformation, Legal Pluralism and Community Justice, 1(2) *Social & Legal Studies* 131–9.

Sauter, Wolf, (1994*a*), 'The ONP Framework: Towards a European Telecommunications Agency' 5 *Utilities Law Review* 140–146.

Sauter, Wolf (1994*b*), 'The Rejection of the ONP Voice Telephony Directive by the European Parliament' 5 *Utilities Law Review* 176–178.

Sbragia, A. M. (1992) (ed.), *Euro-Politics. Institutions and Policymaking in the 'New' European Community* (Washington DC, The Brookings Institution).

Scharpf, F. (1994), 'Community and Autonomy: Multi-Level Policy-Making in the European Union', 1 *Journal of European Public Policy* 219–242.

Schelling, T. (1972), 'The Process of Residential Segregation: Neighborhood Tipping', in Pascal, A. (ed.), *Racial Discrimination in Economic Life* (Lexington, Mass.: Lexington Books).

Schmahl, W. (1991) (ed.), *The Future of Basic and Supplementary Schemes in the EC: 1992 and Beyond* (Baden Baden: Nomos Verlagsgesellschaft).

Schmalensee, R. (1979), 'On the Use of Economic Models in Antitrust: The Realemon Case', 127 *University of Pennsylvania Law Review* 994–1050.

Schmalensee, R. (1982), 'Product Differentiation Advantages of Pioneering Brands', 72 *American Economic Review*, 349–65.

Schmitter, P. C., and Streeck, W. (1991), 'From National Corporatism to Transnational Pluralism: Organized Interests in the Single European Market', 19 *Politics & Society* 133–164.

Schott, Jeffrey (1991), *Trading blocs and the World trading system*, 14:1 The World Economy (March) 1–17.

Schultz, Richard J., and Hudson N. Janisch (1993), *Freedom to Compete-Reforming the Canadian Telecommunications Regulatory System* (Toronto: Bell Canada).

Schumpeter, J. (1943) *Capitalism, Socialism & Democracy* (London: Unwin University Books).

Scoles, E. F., and Hay, P. (1992), *Conflict of Laws* (2nd edn.) (St Paul, Minn: West Publishing Co.).

Scott, Colin (1996), 'Changing Patterns of European Community Utilities Law and Policy: An Institutional Hypothesis.' In Josephine Shaw and Gillian More (eds.), *New Legal Dynamics of European Union* (Oxford: Oxford University Press).

Seattle Times (1993), 'Gay-Travel Expo in Seattle Thursday', 1 August 1993, p. K7.

Seligman, J. (1993), 'The New Corporate Law', 59 *Brooklyn Law Review* 1.

Sen, A. (1986), 'Behaviour and the Concept of Preference', in Elster (1986) *Rational Choice* (New York: NYU Press).

Shepsle, K. A. (1989), 'Studying Institutions: Some Lessons from the Rational Choice Approach', 1 *Journal of Theoretical Politics* 131.

Shepsle, K. A. (1992), 'Congress is a "They," Not an "It": Legislative Intent as Oxymoron', 12 *International Review of Law and Economics* 239.

Shepsle, K. A., and Weingast, B. R. (1985), 'Uncovered Sets and Sophisticated Outcomes with Implications for Agenda Control', 28 *American Journal of Political Science* 48.

Sherman, S. (1992), *Lesbian and Gay Marriage: Private Commitments, Public Ceremonies* (Philadelphia: Temple University Press).

Shleifer, A., and Vishny, R. W. (1994), *Politicians and Firms* (Cambridge: Harvard Institute of Economic Research Discussion Paper No. 1686).

Shocking Gray (1993), *Shocking Gray Fall/Holiday Catalog 1993*.

Sidey, K. (1989), 'Last Temptation Boycott gets Mixed Reviews', *Christianity Today*, 21 April 1989, p. 36.

Siebert, H., and Koop, M. (1993), 'Institutional Competition Versus Centralization: Quo Vadis Europe', 9 *Oxford Review of Economic Policy* 15–30.

Siegrist, H. (1993), 'Les professionnels du droit continentaux: une pluralité de modèles', in Y. Dezalay (ed.), *Batailles territoriales et querelles de cousinage: Juristes et Comptables européens sur le marché du droit des affaires* (Paris: L.G.D.J.).

Sikkink, Kathryn (1993), 'Human Rights, Principled Issue-Networks and Sovereignty in Latin America', 47 *International Organization*, 411–441.

Silva, P. (1991), 'Technocrats and Politics in Chile: From the Chicago Boys to the CIEPLAN Monks', 23 *Journal of Latin American Studies*, 2 (385–410).

Siu-Lun, W. (1988), *Emigrant Entrepreneurs, Shanghai Industrialists in Hong Kong* (Hong Kong Oxford: Oxford University Press).

Skeel, D.A. (1994), 'Rethinking the Line Between Corporate Law and Corporate Bankruptcy', 72 *Texas Law Review* 471–554.

Sklar, M. J. (1988), *The Corporate Reconstruction of American Capitalism, 1890–1916, The Market, The Law and Politics* (Cambridge: Cambridge University Press).

Skog, O. (1994), 'Volonte Generale and the Instability of Spatial Voting Games', 6 *Rationality and Society* 271.

Slaughter, and May (1990), 'The European Community', in *European Corporate Finance Law* (London: Euromoney Publications) 9–38.

Smith, N. C. (1990), *Morality and the Market: Consumer Pressure for Corporate Acountability* (London: Routledge).

Smolla, R. A. (1981), 'Integration Maintenance: The Unconstitutionality of Benign Programs that Discourage Black Entry to Prevent White Flight', 1981 *Duke Law Journal* 891.

Snyder, Francis (1994), 'EMU-Metaphor for European Union? Institut ions, Rules and Types of Regulation' in Dehousee R. (ed.) (1994), *Europe After Maastricht, An Ever Closer Union?* (Munich: Law Books in Europe) pp. 63–9.

Solnik, B. (1991), *International Investments* (New York: Addison Wesley, 2nd edn.).

Spense, A. (1975), 'Monopoly, Quality, and Regulation', 6 *Bell Journal of Economics* 417–29.

Spence, Michael (1979), 'Investment Strategy and Growth in a New Market', 10 *Bell Journal of Economics* 1–19.

Steil, Benn (1993), *Competition, Integration and Regulations in EC Capital Markets* mimeo, Royal Institute of International Affairs (London).

Steil, B., (1994) (ed.), *International Financial Market Regulation* (Chichester: Wiley).

Stein, E. (1971), *Harmonization of European Company Laws* (Indianapolis: Bobbs Merrill).

Steiner, J. (1992), 'Social Security for EC Migrants', 1 *Journal of Social Welfare and Family Law* 33–47.

Stelzer, Irwin M. and Richard Schmalensee (1983) 'Potential Costs and Benefits of Vertical Integration' 52 *Antitrust Law Journal* 249–262.

Sterk, S. E. (1992), 'Competition Among Municipalities as a Constraint on Land Use Exactions', 45 *Vanderbilt Law Review* 831–861.

Stewart, R. B. (1985), 'Federalism: Allocating Responsibility between the Federal and State Courts', 19 *Georgia Law Review* 917–980.

Stewart, R. B. (1993), 'Environmental Regulation and International Competiveness', 102 *Yale Law Journal* 2039.

Stewart, R. B. (1995), 'Markets versus Environment?' No. 19, *Jean Monnett Papers* (Florence: The Robert Schuman Centre at the European University Institute) 1–53.

Stigler, G. (1971), 'The Theory of Economic Regulation', 2 *Bell Journal of Economics and Management Science* 3–31.

Stith, C. D. (1991), 'Note, Federalism and Company Law: A "Race to the Bottom" in the European Community', 79 *Georgetown Law Journal* 1581–1618.

Stone, Katherine Van Wezel (1988), 'Labor and the Corporate Structure', 55 *Chicago Law Review* 173.

Stone, Katherine Van Wezel (1993), 'Policing Employment Contracts Within the Nexus-of-Contracts Firm', 43 *Toronto L. Rev.* 353.

Strain, C. R. (1989) (ed.), *Prophetic Visions and Economic Realities* (Grand Rapids, Mich: Eerdmans).

Strange, S. (1986), *Casino Capitalism* (Oxford: Basil Blackwell).

Strange, Susan (1988), *States and Markets* (Oxford: Basil Blackwell).

Streeck, W. (1995), 'Neo-Voluntarism: A New European Social Policy Regime?, 1 *European Law Journal* 31–59.

Sturm, P. (1992), 'Population ageing and old-age income maintenance: basic facts and problems', in Mortensen, J. (ed.) (1992), *The Future of Pensions in the European Community* (London: Brasseys') 23–38.

Sugarman, D. (1993), 'Qui colonise l'autre? Réflexions historiques sur les rapports entre le droit, les juristes et les comptables en Grande Bretagne', in Y. Dezalay (ed.), *Batailles territoriales et querelles de cousinage: Juristes et Comptables européen sur le marché du droit des affaires*, Paris: L.G.D.J.

Summers, Clyde (1980), 'Worker Participation in the U.S. and West Germany: A Comparative Study from an American Perspective', 28 *American Journal of Comparative Law* 367.

Sun, Jeanne-May, and Pelkmans, Jacques (1995), Regulatory Competition in the Single Market, 33(1) *Journal of Common Market Studies* 67–89.

Sunshine, Steven C. (1994), 'Antitrust Policy Toward Telecommunications Alliances.' Paper presented at American Enterprise Institute for Public Policy Research, July 1994.

Sunstein, C. (1994), 'Incommensurability and Valuation in Law', 92 *Michigan Law Review*, 779–861.

Susskind, L. E. (1992), 'New Corporate Roles in Global Environmental Treaty Making', 27 *Columbia Journal of World Business* 62.

Sutherland, P. (1992), *The Internal Market After 1992: Meeting the Challenge: Report to the EC Commission by the High Level Group on the Operation of the Internal Market* (Sutherland Report), (Brussels: Commission of the European Communities).

Tangonan, S. (1993a), 'Passions Run High as Backers and Foes Clash', *Honolulu Advertiser*, 30 October 1993, p. A1.

Tarlock, A. D. (1981) (ed.), *Regulation, Federalism, and Interstate Commerce* (Cambridge, Mass.: Oelgeschlager, Gunn and Hain).

Tauke, D. (1989), 'Should Bonds Have More Fun? A Re-examination of the debate Over Corporate Bondholder Rights', 1989 *Columbia Business Law Review*, 1–136.

Taylor, Simon M. (1994), 'Article 90 and Telecommunications Monopolies' 15 *European Competition Law Review* 322–334.

Tecce, D. J. (1993), 'The Dynamics of Industrial Capitalism: Perspectives on Alfred Chandler's Scale and Scope', 31 *Journal of Economic Literature* 199–225.

Temin, P. (1991) (ed.), *Inside the Business Enterprise* (Chicago: University of Chicago Press).

Teubner, G. (1987) (ed.), *Juridification of Social Spheres. A Comparative Analysis in the Areas of Labor, Corporate, Antitrust and Social Welfare Law* (Berlin: de Gruyter).

Thatcher, Mark (1992), 'Telecommunications in Britain and France: The Impact of National Institutions' 6 *Communications and Strategies* 35–61.

Thimm, Alfred L. (1992), *America's Stake in European Telecommunication Policies.* Westport (Connecticut: Quorum Books).

Thomson, J. E., and Krasner, S. D. (1989), Global Transactions and the Consolidation of Sovereignty, in E.-O. Czempiel, and J. N. Rosenau (ed.), *Global Changes and Theoretical Challenges* (Lexington, Mass.: Lexington Books).

Tiebout, C. (1956), 'A Pure Theory of Local Expenditures', 64 *Journal of Political Economy* 416–424.

Tilly, R. (1966), *Financial Institutions and Industrialization in the Rhineland, 1815–1870* (Madison: University of Wisconsin Press).

Timmermans, C. (1991), 'Methods and Tools for Integration', in Buxbaum *et al.* (1991), *European Business Law: Legal and Economic Analysis on Integration and Harmonization* (Berlin: de Gruyter) 129–48.

Tinbergen, J. (1954), *International Economic Integration* (Amsterdam: Elsevier).

Tirole, J. (1988), *The Theory of Industrial Organization* (Cambridge, Mass.: MIT Press).

Tollison, R. D. (1982), 'Rent Seeking: A Survey', 35 *Kyklos* 575–602.

Tollison, R. D. (1988), 'Public Choice and Legislation', 74 *Virginia Law Review* 339.

Trachtman, J. P. (1993), 'International Regulatory Competition, Externalization, and Jurisdiction', 34 *Harvard International Law Journal* 47–104.

Trachtman, J. P. (1994), 'Conflict of Laws and Accuracy in the Allocation of Government Responsibility', 26(5) *Vanderbilt Journal of Transnational Law* 975–1057.

Travel Weekly (1994), 'Occupancy Levels at State's Hotels Show Substantial Declines', 27 January 1994, p. H14.

Trebing, Harry M. (1989), 'Telecommunications Regulation—The Continuing Dilemma', in Kenneth Nowotny, David B. Smith, and Harry M. Trebing (eds.), *Public Utility Regulation—The Economic and Social Control of Industry* 93–130 (Boston: Kluwer).

Trubek, D., Dezalay, Y., Buchanan, R., Davis, J. (1994) 'Global restructuring and the law: the internationalization of legal fields and the creation of transnational arenas', 44(2) *Case Western Law Review*.

Trudeau, Gilles, and Vallee, Guylaine (1995), 'Economic Integration and Labour Policy in Canada' in Harry Katz, and Maria Cook (eds.), *Regional Aspects of North American Integration*, 66–79 (Ithaca: Cornell University Press).

Tullock, G. (1980), 'The Welfare Costs of Tariffs, Monopolies, and Theft', in Buchanan, J., Tollison, R., and Tullock, G. (1980), *Toward a Rent-Seeking Society* (College Station: Texas A&M Press).

Tunc, A. (1982), 'A French Lawyer Looks at American Corporation Law and Securities Regulation', 130 *University of Pennsylvania Law Review* 757.

Tunc, A. (1991), 'Corporate Law', in Buxbaum *et al.* (1991), *European Business Law: Legal and Economic Analysis on Integration and Harmonization* (Berlin: de Gruyter) 199–215.

Turley, Jonathan (1990), 'When in Rome': Multinational Misconduct and the Presumption Against Extraterritoriality', 84 *Northwestern University Law Review* 598.

Turner, L. (1992) *Industrial Relations and the Reorganization of Work in West Germany: Lessons for the U.S.*, in Mishel and Voos.

Turner, Lowell (1995), 'Beyond National Unionism?' in Locke, R., and Thelen, K. (eds.), *The Shifting Boundaries of Labor Politics* (Cambridge, Mass: MIT Press).

UK (1990), Report of Mr Rodney Gallagher of Coopers and Lybrand on the Survey of Offshore Finance Sectors in the Caribbean Dependent Territories, House of Commons 1989–90, No. 121.

Underhill, Geoffrey R. D. (1995), 'Keeping Governments Out of Politics: Transnational Securities Markets, Regulatory Cooperation, and Political Legitimacy' 21(3) *Review of International Studies*, 251 (London: HMSO).

Ungerer, Herbert (1992), 'European Policies and Regulation' 16 *Telecommunications Policy* 712–6.

United Nations (1992), *World Investment Report 1992 Transnational Corporations as Engines of Growth* (New York: United Nations).

University of Chicago, The (1989), *The University of Chicago Manual of Legal Style* (Chicago: University of Chicago Press).

US General Accounting Office (1994), *International Banking. Strengthening the Framework for Supervising International Banks*, GAO/GGD-94-68, March 1994.

US Travel Data Center (1991), *Impact of Travel on State Economies, 1989* (Washington DC: US Travel Data Center).

Usher, J. A. (1994*a*), *The Law of Money and Financial Services in the European Community* (Oxford: Clarendon Press).

Usher, John A. (1994*b*) 'The Commission and the Law.' In Geoffrey Edwards and David Spence (eds.), *The European Commission* 146–166 (London: Longman).

Van Hulle, K. (1989), 'The Harmonization of Company Law in the European Community', in Wachter, B. *et al.* (eds.) (1989) 10–30.

Vermulst, E., and Driessen, B. (1995), 'An Overview of the WTO Dispute Settlement System and its Relationship with the Uruguay Round Agreements. Nice on Paper but Too Much Stress for the System?', *Journal of World Trade* 131–62.

Vernon, Raymond (1970), 'Future of the Multinational Corporation', in Charles P. Kindleberger, *The International Corporation* 373 (Cambridge, Mass.: MIT Press).

Vickers, John (1985), 'Pre-emptive Patenting, Joint Ventures, and the Persistence of Oligopoly', 3 *International Journal of Industrial Organization* 261–73.

Vickers, J. (1995), 'Concepts of Competition', 47 *Oxford Economic Papers* 1–23.

von Wilmowsky, P. (1993), 'Waste Disposal in the Internal Market: The State of Play After the ECJ's Ruling on the Wallaoon Import Ban', 30 *Common Market Law Review* 541.

Wachter, B. *et al.* (1989) (eds.), *Harmonization of Company and Securities Laws: The European and American Approach* (Tilburg: Tilburg University Press).

Walker, Dawson, and Jonathan Solomon (1993), 'The Interconnection Imperative: "E Pluribus Unum" ' 17 *Telecommunications Policy* 257–280.

Wallace, Helen, and Woolcock, Stephen (1994), 'European Community regulation and national enterprise' in J. Hayward and Vincent Wright (eds.), *International Enterprise and the State in Western Europe* (Oxford: Oxford University Press).

Wallace, William (1990*a*), *The Transformation of Western Europe* (London: Royal Institute of International Affairs/Pinter Publishers).

Wallace, W., (1990*b*) (ed.), *The Dynamics of European Integration* (London: Pinter).

Wallerstein, M., Mogee, M., and Schoen, R. (1993) (eds.), *Global Dimensions of Intellectual Property* (Washington DC: National Academy Press).

Waters, S. (1993), *The Big Picture* (Rye, New York: Child and Waters Inc.).

Watsons, (1994), *Watsons Pension Summaries* (Guildford: Watsons).

Weale, Albert (1993) *Competition among rules and Environmental Policy*, paper presented to the Royal Institute on International Affairs Study group on the Competition Among Rules (London).

Wedderburn, Lord (1986), *The Worker and the Law* (Harmondsworth: Penguin).

Wehlau, A. (1992), 'The Societas Europea: A Critique of the Commission's Amended Proposal', 29 *Common Market Law Review* 473–510.

Weiler, J. (1993), 'Journal to an Unknown Destination: A Retrospective and Prospective of the European Court of Justice in the Area of Political Integration', 31 *Journal of Common Market Studies* 417–446.

Weingast, B. R. (1984), The Congressional Bureaucratic System: A Principal-Agent Perspective', 44 *Public Choice* 147.

Weingast, B. (1993), 'Constitutions as Governance Structures', 149 *Journal of Institutional and Theoretical Economics* 286–311.

Weingast, B. (1995), 'The Economic Role of Political Institutions: Market Preserving Federalism and Economic Development', 11 *Journal of Law, Economics, and Organization* 1–31.

Weingast , B. R., and Marshall, W. J. (1988), 'The Industrial Organization of Congress; or, Why Legislatures, like Firms are Note Organized as Markets', 96 *Journal of Political Economy* 132.

Weiss, M. (1993), 'The Impact of European Community on Labour Law: Some American Comparisons', 68 *Chicago-Kent Law Review* 1427.

Wenders, John T. (1988), 'The Economic Theory of Regulation and the US Telecoms Industry' 12 *Telecommunications Policy* 16–26.

Whitman, M. von N. (1984), 'Persistant Unemployment: economic policy perspectives in US and Europe', in A. Pierre, *Unemployment and Growth in the Western Economies* (New York, Council on Foreign Relations).

Wilkins, Mira (1970), *The Emergence of International Enterprise* (Cambridge, Mass.: Harvard University Press).

Williamson, Oliver E. (1985), *The Economic Institutions of Capitalism* (New York: Free Press).

Wilson, J. (1980), *The Politics of Regulation* (New York: Basic Books).

Wilson, John D. (1995), 'Diversity in Public Policies of Competing Governments: Lessons from Local Public Economics', forthcoming in Bhagwati and Hudec (eds.) (1995), *Harmonization and Fair Trade: Pre-requisites fore Free Trade?* (MIT Press, Cambridge, Mass, 1996) (forthcoming).

Wilson, T. E. (1983), 'Separation Between Banking and Commerce Under the Bank Holding Company Act—A Statutory Objective Under Attack', 33 *Catholic University Law Review* 163.

Wincott, Daniel (1994), 'Is the Treaty of Maastricht an Adequate "Constitution" for the European Union?' 72 *Public Administration* 573–590.

Winter, R. (1977), 'State Law, Shareholder Protection, and the Theory of the Corporation', 6 *Journal of Legal Studies* 251–92.

Winter, R. (1989), 'The Race for the Top Revisited: A Comment on Eisenberg', 89 *Columbia Law Review* 1526–29.

Woolcock, S. (1993), 'The European acquis and Multilateral Trade Rules: Are they Compatible? 31 *Journal of Common Market Studies* 539–558.

Woolcock, Stephen, Hodges, Michael, and Schreiber, Kristin (1991) *Britain, Germany and 1992: the Limits of Deregulation* (London: Pinter/Royal Institute of International Affairs).

Wooldridge, F. (1991), *Company Law in the United Kingdom and the European Community* (London: Athlone Press).

World Bank (1992), *World Development Report* (Oxford: Oxford University Press).

Wright, M. (1993), 'Avoidance Tactics', *The Atlantic*, October 1993, p. 44.

Wright, M., Robbie, K., and Thompson, S. (1991), 'Corporate Restructuring, Buyouts, and Managerial Equity: The European Dimension', 3 *Journal of Applied Corporate Finance* 46–58.

Wymeersch, E. (1991), 'Groups of Companies', in Buxbaum *et al.* (1991), *European Business Law: Legal and Economic Analysis on Integration and Harmonization* (Berlin: de Gruyter) 227–37.

Young, O. (1972), The Actors in World Politics. In J. Rosenau (ed.), *Analysis of International Politics* 125.

Zakson, Lawrence S. (1984), 'Worker Participation: Industrial Democracy and Managerial Prerogative in the Federal Republic of Germany, Sweden and the United States', 8 *Hastings International and Comparative, Law Review* 93.

Zavvsos, G. (1994), 'Pension fund Liberalization and the Future of Retirement Financing in Europe', 31 *Common Market Law Review* 609–630.

Zdanow, M. (1994), Letter from Marc Zdanow, Operations Manager, Gata Tours, Inc. to Dieter Huckstein, Regional Senior Vice President, Hilton Hotels, 11 February 1994 (copy on file with author).

Zimmerman, James M. (1988), 'Extraterritorial Ampliation of Federal Labour Laws: Congress' Flawed Extension of the ADEA', 21 *Cornell International Law Journal* 103.

Index